This major new work from Quentin Skinner presents a radical reappraisal of the political theory of Hobbes. Using, for the first time, the full range of manuscript as well as printed sources, it documents an entirely fresh interpretation of Hobbes's intellectual development, and re-examines the fundamental shift from a humanist to a scientific culture in European moral and political thought.

The book begins with a detailed and original survey of the reception of classical rhetoric in Renaissance England. One of the central teachings of the Tudor rhetoricians was that the findings of reason must be reinforced by the power of eloquence if they are to have their fullest persuasive effect. Professor Skinner convincingly shows how Hobbes's conception of the civil sciences was shaped by his changing reactions to this precept, and so rescues Hobbes from the intellectual isolation in which he is so often discussed. In his early work, Hobbes reacted against his humanist education, and sought to establish a rigorous and formal science of politics. In the *Leviathan*, however, Hobbes seems to display a clear change of mind. Here he not only advocates the use of persuasion in the human sciences, but makes full use of rhetorical strategies throughout the book. The paradox is resolved when we see that Hobbes is employing the techniques of 'eloquence', but in the service of 'science'.

Quentin Skinner succeeds here in providing both a dramatically new account of this most difficult, pivotal figure in the European political tradition, and a splendid exemplification of the 'Cambridge' contextual approach to the study of intellectual history. The work as a whole highlights two deeply opposed views about the character of moral and political argument: the deductive, scientific model which Hobbes espoused and which has since been largely dominant; and the contrasting humanist model, with its emphasis on dialogue and negotiation, which Quentin Skinner here urges us to reconsider. *Reason and rhetoric* is in this sense the humanist response to the *Leviathan*.

This book will be of interest and importance to a wide range of scholars in history, philosophy, politics and literary theory.

REASON AND RHETORIC IN THE PHILOSOPHY OF HOBBES

REASON AND RHETORIC IN THE PHILOSOPHY OF HOBBES

QUENTIN SKINNER

Professor of Political Science, University of Cambridge

CAMBRIDGE UNIVERSITY PRESS

Published by the Press Syndicate of the University of Cambridge
The Pitt Building, Trumpington Street, Cambridge CB2 1RP
40 West 20th Street, New York, NY 10011–4211, USA
10 Stamford Road, Oakleigh, Melbourne 3166, Australia

First published 1996

Printed in Great Britain at the University Press, Cambridge

A catalogue record for this book is available from the British Library

Library of Congress cataloguing in publication data

Skinner, Quentin.
Reason and rhetoric in the philosophy of Hobbes / Quentin Skinner.
p. cm.
Includes bibliographical references and index.
ISBN 0 521 55436 5 (hc)
1. Hobbes, Thomas, 1588–1679. 2. Reason. 3. Rhetoric.
I. Title.
B1248.R43S55 1996
192–dc20 95–18538 CIP

ISBN 0 521 55436 5 hardback

CE

CONTENTS

PART II HOBBES AND THE IDEA OF A CIVIL SCIENCE

ACKNOWLEDGMENTS

My first thanks are due to the owners and custodians of the manuscript collections I have consulted. I am deeply grateful for the patience and helpfulness of the staff at the Salle des Manuscrits, Bibliothèque Nationale; the Manuscripts Students' Room, British Library; the Manuscripts Reading Room, Cambridge University Library; the Chancery Lane branch of the Public Record Office; and the Library of St John's College Oxford (special thanks to Angela Williams). Above all, I am deeply grateful to his Grace the Duke of Devonshire and the Trustees of the Chatsworth Settlement for permission to study the Hardwick and Hobbes manuscripts now lodged at Chatsworth. I have been made very welcome during my visits, and am conscious of how much I owe to Tom Askey, Michael Pearman and the late T. S. Wragg for their friendliness and knowledgeability.

My research in the printed sources has been conducted in three main places: the North Library and Reading Room of the British Library; the rare books room of the Cambridge University Library; and the Library of the Warburg Institute, University of London. These institutions continue to offer their readers a remarkable service, often in increasingly difficult circumstances, and I am much indebted to all of them. I should also like to record my thanks to Cecil Courtney, Librarian of Christ's College Cambridge, for permitting me to borrow some first editions of Hobbes's works, and to Elliott Shore, Librarian of the Institute for Advanced Study, Princeton, for some crucial last-minute help.

My greatest debt is owed to those scholars who have read and commented on the preliminary studies and earlier drafts of this book. My warmest thanks to David Armitage, Warren Boutcher, Cathy Curtis, Raymond Geuss, Susan James, Noel Malcolm, John Pocock, James Tully and Brian Vickers. They have given unstintingly of their valuable time, and have helped me not only to avoid many errors and obscurities, but also to clarify the direction of my thoughts.

I hope it will not seem invidious if I single out two names. Noel Malcolm has lent me copies over the past several years of the drafts and latterly the proofs of his *Correspondence of Thomas Hobbes.*[1] This definitive edition, which creates for the first time a solid basis for the study of Hobbes's intellectual development, has aided and shortened my own labours immeasurably. For allowing me to make use of his work so far in advance of publication, and for discussing my own work on so many occasions, I am grateful indeed. The other name I want to single out is that of Susan James, to whom I owe most of all. She has read and reread my manuscript in every successive draft, supplying me with numerous references and much indispensable help, and has given me a warmth of support and encouragement for which I can never offer adequate thanks.

I count myself very fortunate in the academic institutions with which I am associated. I never cease to learn from the students in the Faculty of History at the University of Cambridge, and I am deeply indebted to the university for its generous arrangements about sabbatical leave. Meanwhile Christ's College continues to provide excellent secretarial assistance, distinguished intellectual company and the rare benefit of a quiet room in which to work.

I have been glad of the chance to try out various aspects of my argument at several research seminars in Cambridge. My thanks to The B Club (classical philosophy) for patiently listening to me on the subject of ancient eloquence and supplying me with important corrections and references. Thanks also to Ann Barton and John Kerrigan for twice inviting me to speak to their Renaissance seminar, and for providing me on each occasion with bibliographical advice. Finally, my thanks to John Dunn for chairing an exceptionally useful discussion at the Social and Political Thought seminar, as well as for countless acts of friendship over the years.

I have been privileged to test my arguments on a number of equally helpful audiences outside my own university. First I must thank François Furet, at whose invitation I offered a *cours* on English political theory at the Institut Raymond Aron in the spring of 1987. This prompted me to return to the study of Hobbes's philosophy after a long gap, and led me to begin work on the present book.

Next I must mention the Hart Lecture in Jurisprudence, which I gave in the University of Oxford in May 1988. I learned a great deal from the accompanying seminar, an occasion genially chaired by Gerry Cohen. My lecture was on the Hobbesian idea of the state as a moral person, and I recklessly agreed to revise and publish it. When I attempted to do so, however, I found it impossible to get clear enough about the issues

[1] See Hobbes 1994 and Malcolm 1994.

involved. My discussion of Hobbes's theory of legal personality in chapters 8 and 9 embodies as much as I understand about this vital but elusive theme. I can only apologise to the electors for having failed to complete the fuller discussion I initially promised them.

I enjoyed better luck with two further lectures I delivered on Hobbes soon afterwards. I gave the annual Prothero Lecture to the Royal Historical Society in 1989,[2] and am grateful to the Society for permitting me to draw on a section of my published text in chapter 10. I am likewise grateful to the British Academy for inviting me to give the annual Dawes Hicks Lecture in Philosophy in 1990,[3] and for permission to reuse most of my published text in this book.

During November 1992 I served as Cardinal Mercier Visiting Professor at the University of Leuven. One of the lectures I presented was subsequently revised and published as a chapter in the volume I co-edited in 1993 in honour of John Pocock.[4] My thanks to Carlos Steel and the Department of Philosophy at Leuven for their munificent hospitality and memorable seminars, and to the Cambridge University Press for allowing me to incorporate parts of my chapter into the present book.

In September 1993 I contributed a seminar to the series on Proof and Persuasion at the Davis Center for Historical Studies at Princeton University, and used the occasion to surface some materials from chapters 4 and 7. I am especially indebted to Donald Kelley for his incisive commentary on my paper, to Natalie Davis for chairing the session with so much learning and enthusiasm, and to the audience as a whole for many valuable comments.

I delivered the annual F. W. Bateson Memorial Lecture in the University of Oxford in February 1994. I am very grateful to the Fellows of Corpus Christi College for this invitation, and to their President, Keith Thomas, for looking after me with characteristic generosity and panache. I am grateful too to Christopher Ricks and Stephen Wall for publishing my lecture in *Essays in Criticism*,[5] and for allowing me to reprint some of it in chapter 4. I should also like to take this opportunity of thanking Keith Thomas not just for his many kindnesses but for his inspiring example.

I am anxious to reserve a special word of thanks for the Australian National University. It was when I was a Visiting Fellow in the Humanities Research Centre in April 1989 that I first presented for discussion some of

2 See Skinner 1990b.
3 See Skinner 1991.
4 See Skinner 1993.
5 See Skinner 1994.

the themes of this book. I am much indebted to Ian Donaldson for inviting me, and for acting as such a splendid host. My thanks also to Conal Condren for helping to arrange the seminars, and for urging me to make a more systematic study of Renaissance eloquence. I returned to Canberra as a joint Fellow in the Humanities Research Centre and the Research School of Social Sciences in the summer of 1994, where I completed the final draft of the present book in ideal circumstances. My thanks to Geoffrey Brennan, Graeme Clarke and Philip Pettit for acting as equally splendid hosts, and to Conal Condren for arranging a further set of seminars in which I was able to submit some of my text to a final scrutiny.

While I have been writing this book, colleagues and fellow scholars who have become aware of my interests have helped me in many ways. Some have talked to me about my work; some have written to me with advice and criticism; some have sent me books, articles and additional references; some have helped me in all these and other ways too. My grateful thanks to Margaret Atkins, Reinhard Brandt, Annabel Brett, Glenn Burgess, Colin Burrow, Virginia Cox, Edwin Curley, George Garnett, Mark Goldie, Maurice Goldsmith, B. D. Greenslade, Lorna Hutson, Fred Inglis, Jozef Ijsewijn, James Jacob, Lisa Jardine, David Johnston, P. O. Kristeller, Melissa Lane, Joyce Malcolm, Jeremy Maule, Pasquale Pasquino, Markku Peltonen, Raia Prokhovnik, Philip Riley, Christopher Ricks, Isabel Rivers, Paolo Rossi, Paul Seaward, Dominic Scott, David Sedley, Richard Serjeantson, Johann Sommerville, Tom Sorell, A. W. Sparkes, Patricia Springborg, Richard Strier, Paul Thom, Sylvana Tomaselli, Richard Tuck, Martin Windisch and Blair Worden.

Since 1993 I have been Chair of the Faculty of History in the University of Cambridge. Nowadays such posts are far more onerous and less rewarding than they used to be, even if one happens to be blessed (as I am) with the most congenial colleagues. I could never have completed this book while helping to run so large a faculty if I had not had the good fortune to work with an office staff of exemplary dedication and resourcefulness. I should like to pay tribute in particular to Chris Banks, Mary Chalk, Shirley Gilbey and Catharine Kornicki.

No one could possibly ask for a better service than I have received from the Cambridge University Press. Amid his heavy responsibilities as managing director, Jeremy Mynott somehow found time to read sections of my manuscript and to discuss it with me in detail, as well as sustaining me – as he has done over many years – with much-needed advice and encouragement. My editor, Richard Fisher, waited patiently for my manuscript and saw it through the press with wonderful cheerfulness and efficiency, very ably assisted by Ruth Parr. Philip Riley, who meticulously proof-corrected several of my preliminary studies, brought his enviable skills to bear upon my book as well. Lastly, I am pleased to be able to add at proof stage that my text was subedited by Hilary Scannell, who expended an extraordinary amount of care and attention in identifying and sorting out a large number of last-minute difficulties.

NOTES ON THE TEXT

ABBREVIATIONS

DNB stands for *The Dictionary of National Biography*; *OED* for *The Oxford English Dictionary*. No other abbreviations are used.

BIBLIOGRAPHIES

These are simply checklists of the works actually quoted in the text, and make no pretence of being guides to the enormous literature on the themes I discuss. For those needing a conspectus of the literature on Hobbes, several guides are available. Among the most useful are Sacksteder 1982 (especially full on the English-language periodical literature) and Garcia 1986 (more up to date and with a broader linguistic coverage). But neither, of course, takes account of the unprecedented explosion of writings on Hobbes from the past decade. In the bibliography of printed primary sources I refer to anonymous works by title. Where a work was published anonymously but its author's name is known, I place the name in square brackets. The bibliography of secondary sources gives all journal numbers in arabic numerals. It contains no work published after the end of 1994.

CLASSICAL NAMES

All Greek and Roman authors are cited in their most familiar single-name form, both in the text and in the bibliographies. I invariably speak, for example, simply of Livy (not Titus Livius) and of Ovid (not Publius Ovidius Naso).

DATES

I follow my sources in dating by the Christian era. However, I do not follow the early modern English practice of beginning the year on 25 March, but treat the year as beginning on 1 January. This means that I 'redate' several well-known works. For example, the title-page of Thomas Wilson's *The Arte of Rhetorique* states that the book was published 'Anno Domini M.D.L.III. Mense Ianuarii' – that is, in January 1554 according to our style, which I accordingly treat as the date of its appearance.

GENDER

One of the central assumptions of the classical and Renaissance rhetoricians is that the figure of the good orator, whom they equate with the good citizen, is always and necessarily male. I need to stress this feature of their world, because it might otherwise seem that in my text I sometimes say 'he' when what I mean is 'he or she', an unthinkably offensive usage. The reason I am sometimes obliged to speak without qualification of 'he' is of course that the replacement of this pronoun by 'he or she' when presenting the views of the rhetoricians would have the effect of attributing to them a social theory they not only did not hold, but would I think have found almost unimaginable. The exclusion of women from the story is an important part of the story itself.

TITLES

Titles of Greek works are given in their most familiar English form (for example, I speak of Plato's *Republic* and Thucydides' *History*). All other titles are given in the original language.

TRANSCRIPTION

My general rule has been to preserve original spelling and punctuation, except where the best editions happen to be in modernised form (as is the case, for example, with Sir Thomas Elyot among prose writers and Shakespeare among poets). In addition, I have modernised the long 's', silently corrected obvious typographical errors and occasionally allowed myself to thin out capitals, italics and commas. I use 'j' as well as 'i' in English (but not 'j' in Latin), and 'v' as well as 'u' both in Latin and English. Sometimes, when fitting quotations around my own prose, I have allowed myself to change a lower case initial letter to an upper, or vice versa, as the sentence requires. When transcribing early modern Latin I have expanded all contractions, while dropping diphthongs and omitting diacritical marks. When quoting from Hobbes I very occasionally repunctuate to make clearer what I take to be the sense of difficult passages. Hobbes gives his chapter headings in arabic numerals in some of his treatises and in roman numerals in others. I have followed whichever system he uses in each particular case.

TRANSLATIONS

When quoting from the Bible I use the Authorised (or King James) translation of 1611. When quoting from classical sources, and from early modern sources in languages other than English, all translations are my own except where specifically noted. I make extensive use of the editions published in the Loeb Classical Library, all of which contain facing-page versions in English. Even in these instances, however, I have preferred to make my own translations. This is largely because the Loeb renderings are often rather free. One consequence in the case of the ancient rhetorical texts is that their technical vocabulary is sometimes obliterated. But it is essential for this vocabulary to be recovered with as much precision as possible if the views of the rhetoricians are to be fruitfully compared with those of Hobbes. I must stress, however, that I am very grateful for the availability of the Loeb editions, and have generally been guided in my own renderings by the Loeb editors, sometimes even to the extent of adopting turns of phrase. I must also underline the fact that I have made my own translations when quoting from Hobbes's *De Cive.* This is because I find it impossible to believe that the original (and highly inaccurate) English translation of 1651 was wholly or even partly Hobbes's own work, *pace* Warrender's claims to the contrary in the introduction to his critical edition of the text.[1]

1 See Warrender 1983, pp. 4–8.

INTRODUCTION

This book examines the central aspiration of Hobbes's civil philosophy, the aspiration to convert the study of moral and political theory into a scientific discipline. Hobbes emphasises in all his treatises on the nature of the state[1] that his fundamental purpose is to construct a *scientia civilis* or civil science. He first speaks in these terms in *The Elements of Law* in 1640,[2] announcing in his opening epistle that he has discovered the true and only foundations for a science of justice and policy.[3] He makes a similar claim at the start of *De Cive* in 1642, reiterating that he has demonstrated from self-evident arguments the contents of our civil duties,[4] and adding in his preface to the revised edition of 1647 that he has proved as clearly as possible the true principles of a science of justice.[5] The *Leviathan* of 1651 reaffirms that he has 'sufficiently or probably proved' the full range of the theorems relating to 'the Science of Naturall Justice',[6] while the revised Latin edition of 1668 declares once more that moral philosophy, properly understood, amounts to a *scientia* of virtue and vice.[7]

By the time Hobbes began his formal education in the 1590s, the humanists of Tudor England had already put into widespread currency a

1 On Hobbes as a theorist of the state see Skinner 1989, esp. pp. 90, 132. Cf. also Gierke 1957, pp. 60–1.

2 The standard edition of *The Elements*, originally published in 1889, was issued by Ferdinand Tönnies (see Hobbes 1969a). This uses (for good reasons) BL Harl. MS 4235 as its copy text, this being one of three surviving manuscripts signed by Hobbes. (On this mode of authentication see Malcolm 1991, p. 531 and note.) For a full list of surviving manuscripts see Tönnies 1969a, pp. viii–ix. Unfortunately Tönnies's version not only alters Hobbes's spelling and punctuation but contains numerous transcription mistakes. I have therefore preferred to quote directly from BL Harl. MS 4235, although I have added page references to Tönnies's edition. BL Harl. MS 4235 is paginated as well as foliated, but since the pagination has been cancelled I follow the foliation when giving references. The manuscript is in the hand of an unknown amanuensis, but its special authority stems from the fact that it contains many corrections and additions in Hobbes's hand, in addition to his signature ('Tho: Hobbes') at the end of the epistle dedicatory. See BL Harl. MS 4235, fo. 2^{v}, and cf. the similar signature in Chatsworth: Hobbes MS A.2.B, p. iv.

3 BL Harl. MS 4235, fo. 2^{r-v}; cf. Hobbes 1969a, pp. xv, xvi.

4 Hobbes 1983a, p. 76.

5 Hobbes 1983a, pp. 78, 81–2.

6 Hobbes 1991, p. 254.

7 Hobbes 1668, p. 79: 'Scientia autem Virtutum & Vitiorum est Philosophia Moralis.'

distinctive way of thinking about the idea of a civil science. One of my main concerns in part I of this book is to analyse this aspect of Renaissance social thought. As I seek to show, the humanists largely derived their understanding of *scientia civilis* from the classical theorists of eloquence, and above all from the opening sections of Cicero's *De inventione*, a discussion to which they endlessly returned.[8] Cicero begins by assuming that men are the *materia* of cities, and that they need to come together in a union of an honourable and mutually beneficial kind if they are to succeed in realising their highest potentialities.[9] He further assumes that, at some determinate moment, some mighty leader must have recognised this fact and taken it upon himself to mould the available human material into just such a unified shape. This leads Cicero to ask what form of *civilis ratio* or *scientia civilis* must have been possessed by such founding fathers or artificers of cities. He stresses that they must of course have been men of reason and thus of wisdom. But he insists that they must at the same time have been masters of eloquence. 'Wisdom in itself is silent and powerless to speak', so that 'wisdom without eloquence cannot do the least good for cities'.[10] We can thus be sure that 'cities were originally established not merely by the *ratio* of the mind, but also, and more readily, by means of *eloquentia*'.[11] Cicero's conclusion is therefore that there are two indispensable components to the idea of *scientia civilis*. One is reason, the faculty that enables us to uncover the truth. The other is rhetoric, the art that enables us to present the truth with eloquence. The need for rhetoric stems from the fact that, as Cicero repeatedly emphasises, reason lacks any inherent capacity to persuade us of the truths it brings to light. This is why the persuasive force of eloquence must always be added if reason is to be empowered and given effect. 'A large and crucial part' of *scientia civilis* must therefore be occupied by 'that form of artistic eloquence which is generally known as rhetoric, the function of which is that of speaking in a manner calculated to persuade, and the goal of which is that of persuading by speech'.[12]

Hobbes's early published writings reveal a deep absorption in the

8 On reason and eloquence in Cicero see Michel 1960. On the recovery of Cicero's ideal in the Renaissance see Seigel 1968, esp. pp. 176–9, 222–4, 259–60; Skinner 1978, I, pp. 86–7; Vickers 1989, esp. pp. 254–93. On the presumed break between Medieval and Renaissance rhetoric see Murphy 1974, pp. 357–62; for some doubts see Nederman 1992.

9 Cicero 1949a, I.I.I, pp. 4, 6.

10 See Cicero 1949a, I.II.3, p. 6, on *sapientia* as 'tacita' and 'inops dicendi', and cf. I.I.I, p. 2, on how 'sine eloquentia parum prodesse civitatibus'.

11 Cicero 1949a, I.I.I, p. 2: 'urbes constitutas . . . cum animi ratione tum facilius eloquentia'.

12 See Cicero 1949a, I.V.6, p. 14, on 'civilis scientia'; on the fact that 'Eius quaedam magna et ampla pars est artificiosa eloquentia quam rhetoricam vocant'; and that 'Officium autem eius facultatis videtur esse dicere apposite ad persuasionem; finis persuadere dictione.'

rhetorical culture of Renaissance humanism.[13] This is the first claim I attempt to substantiate (chapter 6) when I turn to consider the evolution of Hobbes's thought in part II of this book. As I argue in chapters 7 and 8, however, as soon as Hobbes addressed himself to the topic of *scientia civilis* in the late 1630s he proceeded to pull up his own humanist roots. One of his principal aims in *The Elements* and *De Cive* is to discredit and replace the Renaissance ideal of a union between reason and rhetoric, and hence between science and eloquence. This ambition is reflected with particular clarity in *The Elements*, in which Hobbes prefaces his political arguments with a sketch of his general philosophy. He maintains that, so long as we reason aright from premises based in experience, we shall be able not merely to arrive at scientific truths, but to teach and beget in others exactly the same conceptions as we possess ourselves. He denies, however, that it will ever be necessary to employ the arts of persuasion to bring about these results. He insists that persuasion must be categorically distinguished from teaching, and that the arts of persuasion have no legitimate place in the process of teaching at all. This is because the methods of *recta ratio*, and hence the procedures of all the genuine sciences, serve in themselves to dictate the acceptance of the truths they find out. They supply us with demonstrations evident to the meanest capacity, giving rise to conclusions that admit of no controversy and cannot possibly be gainsaid.[14]

If we turn from these pronouncements of 1640 to the *Leviathan* of 1651, we encounter a remarkable change of mind – a change of mind later consolidated and even extended in the Latin *Leviathan* in 1668.[15] Hobbes now endorses in large measure the humanist analysis of the relations between reason and rhetoric which he had earlier sought to challenge and supersede. He acknowledges that 'the Sciences are small Power', and

13 The relevance of this background is valuably emphasised in Strauss 1963, esp. pp. 30–43, and Reik 1977, esp. pp. 25–34. Recent commentators who have taken up the point include Johnston 1986, pp. 3–25; Tuck 1989, pp. 1–11 (see also Tuck 1993, pp. 279–83), and Schuhmann 1990, pp. 332–6.

14 Hobbes 1969a, esp. pp. 64–7. For a preliminary attempt to sketch this phase of Hobbes's intellectual development see Skinner 1993. Cf. also the valuable chapter in Johnston 1986, pp. 26–65.

15 Hobbes's commentators have paid almost no attention to the fact – and especially the implications of the fact – that the Latin version of *Leviathan* published in 1668 embodies extensive revisions of the English text. As I seek to show in chapters 9 and 10, *Leviathan* in its Latin form is at some points an even more rhetorical text. But it also reveals a pattern of deletions clearly motivated by Hobbes's sense that he had previously gone too far in satirising various religious beliefs. This latter point is of considerable importance in relation to the increasing prevalence of unduly literal-minded readings of *Leviathan* books III and IV. The one scholar who has made a systematic study of the differences between 'the two *Leviathans*' is François Tricaud. See Tricaud 1971, pp. xvi–xxix. I cannot accept Tricaud's thesis that the Latin version formed Hobbes's original draft, but the comparisons he offers are of great value and interest.

cannot hope in themselves to persuade us of the findings they enunciate.[16] He accepts in consequence that, if reason is to prevail, we shall need to supplement and enforce its findings by means of the rhetorical arts.[17] Finally, and most dramatically, he proceeds to practise his own precepts in the body of his texts.[18] The outcome is astonishingly different from the self-consciously scientific austerities of *The Elements* and *De Cive.* The *Leviathan* constitutes a belated but magnificent contribution to the Renaissance art of eloquence – a treatise in which the persuasive techniques of the classical *ars rhetorica* are systematically put to work to amplify and underline the findings of reason and science. The closing two chapters of this book examine these developments, while the conclusion turns to ask what might have prompted Hobbes to change his mind, and in doing so draws on the explanation he himself suggests in *Behemoth,* the history of the civil wars which he completed towards the end of the 1660s.[19]

Hobbes's conception of *scientia civilis* has often been presented as if it constitutes a straightforward application of his views about the character of the natural sciences.[20] This is certainly a plausible way of reading his initial account of what he calls the four steps of science in chapter 6 of *The Elements*, in which he makes no distinction between different types of scientific investigation.[21] As a number of commentators have recently emphasised, however, Hobbes later points to several differences between the methods appropriate to the natural and to the human sciences. He already stresses one distinction at the outset of his Latin manuscript treatise on optics, which he appears to have completed around the time when he was working on *The*

16 Hobbes 1991, p. 63, and cf. pp. 483–4.

17 Hobbes 1991, pp. 483–4.

18 Mathie 1986, p. 282, rightly remarks: 'That the form and even content of *Leviathan* could reflect its author's rhetorical, as well as philosophical purpose is a suggestion frequently advanced but rarely pursued.' I am grateful to Mathie for this observation (and for the title of his article) and try in chapter 10 to pursue the point.

19 The standard edition of *Behemoth* was published by Ferdinand Tönnies in 1889 and reissued in 1969 (see Hobbes 1969b). As his copy text Tönnies used Hobbes's own revised manuscript copy, which is preserved at St John's College Oxford. (See St John's College MS 13 and cf. Tönnies 1969b, pp. ix–x.) Unfortunately – as in his edition of *The Elements of Law* – Tönnies (or his amanuensis) not only altered Hobbes's spelling and punctuation but made numerous transcription mistakes. When citing from *Behemoth* I have therefore preferred to quote directly from the St John's manuscript, although I have added page references to Tönnies's edition. The St John's manuscript has recently been foliated, but it was originally – and still is – paginated. I have followed the original pagination when giving references. The manuscript is in the hand of James Wheldon (or Weldon or Whildon), Hobbes's last amanuensis. On Wheldon see Skinner 1965a, pp. 213–14; on the date of *Behemoth* see Tönnies 1969b, p. vii.

20 Watkins 1965, esp. pp. 66–81; Goldsmith 1966, esp. pp. 228–42; Gauthier 1969, pp. 1–5; Herbert 1989, pp. 21–3, 178–82. For a discussion see Rossini 1988, esp. pp. 204–9; for an excellent critique see Sorell 1986, esp. pp. 4–13.

21 On the '4 stepps' see BL Harl. MS 4235, fo. 25^{v} and cf. Hobbes 1969a, pp. 25–6.

Elements.[22] The manuscript argues that, whereas in civil science it is sufficient to possess a knowledge of definitions and their consequences, in the natural sciences it is necessary in addition to work with hypotheses.[23] A further distinction is introduced in the preface to the 1647 edition of *De Cive.* There we are told that, while the natural sciences are purely mechanistic and anti-teleological in procedure, the artificial bodies investigated by civil scientists are such that it remains inescapable to consider in addition the purposes for which they are brought into existence.[24]

One way of summarising my argument in part II of this book would be to say that I have tried to carry this discussion a stage further. I have tried, that is, to highlight a further sense in which Hobbes eventually distinguished between the methods of the natural and the moral sciences. By the time he came to publish *Leviathan* in 1651, he had arrived at the conclusion that, in the moral but not in the natural sciences, the methods of demonstrative reasoning need to be supplemented by the moving force of eloquence.[25] As I have intimated, this prompted him not merely to give a new account of his theoretical principles but to put them systematically into practice. The outcome, as I seek to show in discussing the rhetorical character of *Leviathan* in chapter 10, is a work in which the humanist ideal of a union between reason and rhetoric is not merely defended but systematically realised.

Having spoken of *Leviathan* as a work of rhetoric, I need to add a word about my use of that much-abused term. There has recently been a great deal of talk about 'the rhetoric of the human sciences'. John S. Nelson and others have edited a collection under that name,[26] while David Johnston has published an important book entitled *The Rhetoric of Leviathan.*[27] This

22 BL Harl. MS 6796, fos. 193^{r}–266^{v}, a Latin treatise in four chapters dealing with light, refractions, convex and concave figures and vision. Brandt 1928, pp. 93–7, and Shapiro 1973, p. 168, both date this manuscript to the mid-1640s, but Tönnies had earlier argued that it 'was written immediately after the first appearance of Descartes' *Dioptrique* in 1637' (see Tönnies 1969a, pp. xii–xiii). Richard Tuck (in Tuck 1988b, pp. 19–27) and Noel Malcolm (in Hobbes 1994, pp. liii–lv and p. 60, note 4) adduce important evidence in favour of an early date. Malcolm has established that the BL copy was made for Sir Charles Cavendish in March 1640. But if we assume that Hobbes completed the manuscript before writing chapter 6 of *The Elements*, it seems strange that *The Elements* makes no use of the important distinction drawn in the manuscript between two different types of science, and instead treats the so-called steps of science in an undifferentiated way. This leads me tentatively to suggest that the early chapters of *The Elements* must have been completed before the writing of the manuscript, and thus to date the latter (following Malcolm in Hobbes 1994, p. liv) specifically to 1640.

23 BL Harl. MS 6796, fo. 193^{r}.

24 Hobbes 1983a, 'Praefatio ad Lectores', pp. 79–80. This distinction is excellently analysed in Malcolm 1990, esp. pp. 148–52.

25 For his most explicit statement see Hobbes 1991, pp. 483–4.

26 Nelson *et al.* 1987. For a discussion of their sense of 'rhetoric' see Munz 1990, esp. pp. 121–2, 126–7.

27 Johnston 1986.

being so, I need to make it clear that my use of the term differs significantly from that of these commentators and the many others who have followed in their wake. When Johnston speaks of Hobbes's rhetoric, he employs the word principally to refer to Hobbes's literary strategies, and more particularly to ask what specific political act Hobbes may have been performing in *Leviathan*.[28] The contributors to Nelson's collection similarly apply the term to describe the various styles of presentation cultivated in the human sciences, especially by those aiming to lend them a spurious or exaggerated air of significance.[29] By contrast, when I speak of Hobbes's rhetoric in *Leviathan* I employ the word in the way that Hobbes himself would I believe have understood it. I use it, that is, to describe a distinctive set of linguistic techniques – those outlined in chapters 4 and 5 – derived from the rhetorical doctrines of *inventio*, *dispositio* and *elocutio*, the three principal *elementa* in classical and Renaissance theories of written eloquence.

It seems important to stress this difference, if only to avoid some increasingly prevalent confusions and ambiguities. Several scholars have recently argued, for example, that in England during the early 1640s the hegemony of common law was replaced by 'a system of discourse that was fundamentally rhetorical and polemical in character', so that even the common law itself became 'one of a variety of rhetorical modes'.[30] If the term 'rhetorical' is being used here to mean something other than would have been understood by the political writers of the time, then I am not sure what is being claimed. But if it is being used as they would have understood it, then the claim is straightforwardly false. To mention only the most obvious counter-example, Hobbes's *De Cive* is arguably the most important work of political theory of the early 1640s, but it is as violently anti-rhetorical a text as Hobbes was capable of making it.

As these observations suggest, my aim in this book is to situate Hobbes's theory and practice of civil science within the intellectual context in which it was formed. I am less interested in Hobbes as the author of a philosophical system than in his role as a contributor to a series of debates about the moral sciences within Renaissance culture.

28 See Johnston 1986, pp. ix, 91, and pp. 128–33, 209–13. I need to stress at the outset, however, that Johnston's book is of exceptional value, and that I am greatly indebted to it. For similarly broad uses of 'rhetoric' in the discussion of Hobbes's thought see Kahn 1985, esp. pp. 157–8, 161; Sorell 1988, esp. pp. 68, 79; Sorell 1990a, esp. pp. 99–104; Cantalupo 1991, esp. pp. 15–24. For a valuable analysis of such usages see Condren 1990, esp. pp. 705–7.

29 See Nelson *et al.* 1987, esp. chapter 6 (pp. 87–110), chapter 10 (pp. 163–83) and chapter 12 (pp. 198–220). This is largely true also of the contributors to part I of Coorebyter 1994. Several contributors to part II of this collection, however, are also interested in the art of rhetoric in its technical sense.

30 Burgess 1992, pp. 224, 225. Cf. also Burgess 1991, p. 67, and Cantalupo 1991, pp. 95–6.

Hobbes has traditionally been portrayed as a lonely eminence, a thinker 'without ancestry or posterity'.[31] Recently, however, there has been a growing disposition to question this assumption, and to try instead to connect his philosophy with his times. Among the present generation of commentators, this process began with the attempt to relate his theory of obligation to the constitutional upheavals of mid-seventeenth-century England.[32] More recently, the effort to contextualise his thought has broadened out to embrace the study of his relationship with scholastic debates about natural law and subjective right,[33] with theological debates about voluntarism and ecclesiology,[34] with methodological debates about the character of the natural sciences,[35] and so forth. I greatly welcome the growing popularity of this approach, and continue to hope that it may eventually become the dominant style in the writing of intellectual history. Meanwhile I have sought to carry it a stage further in the case of Hobbes by offering a contextual account of what I take to be the central concept in his political theory, that of civil science itself.[36]

My argument may thus be said to exemplify a particular approach to the study and interpretation of historical texts. The essence of my method consists in trying to place such texts within such contexts as enable us in turn to identify what their authors[37] were *doing* in writing them.[38] As this implies, I mark a strong distinction between what I take to be two distinguishable dimensions of language. One has conventionally been described as the dimension of meaning, the study of the sense and reference allegedly attaching to words and sentences. The other is best described as the dimension of linguistic action, the study of the range of things that speakers are capable of doing in (and by) their use of words and

31 Trevor-Roper 1957, p. 236.

32 See the pioneering studies of Zagorin 1954, Thomas 1965 and Wallace 1968. I attempted to contribute to this development myself. See Skinner 1964, 1965a, 1965b, 1966a, 1972a and 1972b. I reverted to the topic in Skinner 1988b and 1990b. For other recent studies in a comparable idiom see Baumgold 1988, Metzger 1991, Sommerville 1992. For recent studies of Hobbes and the crisis of 1649 see Burgess 1990 and Goldsmith 1990.

33 See Tuck 1979, Tully 1981 and the conclusion to Brett 1994.

34 On voluntarism see Damrosch 1979, Malcolm 1983, Martinich 1992; on ecclesiology see Pocock 1971, pp. 148–201, Springborg 1975, Eisenach 1982, Whitaker 1988.

35 See Pacchi 1965; Shapin and Schaffer 1985; Sorell 1986, esp. pp. 14–28; Malcolm 1988 and 1990. Cf. also Brandt 1928, a remarkable pioneering work.

36 I am indebted, however, to earlier discussions of Hobbes's conception of a science of politics in Goldsmith 1966 and Sorell 1986.

37 I deliberately cleave to this traditional term, although I sympathise with those who wish to avoid it. Cf. Skinner 1988a, esp. pp. 276–7.

38 For an exposition and defence of this approach see Skinner 1988a, esp. pp. 259–88. I find unrecognisable the position ascribed to me and other so-called 'contextualists' in Lloyd 1992, p. 323. For an important recent defence of an approach similar to my own see Tully 1993, esp. the introduction, pp. 1–6. I should add that I have been greatly influenced by Tully's recent work.

sentences. Traditional hermeneutics has generally, and often exclusively, concentrated on the first of these dimensions; I concentrate very much on the second.[39] I attempt to take seriously the implications of the fact that, as Wittgenstein puts it in *Philosophical Investigations*, 'Words are also deeds.'[40]

What this means in practice is that I treat Hobbes's claims about *scientia civilis* not simply as propositions but as moves in an argument. I try to indicate what traditions he reacts against, what lines of argument he takes up, what changes he introduces into existing debates. This undoubtedly has the effect (to cite the fashionable jargon) of de-centring Hobbes, of questioning his standing as the author of an original and eponymous system of thought. But it is not my aim to bring about his death as an author by drowning him in an ocean of discourse. It is true that I see his view of civil philosophy as largely formed by the language of Renaissance discussions about the nature of the moral sciences. Furthermore, I see no prospect of understanding his thought unless we treat this wider discourse as the primary object of our research. My eventual aim, however, is to return to Hobbes's texts armed with the kind of historical information I regard as indispensable for making sense of them.

The reader may well ask, however, about the value of my approach in the present case. What new insights into Hobbes's civil philosophy does it yield? What existing interpretations does it help us to challenge or supplement?

I should like to end these prefatory remarks by outlining three connected answers, each of which will be taken up at greater length in the body of this book. My first answer I have already indicated: I am able to show how far Hobbes's conception of *scientia civilis* was shaped at all times by his changing reactions to the assumptions and vocabulary of classical and neo-Ciceronian theories of eloquence.[41] This contention can be rephrased, moreover, in a form that gives it a certain polemical edge. An increasing number of commentators have been arguing that Hobbes's major point of reference in working out his civil philosophy was furnished

39 This is not of course to say that I fail to enquire into the meanings of texts and the ambiguities attendant on our attempts to recover and interpret them. It is only to say that a further and discriminable aspect of the hermeneutic enterprise strikes me as having no less importance.

40 Wittgenstein 1958, para. 546, p. 146e.

41 This explains why part I is devoted to the Renaissance revival of the *ars rhetorica* and its teaching in the grammar schools of Hobbes's youth. I hope that these chapters may be of interest to literary scholars, especially as the kind of survey I offer is not, so far as I am aware, available in the literature. (Although some excellent introductions to the *ars rhetorica* in the Renaissance have recently appeared: see Monfasani 1988, Vickers 1989 and Rhodes 1992, pp. 3–65 – the discussion closest to my own concerns.) I am aware, however, that these opening chapters may appear irrelevant to students of Hobbes's philosophy. Perhaps the most important point I am trying to make is that such a reaction would be a mistake.

by the rise of Pyrrhonism in the closing decades of the sixteenth century.[42] It was in the light of his ambiguous feelings about this current of 'sceptical relativism', we are told, that Hobbes worked out his basic principles.[43] I see little evidence, however, that Hobbes was much interested in Pyrrhonism – to say nothing of relativism – in any of his treatises on civil science.[44] He was not primarily responding to a set of epistemological arguments. Rather he was reacting against the entire rhetorical culture of Renaissance humanism within which the vogue for scepticism had developed. Nor was he greatly concerned with the technical claims put forward by self-avowed sceptics, whether of a Pyrrhonian or an Academic stamp.[45] Rather he was seeking to overcome a more generally questioning and anti-demonstrative approach to moral argument encouraged by the emphasis placed by the culture of humanism on the *ars rhetorica,* with its characteristic insistence that there will always be two sides to any question, and thus that in moral and political reasoning it will always be possible to construct a plausible argument *in utramque partem,* on either side of the case.[46]

It was this approach to moral argument which had prompted the classical theorists of eloquence to make a symbolic hero out of the figure of Carneades. Cicero in his *De oratore* and Quintilian in his *Institutio oratoria* both speak of Carneades as a man of famous and surpassing rhetorical powers.[47] Cicero is of course interested in Carneades as a representative of Academic scepticism as well.[48] But his reason for referring to Carneades so admiringly in his rhetorical works – as with Quintilian after him – has little connection with Carneades' epistemological beliefs. Rather his admiration flows from the fact that Carneades managed on a famous occasion to argue convincingly in favour of justice on one day and no less convincingly

42 For pioneering studies see Battista 1966, Popkin 1979. For a list of Popkin's contributions see Watson and Force 1988, pp. 151–62. But Popkin thinks of Hobbes less as replying to scepticism than as impervious to it. See esp. Popkin 1982.

43 For the alleged influence of epistemological scepticism on the development of Hobbes's thought see Pacchi 1965, esp. pp. 63–9, 97–100, 179–83; Battista 1966, esp. pp. 22, 53, 135, 145, 172–5. The argument has been elevated into an orthodoxy by more recent commentators. See Battista 1980; Missner 1983; Sarasohn 1985; Kahn 1985, esp. pp. 154, 181; Sorell 1986, esp. pp. 63–7; Tuck 1988a and Tuck 1989, esp. pp. 64, 93, 102 (and cf. Tuck 1993, pp. 285–98); Hampsher-Monk 1992, esp. pp. 4–6; Hanson 1993, esp. pp. 644–5; Flathman 1993, pp. 2–3, 43–7, 51–2.

44 This doubt is well explored in Sommerville 1992, esp. pp. 168–70, and Zagorin 1993, esp. pp. 512–18.

45 Note that, until the latter part of the sixteenth century, the debate about scepticism centred on Academic rather than Pyrrhonian themes. See Schmitt 1972, esp. pp. 58–9 and 73–4.

46 For preliminary attempts to argue aspects of this case, see Skinner 1991, 1993 and 1994. On the importance of reasoning *in utramque partem* in Cicero see Michel 1960, pp. 158–73.

47 See Cicero 1942a, I.XI.46, p. 34 and Quintilian 1920–2, XII.I.35, vol. IV, p. 374.

48 But we must not connect the Renaissance revival of Ciceronian rhetoric too closely even with Academic scepticism. See Monfasani 1990.

against it on the day following. He thereby demonstrated that, even when discussing the virtues, it will always be possible to uphold the central contention of rhetorical theory, the contention that there are two sides to every question, and thus that one can always argue *in utramque partem.*[49]

My thesis is that, when Hobbes first developed his views about *scientia civilis* in the late 1630s, it was above all against this humanist cast of thought that he sought to define himself and his project. He sought in particular to rescue the concept of justice from the position of jeopardy in which, he believed, the rhetoricians had left it by turning it into a subject of debate. He aimed to challenge their dialogical approach to moral and political reasoning and to replace it with a fully demonstrative civil science.

Once we see this much, we can hope to return to Hobbes's early treatises with a better prospect of understanding a number of their specific arguments. There is a certain polemical value in stressing this point as well, if only because of the widespread tendency to insist that the interpretation of Hobbes's texts and the study of their historical contexts are alternative undertakings, and that we can perfectly well choose to follow one approach rather than the other.[50] I try to demonstrate, by contrast, that there are many elements in Hobbes's science of politics that we have no hope of explicating unless we pay attention to the circumstances out of which they arose.

Consider, for example, Hobbes's views about the concept of citizenship. To raise only the most obvious question, what is the significance of the fact that his earliest published treatise on civil science is entitled *De Cive*, 'The citizen'? The answer lies in grasping what I describe in chapter 2 as the politics of eloquence. The ideal of a rhetorical education became associated in Renaissance England with the aspiration to foster a broader and more inclusive approach to citizenship and civic involvement. To understand Hobbes's views about the duties of the *bonus civis,* we need to recognise the extent to which they are put forward as a hostile commentary on humanist efforts to promote the study of rhetoric as a training for public life.

Consider, similarly, the significance of the fact that Hobbes treats it as one of the chief barriers to the construction of a civil science that, as he observes in chapter 5 of *The Elements*, we find 'scarce two men agreeing, what is to be called good, and what evill, what Liberality, what

49 See Quintilian 1920–2, XII.I.35, vol. IV, p. 374.

50 The contention is well discussed in Baumgold 1988, pp. 15–20 and Martinich 1992, pp. 11–13. For the contention itself see Warrender 1957, esp. pp. viii–ix, and, more recently, Kavka 1986, pp. xiii–xiv; Lloyd 1992, pp. 3–4.

Prodigallity, what Valour, what Temerity'.[51] As I argue in chapter 4, what is especially revealing about this passage is Hobbes's choice of examples. They disclose that what he has in mind at this crucial juncture is the use of a specific rhetorical technique – that of rhetorical redescription – to exacerbate the problems inherent in winning agreement about the right descriptions of moral actions and states of affairs. Once again, our understanding of the way in which Hobbes lays out his argument depends on seeing that he is responding to a problem set by the neo-Ciceronian theory of eloquence.

My investigation of the context in which Hobbes developed his civil science culminates in a particular thesis about what he took himself to have 'demonstrated' about our common life. Hobbes's overriding concern, as he repeatedly reminds us, is to secure peace. What he has demonstrated, he claims, is that the cause of peace is best served by a steady commitment to justice and the full range of the other social virtues. We not only need to act virtuously, but to cultivate a certain kind of virtuous character. Although Hobbes is often portrayed as the creator of an egoistic[52] or a contractarian[53] type of moral theory, I seek in chapters 8 and 9 to argue a strongly contrasting case: that Hobbes is essentially a theorist of the virtues, whose civil science centres on the claim that the avoidance of the vices and the maintenance of the social virtues are indispensable to the preservation of peace.[54] This, I argue, is the position Hobbes takes himself to have proved scientifically, and this in turn explains why he thinks of moral philosophy as 'the science of Vertue and Vice' and more specifically as 'the Science of what is *Good* and *Evill* in the Conversation and Society of man-kind'.[55]

I turn to my second claim about the value of my approach. By concentrating on Hobbes's shifting involvement with humanism, I am able to establish a particular view of his intellectual development. As I have already intimated, this narrative may be said to embody three main episodes. First Hobbes imbibed from his early education a rhetorical understanding of *scientia civilis*; next he devoted himself to repudiating exactly this approach; later he came round to endorsing the very approach

51 BL Harl. MS 4235, fo. 24^r. Cf. Hobbes 1969a, p. 23.

52 Most recently in Kavka 1986, esp. pp. 64–80.

53 For example in Gauthier 1969. I must emphasise, however, that Gauthier's study is extraordinarily perceptive; although his approach is very different from mine, I have learned a great deal from his work.

54 Hobbes's standing as a theorist of the virtues has been recognised in several recent studies. See Sorell 1986, esp. pp. 2–3, 105–8; Boonin-Vail 1994, esp. pp. 106–23, 178–87. Boonin-Vail generously acknowledges (p. 114n.) that I attempted to sketch a similar argument in Skinner 1991. I in turn have learned a great deal from his development of the case.

55 Hobbes 1991, pp. 110–11.

he had earlier repudiated. His final attitude towards the culture of humanism in *Leviathan* reflects a desire to reappropriate much of what he had earlier cast aside.[56]

The significance of these findings is that they too call for a number of modifications to be made to a widely accepted picture of Hobbes's thought. One common assumption has been that, although Hobbes articulated his civil philosophy in several different treatises, his political theory remains 'substantially the same' or 'almost exactly the same', with the changes between its earlier and later versions being 'relatively minor' and 'of secondary importance'.[57] I seek to show, on the contrary, that in his conception of civil science itself – and thus at the core of his civil philosophy – Hobbes presents us not with two different versions of the same theory, but with two different and indeed antithetical theories, as well as with two correspondingly antithetical models of philosophical style.

Another familiar claim has been that, after passing through 'a humanist period' in his youth, Hobbes became 'less and less interested' in 'the formal study of rhetoric' as he became more and more a convert to the cause of science and an opponent of the purely literary culture of humanism.[58] As I try to demonstrate, there is a case for saying that Hobbes became more and more interested in the formal study of rhetoric, and that the composition of *Leviathan* represents the apogee not merely of his theoretical commitment to the *ars rhetorica* but of his willingness to put its precepts into practice. This is not to say (as some have done)[59] that Hobbes's mature statement of his civil philosophy was designed less as a scientific treatise than as a work of rhetoric.[60] It is rather to say that, having initially abandoned rhetoric in favour of science, he eventually sought to found his civil science on combining them.[61]

These considerations bring me to my third and last claim about the value of my approach. By focusing on Hobbes's eventual *rapprochement* with

56 I am very much in agreement with Johnston's account of Hobbes's shifting involvement with the art of rhetoric in Johnston 1986, pp. 24–7, 56–62, 66–7.

57 For these claims see respectively Tuck 1989, p. 28; Raphael 1977, p. 13; Rogow 1986, p. 126; Warrender 1957, p. viii. For similar suggestions see Hampton 1986, p. 5; Baumgold 1988, pp. 3, 11.

58 This argument has come to be associated in particular with Leo Strauss. See Johnston 1986, p. 23 and note, citing Strauss's view. For Strauss's own statement see Strauss 1963, esp. pp. 138–9, 151–70. For discussions see Gray 1978, esp. pp. 205–15, and Rossini 1987, esp. pp. 305–6.

59 For example Taylor 1965, esp. p. 35; Schoneveld 1987.

60 Johnston sometimes seems to incline to this view. See Johnston 1986, p. 91. But for a different emphasis cf. Johnston 1986, p. 67.

61 Hobbes's eventual use of rhetoric to support science has been well discussed in Kahn 1985, esp. pp. 157–8, 177–8, 180–1; Johnston 1986, esp. pp. 66–71; Sorell 1986, pp. 133–7; Prokhovnik 1991, esp. pp. 195–222.

neo-classical theories of eloquence, I am able to provide a new analysis of the rhetorical characteristics of *Leviathan*. I am able, in particular, to point to Hobbes's systematic reliance on the techniques of *ornatus*, and to uncover the purposes for the sake of which he is interested in creating these rhetorical effects. These purposes, I further argue, were largely satirical in character, and help to explain Hobbes's revealing fascination with the phenomenon of laughter and the question of how to provoke it.[62] Hobbes has generally been aligned with such contemporary metaphysicians as Mersenne and Descartes, or placed in a tradition of English empiricism running from Bacon to Locke and Hume. One of the implications of my argument is that Hobbes can be placed with no less justice in a tradition running from Erasmus and More to Rabelais, Montaigne and other Renaissance satirists who dealt with their intellectual adversaries less by arguing with them than by ridiculing their absurdities.

This final point can also be given a polemical edge. Despite the frequency with which commentators have complained about the difficulties and confusions in *Leviathan*, they have generally taken it for granted that, once these are cleared out of the way, we shall be left with a plain and perspicuous text.[63] The possibility that *Leviathan* may be replete with rhetorical codes has scarcely been entertained, and has even been explicitly denied.[64] I attempt to show, however, that to think of Hobbes's prose as a clear window through which we can gaze uninterruptedly at his thought is a serious mistake. Hobbes's thought in *Leviathan* is mediated by a prose in which the techniques of *ornatus* are used to produce a large number of deliberately ambiguous effects. To fail to recognise this fact is to fail to recognise what kind of a work we have in our hands.[65]

It might still be asked whether this really matters. No doubt *Leviathan* is the product of an unfamiliar literary culture, and no doubt it is regrettable that so many of us have shown such insensitivity to the work's literary qualities. But has our ignorance betrayed us into interpreting any of its doctrines in an identifiably erroneous way?

This is not the sort of question to which one can expect a knock-down answer on either side. As I suggest in chapter 10, however, lack of attention to Hobbes's rhetorical strategies has arguably given rise to a number of over-simplified interpretations of his religious beliefs, especially his beliefs

62 Cf. Cantalupo 1991, p. 23.

63 For a recent and strong statement to this effect see Martinich 1992, pp. 15–16. Cf. Adolph 1968, pp. 191, 231–7, for whom Hobbes is an exponent of the so-called new Plain Style.

64 See Hood 1964, p. vii, and Martinich 1992, p. 16, both denying that irony plays any part in Hobbes's interpretation of scripture.

65 This point is excellently made in Condren 1990. See also the valuable observations in Lanham 1976, esp. pp. 33–5, and Kahn 1985, esp. p. 11.

about the veracity of the Bible and the mysteries of the Christian faith. Recent commentators have shown a growing willingness to accept that Hobbes's pronouncements on these matters reveal him not merely to be 'essentially a sincere writer', but 'a Christian of a genuine if eccentric kind'.[66] It is hard to sustain this confidence in the face of the discovery that, when discussing these issues, Hobbes makes systematic use of the various devices specifically recommended by the theorists of eloquence for contriving a tone of irony and ridicule. Hobbes's contemporaries frequently voiced their disquiet at his studied equivocations, as well as their outrage at his skill in using them to evade the charge of speaking with outright scepticism and mockery. It is worth asking whether they may not have been nearer the mark than those modern and literal-minded interpreters who have concentrated on what Hobbes *says* about such topics as the Christian mysteries without paying any attention to his tone and manner of saying it.[67] While assuring themselves that there are no hidden codes to ensnare them, they have, I think, become ensnared in exactly the way that Hobbes intended.[68]

I hope that these reflections may encourage others to reconsider the literary character of further works of early modern social and political philosophy. I say this not because I wish to encourage intellectual historians to work to a greater extent 'across the divide' between literary and other historical texts, but rather because I disbelieve in any such divide. The canon of leading treatises in the history of philosophy is at the same time a canon of major literary texts. Due in part, no doubt, to the influence of Derrida and his followers, this claim is rapidly becoming the commonplace it has always deserved to be,[69] and important work is now being done on the literary conventions in the light of which the major treatises of early modern philosophy were put together.[70] But it remains worth emphasising how much we still need to learn as historians of

66 See Hood 1964, p. vii and Curley 1988, p. 498. Curley powerfully contests this new orthodoxy, prefacing his argument with a list of Hobbes scholars who have espoused it. See Curley 1988, pp. 498–9, note 4. To Curley's list must now be added Lloyd 1992 and, above all, Martinich 1992, esp. pp. 1–2, 336.

67 Martinich 1992, p. 16, makes it his guiding assumption that, in discussing these issues, we can take it that 'for the most part Hobbes meant what he said'.

68 This constitutes my response to the appendix ('Skinner on Hobbes') in Martinich 1992, pp. 354–61, in which I am criticised for suggesting that the reactions of Hobbes's contemporaries might be relevant to the assessment of his thought.

69 See the helpful discussions in Sharpe 1987, pp. ix–xi and Sharpe 1989, esp. pp. 4–9 (although the characterisation of my own views in the latter discussion contains some inaccuracies). Cf. the attempt to apply these considerations specifically to *Leviathan* in Cantalupo 1991, esp. pp. 15–17.

70 See France 1972 (esp. pp. 40–67) and Carr 1990 (esp. pp. 26–61) on Descartes; Walmsley 1990 on Berkeley; Box 1990 on Hume.

philosophy from the disciplines of literary history and literary criticism. While this is a point I have frequently tried to make in general terms,[71] my aim in this present book is to try, perhaps somewhat belatedly, to practise what I preach.

I should like to end by responding to a common line of attack on the sort of approach I have now sketched. I am accused of reducing Hobbes to a figure of merely antiquarian interest, thereby robbing the study of his thought of any philosophical point.[72] Part of my purpose is of course to challenge the depressingly philistine view of historical enquiry presupposed by this line of argument. I am unrepentant in believing that the attempt to gain acquaintance with Hobbes's intellectual world is an undertaking of far greater interest than the attempt to use his texts as a mirror to reflect back at ourselves our current assumptions and prejudices. One reason is simply that, as I hope to illustrate, Hobbes's world is so rich and strange that, if we turn to it merely for answers to our own questions, we shall needlessly impoverish our own intellectual lives. A further reason is that, if we allow ourselves to approach the past with a less importunate sense of 'relevance', we may find our studies taking on a relevance of a different and more authentic kind. We may find, in particular, that the acquisition of an historical perspective helps us to stand back from some of our current assumptions and habits of thought, and perhaps even to reconsider them. The study of the past need not be any the less instructive when it uncovers contrasts rather than continuities with the present.

One such contrast forms the underlying theme of this book. I have tried to highlight the divisions between three rival views about the character of moral and political argument. First there is the view that Hobbes initially defended: that our aim should be to argue deductively in such a way that any rational person who accepts our premises will feel compelled to endorse the conclusions we derive from them. Next there is the view towards which Hobbes eventually inclined: that, even if it is possible to argue deductively about moral and political principles, our arguments will never be persuasive unless we enforce them with the arts of eloquence. Finally, there is the still more rhetorically minded view associated with Renaissance humanism: that our watchword ought to be *audi alteram partem*, always listen to the other side. This commitment stems from the belief that, in moral and political debate, it will always be possible to speak *in utramque partem*, and will never be possible to couch our moral or political theories in deductive form. The appropriate model will always be that of a dialogue, the appropriate stance a willingness to negotiate over rival

71 See Skinner 1966b, esp. pp. 214–15, and Skinner 1988b, esp. pp. 130–2.

72 See Warrender 1979, esp. p. 939, and further examples cited in Skinner 1988a, p. 286.

intuitions concerning the applicability of evaluative terms.[73] We strive to reach understanding and resolve disputes in a conversational way.[74]

This humanist vision has by now been so widely repudiated that the very idea of presenting a moral or political theory in the form of a dialogue has long since lost any serious place in philosophy. I hope, however, that I may have succeeded in presenting more sympathetically the values of the early modern rhetorical culture against which the practice of modern philosophy was to rebel so successfully. I hope I may at the same time have conveyed something of the attractions of its strongly contrasting accounts of rationality and moral argument. I even hope that, by focusing on the historical juncture at which the shift from a dialogical to a monological style of moral and political reasoning took place,[75] I may have succeeded in raising anew the question of which style is more deserving of our intellectual allegiances.

73 On the characteristically 'explorative' (as opposed to 'demonstrative') mode of argument in the English Renaissance see Altman 1978, pp. 13–30. Altman argues (pp. 31–63) that English Renaissance drama largely developed out of the rhetorical emphasis on arguing *in utramque partem.*

74 For an important recent attempt to revive and explore this model of moral argument see Benhabib 1992, esp. pp. 8–9, 31–8, 158–70.

75 This has not been attempted for the English case, but two excellent studies enable us to piece together the earlier but analogous story in the case of Italy: see Marsh 1980 on the rediscovery of Ciceronian dialogue and Cox 1992, pp. 99–113, on the move from open dialogue to the 'closed book' of the later Renaissance.

Part I

CLASSICAL ELOQUENCE IN RENAISSANCE ENGLAND

Chapter 1

THE STUDY OF RHETORIC

THE HUMANIST CURRICULUM

Thomas Hobbes was born in Wiltshire on 5 April 1588[1] and received his early education at a series of local schools. According to John Aubrey, his first biographer, he began by attending the church school in his native village of Westport at the age of four, where he learned to read, write and 'number four figures'.[2] He completed this 'petty' training by the time he was eight[3] after which he was sent to an establishment run by the minister in Malmesbury, the adjoining town.[4] From there he shortly moved back to a private school in Westport where the master, Aubrey tells us, was a gifted young teacher called Robert Latimer, 'newly come from the University'.[5] Hobbes remained under Latimer's tutelage until the age of fourteen, working his way through the six years of study normally required for the completion of the Elizabethan grammar school curriculum.[6] By that time, Aubrey adds, Hobbes had 'so well profited in his learning' that he was judged to be ready for the university, and duly 'went away a good schoole-scholar to Magdalen-hall, in Oxford' at the beginning of 1603, a few months short of his fifteenth birthday.[7]

By the time Hobbes embarked on his secondary schooling in the mid-1590s, there had come to be widespread agreement among the pedagogical theorists of Tudor England about the proper aims of a grammar school education and the best means of attaining them. The most influential

1 Hobbes 1839a, p. xiii. As Aubrey points out, the day was Good Friday. Aubrey 1898, I, p. 327.

2 Aubrey 1898, I, pp. 327–8.

3 For a discussion of 'petty' training and its usual provision by the parish priest see Charlton 1965, pp. 98–105. At Westport the vicar was Hobbes's own father, but according to Aubrey he was barely literate. See Aubrey 1898, I, p. 323.

4 Aubrey 1898, I, p. 328.

5 Aubrey 1898, I, p. 328.

6 Hence the highest form was usually known as the sixth form. See Kempe 1966, p. 237, and cf. Baldwin 1944, I, pp. 429–35, on the curricula of smaller grammar schools.

7 Aubrey 1898, I, p. 328. On Magdalen Hall at this period see McConica 1986.

statement of these principles had been given by a number of writers associated with Erasmus and his circle in the opening decades of the century.[8] Erasmus himself had produced a brief but important sketch of a model curriculum in the course of corresponding with John Colet about the founding of St Paul's School, publishing it in 1512 as *De ratione studii*.[9] Juan Luis Vives, who first arrived in England to teach the *studia humanitatis* at Oxford in 1523,[10] went on to issue a similar but much more ambitious account of the goals and methods of humanist education in his *De tradendis disciplinis* of 1531.[11] Of all the Erasmian handbooks, however, the one that exercised the greatest influence on English schooling was undoubtedly Sir Thomas Elyot's *The Book named the Governor*, also published in 1531.[12] Elyot acknowledged a deep debt to Erasmus, speaking of him as a scholar whom 'all gentle wits are bound to thank and support'.[13] But *The Governor* was at the same time a work of major importance in its own right. Due to his epoch-making decision to abandon the use of Latin in favour of writing 'in our vulgar tongue',[14] Elyot was able to introduce the Erasmian programme to a new and much wider audience, as a result of which *The Governor* remained a standard authority on the upbringing of children throughout the sixteenth century.[15]

The two decades immediately preceding Hobbes's schooldays witnessed a further important development in English educational thought. A number of vernacular treatises appeared in which an attempt was made to apply the general principles of humanist educational theory to the day-to-day running of ordinary grammar schools.[16] There are elements of this aspiration in Roger Ascham's *The scholemaster*, an exceptionally influential[17] if somewhat garrulous guide to the teaching of Latin first printed in 1570,

8 For the Erasmians as a group see McConica 1965, pp. 44–75. For a critique see Fox 1986a. For their influence on education see McConica 1965, pp. 76–105; Simon 1979, pp. 63–73, 102–14; Grafton and Jardine 1986, pp. 136–57. For humanism in school curricula see Dowling 1986, pp. 112–39.

9 For the date of this text see McGregor 1978, p. 662, and for a full analysis see Chomarat 1981, pp. 406–17. On the founding of St Paul's School see Lupton 1909, pp. 154–77, and Simon 1979, pp. 73–80. On Erasmus and Colet see Baldwin 1944, I, pp. 118–33. Colet's statutes are printed in Lupton, 1909, appendix I, pp. 271–84.

10 Noreña 1970, pp. 76–86, 93–5.

11 See Noreña 1970, pp. 116–17, and for an analysis Simon 1979, pp. 106–14.

12 On the date of publication see Hogrefe 1967, pp. 107–8; on Elyot's educational programme see Simon 1979, pp. 148–57.

13 Elyot 1962, p. 34; cf. also p. 40. On Elyot and Erasmus see Major 1964, pp. 77–88.

14 Elyot stresses the innovation himself. See Elyot 1962, p. xiii, and cf. Major 1964, pp. 13–15.

15 It was reprinted on at least seven occasions before 1600. See Hogrefe 1967, p. 107.

16 Simon 1979, pp. 375–83; cf. Cressy 1975, pp. 8–9. For a useful survey of Elizabethan grammar school education see Alexander 1990, pp. 185–207. For a discussion of puritan schools see Morgan 1986, pp. 172–200.

17 It was, for example, the first among the books recommended by Gabriel Harvey for those aiming at 'writing or speaking eloquently or wittely'. See Harvey 1884, pp. 167–8.

two years after Ascham's death.[18] But Ascham never earned his living as a schoolmaster; he spent most of his career as a Fellow of St John's College, Cambridge, apart from his service as tutor to the future Queen Elizabeth from 1548 to 1550, and his diplomatic missions to Germany between 1550 and 1553.[19] For a more down-to-earth view of 'petty' as well as grammar school education, we need to turn to the series of handbooks written by practising schoolmasters that began to appear in the 1580s.[20] One was by Richard Mulcaster, the first headmaster of the Merchant Taylors School,[21] whose *Positions* on the training of children was issued in 1581.[22] A second was by Edmund Coote, briefly master of the school at Bury St Edmunds, whose introduction to 'petty' training entitled *The English Schoole-maister* appeared in 1596.[23] Perhaps the most interesting was by William Kempe, the headmaster of Plymouth Grammar School, whose *Education of children in learning* was published in 1588.[24] Kempe considers in turn 'the dignitie', 'the utilitie' and 'the method' of schooling, providing a convenient summary of the distinctive curriculum as well as the wider social values associated with the English grammar schools by the end of the sixteenth century.

The ultimate goal of education according to all these writers is the mastery of what Elyot and Ascham both describe, in Senecan vein, as the *studia liberalia* or liberal sciences.[25] They further agree that three particular sciences are especially worthy of being characterised as liberal or humane. As soon as they turn to survey these disciplines, their overwhelming debt to the Roman tradition of rhetorical education immediately becomes clear.[26] Quintilian had laid it down in an extraordinarily influential passage from book x of his *Institutio oratoria* that an orator must attempt to master three *scientiae* in addition to rhetoric itself, these being poetry, history and moral philosophy.[27] He had gone on to provide a list of authors especially worthy of study in each of these disciplines. Among the poets he had

18 For its publication see Ryan 1963, p. 250 and note.

19 Ryan 1963, pp. 23–48, 102–12.

20 On this body of writing see Charlton 1965, pp. 104–5.

21 Draper 1962, pp. 12–21. One of Mulcaster's pupils was Edmund Spenser. See Vickers 1989, p. 264.

22 Draper 1962, pp. 22–3.

23 Coote 1968; cf. Simon 1979, pp. 379n. and 383. Coote's main concern is with reading and writing, but his *Schoole-maister* also includes (pp. 72–93) a glossary which has some claim to be regarded as the first English dictionary. Cf. Starnes and Noyes 1946, pp. 11–12, 13–15.

24 On Kempe see Baldwin 1944, I, pp. 436–49; Howell 1956, pp. 258–61.

25 Elyot 1962, pp. 42, 44 and (citing Seneca) p. 226; Ascham 1970b, p. 293. For Elyot and Ascham on Seneca, see Major 1964, pp. 163–6, and Miglior 1975, pp. 204–6. For Seneca's use of the phrase see Seneca 1917–25, I, pp. 248, 426, and Seneca 1935, VI.XV.2, p. 392, and VI.XXIV.2, p. 412.

26 Simon 1979, pp. 60, 103–4.

27 Quintilian 1920–2, X.I.27–36, vol. IV, pp. 16–22.

singled out Homer and Virgil;[28] among the historians he had given pride of place to Thucydides and Herodotus, together with Sallust and Livy among the Romans;[29] and in speaking of moral or civil philosophy he had unhesitatingly added that 'Cicero, who stands out in every form of literary production, is able in this one even to emulate Plato himself.'[30]

It was essentially this Roman vision of the *studia humanitatis* that the English educational theorists of the Renaissance sought to revive.[31] One of the earliest and clearest reflections of this aspiration appears in Elyot's discussion of 'the order of learning' in book I of *The Governor*.[32] Elyot begins with grammar, Greek as well as Latin, since he treats the mastery of these languages as an indispensable propaedeutic to a grasp of the liberal sciences.[33] He then turns to poetry, and above all to Homer, although he later mentions a number of Roman poets whom he takes to be no less instructive.[34] By the age of fourteen, the young gentleman is said to be ready for dialectic and rhetoric, after which he is expected to turn to cosmography and especially history, beginning with Livy and moving on to Caesar, Sallust and Tacitus.[35] Finally, at the age of seventeen it becomes 'needful to read unto him some works of philosophy; specially that part that may inform him unto virtuous manners, which part of philosophy is called moral'.[36] At this juncture he is exhorted to concentrate on Aristotle's *Ethics*, Cicero's *De officiis* and the works of Plato 'above all other'.[37]

This is not to say that Elyot and his contemporaries sought to revive the elements of the *studia humanitatis* in an inert or uncritical style.[38] Elyot in particular is sensitive to the fact that the Roman curriculum stands in obvious need of additions and adjustments if it is to meet the very different social conditions of Tudor England. One specific proposal he makes is that, once a young gentleman has completed his classical training, he should devote himself to the study of English common law.[39] Vives

28 Quintilian 1920–2, X.I.46, vol. IV, p. 28, and X.I.85, vol. IV, p. 48.
29 Quintilian 1920–2, X.I.73, vol. IV, p. 42, and X.I.101, vol. IV, p. 58.
30 Quintilian 1920–2, X.I.123, vol. IV, p. 70: 'Idem igitur M. Tullius, qui ubique, etiam in hoc opere Platonis aemulus exstitit.'
31 Puritan educational ideals mirrored rather than challenged these values. Becon's *Catechism* likewise concentrates on 'liberal sciences', listing their practitioners as 'poets, orators, historiographers, philosophers'. See Becon 1844, p. 382, and cf. Todd 1987, esp. pp. 53–95.
32 As Elyot makes clear, he mainly follows Quintilian. See Elyot 1962, e.g. pp. 27, 28, 50, 57, 58, and cf. Major 1964, pp. 142–3, 160–3.
33 Elyot 1962, p. 29. On the organisation of book I see Major 1964, pp. 20–4.
34 Elyot 1962, pp. 30, 34.
35 Elyot 1962, pp. 34–8.
36 Elyot 1962, p. 39.
37 Elyot 1962, p. 39.
38 For a helpful anthology of their educational ideals see Martindale 1985.
39 Elyot 1962, pp. 52–3. On the place of rhetoric in Tudor legal training see Schoeck 1983. For

suggests an even wider extension of the classical curriculum. Although he begins with the traditional elements of the trivium – grammar, logic and rhetoric[40] – he subsequently places a strong emphasis on mathematics and a number of the practical arts, including the study of medicine.[41]

There can be no doubt, however, that the five-part syllabus of grammar, rhetoric, poetry, history and moral philosophy constituted for every Tudor humanist the essence of the *studia humanitatis*.[42] This emerges very clearly from such handbooks as Ascham's *Scholemaster*. Once a pupil has mastered Latin, he should turn to the 'matter' of his studies and read the best authors in every genus of the liberal arts. Ascham then declares that only four such genera need to be considered: poetry, history, philosophy and oratory.[43] As he emphasises, moreover, he is making a polemical point: he dismisses the claims of mathematics, and he mounts a vehement attack on the sophistries of logic and 'all the barbarous nation of scholemen' who practise it.[44]

By the middle of the sixteenth century, these humanist polemics began to have a marked impact on the syllabuses of even the humbler grammar schools.[45] An early instance can be found in the 1550 statutes of the school at Bury St Edmunds in Suffolk,[46] which call on the master to read over with the highest forms a work of poetry (Virgil's *Aeneid*), a work of history (Caesar's *Commentarii*), a work of moral philosophy (Cicero's *De officiis*) and two works of rhetoric (the *Ad Herennium* and Quintilian's *Institutio oratoria*).[47] An even clearer example is provided by the statutes granted in 1566 to the grammar school at Norwich.[48] Under the heading 'Of Authors to be Redd in the Schoole' we not only find an overwhelming preponderance of writers in 'the Latyn toung'; we also find them divided once more into the five canonical groups: poets, orators, historiographers, grammarians and 'other books of Humanitie', among which 'Officia Ciceronis or eny pt of his philosophie' is particularly singled out.[49]

an attempt to apply the techniques of humanism in legal education, see the orations on civil law delivered by Sir Thomas Smith at Cambridge in CUL MS Mm. 1.48, fos. 394–430.

40 Vives 1913, pp. 90–142, 163–71 and 180–9.

41 Vives 1913, pp. 201–26.

42 They endorsed, that is, the standard Renaissance understanding of the scope of the 'humanistic' disciplines, on which see Kristeller 1979.

43 Ascham 1970b, p. 283.

44 Ascham 1970b, pp. 190, 282–8.

45 Simon 1979, pp. 302–32.

46 Simon 1979, pp. 235–6; cf. Baldwin 1944, I, p. 296n., who notes that the statutes were partly based on those of Winchester College.

47 BL Lansdowne MS 119, no. 2, fo. 14^r. Further authors are recommended, but these make up the primary list. Cf. Leach and Steele Hutton 1907, II, p. 314.

48 Baldwin 1944, I, p. 415. Cf. also the 1580 curriculum of Sandwich School cited in Cressy 1975, p. 82.

49 Saunders 1932, pp. 147–8.

These statutes also make it clear that a liberal education was basically conceived as a matter of studying a canon of what Vives describes as 'set books'.[50] This in turn reminds us that the Renaissance ideal of a training in the humanities had little or no connection with the discovery of new knowledge. It was primarily seen as an exercise in the retrieval and preservation of an ancient form of wisdom more profound than any to which the modern world could aspire. As Vives stresses at the end of *De tradendis disciplinis*, we must recognise that whatever knowledge we possess is entirely owed to others. If we wish to advance our understanding of the humane sciences, we must concentrate on the works in which we find that wisdom expounded, and especially on the major works of antiquity that happen to have survived.[51]

As the humanists concede, however, the sad truth is that this pathway to wisdom is heavily barricaded. Elyot observes that most Greek and Roman authorities 'hold opinion that, before the age of seven years, a child should not be instructed in letters'. But these writers were able to take it for granted that 'all doctrine and sciences were in their maternal tongues', and were thus able to save their pupils 'all that long time which at this day is spent in understanding perfectly the Greek or Latin'. By contrast, 'the infelicity of our time and country' is such that we have no alternative but to begin as early as possible to learn the classical languages. Without acquiring these preliminary skills, we can never hope to enter the house of humane learning and thereby 'attain to wisdom and gravity'.[52]

If the humanists genuinely regretted this difficulty, it might be wondered why they did not devote more energy to translating the wisdom of the ancients into modern English. Some of them evidently felt inhibited by a sense that the most important forms of knowledge ought to remain to some degree esoteric in character.[53] But they also managed to persuade themselves at an early stage that the study of Latin and Greek provides an incomparable training for the mind, a view destined to enjoy an extraordinary longevity in English educational thought.[54] As a result, it soon became the governing assumption of their educational programme that a training in the humanities can virtually be equated with a study of the classical languages.

It is true that some murmurings against this scale of values can already be heard even in the Elizabethan period.[55] These were later to rise to a

50 Vives 1913, p. 45.
51 Vives 1913, e.g. p. 274.
52 Elyot 1962, p. 17.
53 Burton 1989, p. 16, still stresses the importance of not divulging *secreta Minervae*.
54 For this development, and some sceptical reflections on it, see Grafton and Jardine 1986, pp. xi–xvi, 219–20.
55 Simon 1979, pp. 353–4.

shout of disapproval in the educational writings of Hartlib, Comenius and other admirers of Bacon in the first half of the seventeenth century.[56] But as early as the 1580s we find Mulcaster complaining that too much time is spent in learning Latin and Greek.[57] He explicitly criticises Ascham for encouraging this bias, and anticipates the Baconian demand for a more extensive study of the natural sciences.[58] Even Mulcaster concedes, however, that the ancient languages must come first,[59] and most of his contemporaries make the point with greater emphasis.[60] William Kempe's model curriculum of 1588 assigns no more than a single term at the end of the final year to mathematics and the other sciences. The entire timetable is otherwise given over to Latin and Greek.[61] Within a generation, this emphasis had hardened into the assumption that a genuinely liberal education must be wholly linguistic in character. This can be seen most clearly in the leading treatise on grammar school education written in the early Stuart period, John Brinsley's *Ludus Literarius,* first published in 1612 and reprinted in 1627.[62] Brinsley makes no mention of history, devotes only a single chapter to poetry and reduces the discussion of moral philosophy to a simple homily. His account of 'petty' or elementary training is wholly taken up with reading and writing, while his proposed syllabus for the grammar schools is almost wholly centred on the classical languages.[63]

We should finally note that the linguistic training on offer was usually even more specialised than this suggests. Although writers like Elyot stress the need for Greek as well as Latin, in most schools it was Latin alone that was systematically taught.[64] This is not to deny that other ancient languages were occasionally given a place. Kempe and Brinsley both include Greek in their model curricula,[65] and Brinsley even adds a chapter on 'How to get most speedily the knowledge and understanding of the Hebrew'.[66] One example of the high level of proficiency in Greek

56 Webster 1970, esp. pp. 11–21.

57 Collins 1989, pp. 86–8, discusses Mulcaster's doubts.

58 Mulcaster 1888, pp. 239–40.

59 Mulcaster 1888, p. 244.

60 See for example Ascham 1970b, p. 265.

61 Kempe 1966, pp. 226–37.

62 On Brinsley see Campagnac 1917, esp. pp. xxxiii–xxxiv, and Simon 1979, pp. 375, 379–80.

63 Brinsley 1917, esp. pp. 192, 263. As Simon 1979, pp. 379–80, rightly stresses, however, Brinsley was an advocate of using English translations of classical texts. He also acted as a translator himself. See Brinsley 1616.

64 A point valuably emphasised in Charlton 1965, pp. 105, 116–17, 119, and in Grafton and Jardine 1986, pp. 143–5.

65 Kempe 1966, p. 232, and Brinsley 1917, pp. 222–43. As Simon 1979, p. 316, notes, these languages were largely introduced as 'religious instruments'.

66 Brinsley 1917, pp. 244–52.

occasionally attained by really gifted children is provided by Hobbes himself. Aubrey not only informs us that Hobbes's teacher, Robert Latimer, 'was a good Graecian', but adds that the young Hobbes, just before he went up to Oxford, 'turned Euripidis Medea out of Greeke into Latin Iambiques' and presented it to his teacher as a parting gift.[67]

It scarcely needs emphasising, however, that Hobbes must have been an exceptional pupil. He himself appears to have felt in later life that his achievement had been a remarkable one for a boy of fourteen, and he confided to Aubrey that he wished he had kept a copy of his translation to see how he had fared.[68] Few Elizabethan grammar school children embarked on the study of Greek until the fifth form, and most educational manuals make it clear that little was expected of them even at that stage.[69] Kempe merely suggests that, 'if the scholar shall be a Grecian', he should start learning the rudiments of the language at the age of twelve. But there is a strong implication that hardly any will make the attempt.[70] Brinsley similarly observes that he is only concerned with Greek 'so much as it shall be requisite' for the ordinary grammar schools. Again there is a strong implication that it may not be requisite at all.[71]

THE CENTRALITY OF GRAMMAR AND RHETORIC

Despite the wider pretensions of the humanists, the actual practice of the Elizabethan grammar schools was to concentrate overwhelmingly on the teaching of Latin. This process was in turn held to involve two principal steps,[72] a convenient summary of which can be found in the final section of William Kempe's *Education of children in learning.*[73] Kempe begins by reminding us in Shakespearean phrase that 'our life heere is but a short florishing floure'.[74] The first step must accordingly be to learn how to read Latin as early as possible. As we have seen, the young Hobbes embarked on this phase of his education when he was eight. But it appears that he may have done so slightly later than usual. Kempe and Brinsley both assume that the years of petty schooling will be over by the age of seven,[75] and that a child should be ready at that point to enter on the three years of study which, Kempe insists, are required for learning to read Latin with

67 Aubrey 1898, I, pp. 328–9.
68 Aubrey 1898, I, p. 329.
69 Binns 1990, pp. 216–18.
70 Kempe 1966, p. 232. Cf. Ascham 1970b, p. 274.
71 Brinsley 1917, p. 222.
72 Charlton 1965, pp. 104–5; Vickers 1989, pp. 256–65.
73 Kempe 1966, pp. 217–37. Cf. Vives 1913, book III, chapters I and III, pp. 90–9, 107–15.
74 Kempe 1966, p. 217.
75 Kempe 1966, p. 226; Brinsley 1917, p. 9. Cf. Ascham 1970b, p. 222.

any fluency.[76] The first stage in this process, Kempe goes on, consists of getting by heart the parts of speech, the declension of nouns and the conjugation of verbs.[77] After this the child is ready to move up to the second form, in which he is taught 'to practise the precepts of Grammar in expounding and unfolding the works of Latin Authors'.[78] By the time he reaches the third form, at around the age of nine, he is expected to be able to read some moderately difficult Latin texts, among which Kempe especially recommends Jacob Sturm's edition of Cicero's letters.[79]

The young pupil is then ready for his second major step, that of learning to speak and write Latin on his own account.[80] Kempe suggests that this skill should chiefly be inculcated by making translations from English into Latin, an exercise which ought to continue 'with some augmentation of length and hardnes' for the next two years.[81] By the time the pupil reaches the sixth form, in which Kempe recommends he should spend up to three years,[82] he ought to be able to compose Latin 'themes' of his own, brief essays on such worthy topics as the miseries of ambition, the evils of avarice and so forth.[83] These should incorporate the 'artificial instruments' of eloquence he will by then have encountered in reading the best classical authors, among whom Kempe especially mentions Ovid, Virgil and Horace among the poets, Caesar among the historians and Cicero for moral philosophy.[84]

Besides learning to compose themes, some educational theorists added that sixth-form pupils should be taught how to present Latin declamations. This ambitious exercise required the master to raise a controversial question and invite one pupil to speak *pro* and another *contra,* thereby prompting them to produce a rhetorical declamation *in utramque partem.* Kempe makes no mention of this practice, but a number of humanist pedagogues, including Vives, take it for granted that it ought to form the culmination of a grammar school career.[85] Brinsley, while suggesting that such exercises are perhaps 'rather for the Universities', agrees that they can nevertheless be attempted by grammar school pupils, provided they

76 Kempe 1966, p. 230.
77 Kempe 1966, p. 226.
78 Kempe 1966, p. 227.
79 Kempe 1966, p. 229.
80 Charlton 1965, pp. 109–10.
81 Kempe 1966, p. 230. Cf. Brinsley 1917, pp. 147–58.
82 Kempe 1966, p. 237.
83 Kempe 1966, pp. 233–6. Cf. Charlton 1965, p. 106.
84 Kempe 1966, pp. 232–3; cf. p. 237. Pupils were thus expected to be able to recognise the full range of rhetorical devices in the writers they studied. One famous surviving example is of the young John Milton noting, in his copy of Harington's translation of *Orlando Furioso,* over 130 different *figurae* he was able to discriminate. See Clark 1948, pp. 176–7.
85 Vives 1913, pp. 184, 186. Cf. Ascham 1970b, p. 242.

have been 'long exercised' in the writing of simpler themes.[86] That declamations were in fact attempted is clear from a number of Elizabethan grammar school statutes. One exercise prescribed for the highest forms in the Durham statutes of 1593 requires that 'the schoolemaister shall propound a theame or argument which shall have two parties, and two schollers shall be appointed, the one shall take the first part, the other the second'. As the statute points out, this was to ask the boys 'to frame and make an oration according to the precepts of Rhetorick'.[87]

This two-step process of learning Latin was generally equated with the process of mastering the two linguistic elements in the *studia humanitatis*, the *ars grammatica* and the *ars rhetorica*.[88] As Vives observes, we embark on the first of these arts as soon as we begin to study the parts of speech, the declension of nouns and the conjugation of verbs.[89] The humanists generally added that the rudiments of grammar can best be learned in two complementary ways. Erasmus popularised the view that one of these should take the form of scrutinising the most 'correct' classical authors, especially those who wrote during the so-called golden age beginning with Terence and ending after the death of Augustus and the decline into 'silver' Latinity.[90] But even the most enthusiastic proponents of this approach were obliged to admit that the *ars grammatica* consists of a set of rules, and thus that one needs in addition to have recourse to the grammarians themselves. Erasmus and Vives are largely content to recommend the leading classical handbooks, especially those of Donatus and Diomedes,[91] but the writers of the next generation occasionally refer to more recent authorities: Brinsley recommends Lyly,[92] while Ascham mentions both Horman and Whittington.[93]

Having progressed to the writing of themes, the budding scholar was expected to begin to acquire the rudiments of the *ars rhetorica*.[94] This shift of focus was reflected in the fact that in some schools the top classes were

86 Brinsley 1917, p. 185.

87 Leach 1905, pp. 377–8.

88 Baldwin 1944, II, pp. 1, 8–28 stresses this point. On the relations between the teaching of grammar and rhetoric see also Percival 1983. For their analogous place in Roman education see Bonner 1977, pp. 165–327.

89 Vives 1913, pp. 96–7.

90 Erasmus 1978b, pp. 667, 669. (Cf. Vives 1913, p. 132, and Ascham 1970b, p. 286.) For Erasmus on the teaching of grammar see Chomarat 1981, pp. 153–265.

91 Erasmus 1978b, pp. 667, 670; Vives 1913, p. 131, who also mentions some modern writers, including Melanchthon. On the revision and replacement of the ancient grammars see Charlton 1965, pp. 106–7.

92 Brinsley 1917, pp. 71, 72.

93 Ascham 1970b, p. 182. On the rival approaches of Lyly and Whittington see Charlton 1965, pp. 107–8.

94 On the progression from grammar to rhetoric see Charlton 1965, pp. 110–14.

actually known as the rhetoric classes.[95] As Kempe explains, once a student reaches the stage of 'making somewhat of his owne', it ceases to be sufficient for him to consider 'the propertie of speach in the Grammaticall etymologie and syntaxis'. It also becomes necessary for him to consider 'the finenesse of speach in the Rhetoricall ornaments, as comely tropes, pleasant figures, fit pronounciation and gesture'.[96]

As before, the humanists generally concentrate on a list of the most helpful authorities to consult. For the writing of themes, and for the construction of declamations *in utramque partem*, there was one writer whom everyone agreed to be indispensable. This was Aphthonius, a Greek rhetorician of the fourth century, the author of a series of introductory rhetorical exercises entitled *Progymnasmata.*[97] Aphthonius' text first became widely available when Aldus Manutius printed it in 1508 as the opening item in his anthology of ancient Greek treatises on the art of eloquence.[98] It was almost immediately translated into Latin, one of the earliest versions being published in London by Gentian Hervet under the title *Praeexercitamenta* in c.1520.[99] Thereafter it quickly established itself as one of the most popular handbooks for the teaching of rhetoric in schools.[100] Erasmus describes it as the best possible introduction to the subject;[101] Ascham recommends it as an aid to Latin translation;[102] and Brinsley, who similarly recommends it in his *Ludus Literarius*, adds that an English translation is now available.[103] This had been published in 1564[104] by Richard Rainolde, who had been a student at St John's College Cambridge when Roger Ascham's influence was at its height there in the 1540s.[105] Rainolde entitled his book *The Foundacion of Rhetorike*, thereby indicating – in a manner clearly aimed at the grammar schools – that his

95 G., J. 1881, p. 4: 'The boys were divided into six classes, from "Rhetoric" downwards.'

96 Kempe 1966, p. 233.

97 On Aphthonius and other writers of *progymnasmata* (including Hermogenes, author of an almost identical text) see Kennedy 1972, pp. 163–4. On Aphthonius in Tudor England see Johnson 1944 and Plett 1975, pp. 95–8.

98 Aphthonius 1508.

99 Aphthonius c.1520. For the dating see Murphy 1981, p. 19.

100 Further Latin translations were issued by Giovanni Cataneo (1521) and Rudolph Agricola (1540). See Murphy 1981, p. 21. A popular publishing arrangement in the second half of the century was to combine them. More than a dozen such editions appeared, including several at London. See Murphy, 1981, p. 22. For the London printing see Aphthonius 1575. On the centrality of Aphthonius in rhetoric teaching in Tudor schools see Crane 1937, pp. 65–9, 136–8.

101 Erasmus 1978b, p. 679.

102 Ascham 1970b, p. 240.

103 Brinsley 1917, pp. 184–5.

104 The title page reads '1563. Mens. Marcii.vi', i.e. 1564 our style.

105 On Rainolde and his version of Aphthonius see Johnson 1944.

work was intended to cover 'the verie grounde of Rhetorike' in such a way as to enable students to build on it for themselves.[106]

Rainolde's version of Aphthonius consists of a series of fourteen model orations in varying rhetorical styles.[107] Among these, as Brinsley suggests in recommending the book, the one that young scholars can hope to imitate with the greatest benefit is the thesis, a form of declamation in which an inherently disputable question is raised and 'one taketh the Affirmative part, another the Negative'.[108] Rainolde proposes a number of such topics for debate, including 'Whether is it best to marie a wife?' and 'Is warre to be moved upon a juste cause?'[109] He notes that Aphthonius also considers a number of other types of oration in which similar opportunities are offered for arguing *in utramque partem*. One is the *legislatio* in which two opposed speakers mount 'An Oracion either in the defence of a Lawe, or againste a Lawe'.[110] Rainolde offers as an example a discussion for and against the merits of the law 'whiche suffereth adulterie to bee punished with death'.[111] Other exercises of a comparable kind include 'the Destruccion' and 'the Confirmacion', which Rainolde considers together. The speaker of a 'destruccion' presents 'a certain reprehension of any thyng declaimed'. Rainolde gives as an example the contention that 'It is not like to be true, that is said of the battaill of Troie.' We are shown how to convey in a model oration that the story as it has come down to us has probably been exaggerated by 'the vain invention of Poetes'.[112] The speaker of a 'confirmacion' seeks by contrast to demonstrate that it is possible to uphold a proposition that a 'destruccion' may appear to have thrown in doubt. We are shown in this case how to argue that the evidence in favour of the original contention is after all manifest, credible and profitable to be believed.[113]

While this ability to declaim *in utramque partem* was especially prized,[114] it only represented one of a wide range of rhetorical skills that grammar school pupils were expected to acquire. As Kempe explains, the broader goal they were asked to set themselves was that of writing Latin with as much 'finenesse' as possible, deploying all the 'artificiall instruments' of rhetoric to produce the fullest emotional force.[115] As Kempe's phrasing

106 Rainolde 1564, 'To the Reader', sig. a, 3^{v}.
107 The complete list is given at sig. a, 4^{r}.
108 Brinsley 1917, p. 184.
109 Rainolde 1564, fo. liii^{v}.
110 Rainolde 1564, fo. lix^{r}.
111 Rainolde 1564, fos. lix^{r}–lxii^{r}.
112 Rainolde 1564, fos. xxiiii^{v}–xxviii^{v}.
113 Rainolde 1564, fos. xxviii^{v}–xxix^{r}.
114 And helps to explain the re-emergence of dialogue forms in the English Renaissance. See Wilson 1985, esp. pp. 76–107 on Elyot and pp. 109–35 on Ascham.
115 Kempe 1966, p. 233.

intimates, Elizabethan schoolboys were in effect being asked to master the rudiments of the classical Grand Style, the name given by Cicero and Quintilian to the most vehement and powerful form of persuasive speech.[116] This in turn meant that the humanists generally felt it necessary to recommend a series of additional treatises on the *ars rhetorica* to help young scholars meet these not undemanding requirements.

No one doubted that the works principally worth recommending were all composed in antiquity. It is 'onelie in the *Greke* and *Latin* tong', as Ascham declares, that we find 'the trew preceptes, and perfite examples of eloquence'. This means that we must 'seeke in the Authors onelie of those two tonges, the trewe Paterne of Eloquence, if in any other mother tongue we looke to attaine, either to perfit utterance of it our selves, or skilfull iudgement of it in others'.[117] It is true that an element of disquiet is occasionally expressed at God's decision to arrange things in this way. The student must remember, Vives feels obliged to point out, that 'he is wandering amongst the heathen, that is, amongst thorns, poisons, aconite, and most threatening pestilences', and that 'he is to take from them only what is useful, and to throw aside the rest'.[118] Vives and Ascham both stipulate that ancient texts must be selected with the utmost care, and that even those found suitable should if necessary be expurgated for use in schools.[119] However, Vives suggests in more hopeful tones that no genuine science can hinder piety,[120] to which Ascham adds in typically humanist vein that, at least in the crucial instance of Cicero, it pleased God to lighten his darkness so extensively that we can almost count him as a Christian philosopher.[121]

Ascham goes on to announce in emphatic terms his preference for the works of Greek as opposed to Roman antiquity. Voicing a prejudice fundamental to modern classical scholarship, he declares that almost everything of value in Roman literature and philosophy ('Cicero onelie excepted') is 'either lerned, borowed, or stolne, from some one of those worthie wittes of *Athens*'.[122] But this judgment was exceptional, and mainly serves to remind us of the olympian heights from which Ascham surveyed

116 On the Roman ideal of the Grand Style see Quintilian 1920–2, XII.x.58–65, vol. IV, pp. 482–6, and cf. Shuger 1988, pp. 35–41.

117 Ascham 1970b, p. 383.

118 Vives 1913, p. 125. Cf. Becon 1844, p. 382, listing the 'filthy writers' of antiquity who must be avoided.

119 Vives 1913, pp. 88–9, 128; Ascham 1970b, p. 287. The rules for the school at Bury St Edmunds specifically mention the need to exclude obscene poets. See BL Lansdowne MS 119, no. 2, fo. 14[v].

120 Vives 1913, p. 48.

121 Ascham 1970b, p. 293.

122 Ascham 1970b, p. 213.

the needs of Elizabethan schoolmasters and their charges. According to all the other educational theorists we have cited, the list of classical writings on the *ars rhetorica* suitable for use in schools is almost exclusively a list of Roman texts. As Colet declares in his statutes for St Paul's School, the aim is to direct young scholars to 'goode auctors suych as have the veray Romayne eliquence joyned with wisdome'.[123]

The range of these set books is liable to strike a modern reader as impossibly demanding. No doubt, as in any educational system, there was a large gap between the aspirations of the syllabus and the realities of the classroom – a fact acknowledged by several of the writers we have been considering.[124] It is important to remember, however, that the humanists drew a sharp distinction between a schoolmaster's duty to read to his pupils and his pupils' duty to read for themselves. Grammar school students were rarely expected to study more than one or two works of rhetoric on their own account. They were supposed to acquire most of their knowledge from listening to their teachers expounding selected passages from a wider range of texts. When reading, a master was expected to explain technical terms, to underline salient arguments, to suggest headings for notes, to point out useful examples and so forth. As a result, the process of learning was largely a matter of receiving, in Vives's words, a posy of blossoms that the teacher had already picked.[125]

The basic textbook normally recommended for this purpose was the *Rhetorica ad Herennium*.[126] This was widely attributed to Cicero throughout the middle ages, and it was only with the publication of Raffaele Regio's *Ducento problemata* in 1492 that Cicero's authorship was convincingly challenged.[127] It is not clear, however, how far Regio's arguments were initially accepted. Although his scepticism was fully endorsed by such scholars as Erasmus and Vives,[128] the *Ad Herennium* continued to be printed and accepted as a genuinely Ciceronian text throughout the sixteenth century. Whether authentic or not, however, everyone agreed that it was indispensable. Vives recommends it as perhaps the best 'easy and short compendium' to the rules of rhetoric,[129] a judgment widely echoed in the statutes of the Tudor grammar schools. The Bury St Edmunds rules of 1550 require it to be studied in the highest form;[130] the

123 Lupton 1909, appendix I, p. 279.
124 See for example Brinsley 1917, pp. 173–4.
125 Vives 1913, p. 183.
126 On the centrality of this text see Baldwin 1944, II, p. 72, and Charlton 1965, p. 110.
127 Monfasani 1987, pp. 112–15.
128 Vives 1913, p. 183, claims that he cannot understand why Cicero is credited with the text.
129 Vives 1913, p. 183.
130 Leach and Steele Hutton 1907, II, p. 314.

Norwich statutes of 1566 prescribe 'Tullium ad Herenium' for each of the upper forms;[131] while the Rivington School rules of 1576 recommend it as the best possible guide to 'the divers kinds and parts of an Oration'.[132]

The *Ad Herennium* is distinguished by the large amount of space it devotes to *elocutio*, and especially to the classification and explanation of the figures and tropes of speech.[133] This doubtless helps to explain why Tudor educational theorists placed so much emphasis on this topic, on which they sometimes felt it necessary to recommend a number of additional works. Vives, for example, provides a reading list including the *De figuris* of Rutilius Lupus, a near contemporary of Cicero's, as well as Iulius Rufinianus' later work of the same name.[134] He also insists on the need to study various modern authorities. One of these was Antonio Mancinelli, whose *Carmen de Figuris* was first printed in 1493.[135] Another was Petrus Mosellanus, the author of a table of figures entitled *De Schematibus et tropis* which Vives, picking up a hint of Erasmus', proposes should be 'hung up on the wall so that it will catch the attention of the pupil as he walks past it'.[136] Vives and Elyot also warmly recommend Erasmus' own *De copia*, a work containing an extensive analysis of the figures and tropes in addition to its celebrated thesaurus of synonyms and variations of usage.[137]

Besides the *Ad Herennium*, the humanists generally recommended a number of authentically Ciceronian texts. Sometimes they did so without specifying which particular treatises they had in mind. Vives, for example, merely speaks of the need to master Cicero's rhetorical books.[138] When we encounter this description, however, it is usually clear that the writer is following a convention established by the booksellers of the period for referring to this aspect of Cicero's *oeuvre*. The *Ad Herennium* is frequently described as his *Rhetorica nova*,[139] while his youthful (and unquestionably authentic) *De inventione* is described as his *Rhetorica vetus*.[140] It was common practice to publish these two works together under the title *Utraque Ciceronis rhetorica*,[141] or else under the title to which Vives is clearly alluding, *Rhetoricorum libri Ciceronis*.[142] This convention became widespread among

131 Saunders 1932, p. 147.
132 Baldwin 1944, I, p. 349.
133 For a full discussion, noting this emphasis, see Leeman 1963, I, pp. 25–42.
134 Vives 1913, p. 182. On Rutilius Lupus see Kennedy 1972, pp. 121–2, 485.
135 Vives 1913, p. 134; cf. Mancinelli 1493.
136 Vives 1913, p. 134; cf. Mosellanus 1533.
137 Vives 1913, p. 134; cf. Elyot 1962, p. 34.
138 Vives 1913, p. 182.
139 Murphy 1981, pp. 77, 88, 93.
140 Murphy 1981, pp. 77, 93.
141 Murphy 1981, p. 90.
142 Murphy 1981, pp. 89, 91–3.

continental booksellers in the opening decades of the sixteenth century, and was first employed in the printing of Cicero's rhetorical works in England in 1574.[143] It is thus possible to say with some confidence that, when we come upon a general exhortation to study 'Cicero's rhetorical books', we are being directed to the *Ad Herennium* and the *De inventione*.

Within the corpus of Cicero's rhetorical writings, the humanists generally singled out three further treatises. One was the *Topica*, which Elyot particularly admires, although he thinks of it more as a work of logic than of rhetoric.[144] A second was the *De oratore*, which Ascham describes as 'the best booke that ever Tullie wrote',[145] and which Vives regards as so important that he lists it as one of the books a pupil must read for himself as opposed to having it read to him.[146] The third and most popular was the *De partitione oratoria*, which Elyot recommends as the best short introduction to the whole art of rhetoric,[147] while Vives lists it as yet another work that any serious student must be sure to read for himself.[148]

As well as the writings of Cicero, the humanists invariably recommended Quintilian's *Institutio oratoria*, a work they generally cite with even greater reverence. It is true that Ascham again introduces a discordant note at this point, not only criticising Quintilian on many matters of detail but accusing him of spitefully seeking to disparage Cicero's achievement.[149] For most of the writers we are considering, however, Quintilian was the supreme authority not merely on the art of rhetoric but on many broader issues relating to the purposes of a liberal education.[150] Erasmus confesses that, in writing about methods of learning, he may well be accused of sheer impertinence, given that the great Quintilian has already written on the same theme.[151] Elyot suggests that one way of learning the whole art of rhetoric would simply be to read Quintilian.[152] And Vives, who continually cites Quintilian as his own principal authority,[153] recom-

143 See Cicero 1574, published by John Kingston. Murphy 1981 misses this edition, but notes (p. 94) a similar edition in 1579.

144 Elyot 1962, p. 34, endorsing Agricola's view of 'topical' logic, on which see Jardine 1977.

145 Ascham 1970b, p. 269.

146 Vives 1913, p. 183.

147 Elyot 1962, p. 34.

148 Vives 1913, p. 183; cf also Ascham 1970b, p. 285.

149 Ascham 1970b, pp. 243–4, 271.

150 For Quintilian as 'the supreme authority' see Baldwin 1944, II, p. 197. The humanists' admiration turned it into one of the bestsellers of the first age of the printed book. After its *editio princeps* (Rome, 1470) it was reprinted at the rate of at least one new edition every year throughout the ensuing century. See Murphy 1981, pp. 230–4.

151 Erasmus 1978b, p. 672.

152 Elyot 1962, p. 34.

153 See for example Vives 1913, pp. 64–5, 66–7, 79, 81, 98, etc.

mends the *Institutio oratoria* as yet another treatise that any serious student must be sure to read for himself.[154]

As will by now be evident, the reading lists suggested by the humanists generally converge on three principal authorities. These are listed with admirable terseness in the 1566 statutes of the Norwich Grammar School, the provisions of which constitute an unusually valuable insight into Elizabethan grammar school practice.[155] Under the heading 'Of Authors to be Redd in the Schoole' we learn that the headmaster is expected to 'reade to the highest fourme' just three works on the theory of rhetoric: 'Tullium ad Herenium. Quintilianum. Apthonii Progymnasmata'.[156]

Reflecting on this list, we can hardly fail to be struck by one omission: no mention is made of Aristotle's *Art of Rhetoric*. This neglect, which extends to virtually all the writers we have been considering, is undoubtedly due in part to the fact that Aristotle's text was hardly available outside Italy for much of the sixteenth century.[157] Although George of Trebizond's Latin translation of 1445 had been in print since 1472,[158] and although a further translation by Ermolao Barbaro was published in 1545,[159] it was not until Jacob Sturm's long-meditated edition appeared at Strasbourg in 1570 that an accurate Latin version became widely available in northern Europe.[160] Even more important, it was only after Theodore Goulston's facing-page translation was published in London in 1619 that a Latin version began to circulate at all widely in England.[161]

It would be misleading, however, to imply that it was wholly or even chiefly due to ignorance that the writers we have been considering failed to recommend Aristotle's *Rhetoric*. Even the earliest English vernacular theorists of rhetoric appear to have had some acquaintance with his text.[162] This is certainly true of Roger Ascham, who corresponded with Sturm about the drafts of his translation in the early 1550s,[163] and who refers familiarly to 'Aristotle in his Rhetoricke' at several points in *The*

154 Vives 1913, p. 183.

155 As noted in Baldwin 1944, I, p. 416.

156 Saunders 1932, p. 147.

157 On its marginal status in the west before the end of the sixteenth century see Vickers 1989, pp. 229, 297, and Green 1994, esp. pp. 1–2.

158 On George of Trebizond's *Rhetoricorum Libri v* and his translation of Aristotle's *Art of Rhetoric* see Monfasani 1983 and Green 1994, pp. 3–5.

159 Green 1994, pp. 7–11, 22.

160 Murphy 1981, p. 29; cf. Herrick 1926.

161 Goulston 1619; cf. Binns 1990, p. 237.

162 See for example Cox c.1530, sig. A, 3^{r}; Sherry 1961, p. 88; Wilson 1554, fo. 9^{v}. Cf. Herrick 1926, pp. 248–9. Vives recommends the text, as Green 1994 points out, p. 5. Stern 1979, p. 21, notes that Gabriel Harvey was closely annotating Aristotle's *Rhetoric* in the early 1570s.

163 See their correspondence of 1550–52 in Ascham 1864–65, I, pp. 198, 227, 301, 305, 315, 324. John Astely wrote to Ascham in 1552 to recall their habit of 'readyng together *Aristotles* Rethorike'. See Ascham 1970a, p. 123.

scholemaster.[164] The same applies to Ascham's pupil Richard Rainolde, who opens his *Foundacion of Rhetorike* by invoking the authority of 'Aristotle the Philosopher in his Booke of Rhetorike'.[165] Nor was a detailed knowledge of Aristotle's treatise confined to Ascham's circle at Cambridge. When John Rainolds took up his appointment as Greek Reader at Corpus Christi College Oxford in 1572, he chose Aristotle's *Art of Rhetoric* as the main work on which to comment in his lectures.[166] Soon afterwards Sir Philip Sidney, a student at Oxford during the same period, made what appears to have been the first English translation of Aristotle's text.[167] Sidney's drafts remained unpublished, but John Hoskins assures us in his *Directions for Speech and Style* that he once saw 'the first two books Englished by him in the hands of the noble studious Henry Wotton'.[168]

One reason for the relative lack of interest in Aristotle's *Rhetoric* may well have been that many of his claims appeared commonplace to sixteenth-century humanists nurtured on Roman theories of eloquence. Cicero and Quintilian had both been deep students of Aristotle's text, and both were content to reiterate his arguments at many important points. As a result, many of Aristotle's classifications and typologies became part of the common stock. A second and strongly contrasting reason is that, to anyone brought up on Cicero and Quintilian, much of what Aristotle says about the scope and character of the *ars rhetorica* must have seemed hard to assimilate. Aristotle begins by declaring that, if there is a genuine 'art' of rhetoric, it cannot simply consist of a series of devices for enabling us to improve the elegance and persuasiveness of our speech; it must on the contrary consist of a distinctive art of reasoning. This leads him to enunciate perhaps his most important thesis: that the 'art' in question is essentially that of learning to manipulate a rhetorical form of syllogism, the so-called enthymeme, in which the premises are merely probable and the point of deploying them is to arouse emotion as well as to furnish proofs.[169] By contrast, Cicero, Quintilian and their Renaissance disciples treat the art of rhetoric as fundamentally concerned with enabling us to speak and write in an elegant and persuasive style.[170] They have almost nothing to say about rhetorical syllogisms, and instead concentrate on explaining how the figures and tropes can be used as persuasive devices, a

164 Ascham 1970b, pp. 240, 275.
165 Rainolde 1564, fo. 1^r.
166 Green 1988, p. 10 and Green 1994, pp. 12–15. On Rainolds's humanist approach to Aristotle see also Schmitt 1983, pp. 70–1.
167 Wallace 1915, p. 327.
168 Hoskins 1935, p. 41.
169 Aristotle 1926, I.I.1–11, pp. 2–10.
170 See for example Elyot 1962, p. 34, stressing this aspect of rhetoric and the need to concentrate on it.

topic on which Aristotle scarcely touches at all. Furthermore, Aristotle's emphasis on the use of enthymemes to arouse emotion prompts him to devote a great deal of attention to the analysis of the passions and the question of how they should be classified.[171] This again stands in marked contrast with the outlook of the Roman theorists and their Renaissance followers, few of whom exhibit any serious interest in this predominantly psychological theme.

This is not to say that Aristotle's *Rhetoric* totally lacked for serious readers in Tudor and early Stuart England. To round off these preliminary remarks about the reception of classical eloquence in Renaissance England, a word should be said about those secular rhetoricians who made a close study of Aristotle's text. One deep admirer was John Hoskins, the author of *Directions for Speech and Style*. Hoskins's handbook, which he completed at some point in the 1590s,[172] includes a fascinating encomium on Aristotle's text. It is striking, however, that Hoskins thinks of it less as a work on rhetoric than as a psychological treatise on how to understand the 'motions' of the will. Nowadays, Hoskins maintains, we particularly stand in need of such an understanding, because 'as Machiavelli saith, perfect virtue or perfect vice is not seen in our time, which altogether is humorous and spurting'.[173] Given this feature of the age, we need to gain some insight into the character of the humours involved. And it is Hoskins's contention that, if we wish to acquire 'the directest means of skill to describe, to move, to appease or to prevent any motion whatsoever', the work we ought above all to consult is Aristotle's *Art of Rhetoric*.[174]

A second writer who speaks admiringly of Aristotle's *Rhetoric* – and indeed of Machiavelli's politics[175] – is Francis Bacon, who discusses Aristotle's text in *The Advancement of Learning* in 1605. But he too thinks of it mainly as a work on the 'affections' or passions of the soul, and examines it in connection with his treatment of that topic in book II. Bacon professes to find it strange that Aristotle 'should have written divers volumes of ethics, and never handled the affections, which is the principal subject thereof'. But he notes that Aristotle made good the omission when he turned in the *Rhetoric* to consider how the affections 'may be moved by speech'. And although Bacon complains that this was hardly the best place

171 Aristotle 1926, esp. II.II.2 to II.XI.7, pp. 172–246. Vickers 1989, pp. 229–30, and Green 1994, esp. pp. 11, 15, both note the sixteenth-century tendency to regard Aristotle's text as a treatise on the passions of the soul.

172 Murphy 1981, p. 176, suggests 1599 as the date of the manuscript.

173 Hoskins 1935, p. 41. For Machiavelli's observation see Machiavelli 1960, I.26, p. 194.

174 Hoskins 1935, p. 41.

175 Bacon 1915, pp. 165, 186.

in which to offer an analysis of the emotions, he allows that Aristotle 'handleth them well'.[176]

It is Hobbes, however, who provides the best example of a secular rhetorician from this period who clearly possessed an intimate knowledge of Aristotle's *Rhetoric*, but who made use of it only in connection with analysing the passions of the soul. Hobbes was in general no friend to Aristotle, whom he denounced to Aubrey as 'the worst teacher that ever was, the worst polititian and ethick'.[177] But he shared Bacon's judgment that in the *Rhetoric* Aristotle had surpassed himself.[178] He told Aubrey that he regarded the work as rare,[179] and at various times he devoted a great deal of attention to it. He first appears to have studied it closely in the early 1630s, at the time when he was serving as tutor to the third earl of Devonshire. A Latin version of the text survives, written in the young earl's hand, with copious insertions and corrections by Hobbes,[180] suggesting that the latter may originally have dictated the work to his pupil as a series of Latin comprehension exercises.[181] Soon afterwards Hobbes translated his paraphrase into English, publishing it anonymously as *A Briefe of the Art of Rhetorique* in 1637.[182] But Hobbes's most interesting engagement with the *Rhetoric* dates from 1640, the year in which he completed the first draft of his general philosophy, *The Elements of Law*. When he turns in chapters 8 and 9 to discuss the 'affections', he not only draws on a number of Aristotle's assumptions, but enunciates several of his own definitions in the form of virtual quotations from his own translation of Aristotle's text.[183]

Hobbes's analysis begins with the concept of honour, which he equates with 'acknowledgment of power'. Among the actions usually judged honourable he lists 'Victory in Battail or Duell', and among signs of honourable riches he mentions 'Giftes, Costs and Magnificence of Houses'.[184] These observations already echo Aristotle, whose list of honourable things includes 'victory', 'things that excell' and 'Possessions

176 Bacon 1915, p. 171.
177 Aubrey 1898, I, p. 357.
178 Bacon 1915, p. 146.
179 Aubrey 1898, I, p. 357.
180 Chatsworth: Hobbes MS D.I.
181 A suggestion originally put forward in Robertson 1886, p. 29 and note.
182 The first edition ('printed by Tho. Cotes, for Andrew Crook') is undated. See [Hobbes] 1637(?) and cf. Macdonald and Hargreaves 1952, pp. 7–8. The work was entered in the Register of the Company of Stationers on 1 February 1636 (i.e. 1637 our style) and ascribed to 'T. H.'. See Arber 1875–94, IV, p. 372. Aubrey 1898, I, p. 359, notes that the *Briefe* is Hobbes's work, 'though his name be not to it'.
183 This point is valuably emphasised in Strauss 1963, who prints parallel passages at pp. 36–41. See also Zappen 1983.
184 BL Harl. MS 4235, fo. 31^{r-v}. Cf. Hobbes 1969a, pp. 34–5.

we reap no profit by'.[185] When Hobbes reverts to the topic of the affections in chapter 9, he begins by considering the concept of glory and the emotions associated with it. One is anger, which as Hobbes notes is 'commonly defined to be griefe proceeding from an opinion of Contempt'.[186] Here too he closely echoes his own translation of Aristotle, in which anger had been defined as 'desire of revenge, joyned with greefe for that He, or some of his, is, or seemes to be *neglected*'.[187] Hobbes goes on to contrast anger and vengefulness with pity, which he defines as 'Imagination or Fiction of Future Calamity to ourselves proceeding from the Sense of another mans present Calamity'.[188] Again the definition is remarkably close to Aristotle's, for whom pity 'is a perturbation of the mind, arising from the apprehension of hurt, or trouble to another that doth not deserve it, and which he thinkes may happen to himselfe or his'.[189] Hobbes next contrasts pity with indignation, which he defines as 'that Grief which consisteth in the Conception of good successe happening to them whom they think unworthy thereof'.[190] This too is virtually a quotation from Aristotle, for whom indignation is 'Opposite in a manner to *Pitty*' and consists in 'griefe for the prosperity of a man unworthy'.[191] The last in this group of passions according to Hobbes is emulation, which he takes to be 'Griefe arising from seeing ones selfe exceeded or excelled by his Concurrent, together with hope to equall or exceed him in tyme to come'.[192] Once more there is an obvious parallel with Aristotle, according to whom '*Emulation* is griefe arising from that our Equals possesse such goods as are had in honour, and whereof we are capable, but have them not'.[193]

There is a final point worth underlining by way of rounding off these observations about the teaching of rhetoric in the grammar schools of Hobbes's youth. This concerns the attitude of the writers we have been considering towards the classical treatises they recommended. It is commonly said that one of the distinctive achievements of Renaissance humanism was to recognise and accentuate the distance between classical and later times, thereby initiating the modern project of seeking to appraise the culture of antiquity on its own terms.[194] It is arguable that

185 Hobbes 1986, p. 53.
186 BL Harl. MS 4235, fo. 34^r^. Cf. Hobbes 1969a, pp. 38–9.
187 Hobbes 1986, p. 69.
188 BL Harl. MS 4235, fo. 34^v^. cf. Hobbes 1969a, p. 40.
189 Hobbes 1986, p. 80.
190 BL Harl. MS 4235, fo. 35^r^. Cf. Hobbes 1969a, pp. 40–1.
191 Hobbes 1986, p. 81.
192 BL Harl. MS 4235, fo. 35^v^. Cf. Hobbes 1969a, p. 41.
193 Hobbes 1986, p. 84.
194 See Levy 1967, pp. 36–7; Dean 1988.

this generalisation stands in need of some reconsideration in the light of the humanists' attitude towards the major texts of classical eloquence.[195] It is of course true that they viewed them as products of a different culture in the sense that they felt the need to occupy themselves with such historically minded tasks as producing improved editions, raising questions about authorship and so forth.[196] What is striking, however, is the extent to which they nevertheless lack any sense of the past as a foreign country. Having dusted down the ancient texts, they exhibit almost no interest in reconstructing their historical contexts as a way of making better sense of them. On the contrary, they approach them as if they are contemporary documents with an almost wholly unproblematic relevance to their own circumstances. This in turn means that there is nothing unhistorical about yoking Cicero and Quintilian together with the vernacular rhetoricians of Tudor England – as I shall have cause to do throughout part I of this book – and treating them as if they were all contributing to the same argument. To do so is simply to reflect the extraordinarily strong sense of cultural unity with which the Tudor humanists confronted their classical authorities.

THE ELEMENTS OF CLASSICAL RHETORIC

When the educational theorists of Tudor England issued their lists of set books for the study of the *ars rhetorica,* they generally coupled their recommendations with an indication of the topics and arguments that schoolmasters ought particularly to draw to the attention of their pupils. Teachers were asked in the first place to ensure that the different genera of rhetorical writing and speech were thoroughly understood. This is the first point Erasmus makes when discussing the writing of themes in his *De ratione studii.* If a theme is to be properly handled, the student must bring to it an awareness of 'the different kinds of formal oratory' and 'the nature of each type'.[197] Vives reiterates the same demand at greater length, claiming that one of the main reasons for turning to classical theories of eloquence is to gain an appreciation of the different forms of oratory and the different 'precepts concerning the kinds of speeches' and their characteristic arguments.[198]

195 These remarks apply only to secular rhetorics: Shuger 1988, pp. 55–117, persuasively argues that exponents of the Christian Grand Style in the Renaissance were committed to a more historically minded approach, concerned as they were with the changes wrought by the rise of Christianity.

196 On these aspects of Renaissance humanism see Burke 1969b, esp. pp. 50–76.

197 Erasmus 1978b, p. 680.

198 Vives 1913, p. 182.

Teachers were also instructed to indicate the different steps – or, to put it another way, the different rhetorical skills – required for speaking or writing persuasively in any of the recognised genres. A useful summary of these further points can also be found in Erasmus' *De ratione studii*. The student must first consider how many propositions he wants to discuss, how many reasons he wants to put forward and what kinds of proof he wants to adduce. He must then turn to his classical authorities for an understanding of how to 'amplify' his arguments. Finally, he must seek their guidance on how his arguments should be 'disposed': how the different parts of his oration should be joined together, how the transitions from one part to another should be managed.[199] The educational theorists of the next generation offer very similar advice. Ascham speaks of the need to study the ancient orators with a view to discovering the best arguments to employ on any given occasion, the best order in which to 'dispose' them and the most comely figures with which to enhance their persuasive effect.[200] Kempe similarly insists on the value of the ancient rhetoricians as a guide to 'method', to 'examples of the arguments' and to ways of ornamenting them by 'every trope, every figure, as well of words as of sentences'.[201]

A diligent student who consulted the approved classical authorities on each of these topics would have found a reassuring measure of agreement. They almost all agree in the first place about the range of genera into which rhetorical utterances should be classified. This consensus was largely due, as Quintilian notes, to the fact that most Roman rhetoricians simply accepted the typology originally proposed by Aristotle.[202] Aristotle had laid it down in book I, chapter 3, of his *Rhetoric* that – in the words of Hobbes's translation – 'there are three kinds of *Orations*; *Demonstrative*, *Judicial*, *Deliberative*', and that a certain time is appropriate to each: 'To the *Demonstrative*, the *Present*. To the *Judiciall*, the *Past*, and to the *Deliberative*, the *time to come*.'[203]

Cicero admittedly seeks at one point to cast doubt on the adequacy of these categories. In his early *De inventione* he lists the three genera and praises Aristotle for having distinguished them.[204] But in his later *De oratore* he speaks slightingly of the classification, and the figure of Antonius is made to imply that the number of different types may be incalculable.[205]

199 Erasmus 1978b, pp. 680–1.
200 Ascham 1970b, p. 245.
201 Kempe 1966, p. 233.
202 Quintilian 1920–2, III.IV.1, vol. I, p. 390.
203 Hobbes 1986, p. 41.
204 Cicero 1949a, I.V.7, pp. 14–16, and I.IX.12, p. 26.
205 Cicero 1942a, II.X–XII, vol. I, pp. 226–36. Cf. II. LXXXI.333, vol. I, p. 450.

By and large, however, Aristotle's distinctions were accepted by the Roman rhetoricians as an important clarification of their subject. The *Ad Herennium* opens by repeating them without qualification, agreeing that 'there are three genera of causes', and that these can be listed as the *genus demonstrativum*, the *genus deliberativum* and the *genus iudiciale*.[206] Quintilian adopts the same classification, commending Aristotle at the same time 'for establishing this tripartite division of oratory into the judicial, the deliberative and the demonstrative'.[207] He also allows himself, in a rare moment of asperity, to express some impatience with Cicero for having tried to establish that there are more than three genera when he ought to have reflected that 'all those of the greatest authority among ancient writers, following Aristotle, have been content to accept this division'.[208]

The classical rhetoricians almost invariably begin by discussing the *genus demonstrativum*. Aristotle lays it down that (in the words of Hobbes's translation) the proper office of such epideictic orations is '*Praysing* and *Dispraysing*', while their proper ends are to point out what is '*Honourable*, or *Dishonourable*'.[209] It is true that the Roman theorists seldom find much to say about orations of this type.[210] The *Ad Herennium* observes that we rarely encounter them in everyday life,[211] while the figure of Antonius in the *De oratore* even suggests that 'because we no longer have much use for such panegyrics, it seems appropriate that I set this topic entirely to one side'.[212] When the Roman writers trouble to examine the category, however, they generally associate themselves with Aristotle's account. If we turn to the author of the *Ad Herennium*, for example, we find him agreeing that the *genus demonstrativum* is principally concerned with *laus et vituperatio*, and that we normally reserve our commendations for things we find honourable. These include such goods of fortune as wealth, power and glory, such bodily qualities as agility, strength and dignity and such attributes of character as prudence, justice, courage and modesty.[213]

Quintilian later introduced one refinement in the course of considering

206 *Ad C. Herennium* 1954, I.II.2, p. 4: 'tria genera sunt causarum ... demonstrativum, deliberativum, iudiciale'.

207 Quintilian 1920–2, II.XXI.23, vol. I, p. 366: 'Aristoteles tres faciendo partes orationis, iudicialem, deliberativam, demonstrativam'.

208 Quintilian 1920–2, III.IV.I, vol. I, p. 390: 'omnes utique summae apud antiquos auctoritatis scriptores Aristotelem secuti ... hac partitione contenti fuerant'.

209 Hobbes 1986, p. 41.

210 On the marginal status of epideictic oratory in Rome see Kennedy 1972, pp. 21–3, 428–9.

211 *Ad C. Herennium* 1954, III.VIII.15, p. 182.

212 Cicero 1942a, II.LXXXIV.341, vol. I, p. 456: 'nos laudationibus non ita multum uti soleremus, totum hunc segregabam locum'.

213 *Ad C. Herennium* 1954, III.VI to III.VIII, pp. 172–84.

the range of things that can properly be praised or blamed. Whereas Cicero and the author of the *Ad Herennium* had both assumed that, as the latter puts it, *laus* or *vituperatio* can only be heaped upon 'some particular person',[214] Quintilian sees no reason why our praises should not be scattered more widely, and specifically mentions that they can encompass animals, inanimate objects, public works, individual places and 'every other kind of thing'.[215] This more inclusive understanding was later adopted by a number of Renaissance rhetoricians, several of whom exhibit a special interest in re-establishing the genus of panegyric both in prose and verse.[216] Rainolde, for example, assures us in his account of 'the parte of Rhetorike, called praise' that 'All thynges that maie be seen, with the iye of man, touched, or with any other sence apprehended' can equally well be praised or dispraised: 'as Manne. Fisshe. Foule. Beaste. Orchardes. Stones. Trees. Plantes. Pettals. Citees. Floodes. Castles. Toures. Gardeins. Stones. Artes. Sciences'.[217]

The second form of utterance to which the classical rhetoricians address themselves is the *genus deliberativum.* Aristotle lays it down that the office of such speeches is '*Exhortation* and *Dehortation*', and that their proper end is 'to proove a thing *Profitable*, or *Unprofitable*'.[218] The implication that an orator who deliberates must in effect be counselling was subsequently taken up by all the leading Roman writers on the rhetorical arts.[219] They further accept that, in the words of the *Ad Herennium*, the purpose of offering such counsel is normally *suasio et dissuasio*, to persuade or dissuade someone from acting in some particular way.[220] The only point at which they express any doubts about Aristotle's analysis is in considering his claim that the goal of deliberative oratory is to indicate which of various possible actions should be treated as especially advantageous or profitable. As Cicero puts it in the *De inventione*, 'whereas Aristotle is content to regard *utilitas* or advantage as the aim of deliberative oratory, it seems to me that our aim should be *honestas et utilitas*, honesty allied with advantage'.[221]

214 *Ad C. Herennium* 1954, I.II.2, p. 4: 'Demonstrativum est quod tribuitur in alicuius certae personae laudem vel vituperationem.'

215 Quintilian 1920–2, III.VII.6, vol. I, p. 466; III.VII. 26–7, vol. I, p. 476, and III.VII.27, vol. I, p. 478 on 'rerum omnis modi'.

216 For the origins of this development see Skinner 1990c, pp. 125–6. On epideictic oratory in the Renaissance see Hardison 1962 and McManamon 1989.

217 Rainolde 1564, fo. xxxvii^r. Cf. Day 1967, p. 42.

218 Hobbes 1986, p. 41.

219 See for example *Ad C. Herennium* 1954, III.II.2–3, pp. 158–60; Cicero 1942b, XXIV.83, p. 372.

220 *Ad C. Herennium* 1954, I.II.2, p. 4. Cf. Cicero 1949a, II.IV.12, p. 176 and Quintilian III.VIII.6, vol. I, pp. 480–2.

221 Cicero 1949a, II.LI.156, p. 324: 'In deliberativo autem Aristoteli placet utilitatem, nobis honestatem et utilitatem.' Cf. Cicero 1949a, II.LV.166, p. 332. See also *Ad C. Herennium* 1954, III.II.3, p. 160, and Quintilian 1920–2, III.VIII.22, vol. I, p. 490.

Aristotle had added that 'the subject of Deliberatives' will always be 'something in our owne power, the knowledge whereof belongs not to *Rhetorique*, but for the most part to the *Politiques*'.[222] The Roman theorists expand these observations into the claim that, as the figure of Crassus puts it at the beginning of the *De oratore*, the chief forum for deliberative oratory will normally be the Senate or the assemblies of the people.[223] Quintilian later underlines the same point, although he also stresses – in a reflection of his different political circumstances – that one of the most important occasions on which a citizen may be asked to speak in deliberative vein may be in proffering advice to the emperor or some other supreme magistrate.[224]

The point on which everyone agrees is that deliberative oratory represents the central and inescapable idiom of *scientia civilis*. As Cicero puts it at the start of the *De inventione*, 'it is in the giving of an opinion in political argument that the deliberative genus has its characteristic place'.[225] Aristotle had added the influential suggestion that 'the subject of Deliberatives' may be 'referred in a manner to these five heads': 'Of levying of money'; 'Of Peace, and Warre'; 'Of the safeguard of the Country'; 'Of Provision'; and 'Of making Lawes'.[226] Cicero mounts a similar argument in considering the themes of advantage and efficiency in the *De partitione oratoria*, in the course of which he notes that among the main topics falling under these headings are arms, money and systems of alliances.[227] From these observations it proved a short step to the conclusion reached by so many Renaissance writers to the effect that what is *onesto* and what is *utile* in relation to arms, money and alliances may be said to form the central questions of political science.[228] From there it proved an even shorter step to Machiavelli's subversive suggestion that the question of what is *utile* in such matters of statecraft may have no connection with what is *onesto* at all.[229]

The last form of utterance discussed by the Roman rhetoricians is the *genus iudiciale*. Once again they generally take their definitions from Aristotle's *Rhetoric*, in which the office of judicial oratory had been described as that of '*Accusation* and *Defence*' and its goal as that of

222 Hobbes 1986, p. 42.
223 Cicero 1942a, I.XIV.60, vol. I, p. 44.
224 Quintilian 1920–2, XI.III.150, vol. IV, p. 324.
225 Cicero 1949a, I.V.7, p. 16: 'deliberativum, quod positum in disceptatione civili habet'. Cf. II.LV.167, p. 34.
226 Hobbes 1986, pp. 42–3.
227 Cicero 1942b, XXVII.95, p. 380.
228 See, most obviously, Botero 1956, esp. books VI to IX, pp. 117–207.
229 See especially Machiavelli, *Il Principe*, chapter 15, on his desire 'scrivere cosa utile', and on how it is often necessary 'essere non buono'. Machiavelli 1960, p. 60.

discovering in some particular instance what is '*Just*, or *Unjust*'.[230] Among the Roman writers, Cicero provides the fullest restatement of these categories. A pleader of causes for most of his career, Cicero is principally concerned with the problems of forensic oratory, and in *De inventione* he goes so far as to relegate the discussion of deliberative and demonstrative speech to a few pages at the end.[231] For all his emphasis on the *genus iudiciale*, however, he has little to add to Aristotle's basic definitions. He agrees that the proper place for judicial oratory is in the courts of law; he agrees that the genus itself takes the form of accusation and defence;[232] and he agrees that 'in trials the question at issue is always what is equitable'.[233]

We have seen that, besides mastering the different genera of rhetorical utterance, sixth-form pupils in Elizabethan grammar schools were asked to carry away a second and even more important lesson from their studies of classical eloquence. A truly conscientious student was expected to learn the full range of skills required for writing or speaking in the Grand Style with the maximum degree of clarity, elegance and emotional force.

The classification of these skills had generally provided the Roman rhetoricians with the overarching framework of their treatises.[234] There was some dispute, however, as to what exactly they took themselves to be classifying. According to the *Ad Herennium* they were listing the duties (*officia*) or alternatively the faculties (*res*) of those who practise the art of oratory with success.[235] But according to Cicero and Quintilian they were listing the *materia* – the various *partes* or *elementa* – of the *ars rhetorica* itself.[236] Whatever view was taken, however, there was widespread agreement as to the number of these elements and the order in which they ought to be discussed. For the briskest summary of the conventional wisdom we cannot do better than turn to the opening pages of the *Ad Herennium*. There it is laid down without preamble that we need to distinguish five separate faculties which any successful orator must possess. The first is *inventio*, 'the capacity to find out the considerations, true or plausible, that may serve to make our cause appear probable'.[237] The second is *dispositio*, the capacity

230 Hobbes 1986, p. 41.
231 Cicero 1949a, II.LI–LIX, pp. 322–44.
232 Cicero 1949a, I.V.7, p. 16.
233 Cicero 1949a, II.IV.12, p. 176: 'in iudiciis quid aequum sit quaeritur'.
234 Kennedy 1969, pp. 59–100, stresses this point in the case of Quintilian.
235 See *Ad C. Herennium* 1954, I.II.3, p. 6, on *res* and I.III.4, p. 10, on *officia*.
236 See Cicero 1949a, I.VII.9, p. 18, on *materia* and Quintilian 1920–2 III.III.1, vol. I, p. 382, on *partes*.
237 *Ad C. Herennium* 1954, I.II.3, p. 6: 'Inventio est excogitatio rerum verarum aut veri similium quae causam probabilem reddant.'

'to order and distribute the things we have found out in such a way as to indicate how they can best be placed'.[238] The next is *elocutio*, 'the application of appropriate thoughts and words to describe the things we have found out'.[239] The fourth is *memoria*, 'the capacity to hold firmly in the mind the things we have found out, the words in which we wish to express them, and the order in which we wish to present our arguments'.[240] The last is *pronuntiatio*, 'the regulation of voice, countenance and gesture in a temperate and elegant style'.[241]

This is not to say that these *res* or *partes* were accorded equal weight. Aside from Quintilian, few Roman writers find much to say about *memoria*, while fewer still address the problems of *pronuntiatio* at any length. The relative lack of interest in the latter topic may well have stemmed from the fact that, as Aristotle had originally remarked, '*Oratoricall Action* has not beene hitherto reduced to *Art*'[242] – the implication being that little can usefully be said about it in general terms. A further reason may have been that, as the Roman theorists sometimes imply, the faculties of memory and voice production are only important in spoken oratory, whereas the basic rules of the *ars rhetorica* are expected to apply to the written no less than the spoken word.

If we turn, by contrast, to *inventio*, *dispositio* and *elocutio*, we find the Roman rhetoricians treating them at considerable length. They invariably begin with *inventio*, a concept that reappears in English rhetorical theory as the 'invention' of arguments. It is worth signalling at the outset, however, that this is perhaps an unfortunate rendering, suggesting as it does to modern ears the idea of 'making up' a case. This is very far from the classical conception, according to which the faculty of invention is that of discovering the 'places' in which suitable arguments can be found with a view to presenting them in the most persuasive style.[243] As the author of the *Ad Herennium* stresses, this in turn means that, 'of the five tasks of the orator, that of *inventio* is not only the first in order of importance but is also by far the most difficult'.[244] Cicero reaffirms this judgment in the *De*

238 *Ad C. Herennium* 1954, I.II.3, p. 6: 'Dispositio est ordo et distributio rerum, quae demonstrat quid quibus locis sit conlocandum.'

239 *Ad C. Herennium* 1954, I.II.3, p. 6: 'Elocutio est idoneorum verborum et sententiarum ad inventionem adcommodatio.'

240 *Ad C. Herennium* 1954, I.II.3, p. 6: 'Memoria est firma animi rerum et verborum et dispositionis perceptio.'

241 *Ad C. Herennium* 1954, I.II.3, p. 6: 'Pronuntiatio est vocis, vultus, gestus moderatio cum venustate.'

242 Hobbes 1986, p. 107.

243 Cicero 1942b, II.5, pp. 312–14.

244 *Ad C. Herennium* 1954, II.I.2, p. 58: 'De oratoris officiis quinque inventio et prima et difficillima est'.

inventione, in which he not only declares at the outset that invention 'is the most important of all the parts of oratory'[245] but subsequently devotes the whole of his attention – as his title indicates – to this theme alone.

Having discovered which arguments to use, the orator must learn to 'dispose' or 'distribute' them in the most effective way. While agreeing that *dispositio* constitutes the second part of rhetoric, however, the Roman theorists disagree in a number of ways about its character and significance. Some declare that the question of how to organise an oration should be handled under the heading of invention and not treated as part of disposition at all. The author of the *Ad Herennium* insists on this view, in consequence of which he reduces the category of *dispositio* almost to vanishing point.[246] Cicero challenges this approach in the *De oratore*, in which the figure of Antonius provides a full analysis of what it means to speak of effective disposition, a topic he explicitly distinguishes from the invention of arguments.[247] But Quintilian self-consciously reverts to the opposite point of view, observing in the preface to his *Institutio oratoria* that his opening five books will be given over entirely to *inventio*, immediately adding that 'I include the topic of *dispositio* within this account'.[248]

A second disputed question related to the number of sections in a properly organised speech. According to Aristotle 'there bee four *Parts* of an *Oration*': in the words of Hobbes's translation, these are 'the *Proeme*, the *Proposition*, or (as others call it) the *Narration*; the *Proofes* (which containe *Confirmation*, *Confutation*, *Amplification*, and *Diminution*;) and the *Epilogue*'.[249] According to the *Ad Herennium*, however, this scheme needs to be expanded into six distinct parts: the *exordium*, the *narratio*, the *divisio*, the *confirmatio*, the *confutatio* and the *conclusio*.[250] Quintilian goes even further, arguing that we need to think in terms of a partly contrasting and still more elaborate scheme involving seven separate elements: the *proemium*, the *narratio*, the *confirmatio*, the *propositio*, the *partitio*, the *refutatio* and the *peroratio*.[251]

The last major talent that orators were asked to cultivate was *elocutio*, the ability to write and speak with full expressiveness and thus in the most commanding way. It was generally agreed that there are two main aspects

245 Cicero 1949a, I.VII.9, p. 20: 'inventio, quae princeps est omnium partium'. Cf. also II.LIX.178, p. 344.

246 The issue is disposed of in a couple of pages. See *Ad C. Herennium* 1954, III.IX.16–18, pp. 184–8.

247 Cicero 1942a, II.LXXVI–LXXXV, vol. I, pp. 432–62.

248 Quintilian 1920–2, Proemium, 22, vol. I, p. 16: 'Quinque deinceps inventioni (nam huic et dispositio subiungitur).'

249 Hobbes 1986, p. 119.

250 *Ad C. Herennium* 1954, I.III.4, p. 8; cf. Cicero 1949, I.XIV.19, p. 40.

251 Quintilian 1920–2, IV.I.I, vol. II, p. 6; IV.II.I, vol. II, p. 48; IV.III.I, vol. II, p. 120; IV.IV.I, vol. II, p. 130; IV.V.I, vol. II, p. 136; V.XIII.I, vol. II, p. 310; VI.I.I, vol. II, p. 382.

of *elocutio*, and hence two characteristic elements in a fully persuasive Grand Style. The first, as the *Ad Herennium* puts it, is the ability to speak 'purely and clearly', 'with clearness and lucidity'.[252] Cicero prefers to express the point in negative terms, warning us to prevent our speech from becoming contorted, to avoid lapsing into obscurity and above all to abstain from troubling our listeners with riddles or enigmas.[253] Quintilian later reiterates the point in still more forthright terms:

> My own view is that perspicuity is the very first virtue of a good style, and that it requires suitable words to be used, their order to be appropriate, no excessive deferment of our conclusion, and nothing that seems either inadequate or superfluous.[254]

Contrary to their later reputation, the Roman rhetoricians all insist on plainness as an indispensable element of true eloquence.[255]

The other feature of a good style is said to be *ornatus*.[256] The figure of Crassus is made to yoke the two together in discussing *elocutio* in the final book of the *De oratore*:

> Whom do people stare at in astonishment when he speaks? Whom do they applaud? Whom do they regard, as I might put it, as a god among men? Those who speak distinctly, explicitly and copiously, whose words and arguments are presented with complete clarity, and who in delivering a speech are able to attain a kind of rhythm, speaking in the manner I call ornate.[257]

Quintilian echoes the same sentiment in declaring that a mastery of *ornatus* and of the *ornamenta* may be said to represent the climax of an orator's skills. 'A capacity for *inventio*', he observes at the outset of his analysis in book VIII, 'is often displayed even by the untrained, while a capacity for *dispositio* can be acquired with only a modicum of learning; it is thus through refinement and *ornatus* that a speaker commends himself above all.'[258]

It is easy to misunderstand the significance of these claims about *ornatus* and *ornamenta*, especially if these terms are translated (as they often are) as

252 See *Ad C. Herennium* 1954, IV.XII.17, pp. 268–70, on the value of speaking 'pure et aperte', and the need to sound 'apertam et dilucidam'.

253 Cicero 1942a, III.XIII.49–50, vol. II, pp. 38–40, and III.XLII.167, vol. II, p. 130. See also Cicero 1949a, I.XX.29, p. 58.

254 Quintilian 1920–2, VIII.II.22, vol. III, p. 208: 'Nobis prima sit virtus perspicuitas, propria verba, rectus ordo, non in longum dilata conclusio, nihil neque desit neque superfluat.'

255 A point valuably stressed in Vickers 1989, pp. 1–3.

256 On the importance of *ornatus* for Cicero see Michel 1960, pp. 328–62.

257 Cicero 1942a, III.XIV.53, vol. II, p. 42: 'Quem stupefacti dicentem intuentur? In quo exclamant? Quem deum, ut ita dicam, inter homines putant? Qui distincte, qui explicate, qui abundanter, qui illuminate et rebus et verbis dicunt, et in ipsa oratione quasi quemdam numerum versumque conficiunt – id est quod dico ornate.'

258 Quintilian 1920–2, VIII.III.2, vol. III, pp. 210–12: 'Inventio cum imperitis saepe communis, dispositio modicae doctrinae credi potest ... Cultu vero atque ornatu se quoque commendat.'

'ornamentation' or 'embellishment'. This tends to convey the impression that the theorists we have been considering were only interested – as several recent critics have complained – in 'superficial elocutionary devices' or 'gratuitous verbal ornament'.[259] This misses the metaphorical force of their argument, much of which turns on the fact that, in classical Latin, the term *ornatus* is the word ordinarily used to describe the weapons and accoutrements of war.[260] To be properly *ornatus* is to be equipped for battle, powerfully armoured and protected. What the rhetoricians are claiming is that the 'ornaments' characteristic of the Grand Style are *not* mere decorations or embellishments; they are the weapons an orator must learn to wield if he is to have any prospect of winning the war of words, and thus of gaining victory for his side of the argument.[261]

The suggestion that an orator who deploys the right *ornamenta* is someone in battle array is strongly emphasised by all the Roman writers on eloquence. The author of the *Ad Herennium* portrays him as a man brandishing a sword with the aim of wounding his adversaries as grievously as possible.[262] The normally mild-mannered Quintilian invokes the same image of the *vis verborum* or force of words with still greater ferocity. He not only compares the orator whose speech is *ornatus* with a man wielding a sword that brings terror to the eyes;[263] he also refers on all possible occasions to the weapons of oratory,[264] the battles of the assemblies and law courts,[265] the fights of contending parties,[266] the unending struggle for conquest and victory.[267] Writing a few years after the appearance of Quintilian's great work, Tacitus in his *Dialogus de oratoribus* reworks the same metaphors with characteristic savagery. As the figure of Aper stresses, the great advantage of mastering the art of rhetoric is that 'it leaves you perpetually armed', able 'to strike fear and terror into malignant enemies'.[268] A man of eloquence possesses 'a means of security as well as a weapon of attack, one of equal value in assault as well as in defence'.[269]

259 Kennedy 1978, pp. 1, 4. Cf. Watson 1955, p. 562, Shapiro 1983, pp. 228–9.

260 Ong 1958, p. 277. Cf. Whigham 1984, pp. 139–41; Vickers 1989, pp. 283–4, 314–15; Skinner 1993, pp. 73–4.

261 For the Roman emphasis on the sheer power of the grand style (in contrast to the Hellenistic and later the Christian emphasis on sublimity) see Shuger 1988, pp. 21–41.

262 *Ad C. Herennium* 1954, IV.XIX.26, p. 296, and IV.XXVIII.38, p. 324.

263 Quintilian 1920–2, VIII.III.5, vol. III, p. 212.

264 Quintilian 1920–2, II.XVI.10, vol. I, p. 322; V.VII.8, vol. II, p. 172; XII.I.2, vol. IV, p. 356.

265 Quintilian 1920–2, II.X.8, vol. I, p. 276; VI.IV.15–17, vol. II, p. 510; X.V.17, vol. IV, p. 122.

266 Quintilian 1920–2, V.XIII.11, vol. II, p. 318; X.I.4, vol. IV, p. 4.

267 Quintilian 1920–2, II.XVII.23, vol. I, p. 334; V.III.1, vol. II, p. 190; VII.I.44, vol. III, p. 30; VIII.III.11, vol. III, p. 21; X.II.27, vol. IV, p. 90.

268 Tacitus 1970, 5.5–6, p. 240: as an orator you are 'semper armatus', so that 'invidis vero et inimicis metum et terrorem ultro feras'. Cf. also 37.8, pp. 334–6.

269 Tacitus 1970, 5.6, p. 240: 'praesidium simul ac telum, quo propugnare pariter et incessare'.

When the Roman rhetoricians unpack their master metaphors of 'winning' and 'disarming' speech, they generally make it clear that they have in mind two distinct methods of ornamenting our utterances. One consists of challenging some proffered definition or description of an action or state of affairs in such a way as to defend or support or strengthen whatever interpretation we may wish to give of it. The other, to which they devote far more of their attention, takes the form of recasting or illuminating or amplifying our arguments by means of the figures and tropes of speech. The discussion of this latter aspect of *ornatus* represents one of the most distinctive and important legacies of Roman rhetorical theory, and again it is Quintilian who provides the fullest and best-organised account.

First of all, it is Quintilian who places on a firm footing the basic distinction between figures and tropes.[270] According to his definition, a trope or 'turning' of speech 'is an alteration of a word or phrase from its proper signification to a different one in an especially powerful way'.[271] He lists a dozen different 'translations' of this kind, eight of which are said to involve a straightforward change of meaning, while the rest are said to achieve the same effect – that of ornamenting and augmenting our utterances – through a transfer of usage rather than a direct alteration of sense.[272]

After surveying these *tropi* in book VIII, Quintilian turns in book IX to consider the range of *figurae* or artistic 'shapes' of speech (although he sometimes prefers the equivalent Greek term *schemata*).[273] The difference between the tropes and figures is said to be that, in the case of the latter, no change of meaning is involved. When we write or speak figuratively, we merely give 'a certain unusual configuration to our speech'.[274] Picking up a distinction already suggested by the author of the *Ad Herennium*,[275] Quintilian goes on to contrast *figurae sententiarum* or figures of thought with *figurae verborum* or figures of speech in the strict sense.[276] We employ a figure of thought whenever we express an idea in an indirect or challenging way, for example by asking a rhetorical question instead of merely making the equivalent statement.[277] By contrast, we employ a figure of

270 But the distinction is already adumbrated in *Ad C. Herennium* 1954, IV.XXXI.42, p. 332.

271 Quintilian 1920–2, VIII.VI.1, vol. III, p. 300: 'Tropus est verbi vel sermonis a propria significatione in aliam cum virtute mutatio.'

272 For the first class, see Quintilian 1920–2, VIII.VI.1–39, vol. III, pp. 300–22; for the second, VIII.VI.40–76, vol. III, pp. 322–44.

273 For this usage see Quintilian 1920–2, IX.I.1, vol. III, p. 348.

274 Quintilian 1920–2, IX.I.4, vol. III, p. 350: 'conformatio quaedam orationis remota a communi'.

275 *Ad C. Herennium* 1954, IV.XIII.18, p. 274.

276 For a discussion of the distinction see Vickers 1989, pp. 315–16.

speech whenever we rely on some purely linguistic configuration to give our observations a novel appearance or emphasis.[278] To illustrate this final category, Quintilian introduces a further distinction between rhetorical and grammatical figures of speech.[279] The former, including such devices as antithesis and epanodos, depend on the use of patterned or unusual word order to convey an arresting effect. The latter, of which zeugma would be an obvious example, instead rely on the use of non-standard grammatical forms to produce the same result.[280]

The significance of all these devices according to Quintilian is that they serve in different ways to improve the fighting qualities of our speech. To arm and equip ourselves with any of these 'ornaments' is automatically to increase the *vis* or emotional power of our utterances.[281] The same crucial conclusion had already been drawn by the author of the *Ad Herennium.* The value of the *figurae* lies in helping us to force our hearers to accept our point of view.[282] They provide us with perhaps the most important means of attaining the ultimate goal of oratory: that of persuading our listeners not merely, or even primarily, by the force of argument, but rather by exploiting the persuasive resources inherent in language itself.

THE TUDOR RHETORICIANS

The decades immediately preceding Hobbes's schooldays in the 1590s witnessed perhaps the most important development in the history of English rhetorical thought. The educational theorists we have so far been considering had largely confined their attention to the major Roman treatises on the *ars rhetorica*, with occasional references to such modern Latin handbooks as those of Mancinelli, Mosellanus and especially Melanchthon.[283] But in the second half of the sixteenth century a number of English rhetoricians began to produce their own vernacular treatises, thereby introducing the principles of ancient secular eloquence to a new and much broader audience.[284]

277 Quintilian 1920–2, IX.II.1, vol. III, p. 374.

278 Quintilian 1920–2, IX.III.27, vol. III, p. 460, and IX.III.46, vol. III, p. 472.

279 For the introduction of this distinction see Quintilian 1920–2, IX.III.1, vol. III, p. 442.

280 Quintilian 1920–2, IX.III.35, vol. III, p. 464, and IX.III.81, vol. III, p. 494.

281 Quintilian 1920–2, IX.I.1, vol. III, p. 348: 'nam et vim rebus adiiciunt et gratiam praestant'.

282 On the 'forceful' effect of the figures, see *Ad C. Herennium* 1954, IV.XVIII.26, p. 292, and IV.XXVIII.38, p. 324.

283 Vives 1913, p. 183, and Ascham 1970b, p. 271, particularly recommend Melanchthon among modern authorities. Cf. Meerhoff 1994, esp. pp. 49–56.

284 These writers frequently allude to the desirability of appealing to a broader audience, and hence of writing in English. See for example Sherry 1961, p. 8; Wilson 1554, fo. 7r; Peacham 1971, sig. A, 3v; Fenner 1584, sig. A, 2r.

This indigenous literature in turn evolved in two contrasting ways. One group of writers sought to popularise an authentically classical conception of the *ars rhetorica* and its place in the traditional scheme of the liberal sciences. The pioneer of this approach was Thomas Wilson, a student at King's College Cambridge in the 1540s and a pupil of Sir John Cheke.[285] Cheke in turn brought Wilson to the attention of Roger Ascham and others of his circle in Cambridge, including Sir Thomas Smith.[286] Under the guidance of these teachers Wilson seems to have turned to the study of rhetoric at an early stage. The outcome was the publication in 1554[287] of his major vernacular treatise, *The Arte of Rhetorique,* the earliest work in which a classical understanding of the scope and value of the rhetorical arts was 'sette forth in English' (as the title page boasts) 'for the use of all suche as are studious of eloquence'.[288]

Although Wilson speaks of his *Arte of Rhetorique* as an original work, he follows his Roman authorities so faithfully as to remind us that the lines between authorship and compilation were rather differently drawn in the Renaissance. He begins by reiterating the classical assumption that all forms of oratory can be divided into 'three kyndes of causes', the demonstrative, the deliberative and the judicial.[289] He goes on to observe that the art of writing or speaking in any of these genera embodies five main subdivisions, and takes sides with the author of the *Ad Herennium* in adding that these must be viewed as faculties of those who practise rhetoric rather than elements of the art itself.[290] He lists these faculties in the usual way as 'Invencion of matter, Disposition of the same, Elocution, Memorie, Utteraunce', and in explicating these concepts he simply translates the definitions given in the *Ad Herennium.*[291] He then turns in book II to consider 'the partes of every Oracion', at which point he closely echoes Quintilian's arguments.[292] He agrees that the question of how to organise an oration must be treated as an aspect of invention, and endorses Quintilian's distinctive claim that any oration must be capable of being broken down into seven separate parts. He apportions much of book II to describing and illustrating this structure, the features of which he itemises

285 For biographical details on Wilson see Wagner 1960, p. 3.

286 On the relations between Wilson and Cheke's circle see Wagner 1960, pp. 4–7. On Cheke and Smith see Dewar 1964, pp. 12–13.

287 The title page reads 'M.D.LIII. Mense Januarii.' i.e. 1554 our style. See Wilson 1554 and cf. Wagner 1929.

288 For the full title see Wilson 1554. For a discussion see Howell 1956, pp. 98–110.

289 Wilson 1554, fo. 6^{r}. The three kinds are discussed at fos. 6^{v}–16^{r}, 16^{r}–47^{r} and 47^{r}–54^{v}.

290 See Wilson 1554, fo. 3^{v}, speaking of the 'five thynges [cf. *Ad C. Herennium* on *res*] to be considered in an Orator'.

291 Wilson 1554, fos. 3^{v}–4^{r}; cf. *Ad C. Herennium* 1954, I.II.3, p. 6.

292 Wilson 1554, fo. 55^{r}.

(in resonant translations of Quintilian's terminology) as 'Enteraunce', 'Narration', 'Division', 'Proposicions', 'Confirmacion', 'Confutacion' and 'Conclusion'.[293] Wilson's third and final book surveys the remaining three faculties or 'thynges' required of an orator: 'Elocucion', 'Memorie' and 'Pronunciation'.[294] His discussion ends with pronunciation, by which he means 'an apte orderinge' not merely of the voice but of 'countenance and all the whole bodye' in such a way as to lend special emphasis to what is said.[295] But he is true to his Roman authorities in assigning most of his space to elocution, which he takes to include four distinct elements, 'plainnesse, aptenesse, composicion, exornacion'.[296] Among these, 'exornacion' is said to be by far the most important, and in handling this topic Wilson again relies on Quintilian, first dividing the methods of exornation into tropes and figures and finally subdividing the latter into figures of words and figures of sentences.[297]

Wilson's understanding of eloquence as a five-fold art proved to be the starting-point of a major tradition in English rhetorical thought.[298] His own treatise was reprinted at least eight times in the reign of Elizabeth,[299] and according to Gabriel Harvey it became 'the dailie bread of owr common pleaders & discoursers'.[300] Meanwhile Wilson's approach was taken up by a number of prominent writers of rhetorical textbooks in the early seventeenth century. Thomas Vicars, who became a Fellow of Queen's College Oxford in 1616,[301] restates the same view of rhetoric as an art with five *elementa* in his *Cheiragogia*, a popular question-and-answer manual first published in 1619 and reprinted on at least three occasions in the 1620s.[302] Thomas Farnaby adopts a similar approach in his *Index Rhetoricus* of 1625, by far the most widely used textbook of the early Stuart period.[303] Farnaby omits the category of *memoria*, but his approach to the

293 Wilson 1554, fos. 55^{r}, 58^{v}, 60^{r}, 61^{r}, 61^{v}, 62^{r}, 63^{r}.

294 Wilson 1554, fos. 85^{v}, 111^{v}, 116^{v}.

295 Wilson 1554, fo. 116^{v}.

296 Wilson 1554, fo. 86^{r}.

297 Wilson 1554, fos 90^{v}, 94^{r}.

298 Not the sole starting-point, as the five elements had already been discriminated by Stephen Hawes in his vernacular poem of 1509, *The Pastime of Pleasure*. But Hawes's poem is intended not as a work of rhetoric but a guide to courtliness. See Hawes 1928, lines 701–1295, and cf. Howell 1956, pp. 48–9, 81–8.

299 Wagner 1929, pp. 427–8.

300 Harvey 1913, p. 122.

301 For biographical details on Vicars see Howell 1956, pp. 320–1.

302 The first edition is extremely rare: see Murphy, 1981, p. 298. I quote from the second edition, 1621. For the printing history see Murphy 1981, p. 298. (But Murphy has missed an 'editio nova', London, 1624.) On rhetoric as a five-fold art see Vicars 1621, p. 1, paraphrasing Cicero 1949a, I.VII.9, p. 18.

303 On Farnaby and his adventurous life (he sailed with Drake and fought in the Netherlands) see Nadeau 1950, pp. 34–44. Farnaby achieved fame as an editor, his versions of Ovid, Virgil,

ars rhetorica is otherwise entirely classical, encompassing in turn the three genera of oratory and the four elementa of *inventio*, *dispositio*, *elocutio* and *pronuntiatio*.[304]

As Gabriel Harvey's comment suggests, the popularisation by Wilson and his contemporaries of a fully Ciceronian conception of the rhetorical arts soon had a marked impact on the development of English prose. Perhaps the most remarkable attempt to put into practice the full range of Ciceronian precepts can be found in John Lyly's *Euphues*, which caused a sensation on its publication in 1579 and went through several editions before Sir Philip Sidney in his *Defence of Poesie* led a reaction against its remorselessly 'schematising' style.[305] Lyly recounts the story of the young Euphues' quest for a form of education and a way of life suitable for a gentleman. The hero – whose name appears to be taken from Ascham's *Scholemaster*[306] – begins by devoting himself to sexual intrigue in 'Naples', which evidently stands for London and its corrupt Italianate ways. He soon exchanges his worldly life for that of a scholar in Oxford ('Athens'),[307] where Lyly himself had been a student in the early 1570s.[308] The values of scholarship are in turn transcended when Euphues forsakes the pagan *studia humanitatis* to dedicate himself to a life of divinity. Lyly presents his text as a narrative, but he mainly develops his argument in the form of a sequence of rhetorical exercises.[309] These include formal epistles and orations exploiting every device of *ornatus*, as well as a number of declamations in which the moral problems raised by Euphues' progress are debated *in utramque partem*, including the advisability of marriage, the virtues and vices of women, the merits of studying the humanities and finally, and most daringly, the existence of God.[310] By these means Lyly provided his readers with an exemplification of the uses – and possible misuses[311] – of virtually all the elements we have so far been examining in the classical theory of eloquence. The virtuosity of the performance was not lost on his contemporaries. As William Webbe remarks in his *Discourse*

Seneca and Juvenal being used throughout the century. See Binns 1990, pp. 194–5. Farnaby's *Index*, designed as its title page says 'for the instruction of those of tender age' went through at least six editions by the middle of the century. See Murphy 1981, pp. 143–4.

304 Farnaby 1970, pp. 2–8, 8–16, 16–30, 30–1. Howell 1956, p. 321, classifies Farnaby as a 'Neo-Ciceronian'. Farnaby's approach was in turn adopted by several leading textbooks of the next generation. See Stephens 1648 and Walker 1682 (the latter first issued in 1659).

305 See Hunter 1962, pp. 48, 72, 286–9, and Croll 1966, pp. 241–95, on Lyly's sources.

306 See Ascham 1970b, p. 194. On Lyly and Ascham see Miglior 1975, pp. 257–72.

307 On 'Naples' and 'Athens' see Kinney 1986, pp. 138–9.

308 Hunter 1962, pp. 39–40.

309 For an analysis of *Euphues* stressing its exemplifications of rhetorical theory see Kinney 1986, pp. 133–80.

310 Lyly 1868, pp. 83–5, 106–21, 128–57, 160–77.

311 As emphasised in Hutson 1993, p. 93.

of English Poetrie of 1586, Lyly's writings not only exhibit 'singuler eloquence' but 'make tryall thereof thorough all the partes of Rethorike'.[312]

During the second half of the sixteenth century, however, most English treatises on the *ars rhetorica* began to present a more restricted view of the discipline. This development can in part be explained in terms of the overwhelming influence of the Roman rhetorical tradition we have so far discussed. Several classical treatises – most obviously Cicero's *De inventione* – had chiefly concentrated on invention and disposition, and a number of English rhetoricians simply followed their lead. One such writer was Leonard Cox, the author of the earliest work on rhetoric to be published in English, the black-letter treatise of c.1530 entitled *The Arte or Crafte of Rhethoryke.*[313] But the same approach can also be found in a number of later and more sophisticated guides to the rhetorical arts. A good example is provided by the work of William Pemble, a younger contemporary of Hobbes's at Magdalen Hall Oxford.[314] Pemble's *Enchiridion Oratorium,* posthumously published in 1633, is modelled more closely even than Cox's treatise had been on Cicero's *De inventione.* Pemble begins by itemising the five *partes* of the *ars rhetorica,*[315] after which he divides his analysis into two books. Book I surveys the three genera of oratory,[316] while book II is wholly given over to listing the elements of an ideal speech.[317] The topics of *inventio* and *dispositio* are thus taken to cover the entire field of the rhetorical arts.

As we have seen, however, the main element of specialisation already present in the Roman tradition had consisted of emphasising the importance of *elocutio.* The author of the *Ad Herennium* had assigned the whole of his final book to the topic, while later writers such as Rutilius Lupus and Iulius Rufinianus had confined themselves to *elocutio* alone. Here again a number of English rhetoricians simply followed their lead, although they were able to draw at the same time on various modern treatises already published on the continent. Among the earliest of these had been Mancinelli's *Carmen* and Mosellanus' *De Schematibus,* but by far the most popular was Johann Susenbrotus' *Epitome troporum ac schematorum,* the first edition of which had appeared at Zurich in 1535.[318] A schoolmaster in Regensburg, Susenbrotus remains a shadowy figure,[319] but his *Epitome*

312 Webbe 1904, p. 256; cf. Kinney 1986, p. 134.
313 See Cox c.1530. On Cox see Howell 1956, pp. 90–2.
314 On Pemble see Howell 1956, pp. 323–4.
315 Pemble 1633, sig. A, 3^v.
316 Pemble 1633, book I, pp. 1–57.
317 Pemble 1633, book II, pp. 58–78.
318 Murphy 1981, p. 280.
319 But see Brennan 1953 for an edition and commentary and cf. Brennan 1960.

seems to have won him an immediate and extensive English following. It was printed in London as early as 1562,[320] and rapidly established itself as one of the most widely used guides to *elocutio* in the Elizabethan grammar schools.[321]

Given this background, it is not surprising that a similar tendency to focus exclusively on *elocutio* appeared at an early stage in English rhetorical thought.[322] Richard Sherry, headmaster of Magdalen College School in the 1530s,[323] published the first specialised manual of this kind in 1550, entitling it *A Treatise of Schemes and Tropes*.[324] The next English rhetorician to concentrate on *elocutio* was Henry Peacham, the otherwise unknown rector of a parish in Lincolnshire.[325] Peacham's treatise, *The Garden of Eloquence*, which was first issued in 1577 and reprinted in a much revised and expanded form in 1593,[326] was also concerned exclusively with defining and illustrating the figures and tropes of speech.[327] A further study of *elocutio*, partly dependent on Sherry and Peacham,[328] appeared in the well-known treatise on poetics, *The Arte of English Poesie*, which was first published in 1589.[329] The *Arte* appeared anonymously, but has generally been attributed to George Puttenham, a nephew of Sir Thomas Elyot.[330] Puttenham divides his text into three sections, the first of which considers the standing of poets and poetry, while the second applies the Ciceronian ideal of decorum to the writing of English verse. But the third and longest part, entitled 'Of ornament', is as much concerned with rhetoric as with the theory of poetry, and is largely given over to a further analysis of the figures and tropes.[331] This renewed emphasis on *elocutio* was echoed soon afterwards in Sir Philip Sidney's *Defence of Poesie*, first printed in 1595,[332]

320 Murphy 1981, p. 280.

321 For its use in schools see Baldwin 1944, I, pp. 370–1, 405–6, 413.

322 Vickers 1988, pp. 742–4.

323 On Sherry see Howell 1956, pp. 125–31.

324 See Sherry 1961. As Crane 1965 notes, Sherry depends heavily on Mosellanus (esp. pp. 25–46) and the *Ad Herennium* (esp. pp. 47–61). Note that this concentration on *elocutio* predates by a generation the reception of Ramism in England. Cf. Howell 1956, pp. 254, 257, who is inclined to see in Ramism the explanation for this development.

325 On Peacham see Pitman 1934 and Howell 1956, pp. 132–7. Peacham held the living of North Leverton from 1578.

326 See respectively Peacham 1971 and Peacham 1593.

327 Peacham draws particularly on Susenbrotus and Sherry. See Crane 1965, p. 219, and Howell 1956, p. 135 and note.

328 See the appendix on sources in Willcock and Walker 1970, pp. 319–22.

329 On its composition and publication see Willcock and Walker 1970, pp. xliv–liii. The *Arte* is usually classified as a treatise on poetics, but rhetoric and poetics were scarcely distinguished at this time. See Sloan 1974, Vickers 1989, pp. 278–9, Norbrook 1992, pp. 51–60.

330 For this attribution see Willcock and Walker 1970, pp. xi–xliv. For biographical details see Willcock and Walker, pp. xviii–xxxi.

331 Puttenham 1970, pp. 137–308. Cf. Howell 1956, pp. 327–9.

332 It is generally accepted, however, that Sidney had composed his *Defence* some fifteen years

itself a carefully crafted exercise in the *genus demonstrativum* that follows Quintilian's seven-fold analysis of *dispositio* to the letter.[333] The last Elizabethan to produce a treatise wholly devoted to this topic was the humbler figure of Angel Day, whose other productions were mainly in the epideictic genre of commendatory verse.[334] In 1586 Day published *The English Secretary*,[335] a formulary or book of model letters[336] conceived on the age-old humanist pattern of the *ars dictaminis*.[337] When this was reprinted in 1592, he added a section entitled 'A Declaration of such Tropes, Figures or Schemes, as for excellencie and ornament in writing, are specially used in this Methode'.[338] Whereas his original text had merely drawn attention in a series of marginal scholia to the figures and tropes contained in his model letters, Day's new section offered what amounted to an independent treatise on the same subject. Although it consisted of little more than a paraphrase of Susenbrotus' *Epitome*, it nevertheless enjoyed a considerable vogue, and went through at least five editions within the next twenty years.[339]

We also need to consider a second and more important reason for the growing specialisation of English rhetorical theory in the latter part of the sixteenth century. This was partly a reflection of wider changes affecting the classification of the liberal arts. One such change took the form of the claim that the art of memory should be treated not as an aspect of rhetoric but as a *scientia* in its own right. The increasing acceptance of this assumption[340] undoubtedly helps to explain why the analysis of memory virtually disappeared from English rhetorical textbooks by the end of the century.[341] We encounter the assumption itself as early as 1548, the year in which Robert Copland published his treatise entitled *The Art of Memory*.[342]

earlier. See Hamilton 1977, pp. 107–8, and Weiner 1978, p. 197. For a discussion of the *Defence* in relation to courtly ideals of self-presentation see Javitch 1978, pp. 93–104.

333 Sidney 1923, esp. pp. 9, 14–16, 29–30, on the figures and images of poetry. On the rhetoric of Sidney's own text see Myrick 1935, pp. 46–83.

334 These included a prefatory sonnet in William Jones's translation of Nennio's *Treatise of nobility*. See Jones 1967, sig. ¶, 2v. For biographical details see Evans 1967.

335 The edition I use is Day 1967, which reprints the version of 1599.

336 Day 1967 lists twelve main forms of epistle, with examples ranging from the descriptive to the amatory.

337 On the *ars dictaminis* and the origins of humanism see Skinner 1990c, esp. pp. 123–4 and references cited there. On the *ars* in medieval rhetoric see Murphy 1974, pp. 194–268.

338 See Day 1592. Day's modern editor appears unaware of this edition (see Evans 1967, pp. vi–vii). He instead reprints the *Declaration* from the 1599 edition. See Day 1967, pp. 75–100.

339 Murphy 1981, p. 109.

340 When, for example, Bacon classifies the sciences he takes it for granted that memory is a distinct science. See Bacon 1915, pp. 135–6.

341 The element of memory is omitted from such early Stuart textbooks as those of Pemble and Farnaby. For an explicit statement to the effect that rhetoric has only four parts, see Pemble 1633, sig. A, 3v.

342 Copland c.1548; for the suggested date of publication see Yates 1966, p. 112n. Copland's work

Copland presents his findings not as a contribution to rhetoric but rather as an introduction to a separate discipline which, as his title page insists, is 'behovefull and profytable to all professours of scyences', among whom Copland numbers not merely students of eloquence but also 'legystes, phylosophres & theologiens'.[343] The same attitude is even more clearly mirrored in William Fulwood's *The Castel of Memorie* of 1562.[344] Fulwood's closing chapter takes the form of a conventional discussion – much indebted to the *Ad Herennium*[345] – of how the memory can be artificially 'admonished' by associating what needs to be recalled with places and images. But as Fulwood stresses, this does not mean that he thinks of his study as a contribution to the theory of eloquence. Rather he treats the investigation of memory as a distinct science of an essentially medical character, and devotes his earlier chapters to considering what serves to damage its powers, what cures are available and what 'medicinable compounded remedies' may be capable of increasing its capacity.[346]

A second change in the classification of the liberal arts arose out of the new view of dialectic put forward by Lorenzo Valla and later by Rudolph Agricola and his numerous disciples in the early years of the sixteenth century.[347] The essence of their argument was that *inventio* and *dispositio* must be treated as aspects of the *ars dialectica*.[348] This too had the effect of limiting the scope of rhetoric, restricting it to the remaining three elements of *elocutio*, *memoria* and *pronuntiatio*. We already find Sir Thomas Elyot endorsing these new lines of demarcation in *The Governor*, in which he specifically recommends Agricola as a dialectician 'whose work prepareth invention, telling the places from whence an argument for the proof of any matter may be taken'. Elyot adds that the study of *inventio* forms a part of logic, and must therefore be distinguished from the art of rhetoric which, he suggests, should be taught immediately after the rudiments of logic have been acquired.[349]

The main impetus, however, behind the reduction in the scope of the *ars rhetorica* undoubtedly came from the Ramist programme for the reorganisation of the liberal arts. It was Pierre de la Ramée – better

is a translation of Peter of Ravenna 1541, first printed in 1491. See Yates 1966, p. 112 and note.

343 Copland 1548, title page.

344 A translation of Guglielmo Grataroli, *De memoria* (1554), as Fulwood explains on his crowded title page. See Grataroli 1562 and cf. Howell 1956, p. 143.

345 Grataroli 1562, sig. G, 6[v].

346 Grataroli 1562, esp. chapter 5, sig. E, 3[r].

347 On Valla, Agricola and their influence see Vasoli 1968, esp. pp. 28–77, 147–82, 249–77.

348 On these changes see Vasoli 1968, esp. 28–77; Jardine 1974, pp. 13–14, 73–4; Jardine 1977; and for a summary Jardine 1988.

349 Elyot 1962, p. 34.

known in his Latinised style as Petrus Ramus – who gave his name to these reforms.[350] Born in c.1515 and educated at the University of Paris, Ramus gained his master's degree at the age of twenty-one for a defence of the thesis that 'everything affirmed on the authority of Aristotle is artificial and contrived'.[351] So began a career of unremitting polemical violence that came to a correspondingly violent end when Ramus, an early convert to Huguenotism, was murdered in the massacre of St Bartholomew's Day in 1572.[352] Ramus' proposed reorganisation of the arts was rooted in his perception that the traditional curriculum, and especially the teaching of the trivium (grammar, rhetoric, logic), had become filled with redundancies and overlapping categories. He mainly concentrated on the simplification of logic or dialectic, while the place of rhetoric in the new scheme of things was clarified by his associate Omar Talon. Ramus first announced his new approach to logic in his *Dialecticae Partitiones* of 1543, while Talon went on to produce his complementary *Rhetorica* five years later,[353] although Ramus may have had a hand in the production of the latter text as well.[354] Subsequently Ramus rounded off his exposition of the new programme by producing a vernacular digest of his logic, the *Dialectique*, in 1555.[355]

According to the *Dialectique*, 'the parts of logic are two in number, Invention and Judgment'.[356] Invention seeks to discover 'reason, proof and argument', while judgment ('which is also called Disposition') 'shows the ways and means of organising arguments'.[357] The art of memory forms an aspect of disposition or judgment, since ease of recollection depends essentially on logical arrangement. The discussion of these two themes takes up the two corresponding books into which Ramus' treatise is divided. Book I considers the various aspects of invention, including cause and effect, subject and circumstance, similarities, dissimilarities and the like. Book II examines the topic of disposition or arrangement, focusing on the characteristically Ramist concept of *La méthode*[358] and arguing that,

350 On Ramism see Vasoli 1968; Bruyère 1984; Grafton and Jardine 1986, pp. 161–70; and for a summary Jardine 1988, pp. 184–6.

351 'Quaecunque ab Aristotele dicit, commentitia esse'. On this translation see Duhamel 1952, p. 1036.

352 Ong 1958a, pp. 28–9. For a survey of Ramus' academic quarrels see Ong 1958b, pp. 492–506.

353 Murphy 1981, p. 244. For a listing of Ramus' works see also Ong 1958b, pp. 37–40. When quoting Talon's *Rhetorica* I use the first Cambridge edition.

354 Ong 1965, p. 228.

355 Dassonville 1964, pp. 43–6.

356 Ramus 1964, p. 63: 'Les parties de Dialectique sont deux, Invention et Jugement.'

357 Ramus 1964, pp. 53–4: invention is concerned with 'raison, preuve, argument' while judgment – 'aussi nommé disposition' – 'monstre les manières et espèces de les disposer'.

358 Vasoli 1968, pp. 498–511.

whereas logic follows a natural method, rhetoric follows 'the method of prudence'.[359]

If invention and disposition constitute the twin elements of natural logic, it would seem that neither of these topics can figure in a separate art of rhetoric. Moreover, if the best method of strengthening the memory is simply to organise what needs to be recollected in the most logical manner, it would seem that the idea of memory as a further element of rhetoric must similarly drop away.[360] That these were indeed the inferences Ramus and his followers wished to draw becomes clear as soon as we turn to Talon's *Rhetorica.* 'Rhetoric', Talon begins, 'is the art of speaking well.' This being so, 'the parts of rhetoric are two: *elocutio* and *pronuntiatio*.'[361] With this opening declaration Talon announces a drastic reduction in the scope of the rhetorical arts: the other three traditional elements – *inventio, dispositio* and *memoria* – simply disappear. Lest the moral be missed, Ramus later spelled it out as unambiguously as possible at the end of his *Dialectique.* 'The tropes and figures of elocution, together with the graces of action, form the entirety of Rhetoric as a true art distinct from Dialectic.'[362]

These inroads upon the traditional province of rhetoric were at first opposed by English humanists with considerable warmth.[363] Roger Ascham not only denounces Ramus and Talon for their 'singularitie in dissenting from the best mens judgementes', but adds that their attitude 'is moch misliked of all them that joyne with learning discretion and wisedome'.[364] Unrepentantly he maintains that 'even as far as *Tullie* goeth beyond *Quintilian, Ramus* and *Talaeus* in perfite Eloquence, even so moch, by myne opinion, cum they behinde *Tullie,* for trew judgement in teaching the same'.[365] To a younger generation of teachers, however, Ramus' proposed simplifications of the curriculum clearly came as an exciting development.[366] The University of Oxford at first resisted, but a number of enthusiasts at Cambridge soon began to speak out in his support.[367] One of the earliest was

359 See Ramus 1964, pp. 145, 150 contrasting 'méthode de nature' with 'méthode de prudence'. For a discussion see Bruyère 1984, pp. 139–41.

360 Howell 1956, p. 269.

361 Talon 1631, pp. 1–2: 'Rhetorica est ars bene dicendi ... Partes Rhetoricae duae sunt; Elocutio & Pronunciatio.'

362 Ramus 1964, p. 152: 'tous les tropes et figures d'élocution, toutes les grâces d'action, qui est la Rhétorique entière, vraye et séparée de la Dialectique'.

363 For similar resistance in Paris see Scott 1910, esp. pp. 99–100.

364 Ascham 1970b, p. 243.

365 Ascham 1970b, p. 244.

366 On the popularity of Ramist texts in the generation following Ramus' death see Maclean 1990.

367 Simon 1966, pp. 319–20.

Gabriel Harvey,[368] who took up the post of University Praelector in Rhetoric in 1574.[369] His inaugural lecture was published in 1577 under the title *Rhetor*, while his opening lecture of 1576 was issued at the same time as *Ciceronianus*.[370] Both orations indicate that Harvey had introduced his audiences to a purely Ramist understanding of the rhetorical arts. The *Ciceronianus* goes so far as to compare Roger Ascham unfavourably with Ramus, whom Harvey punningly hails not merely as a branch (*ramus*) but as a principal root from which the new approaches to logic and rhetoric have sprung.[371] The *Rhetor* gives an account of the new approaches themselves, ending with an unambiguous summary of the drastically limited role assigned to rhetoric in the Ramist scheme of things:

> Dialectic has two parts, one being invention, the other judgment. But these have been elaborated not by the rhetoricians but rather by Aristotle and the Stoics. Moreover, memory is common to many of the arts. So the proper praise of an orator must derive from his elocution, to which must be added an eloquence of bodily movement.[372]

As in Talon's account, *elocutio* and *pronuntiatio* are thus taken to constitute the whole of the *ars rhetorica.*

The next work of Ramist inspiration to be published by an English rhetorician was the brief but influential treatise entitled *The Artes of Logike and Rethorike*, which first appeared in 1584.[373] This was the work of Dudley Fenner, one of the most uncompromising of the early puritan divines.[374] A graduate of Peterhouse, where he matriculated in 1575, Fenner may well have heard Gabriel Harvey lecture in the course of that year in praise of Ramus and Talon.[375] Certainly Fenner's own treatise is wholly Ramist in character, in addition to being the earliest work in English in which a Ramist understanding of logic and rhetoric are placed side by side in such a way as to enable the 'natural' approach to both subjects to be compared. Fenner begins with logic, describing it as an art of reasoning in two parts.

368 On Harvey and his Ramism see Jardine 1986, esp. pp. 42–8; Grafton and Jardine 1986, pp. 184–96.

369 Stern 1979, p. 28.

370 Stern 1979, pp. 21, 28, 30. On the *Ciceronianus* see Binns 1990, pp. 278–82.

371 Harvey 1577a, p. 33: 'dic ornatissime Rame, tuum quod sit tam illustre fundamentum'. Ascham is criticised by name at pp. 55, 57.

372 Harvey 1577b, sig. E, iiii^{r-v}: 'Dialecticam duas habere partes: unam inveniendi, alteram iudicandi; in quibus non Rhetores, sed Aristoteles & Stoici elaboraverunt; Memoriam esse communem multarum artium; Oratoris propriam laudem esse in elocutione; ... [et] eloquentiam illam corporis Actionem adiungat.'

373 As Ong 1951 (p. 263 and note) rightly noted, there were two different printings in 1584. Fenner's name was only added in the posthumous reprinting of 1588.

374 On Fenner see Collinson 1967, pp. 266, 274, 434.

375 Howell 1956, p. 255 and note.

The first, which 'doth helpe muche to the finding out of reasons' is said to be invention; the second, 'concerning the ordering of reasons', is said to be judgment.[376] This means that, by the time we come to the chapters on rhetoric, Fenner has already disposed of two of its traditional elements. Closely paraphrasing Talon's *Rhetorica*, he goes on to draw the characteristically Ramist conclusion that rhetoric is also an art with only two parts: 'Garnishing of speech, called Eloquution' and 'Garnishing of the maner of utterance, called Pronunciation'.[377]

The closing years of Elizabeth's reign saw the publication of two further treatises in which a similar understanding of rhetoric acquired an even wider currency. The first of these, the work of Abraham Fraunce, appeared under the title *The Arcadian Rhetoric* in 1588. Like Fenner, Fraunce had been a student at Cambridge in the 1570s and may well have heard Gabriel Harvey lecture on Ramism.[378] His own work is basically a paraphrase of Talon's *Rhetorica*,[379] although he supplements the dry classifications typical of Ramism with many illustrations drawn from ancient and modern poetry, even quoting from Edmund Spenser's then unpublished *Faerie Queene*.[380] The last of the Elizabethan Ramists was Charles Butler, whose *Rhetoricae Libri Duo* first appeared in 1598.[381] A rare instance of an Oxford convert to Ramism, Butler took his degree at Magdalen Hall only a few years before Hobbes became an undergraduate there.[382] Although Butler's treatise amounts to little more than a further reworking of Talon's *Rhetorica*, it proved extremely successful in its own right, and probably served more than any other work to popularise the tenets of Ramist rhetoric in England.[383] As we have seen, these tenets can essentially be reduced to two, and in stating them Butler may be said to summarise a whole generation of argument. The first claims that 'there are only two parts of rhetoric, *elocutio* and *pronuntiatio*';[384] the second adds that *elocutio*, by far the more important element, 'can be equated with the internal exornation of speech', and thus 'with a trope or a figure'.[385]

As well as encouraging this drastically simplified equation between

376 Fenner 1584, sig. B, 1^r and sig. C, 1^r.
377 Fenner 1584, sig. D, 1^v.
378 On Fraunce see Seaton 1950, pp. viii–xii and Howell 1956, pp. 257–8.
379 As Seaton 1950 notes, pp. ix–x.
380 Seaton 1950, p. xl.
381 For publishing details see Howell 1956, pp. 262–3. I quote from the first London edition.
382 On Butler see Howell 1956, pp. 262–9.
383 Howell 1956, pp. 258–65; Simon 1979, p. 320. Butler's text went through at least eight editions in its first fifty years. See Murphy 1981, pp. 57–8.
384 Butler 1629, sig. B, 1^r: 'Partes rhetoricae duae sunt. Elocutio & Pronunciatio.'
385 See Butler 1629, sig. B, 1^r for the claim that 'Elocutio est interna exornatio orationis', and thus that 'Elocutio est tropus aut figura.'

eloquence and *elocutio*, the Ramists were responsible for introducing one further simplification into English rhetorical theory in the latter part of the sixteenth century. This stemmed from their characteristic insistence on the need to reorganise the constituent elements of the different disciplines and present them in a more 'methodical' style. Applied to the topic of *elocutio*, this led the Ramists to put forward a more straightforward and purportedly 'natural' set of categories for the classification and explanation of the figures and tropes of speech.

Earlier English writers on *elocutio* had largely derived their classifications from Quintilian's analysis in book VIII of the *Institutio oratoria*. Sherry's pioneering discussion had employed the same basic distinction between a 'figure of worde' and 'figures of sentence', as well as contrasting the full range of these figures with the separate concept of a trope.[386] Sherry's immediate successors continued to use the same categories, although they began to add a number of complications to Quintilian's account. One refinement, introduced by Peacham in 1577 and later developed by Day, consisted of applying to the tropes the distinction already drawn by Quintilian in the case of the figures between *verba* and *sententiae*.[387] A further refinement took the form of laying much greater emphasis on the purely grammatical figures of speech. These 'figures of construccion', as Sherry had called them,[388] came to seem so important that John Stockwood devoted almost the entirety of his *Treatise of the Figures* of c.1590 to their exposition,[389] concentrating on such rarefied instances as antiptosis, epergesis, evocatio and syllepsis in addition to such well-known figures as zeugma.[390]

Once the grammatical and rhetorical figures had been discriminated, a number of writers introduced further subdivisions under each of these categories. But the main effect of introducing so many new distinctions was simply to exacerbate the problem to which the use of the traditional classifications had already given rise: no one could agree on how many figures and tropes needed to be discriminated. Sherry had begun by suggesting a list of fifteen different tropes,[391] but Day raised the number to sixteen, finding seven tropes of words and nine of sentences.[392] A year later Peacham raised the number yet again, finding a further trope under each of Day's categories.[393] Similar problems beset the itemising of the

386 Sherry 1961, pp. 25–6, 39, 62.
387 Peacham 1971, sig. B, 1r; Day 1967, pp. 77, 79.
388 Sherry 1961, p. 28.
389 Stockwood 1713, sig. A, 6r to sig. C, 7r.
390 Stockwood died in 1610, but his treatise remained unpublished until 1672. See Murphy 1981, p. 276. I cite from the London edition of 1713.
391 Sherry 1961, pp. 3–46.
392 Day 1967, pp. 77–80.
393 Peacham 1593, pp. 3–25, 25–40.

figures or schemes. Sherry had begun by distinguishing over forty 'figures Rethoricall',[394] but Day increased the number to over fifty,[395] while Puttenham proposed a list of 'Figures sententious otherwise called Rhetoricall' encompassing over sixty separate elocutionary techniques.[396]

This was the scene of confusion upon which the Ramists launched their call for a more 'methodical' approach.[397] Their first simplifying move was to claim that there were only four genuine tropes.[398] Omar Talon makes the point with much polemical force at the outset of his *Rhetorica*. First he complains that an excessive amount of obscurity and redundancy currently distort the handling of this theme. Then he goes on to isolate the four tropes alone worthy of the name: metonymy, irony, metaphor and synecdoche.[399] The impact of his proposal was immediate. While some of his English disciples proposed a different ordering,[400] no one of Ramist sympathies ever subsequently dissented from his basic contention that, as Fenner expresses it, metonymy, irony, synecdoche and metaphor are the sole instances in which 'one worde is drawen from his first proper signification to another' in such a way as to produce a rhetorical effect.[401]

The Ramists adopted a similar policy in analysing the figures or schemes of speech. First they removed any mention of the so-called grammatical schemes. This simply followed from their basic assumption that each of the liberal arts must possess its own autonomous subject matter: if there are any figures whose distinguishing marks are entirely grammatical, they must obviously be studied under the heading of grammar and not of rhetoric. At the same time they reorganised and greatly abbreviated the remaining lists of figures or schemes. Talon put forward a completely new classification at this point, and its typically Ramist bifurcations were subsequently taken up by all his English followers. Talon's system is based on accepting the traditional distinction between figures of words and figures of sentences. Under the former

394 Sherry 1961, pp. 47–61.
395 Day 1967, pp. 84–100.
396 Puttenham 1970, pp. 196–249.
397 On pre-Ramist confusions see Hudson 1935, esp. pp. xviii–xix. On Ramism and 'the method of method' see Ong 1958a, pp. 245–69. To modern scholars it seems obvious that the only methodical way of listing the figures and tropes is alphabetically. See for example Vickers 1989, pp. 491–8. But the first English rhetorician to employ this approach was Smith in 1657. See Smith 1969.
398 For this development see Vickers 1989, p. 439 and note.
399 Talon 1631, pp. 2–3, 3–17.
400 See for example Fenner 1584, sig. D, 1^{v}–2^{v}.
401 Fenner 1584, sig. D, 1^{v}. Cf. Fraunce 1950, p. 4, and Butler 1629, sig. B, 2^{r}. This view of the tropes was eventually accepted even by non-Ramist writers. See Vicars 1621, p. 69; Farnaby 1970, p. 20; Stephens 1648, p. 7; Smith 1969, pp. 2–3. For the view that there are only four tropes, and that their order – metaphor, metonymy, synecdoche and irony – bears a metaphysical significance, see Vico 1948, pp. 116–18, and cf. Mooney 1985, pp. 206–32.

heading, however, he and his disciples included only those figures dependent on the use of different sounds (such as paranomasia and polyptoton) and those dependent on the repetition of similar sounds (such as anaphora, climax and epanados).[402] Under the latter heading they proposed a further simplification based on their characteristic interest in the objects of speech, arriving at a basic distinction between what Fenner and Fraunce both describe as 'speech alone' as opposed to speech in the form of 'conference or debate'.[403] As in the case of the figures of words, the effect was greatly to shorten the long and undifferentiated lists favoured by the neo-Ciceronian writers. These were finally reduced in the works of Talon and his followers to a set of at most eighteen principal figures of speech.[404]

These simplifications clearly came as a liberation to those attempting to teach the rudiments of rhetoric in the Elizabethan grammar schools. As we have seen, it had seemed unavoidable to an earlier generation that schoolmasters should concentrate on the major Roman texts. But by the time John Brinsley came to publish his *Ludus Literarius* in 1612 the situation had greatly changed. Turning in chapter 16 to advise teachers on how to explain 'any needefull question of Grammar or Rhetoricke', Brinsley has two suggestions to make. One is that 'you may if you please make them perfect in *Talaeus* Rhetoricke, which I take to be most used in the best Schooles'; the other is that 'in stead of *Talaeus*, you may use Master *Butler*'s Rhetoricke, of *Magdalens* in Oxford'.[405] This is a new book, Brinsley adds, and not an expensive one, but its value 'will be found to be farre above all that ever hath beene written of the same'.[406]

402 Talon 1631, pp. 30–7. Cf. Fenner 1584, sig. D, 3^v–4^r; Fraunce 1950, table following p. 136; Butler 1629, sig. K, 4^r.

403 Fenner 1584, sig. D, 4^r; Fraunce 1950, table following p. 136.

404 See for example the tabulation in Butler 1629, sig. E, 2^r.

405 Brinsley 1917, p. 203.

406 Brinsley 1917, p. 204, and cf. Simon 1979, pp. 379–80.

Chapter 2

THE POLITICS OF ELOQUENCE

THE IDEAL OF THE *VIR CIVILIS*

When Thomas Wilson first made available to English readers a Roman conception of the *ars rhetorica*, he saw himself as engaged on an undertaking of far wider significance than that of merely outlining the various definitions and typologies we have so far discussed. He saw himself as retrieving a classical understanding of why it should be regarded as a matter of cultural importance to acquire a mastery of those precise definitions and typologies.

It is true that, according to Wilson and most of his contemporaries, part of the point of studying the *ars rhetorica* was to advance the cause of Christian as opposed to classical culture. One of the claims that Cox, Wilson and Sherry all emphasise in their pioneering treatises is that, as Sherry puts it, an understanding of rhetoric greatly profits us 'in the readinge of holye scripture, where if you be ignoraunte in the fygurative speches and Tropes, you are lyke in manye greate doubtes to make but a slender solucion'.[1] Wilson offers a dramatic example in the course of illustrating the trope of synecdoche, the trope he takes to be in play whenever 'by the signe we understande the thyng signified'.[2] One catastrophic theological error stemming from ignorance of this device is the failure to recognise that, when we eat the bread at communion, we merely 'remember Christes death, and by Faith, receive hym spiritually'. According to Wilson, the Catholic doctrine of the eucharist amounts to nothing more than a misunderstanding of rhetorical speech: *hoc est corpus* is not the report of a miracle; it is simply a synecdoche.[3]

Of scarcely less significance for Wilson and his generation was the possibility that a better understanding of rhetoric might help to improve

1 Sherry 1961, p. 14. Cf. Cox c.1530, sig. A, ii^v. On the rhetorical characteristics of puritan language see Smith 1989, esp. pp. 14–17.
2 Wilson 1554, fo. 93^r.
3 Wilson 1554, fo. 93^v. Cf. Wildermuth 1989.

the quality of preaching.[4] Wilson, Fenner and Peacham were all strong defenders of the Protestant faith, and all of them clearly felt that the increased prominence accorded to the art of preaching by the Reformers cried out for the development of matching rhetorical skills.[5] As Wilson complains, there are many pastors who 'mynd so muche edefiyng of soules, that thei often forget, we have any bodies'. The result is that 'some doo not so muche good with tellyng the truthe, as thei doe harme with dullying the hearers, beyng so farre gone in their matters, that oftentymes thei cannot tell when to make an ende'.[6] Wilson expresses the earnest hope that some of what he says 'maye well helpe those that preache Goddes truthe and exhorte men in open assemblies to upright dealing'.[7] Otherwise there is a danger that they 'are like some tymes to preache to the bare walles'.[8]

This preoccupation with the art of preaching eventually helped to foster a distinctive rhetorical style, a style derived more from Hellenistic sources than from the Roman authorities on whom we have so far concentrated.[9] Meanwhile, however, the schoolboys of late Tudor and early Stuart England continued to be drilled in a basically Roman tradition of secular rhetoric, according to which the point or purpose of studying the *ars rhetorica* was civic and political in character. Without a mastery of this art, it was argued, no one can hope effectively to discharge the most important duties of nobility or citizenship. The opening epistle in Wilson's *Arte of Rhetorique*, addressed to the earl of Warwick, presents a ringing reaffirmation of this Ciceronian theme. So worthy a thing is rhetoric, Wilson declares, 'that no man oughte to be withoute it, which either shall beare rule over manye, or must have to do wyth matters of a realm'. This is why, considering 'your Lordshyps hyghe estate & worthy callyng' nothing could be 'more fittynge wyth your honoure, then to the gyfte of good reason and understandynge, wherwith we see you notably endued, to ioyne the perfection of Eloquente utteraunce'.[10]

To see how Wilson and others of his generation arrived at this lofty view of rhetoric and its political significance, we need to begin by asking what conception of citizenship they inherited from the rhetorical theorists

4 Vives 1913, p. 199, had already made the same point, but in sixteenth-century England the aspiration became associated with the puritan movement. See Morgan 1986, pp. 108–9, 128–32.

5 On the *ars rhetorica* and sixteenth-century preaching see O'Malley 1983.

6 Wilson 1554, fo. 75^{r}.

7 Wilson 1554, fo. 58^{r}.

8 Wilson 1554, fo. 2^{v}.

9 For a brilliant study of the Christian Grand Style in the Renaissance see Shuger 1988, esp. pp. 55–117.

10 Wilson 1554, sig. A, 1^{v}. Cf. Ascham 1970b, p. 282.

of ancient Rome. One of the most important claims on which their Roman authorities had always insisted in discussing the figure of the *civis* was a negative one. If we wish to be of benefit to our community, we must never withdraw from public life and dedicate ourselves to abstruse or speculative pursuits. Cicero speaks dismissively of the life of *otium*, of contemplative leisure, at many points in his rhetorical works. He goes even further in *De officiis*, his treatise on the obligations of citizenship, in which he expresses his preference for the life of *negotium* or public activity in sternly moralistic terms. 'It is actually a vice', he declares, 'when people devote too much study and effort to obscure and difficult matters and those which are not necessary.'[11] This is because 'allowing ourselves to be carried away from public affairs is contrary to our duty, since the whole praise of virtue consists in activity'.[12] Quintilian later speaks no less disparagingly of those who withdraw from public life in the name of acquiring wisdom. 'It is the truly civic man,' he retorts, 'who is at the same time truly wise – the man who does not devote himself to useless disputations, but instead dedicates himself to the administration of the commonwealth, the very activity from which those who like to be called philosophers have withdrawn themselves as far as possible.'[13]

The same preference for *negotium* at the expense of *otium* is even more vehemently expressed by the educational theorists of Tudor England. Vives opens his *De tradendis disciplinis* by expressing frank scepticism about the value of such purely scientific pursuits as 'an investigation as to the measure or material of the heavens, or the virtues of plants or stones'.[14] A liberal education must avoid such 'difficult, hidden and troublesome knowledge'; it must never breed students who have no time for civic affairs or family life.[15] A generation later, we find Ascham in his *Scholemaster* discouraging the study of mathematics on the grounds that it unfits us for the duties of citizenship. If we 'marke all Mathematicall heades, which be onely and wholy bent to those sciences', we can hardly fail to be struck by 'how solitarie they be themselves, how unfit to live with others, & how unapte to serve in the world'.[16] Ascham would have felt it wholly appropriate that a ruler such as Prospero, more interested in his books

11 Cicero 1913, I.VI.19, p. 20: 'est vitium, quod quidam nimis magnum studium multamque operam in res obscuras atque difficiles conferunt easdemque non necessarias'.

12 Cicero 1913, I.VI.19, p. 20: 'cuius studio a rebus gerendis abduci contra officium est. Virtutis enim laus omnis in actione consistit.'

13 Quintilian 1920–2, XI.I.35, vol. IV, p. 174: 'At vir civilis vereque sapiens, qui se non otiosis disputationibus, sed administrationi rei publicae dediderit, a qua longissime isti, qui philosophi vocantur, recesserunt.'

14 Vives 1913, p. 17. Cf. also p. 38 on the need for knowledge to be 'for use'.

15 Vives 1913, pp. 18, 27. Cf. also p. 277 on the need to avoid inane contemplation.

16 Ascham 1970b, p. 190.

than in governing his duchy of Milan, should have suffered deposition and banishment.[17]

The positive image of citizenship put forward by the Roman rhetoricians centred on the figure of the *bonus civis* or *vir civilis*, the man who knows how to plead in the law courts for justice and to deliberate in the councils and public assemblies of the *res publica* in such a way as to promote policies at once advantageous and honourable. This is the figure who emerges as the hero of Cicero's *De officiis*. 'While the life of those who cultivate *otium* is undoubtedly easier, safer, and less of a burden or trouble to others, the life of those who apply themselves to public affairs and the handling of great matters is at once more valuable to mankind and is better suited to winning us greatness and fame.'[18] Quintilian reaffirms the same values in outlining his ideal of the *vir civilis* in the preface to his *Institutio oratoria*. 'The man who is truly civic, the true *vir civilis*, is the man who is suited to the administration of public as well as private affairs, who is capable of ruling cities with his advice, maintaining them with laws and reforming them by means of legal judgments.'[19] He subsequently restates the commitment at the end of his final book. 'I want the person whom I am educating to be wise in the truly Roman sense, and thus to be capable of showing himself a true *vir civilis* in the work and experience of government, and not merely in disputations of a purely private kind.'[20] Specifically, Quintilian adds, the *vir civilis* must be 'a frequent pleader in the courts, an outstanding speaker in the assemblies'.[21] He must ensure that the verdicts delivered in the courts are just and the decisions made by the public assemblies of benefit to the community as a whole.

Whereas Cicero concentrates on the *res publica*, Quintilian also considers the duties of a *bonus civis* under a monarchy,[22] and does so in a way that clearly made his analysis seem even more relevant to his Renaissance audience. As well as pleading 'before judges who are obliged to give judgment according to the law', we may find ourselves 'in attendance upon the emperor or some other magistrate who has discretion to arrive at

17 On Prospero as 'a bad humanist' see Bate 1994, esp. p. 10.

18 Cicero 1913, I.XXI.70, p. 72: 'sed et facilior et tutior et minus aliis gravis aut molesta vita est otiosorum, fructuosior autem hominum generi et ad claritatem amplitudinemque aptior eorum, qui se ad rem publicam et ad magnas res gerendas accommodaverunt'.

19 Quintilian 1920–2, I, Proemium, 10, vol. I, p. 10: 'vir ille vere civilis et publicarum privatarumque rerum administrationi accommodatus, qui regere consiliis urbes, fundare legibus, emendare iudiciis possit'.

20 Quintilian 1920–2, XII.II.7, vol. IV, p. 384: 'Atqui ego illum, quem instituo, Romanum quendam velim esse sapientem, qui non secretis disputationibus, sed rerum experimentis atque operibus vere civilem virum exhibeat.'

21 Quintilian 1920–2, XII.II.7, vol. IV, p. 384: 'in iudiciis frequens aut clarus in contionibus'.

22 See Michel 1962, pp. 71–96, and Kennedy 1969, pp. 24–6.

his own verdict'.[23] When this happens, we must follow a different approach, presenting our arguments less in forensic style than in the manner of someone offering advice about the most useful course of action to pursue. Quintilian subsequently extends these remarks to include the whole question of the appropriate demeanour for a citizen to adopt in pleading before a prince. We must never forget 'that it will by no means be appropriate even to use the same voice, the same gestures and the same bearing as we would when appearing before the senate, the people or their magistrates'.[24] Tacitus was later to strike a similar note – with a disconcerting hint of irony – at the end of his *Dialogus de oratoribus*,[25] in which the figure of Maternus brings the discussion to a sudden close by remarking that nowadays there is much less scope for oratory, since 'what is the use of making numerous speeches before the populace, given that public issues are no longer considered by the uneducated multitude, but rather by a single individual who is supremely wise?'[26]

These observations were absorbed and extended by the educational theorists of Tudor England in such a way as to give rise to two complementary views about the value of an education in the humanities. The humanists liked to think of themselves in the first place as peculiarly well fitted to serve as personal advisers or counsellors to the leaders of their communities, princes and nobles alike.[27] Richard Mulcaster takes it for granted in his *Positions* of 1581 that 'the highest degree to which learned valure doth prefer' will be that of becoming 'a wise *counsellor* whose learning is learned pollicie'.[28] George Puttenham likewise assumes that the purpose of acquiring a humanistic education will be to fit oneself to act as an adviser or counsellor, preferably to one's sovereign, in which capacity 'it is neither decent to flatter him, for that is servile, neither to be rough or plaine with him, for that is dangerous, but truly to Counsell & admonish, gravely not grevously, sincerely not sourly'.[29]

23 Quintilian 1920–2, V.XIII.6–7, vol. II, p. 314, contrasts pleading 'apud iudices quidem secundum legem dicturos sententiam' with appearing 'apud principum aliumve, cui utrum velit liceat'.

24 Quintilian 1920–2, XI.III.150, vol. IV, p. 324: 'Neque eadem in voce, gestu, incessu, apud principem, senatum, populum , magistratus'.

25 On this dialogue and its date (AD 101) see Kennedy 1972, pp. 515–26.

26 Tacitus 1970, 41.4, p. 344: 'Quid multis apud populum contionibus ... cum de re publica non imperiti et multi deliberent, sed sapientissimus et unus?'

27 On humanism and the importance of 'counsel', see Lehmberg 1961; Ferguson 1965, esp. pp. 162–99; Skinner 1978, I, pp. 213–21; Guy 1993, esp. pp. 13–22, and, more specifically, Simon 1979, pp. 150–6, on Elyot; Logan 1983, pp. 39–47, 66–74, 111–23, on More; Mayer 1989a, esp. 106–38, on Starkey.

28 Mulcaster 1888, p. 202.

29 Puttenham 1970, p. 295. On Puttenham and Castiglione see Javitch 1972.

One consequence of this emphasis on counsel was that many humanists came to see their role specifically as teachers – as tutors and mentors to the children of the gentry and aristocracy or as lecturers on the *studia humanitatis* in the schools and universities.[30] They also saw themselves, more ambitiously, as confidential advisers capable of helping their royal or aristocratic patrons in the administration of their affairs. We already find these aspirations reflected in the first generation of humanist discussions about the reformation of the English commonwealth. They underlie the debate about *otium* and *negotium* in book I of Sir Thomas More's *Utopia* of 1516,[31] and recur in Thomas Starkey's *Dialogue between Pole and Lupset* in the early 1530s,[32] which opens with a paraphrase both of the start of the *De inventione* and of Cicero's praise for the life of *negotium* in *De officiis*.[33] The same aspirations help to account for the growing popularity of foreign treatises on the importance of courtiers and counsellors in later sixteenth-century England.[34] Sir Thomas Hoby's translation of Castiglione's *Il libro del cortegiano*, first issued in 1561,[35] put into circulation an eloquent plea for the perfect courtier to be educated 'in those studyes which they call Humanitie',[36] and for the courtier to treat the goal of his studies as that of advising his prince, 'that he may breake his minde to him, and alwaies enfourme hym francklye of the trueth of everie matter meete for him to understande'.[37] Thomas Blundeville's version of Federigo Furio's treatise on counsel, published as *A very Briefe and profitable Treatise* in 1570,[38] offers a more workaday restatement of the same themes. Blundeville lays it down that 'the qualities of the minde requisite in anye counseler' are 'To be wise' and 'To be eloquent', so that 'he may be able to perswade or diswade, to accuse or to defende, to prayse, or disprayse'.[39] The clear implication is that princes must surround themselves with advisers who have followed the kind of rhetorical training that fosters these precise qualities. The same implication underlies John Thorius' translation of Bartolome Felippe's treatise on counsel, which he issued as *The Counseller: A Treatise of Counsels and Counsellers of Princes* in 1589. Here too we are assured that

30 See Simon 1979, pp. 204–6, on Cheke and Ascham; Dewar 1964, esp. pp. 12–25, on Smith.

31 More 1965, pp. 54–60. For a discussion see Norbrook 1984, pp. 23–31, and Skinner 1987, pp. 125–35. On Elyot's approach to the same theme see Fox 1986b and Conrad 1992.

32 For the date of the *Dialogue* see Mayer 1989b, pp. x–xii. (But cf. Guy 1993, p. 15n.)

33 Starkey 1989, pp. 1–3.

34 On Castiglione see Anglo 1977, pp. 36–44, and on the reception of his text pp. 44–53.

35 On Hoby's translation see Javitch 1978, pp. 23–6, and cf. Cox 1994, pp. xxix–xxxi.

36 Castiglione 1994, p. 80.

37 Castiglione 1994, p. 295. On the relations between courtiers and princes see Javitch 1983.

38 Blundeville himself tells us (sig. A, 2^r) that Furio is his source.

39 Blundeville 1570, sig. D, 2^v and sig. E, 2^v.

those with a training in the *studia humanitatis* are best equipped to serve as wise and prudent advisers to the princes and nobility of the age.[40]

The other role the humanists saw themselves as especially well fitted to discharge was that of acting as public and political figures in their own right.[41] This confidence was associated with their reinstatement of the classical ideal of the *civis* or citizen, with its implicit challenge to the more familiar concept of the *subditus* or subject. They saw themselves not merely as subjects of princes and their laws, but rather as *viri civiles* with an active and supremely honourable role to play as judges and legislators in the creation and maintenance of the *res publica* or commonwealth. They aspired in consequence to serve not merely as courtiers and counsellors but as secretaries of state – a term that came into general use for the first time in the latter part of the sixteenth century.[42]

We already find these ambitions reflected – as his title indicates – in Sir Thomas Elyot's *Book named the Governor*. As Elyot explains in his opening proem, his aim is to offer advice not merely to princes and nobles but to anyone 'studious about the public weal'.[43] He hopes to encourage the aristocracy and gentry to master the *genus iudiciale* and associate themselves with their sovereign as 'inferior governors' in 'the distribution of justice'.[44] He also calls on them to master the *genus deliberativum* and to offer honourable and expedient 'consultations' about the best methods of ruling and reforming the commonwealth. They must be ready to 'bear with them out of the counsel house, as it were on their shoulders, not only what is to be followed and exploited, but also by what means or ways it shall be pursued, and how the affair may be honourable; also what is expedient and of necessity'.[45] With these ends in view, Elyot outlines a form of education suitable for gentry and nobility alike, urging them to put their training to use in such a way that 'by the noble example of their lives and the fruit thereof coming, the public weal that shall happen to be under their governance shall not fail to be accounted happy, and the authority on them to be employed well and fortunately'.[46]

The same concern to encourage an active political elite is no less marked among the humanist educational writers of the next generation. Ascham assures us in his *Scholemaster* that the studies he recommends will

40 Felippe 1589, esp. discourse 3, sig. B, 2^r *et seq.* and discourse 6, sig. C, 3^v *et seq.*

41 For a classic study of this theme see Hexter 1961, pp. 45–7. See also Slavin 1970, esp. pp. 311–13; Elton 1973, pp. 14–37. For specific cases, see Guy 1980, esp. pp. 37–79, on More; Hogrefe 1967, esp. pp. 84–101 and 157–70, on Elyot; Dewar 1964 esp. pp. 25–32, 171–84, on Smith.

42 James 1986, pp. 375–83.

43 Elyot 1962, p. xiii.

44 Elyot 1962, p. 13.

45 Elyot 1962, p. 237.

46 Elyot 1962, p. 95. Cf. Vives 1913, pp. 72, 199.

produce men 'deepe of judgement, whether they write, or give counsell in all waightie affaires'.[47] Kempe similarly maintains in his *Education of children* that an upbringing in the disciplines he describes will enable us to serve not merely as 'discreet and wise Councellers', but as 'Judges, Justices and Rulers in the Common wealth'.[48] Peacham in his *Garden of Eloquence* speaks with even greater magniloquence, declaring that anyone who follows his precepts will become 'fit to rule the world with counsell, provinces with laws, cities with pollicy & multitudes with persuasion'.[49]

As will by now be evident, part of the attraction of the ideal of the *vir civilis* for the humanists of Tudor England was that it helped them to claim a place for educated laymen in the conduct of government.[50] These aspirations have often been dismissed as irrelevant to the political circumstances in which they found themselves.[51] But in fact the humanists we have been considering were conspicuously successful at claiming a place in public life on their own behalf. They were prominent first of all as teachers of the *studia humanitatis* and as tutors and mentors to the princes and nobility of the age. This applies in particular to the group of young scholars, including Roger Ascham and Thomas Wilson, who studied under Sir John Cheke and Sir Thomas Smith at Cambridge in the 1540s. Cheke began lecturing on the humanities at St John's College as early as 1529, where he was joined by Ascham as a colleague in 1534, the year in which Smith embarked on teaching Greek at Queens' College.[52] The first position gained by Thomas Wilson after graduating from Cambridge in 1549 was as tutor to the sons of the duchess of Norfolk,[53] while Cheke and Ascham both served in addition as tutors and mentors to the royal family, Cheke taking charge of the future Edward VI's education in 1544 while Ascham taught the future Queen Elizabeth I between 1548 and 1550.[54]

A number of these scholars also succeeded in making the coveted transition to the world of public affairs. Sir Thomas Elyot acted as clerk to the Privy Council between c.1522 and 1530 and ambassador to the court of Charles V in the early 1530s.[55] Still more imposingly, Sir Thomas More became a member of Parliament in 1504, Speaker of the House of

47 Ascham 1970b, p. 191. Cf. p. 280 on offering 'Civill service' to prince and country.
48 Kempe 1966, p. 215.
49 Peacham 1593, sig. AB, iii^{v}.
50 See Hexter 1961 and the discussion of 'pragmatic' humanism in Jardine 1986 and in Grafton and Jardine 1986.
51 See Shuger 1988, pp. 12–13; Vickers 1994, pp. 83–4. But for a corrective see Norbrook 1992, pp. 12–20, and Norbrook 1994, esp. pp. 141 and 154–9.
52 Charlton 1965, pp. 142, 159; Simon 1979, pp. 203–9.
53 Schmidt 1959–60, p. 51.
54 Simon 1979, pp. 209, 269. See also Slavin 1970, p. 311.
55 Hogrefe 1967, pp. 84–101, 157–70.

Commons in 1523 and Lord Chancellor in 1529.[56] The same ideal of serving the commonwealth was no less impressively upheld in the next generation. Sir Thomas Smith became a secretary of state as early as 1548, with Sir John Cheke following him some five years later.[57] Thomas Wilson was elected to Parliament in 1572, and on Smith's death in 1577 took his place on the Privy Council with the same title of secretary, a post he continued to hold until his death in 1581.[58] They all managed, in short, to sustain the ideal of the *vir civilis* in their lives no less than their works.

THE QUALITIES OF THE *VIR CIVILIS*

As well as formulating the ideal of the *vir civilis*, the Roman rhetoricians bequeathed a no less influential account of the qualities that distinguish those capable of pleading and counselling effectively in the law courts and public assemblies of a commonwealth. The true *vir civilis* must above all be a good man, someone possessed of all the virtues requisite for civic life. Listing the heroes of the early republic at the outset of his *De inventione*, Cicero observes that 'these were men who not only possessed the highest virtue but also possessed an authority amplified by such high virtue'.[59] Quintilian similarly argues in the proem to his *Institutio oratoria* that 'the true citizen who is best suited to the administration of public as well as private affairs' will be a *vir bonus*, a good man endowed with 'all the virtues of the mind' together with 'a true understanding of an upright and honourable life'.[60]

The Roman writers begin by focusing on the intellectual virtues needed for effective citizenship. They insist that a *vir civilis* must be capable in the first place of instructing his fellow citizens in the truth, and must therefore be a man of *sapientia*, the talent required by those who aspire to teach. Cicero observes at the beginning of *De officiis* that, if our aim is the hunting and discovery of truth, the qualities we chiefly need are wisdom and prudence.[61] He confirms at the outset of *De inventione* that wisdom is the key quality that every founding father of a *civitas* must have possessed.[62] Later he reiterates the argument in book III of *De oratore*, in which the

56 Marius 1985, pp. 50–1, 205–11, 360–4.
57 Dewar 1964, pp. 32, 36–55.
58 Schmidt 1959–60, pp. 49–50, 56, 59.
59 Cicero 1949a, I.IV.5, p. 10: 'quibus in hominibus erat summa virtus et summa virtute amplificata auctoritas'.
60 Quintilian 1920–2, Proemium, 9–10, vol. I, pp. 8–10: on the 'vir ille vere civilis et publicarum privatarumque rerum administrationi accommodatus' as a 'vir bonus' possessed of 'omnes animi virtutes' and 'rationem rectae honestaeque vitae'.
61 Cicero 1913, I.V.15, p. 16.
62 Cicero 1949a, I.II.2, p. 4.

figure of Crassus remarks that *sapientia* is so vital for instructing and informing an audience that 'I shall not object if people prefer to characterise the orator I am describing as a philosopher'.[63]

If a citizen is to teach wisely and well, he must in turn possess sufficient *ratio* or powers of reasoning to enable him to acquire the necessary *scientia* or knowledge of the subjects on which he proposes to speak. Discussing the origins of *civitates* at the start of *De inventione*, Cicero maintains that *ratio* is of even greater significance than *sapientia*, since it is only through the exercise of reason that founding fathers can hope to counsel their fellow citizens with wisdom.[64] He underlines the argument when speaking in his own person at the beginning of *De oratore*. In the absence of *ratio*, and hence of *scientia*, even the most fluent orator will quickly find himself reduced to worthless garrulity. 'A knowledge of very many issues must be acquired, for in the absence of such *scientia* the flow of our words will be nothing better than inane and laughable.'[65]

This emphasis on reason as the ultimate source of wisdom is no less marked among the humanist educational writers of Tudor England.[66] Vives opens his *De tradendis disciplinis* with a powerful defence of reason, prudence and wisdom as crucial to the formulation of effective policies, and later echoes Cicero by adding that mere fluency in the absence of such wisdom amounts to nothing more than empty verbiage.[67] Elyot writes in similar vein at the outset of *The Governor*, insisting that what matters most in a public weal is that it should be 'governed by the rule and moderation of reason'.[68] Those who excel 'in knowledge and wisdom' and 'influence of understanding' are therefore urged to employ these talents 'to the detaining of other within the bounds of reason'.[69] Governors are particularly exhorted to employ their knowledge to establish 'a disposition and order according to reason' throughout the whole fabric of society.[70] The same commitment is reaffirmed when Elyot discusses 'that part of sapience that of necessity must be in every governor' towards the close of book III.[71] The maintenance of 'disposition and order' in government is

63 Cicero 1942a, III.XXXV.142, vol. II, p. 112: 'sive hunc oratorem ... philosophum appellare malit, non impediam'. As Vickers 1989, p. 30, notes, Crassus is for much of the time Cicero's mouthpiece. For a discussion of the figures in the dialogue see Vickers 1989, pp. 30–6.

64 Cicero 1949a, I.II.2, pp. 4–6. Cf. Cicero 1942a, I.XXXVI.165, vol. I, pp. 112–14.

65 Cicero 1942a, I.V.17, vol. I, pp. 12–14: 'Est enim et scientia comprehendenda rerum plurimarum, sine qua verborum volubilitas inanis atque irridenda est.' Cf. also I.VI.20, vol. I, p. 16; I.XII.51, vol. I, p. 38.

66 See for example Crosse 1603, sig. B, 1v.

67 Vives 1913, pp. 14–15, 296; cf. pp. 181, 229.

68 Elyot 1962, p. 1.

69 Elyot 1962, p. 4. Cf. Ascham 1970, pp. 205–6.

70 Elyot 1962, p. 5.

71 Elyot 1962, book III, chapter 13, 'Of sapience, and the definition thereof', p. 218.

impossible in the absence of 'sovereign knowledge, proceeding of wisdom'.[72] Those who aspire to act as governors must therefore devote themselves to the acquisition of 'science' and the wisdom or sapience stemming from it. Anyone who seeks to plead or offer counsel in the absence of such knowledge will merely find himself making 'a sound without any purpose'.[73] And as Elyot adds, closely paraphrasing Cicero, 'what is so furious or mad a thing as a vain sound of words of the best sort and most ornate, containing neither cunning nor sentence?'[74]

Besides possessing the talents necessary for discovering the truth, the Roman rhetoricians stress that the *vir civilis* must cultivate a range of moral virtues. As Cicero puts it at the start of *De officiis*, the qualities needed are those on which the preservation of civic life may be said to depend.[75] According to Cicero there are three such qualities: he lists them as justice, fortitude and temperance, and he devotes the whole of book I of *De officiis* to anatomising them.[76] No one subsequently doubted that these, together with wisdom or prudence, must be regarded as the four 'cardinal' virtues, and most moralists and rhetoricians of later antiquity simply repeated the list. Quintilian, for example, acknowledges in the proem to his *Institutio oratoria* that in speaking of the virtues he will draw on the usual philosophical textbooks, and that this will mean focusing on justice, temperance and fortitude as the principal foundations of social life.[77]

These claims were likewise taken up by the humanists and educational writers of Tudor England. Some of them provided translations of the leading Roman treatises, concentrating in particular on Cicero's *De officiis*.[78] They also created a virtual subgenre of moral philosophy out of their own neo-Ciceronian reflections on the cardinal virtues. Elyot organises the whole of book III of *The Governor* around the discussion of justice, fortitude and temperance, bringing his work to an end with a consideration of the intellectual virtue of sapience.[79] Cornelius Valerius' treatise on the cardinal virtues, anonymously translated in 1571 as *The Casket of Jewels*, is likewise organised around the analysis of prudence,

72 Elyot 1962, p. 218.
73 Elyot 1962, p. 45.
74 Elyot 1962, p. 45, evidently alluding to Cicero 1942a, I.XII.51, vol. I, p. 38.
75 Cicero 1913, I.V.17, p. 18.
76 Cicero 1913, I.VII.20, pp. 20 *et seq.* (justice); I.XVIII.61, pp. 62 *et seq.* (fortitude); I.XXVII.93, pp. 94 *et seq.* (temperance).
77 Quintilian 1920–2, Proemium, 12, vol. I, p. 10.
78 For the first English translation, by Robert Whytinton, see Cicero 1534. Nicolas Grimalde issued a new version in 1556, claiming to have achieved 'sommewhat the more'. See Cicero 1566, sig. CC, v^{v}. Richard Brinsley issued a further translation of book I in 1616, stressing that his work was intended 'for the perpetuall benefit of Schooles'. See Brinsley 1616, sig. [A], 5^{r}.
79 Elyot 1962, pp. 159 *et seq.* (justice); pp. 183 *et seq.* (fortitude); pp. 209 *et seq.* (temperance); pp. 218 *et seq.* (sapience).

justice, fortitude and temperance.[80] Thereafter the theme was taken up by numerous Elizabethan humanists in a multitude of different ways. Richard Robinson's *The Vineyarde of Vertue* of c.1579 concludes with a similar survey of 'the foure moste excellent vertues called cardinall vertues';[81] Simon Haward's *Encheiridion Morale* of 1596 turns the discussion into Latin, singling out (in the words of its title page) *Virtutes quatuor (ut vocant) Cardinales*;[82] William Leighton in his *Vertue Triumphant* of 1603 presents the same theme in verse, examining in turn the qualities of prudence, temperance, fortitude and justice and reminding us that 'These Morall Vertues Cardinall are nam'd'.[83]

Besides examining these leading virtues, the Roman moralists and rhetoricians considered a further range of attributes required for the proper conduct of civic life. They generally focused on three additional qualities, all of which were made the subjects of specialised treatises. One was *fides* or mutual trust, and hence the value of *amicitia* or friendship, the unique excellence of which was held to lie in the feelings of loyalty to which it gives rise. The most frequently cited treatise on this theme was Cicero's address to Laelius, the *De amicitia*, in which the value of friendship is associated with constancy, unswerving devotion and a concern for justice, all grounded on the basic value of *fides* or mutual trust. 'The ultimate foundation', as Cicero explains, 'of that stability and steadfastness which we look for in friendship is *fides*, for nothing can ever be stable which involves disloyalty.'[84]

A second crucial value was said to be humanity, the cultivation of kindly or philanthropic feelings, and hence the exercise of liberality, generosity, gratitude. These attributes are also important to Cicero, who uses the term *humanitas* in the *De oratore* to summarise Crassus' finest qualities, and associates the ideal of humanity with dutiful respect and a capacity for gratitude.[85] But the classic treatment of this theme was owed to Seneca, whose *De beneficiis* is largely given over to celebrating exactly these virtues. We are admonished in book II to ensure that every kind of humane feeling accompanies our acts of generosity and beneficence,[86] and told in book III

80 Valerius 1571, sig. D, iv^{v} *et seq.* (prudence); sig. F, iii^{r} *et seq.* (justice); sig. H, vi^{v} *et seq.* (fortitude); sig. J, v^{r} *et seq.* (temperance).

81 Robinson c.1579, sig. H, 6^{v} *et seq.*

82 Haward 1596 discusses prudence (pp. 9–36); justice (pp. 37–63); fortitude (pp. 63–99); temperance (pp. 99–150).

83 Leighton 1603, sig. A, 8^{v}. Cf. also Crosse 1603, sig. B, 2^{r} and, for the fullest analysis, closely following Cicero, Barnes 1606.

84 Cicero 1923, XVIII.65, p. 174: 'Firmamentum autem stabilitatis constantiaeque est eius quam in amicitia quaerimus fides est; nihil est enim stabile, quod infidum est.'

85 Cicero 1942a, II.LXXXIX.362, vol. I, p. 472.

86 Seneca 1935, II.XI.4, p. 68.

that the giving of benefits and the receiving of them with proper gratitude constitute the two most beautiful elements in a true *vita humana*, a genuinely humane life.[87]

The other value particularly singled out by the Roman moralists was *clementia* or *misericordia*. By these terms they understand a readiness to avoid undue severity, to abate feelings of anger, and hence to display mercy, compassion, a willingness to pardon and excuse. These qualities were sometimes linked with *humanitas*, as they are by the author of the *Ad Herennium*, who argues that we can always hope to develop a powerful line of defence in a court of law by reminding our judges of 'the *clementia*, the *humanitas* and the *misericordia* we ourselves have displayed towards others'.[88] These too are important qualities for Cicero, who declares in book I of his *De officiis* that 'nothing is more laudable, nothing is worthier in a great and outstanding man than forbearance and *clementia*'.[89] Again, however, it is Seneca who provides the fullest analysis. He continually preaches in *De ira* about the evils of rage, the importance of extirpating it from our lives and the need to avoid behaving implacably.[90] Correspondingly, he devotes the whole of *De clementia* to commending the qualities of mercy, true compassion and placability. Although he sternly warns us in Stoic vein against a sentimental excess of pity,[91] he considers true clemency the most humane of all the virtues. No quality is more valuable in a prince, none is of greater importance for the harmonious functioning of civic life.[92]

These further arguments were also taken up by the humanists and rhetoricians of Renaissance England. As before, they showed considerable interest in translating the Roman treatises in which these attributes had been singled out,[93] but at the same time they developed their own accounts of the virtues involved. An early and important example is provided by Elyot's *Governor*, the central book of which is almost wholly given over to examining these additional qualities. The discussion opens in chapter 6 with a consideration of clemency and placability. A governor

87 Seneca 1935, III.VII.2–6, pp. 136–8.

88 *Ad C. Herennium* 1954, II.XXXI.50, p. 152: 'si de clementia, humanitate, misericordia nostra qua in alios usi sumus'.

89 Cicero 1913, I.XXV.88, p. 88: 'nihil enim laudabilius, nihil magno et praeclaro viro dignius placabilitate atque clementia.'

90 Seneca 1928b, esp. II.XIII.1–3, pp. 194–6, and II.XXXIV.1–5, pp. 242–4.

91 Seneca 1928a, II.IV.4, pp. 436–8.

92 Seneca 1928a, esp. I.III. 2–3, pp. 364–6, and I.V.1–7, pp. 370–2.

93 Tiptoft's version of Cicero's *De amicitia* was printed by Caxton. See Cicero 1481 and cf. Gray 1990, esp. pp. 27–8. Further versions were published by John Harryngton (Cicero 1550) and Thomas Newton (Cicero 1577). Nicholas Haward issued a translation of the first three books of Seneca's *De beneficiis* (Seneca 1569), followed by Arthur Golding's translation of the whole treatise (Seneca 1578). Sir Thomas Lodge included a further version, together with translations of *De ira* and *De clementia*, in his edition of Seneca's *Workes* (Seneca 1614).

must never lapse into wrath or cruel malignity, since wrath is inhuman and cruelty the most odious vice of all.[94] The next three chapters discuss the virtue of humanity, the three principal elements of which are benevolence, beneficence and liberality, qualities that bring 'much commodity' as well as honour to those possessing them.[95] Chapters 11, 12 and 13 deal with the concept of amity, the virtue associated with mutual trust and friendship.[96] Here the governor is exhorted above all to avoid the least sign of ingratitude, this being the most damnable of the vices and the one most liable to undermine the harmony of civic life.[97]

These themes recur in most of the moral treatises of the next generation. The anonymous translator of Valerius' *Casket of Jewels* describes the cardinal virtue of justice as having six parts, one of which is friendship and the 'perfect accord' it manifests, a second of which is liberality and generosity, while a third is compassion or true clemency.[98] Richard Robinson in his *Vineyarde of Vertue* makes a number of similar claims in developing his running metaphor about the virtues as fruitful plants. Among the plants of a good life, the fifteenth is 'Amitie or friendship', while the sixteenth is 'gratitude or thankfulness', the seventeenth hospitality, the eighteenth liberality, the nineteenth mercy and the twentieth innocence.[99] Joseph Hall associates a similar set of qualities with the nine worthies he portrays in his *Characters of Vertues and Vices* of 1608.[100] He stresses the value of clemency in sketching the character of the patient man, who is calm and gentle, void of fury and rage[101] He refers to the ideal of humanity in describing the man of true nobility, who is open and bounteous, benevolent and full of pity for the distressed.[102] And he points to the values of trust and amity in speaking of the true friend, who is recognisable by his constancy and unswerving faithfulness.[103]

The Tudor moralists also focus on one further group of virtues which they regard as perhaps the most important of all. These are modesty, moderation and humility, the characteristics of those who know how to act

94 Elyot 1962, pp. 111–15. The succeeding chapter distinguishes, in neo-Stoic vein, between true mercy and 'vain pity', pp. 115–20.

95 Elyot 1962, pp. 120–32.

96 Elyot 1962, pp. 132–54, chapter 12, relates, from Boccaccio's *Decameron*, 'the wonderful history of Titus and Gisippus', a story of perfect friendship. For Elyot's use of Boccaccio see Major 1964, pp. 257–8.

97 Elyot 1962, chapter 13, pp. 152–4.

98 Valerius 1571, sig. G, 5^r–7^v.

99 Robinson c.1579, sig. E, 4^r to F, 5^v.

100 On Hall see Crane 1937, pp. 152–6; on his use of Theophrastus as a model see Lechner 1962, pp. 221–2.

101 Hall 1608, pp. 39–44.

102 Hall 1608, pp. 51–6.

103 Hall 1608, pp. 45–50.

with affability and avoid all displays of hauteur, arrogance and pride. These attributes had not been much respected by their Roman authorities, for whom the term *humilitas* had been the name of an undesirable quality of abjectness and subservience.[104] Among the moralists of the Renaissance, however, only Machiavelli dares to suggest that humility may not be the name of a virtue nor pride of a vice.[105] The writers we have been considering all regard the sin of pride as the deadliest of the seven deadly sins, while the qualities of humility, moderation and even *sprezzatura*[106] are especially prized.

An early statement of these commitments can be found in the closing pages of Sir Thomas More's *Utopia*, where the traveller to Utopia, Raphael Hythloday, suddenly bursts out in a bitter invective against the vice of *superbia*. The source of all the evils now afflicting Europe can be traced to 'one single monster, pride, the leader and parent of every other plague'.[107] A similar claim recurs in Elyot's *Governor*, possibly reflecting Elyot's direct acquaintance with More's text. When Elyot turns in book II to anatomise the leading virtues of civic life, the first quality he mentions is affability and the avoidance of pride. A governor must always be approachable, modest in demeanour, capable of sufferance. He must never exhibit a haughty countenance nor act contemptuously towards his social inferiors, these being detestable vices that breed hatred and often lead to unrest and rebellion.[108]

The same claims are widely repeated by the moralists of the next generation. Thomas Blundeville's treatise on counsellors particularly mentions the importance of affability.[109] The translator of Valerius' *Casket of Jewels* stresses the value of modesty, treating it as an aspect of the cardinal virtue of temperance.[110] Richard Robinson's *Vineyarde of Vertue* opens with a discussion of humility, warning us against 'pride of hearte and overmuch disdaining others'.[111] Henry Crosse's *Vertues Common-wealth* speaks out even more fiercely against 'pride, contempt, disdaine, self-love, and the very fire that burneth up all good motions, if not quenched with moderation'.[112] Picking up an argument already stressed by Crosse, Joseph Hall in his *Characters of Vertues and Vices* adds that persons of true nobility are always

104 See for example Cicero 1913, III.XXXII.115, p. 396; Cicero 1949a, I.LVI.109, p. 160.
105 See for example Machiavelli 1960, II.II, pp. 282–3.
106 For this quality of aristocratic offhandedness, emphasised by Castiglione and translated by Hoby as 'reckelesness', see Castiglione 1994, p. 53, and for a full discussion see Saccone 1983.
107 More 1965, p. 242: 'una tantum belua, omnium princeps parensque pestium superbia'.
108 Elyot 1962, pp. 106–11.
109 Blundeville 1570, sig. D, 3v.
110 Valerius 1571, sig. K, 1v.
111 Robinson c.1579, sig. C, 2v.
112 Crosse 1603, sig. D, 4v.

recognisable by their courtesy and affability.[113] Concerned as they are to civilise an elite, the thought that all these writers wish to leave with us is that *noblesse oblige.*

This emphasis on the need to cultivate the virtues in turn explains why the educational theorists we have been considering always insist that, after acquiring the rudiments of grammar and rhetoric, the disciplines to which an aspiring *vir civilis* must devote himself are history and moral philosophy. They take from their classical authorities the belief that these are the academic subjects from which we can best hope to learn about the qualities we need for playing an effective role in public life. Quintilian had particularly emphasised the point in outlining, in book x of his *Institutio oratoria*, the syllabus of reading that young orators should set themselves. He begins by discussing the poets, who are able to provide us with inspiring instances of language at its most sublime.[114] But he places his main emphasis on the historians and moral philosophers. The former are equipped to furnish us with a knowledge of facts and precedents, while the latter are particularly able to instruct us in matters of justice, honesty and advantage.[115]

Taking up these suggestions, the Tudor educational theorists agree in the first place that history and moral philosophy supply us with a full account of the moral virtues required in public life. This is obvious, they think, in the case of moral philosophy, which as Elyot observes in *The Governor* is largely preoccupied with the need to give instruction and information about virtuous manners.[116] But the same is true of history, which is full of valuable illustrations of 'the good and evil qualities of them that be rulers, the commodities and good sequel of virtue, the discommodities and evil conclusion of vicious license'.[117]

The same writers are even more insistent on the value of history and moral philosophy as sources of wisdom and the other intellectual virtues. Again they regard it as obvious that moral philosophy is capable of supplying us with the insights we require. As Elyot puts it, there is no greater storehouse of 'profitable counsel joined with honesty' than the moral treatises of writers such as Plato and Cicero, who introduce us to 'absolute virtue with pleasure incredible'.[118] As before, however, they are equally emphatic about the value of history as a teacher of wisdom or

113 Hall 1608, pp. 51–6, esp. p. 52.
114 Quintilian 1920–2, x.i.27–30, vol. iv, pp. 16–18.
115 Quintilian 1920–2, x.i.34–6, vol. iv, pp. 20–2, stresses these points, although (as he notes) they are strictly speaking irrelevant to his argument at that juncture, which is concerned with examples of good style.
116 Elyot 1962, p. 39.
117 Elyot 1962, p. 38.
118 Elyot 1962, p. 39.

sapience. Vives in his *De tradendis disciplinis* quotes the famous passage from the *De oratore* in which Cicero ('that wisest of men') had spoken of history as the light of truth, adding that no science is of more importance 'for the government of the commonwealth and the administration of public business'.[119] Elyot speaks even more fulsomely, devoting a special chapter in *The Governor* to 'a defence of histories', in which he begins by observing that the attainment of wisdom depends on experience, and that 'the knowledge of this experience is called example, and is expressed by history'.[120] History must accordingly be acknowledged the primary teacher of the kind of wisdom or ('in a more elegant word')[121] the kind of sapience that good citizens require.[122] Ascham draws the moral in the introduction to the *Report and Discourse* on 'the affaires and state of Germany' which he wrote after returning from his diplomatic mission to the court of Charles V.[123] It is the special duty of anyone 'that would well and advisedly write an history', he declares, 'to marke diligently the causes, counsels, actes, and issues in all great attemptes', with the underlying purpose of noting 'some generall lesson of wisdome & warines'.[124]

The idea of history as a storehouse of wisdom for the *vir civilis* soon became a humanist article of faith. When Thomas Blundeville issued his version of Federigo Furio's treatise on counsel in 1570,[125] he declared that anyone desirous of becoming a wise counsellor must turn himself not merely into 'a good Moral Philosopher' but into 'a good Historiographer', since 'nothing is more necessary for a counseler, than to be a diligent reader of Hystories'.[126] When he published his own treatise on *The true order and Methode of wryting and reading Hystories* four years later, he proclaimed still more emphatically that 'by reading Hystories' we can hope not only 'to make our selves more wyse, as well to direct our owne actions as also to counsell others'; we can also hope 'to beautify our owne speache with grave examples, when we discourse of anye matters, that therby it may have the more aucthoritie, waight, and credite'.[127] Francis Bacon reaffirmed the same beliefs in discussing the value of history in his *Advancement of Learning* in 1605.[128] He insists that 'the use and end' of

119 Vives 1913, p. 231. On history as 'the light of truth' see Woolf 1990.
120 Elyot 1962, pp. 228–31, esp. p. 228.
121 Elyot 1962, p. 218.
122 For similar references to 'Wisdom or Sapience', see Bacon 1915, p. 36.
123 Levy 1967, pp. 74–7.
124 Ascham 1970a, p. 126.
125 On Blundeville see Ferguson 1979, esp. pp. 24–6.
126 Blundeville 1570, sig. D, 3^r and sig. F, 2^v.
127 Blundeville 1574, sig. H, 2^v–3^r.
128 For Bacon on history and counselling see Fussner 1962, esp. pp. 261–4, and Woolf 1990, pp. 141–58.

historical study is not merely to satisfy our curiosity; it also serves 'a more serious and grave purpose', that of making 'learned men wise in the use and administration of learning'.[129] He puts the point rather more laconically in his essay 'Of studies', in which he assures us that 'Histories make men wise.'[130]

According to the argument we have been considering, the true *vir civilis* must in the first instance be a man of *ratio* and hence of *sapientia.* The humanists' primary aim is to fashion the very figure whom the puritans were later to denounce: the figure of Mr Worldly Wiseman. A further and distinctive claim of these writers, however, is that the possession of worldly wisdom, even in association with the leading moral virtues, will never be sufficient in itself to enable us to play an active and effective role in the government of our commonwealth. If we are to plead successfully for justice in the law courts and for useful and beneficial policies in the public assemblies, it will never be enough to argue wisely and honourably about the issues involved; it will always be necessary in addition to move or impel our hearers to accept our arguments. This in turn means that, besides being a wise man capable of reasoning aright, the true *vir civilis* must be a man of the highest eloquence, capable of persuading his listeners by the sheer force of his 'winning' speech to acknowledge the truths that his reasoning brings to light.

The *vir civilis* accordingly stands in need of two crucial qualities: *ratio* to find out the truth and *eloquentia* to make his hearers accept it. The possession of these qualities is in turn said to make the *vir civilis* a master of *scientia civilis*, the two principal elements of which are *ratio atque eloquentia*, reason joined with eloquence. Perhaps the most influential statement of these fundamental beliefs is furnished by Cicero in the opening pages of his *De inventione.* He concedes that 'eloquence in the absence of wisdom is frequently very disadvantageous and is never of the least advantage to civil communities'.[131] But he insists that, since 'wisdom in itself is silent and powerless to speak', wisdom in the absence of eloquence is of even less use.[132] What is needed 'if a commonwealth is to receive the greatest possible benefit' is *ratio atque oratio*, powerful reasoning

129 Bacon 1915, p. 70. On Bacon's theory of civil history see Dean 1968, esp. pp. 219–21, and Ferguson 1979, esp. pp. 45–7.

130 Bacon 1972, p. 151.

131 Cicero 1949a, I.I.1, p. 2: 'civitatibus eloquentiam vero sine sapientia nimium obesse plerumque, prodesse nunquam'.

132 Cicero 1949a, I.I.1 and I.II.3, pp. 2 and 6: *sapientia* is 'tacita' and 'inops dicendi', so that 'sapientiam sine eloquentia parum prodesse civitatibus'.

allied with powerful speech.[133] We can thus be sure that 'cities were originally established not merely by the *ratio* of the mind but also, and more readily, by means of *eloquentia*'.[134] These are the qualities that enabled the first lawgivers to persuade our forefathers to adopt a civilised way of life, and these remain the qualities that civic leaders must possess above all. This is why 'a large and crucial part' of *scientia civilis* must be occupied by the art of eloquence, and especially by 'that form of artistic eloquence which is generally known as rhetoric, the function of which is that of speaking in a manner calculated to persuade, and the goal of which is that of persuading by speech'.[135]

Cicero later summarises these commitments in a much quoted section of the *De partitione oratoria* in which he proclaims that 'eloquence is nothing other than wisdom speaking copiously'.[136] The same argument is subsequently invoked by Quintilian in a highly charged passage from the proem to his *Institutio oratoria* in which he asks what distinguishes the *vir ille vere civilis*, the truly and completely civic man. 'As Cicero has indicated as clearly as possible', he replies, such citizens 'unite together both by nature and in the discharge of their civic duty the qualities at once of *sapientes*, men of wisdom, and *eloquentes*, men of eloquence.'[137] These are the talents that make a citizen 'fit to administer both public and private affairs'.[138]

Quintilian further develops these remarks in the course of discussing, at the end of book IV, the need for orators to persuade as well as instruct their fellow citizens.[139] By the end of his final book, he has arrived at the conclusion that the highest task of oratory can therefore be defined as a matter of knowing how to teach or instruct, while knowing at the same time how to delight and persuade an audience. This in turn explains why, after anatomising the three different styles of oratory, he concludes that the Grand Style is alone capable of scaling the heights of eloquence. The Plain Style merely enables us to teach; the Intermediate Style enables us to

133 Cicero 1949a, I.II.3, p. 6 on 'ratio atque oratio'; cf. also I.IV.5, p. 12, on how, if *eloquentia* is added to *sapientia*, 'ad rem publicam plurima commoda veniunt'. Cf. Cicero 1942a, III.XXXV.142, vol. II, p. 112.

134 Cicero 1949a, I.I.1, p. 2: 'urbes constitutas ... cum animi ratione tum facilius eloquentia'.

135 Cicero 1949a, I.V.6, pp. 12–14: on 'civilis scientia' and the fact that 'Eius quaedam magna et ampla pars est artificiosa eloquentia quam rhetoricam vocant', and that 'Officium autem eius facultatis videtur esse dicere apposite ad persuasionem; finis persuadere dictione.'

136 Cicero 1942b, XXIII.79, p. 368: 'Nihil enim est aliud eloquentia nisi copiose loquens sapientia.'

137 Quintilian 1920–2, Proemium, 13, vol. I, p. 10: 'ut Cicero apertissime colligit, quemadmodum iuncta natura sic officio quoque copulata, ut iidem sapientes atque eloquentes haberentur'.

138 Quintilian 1920–2, Proemium, 10, vol. I, p. 10: 'et publicarum privatarumque rerum administrationi accommodatus'.

139 Quintilian 1920–2, IV.V.6, vol. II, pp. 138–40. Cf also IV.II.31, vol. II, p. 66.

teach and persuade; the Grand Style enables us to teach, delight and persuade our hearers all at once.[140]

The humanists of Tudor England seize on these arguments with the utmost eagerness. They agree in the first place that, in order to discharge our civic duties, we must learn how to persuade as well as instruct. Elyot follows Quintilian in defining oratory as the art 'wherein is the power to persuade, move and delight',[141] and Wilson similarly lays it down at the outset of his *Arte of Rhetorique* that 'three thynges are required of an Orator', these being 'to teache, to delight and to perswade'.[142] They further agree that, in order to argue persuasively, the talent we must cultivate is that of speaking with eloquence. Elyot simply refers us at this point to the opening sections of the *De inventione*, laying particular emphasis on Cicero's claim that the earliest commonwealths must have arisen when a great leader 'helped by sapience and eloquence' assembled the people 'and persuaded to them what commodity was in mutual conversation and honest manners'.[143] Wilson opens his *Arte of Rhetorique* with an even closer paraphrase of the same passage, arguing that we cannot hope to explain how men 'coulde have bene broughte by anye other meanes to lyve together in felowshyppe of life, to mayntayne Cities, to deale trulye, and willyngelye to obeye one another, if menne at the first hadde not by Art and eloquence perswaded that which they ful oft found out by reason'.[144] Thomas Nashe alludes to the same passage yet again in his *Anatomie of Absurditie* in the course of ridiculing those who aim to persuade without having mastered the art of speech:

> A man may baule till his voice be hoarse, exhort with teares till his tongue ake and his eyes be drie, repeate that he woulde perswade, till his stalenes dooth secretlie call for a Cloake bagge, and yet move no more then if he had been all that while mute, if his speech be not seasoned with eloquence and adorned with elocutions assistance.[145]

Nashe's burlesque version of the argument suggests that by this stage it had become familiar to the point of tediousness.

Like their Roman authorities, the Tudor humanists summarise these commitments by speaking of the need for an alliance between reason, wisdom and eloquence. Sir Thomas Smith explains in one of his orations on the value of studying the law that, if we wish to speak persuasively, we must learn to combine our expert knowledge with a grasp of the techniques employed by 'those orators who have displayed the greatest

140 Quintilian 1920–2, XII.II.10–11, vol. IV, pp. 386–8, and XII.X.58–65, vol. IV, pp. 482–6.
141 Elyot 1962, p. 46; cf. Erasmus 1978a, p. 648.
142 Wilson 1554, sig. A, 1ᵛ.
143 Elyot 1962, pp. 45–6.
144 Wilson 1554, sig. A, 3ʳ.
145 Nashe 1958, p. 45. On Nashe's admiration for Ascham see Crewe 1982, pp. 24–5.

copiousness and eloquence'.[146] Ascham similarly argues in *The scholemaster* that the most important reason for concentrating on Greek and Roman literature is that these sources alone provide us with what we chiefly require, 'wisdome and eloquence, good matter and good utterance never or seldom a sonder'.[147] Peacham in his *Garden of Eloquence* carries us back to Cicero, citing his dictum to the effect that 'eloquence is the light and brightnesse of wisdome' and adding that this 'both expresseth the singular praises of two most worthie vertues, and also enforceth the necessitie and commendeth the utilitie of their excellent conjunction'.[148]

The belief that even the wisest reasoning needs to be underpinned by the force of eloquence helps in turn to explain why these writers insist that, before turning to the study of history and moral philosophy, the discipline that any aspiring *vir civilis* must be sure to master is the *ars rhetorica*. If and only if we study this art, learning in particular how to deploy the affective power inherent in the Grand Style, can we hope to speak with sufficient eloquence to persuade our fellow citizens of the truths that reason finds out. The art of rhetoric is seen, in short, as the key to eloquence. As Quintilian explains in book II of the *Institutio oratoria*, referring yet again to the opening pages of Cicero's *De inventione*, rhetoric can actually be defined as the art of eloquence,[149] since its exponents are those who have succeeded in reducing the precepts of eloquence to an art that can be taught.[150]

The first Tudor humanist to repeat this crucial claim is Vives in his *De tradendis disciplinis*. He opens his chapter on rhetoric by defining it as the art that leads to eloquence, and hence as the discipline that good and wise citizens can least afford to neglect.[151] Elyot in his chapter on the decay of learning in book I of *The Governor* likewise explains that the value of rhetoric stems from the fact that it shows us how to speak with eloquence, 'wherein is the power to persuade, move, and delight'.[152] Nashe goes even further in his encomium on rhetoric in *The Anatomy of Absurditie*, proclaiming that 'amongst all the ornaments of Artes, Rethorick is to be had in highest reputation, without the which all the rest are naked, and she onely garnished'. A mastery of rhetoric alone enables us to speak with eloquence, while eloquence alone enables us to hold the attention of an audience. By contrast, 'nothing is more odious to the Auditor then the artlesse tongue'

146 On the need to study 'oratores copiosi et facundi' see Smith, *Oratio*, CUL MS Mm. 1.48, p. 410.
147 Ascham 1970b, p. 265.
148 Peacham 1593, sig. AB, ii^{v}; cf. Sherry 1961, p. 96.
149 Quintilian 1920–2, II.XVII.2, vol. I, p. 326.
150 Quintilian 1920–2, II.I.I, vol. I, p. 204.
151 Vives 1913, pp. 180–1.
152 Elyot 1962, p. 46.

of someone unversed in rhetoric, the effect of which 'dulleth the delight of hearing, and slacketh the desire of remembring'.[153] As so often, however, it is Henry Peacham who summarises the argument with the greatest assurance. He declares in the prefatory epistle to his *Garden of Eloquence* that 'this happie union (I meane of wisdom & eloquence)' is so powerful that the orator is second only 'to the omnipotent God in the power of perswasion'. To which he adds that 'the principal instruments of mans help in this wonderfull effect' are all provided by the art of rhetoric, and above all by 'the frutefull branches of eloquution' on which he therefore chooses to concentrate.[154]

THE POWERS OF THE ORATOR

We can now see why the theorists we have been considering place such an extraordinarily high value on the *ars rhetorica.* A mastery of the art of rhetoric, and above all of the Grand Style, is said to be a necessary condition of writing and speaking with persuasive eloquence. But the ability to write and speak with eloquence is in turn said to be a necessary condition of pleading and deliberating effectively in the law courts and public assemblies of a commonwealth. An understanding of the seemingly humble tricks of the rhetorician's trade is accordingly held to be indispensable for discharging the most important duties of citizenship. If and only if we learn the proper methods of inventing, disposing and ornamenting our utterances can we hope to act as true *viri civiles*, persuading our fellow citizens of the truths that reason brings to light.

If we reflect on the specific duties of the *vir civilis*, moreover, we find that these writers are arguing for an even closer connection between a mastery of rhetoric and a capacity for good citizenship. The citizen's principal obligation is to plead for justice in the law courts and to offer honest and profitable counsel in the assemblies. But to plead in the law courts with the aim of securing justice is at the same time to practise one of the two leading genres of rhetorical utterance, the *genus iudiciale.* And to offer counsel in such a way as to show that a given course of action is at once honest and profitable is to practise the other leading genre, the *genus deliberativum.* What is being claimed is thus that the most important activities of a good citizen are essentially rhetorical in character; a *vir civilis* who dedicates himself to the execution of his principal duties will at the same time be acting as an exponent of the rhetorical arts.

According to the Roman rhetoricians, it follows that the person capable

153 Nashe 1958, p. 45. On Nashe's view of rhetoric see Crewe 1982, pp. 45–7.
154 Peacham 1593, sig. AB, iii^{v}.

of embodying in the highest degree the qualities necessary for good citizenship will be the orator, the man whose mastery of rhetoric enables him to empower his wisdom with eloquence. It is crucial to these theorists that to write *de oratore*, about the perfect orator, is at the same time to write *de cive*, about the ideal of citizenship. It is the figure of the orator who consequently features as the hero of all the Roman treatises we have so far discussed. A rousing affirmation of his heroic status appears at the start of Cicero's *De oratore*, where Crassus asserts that 'by the moderation and wisdom of the perfect orator, not only his own dignity but the safety of very many private individuals and of the entire commonwealth are upheld to the greatest possible degree'.[155] He later develops these observations into an almost Miltonic tribute to the orator's capacities:

> Who else is able, by his power of speaking, to expose the crimes and frauds of evil men to the hatred of his fellow citizens and coerce them by punishment; who else can liberate the innocent from the penalty of the laws by the protection of his talent; who else can arouse a languishing and failing people to a sense of what is honourable, or lead them away from the paths of error, or inflame them against the wicked, or calm them down when they have been incited against the good?[156]

Quintilian goes even further, devoting much of the closing book of his *Institutio oratoria* to arguing that the good orator can be identified so closely with the good citizen that we cannot even conceive of a traitor or a criminal as a master of the oratorical arts.[157] His positive contention is not merely 'that the figure of the orator ought to be a good man; it is rather that, unless you are a good man, you will find it impossible to be a good orator'.[158]

These commitments prompt the Roman rhetoricians to describe the ideal orator as a figure of extraordinary power and ascendancy.[159] Crassus opens the *De oratore* by describing how a great orator 'can turn an entire Senate in a particular direction by means of a single speech'.[160] The suggestion that eloquence enables us to guide or deflect an audience along

155 Cicero 1942a, I.VIII.34, vol. I, p. 26: 'perfecti oratoris moderatione et sapientia non solum ipsius dignitatem, sed et privatorum plurimorum, et universae reipublicae salutem maxime contineri'.

156 Cicero 1942a, I.XLVI.202, vol. I, p. 142: 'qui scelus fraudemque nocentis possit dicendo subicere odio civium, supplicioque constringere; idemque ingenii praesidio innocentiam iudiciorum poena liberare; idemque languentem labentemque populum aut ad decus excitare, aut ab errore deducere, aut inflammare in improbos, aut incitatum in bonos, mitigare'.

157 Quintilian 1920–2, XII.I.9, vol. IV, p. 360; XII.I.23–4, vol. IV, p. 368.

158 Quintilian 1920–2, XII.I.3, vol. IV, p. 356: 'eum, qui sit orator, virum bonum esse oportere, sed ne futurum quidem oratorem nisi virum bonum'.

159 On this theme see Vickers 1983.

160 See Cicero 1942a, I.VIII.31, vol. I, p. 24: on how the Senate can be 'unius oratione converti'.

whatever paths we choose is one that many Tudor poets and rhetoricians take up. Rainolde alludes at the start of his *Foundacion of Rhetorike* to the special ability of trained orators to 'drawe unto theim the hartes of a multitude' and turn them into followers.[161] Puttenham likewise speaks at several points about the orator's power to 'lead on' an audience, to make them take whatever turning he wishes and thereby 'serve his owne turne'.[162] Samuel Daniel draws even more extensively on the same imagery in his verse dialogue, *Musophilus*, which he completed in 1599:[163]

> Powre above powres, O heavenly Eloquence,
> That with the strong reine of commanding words,
> Dost manage, guide, and master th'eminence
> Of mens affections, more then all their swords:
> Shall we not offer to thy Excellence,
> The richest treasure that our wit affords?[164]

Musophilus' rhetorical question brings to a resounding close his response to the worldly figure of Philocosmos, who had opened the poem by mocking Musophilus for his preoccupation with 'ungainful Art' in 'this wiser profit-seeking age'.[165]

A second and even more prominent metaphor points to the orator's capacity to shift or move an audience. The characters in Cicero's *De oratore* repeatedly point to the power of eloquence to drive or impel people, to sway or move them, to press or coerce them into adopting some specific point of view.[166] The figure of Antonius even adds that, should an orator find himself confronting a judge 'who is actively hostile to his cause and friendly to his adversary', he should 'try to swing him round as if by some kind of machinery'.[167] The idea of persuading people by the 'machinations' of eloquence greatly appealed to the poets and rhetoricians of Tudor England. Wilson refers to the orator's ability to 'stir' his hearers, to press or push them towards some particular standpoint.[168] Peacham resorts to even more physical language, describing the power of rhetorical amplification to 'prevaile much in drawing the mindes' of our listeners, to 'winde them from their former

161 Rainolde 1564, fo. i^v.
162 Puttenham 1970, e.g. pp. 147, 151, 189.
163 For a discussion of the poem see Rhodes 1992, pp. 57–8.
164 Daniel 1963, p. 255. Musophilus' *laudatio* occupies lines 523–994, pp. 242–56. See also in Gardner 1972, p. 122.
165 Daniel 1963, p. 225.
166 See Cicero 1942a, e.g. at I.VIII.30, vol. I, p. 22; II.XLII.178, vol. I, p. 324; III.VI.23, vol. II, p. 18; III.XIV.55, vol. II, p. 44.
167 Cicero 1942a, II.XVII.72, vol. I, p. 252: when the judge is 'amicus adversario et inimicus tibi', then 'tanquam machinatione aliqua ... est contorquendus'.
168 Wilson 1564, e.g. fo. 63^r. Cf. also Rainolde 1564, fo. i^v; Bacon 1859, p. 77.

opinions', and above all to help the orator 'move them to be of his side, to hold with him, to be led by him'.[169] Daniel calls on a similar set of images in his encomium on rhetoric at the end of *Musophilus*:

> Thou that canst doe much more with one poore pen
> Then all the powres of Princes can effect:
> And draw, divert, dispose and fashion men
> Better then force or rigour can direct:
> Should we this ornament of Glory then
> As th'unmateriall fruits of shades, neglect?[170]

Daniel offers the most hyperbolical restatement of the shared assumption that the pen is mightier than the sword.

Once eloquence came to be seen as a power mightier than might itself, the orator was in turn described as a figure of violent energies and strength. One range of images portrays his ability to seize or captivate an audience, to hold them in the palm of his hand. The *Ad Herennium* begins by arguing that we must always ensure, especially at the start of an oration, that we speak 'in such a way that we manage to seize the attention of our hearers and render them docile and benevolent'.[171] When Crassus opens the discussion in the *De oratore*, he similarly declares that 'nothing seems to me more splendid than the capacity, by means of oratory, to seize hold of an assembly, draw their minds and impel their wills in whatever direction one wants'.[172] A second set of images depicts the orator's power, after captivating and enthralling his audience, to abduct or carry them off. The *Ad Herennium* stresses the need to 'transport' our hearers by amplifying our speech 'in such a way as to induce them to feelings of rage, or lead their minds towards feelings of pity'.[173] The figure of Antonius in the *De oratore* likewise speaks of the orator's ability to 'carry off' the members of a tribunal, and claims for himself the capacity 'to shift or impel the minds of judges' in any direction he wants.[174]

These images proved especially attractive to the rhetoricians of Tudor England. 'What greater delite do we know', Wilson asks, 'then to see a whole multitude with the onely talke of a man ravished & drawen whiche waye him liketh best to have them?'[175] Ascham similarly describes the

169 Peacham 1593, p. 121.

170 Daniel 1963, p. 255. See also in Gardner 1972, p. 123.

171 *Ad C. Herennium*, I.IV.6, p. 12: 'ita sumitur ut adtentos, ut dociles, ut benivolos auditores habere possimus'. Cf. also Cicero 1942a, II.XIX.80–3, vol. I, pp. 256–8.

172 Cicero 1942a, I.VIII.30, vol. I, p. 22: 'Neque vero mihi quidquam ... praestabilius videtur, quam posse dicendo tenere hominum coetus, mentes allicere, voluntates impellere quo velit.'

173 *Ad C. Herennium*, III.XIII.23, p. 196: 'aut in iracundiam inducit, aut ad misericordiam trahit auditoris animum'.

174 Cicero 1942a, II.XLIV.185, vol. I, p. 330: 'mentes iudicum permovet, impelletque'.

175 Wilson 1554, sig. A, i^{v}.

ideal schoolmaster as a man able 'to teach plainlie, to delite pleasantlie, and to cary away by force of wise talke, all that shall heare or read him'.[176] Puttenham invokes the same imagery with much greater violence, referring to the orator's power to ravish, to assail, to conquer and vanquish the mind.[177] With less fortunate results, Angel Day extends the same metaphor, describing the man of eloquence as capable of ensuring that his hearers are 'egged forward' in any direction he may desire.[178]

By defining the good orator as someone who forces us to do what reason commands, the Roman rhetorical theorists present him as a figure of almost magical potency.[179] His art, like that of the musician, is said to be a bewitching one, with the power of a *carmen* to charm or a *cantus* to enchant.[180] The Tudor poets and rhetoricians frequently embroider the same analogies. Wilson thinks that 'thynges wittely devised, and pleasauntly set furthe' have no less grace than 'the sound of a lute or any suche instrument doeth give'.[181] Puttenham describes 'the harmonicall speaches of oratours' and commends 'the well tuning of your words and clauses to the delight of the eare'.[182] Most fulsomely of all, Thomas Edwards invokes the same metaphors at the start of his eulogy of 1595 on the young William Shakespeare:

> Well could his bewitching pen,
> Done the Muses objects to us
> Although he differs much from men
> Tilting under Frieries,
> Yet his golden art might woo us
> To have honored him with baies.[183]

The orator, like the magus, is seen as someone with 'Spirits to enforce, art to enchant'.[184]

Besides portraying the orator as a magician, the Roman rhetoricians liked to draw on one final and even more high flown piece of imagery. The ideal orator, Quintilian suggests, should be thought of as nothing less than a force of nature. On three occasions Quintilian quotes Aristophanes' remark to the effect that the impact of Pericles' oratory felt like a

176 Ascham 1970b, p. 283.

177 Puttenham 1970, p. 197. For other references to the orator's power to ravish see Nashe 1985, p. 267; Bacon 1915, p. 50; Shakespeare 1988, *Love's Labour's Lost*, II.i.75, p. 285.

178 Day 1967, p. 5.

179 On Renaissance word magic see Rhodes 1992, pp. 8–12.

180 Cicero 1942a, II.VIII.34, vol. I, p. 222; Quintilian 1920–2, II.VIII.15, vol. I, p. 270, and IX.II.6, vol. III, p. 376.

181 Wilson 1564, fo. 2^{r}.

182 Puttenham 1970, pp. 171, 197. Cf. also Peacham 1593, sig. AB, iii^{r} and pp. 48, 49, 59.

183 Ingleby 1879, p. 18.

184 Shakespeare 1988, *The Tempest*, Epilogue, l. 14, p. 1189.

thunderstorm.[185] Quintilian assures us that 'this indicates the power of true eloquence',[186] adding 'is it not a splendid thing that, simply by employing ordinary intelligence and the words everyone uses, we can gain such praise and glory that we appear not to speak and orate, but rather, as was said of Pericles, to thunder and flash like lightning?'[187] Among the Tudor rhetoricians, Henry Peacham lays particular emphasis on the same range of images, introducing his discussion of amplification by declaring that 'the Orator by helpe hereof either renteth all in pieces like the thunder: or else by little and little, like the flowing water creepeth by gentle meanes into the consent of his hearers'.[188] Soon afterwards Sir Philip Sidney in his *Defence of Poesie* applied the same simile to Cicero, observing that 'When he was to drive out *Catiline*', he did so 'as it were with a thunderbolt of eloquence'.[189] Eventually the comparison became so hackneyed that the idea of thundering at an audience slipped from being a simile to being a mere synonym for speaking with terrifying eloquence.

By way of summarising these images, the Tudor rhetoricians frequently compared the orator with different mythical figures. Sometimes they referred to Orpheus,[190] but their most frequent comparison was with the figure of Hercules. Generally they draw on Lucian's version of the fable, thereby calling attention to their familiarity with one of the writers most admired by Erasmus and his circle.[191] Wilson offers an interpretation of Lucian's account of the story in the preface to his *Arte of Rhetorique*. 'Hercules being a man of greate wisdome had all men lincked together by the eares in a chaine to draw them and leade them even as he lusted.'[192] But the chain was a metaphorical one, taking as it did the form of Hercules' eloquence. 'For his witte was so greate, his tongue so eloquente & his experience suche that no one man was able to withstand his reason, but everye one was rather driven to do that whiche he woulde and to wil that whyche he did.'[193] Puttenham similarly tells us about the 'pretie

185 Quintilian 1920–2, II.XVI.19, vol. I, p. 324; XII.X.24, vol. IV, p. 462; XII.X.65, vol. IV, p. 486. On Pericles as the ideal of an eloquent citizen see also Cicero 1942a, I.L.216, vol. I, p. 152, and II.XXII.93, vol. I, p. 266.

186 Quintilian 1920–2, XII.X.65, vol. IV, p. 486: 'haec est vere dicendi facultas'.

187 Quintilian 1920–2, II.XVI.19, vol. I, p. 324: 'nonne pulcrum vel hoc ipsum est, ex communi intellectu verbisque, quibus utuntur omnes, tantum adsequi laudis et gloriae, ut non loqui et orare sed, quod Pericli contigit, fulgurare ac tonare videaris?' Cf. Tacitus 1970, 8.2, p. 246.

188 Peacham 1593, p. 121.

189 Sidney 1923, p. 42.

190 Peacham 1593, sig. AB, iii^v; Kempe 1966, p. 199. On the use of the myth see Rhodes 1992, pp. 3–8.

191 See Wilson 1564, fo. 106^r on Lucian and Sir Thomas More. For a discussion of Lucian's version of the fable, and of its iconography, see Jung 1966, pp. 73–93. Lucian's account is finely illustrated in emblem 43, 'Gallorum Hercules', in Haechtanus 1579.

192 Wilson 1564, sig. A, iii^v.

193 Wilson 1564, sig. A, iii^v–iv^r.

devise or embleme that *Lucianus* alleageth he saw in the pourtrait of *Hercules* within the Citie of Marseills'.[194] The portrait was that of 'a lustie old man with a long chayne tyed by one end at his tong, by the other end at the peoples eares, who stood a farre of and seemed to be drawen to him by the force of that chayne fastned to his tong'.[195] The moral of the story is that, although Hercules was not literally pulling the people along, he was pulling them nevertheless, since he was doing so 'by force of his perswasions'.[196]

THE NEED FOR ELOQUENCE

'The true *vir civilis*', Quintilian concludes, 'is none other than the figure of the orator', the man who knows how to gain a hearing for his wisdom by means of his eloquence.[197] While this brings us to the heart of the argument we have been considering, it remains to explain why the Roman rhetoricians are so insistent that, in the absence of eloquence, even the wisest reasoning can never hope to prevail. What makes it impossible to rely on the force of reason to carry us to victory in the law courts and public assemblies of the commonwealth?

The problem is held to be especially acute in the case of deliberative oratory. As we have seen, to write or speak in the *genus deliberativum* is to advise or counsel that a certain line of policy should be pursued, a line of policy at once advantageous and honourable. The speaker's aim is consequently to reason in such a way as to persuade his fellow citizens to follow one course of action rather than another. According to the writers we have been considering, however, even an orator who provides his fellow citizens with good reasons for acting in some particular way can never hope by force of reason alone to motivate them so to act. Cicero gives powerful expression to this difficulty at the start of his *De inventione*, in the course of considering how the first commonwealths came to be formed. As we have seen, he postulates that, 'at a time when men were living dispersed in fields and hidden in woods', there must have arisen a great founder or lawgiver, 'a man at once mighty and wise', who possessed the vision to see 'that there was an opportunity for men to achieve the greatest things' if only they would alter their brutish way of life.[198] The

194 Puttenham 1970, p. 142.

195 Puttenham 1970, p. 142. This is how Hercules is portrayed in emblem 181 of Alciati's *Emblemata*. See Alciati 1621, p. 751.

196 Puttenham 1970, p. 142. Cf. also Harvey 1913, p. 155. For further references to the meaning of the story see Skinner 1990b, p. 137n.

197 Quintilian 1920–2, Proemium, 10, vol. I, p. 10: 'vir ille vere civilis ... non alius sit profecto quam orator'. Cf. Cicero 1942a, I.VIII.34, vol. I, p. 26.

198 See Cicero 1949a, I.II.2, pp. 4–6 on the 'magnus videlicet vir et sapiens' who, when men were

wisdom of this visionary figure enabled him to perceive that men needed in particular to abandon their lawless reliance on natural ferocity in favour of learning 'to keep faith, to recognise the need to uphold justice and be ready to submit their wills to others'.[199] As Cicero adds, however, it is impossible to believe that such a lawgiver could ever have induced an uncivilised multitude to change their settled habits simply by reason and argument. We can be sure that 'at first they cried out against him because of the unfamiliarity of his plans', even though it was undoubtedly in their interests to accept them.[200]

This in turn explains why successful counsellors and lawgivers must be men of eloquence. They need to call on something more powerful than 'mute and voiceless wisdom' if they are to alter our behaviour;[201] they need to supply us in addition with a desire to act rationally. But the only means of empowering wisdom in this way is to lend it the force of eloquence. 'Eloquence', Cicero concludes, 'is indispensable if men are to persuade others to accept the truths that reason finds out.'[202] This is why 'I find that many cities have been founded, and even more wars have been ended, while the firmest of alliances and the most sacred of friendships have been established not simply by rational argument but also, and more readily, by means of eloquence.'[203]

Cicero's *De oratore* repeats these claims about the powerlessness of reason to motivate us,[204] and the same arguments resurface in a number of Renaissance treatises. Henry Peacham insists on 'the great necessitie' of a conjunction between wisdom and eloquence on the grounds that 'to possesse great knowledge without apt utterance is as to possesse great treasure without use'. It is crucial to be 'well furnished with both', in the manner of 'those men in times past, who by their singular wisdom and eloquence made savage nations civil, wild people tame'.[205] The same assumptions recur in Francis Bacon's discussion of the art of rhetoric in

'in agros et in tectis silvestribus abditos' recognised 'quanta ad maximas res opportunitas in animis inesset hominum'.

199 Cicero 1949a, I.II.3, p. 6: 'fidem colere et iustitiam retinere discernunt et aliis parere sua voluntate consuescerent'.

200 Cicero 1949a, I.II.2, p. 6: 'primo propter insolentiam reclamantes'.

201 See Cicero 1949a, I.II.3, p. 6 on *sapientia* as 'tacita' and 'inops dicendi'.

202 See Cicero 1949a, I.II.3, p. 6 on the need for 'homines ea quae ratione invenissent eloquentia persuadere'.

203 Cicero 1949a, I.I.1, p. 2: 'multas urbes constitutas, plurima bella restincta, firmissimas societates, sanctissimas amicitias intelligo cum animi ratione tum facilius eloquentia comparatas'.

204 Cicero 1942a, I.VIII.33–4, vol. I, pp. 24–6. Cf. also Quintilian 1920–2, II.XVI.9–10, vol. I, pp. 320–2, strongly alluding to the opening of the *De inventione*.

205 Peacham 1593, sig. AB, iii^{r-v}.

inferior to wisdom', nevertheless 'with people it is the more mighty'.[218] He later explains that this is due to its popular appeal, repeating the adage that 'logic differeth from rhetoric' as 'the fist from the palm, the one close, the other at large'.[219] The difference stems from the fact that, whereas logic 'handleth reason exact and in truth', rhetoric 'handleth it as it is planted in popular opinions and manners'. We may therefore speak of a 'politic part of eloquence', the force of which derives from its capacity to help a speaker adjust his arguments to suit different audiences.[220]

The Roman rhetoricians end by pointing to a yet further and even more conclusive reason for doubting whether wisdom in the absence of eloquence can ever hope to win people round to the cause of justice and truth. This additional difficulty becomes obvious as soon as we reflect on the subject matter of forensic or deliberative speech. An orator practising the *genus iudiciale* will be engaged in prosecuting or defending in circumstances in which it will often be possible for a skilful adversary to mount a no less plausible case on the other side. An orator practising the *genus deliberativum* will similarly be attempting to show that some particular course of action ought to be followed in circumstances in which it will often be no less rational to propose a contradictory policy. In such situations there will be no possibility of demonstrating beyond question that one side is in the right. As Quintilian puts it in his chapter on the nature of rhetoric, these are the sort of cases 'in which two wise men may with just cause take up one or another point of view, since it is generally agreed that it is possible for reason to lead even the wise to fight among themselves'.[221] These are instances, in other words, in which 'the weapons of powerful speech can always be used *in utramque partem*, on either side of the case'.[222] The situation is such a familiar one, Quintilian adds, that when we speak of 'the general question at issue' in an oratorical argument we are usually describing 'that which it is possible to speak about with plausibility *in utramque partem* or even on many different sides'.[223]

By the time Cicero came to write his *De oratore*, he had reached the conclusion that the subject matter of oratory makes the capacity to speak *in utramque partem* the most important skill of all. The figure of Crassus insists in book III that 'we ought to have enough intelligence, power and

218 Bacon 1915, p. 146.
219 Bacon 1915, p. 148.
220 Bacon 1915, p. 148.
221 Quintilian 1920–2, II.XVII.32, vol. I, p. 338: 'duos sapientes aliquando iustae causae in diversum trahant (quando etiam pugnaturos eos inter se, si ratio ita duxerit, credunt)'.
222 Quintilian 1920–2, II.XVI.10, vol. I, p. 322: 'in utramque partem valet arma facundiae'.
223 Quintilian 1920–2, III.XI.1, vol. I, p. 522: the *quaestio* will usually be 'de qua in utramque partem vel in plures partes dici credibiliter potest'.

art to speak *in utramque partem*' on all the leading commonplaces: 'on virtue, duty, equity, goodness, dignity, benefit, honour, ignominy, reward, punishment and all the rest'.[224] Shortly after this point in the dialogue, the youthful Cotta is made to exclaim that, after listening to Crassus, he now realises where his own ambitions lie. 'I shall never allow myself to be overcome nor shall I give up through exhaustion until I understand the method of debating *pro* and *contra* in every possible case.'[225]

This in turn explains why the ideal of the perfect orator is always symbolised for the Roman rhetoricians by the figure of Carneades. As Quintilian reminds us in book XII, it was Carneades who shocked and astonished Cato the Censor by coming to Rome and 'speaking against the virtue of justice on one day with no less strength than he had spoken in favour of it the day before'.[226] Crassus underlines the significance of Carneades' performance in the course of his long speech about style in book III of the *De oratore*. What Carneades recognised was that, in all matters pertaining to *scientia civilis*, it will always be possible to argue against any proposition put forward, and thus to construct a plausible case *in utramque partem*.[227] If anyone were now to cultivate this talent to the full, Crassus adds, he would be entitled to be hailed as 'the true, the perfect, the one and only ideal orator'.[228]

We can now see how this view about the character of *scientia civilis*, and hence about the subject matter of oratory, prompts the Roman rhetoricians to conclude that, even if we learn to speak with the deepest wisdom and the highest philosophical abilities, we can never hope to win the war of words by these means alone. Given that there are many questions on which we can hope to speak with equal plausibility *pro* and *contra*, it will never be sufficient to reason wisely in order to win over an audience. It will always be necessary to add the *vis* or moving force of eloquence to press or impel them to desert the opposition and come round to our side. It is true that these considerations are not thought to apply in the exact as opposed to the moral sciences. As the figure of Scaevola concedes at the start of the *De oratore*, 'we can pass over the mathematicians, the grammarians and the followers of the muses, with whose arts this capacity

224 Cicero 1942a, III.XXVII.107, vol. II, pp. 84–6: 'de virtute, de officio, de aequo et bono, de dignitate, utilitate, honore, ignominia, praemio, poena similibusque de rebus in utramque partem dicendi animos et vim et artem habere debemus'.

225 Cicero 1942a, III.XXXVI.145, vol. II, p. 114: 'nunquam conquiescam neque defatigabor ante quam ... pro omnibus et contra omnia disputandi percepero'.

226 Quintilian 1920–2, XII.I.35, vol. IV, p. 374: 'non minoribus viribus contra iustitiam ... disseruisse quam pridie pro iustitia dixerat'. For an account of the occasion see Kennedy 1972, pp. 53–5.

227 Cicero 1942a, III.XXI.80, vol. II, p. 64.

228 Cicero 1942a, III.XXI.80, vol. II, p. 80: 'is sit verus, is perfectus, is solus orator'.

for powerful speaking has no connection at all'.[229] But Scaevola's main contention is that, in cases where we cannot look for certainty – as in most of the arguments characteristic of civic life – the need for eloquence becomes paramount. You cannot do without it, he declares, 'if you want the case you are pleading in the courts to seem the better and more plausible one, or if you want the speeches you deliver in the assemblies to have the greatest persuasive force, or if you merely want your utterances to appear truthful to the uninstructed and skilful to the wise'.[230] If, in short, your arguments fall in any way within the purview of *scientia civilis*, you will always find it necessary to supplement your reasoning with the force of eloquence.

The same assumptions recur with even greater emphasis in the Renaissance, in the course of which we encounter an unparalleled degree of interest in the exploration of paradoxes, dialogues and other forms of argument lacking obvious closure.[231] The dictum that there will always be two sides to any question eventually became proverbial, and already underpins the treatment of proverbs and *loci communes* in many writers of the English Renaissance. As Bacon expresses the point in *The Advancement of Learning*, one of the crucial offices of moral virtue is that of 'acquainting the mind to balance reasons on both sides'.[232] The poets and dramatists are especially alert to such dialectical possibilities, and such poets as Michael Drayton and Samuel Daniel reveal a close acquaintance with the rhetorical ideal of arguing *in utramque partem*.[233] The moral, everyone agreed, is that if we are to persuade an audience to accept one side of an argument rather than the other, it will always be necessary to supplement even the deepest wisdom with the force of eloquence. Among the Tudor rhetoricians it is Peacham in *The Garden of Eloquence* who draws the conclusion with the greatest emphasis. It will always be due in part to 'the secret and mightie power of perswasion' that 'wisdome appeareth in her beautie, sheweth her maiestie and exerciseth her power'. If we are to ensure that 'the precious nature and wonderfull power of wisedome' is 'produced and brought into open light', we can never dispense with 'the commendable Art and use of eloquence'.[234]

229 Cicero 1942a, I.x.44, vol. I, p. 32: 'Missos facio mathematicos, grammaticos, musicos, quorum artibus vestra ista dicendi vis ne minima quidem societate contingitur.'

230 Cicero 1942a, I.x.44, vol. I, pp. 32–4: 'ut in iudiciis ea causa, quamcumque tu dicis, melior et probabilior esse videatur; ut in concionibus et sententiis dicendis ad persuadendum tua plurimum valeat oratio; denique ut prudentibus diserte stultis etiam vere dicere videaris'.

231 On paradox see Colie 1966; on dialogue see Marsh 1980, Wilson 1985, Cox 1992.

232 Bacon 1915, p. 55.

233 See for example Drayton's sonnet 'To proverbe', in which *loci communes* are debated *in utramque partem*. Drayton 1953, p. 16.

234 Peacham 1593, sig. AB, iii[r].

THE STANDING OF THE *ARS RHETORICA*

The essence of the argument we have been considering is that a mastery of the *ars rhetorica* enables us to speak with eloquence, and that the power of eloquence enables us to speak in a 'winning' style. As Quintilian acknowledges in book II, however, there is something misleading about defining rhetoric in these terms. On the one hand, there are many other ways of being persuasive besides speaking eloquently; and on the other hand, there is always the possibility that we may succeed in speaking eloquently without being persuasive.[235] Quintilian accordingly prefers to define the art of rhetoric simply by reference to the distinctive skills it involves, and not by reference to its intended effects. This yields the rather more modest conclusion that 'rhetoric is to be defined as the science of speaking well'.[236]

Even Quintilian concedes, however, that our purpose in studying this science will normally be to learn how to impel or persuade an audience to come round to our point of view. 'The aim of a speaker will of course be to secure victory, despite the fact that someone who speaks well may be said to be practising the art of rhetoric, even though he may not succeed in winning the argument.'[237] Despite his scruples, Quintilian accordingly arrives at a conclusion not unlike Cicero's in *De inventione*. We need to distinguish, Cicero had argued, between the *officium* or task of rhetoric and its *finis* or goal. While we may be said to have discharged our task if we succeed in speaking in the manner we judge most likely to persuade, we can hardly be said to have attained our goal unless our auditors are in fact persuaded.[238] As the author of the *Ad Herennium* had more brutally put it, 'the proper disposition of topics, like the proper drawing up of troops, is what will most easily gain what you want in speaking, as in fighting, which is victory'.[239]

The Roman theorists were highly conscious of the fact that, in treating rhetoric as the art enabling us to persuade as well as instruct, they were taking sides in a bitter and long-standing dispute.[240] It had often been retorted that, if someone seeks to persuade, it follows that they cannot be said to teach. The figure of Crassus in book III of the *De oratore* singles out Socrates as 'the leading figure among those who have denounced and

235 Quintilian 1920–2, II.XV.1–16, vol. I, pp. 300–6.

236 Quintilian 1920–2, II.XV.38, vol. I, p. 316: 'Dicam enim ... rhetoricem esse bene dicendi scientiam'. For a discussion of Cicero's views on the same issue see Michel 1960, pp. 39–42.

237 Quintilian 1920–2, II.XVII.23, vol. I, p. 334: 'Tendit quidem ad victoriam qui dicit; sed cum bene dixit, etiamsi non vincat, id quod arte continetur effecit.'

238 Cicero 1949a, I.V.6, p. 14. Cf. Cicero 1942a, II.XVII.72, vol. I, pp. 250–2.

239 *Ad C. Herennium* 1954, III.X.8, p. 188: 'dispositio locorum, tamquam instructio militum, facillime in dicendo, sicut illa in pugnando, parere poterit victoriam'.

240 For a survey of philosophy's dispute with rhetoric see Ijsseling 1976, esp. pp. 7–17.

condemned the art of speaking' in exactly this way.[241] He adds that Socrates 'introduced into his disputations a separation between the science of thinking wisely and speaking eloquently', although Crassus maintains that 'in fact these two things go together'.[242] Quintilian later fixes on the same aspect of Socrates' teaching when comparing the various definitions of rhetoric in book II of the *Institutio oratoria*. He first notes that 'when Gorgias in Plato's dialogue says that he is a master of the art of persuasion both in the law courts and in other public assemblies, Socrates in his response allows that Gorgias has the capacity to persuade but not the capacity to teach'.[243] He goes on to mention that Plato in the *Gorgias* puts into the mouth of Socrates the claim that 'rhetoric can be described as nothing better than a sophistical means of quibbling about justice'.[244] Once again, the reason for Socrates' hostility is that he thinks of rhetoric as a means to instigate beliefs as opposed to engendering them by genuine argument.

These anxieties about the potentially deceiving character of eloquence are not wholly absent even from Roman discussions of the rhetorical arts. Cicero expresses a momentary qualm at the beginning of the *De inventione* as to 'whether more harm than good has come to men and cities from powerful speaking and the deepest study of eloquence',[245] while Sallust depicts the art of rhetoric in his *Bellum Catilinae* in such a way as to suggest that the balance sheet is all too liable to come out on the side of harm. He not only portrays the figure of Catiline as 'a man of great eloquence but of small wisdom',[246] but uses the example of Catiline's conspiracy to illustrate how easily the art of speaking can be used to undermine the stability of commonwealths.

According to most of the Roman theorists, however, the objection that we cannot teach and persuade at the same time can easily be overcome. The two activities, they insist, can perfectly well be combined.[247] Quintilian in particular emphasises that, while a good orator aims at victory, he always aims at victory for the cause of justice and truth. He

241 See Cicero 1942a, III.XVI.59–60, vol. II, p. 48, speaking of those who 'hanc dicendi exercitationem exagitarent atque contemnerent', among whom 'princeps Socrates fuit'. For Socrates' attack on rhetoric, especially in the *Gorgias*, see Vickers 1989, pp. 83–113.

242 Cicero 1942a, III.XVI.60, vol. II, p. 48: 'sapienterque sentiendi et ornate dicendi scientiam re cohaerentes disputationibus suis separavit'.

243 Quintilian 1920–2, II.XV.18, vol. I, p. 308: 'Gorgias apud Platonem suadendi se artificem in iudiciis et aliis coetibus esse ait ... cui Socrates persuadendi, non docendi concedit facultatem.'

244 Quintilian 1920–2, II.XV.25, vol. I, p. 310: 'cavillatricem iustitiae rhetoricem [vocet]'.

245 Cicero 1949a, I.I.1, p. 2: 'bonine an mali plus attulerit hominibus et civitatibus copia dicendi ac summum eloquentiae studium'.

246 Sallust 1921a, V.5, p. 8: 'satis eloquentiae, sapientiae parum'.

247 Maclean 1992, pp. 75–7.

deploys the Grand Style to fight for honourable and profitable decisions in the assemblies and for equitable verdicts in the courts. 'Since his behaviour springs from a good motive', Quintilian adds, 'there is nothing disgraceful about what he does.'[248] Quintilian is even prepared to go much further, declaring that 'it is permitted on some occasions for a wise man to tell a lie if he can see no other way to lead a judge to arrive at an equitable verdict'.[249] The justification for such dissimulation lies in the fact that 'so much evil opposes the truth' that 'we must fight with all our art and make use of anything that will advance our cause'.[250] The good orator is accordingly seen as someone who seeks so far as possible to teach the truth, but who seeks at the same time by every possible means to impel or persuade us to accept it.

It is true that Cicero intermittently acknowledges that such an art might be thought to have a somewhat dubious character. One concession he makes is to question whether rhetoric can genuinely be regarded as an *ars*, a subject of true *scientia* or knowledge. At the beginning of the *De inventione* he asks himself whether eloquence may not be a mere gift of nature,[251] and in book I of the *De oratore* he develops the suggestion at some length. The figure of Crassus, answering a doubt raised by Scaevola, announces that 'it seems to me that either there is no art of speaking at all, or at best a very attenuated one'.[252] He begins by explaining that 'natural ability and intelligence lend by far the greatest force to successful oratory'.[253] But his scepticism is principally rooted in his views about the genuine arts and sciences. 'If an art is defined as something which has as its subject-matter things that are clearly perceived and plainly understood, that are detached from the arbitrariness of mere opinion and are capable of being made a subject of exact knowledge, then it seems to me that the art of oratory cannot be accounted a genuine art at all.'[254] The reason is that 'all the *genera* of public speaking we employ are not only changeable in themselves, but have to be

248 Quintilian 1920–2, II.XVII.27, vol. I, p. 336: 'cum ex bona ratione proficiscitur, ideoque nec vitium'.

249 Quintilian 1920–2, II.XVII.27, vol. I, p. 336: 'Nam et mendacium dicere etiam sapienti aliquando concessum est . . . si aliter ad aequitatem perduci iudex non poterit.'

250 Quintilian 1920–2, II.XVII.29, vol. I, p. 338: 'tot malis obnoxia veritas, arte pugnandum est et adhibenda quae prosunt'.

251 Cicero 1949a, I.II.2, p. 4.

252 Cicero 1942a, I.XXIII.107, vol. I, p. 76: 'mihi dicendi aut nullam artem, aut pertenuem videri'.

253 Cicero 1942a, I.XXV.113, vol. I, p. 80: 'naturam primum, atque ingenium ad dicendum vim afferre maximam'. Cf. Antonius' similar comments at II.XXXV.147, vol. I, p. 304.

254 Cicero 1942a, I.XXIII.108, vol. I, p. 76: 'Nam si ars ita definitur . . . ex rebus penitus perspectis planeque cognitis, atque ab opinionis arbitrio seiunctis, scientiaque comprehensis, non mihi videtur ars oratoris esse ulla.' Cf. Antonius' similar comments at II.VII.30, vol. I, p. 218.

accommodata – adapted or accommodated – to the understanding of the uneducated and the populace at large'.[255]

A second and related concession – put forward by Quintilian as well as Cicero – acknowledges that the art of rhetoric stands in an equivocal relationship with the truth. As we have seen, both writers assume that, in any argument about civil affairs, it will generally be possible to construct a plausible case *in utramque partem*. It follows that the idea of a fully demonstrative *scientia civilis* is nothing more than an oxymoron. An orator can never hope to prove or demonstrate his conclusions beyond doubt (*demonstrare*); he can only hope to discuss and debate the rival merits of different points of view (*disserere*).[256] But this means that an orator aiming at victory cannot primarily commit himself to the statement of plain and unvarnished truths. While a good orator will of course stick to the truth as far as possible, he cannot fail to be more interested in working out what lines of argument are likely to sound most plausible and persuasive, emphasising such considerations as much as possible while minimising anything capable of being said against them. As Antonius summarises in book II of Cicero's *De oratore*, while the orator must be sure to give a proper *narratio* of the facts, he must never forget 'that one of the greatest virtues of any such narrative lies in its capacity to present the facts in a manner *accommodata* or calculated at once to delight and to persuade'.[257]

Despite these concessions, neither Cicero nor Quintilian ever seriously doubts that the *ars rhetorica* is a genuine art.[258] After laying out his sceptical arguments, the figure of Crassus in the *De oratore* undercuts them by observing that 'I do not understand why oratory should not be seen as an art, not perhaps according to the subtlest definition, but certainly according to its commonly received sense.'[259] Having spoken at the outset in even more disparaging terms, Antonius subsequently indicates that he too has been arguing *in utramque partem*, putting forward at least some of his misgivings as a preliminary to countering them in best rhetorical style.[260] 'While I have acknowledged', he observes, 'that the art of oratory may not

255 Cicero 1942a, I.XXIII.108, vol. I, p. 76: 'Sunt enim varia, et ad vulgarem popularemque sensum accommodata omnia genera huius forensis nostrae dictionis.'

256 Cicero 1942a, III.XXI.80, vol. II, p. 64 and III.XXVII.107, vol. II, pp. 84–6. Cf. Quintilian 1920–2, XII.I.35, vol. IV, p. 374 and XII.II.25, vol. IV, p. 396.

257 Cicero 1942a, II.LXXX.326, vol. I, p. 444: 'quod eam virtutem quae narrationis est maxima, ut iucunda et ad persuadendum accommodata sit'.

258 Nor does the author of the *Ad Herennium*. See *Ad C. Herennium* 1954, IV.II.3 (p. 232), IV.III.4 (p. 234) and IV.IV.7 (p. 240).

259 Cicero 1942a, I.XXIII.109, vol. I, p. 76: 'non intellego, quam ob rem non, si minus illa subtili definitione, at hac vulgari opinione, ars esse videatur'.

260 On Antonius' apparent change of mind overnight (i.e. between books I and II) see Kennedy 1972, pp. 206–7. For Antonius' admission see Cicero 1942a, II.X.40, vol. I, pp. 226–8.

be the greatest of the arts, I nevertheless affirm that it is possible to offer a number of extremely shrewd precepts for directing other people's opinions and forming their wills.'[261] To which he immediately adds that 'should anyone wish to claim that a knowledge of this technique amounts to an art of major importance, I shall certainly not seek to deny that this is the case'.[262]

Nor are Crassus and Antonius even willing to admit that rhetoric stands in an equivocal relationship with the truth.[263] Although they allow that the truth may sometimes need to be varnished, and although they regard the ideal practitioner of the Grand Style as a figure of powerfully coercive abilities, they insist at the same time on the contrasting claim – so unfamiliar to modern readers as to be difficult to grasp[264] – that ornamentation is an inherently veracious process, one that may be said to track the truth. As Crassus insists in summarising his views about *ornatus* in book III of the *De oratore*, the addition of effective ornamentation to our speech is not simply a matter of adding alluring dress or colouring; it is a matter of dressing or colouring things in their truest style, thereby presenting or revealing their essential nature or character.[265] It follows that the process of ornamentation not only sits more easily with the truth than with falsehood, but that it is almost impossible to ornament falsehoods successfully.[266] As Quintilian later expresses the point – at the same time disclosing its Aristotelian provenance[267] – the process of ornamentation consists of perfecting rather than embellishing nature.[268] The techniques of the rhetorician are held to stand in a non-contingent relationship with the furtherance of truth.

With the rise of the Christian Grand Style in the Renaissance, a yet further defence became available against the accusation that rhetoric is merely a technique for using emotional appeals to defeat or varnish the truth. This stemmed from the Augustinian assumption that human nature is not merely inherently spiritual, but that human spirituality is inherently

261 Cicero 1942a, II.VIII.32, vol. I, p. 220: 'sum confessus ... artem esse non maximam, sic illud affirmo, praecepta posse quaedam dari peracuta ad pertractandos animos hominum et ad excipiendas eorum voluntates'.

262 Cicero 1942a, II.VIII.32, vol. I, p. 220: 'Huius rei scientiam si quis volet magnam quamdam artem esse dicere, non repugnabo'. Cf. Quintilian 1920–2, II.XVII.11–15, vol. I, pp. 330–2, invoking Aristotle's authority for the view that rhetoric is a genuine *ars*.

263 For reasons excellently discussed in Briggs 1989, pp. 79–85.

264 Briggs 1989, pp. 85–6, gives examples of such incomprehension.

265 See Cicero 1942a, III.LII.199–201, vol. II, pp. 158–60, and the opening of the discussion of *actio* at III.LVII.215, pp. 170–2.

266 This forms an important part of Quintilian's argument in book XIII to the effect that good orators are necessarily good men. See Quintilian 1920–2, XII.I.1–13, vol. IV, pp. 354–62.

267 Aristotle 1926, I.I.12, pp. 10–12.

268 Quintilian 1920–2, IX.III.3–9, vol. III, pp. 506–10.

affective and passionate, founded as it is on such profound emotions as joy and sorrow, hope and fear, hatred of sin and love of God. With its techniques for exciting the emotions, the ancient *ars rhetorica*, and especially the classical Grand Style, accordingly came to be viewed as a method for expressing human spirituality, and hence as a method for illuminating and directing us towards the truth, not for deflecting us from it.[269]

While this highflown defence of the *ars rhetorica* was scarcely available to secular rhetoricians of the English Renaissance, preoccupied as they were with law courts and public assemblies, they nevertheless contrived to defend the value and importance of their discipline with equal assurance.[270] It is true that Puttenham allows himself a moment of grand condescension when he dismisses 'the toyes of this our vulgar art' in the closing lines of his *Arte of English Poesie*.[271] But this turns out to be *sprezzatura*, for he also stresses that 'there be artes and methodes both to speake and to perswade and also to dispute', and that 'those artes of Grammer, *Logicke*, and *Rhetorick*' can be 'reduced into perfection, and made prompt by use and exercise'.[272] Angel Day speaks even more confidently in *The English Secretary* of the fact that, although 'every one naturallye can speake or in some sort or other set down their meaning', there is nevertheless an art of rhetoric enabling everything to be 'beautified, adorned and as it were into a new shape transmuted by such kind of knowledge'.[273] Bacon develops a similar argument in *The Advancement of Learning*, insisting that 'it was great injustice in Plato, though springing out of a just hatred of the rhetoricians of his time, to esteem of rhetoric but as a voluptuary art'.[274] Although Bacon has a number of criticisms to make of the contemporary state of the subject, and offers 'to stir the earth a little about the roots of this science', he nevertheless thinks it indisputable that rhetoric is 'a science excellent, and excellently well laboured'.[275] As he had earlier insisted, 'it is a thing not hastily to be condemned, to clothe and adorn the obscurity even of Philosophy itself with sensible and plausible elocution'.[276] He concedes that the value of rhetoric

269 See the fascinating account in Shuger 1988, esp. pp. 242–50.

270 For an analysis of humanist discussions about the concept of an *ars* in Cicero and Quintilian, see Gilbert 1960, pp. 67–73. For the fact that Renaissance defences of the *ars* include the claim that *ornatus* has an affinity for truth see Tuve 1947, pp. 27–31, and Briggs 1989, pp. 86–95.

271 Puttenham 1970, p. 308, echoing the closing lines of the *Ad Herennium*. Cf. *Ad C. Herennium* 1954, IV.LVI.69, pp. 408–10.

272 Puttenham 1970, p. 30.

273 Day 1967, pp. 1–2. Cf. Day 1592, 'To the curteous Reader', announcing (sig. M, 2^{v}) that the ensuing discussion is designed for 'all favourers of science'.

274 Bacon 1915, p. 147.

275 Bacon 1915, p. 146. For commentary on this crucial passage see Shapiro 1983, p. 235, and Briggs 1989, pp. 150–1.

276 Bacon 1915, p. 25.

may be doubtful in the case of the exact sciences, in which it may act as 'some hindrance' to 'the severe inquisition of truth'. But he accepts that, in the moral if not in the natural sciences, it is worth recognising that, 'if a man be to have any use of such knowledge in civil occasions, of conference, counsel, persuasion, discourse, or the like; then shall he find it prepared to his hands in those authors which write in that manner'.[277]

We need finally to note that, in a further gesture of pride in their discipline, the Roman rhetoricians put forward one further and even more elevated claim about the *ars rhetorica.* The man of eloquence, they declared, is not merely the model of a good citizen; he is nothing less than the embodiment of humanity in its highest form.[278] Cicero first permits himself this boast at the beginning of *De inventione*,[279] and later puts the same sentiment into the mouth of Crassus in book I of the *De oratore.* 'The one way in which above all others we excel wild animals is that we are able to talk with each other and explain our impressions in speech.'[280] But if this is so, 'who would not rightly admire this ability, and who would not judge it right to devote himself to acquiring it as much as possible, in order to excel all other men in that very respect in which men above all surpass the beasts?'[281]

The implication, as Crassus expresses it in the final book of the *De oratore*, is that 'the power of eloquence must accordingly be regarded as one of the highest virtues':[282] the virtues of speech are elevated even above the capacity for reasoning.[283] Quintilian in book II of the *Institutio oratoria* refers us directly to this passage from the *De oratore*, adding that 'Cicero was right to make Crassus talk in this way'.[284] Not only is eloquence a supreme virtue, but 'I do not see why we should not hold that the virtue of man resides as least as much in eloquence as in his reasoning ability.'[285] Crassus had already voiced a similar belief in even more grandiloquent terms. 'What is more powerful, what is more splendid than that one man

277 Bacon 1915, p. 25.

278 On this claim and its influence see Vickers 1989, pp. 271–2.

279 Cicero 1949a, I.IV.5, p. 12.

280 Cicero 1942a, I.VIII.32, vol. I, p. 24: 'Hoc enim uno praestamus, vel maxime feris, quod colloquimur inter nos, et quod exprimere dicendo sensa possumus.' Quintilian frequently makes the same point. See for example Quintilian 1920–2, II.XVI.11–13, vol. I, p. 322, and II.XX.9, vol. I, p. 354. See also Tacitus 1970, 6.3, p. 242.

281 Cicero 1942a, I.VIII.33, vol. I, p. 24: 'quis hoc non iure miretur, summeque in eo elaborandum esse arbitretur, ut, quo uno homines maxime bestiis praestent, in hoc hominibus ipsis antecellat'.

282 Cicero 1942a, III.XIV.55, vol. II, 42: 'Est enim eloquentia una quaedam de summis virtutibus'.

283 On this implication see Chomarat 1981, pp. 62–6.

284 Quintilian 1920–2, II.XX.9, vol. I, p. 354: 'recte hoc apud Ciceronem dixerit Crassus'.

285 Quintilian 1920–2, II.XX.9, vol. I, p. 354: 'cur non tam in eloquentia quam in ratione virtutem eius esse credamus'. Cf. Quintilian 1920–2, I.XII.16, vol. I, p. 198, on eloquence as the most beautiful thing in the world.

should be able to affect the movements of the people, the scruples of judges, the gravity of the Senate by means of oratory?'[286] 'Furthermore', he goes on, 'what could be more regal, more liberal, more munificent'[287] than this art of rhetoric, the art enabling us 'to grant supplications, to raise up the afflicted, to guarantee safety, to free people from dangers and maintain them in a civil state?'[288]

The Tudor rhetoricians draw on these passages with much enthusiasm when discussing the standing of the *ars rhetorica*. Wilson opens his *Arte of Rhetorique* by repeating that, while 'menne are in manye thynges weake by Nature, and subjecte to much infirmitye', it cannot be denied that 'in this one point they passe all other Creatures livynge, that they have the gift of speache and reason'.[289] He goes on extol the power of eloquence in awestruck tones that recall Quintilian. 'And amonge all other, I thinke him most worthye fame, and amongest menne to be taken for halfe a God, that therein dothe chiefelye, and above all other, excell menne, wherin men do excell beastes.'[290] Peacham speaks in still more religious terms in the epistle dedicatory to the first edition of his *Garden of Eloquence*. 'For the common use & utillity of mankind, the Lord God hath joyned to the mind of man speech, which he hath made the instrument of our understanding & key of conceptions.'[291] Appealing once more to Cicero, he adds that 'herein it is that we do so far passe and excell all other creatures, in that we have the gifte of speech and reason, and not they'.[292] This prompts a further effusion in praise of eloquence and the art that produces it. 'How worthy of high commendations are those men that perceiving this do bestowe their studyes, their travayle and their tyme to obtayne Wysedome and Eloquence, the onelye Ornamentes whereby mannes lyfe is bewtifyed and a prayse most precyous purchased.' [293]

It is important, moreover, not to underestimate the scope assigned by these writers to the art of rhetoric by taking too literally their claim to be describing an art of speech. It is of course true that their main preoccupation is with the figure of the orator, and thus with the topic of spoken eloquence. Cicero characterises his *De inventione* as a manual on the art of

286 Cicero 1942a, I.VIII.31, vol. I, pp. 22–4: 'Aut tam potens, tamque magnificum, quam populi motus, iudicium religiones, Senatus gravitatem, unius oratione converti?'
287 Cicero 1942a, I.VIII.32, vol. I, p. 24: 'Quid tam porro regium, tam liberale, tam munificum'.
288 Cicero 1942a, I.VIII.32, vol. I, p. 24: 'ferre supplicibus, excitare afflictos, dare salutem, liberare periculis, retinere homines in civitate'.
289 Wilson 1554, sig. A, iii^r.
290 Wilson 1554, sig. A, iii^r. Cf. Harvey 1913, p. 192, commending those who 'treat speech as man's supreme glory'.
291 Peacham 1971, sig. A, ii^r.
292 Peacham 1971, sig. A, ii^r.
293 Peacham 1971, sig. A, ii^r.

speaking, and Quintilian declares at the start of his *Institutio oratoria* that his aim is to write *de ratione dicendi*, about the principles of speech.[294] Nevertheless, they think of this art as having extensive boundaries. They are clear in the first place that eloquence can take a written as much as a spoken form. Cicero, for example, makes the figure of Antonius say in the *De oratore* that Thucydides' *History* entitles him to be ranked among the most eloquent men of Greece.[295] To this Cicero adds the stronger claim that anyone who aspires to speak effectively must first learn to write with eloquence. The figure of Crassus in the *De oratore*, replying to a question put by Sulpicius, insists that 'the pen is the best and most outstanding source and teacher of powerful speech'.[296] We not only find that 'all the thoughts we need and all the words most brilliant of their kind come to us at the point of our pen';[297] we also find that 'the gathering and arrangement of these words is rendered perfect in the course of writing them'.[298] Crassus concludes that 'none of the qualities that bring clamour and applause to good orators can possibly be acquired by anyone who has not devoted himself long and frequently to the written word'.[299]

The Tudor rhetoricians are no less confident that the leading prescriptions of the *ars rhetorica* apply as much to the written as to the spoken word. Sherry professes an equal interest in 'speakynge and wrytynge', in 'the writing and speaking of eloquente English men'.[300] Wilson emphasises that the rules he lays down can be used 'both in writyng, and also in speakyng'.[301] But it is Angel Day who takes most seriously the claim that writing is a form of speech.[302] Although his *English Secretary* is wholly concerned with the written word, he makes it clear that part of his purpose is to demonstrate that the rules of good writing and successful oratory are basically the same. When he discusses the different types of letter, he classifies them in the manner of speeches as demonstrative, deliberative and judicial.[303] When he surveys the qualities of good letter writers, he

294 Cicero 1949a, II.II.4, p. 168; Quintilian 1920–2, Proemium, I, vol. I, p. 4.

295 Cicero 1942a, II.XIII.56, vol. I, p. 238.

296 Cicero 1942a, I.XXXIII.150, vol. I, p. 102. 'Stilus optimus et praestantissimus dicendi effector ac magister [est]'. Quintilian 1920–2, X.III.1–4, vol. IV, pp. 90–2, quotes this remark and endorses it.

297 Cicero 1942a, I.XXXIII.151, vol. I, p. 104: 'omnesque sententiae, verbaque omnia, quae sunt cuiusque generis maxime illustria, sub acumen stili subeant'.

298 Cicero 1942a, I.XXXIII.151, vol. I, p. 104: 'collocatio conformatioque verborum perficitur in scribendo'.

299 Cicero 1942a, I.XXXIII.152, vol. I, p. 104: 'Haec sunt, quae clamores et admirationes in bonis oratoribus efficiunt; neque ea quisquam, nisi diu multumque scriptitarit.'

300 Sherry 1961, pp. 12, 13. See also pp. 25–6, 36, 39, for repetitions of the 'writing or speaking' formula.

301 Wilson 1554, fo. 2^v; cf. also fos. 3^r, 48^r, 108^v.

302 On epistolary theory in the English Renaissance see Plett 1975, pp. 56–66.

303 Day 1967, p. 20.

lists them in oratorical style as a capacity for invention, disposition and elocution.[304] When he explains how to compose a letter in the most persuasive style, he suggests that it ought to be divided like a speech into five separate parts, duly labelling them the 'Exordium', 'Narratio', 'Confirmatio', 'Confutatio' and 'Peroratio'.[305] His entire approach depends, as he says at the outset, on treating letter writing as a form of 'familiar speach'.[306]

The assumption that writing is a form of speech[307] eventually found expression in a range of metaphors still lodged in the English language to this day. Some imply that the written word can be viewed not merely as an analogue of conversation but an instance of speech. We already encounter this *façon de parler* in Wilson's *Arte of Rhetorique*, which begins by declaring that the rules of rhetoric apply only to speech or utterance, but later classifies various forms of writing as 'utteraunces'.[308] Puttenham refers to 'good utterance be it by mouth or by writing',[309] and Ascham similarly yokes together 'utterance either by pen or taulke', describing his own book as an attempt 'to utter theis my thoughts'.[310] Still more emphatic are the metaphors directly equating the act of writing with speech. Wilson makes frequent use of these,[311] while Puttenham appeals to them even more extensively, describing one of the poems he analyses as 'speaking' of a particular theme, and referring to his own treatise as 'speaking' about the figures and tropes.[312]

It is worth observing in conclusion that this growth of interest in written eloquence may in turn help to account for some of the changes that overtook the study of rhetoric in the course of the sixteenth century, including the rise in the popularity of Ramism. As we have seen, it has usually (and no doubt rightly) been argued that, when the Ramists sought to restrict the teaching of rhetoric to *elocutio* and *pronuntiatio*, they were primarily motivated by a desire to remove a number of redundancies from the syllabus of the liberal arts. But this falls short of explaining why so many Ramists went on to treat the topic of *pronuntiatio* – the analysis of

304 Day 1967, p. 9.
305 Day 1967, p. 11.
306 Day 1967, p. 1.
307 Ong 1982, pp. 108–12, sees in academic rhetoric the prime cause of the preservation of an interaction between writing and orality, and associates their eventual separation with the decline of rhetoric. On the importance of speech for Tudor humanists, and on the growing authority of written texts, cf. Elsky 1989, esp. pp. 110–46.
308 Wilson 1564, fos. 1^{r-v} and 78^{r}.
309 Puttenham 1970, p. 155.
310 Ascham 1970b, pp. 263, 278.
311 See for example Wilson 1564, fos. 96^{v}, 99^{v}, 100^{r}, 101^{v}.
312 Puttenham 1970, pp. 210, 211, 226, 230.

voice and gesture – in such a residual fashion that it sometimes dropped out of sight altogether.[313] This further specialisation can readily be explained, however, if we take it that the Ramists were primarily interested in the phenomenon of written as opposed to spoken eloquence. Without necessarily being fully conscious of the fact, they seem to have been engaged in adjusting the art of rhetoric to the age of the printed book.[314]

313 As it does, for example, in Fenner 1584, as Fenner himself notes, sig. E, 1v.

314 On Ramism and printing as 'related phenomena' see Ong 1958a, pp. 307–14.

Chapter 3

THE MEANS OF PERSUASION

The promise of classical rhetoric is that, if we succeed in mastering the *ars rhetorica*, we shall be able to speak and write with complete persuasiveness. We shall be able, that is, to shift or move even a hostile or sceptical audience towards the acceptance of our point of view. But it remains for the rhetoricians to explain how this can be done. What are the specific techniques that enable us to speak and write in a 'winning' style? This is the question with which the following three chapters will be concerned.

THE INVOCATION OF COMMONPLACES

According to the classical rhetoricians, certain types of argument may be said to possess an inherently persuasive character. The first task of the orator is to find them out (*invenire*) and learn how to apply them in individual cases. This is the contention examined by the Roman theorists of eloquence under the heading of *inventio*, which in turn explains why they invariably insist that, as the *Ad Herennium* puts it, 'among the five tasks of the orator, the mastery of invention is both the most important and the most difficult of all'.[1]

Some arguments are not in this sense 'artificial'; they are not dependent, that is, on the art of rhetoric for their persuasiveness. Aristotle originally introduced this terminology in book I of the *Rhetoric*, in which he contrasts (in Hobbes's rendering) 'Artificial Proofes' with 'Inartificiall Proofes, which we invent not'.[2] Quintilian elaborates the distinction at the start of book V when he first turns to consider the topic of proofs. He begins by noting that 'this division, originally proposed by Aristotle, has won the acceptance of almost everyone'.[3] The division itself acknowledges the fact that 'there are some proofs which the orator accepts from outside the art of

1 *Ad C. Herennium* 1954, II.I.I, p. 58: 'De oratoris officiis quinque inventio et prima et difficillima est.' Cicero 1949a, II.LIX.178, p. 344, speaks in almost identical terms.

2 Hobbes 1986, p. 64.

3 Quintilian 1920–2, V.I.I, vol. II, p. 156: 'illa partitio ab Aristotele tradita consensum fere omnium meruit'.

speaking'.[4] Such inartificial proofs merely need to be reported, in consequence of which their presentation 'calls for the exercise of no particular skill'.[5] Like Aristotle, Quintilian takes these proofs to be of special importance in judicial oratory, and goes so far as to claim that the majority of forensic arguments consist of nothing else. Among the examples he offers, he includes the evidence of rumour, the judgments of earlier courts, the kinds of testimony that result from the use of torture and the various sorts of purely factual information to be gleaned from documents, depositions and witnesses.[6]

By contrast with such matters of fact and law, Quintilian turns in the second half of book v to 'the other aspect of proof', the aspect Aristotle had designated as 'artificial' or 'wholly dependent on the art of rhetoric'.[7] Aristotle himself had placed almost all his emphasis at this juncture on the topic of enthymemes. He had defined the enthymeme as a distinctive form of rhetorical syllogism in which the premises are generally no more than probable, and had argued that the chief skill of the rhetorician lies in manipulating such incomplete forms of reasoning in persuasive ways.[8] As we saw in chapter 1, however, there is a sharp contrast at this point between the Aristotelian and the Roman approaches to the issue of rhetorical proofs. The leading Roman textbooks have almost nothing to say about enthymemes, a topic on which the *Ad Herennium* remains completely silent, and on which Cicero and Quintilian offer little more than brief and seemingly bewildered references to Aristotle's analysis.[9] When they consider the theme of artificial proofs, they instead place all their stress on the concept of *loci communes* or common 'places' of rhetorical argument, virtually equating the manipulation of commonplaces with the ability to 'invent' artificial proofs.[10]

As Quintilian intimates at the outset of his discussion,[11] there are two senses in which rhetoricians speak about the *loci* or places in which

4 Quintilian 1920–2, v.i.1, vol. ii, p. 156: 'alias esse probationes, quas extra dicendi rationem acciperet orator'.

5 Quintilian 1920–2, v.i.1, vol. ii, p. 156: 'per se carent arte'.

6 Quintilian 1920–2, v.i.1, vol. ii, p. 156. For a similar account see Cicero 1942a, ii.xxvii.114–17, vol. i, pp. 280–2. Both appear closely dependent on Aristotle 1926, i.ii.2, p. 14. On 'inartificial' proofs in Renaissance rhetoric see Joseph 1966, pp. 309–12.

7 Quintilian 1920–2, v.viii.1, vol. ii, p. 190: 'pars altera probationum, quae est tota in arte'.

8 Aristotle 1926, i.i.11, pp. 8–10; ii.xxii.1–3, pp. 288–90; ii.xxv.8, pp. 336–8.

9 Cicero 1949a, i.xxxiv.5, pp. 98–100; Quintilian 1920–2, v.x.1–8, vol. ii, pp. 202–6. Kennedy 1972, p. 222, suggests that Roman rhetorical writers of this period may have known Aristotle's *Art of Rhetoric* only in an incomplete form.

10 For example Cicero 1942b, ii.5, p. 312.

11 Quintilian 1920–2, v.x.20, vol. ii, p. 212.

persuasive arguments can be found.[12] Sometimes they use the term to refer to general forms of reasoning that we can hope to master in the abstract and apply to individual cases. This is the understanding of the concept explored in Cicero's *Topica*, an account to which Quintilian's analysis appears to be heavily indebted.[13] The examples Cicero gives include the possibility of showing that the case we are arguing falls under some widely accepted definition, or is an instance of some well-known genus of argument, or is sufficiently analogous to count as an instance, and so forth.[14] The commonplaces are thus equated in effect with the broadest forms of persuasion and argument.[15]

Quintilian acknowledges, however, that most people have something simpler in mind when they speak of commonplaces. According to the more conventional view, we can always hope in any argument to call on various general maxims or stock themes which we can hope to apply in addition to the considerations specific to the case.[16] A mastery of the *loci* thus came to be equated with a knowledge of the places in which such maxims can be found, together with an ability to apply them tellingly to the case in hand. The metaphors used to describe this ability usually speak of the *sedes* or seats of arguments, or else of the hiding places from which the required apophthegms need to be hunted out and brought to light.[17]

Aristotle gestures at this simpler doctrine when contrasting the arts of rhetoric and logic at the outset of book I of *The Art of Rhetoric*. As Hobbes's translation puts it, 'The *Principles* of *Rhetorique*' must derive from the 'colours',[18] that is, from 'the *common opinions* that men have concerning *Profitable* and *Unprofitable*, *Just* and *Unjust*, *Honourable* and *Dishonourable*, which are the points in the severall kinds of *Orations* questionable'.[19] It is in the early Roman textbooks, however, that we find this understanding of *loci communes* most fully explored.[20] Cicero offers a classic analysis in book

12 Helpfully distinguished in Lechner 1962, esp. pp. 227–30. But as Lechner rightly warns, there is considerable unsteadiness in the application of the distinction by the Roman theorists.

13 See Cicero 1949b, II.7, p. 386; cf. Quintilian 1920–2, V.X.20, vol. II, p. 212, who appears to allude to this passage.

14 Cicero 1949b, II.9–10 and III.11–17, pp. 388–92. On *sedes* in legal argument, see Maclean 1992, pp. 78–82.

15 See Lechner 1962, pp. 101–10; 201–25.

16 As this suggests, however, the two meanings of *loci* distinguished by Quintilian cannot easily be kept apart. Renaissance rhetoricians frequently complain about the resulting confusions: see for example Sherry 1961, p. 88.

17 Lechner 1962, pp. 131–52. Cf. also Moss 1993, stressing (esp. pp. 203–4) that collections of commonplaces were correspondingly viewed as 'storehouses'.

18 For this equation between common opinions and the 'colours' of arguments (that is, their outward appearances) see Hobbes 1986, p. 45, and cf. pp. 47, 51, 56, 63.

19 Hobbes 1986, p. 41.

20 Quintilian, however, is not much interested in this vulgar understanding of commonplaces, as

II of the *De inventione*, where he begins by marking a strong distinction between two different types of argument. The first 'is solely joined to the cause being debated, and is so closely related to it that it is not possible for it to be transferred effectively to any other kind of case'.[21] But the second 'is much more wide-ranging, and can be adapted for use in all or at least in very many cases of the same character'.[22] When we speak of *loci communes*, we are referring 'to these second types of argument, which can be transferred and applied in many different cases'.[23] To speak of the 'places' in which such arguments can be found is thus to speak – as Antonius later explains in the *De oratore* – of the headings or *capita* we need to keep in mind if we are to have the best hope of recalling the general maxims apposite to our cause.[24]

The *De inventione* and the *Ad Herennium* both provide examples of the *loci* in which we can hope to discover such wise saws and modern instances. First they consider the predicament of the judicial orator, whose concern is either with prosecution or defence. Among the headings under which he is advised to search for general maxims are the following. Should we consider only the crime itself, or also the motives for committing it?[25] Should we consider only the text of the law or also the intentions of the legislator?[26] Should we always follow court procedures or is there room for flexibility?[27] Both Cicero and the *Ad Herennium* consider in addition the position of the deliberative orator whose goal is to ensure that a given course of action is followed or avoided, and whose aim must therefore be to find, as the *Ad Herennium* puts it, 'places either of persuasion or dissuasion'.[28] Suppose, the *Ad Herennium* goes on, you are proposing that a given action ought to be undertaken on the grounds that it is just. You must try to find a number of maxims under the *topos* or heading of justice which are at once widely accepted and at the same time relevant to your

he calls it, and claims that a full discussion would be an endless and fruitless task. Quintilian 1920–2, V.X.20, vol. II, p. 212, and V.XII.15–16, vol. II, p. 306.

21 Cicero 1949a, II.XIV.47, p. 208: 'est adiuncta ei causa solum quae dicitur, et ex ipsa ita ducta ut ab ea separatim in omnes eiusdem generis causas transferri non satis commode possit'.

22 Cicero 1949a, II.XIV.47, p. 208: 'est pervagatior et aut in omnes eiusdem generis aut in plerasque causas accommodata'.

23 Cicero 1949a, II.XV.48, p. 208: 'Haec ergo argumenta, quae transferri in multas causas possunt, locos communes nominamus.'

24 Cicero 1942a, II.XXXIV.146, vol. I, p. 304. Lechner 1962, p. 229, distinguishes between this view and a more 'analytic' understanding of *loci* as concepts useful in helping us to ask questions about a given topic as a way of generating ideas about it. As Lechner herself acknowledges, however, it is not clear that the Roman theorists employed this further distinction consistently.

25 *Ad C. Herennium* 1954, II.XVI.24, p. 102; Cicero 1949a, II.XXVI.77, p. 242.

26 *Ad C. Herennium* 1954, II.IX.13–14, pp. 80–4; Cicero 1949a, II.XLVIII.143, pp. 310–12.

27 Cicero 1949a, II.XX.61, p. 224.

28 See *Ad C. Herennium* 1954, III.III.4, p. 164 on *loci* 'ad suadendum et ad dissuadendum'.

case. These may include such propositions as that we ought to pity the innocent, to punish the guilty, to keep our promises, to uphold the laws of our community, and so on.[29] You must show that the course of action you are advising ought to be acceptable to anyone who already endorses such general principles. The *loci* are thus treated as storehouses of material for the amplification of our case.

Among English rhetoricians of the Renaissance, this Ciceronian understanding of *loci communes* was widely taken up. The prevalence of this interpretation was doubtless due in part to the influence of Erasmus, who speaks in characteristically homely vein in *De copia* of the value of knocking on the door of every topic to see whether any arguments relevant to the case in hand can be induced to emerge.[30] When Elyot in *The Governor* insists on the importance of rhetoric in the education of lawyers, he too speaks of the need to master 'the places whereof they shall fetch their reasons, called of orators *loci communes*'.[31] Sherry's discussion of 'places' at the end of his *Treatise of Schemes and Tropes* similarly observes that the term is primarily used to denote those arguments which 'indifferentlye apperteyne to all kyndes and partes of causes'.[32] This means that we can also think of them, he adds, as 'seates of argumentes, whyche the Rethoricianes do applie to eche kyndes of causes'.[33]

Of all the English writers who discuss *loci communes*, it is Francis Bacon who offers perhaps the most interesting account. Bacon thinks of the issue as having a special salience in relation to persuasion and dissuasion, and hence considers it principally as an aspect of deliberative oratory. His main discussion appears in the fragment entitled 'Of the colours of good and evil', which he first appended to the original edition of the *Essays* in 1597 and eventually incorporated into the *De Augmentis* in 1623.[34] When Bacon speaks of good and evil as having 'colours', what he chiefly has in mind is the Aristotelian suggestion[35] that they may be said to have certain outward and accepted appearances or, as he usually prefers to put it, certain 'popularities'.[36] As Hobbes explains in his translation of Aristotle's *Rhetoric* – in a striking echo of Bacon's phraseology – we may therefore

29 *Ad C. Herennium* 1954, III.III.4, p. 164.
30 Erasmus 1978a, p. 606.
31 Elyot 1962, p. 54.
32 Sherry 1961, p. 86.
33 Sherry 1961, p. 88.
34 See *Exempla Colorum Boni et Mali* in Bacon 1857b, pp. 674–88. For discussions see Jardine 1974, pp. 219–24, and Briggs 1989, pp. 69–72. Briggs stresses (pp. 72–9) the alchemical background to the emphasis on tinctures and colouring.
35 For Bacon's reliance on Aristotle's *Rhetoric* at this point see Jardine 1974, pp. 221–2.
36 Bacon 1859, p. 77. See also Bacon 1915, p. 148, on 'the popular signs and colours of good and evil'.

speak of 'the *Colours*, or *common opinions* concerning *Good* and *Evil*'.[37] Bacon's point is that, by invoking such common opinions, we can hope to lend additional weight to our case whenever we find ourselves debating whether or not some particular course of action ought or ought not to be followed.[38] The appeal to such 'popularities' can be used, in other words, to increase the power and persuasive force of our arguments by improving their 'colourability'.

This is to say that, in discussing the colours, we are in effect discussing the contents of the arguments to be found in the 'places' we are urged to investigate. It follows for Bacon that rhetorical 'colouring' is not, as it generally was for neo-Ciceronian rhetoricians, a mere synonym for *ornatus*; when Bacon speaks of the colours, what he usually has in mind are general precepts of argument.[39] As he confirms in his 1597 fragment – in an evident allusion to the *Ad Herennium* – he is offering 'a table of colours or appearances of good and evil, and their degrees, as places of persuasion and dissuasion'.[40] He recurs to the point in *The Advancement of Learning*, in which he stresses once more that 'the ancient writers of Rhetoric do give it in precept, "that pleaders should have the Places, whereof they have most continual use, ready handled" '.[41] As an example of such a 'place', he offers – as Cicero and the *Ad Herennium* had done before him – the question of whether the literal interpretation of a law should always be upheld.[42]

The Roman rhetoricians had invariably assumed that the maxims or general principles we can hope to find in such *loci* will almost by definition be merely 'probable'. They will thus be susceptible of being used *in utramque partem*, depending on whether one happens to be engaged in attack or defence.[43] By way of illustration, Cicero in his *De inventione* considers the following judicial *topos*: should intentions be considered in the assessment of blame, or should acts alone be judged? If you are engaged in prosecuting, one of the maxims you can hope to take from this 'place' will be the one stating that, if a deed is very base, it ought in no way to be mitigated or excused. If you are defending, one of the maxims you can instead hope to invoke with no less plausibility will be the one stating that the character of a deed can never be known without examining the

37 Hobbes 1986, p. 45.

38 As Briggs 1989, pp. 150–1, notes, Bacon's argument depends on the rhetorical assumption that the prevalence of common opinions implies some connection with the truth.

39 On 'colours' as precepts see Jardine 1974, p. 219.

40 Bacon 1859, p. 78. Cf. note 28, *supra*, for the same phrase in the *Ad Herennium*.

41 Bacon 1915, p. 128.

42 Bacon 1915, p. 128.

43 See *Ad C. Herennium* 1954, II.VI.9, p. 72; Cicero 1949a, II.XLVIII.143, p. 310; Cicero 1942a, III.XXVII.107, vol. II, p. 84. Cf. Lechner 1962, pp. 84–6.

intentions underlying it.[44] Consider similarly, Cicero later suggests, the question of whether a court should always follow the letter of the law. If the case you are arguing obliges you to attack this principle, you should single out such maxims as the one telling us that 'the worth of laws consists not in words but in the upholding of the common good'.[45] If you are instead appearing for the defence, you should emphasise such maxims as the one telling us that 'nothing ought to be held in higher reverence than the laws themselves'.[46]

This doctrine of *loci communes* clearly presupposes a particular view about the nature of the argumentative skills we need to cultivate. We must recognise, as Crassus reminds Antonius in book II of the *De oratore*, that 'although you yourself are able to speak with novelty and brilliance, the *loci* from which you derive what you say are nevertheless the sources of familiar maxims and widely accepted principles'.[47] The most effective orator will therefore be the one who knows best how to select and appeal to such 'popularities' and apply them to uphold his own cause. The skill required, as Quintilian repeatedly emphasises, is that of knowing how to relate our views to popular opinion (*vulgi opinione*),[48] how to make use of assumptions that are generally accepted (*publice recepta*)[49] and how if necessary to make straightforward appeals to the prejudices of our audience.[50]

The aim, in short, is that of 'accommodating' our arguments so far as possible to received opinions and beliefs. 'What is indispensable to the orator', Crassus declares at the outset of the *De oratore*, is that he should be able to speak 'in a style accommodated to the minds and general sensibilities of mankind'.[51] He later reiterates the commitment in response to a question from Mucius. 'In every genus of public speaking, what we say must be accommodated to the ordinary outlook and understanding of the populace.'[52] Antonius subsequently underlines the point in the course of giving his views about the ideal orator towards the end of book I. 'I take the orator to be a man capable of using language acceptable to his hearers

44 Cicero 1949a, II.XXVI.77, p. 242.

45 Cicero 1949a, II.XLVIII.143: 'leges in . . . utilitate communi, non in verbis consistere'.

46 Cicero 1949a, II.XLVIII.143: 'legibus antiquius haberi non oportere'.

47 Cicero 1942a, II.XXIX.127, vol. I, p. 288: 'ex locis ea, quae dicenda sunt in causis, reperiantur; quae quamquam a te novo quodam modo praeclareque dicuntur, sunt tamen et re faciliora et praeceptis pervagata'.

48 Quintilian 1920–2, III.VIII.39, vol. I, p. 498.

49 Quintilian 1920–2, III.VII.23, vol. I, p. 474.

50 Quintilian 1920–2, III.VIII.1–3, vol. I, pp. 478–80.

51 Cicero 1942a, I.XII.54, vol. I, p. 40: 'Hoc enim est proprium oratoris', namely a style 'et hominum sensibus ac mentibus accommodata'.

52 Cicero, 1942a, I. XXIII.108, vol. I, p. 76: 'ad vulgarem popularemque sensum accommodata omnia genera huius forensis nostrae dictionis'.

and of using such arguments as are best accommodated to the establishment of his case.'[53]

The belief that we must speak and write in such a way as to maximise our use of popular maxims and familiar arguments was carried even further in the Renaissance.[54] One consequence was the rise to a new level of prominence of a special subgenre known as the *cento*. William Camden offers a useful definition and exemplification of this form of writing at the beginning of his *Remains* in 1605. He concludes his opening chapter – which discusses the inhabitants of Britain – with a Latin poem 'in praise of the English Nation', a poem which he describes as 'quilted as it were out of shreds of divers Poets, such as Schollers do call a *Cento*'.[55] One notable example of such a *cento* from the political literature of the period is the translation of Justus Lipsius' *Sixe Bookes of Politickes* issued by William Jones in 1594. As Lipsius explains at the outset, his aim is to offer instruction 'not by my owne sayings, but by the precepts of ancient authors, delivered also in their own wordes'.[56] The outcome is a patchwork of precisely the kind that Camden describes, a work composed almost entirely of quotations from the classical writers whom Lipsius judges to be 'of best worth'.[57] Of all such writings from this period, however, the most remarkable is Robert Burton's introduction to his *Anatomy of Melancholy* of 1621. Insisting that 'we can say nothing but what hath beene said',[58] Burton explains that this has helped to determine the type of work he has produced:

> *Omne meum, nihil meum*, 'tis all mine and none mine. As a good hous-wife out of divers fleeces weaves one peece of Cloath, a bee gathers Wax and Hony out of many Flowers, and makes a new bundle of all, *Floriferis ut apes in saltibus omnia libant*, I have laboriously collected this *Cento* out of divers Writers, and that *sine injuria*, I have wronged no Authors, but given every man his owne.[59]

Burton cunningly points to the method in his madness, implying that the successful weaving together of such a *cento* provides the best means of persuading one's readers while revealing the depths of one's own learning and literary sensibility.[60]

To Burton and his contemporaries, the doctrine of commonplaces

53 Cicero 1942a, I.XLIX.213, vol. I, p. 150: 'puto esse [oratorem], qui verbis ad audiendum iucundis, et sententiis ad probandum accommodatis uti possit'. Cf. Antonius' comments in Cicero 1942a, II.XXVII.114, vol. I, p. 280. The point is summarised in Cicero 1942b, XXV.90, p. 377, and taken up in Quintilian 1920–2, X.I.69, vol. IV, p. 40 and XI.I.1–2, vol. IV, p. 154.

54 On this 'rhetoricisation' of ethics, see Cox 1992, esp. on Castiglione, pp. 57–60.

55 Camden 1605, p. 11.

56 Lipsius 1594, p. 1.

57 Lipsius 1594, sig. A, v^{r}.

58 Burton 1989, p. 11.

59 Burton 1989, p. 11.

60 Vicari 1989, pp. 186–96.

appeared so closely related to the idea of endorsing received beliefs that they eventually arrived at a new understanding of the term itself. They began to use it to refer not to the places or headings under which general maxims should be sought, but rather to the maxims themselves.[61] The change can already be observed in the epistle dedicatory to the *Booke of Notes and Common places* issued by John Marbeck in 1581. A vehement enemy of the Catholic Church, Marbeck informs us that he so much fears the renewal of its ascendancy in England that he has made a collection of the most profound sayings by the most godly and learned writers about the true nature of Christianity. He describes these sayings themselves as 'common places', and expresses the hope that those who study them may find that 'some sparke of Gods true knowledge' may 'kindle a right understanding in them'.[62]

As Marbeck's earnest tone reveals, he takes it for granted that a commonplace is a maxim or apophthegm which, while expressing a widely shared belief, presents it in an exceptionally vivid or memorable form. The whole purpose of assembling books of commonplaces was to build up stores of sententious generalities with which to amplify specific arguments.[63] As Thomas Cooper puts it in introducing his *Thesaurus* of 1565,[64] the contents of a 'common place booke' should be such that 'a studious yong man' can 'gather to himself good furniture both of words and approved phrases and fashions of speaking for any thing he shall eyther write or speake of'.[65] It is thus a somewhat melancholy reflection on the contents of such compilations that, within a generation, the term 'commonplace' came to be used instead to refer to excessively obvious or well-worn platitudes. We already encounter this disparaging usage – with its underlying scepticism about this aspect of the *ars rhetorica* – in one of Bacon's observations from his essay 'Of discourse'. He mentions that 'some have certain common places and themes wherein they are good, and want variety; which kind of poverty is for the most part tedious, and, when it is once perceived, ridiculous'.[66] By the time we come to Ben Jonson's *Epicoene* of 1609, in which the figure of Jack Daw dismisses Aristotle as 'a mere commonplace fellow', we find the doctrine being humorously invoked to mock the philosopher credited with inventing it.[67]

61 On commonplaces in this sense see Crane 1937, pp. 33–48.
62 Marbeck 1581, sig. A, iii^{v}.
63 See, for instance, the discussion and examples in Brinsley 1917, pp. 188–9, and cf. Moss 1993.
64 On Cooper and his *Thesaurus* see Lechner 1962, pp. 184–5.
65 Cooper 1565, sig. *, 4^{v}.
66 Bacon 1972, p. 102. Cf. Bacon 1859, p. 91 and Bacon 1915, p. 15.
67 Jonson 1971, II.iii.54, p. 57.

THE AROUSAL OF EMOTION

Despite their emphasis on 'inventing' rhetorically persuasive arguments, the Roman theorists of eloquence are far from supposing that an orator should rely exclusively or even primarily on such powers of invention to win a case. The orator's most powerful weapon, they all agree, is his ability to manipulate the emotions of his audience and enlist them on his side. They accordingly focus their main attention on the question of how to add *pathos* to *logos*,[68] how to appeal to the passions or affections of our auditors in such a way as to excite them against our opponents and in favour of our own cause.

When considering the range of feelings we must seek to arouse, the Roman rhetoricians generally begin by emphasising the importance of soothing and mollifying our hearers to secure a certain kind of docility and receptiveness. It should be our first aim, Antonius stresses in book II of the *De oratore*, 'to conciliate those who are listening to us'.[69] He later adds in reply to Catulus that 'nothing is in fact of greater importance in public speaking than that the orator should succeed in winning the favourable attention of his audience'.[70] Quintilian elaborates the point in discussing how to compose an exordium in book IV. 'The opening of a speech has no other purpose', he maintains, 'than to prepare our auditors to listen with greater receptiveness to the rest of what we shall have to say.'[71] He goes on to explain that 'according to the vast majority of authorities, there are three things that most of all conduce to this effect, these being that we should arouse in our audience feelings of benevolence, of attentiveness and of readiness to be instructed'.[72] This in turn requires that the tone of our exordium should be as conciliatory as possible. We need to remember that 'if the case offers us any material at all for winning the favour of the judge, it is vital that anything which appears to be particularly conducive to this end should be introduced at the start'.[73]

68 Kennedy 1972, pp. 208, 212–13, 219–22.

69 See Cicero 1942a, II.XXVII.115, vol. I, p. 280 on the need 'ut conciliemus eos nobis, qui audiunt'. Cf. also II.XXIX.128, vol. I, p. 290.

70 Cicero 1942a, II.XLII.178, vol. I, p. 324: 'Nihil est enim in dicendo, Catule, maius, quam ut favet oratori is, qui audiet.'

71 Quintilian 1920–2, IV.I.5, vol. II, p. 8: 'causa principii nulla alia est, quam ut auditorem, quo sit nobis in ceteris partibus accommodatior, praeparemus'.

72 Quintilian 1920–2, IV.I.5, vol. II, p. 8: 'Id fieri tribus maxime rebus inter actores plurimos constat, si benevolum, attentum, docilem fecerimus.' On benevolence and attentiveness see IV.I.42, vol. II, p. 28; on docility and a readiness to be instructed see IV.I.38, vol. I, p. 26. On the need to render judges 'benevolem, attentum, docilem' see too IV.I.51, vol. II, p. 34.

73 Quintilian 1920–2, IV.I.23, vol. II, p. 16: 'Si causa conciliandi nobis iudicis materiam dabit, ex hac potissimum aliqua in usum principii, quae maxime favorabilia videbuntur, decerpi oportebit.' Cf. also IV.I.26, vol. II, p. 18.

Cicero and Quintilian both emphasise, however, that the feelings we must principally seek to arouse need to be of a more violent and turbulent kind.[74] Crassus lays it down in book II of the *De oratore* that 'although you must initially seek to conciliate your hearers, and then instruct them, your third aim must be to excite and agitate them'.[75] Antonius later announces the same commitment with disarming frankness. After winning the attention of your listeners, 'you must try to shift or impel them so that they become ruled not by deliberation and judgment but rather by sheer impetus and perturbation of mind'.[76] Quintilian develops a similar argument at the start of book VI, where he rounds off his survey of the elements of an ideal speech by considering the peroration. He has already explained that there is little scope for emotional appeals in the confirmation or refutation;[77] he now declares that the peroration is the place where, 'in a wider and fuller style', we must seek 'either to excite or to calm down the feelings of the judge'.[78] If we are engaged in prosecuting, 'the best way of arousing his emotions will be by making the objection we are raising seem as atrocious or, if possible, as utterly disgraceful as possible'.[79] If we are serving as counsel for the defence, 'we must appeal to his emotions even more fully and frequently, since our aim is not to excite him but to turn aside his wrath'.[80] We must recognise, in short, that 'the Peroration is the point at which, if anywhere, it becomes appropriate to open up every possible fountain of eloquence'.[81]

Aristotle had conceded in his *Art of Rhetoric* that one way in which an orator can procure belief will always be, as Hobbes's translation puts it, 'from the *passions* of the *Hearer*'.[82] As we have seen, however, Aristotle had insisted that the 'art' of rhetoric ought not to be viewed principally

74 Cicero 1962, XXI.82, pp. 74–6, singles out Galba as the first Roman orator to recognise the importance of such emotional appeals. Cf. Kennedy 1972, pp. 72–3.

75 Cicero 1942a, I.XXIX.128, vol. I, p. 290: 'una conciliandorum hominum, altera docendorum, tertia concitandorum'. Cf. Kennedy 1972, pp. 219–20, who plausibly regards the emphasis on emotional appeals as a statement of Cicero's own beliefs.

76 Cicero 1942a, II.XLII.178, vol. I, p. 324: 'ipse sic moveatur, ut impetu quodam animi et perturbatione, magis quam iudicio aut consilio regatur'.

77 Quintilian 1920–2, V.XIII.1–2, vol. II, p. 310.

78 Quintilian 1920–2, VI.I.9–11, vol. II, p. 388: 'liberiora plenioraque ... iudicem concitare adfectus et componere'. For Quintilian's dependence on Cicero at this juncture see Kennedy 1972, pp. 505–6.

79 Quintilian 1920–2, VI.I.15, vol. II, p. 390: 'Summa tamen concitandi adfectus ... est, ut id, quod obiecit, aut quam atrocissimum aut etiam, si fieri potest, quam maxime miserabile esse videatur.'

80 Quintilian 1920–2, VI.I.9, vol. II, p. 386: 'ille saepius ac magis, nam ... illi [sc. adfectus] flectere convenit'.

81 Quintilian 1920–2, VI.I.52, vol. II, p. 414: 'At hic [viz., in the *peroratio*], si usquam, totos eloquentiae aperire fontes licet.'

82 Hobbes 1986, p. 69.

as a method of arousing emotions; it ought rather to be viewed as a method of reasoning, or else it cannot be counted as a genuine art at all. John Rainolds, delivering his pioneering lectures on Aristotle's *Rhetoric* at Oxford in the 1570s, was to open his analysis of book I, chapter 2, with an emphatic commentary on this very point. Aristotle 'teaches the would-be persuader that the "art of rhetoric" concerns itself with just one thing, finding arguments and proofs with which to demonstrate the point at issue'.[83] So strongly does Aristotle make this claim, Rainolds goes on, that 'in this section of the *Rhetoric*, using a variety of reasons, he criticizes and refutes those rhetoricians who were of the opinion that the skill of speaking depends upon emotions more than upon arguments'.[84]

It is at this juncture, however, that the Roman rhetoricians and their Renaissance followers part company most decisively with Aristotle's approach. They not only insist that an ability to excite the emotions forms an indispensable part of the orator's equipment; they think of this ability as constituting the heart and core of the *ars rhetorica*, and above all of the vehemently affective Grand Style.[85] Cicero initially makes the point when speaking in his own person at the outset of the *De oratore*. 'It is in calming down or rousing up the minds of those who are listening to us that the full force and skill of our oratory need to be expended.'[86] Later in the dialogue the figure of Antonius is made to express his full agreement with this point of view. 'It is in inflaming the feelings of our listeners by our speech, or else in quietening them down after they have been inflamed, that the power of oratory and its greatness can above all be discerned.'[87] Quintilian reiterates the argument in the form of an evident allusion to Aristotle's contrasting argument. 'There have been a number of celebrated authorities to whom it has seemed that the sole duty of the orator is to teach, and who have therefore thought that all emotional appeals must be excluded.'[88] He makes it clear, especially when discussing the role of emotions in book VI, that this view of oratory is as far as possible from his own. It is in arousing passion, he retorts, 'that the force of oratory is able

83 Rainolds 1988, p. 117.

84 Rainolds 1988, p. 11.

85 For an excellent discussion of the division between the Roman ideal of an affective Grand Style, and a different – originally Hellenistic – ideal of a rhetorical yet philosophical prose, see Shuger 1988, esp. pp. 3–10.

86 Cicero 1942a, I.V.17, vol. I, p. 14: 'omnis vis ratioque dicendi in eorum, qui audiunt, mentibus, aut sedandis, aut excitandis expromenda est'.

87 Cicero 1942a, I.LI.219, vol. I, p. 154: 'aut inflammare dicendo, aut inflammatas restinguere, cum eo maxime vis oratoris magnitudoque cernatur'. Cf also II.IX.35, vol. I, p. 222.

88 Quintilian 1920–2, V, Proemium, 1, vol. II, p. 154. 'Fuerunt et clari quidem auctores, quibus solum videtur oratoris officium docere; namque et adfectus . . . excludendos putabant.'

to display itself to the greatest effect'.[89] Speaking with growing passion himself, he declares that 'this is the power which dominates the courts, this is the style of eloquence which rules over all'.[90] He concludes with a direct reversal of Aristotle's priorities. 'While it is of course true that proofs possess the capacity to make judges think our case the better one, appeals to their emotions are capable of doing much more, for they are capable of making them desire that this should be so; and what they desire they will also come to believe.'[91]

Among the Tudor rhetoricians we encounter an even stronger tendency to emphasise the purely emotional aspects of the orator's art. These writers generally find much less to say about *inventio* and much more about the orator's almost magical ability to 'draw' or enchant an audience.[92] As Elyot puts it in *The Governor*, we recognise the presence of 'very eloquence' when we find that 'sentences be so aptly compact that they by a virtue inexplicable do draw unto them the minds and consent of the hearers'.[93] When Sir Thomas North issued his translation of Plutarch's *Lives* in 1580, his version of the life of Pericles gave still wider currency to this view of eloquence. Pericles 'manifestly proved' by the use of his oratorical skills in government 'that rethorike and eloquence (as *Plato* sayeth) is an arte which quickeneth mens spirites at her pleasure, and her chiefest skill is, to knowe howe to move passions and affections throughly, which are as stoppes and sounds of the soule, that would be played upon with a fine fingered hande of a conning master'.[94] By the time Shakespeare was writing *Love's Labour's Lost* in the early 1590s, this understanding of rhetoric had become firmly entrenched. When Longueville recites the sonnet he has composed in honour of the lady Maria, he begins his lover's complaint with a question:

> Did not the heavenly rhetoric of thine eye,
> 'Gainst whom the world cannot hold argument
> Persuade my heart to this false perjury?[95]

It is characteristic of the rhetorician, Longueville implies, to persuade by moving the emotions rather than by genuine argument.[96]

89 Quintilian 1920–2, VI.II.2, vol. II, p. 416: 'quo nihil adferre maius vis orandi potest'.
90 Quintilian 1920–2, VI.II.4, vol. II, p. 418: 'Atque hoc est quod dominetur in iudiciis, haec eloquentia regnat.'
91 Quintilian 1920–2, VI.II.5, vol. II, p. 418: 'Probationes enim efficant sane ut causam nostram meliorem esse iudices putent, adfectus praestant ut etiam velint; sed id quod volunt credunt quoque.'
92 For example, Wilson 1554 has no discussion of enthymemes, and treats rhetoric almost exclusively as an art of persuasion.
93 Elyot 1962, p. 45.
94 Plutarch 1580, p. 177.
95 Shakespeare 1988, *Love's Labour's Lost*, IV.iii. 57–9, p. 293. Cf. also Jonson 1947, p. 640.
96 On rhetorical techniques in *Love's Labour's Lost* see Trousdale 1982, pp. 95–113.

A deliberate ambiguity in the use of the word *move* may thus be said to lie at the heart of the Roman and neo-Roman conceptions of the rhetorical arts. The essential task of the orator is that of shifting or moving his audience to come round to his point of view. But the surest means of accomplishing this task is by speaking in such a way that his audience is not merely convinced but 'greatly moved'. If and only if we move our hearers emotionally can we hope to move them to our side. This is the point Antonius makes in book II of the *De oratore* when he first turns from discussing *loci communes* to considering other and more powerful means of winning over an audience. Besides appealing to proofs, 'we must add that very different method of speaking which, in a contrasting way, moves and thereby impels the minds of our judges'.[97] He develops the argument in responding to Catulus towards the end of book II. 'There are three methods of bringing people round to accepting our point of view: either by teaching them or by conciliating them or else by moving them emotionally.'[98] The highest art of the rhetorician consists of deploying the Grand Style in such a way that, while appearing merely to teach, we are able to arouse the emotions of our audience and persuade them at the same time.[99] Some sections of our speech will of course offer proofs, but 'they should at the same time have the power as much as possible to move the minds of those among whom we are speaking'.[100] Moreover, 'there will be other sections which, even though they teach nothing at all by means of argument, will aid our cause very greatly by persuading and moving the minds of our listeners'.[101] Cicero later summarises the point with epigrammatic economy when speaking in his own person in the *De partitione oratoria*. 'That speech which has the greatest effect in shifting or moving our hearers will be the one that serves to move their minds.'[102]

Quintilian slides back and forth in a similar way between the literal and metaphorical senses of 'moving' an audience. He first exploits the ambiguity when discussing the topic of narrative in book IV. If we are to succeed in shifting or moving a hostile judge to come round to our point of view, we

97 Cicero 1942a, II.XLIV.185, vol. I, p. 330: 'illa dispar adiuncta ratio orationis, quae alio quodam genere mentes iudicium permovet, impellitque'.

98 Cicero 1942a, II.LXXVII.310, vol. I, p. 434: 'tribus rebus homines ad nostram sententiam perducimus, aut docendo, aut conciliando aut permovendo'.

99 This point is developed in Cicero 1942a, II.LXXXI.331–3, vol. I, pp. 448–50.

100 Cicero 1942a, II.LXXVII.310, vol. I, p. 434: 'habere hanc vim magnopere debent, ut ad eorum mentes apud quos agetur movendas pertinere possint'.

101 Cicero 1942a, II.LXXVII.311, vol. I, p. 434: 'sed his partibus orationis quae, et si nihil docent argumentando, persuadendo tamen et commovendo proficiunt plurimum'.

102 Cicero 1942b, VI.22, p. 328: 'maximeque movet ea quae motum aliquem animi miscet oratio'. Cf. Cicero 1942b, XIII.46, p. 346; Cicero 1949a, I.LV.106–9, pp. 156–62.

must be prepared if possible to move him to tears.[103] He puts forward a similar claim when explaining how to compose a peroration in book VI. He now suggests that this is the juncture above all at which an orator must aim to shift or move his audience by moving them emotionally.[104] He summarises the doctrine when comparing the different styles of oratory at the end of his closing book. The Plain Style merely enables us to teach; the Intermediate Style enables us to teach and delight; but the Grand Style enables us to teach, delight and move an audience to accept our point of view.[105] The central importance of the Grand Style accordingly derives from the fact that, 'if you wish to guide people's minds, especially if they are uneducated, you must make sure that they are profoundly moved'.[106]

The suggestion that the best method of altering people's behaviour is to move their emotions is of no less importance to the poets and rhetoricians of the Renaissance. Among the poets Sir John Davies in his *Gulling Sonnets* offers one of the most elaborate meditations on the theme:

> What eagle can behold her sunbright eye,
> Her sunbright eye that lights the world with love,
> The world of love wherein I live and die,
> I live and die and divers changes prove;
> I changes prove, yet still the same am I,
> The same am I and never will remove,
> Never remove until my soul doth fly,
> My soul doth fly and I surcease to move;
> I cease to move which now am moved by you,
> Am moved by you that move all mortal hearts,
> All mortal hearts whose eyes your eyes doth view,
> Your eyes doth view whence Cupid shoots his darts,
> Whence Cupid shoots his darts and woundeth those
> That honour you, and never were his foes.[107]

These ambiguities are no less confidently handled by the rhetoricians of the period. The orator, as Sherry puts it, must be 'appoynted and readye thorowlye to move and turne mens myndes'.[108] Wilson agrees that he 'muste perswade, and move the affeccions of his hearers' if he is to ensure 'that thei shalbe forced to yelde unto his saiying'.[109] Peacham likewise

103 Quintilian 1920–2, IV.II.77, vol. II, pp. 90–2. See also IV.II.115, vol. II, p. 112.
104 Quintilian 1920–2, VI.II.1, vol. II, p. 416.
105 Quintilian 1920–2, XII.X.58–60, vol. IV, pp. 482–4.
106 Quintilian 1920–2, XII.X.50, vol. IV, p. 478: 'commovendos enim esse ducendosque animos imperitorum'. Cf. XII.X.61–5, vol. IV, pp. 484–6.
107 Davies 1992, p. 664.
108 Sherry 1961, p. 22; cf. p. 40, on how the orator 'moveth more mightily the affeccions'.
109 Wilson 1554, fo. 2^v. Cf. fo. 58^r on the need 'to move the hartes of menne' and fo. 72^v on 'movyng affections'.

stresses at many points that one of the orator's principal aims in using the figures and tropes must be to shift or move his listeners to accept his version of events by seeking 'to move the like affections', to 'move to the love of the thing', to 'force and move the mind forward to a willing consent'.[110]

For all the importance they assign to arousing the affections, however, few of these writers exhibit much interest in the analysis and classification of the passions of the soul. Aristotle had been greatly concerned with this topic in the *Rhetoric*, but Cicero and Quintilian content themselves with making one basic distinction which Quintilian in particular explores: the distinction between the calmer passions and the emotions in their fullest and strongest sense.[111] As we have seen, both Cicero and Quintilian think it important that a rhetorician should know how to stimulate the calmer passions, and regard it as the main purpose of an exordium to win the attention, the sympathy and the benevolence of an audience. But they take the principal task of the rhetorician to be that of stirring far deeper feelings, among which Cicero singles out two contrasting ranges of emotion that need above all to be activated. On the one hand, we must seek to excite feelings of love and compassion on behalf of those we are trying to defend; on the other hand, we must seek to discredit our opponents by arousing against them feelings of anger, hatred and contempt.[112]

Among the Tudor rhetoricians, these arguments are taken up and summarised in two pervasive figures of speech. One draws on the idea of the stronger passions as passive and hence malleable, and calls on the orator to mould his audience, to manipulate or 'work them up'. Peacham speaks in *The Garden of Eloquence* of the rhetorician as 'working in the minde of the hearer',[113] while Bacon in *The Advancement of Learning* not only refers to 'persuasions that are wrought by eloquence', but describes the orator as someone capable of setting the people 'in working and agitation'.[114] The second range of images draws on the medical understanding of the passions as products of bodily heat, and invites the orator to inflame his hearers or 'fire them up'.[115] Vives opens his chapter on rhetoric in *De tradendis disciplinis* by speaking of the passions as torches capable of being

110 Peacham 1593, pp. 63, 65, 77.

111 For the most explicit statement of the distinction see Quintilian 1920–2, VI.II.8–24, vol. II, pp. 420–30. Cf. Kennedy 1972, pp. 222–4 (on Cicero) and pp. 505–6 (on Quintilian).

112 Cicero 1942a, I.XII.53, vol. I, p. 40; II.LI.206, vol. I, p. 348; II.LIII.216, vol. I, p. 356. Cf. Cicero 1942b, V.15, p. 322; XVI.56, p. 352; XXXVI.128, p. 408.

113 Peacham 1593, sig. AB, iii^r.

114 Bacon 1915, pp. 121, 171.

115 This image is already prominent in the classical texts. See Cicero 1942a, I.XIV.60, vol. I, p. 44; I.LI.219, vol. I, p. 154; II.XLV.190, vol. I, p. 334. See also Quintilian 1920–2, XI.III.2–3, vol. IV, pp. 242–4.

set ablaze by the sparks of eloquent speech.[116] Abraham Fraunce explains that the value of many of the figures and tropes derives from their capacity to help the orator speak heatedly.[117] Wilson similarly declares in his section on the elements of an ideal speech that one of the chief goals of a peroration should be to 'set the Judges on fire, and heate them earnestly against the wicked offendor'.[118] Recurring to the same thought at the end of his treatise, he reminds us once again (although on this occasion with somewhat unfortunate bathos) that by these means we can hope to make our writings and speeches 'as hote as a tost'.[119]

THE ESTABLISHING OF ETHOS

The question we are left confronting is how we can hope in practice to inflame or work upon an audience in such a way as to move them to accept our point of view. When the Roman rhetorical theorists turn to this absolutely central theme, they generally begin by reverting to their conception of the passions as inherently unstable and hence pliable. As Antonius puts it in book II of the *De oratore*, the orator commonly finds himself speaking before a fickle crowd who are not only liable to be swayed by their emotions but are liable as a result 'to believe and judge differently at different times about the very same things'.[120] The Roman moralists frequently underline the same point. When Seneca, for example, urges us in his *De vita beata* not to follow the opinions of the multitude, he reminds us that the outcome of doing so will merely be that 'we approve at one point of the very same things that at another point we condemn'.[121]

If we turn to the admirers of Seneca and Cicero in the Renaissance[122] we find them articulating a very similar understanding of the power and volatility of the passions. One such admirer was Castiglione, who raises the issue at the outset of his *Libro del cortegiano*. When the figure of the count is urged to describe the perfect courtier, he begins by conceding that he cannot hope to furnish anything like an indefeasible or even an unambiguous account. Modestly applying to himself Antonius' remarks in the *De oratore* about the fickleness of the crowd, he acknowledges that (in the words of Hoby's translation) 'not onelye one thynge maie seme unto you, and an other to me, but also unto my self it may appere sometime one

116 Vives 1913, p. 180.
117 Fraunce 1950, p. 78.
118 Wilson 1554, fo. 63^{r}.
119 Wilson 1554, fo. 106^{r-v}.
120 Cicero 1942a, II.VII.30, vol. I, p. 218: 'illi alias aliud eisdem de rebus et sentiunt et iudicant'.
121 Seneca 1932, I. 5, p. 102: 'Eadem probamus, eadem reprehendimus.'
122 On whom see Salmon 1989.

thing, sometime another'.[123] Montaigne draws extensively on the same Stoic doctrines about the mutability of the passions in his *Essais*, and with the appearance of Florio's translation in 1603 these observations entered the mainstream of English moral thought. Montaigne considers the issue most fully in the course of his longest and perhaps most celebrated essay, the 'Apology' for the Spanish theologian Raymond Sebond. There he insists that our beliefs are so deeply affected by our passions, and our passions so wayward in themselves, that even in legal arguments 'an exceeding confusion of judgements must arise'.[124] The inevitable outcome is that 'what one company hath judged another will adjudge the contrary, and the very same will another time change opinion'.[125] John Lyly had meanwhile introduced the same arguments to English readers in his *Euphues* of 1579. 'So many men so many words' is the young Euphues' way of dismissing the worthy old gentleman who reproves his careless mode of life. Many forms of behaviour, he goes on, 'may seeme in your eye odious, which in anothers eye may be gracious'. Rather than attempting to reform others, we should recognise that 'though all men bee made of one mettall, yet they bee not cast all in one moulde'.[126]

Even if our passions are diverse and pliable, the orator still faces the problem of how to shape them to suit his own ends. One way in which this can be done, according to the classical rhetoricians, is by the process originally described by Aristotle as that of establishing a good ethos.[127] Quintilian devotes part of book VI of his *Institutio oratoria* to examining and extending Aristotle's arguments. He begins by observing that the topic is somewhat confused, partly because the Greek word ἦθος lacks a Latin counterpart, and partly because the concept has never been clearly analysed.[128] The analysis he goes on to offer can hardly be said to meet his own accustomed standards of clarity, but he appears to have two closely related points in mind. One is that the creation of a good ethos is partly a matter of presenting a good image or impression of ourselves. 'If the term ethos refers to disposition or character', he suggests, 'then our speeches must themselves reflect good character when we are portraying those who possess it.'[129] He also maintains that the term refers to the feelings an

123 Castiglione 1994, p. 36.
124 Montaigne 1893, p. 299.
125 Montaigne 1893, p. 299.
126 Lyly 1868, p. 40.
127 Aristotle 1926, I.II.3, p. 16 and II.I.1–4, pp. 168–70. For a discussion of Aristotle's view, with excellent references, see Joseph 1966, pp. 393–5, and Wisse 1989, pp. 29–36. For a survey of ethos in classical rhetoric, see Johnson 1984. On the reception of Aristotle's analysis in Roman rhetoric see Wisse 1989, esp. pp. 222–49.
128 Quintilian 1920–2, VI.II.8 and 12, vol. II, pp. 420–2.
129 Quintilian 1920–2, VI.II.17, vol. II. p. 426: 'Nam si ἦθος mores sunt cum hos imitamur, ex his

orator can hope to arouse if he is successful in presenting an attractive image of himself. By these means an orator can hope to excite a number of calmer passions, prompting his auditors to view his cause with a heightened sense of attention and docility, and even with an increased feeling of benevolence and friendliness.[130]

As we have seen, Quintilian takes the sole purpose of the proem or exordium to be that of establishing one's character in this way, thereby putting one's audience in a receptive frame of mind. Like the author of the *Ad Herennium*, this leads him to consider the means of establishing a good ethos as part of his survey of the 'invention' of arguments.[131] His reason for following this procedure stems from his acceptance of the *Ad Herennium*'s claim that the question of how to construct an exordium is the first topic to be handled under the heading of *inventio*.[132] It follows for Quintilian that this must be the proper place in which to discuss the question of ethos, even though he acknowledges that the orator's aim in establishing his ethos will not be to invent arguments, but rather to embark on the complementary task of manipulating the emotions of his audience.[133]

The classical rhetoricians generally focus on two distinct methods by which we can hope to establish our ethos and thereby excite a range of calmer passions. One is by promising our auditors to inform them of something at once novel and of public importance. As Aristotle puts it (in Hobbes's translation), we must seek to benefit from the fact that '*Hearers* use to bee attentive' to '*things* that are of *great Consequence*, or that *concerne themselves*, or that are *strange*, or that *delight*'.[134] The *Ad Herennium* agrees that 'we shall guarantee attentive hearers if we promise to treat of great or new or unusual affairs, or such as concern the commonwealth'.[135] Quintilian similarly observes in his chapter on the exordium that 'nothing makes a judge more attentive than the sense that the issue about to be discussed is novel, important, atrocious, relevant to setting a precedent, or above all something that concerns either him personally or the good of the community'.[136]

The other and even more efficacious way of creating a good ethos is, as

ducimus orationem.' This clearly draws on Aristotle's understanding of ethos as a matter of persuading by establishing one's good character, on which see Vickers 1989, pp. 19–20.

130 Quintilian 1920–2, VI.II.13–19, vol. II, pp. 422–6.

131 Cf. *Ad C. Herennium* 1954, I.III.4, p. 8.

132 Quintilian 1920–2, IV.I.5–79, vol. II, pp. 8–48.

133 Quintilian 1920–2, IV.I.5, vol. II, p. 8.

134 Hobbes 1986, p. 120.

135 *Ad C. Herennium* 1954, I.IV.7, p. 14: 'Adtentos habebimus, si pollicebimur nos de rebus magnis, novis, inusitatis verba facturos, aut de iis quae ad rem publicam pertineant.'

136 Quintilian 1920–2, IV.I.33, vol. II, p. 22; 'plerumque attentum iudicem facit, si res agi videtur

Hobbes's translation of Aristotle adds, for the orator directly to emphasise 'the *probitie* of his owne *person*'.[137] According to the *Ad Herennium*, we must seek above all to create an impression of modesty, praising ourselves if possible but taking care to do so without any trace of arrogance.[138] We must seek at the same time to ingratiate ourselves with our audience, and if we are appearing before a panel of judges we must take particular care 'that their goodwill is won by pointing out to them that their previous judgments have been given courageously, wisely, humanely and with nobility'.[139]

Quintilian first develops these suggestions in his chapter on the exordium, later discussing them in greater detail at the start of book VI. He begins by stressing that we must always speak in such a way as to appear calm, placating, courteous and humane.[140] We must give an impression of complete impartiality, 'making it seem that everything we say arises simply out of the facts of the case and the characters of the persons involved'.[141] We must in addition 'express approval of the virtues of the plaintiff on whose behalf we are appearing, and ensure that we possess or at least appear to possess the same virtues, because if the orator seems to be undertaking cases out of the goodness of his heart, this will greatly benefit him in most of the cases he undertakes'.[142] Finally, we must be sure to speak with moderation and modesty, avoiding the least sign of anger or hatred as well as any trace of self-importance or loftiness. We must remember that 'anyone who, in the process of speaking, appears to be a bad man can already be said to be speaking incompetently'.[143]

The *Ad Herennium* adds the contrasting point that, besides establishing the excellence of our own character, we must take advantage of the fact that 'the benevolence of our audience can also be won if we can manage to bring the character of our adversaries into hatred, odium and

nova, magna, atrox, pertinens ad exemplum, praecipue tamen, si iudex aut sua vice aut reipublicae commovetur.'

137 Hobbes 1986, p. 120.

138 *Ad C. Herennium* 1954, I.V.8, p. 14. On establishing character by tropes of modesty see Janson 1964, esp. pp. 124–48.

139 *Ad C. Herennium* 1954, I.V.8, p. 16: 'benivolentia colligitur si res eorum fortiter, sapienter, mansuete, magnifice iudicatis proferemus'.

140 Quintilian 1920–2, VI.II.13, vol. II, pp. 422–4.

141 Quintilian 1920–2, VI.II.13, vol.II, p. 424: 'ut fluere omnia ex natura rerum hominumque videantur'.

142 Quintilian 1920–2, VI.II.18, vol. II, p. 426: 'Quas virtutes cum etiam in litigatore debeat orator, si fieri potest, approbare, utique ipse aut habeat aut habere credatur. Sic proderit plurimum causis, quibus ex sua bonitate faciet fidem.'

143 Quintilian 1920–2, VI.II.18, vol. II, p. 426: 'Nam qui, dum dicit, malus videtur, utique male dicit.'

contempt'.[144] To Quintilian this seems a dangerous as well as an unworthy enterprise, and he reminds us of the need 'to avoid appearing abusive, malignant, arrogant or slanderous to any individual or body of people'.[145] To the author of the *Ad Herennium*, however, such opportunities for invective clearly seemed too good to miss, and he speaks with evident relish of what he has in mind. We can hope to provoke hatred of our antagonists 'if we can point to some base, proud, perfidious, cruel, arrogant, malicious or disgraceful act they have committed'.[146] We can hope to turn them into objects of odium 'if we can pin on them such attributes as violence, lust for power, factiousness, excessive wealth and promiscuousness'.[147] And we can hope to bring them into contempt 'if we are able to draw attention to their idleness, their cowardice, their inactivity and their luxuriousness'.[148]

By the beginning of the sixteenth century, an important supplement to these accounts of ethos had become available in the form of the *ars rhetorica* originally produced by Hermogenes of Tarsus in the second century. First printed in Aldus Manutius' collection of *Rhetores* in 1508, and reprinted on at least a dozen occasions in the course of the sixteenth century,[149] Hermogenes' rhetoric included an account of ethos as one of the seven 'ideas of style'. To possess a good ethos, he suggests, is a matter of possessing simplicity, sweetness, subtlety and modesty, all of which he treats as an expression of character and at the same time as a means of winning the goodwill of an audience.[150]

Among the Tudor rhetoricians, it is Thomas Wilson in *The Arte of Rhetorique* who re-examines the concept with the greatest seriousness. Like his classical authorities, he regards the establishment of ethos as one of the main functions of the exordium, and accordingly discussed the issue in his section on 'Enteraunce'. He accepts that our first concern must be to 'make the people attentive, and glad to heare us'.[151] Unless we begin by 'gettyng them to give good eare' we can never hope to succeed 'in winnyng their favour' and thereby succeed in 'the winnying of victorie'.[152]

144 *Ad C. Herennium* 1954, I.v.8, p. 14: 'Ab adversariorum persona benivolentia captabitur si eos in odium, in invidiam, in contemptionem adducemus.'

145 Quintilian 1920–2, IV.I.10, vol. II, p. 10: 'Vitandum etiam, ne contumeliosi, maligni, superbi, maledici in quemquam hominem ordinemve videamur.'

146 *Ad C. Herennium* 1954, I.v.8, pp. 14–16: 'si quid eorum spurce, superbe, perfidiose, crudeliter, confidenter, malitiose, flagitiose factum proferemus'.

147 *Ad C. Herennium* 1954, I.v.8, p. 16: 'si vim, si potentiam, si factionem, divitas, incontinentiam ... proferemus'.

148 *Ad C. Herennium* 1954, 'si inertiam, ignaviam, desidiam, luxuriam ... proferemus'.

149 Patterson 1970, pp. 219–20.

150 Patterson 1970, pp. 57–64; Shuger 1988, pp. 155–64.

151 Wilson 1554, fo. 55^r (*recte* fo. 56^r).

152 Wilson 1554, fo. 55^v.

It is thus of the greatest importance 'to wynne their good willes' at the outset by putting them in a receptive and benevolent frame of mind.[153]

Wilson agrees with the *Ad Herennium* that one way of achieving these ends will be by assuring our audience that we plan 'to speake of weightie matters, of wholsome doctrine suche as thei have heretofore wanted'.[154] He is confident that 'if we promise to tell them thynges concernyng either their awne profite or thadvauncement of their countrey, no doubte wee shall have them diligent hearers'.[155] He also considers how we should proceed if we know that they 'like not to heare weighty affairs'. In that case we ought to 'promise theim straunge newes, and perswade them we wil make them laugh'. Having allowed them an opportunity 'to heare a tale of a Tubbe, and thus havyng them attentive', we may find it possible to persuade them after all to listen to 'matters of great importaunce'.[156]

Following his classical authorities once more, Wilson goes on to argue that an even more effective way of putting an audience in a friendly and receptive frame of mind will be to persuade them of our excellence of character. We must take care in the first place to present ourselves as persons of moderation and modesty. Wet must 'declare our goodnes', but we must be careful to do so 'without all ostentation'; we must 'modestly set furthe our bounden duties and declare our service doen without all suspicion of vauntyng'.[157] Next, as the *Ad Herennium* had emphasised, we must try to ingratiate ourselves with our audience. If we are appearing before a group of judges, we must be sure to 'commende their worthy dooynges and praise their just dealyng and faithfull execucion of the law'.[158] Finally, Wilson agrees with the *Ad Herennium* that we must seek at the same time to undermine the characters of our adversaries. We must speak of them in such a way that our judges 'hate to heare of them'. This we can hope to do 'if we shewe and set furth some naughtie deede of theirs and declare how cruelly, how vilie, and how maliciously they have used other men heretofore'. We must also seek to make our judges 'altogether despise theim'. This can best be done by showing 'how unthriftely thei live, how thei do nothyng from daie to daie but eate, drinke and slepe' and how in consequence they are persons of no value 'either in profityng their countrey, or in tenderying their awne commoditie'.[159]

153 Wilson 1554, fo. 55^r.
154 Wilson 1554, fo. 55^r (*recte* fo. 56^r).
155 Wilson 1554, fo. 55^r (*recte* fo. 56^r).
156 Wilson 1554, fo. 55^r (*recte* fo. 56^r).
157 Wilson 1554, fo. 56^v.
158 Wilson 1554, fo. 56^v.
159 Wilson 1554, fo. 56^v.

To these general observations Henry Peacham later added in his *Garden of Eloquence* that a number of rhetorical figures are particularly well adjusted to enabling a good ethos to be established.[160] By the figure of syngnome we can hope to present a subtle commendation of our own charity and mercy;[161] by the figure of parrhesia we can similarly hope to contrive a tone of 'humble submission and modest insinuation', thereby forestalling any displeasure and offence at our speech.[162] Conversely, by the figure of onedismus we can seek to undermine the character of our adversaries by way of upbraiding them for ingratitude and impiety,[163] while the figure of syngnome can likewise be used 'to note the impiety' of our opponents by comparison with ourselves.[164]

THE AMPLIFICATION OF ARGUMENTS

While the Roman rhetoricians treat the establishing of ethos as a method of arousing the emotions, they generally accept that the most we can hope to achieve by these means is an intensification of the calmer passions of an audience. It is true that according to the *Ad Herennium* we may be able to excite much stronger feelings if we can manage at the same time to denigrate our adversaries. But Quintilian more soberly concludes that we can rarely hope for more than an increase 'in benevolence, attention and docility'.[165] As we have seen, however, the central contention of these writers is that an orator must learn how to move the deepest and most powerful emotions of his audience if he is to have any prospect of winning them round to his side. The question that still remains is accordingly how we can hope to speak with sufficient eloquence to stir our listeners to their very depths.

Not without some misgivings, the Roman theorists answer that there is only one possible way. We must find some means of presenting the facts in a manner more favourable to our side than they are in strict truth. As the figure of Antonius puts it in a crucial passage in book I of *De oratore*, the principal means by which successful orators work upon the feelings of their hearers is 'by succeeding, through their use of words, in making all those things which in ordinary life are felt to be bad, troublesome and thus to be avoided seem very much graver and more irksome, while managing at the

160 A point well brought out in Joseph 1966, pp. 396–8.
161 Peacham 1593, p. 98.
162 Peacham 1593, p. 113.
163 Peacham 1593, p. 73.
164 Peacham 1593, p. 98.
165 See Quintilian 1920–2, IV.I.5, vol. II, p. 8, on making an audience 'benevolum, attentum, docilem'.

same time by their manner of speaking to amplify and embellish all those things which are generally felt to be most desirable and worthwhile'.[166] Quintilian makes the same point still more forthrightly in the course of conceding that, as critics of the *ars rhetorica* complain, 'this is an art which relies on moving the emotions by saying that which is false'.[167] He allows that such methods can only be justified 'if there is no other possibility of ensuring that the judge is led to arrive at a fair verdict'.[168] But he freely acknowledges that, 'since those who sit in judgment are often ignorant, it will often be necessary to speak in such a way as to deceive them if they are not to make mistakes'.[169] He later repeats his conclusion in tones of some defiance when considering the scruples habitually expressed by moral philosophers about the use of bad means to attain worthy ends. 'While it seems to them contrary to good practice to distract a judge from the truth, and inappropriate that a virtuous man should make use of such evil methods, they are nevertheless forced to concede the indispensability of such emotional appeals if there is no other way of advancing the cause of truth, justice and the common good.'[170]

These somewhat Machiavellian commitments are no less frankly avowed by the leading rhetoricians of the English Renaissance. As Wilson puts it in discussing the composition of perorations, the best way to arouse our hearers is to 'encrease muche the matter' and 'moste copiouslye to exaggerate'.[171] Puttenham similarly recognises that, if we wish 'to excuse a fault', we may find ourselves committed to using 'a terme more favorable and of less vehemencie then the troth requires'.[172] Bacon likewise marks a strong distinction in *The Advancement of Learning* between 'amplification' on the one hand and 'positive and measured truth' on the other,[173] and later speaks unapologetically of the need for rhetorical amplification in the course of discussing antithetical arguments in the *De Augmentis*. The special value of antitheses, he claims, stems from the fact that they help an orator in his indispensable task of exaggerating his case in one direction or the

166 Cicero 1942a, I.LI.221, vol. I, p. 156: 'Orator autem omnia haec, quae putantur in communi vitae consuetudine, mala, ac molesta, et fugienda, multo maiora et acerbiora verbis facit; itemque ea, quae vulgo expetenda atque optabilia videntur, dicendo amplificat atque ornat.'

167 Quintilian 1920–2, II.XVII.26, vol. I, p. 336: 'et falsum dicat et adfectus moveat'.

168 Quintilian 1920–2, II.XVII.27, vol. I, p. 336: 'si aliter ad aequitatem perduci iudex non poterit'.

169 Quintilian 1920–2, II.XVII.28, vol. I, p. 336: 'Imperiti enim iudicant et qui frequenter in hoc ipsum fallendi sint, ne errent'.

170 Quintilian 1920–2, VI.I.7, vol. II, p. 386: 'nec boni mores videntur, sic a vero iudicem averti, nec convenire bono viro vitiis uti. Necessarios tamen adfectus fatebuntur, si aliter obtineri vera et iusta et in commune profutura non possint.'

171 Wilson 1554, fos. 63^v, 65^r.

172 Puttenham 1970, p. 220.

173 Bacon 1915, p. 2.

other, even to the point of speaking 'unfairly and altogether beyond the truth'.[174]

The Roman theorists had laid it down that there are two complementary ways in which an orator can hope to stretch the truth in such a way as to arouse the deepest and most powerful feelings of an audience. He must first of all present his own case so as to minimise or gloss over any weaknesses in it, thus making it appear as plausible and attractive as possible. The verb generally used in this context is *minuere* – to lessen, to diminish, to extenuate. The figure of Antonius makes the point with remarkable bluntness in summarising his own oratorical practice in book II of the *De oratore.* 'My usual method of constructing a speech', he confesses, is 'to keep away from any weak or bad elements in the case as far as posssible, not in such a way as to appear to be evading them, but certainly in such a way as to cover them up'.[175] Quintilian reiterates the suggestion when he observes in the course of analysing the exordium in book IV that 'anything which is liable to seem damaging must at the very least be extenuated and preferably set aside altogether in the statement of our case'.[176]

The orator's other and even more important task is to magnify everything that can plausibly be said in favour of his own cause and against that of his adversaries. The verb used by the Roman rhetoricians in this contrasting context is *augere* – to increase, to strengthen, to intensify or enhance. The *Ad Herennium* insists in discussing *loci communes* that we must aim to deploy them 'with exaggeration and an enumeration of the sins of our adversaries'.[177] Cicero speaks at the end of book I of *De inventione* of the need for everything pertinent to the case we are arguing 'to be presented with an exaggeration born of indignation'.[178] The figure of Antonius elaborates the claim with his usual frankness in book I of the *De oratore*, in which he declares that his invariable practice 'is to fix on the good points in my case, after which I increase them, embellish them, exaggerate them, speak at length on them, dwell on them, stick to them'.[179] Quintilian recurs to the argument in the passage from book IV in which he also stresses the need to diminish or extenuate anything that can be said against

174 See Bacon 1857b, p. 688, on speaking 'tanquam improbe et prorsus praeter veritatem'.

175 Cicero 1942a, II.LXXII.292, vol. I, p. 420: 'mea autem ratio in dicendo haec esse solet ... a malo autem vitioque causa ita recedam non ut me id fugere appareat sed ut ... obruatur'.

176 Quintilian 1920–2, IV.I.27, vol. II, p. 20: 'ita quod laedit aut omnino repellere aut certe minuere ex causa est'.

177 See *Ad C. Herennium* 1954, II.XVII.26, p. 104, on the need to speak 'cum amplificatione et enumeratione peccatorum'.

178 Cicero 1949a, I.LIII.101, p. 152: 'cum amplificatione per indignationem ostenditur'.

179 Cicero 1942a, II.LXXII.292, vol. I, p. 420: 'ut boni quod habeat id amplectar, exornem, exaggerem, ibi commorer, ibi habitem, ibi haeream'.

us. We must aim at the same time to find out and then attempt to increase and intensify – *augere* – everything that can be said in favour of our side.[180]

The nearest the classical theorists come to encapsulating this doctrine in a single concept is when they speak of the process of *amplificatio.* It is true that they employ this term in various ways to refer to a number of different devices of emphasis, not all of which are of great significance. But they frequently speak of *amplificatio* as the general means by which an orator can hope to develop his case in such a way as to enlist the emotional support of his audience.[181] There is a hint of this doctrine in Aristotle's *Rhetoric*,[182] but it first becomes fully explicit in the leading Roman treatises. The author of the *Ad Herennium* observes that, when we speak of amplification, we generally mean 'that type of speech which either moves the mind of a listener to pity or incites them to wrath'.[183] The figure of Crassus in book III of the *De oratore* makes a similar point when he declares that 'the very highest praise of eloquence comes from our being able to amplify our case by embellishing it, since it is amplification which serves not merely to augment whatever we are saying and raise it to a higher plane, but also to extenuate objections and disparage the opposing side'.[184] Consequently, 'when we wish to rouse up an audience, it is amplification which is best able to achieve this effect, with the result that this is the talent for which orators are praised more than for anything else'.[185]

This use of the term 'amplification' to cover the whole process of arousing the emotions by way of stretching the truth recurs even more prominently among the English rhetoricians of the Renaissance. Sherry assigns the topic a separate section in his pioneering *Treatise of Schemes and Tropes*, placing it before (and implicitly contrasting it with) the notion of rhetorical proofs. His main contention is that amplification comprises 'a greate parte of eloquence', since an orator will always and inevitably be concerned with 'increasing and diminyshing' the facts of any case.[186] Wilson in his *Arte of Rhetorique* agrees that the best means of 'stirryng the hearers by large utteraunce' and so achieving an 'apte movyng of affections' is by means of 'Amplificacion', the term he employs for the

180 Quintilian 1920–2, IV.I.2, vol. II, p. 20.
181 See Kennedy 1972, p. 228.
182 See, for example, the section translated in Hobbes 1986, p. 105, and cf. pp. 119, 128.
183 *Ad C. Herennium* 1954, III.XIII.23, p. 196: 'Amplificatio est oratio quae aut in iracundiam inducit, aut ad misericordiam trahit auditoris animum.'
184 Cicero 1942a, III.XXVI.104, vol. II, p. 82: 'Summa autem laus eloquentiae est amplificare rem ornando, quod valet non solum ad augendum aliquid et tollendum altius dicendo sed etiam ad extenuandam atque abiciendum.'
185 Cicero 1942a, III.XXVII.104, vol. II, pp. 82–4: 'cum concitamus ... amplificatio potest plurimum, eaque una laus oratoris est proprie maxime'.
186 Sherry 1961, p. 70.

methods of 'augmentyng and vehemently enlargyng' our arguments so as to 'set the Judge or hearers in a heate, or els to mitigate and asswage displeasure conceived'.[187] Peacham in *The Garden of Eloquence* later develops a similar understanding of the term. He begins by marking an apparent contrast between those figures which 'attend upon affections' and those which merely serve 'to amplifie & garnish' our speech.[188] But when he turns to the latter – to which he devotes the bulk of his book – he declares that amplification is not merely the name of a figure, but is rather the general term for the entire process of 'increasing and diminishing' the force of an argument.[189] When Francis Bacon, a few years later, went on to describe his ambition as that of bringing about an advancement of learning, an augmentation of the sciences, he was thus presenting his scientific programme in language drawn from classical and Renaissance theories of eloquence.[190] He appears to endorse the resounding conclusion already reached by Peacham in his *Garden of Eloquence* to the effect that the processes of amplification and augmentation provide us with the means 'whereby the hearers might the sooner be moved to like of that which was spoken'.[191] These are the means by which the orator can hope to 'prevaile much in drawing the mindes of his hearers to his owne will and affection; he may winde them from their former opinions, and quite alter the former state of their mindes'.[192]

187 Wilson 1554, fos. 63^r^ and 71^v^.
188 Peacham 1593, p. 120.
189 Peacham 1593, pp. 120, 121; cf. also pp. 146, 156.
190 As noted in Briggs 1989, pp. 153–4.
191 Peacham 1593, p. 121.
192 Peacham 1593, p. 121; cf. also pp. 140, 143–4.

Chapter 4

THE TECHNIQUES OF REDESCRIPTION

If we need to amplify our arguments to arouse our hearers, and if we need to arouse our hearers to win the war of words, we next need to know what specific rhetorical techniques enable this crucial process of amplification to be carried out. It was widely accepted in the first place that a mastery of *inventio* can help us to stretch the truth in the required ways. As Cicero in particular stresses, we can often invoke a number of *loci communes* not merely as forms of rhetorical proof but as means of exciting an audience, especially if we draw on such *topoi* as those which emphasise the weakness of humanity, the fickleness of fortune and so forth.[1] It was also agreed that, in the case of spoken oratory, the element of *pronuntiatio* can likewise be used to engender powerful emotional effects. On the one hand, as Cicero observes in *De partitione oratoria*, 'it is possible to rouse a judge to feelings of hatred merely by adopting a tone of indignant complaint'.[2] And on the other hand, as Quintilian later adds, 'we can seek to rouse a judge's compassion as well as indignation simply by using a particular modulation of the voice'.[3]

It was generally accepted, however, that the power to amplify, and hence to arouse emotion, depends above all on effective *elocutio*, and especially on the apt use of *ornatus*. This is not to say that a desire to excite emotion was taken to be the sole reason for speaking in the Grand Style. As Quintilian frequently insists, *ornatus* has many other uses, including the avoidance of monotony,[4] the improvement of clarity[5] and especially the addition of beauty and grace to our speech.[6] Quintilian's Renaissance admirers make the same point with even firmer emphasis. Wilson observes that such ornaments as similitudes are 'not onelye used to amplifie a

1 Cicero 1949a, I.LV.106, pp. 156–8. Cf. *Ad C. Herennium* 1954, II.XXX.47, pp. 144–6.

2 Cicero 1942b, XXXIX.137, p. 416: 'retrahatur in odium iudiciis cum quadam invidiosa querela'.

3 Quintilian 1920–2, I.X.25, vol. I, p. 170: 'et vocis . . . modulatione concitationem iudicis, alia misericordiam petimus'. Cf. IV.II.77, vol. II, p. 92.

4 Quintilian 1920–2, IX.I.21, vol. III, p. 358.

5 Quintilian 1920–2, VIII.III.61–2, vol. III, p. 244.

6 Quintilian 1920–2, IX.III.58, vol. III, p. 478; IX.III.74, vol. III, p. 488; IX.III.80, vol. III, p. 492.

matter, but also to beautifie the same, to delite the hearers, to make the matter playne, and to shewe a certaine maiestye'.[7] Fraunce ingenuously adds that *ornatus* may be said to lend 'bravery' to speech, contributing 'delight and pleasant grace' by ensuring that our words 'do sweetlie and fitly sound'.[8] Peacham even suggests that a range of 'ornaments' can be distinguished which have no particular power to affect the feelings, but are merely employed to garnish our utterances in a manner pleasing to the ear.[9]

It was the view of all these writers, however, that the principal value of *ornatus* lies in providing the orator with the means to arouse the emotions of an audience. Hence the crucial importance of the Grand Style, the style defined by its preoccupation with the use of *ornamenta* to produce emotional effects.[10] As Crassus puts it in book III of the *De oratore*, 'the greatest praise for eloquence is reserved for the amplification of argument by means of *ornatus*',[11] and it is by means of such amplifications 'that we are either able to conciliate the minds of our listeners or else excite them'.[12] We accordingly find that, when they turn to examine the nature of the rhetorical techniques by means of which we can hope to produce these effects, the Roman rhetoricians and their Renaissance followers alike concentrate on the topic of *ornatus* above all.

As we saw in chapter I, there were held to be two principal ways in which *ornatus* can be used to amplify and empower our utterances. One is by enabling us to redescribe actions or states of affairs in such a way as to lend additional force to whatever interpretation we may wish to put upon them. The other is by colouring or enhancing our arguments by means of the figures and tropes of speech. The present chapter will accordingly be concerned with the various techniques of redescription recommended for arousing the feelings of an audience. Chapter 5 will examine the contribution made to the same end by the figures and tropes of speech.

QUESTIONING DEFINITIONS AND DESCRIPTIONS

The classical theorists of eloquence single out two contrasting ways in which we can hope, simply by offering a redescription of an action or state of affairs, to excite the emotions of our listeners and enlist them on our

7 Wilson 1554, fo. 101^{r-v}; cf. also fos. 85^{v}, 810^{v} (*recte* 90^{v}).
8 Fraunce 1950, pp. 3, 26.
9 Peacham 1593, pp. 44, 54, 55.
10 As Quintilian stresses in book XII. See Quintilian 1920–2, XII.X.61–5, vol. IV, pp. 484–6.
11 Cicero 1942a, III.XXVI.104, vol. II, p. 82: 'Summa autem laus eloquentiae est amplificare rem ornando.'
12 Cicero 1942a, III.XXVII.104, vol. II, p. 82: 'vel cum conciliamus animos vel cum concitamus'.

side. The first is by claiming that an existing description ought to be rejected on the grounds that one or other of the terms used to state it has been misleadingly defined. Aristotle discusses this technique at the end of book I of *The Art of Rhetoric,* where he considers how someone accused of an offence may be able to admit the facts while denying the description underpinning the charge. To cite Aristotle's own examples, he may be willing to admit that he took something while denying that this was an act of theft; that he killed someone while denying that this was an act of homicide; that he had sexual relations with someone while denying that this was an act of adultery; or that he stole a sacred object while denying that this was an act of sacrilege. As Aristotle adds, the only way to block this type of defence and establish that an offence has in fact been committed is to gain agreement at the outset about the proper definitions to be given to such key terms as theft, homicide, adultery and sacrilege.[13]

Cicero makes the same point in his important discussion of definitions[14] at the start of the *De inventione.* 'One controversy about the name to be given to an act arises when there is agreement about a fact and the question is by what name the fact should be described.'[15] The only way to avoid such disputes 'is for the issue to be properly defined in words and then briefly illustrated'.[16] For example, 'suppose a sacred object has been stolen from a private house, the question arises as to whether this should be judged an act of theft or rather of sacrilege'.[17] If we are to prevent our opponents from getting the better of us, 'it will be necessary to define what constitutes theft, what constitutes sacrilege, and to show by our own description that the act in question ought to be called by a different name from that which our adversaries have assigned to it'.[18]

Later Roman writers on eloquence were largely content to model their discussions of definition on Cicero's analysis and examples.[19] When Quintilian turns to the topic in book VII, he begins by offering a similar account of how the manipulation of definitions can be used as a rhetorical device. 'A defendant who cannot claim that he has done nothing has the possibility of saying that he has not committed the particular act with

13 Aristotle 1926, I.XIII.9–10, p. 142.

14 On which see Michel 1960, pp. 190–7.

15 Cicero 1949a, I.VIII.II, p. 22: 'Nominis est controversaria, cum de facto convenit et quaeritur, id quod factum est quo nomine appellatur.'

16 Cicero 1942a, I.VIII.II, p. 24: 'definienda res erit verbis et breviter describenda'.

17 Cicero 1942a, I.VIII.II, p. 24: 'ut, si quis sacrum ex privato surripuerit, utrum fur an sacrilegus sit iudicandus'.

18 Cicero 1942a, I.VIII.II, p. 24: 'necesse erit definire utrumque, quid sit fur, quid sacrilegus, et sua descriptione ostendere alio nomine illam rem de qua agitur appellari oportere atque adversarii dicunt'.

19 As were the rhetoricians of the English Renaissance. See Joseph 1966, pp. 312–13.

which he is charged.'[20] One way of doing this is to question whether the terms used to frame the accusation have been employed in virtue of their accepted definitions. For example, perhaps the defendant can hope to deny a charge of adultery by claiming that, since the act took place in a brothel, it escapes the ordinary understanding of the term.[21] Or perhaps he can evade a charge of sacrilege by claiming that, although he admittedly stole from a temple, the item he stole was not itself a sacred object.[22]

The one leading Roman rhetorician with something further to say about definition is the author of the *Ad Herennium*. He is explicit in claiming in the first place that the technique of 'elevating' or 'depreciating' actions by challenging definitions should be classified as an aspect of *ornatus*. Specifically, he suggests that it should be treated as a figure of speech.[23] His account is also notable for illustrating the technique with an unusually rich array of examples. Besides alluding to Aristotle's discussion of theft,[24] he considers the proper definitions of such central moral concepts as justice, courage and avarice.[25] He also provides an especially clear account of how one can hope to raise questions about definitions in such a way as to augment or extenuate the alleged significance of a particular action or state of affairs. Focusing on the example of courage, he imagines a situation in which a given action has been described and commended as courageous on the grounds of 'the agent's willingness to suffer dangers in the manner of a gladiator without any consideration of the pains involved'.[26] One way of challenging this description will be to retort that 'this act you are describing is not in fact a case of courage but rather of sheer temerity, because what it means to be courageous is to show contempt for toil and danger with a clear understanding of the usefulness of the act and a consideration of its advantages'.[27] The rhetorical significance of the proposed redefinition is that it serves to place the action in a new moral light. We not only come to see that the term used to evaluate it was misleadingly applied; we also come to see that the action

20 Quintilian 1920–2, VII.III.1, vol. III, p. 82: 'Nam, qui non potest dicere nihil fecisse, proximum habebit, ut dicat, non id fecisse, quod obiiciatur.'

21 Quintilian 1920–2, VII.III.6, vol. III, p. 86.

22 Quintilian 1920–2, VII.III.10, vol. III, p. 88.

23 *Ad C. Herennium* 1954, IV.XXV.35, p. 316.

24 *Ad C. Herennium* 1954, I.XII.21–2, pp. 38–40.

25 *Ad C. Herennium* 1954, IV.XXV.35, p. 316.

26 *Ad C. Herennium* 1954, IV.XXV.35, p. 316: 'cum inconsiderata dolorum perpessione gladiatoria periculorum susceptio'.

27 *Ad C. Herennium* 1954, IV.XXV.35, p. 316: 'Non est ista fortitudo, sed temeritas, propterea quod fortitudo est contemptio laboris et periculi cum ratione utilitatis et conpensatione commodorum.'

falls under a different description which evaluates it in a much less favourable way.

As the Roman theorists appear to recognise, however, the manipulation of definitions obviously constitutes a somewhat crude and inflexible rhetorical device. They generally devote far more attention to a second and contrasting way in which we can hope to augment or extenuate the significance of actions by redescribing them. We can argue, they claim, that a given action has been wrongly assessed not because the terms used to describe it have been misdefined, but rather because the action itself has a different moral complexion from that which the terms used to describe it suggest.

When Cicero considers this alternative technique at the beginning of *De inventione*, he goes so far as to argue that, if we cannot hope to challenge our opponents over a matter of fact or law, we can only hope to repudiate their view of the basic question at issue – the *constitutio* – in one of two ways.[28] One will be to raise questions about definition; the other will be to use this second method of attempting, as Cicero puts it, to raise 'qualitative' questions about the *constitutio generalis* by attempting to show that the action in question possesses a different 'value' or 'quality' or 'character' from the one alleged by our adversaries.[29] Quintilian takes up the point in discussing the topic of refutations in book v and again in his technical discussion of *constitutiones* in book vi. If you are seeking to rebut an opponent, and cannot hope to deny the facts of the case, you must aim to restate them in such a way as to excuse or pardon or soften or extenuate or turn aside the charge.[30] You must try 'to show in some way that the action in question does not have the character alleged'.[31] More specifically, you must try to redescribe it in such a way as to suggest 'that it has a lesser significance than your adversary has claimed for it'.[32]

Cicero admittedly offers a somewhat confusing account of these contrasting rhetorical techniques. He appears to suggest that it is only in the case of a dispute about definitions that we shall find ourselves arguing over which of two rival descriptions ought to be applied.[33] As other writers

28 On the organisation of the *ars rhetorica* – and especially the *genus iudiciale* – around 'basic issues' or *constitutiones*, see Kennedy 1972, p. 61, and Vickers 1989, pp. 26–7.

29 See Cicero 1949a, I.VIII.10, pp. 20–2, on the *constitutio definitiva* and the *constitutio generalis*, and on the latter as concerned with the *vis* and *genus* of the act, and on *qualis sit res*.

30 Quintilian 1920–2, V.XIII.2, vol. II, pp. 310–12.

31 See Quintilian 1920–2, V.XIII.7, vol. II, p. 314, on the attempt to show 'non hoc esse, quod factum sit'.

32 See Quintilian 1920–2, V.XIII.10, vol. II, p. 316, on showing that 'minus est quam adversarius dicat'.

33 Cicero 1949a, I.VIII.11, p. 23 and II.XXI.62, p. 224. Cf. Cicero 1942b, XXIX.102, p. 388.

make clear, however, the difference between the two methods is not that one involves word substitution while the other does not, but rather that the process of substitution operates in the two cases in different ways. The nature of the distinction is drawn with admirable clarity by the author of the *Ad Herennium* in discussing the case of courage. As we have seen, he accepts that one type of dispute as to whether a given action should be appraised as courageous can certainly arise in consequence of a disagreement over the definition of the term. To repeat his own example, one party may seek to insist, while the other attempts to deny, that genuine courage always presupposes heedfulness. But the two parties may still find themselves in disagreement even if they both accept that heedless courage is really recklessness. For they may disagree about whether the action in question can properly be said to have been done with heed. If the orator's aim is to 'augment' the significance of the action with a view to arousing the admiration of his audience, he will seek to establish that the action embodied a sufficient degree of forethought. But if he wishes to arouse their hostility, he will seek to deny that it reflected any such quality. He will instead attempt, as the *Ad Herennium* puts it, to 'diminish' the value of the action by suggesting 'that the very same conduct which our opponent has described as courageous we say ought to be described as mere gladiatorial and inconsiderate temerity'.[34] The purpose of the redescription, as the *Ad Herennium* adds, is to suggest 'that the virtue of courage consists in qualities other than those displayed in the action concerned', so implying that the action under investigation lacks the virtuous character assigned to it by our adversaries.[35]

Quintilian later discusses this second method of redescription in similar terms. He first turns to the topic in book IV, in the course of considering how best to present a narrative of facts. Suppose we find ourselves facing an opponent who has managed to recount the facts of a case 'in such a way as to rouse up the judges and leave them full of anger against us'.[36] If we cannot hope to deny that some act has taken place, we shall find ourselves in serious difficulties. 'What then should we do? Should we simply restate the same facts?'[37] Quintilian responds that 'we must indeed restate them, but not at all in the same way; we must assign different causes, a different state of mind and a different motive for what was

34 *Ad C. Herennium* 1954, II.III.6, pp. 166–8: 'quam ille fortitudinem nominarit, eam nos gladiatoriam et inconsideratam appellabimus temeritatem'.

35 *Ad C. Herennium* 1954, III.II.6, p. 166: 'in contrariis potius rebus quam in his virtus [sc. fortitudo] constare quae ostendantur'.

36 Quintilian 1920–2, IV.II.75, vol. II, p. 90: 'incendit [iudices] et plenos irae reliquit'.

37 Quintilian 1920–2, IV.II.76, vol. II, p. 90: 'Quid ergo? eadem exponemus?'

done'.[38] Above all 'we must try to elevate the action as much as possible by the words we use: for example, prodigality must be more leniently redescribed as a case of liberality, avarice as a case of carefulness, negligence as a case of simplicity of mind'.[39]

Quintilian recurs to the topic in book VIII, where he adds a helpful characterisation of the rhetorical technique involved. Strictly speaking, he observes, we ought not to label the act of redescribing prodigality as liberality as a case of substituting one word for another, as some experts have done. For what we are claiming is that the *res* – the actual behaviour involved – possesses a different moral character from that which has been claimed for it. Rather than speaking of substituting one word for another, *verbum pro verbo*, we ought therefore to speak of substituting one thing for another, *res pro re*.[40] 'For no one supposes that the words prodigality and liberality mean the same thing; the difference is rather that one man calls something prodigal which another thinks of as liberality.'[41]

It is this second technique that the Roman rhetoricians take to be of cardinal importance, and it is Quintilian who exhibits the most systematic interest in it. It is true that he warns us not to make excessive use of the device, and criticises his elder contemporary Cornelius Celsus for having over-emphasised it in his rhetorical works.[42] But he agrees that it constitutes one of the most potent means of amplifying our utterances,[43] and it is to him that we must turn for the fullest account of how to use it to arouse the emotions of an audience.

As Quintilian intimates at a number of points, we must first take note of a crucial fact about moral language which helps to explain the possibility of arousing the emotions by substituting *res pro re*. This is the fact that, if we can manage to challenge the description of a given action or state of affairs, we can often manage, *eo ipso*, to challenge its moral appraisal at the same time. Quintilian makes the point explicitly in book XI, in the course of discussing the best methods of speaking with decorum and appropriateness:

If there is anything unpleasant about the topic on which you have to speak, it is usual to lessen the force of what you say by the moderation of the words you use. If you are

38 Quintilian 1920–2, IV.II.76, vol. II, p. 90: 'eadem sed non eodem modo; alias causas, aliam mentem, aliam rationem dabo'.

39 Quintilian 1920–2, IV.II.77, vol. II, pp. 90–2: 'Verbis elevare quaedam licebit; luxuria liberalitatis, avaritia parsimoniae, negligentia simplicitatis nomine lenietur.'

40 Quintilian 1920–2, VIII.VI.36, vol. III, pp. 320–2.

41 Quintilian 1920–2, VIII.VI.36, vol. III, p. 322: 'neque enim quisquam putat luxuriam et liberalitatem idem significare; verum id quod fit alius luxuriam esse dicit, alius liberalitatem'.

42 Celsus' rhetorical works have not survived. See Fabricius 1703, pp. 54–6, and Kennedy 1972, pp. 483–6. For Quintilian's strictures see Quintilian 1920–2, III.VII.25, vol. I, p. 476.

43 Quintilian 1920–2, VI.II.23–4, vol. II, p. 430.

speaking of a cruel man, you can say he is really only somewhat severe; if you are speaking of someone who is unjust, you can say he has been misled by prejudice; if you are speaking of someone who is extremely obstinate, you can say he is a person of exceptional tenacity.[44]

The point of Quintilian's examples is that the proposed redescriptions serve in every case to re-evaluate what was done: someone who had seemed liable to condemnation is at least partly exonerated.

There is no categorical distinction, in other words, between descriptive and evaluative terms: some descriptions serve at the same time to evaluate. Given this crucial fact about normative language, it is easy according to Quintilian to see how the technique of substituting *res pro re* can be used to express and solicit an 'augmented' or 'extenuated' emotional response to a given action or state of affairs. We simply replace whatever descriptions our opponents may have offered with a different set of terms that serve to describe the action with no less plausibility, but place it at the same time in a different moral light. We seek to persuade our hearers to accept our redescription, and hence to adopt a new emotional attitude towards the action involved – either one of increased sympathy or acquired moral outrage.[45]

Quintilian first presents the issue in these terms when he turns to the topic of emotional appeals in book VI. One way, he suggests, in which we can hope to exaggerate an injury done to us is 'by speaking of things which people usually tolerate in such a way as to make them appear far graver'.[46] For instance, when someone has been struck we can claim that they have really been wounded. By our choice of words 'we lend additional force to our claims about the injustice or cruelty or hatefulness of things'.[47] As Quintilian himself notes, however, the most appropriate point at which to examine this technique is under the heading of *amplificatio*, and it is accordingly in discussing that topic in book VIII that he gives his main examples. 'The primary method of amplification or extenuation', he declares at that juncture, 'is to be found in the actual

44 Quintilian 1920–2, XI.I.90, vol. IV, p. 208: 'verborum etiam moderatione detrahi solet, si qua est rei invidia: si asperum dicas nimium severum, iniustum persuasione labi, pertinacem ultra modum tenacem esse propositi'.

45 It is perhaps worth underlining the strong analogy with current attempts to reformulate Kantian principles of universalisability by appealing to models of moral dialogue. See for example Benhabib 1992, p. 163: 'When we morally disagree, for example, we do not only disagree about the principles involved; very often we disagree because what I see as a lack of generosity on your part you construe as your legitimate right not to do something; we disagree because what you see as jealousy on my part I view as my desire to have more of your attention.' This is to restate Quintilian's point (and one of his examples).

46 Quintilian 1920–2, VI.II.23, vol. II, p. 430: 'quae toleranda haberi solent, gravia videantur'.

47 Quintilian 1920–2, VI.II.24, vol. II, p. 430: 'rebus indignis, asperis, invidiosis addens vim oratio'.

term we use to describe something.'[48] He proceeds to offer a number of examples that were widely taken up:

> We may say of someone who has been struck down that he was really *murdered*, or of someone of doubtful probity that he is really a *robber*. On the other hand, we may say of someone who has struck someone else that he really only *touched* him, or of someone who has inflicted a serious wound that it was really only *a slight hurt*.[49]

Citing Cicero as an exemplary practitioner, Quintilian makes a further point about the way in which we can use this device to arouse an audience and intensify its emotional response:

> This method of amplification can be increased and made more manifest if the words of greater force are explicitly compared with those we propose to substitute, the method Cicero uses in his prosecution of Verres: '*We have brought before you for judgment not a thief but a plunderer, not an adulterer but a rapist, not a committer of sacrilege but an enemy of everything sacred and religious, not an assassin but someone who has actually butchered allies and fellow-citizens with the utmost cruelty*.'[50]

For the most powerful effects, Quintilian is suggesting, the technique of substituting *res pro re* should be combined with the *figura* of climax.

Quintilian also makes it clear – following a number of earlier authorities – that we can hope to employ this technique with equal effectiveness in all the different genera of rhetorical speech. Its value is perhaps most evident in epideictic or demonstrative oratory, since the main purpose of such orations is to commend or criticise. This point had originally been made by Aristotle, who examines the technique in the course of discussing the category of epideictic speech in book I of *The Art of Rhetoric*, giving a number of examples later adopted by almost everyone. A rude or angry person can be redescribed as frank and open, an arrogant person as magnificent and dignified, a reckless person as courageous, a prodigal person as exhibiting exceptional liberality.[51] Cicero observes in *De partitione oratoria* that this method of redescribing actions is at its most effective in eulogies,[52] while Quintilian in his analysis of panegyrics in book III not only refers us back to Aristotle's discussion but repeats a number of his

48 Quintilian 1920–2, VI.IV.1, vol. III, p. 262: 'Prima est igitur amplificandi vel minuendi species in ipso rei nomine.'

49 Quintilian 1920–2, VIII.IV.1, vol. III, p. 262: 'ut cum eum, qui sit caesus, *occisum*, eum, qui sit improbus, *latronem*, contraque eum, qui pulsavit, *attigisse*, qui vulneravit, *laesisse* dicimus'.

50 Quintilian 1920–2, VIII.IV.2, vol. III, p. 262: 'Hoc genus [amplificationis] increscit ac fit manifestius, si ampliora verba cum ipsis nominibus, pro quibus ea posituri sumus, conferantur: ut Cicero in Verrem, *Non enim furem sed ereptorem, non adulterum sed expugnatorem pudicitiae, non sacrilegum sed hostem sacrorum religionumque, non sicarium sed crudelissimum carnificem civium sociorumque in vestram iudicium adduximus*.'

51 Aristotle 1926, I.IX. 28–9, p. 96.

52 Cicero 1942b, XXIII.82, p. 370.

examples. If we are trying to praise someone, we can hope 'to call them courageous rather than reckless, liberal rather than prodigal, careful rather than avaricious', while in pronouncing a vituperation 'we can use the same means to opposite ends'.[53]

The same device is held to be no less valuable in the genus of deliberative speech. Quintilian initially turns to this topic in book III, chapter 8, where he notes that, in deliberating over which of various possible actions may be the most honourable and expedient, it is usual to employ this technique to modify the names of things. But he also notes that the same method can equally well be employed against us. 'For that which we call honourable our opponents may succeed in calling vain, ambitious and insensible.'[54] The *Ad Herennium* lays even greater emphasis on the value of such redescriptions in deliberative speech. When we advise or deliberate, we are normally trying to show that a proposed course of action is *honestus* and can at the same time be expected to bring security. But to speak of an action as *honestus* is to claim that it embodies one or other of the cardinal virtues. It follows that, in order to gain a hearing for our side, and to undermine our opponents at the same time, we must try to show that the actions they consider honourable deserve to be seen in a different moral light:

> What the person speaking against us designates as justice we shall prove to be cowardice, and a lazy and corrupt form of liberality; what he calls prudence we shall speak of as foolish, indiscreet and offensive cleverness; what he speaks of as temperance we shall speak of as lazy and dissolute negligence; what he names courage we shall call the heedless temerity of a gladiator.[55]

By means of such redescriptions we can hope to discredit whatever policies are being advocated.

Quintilian also stresses that such redescriptions are of equal value in the third genus of rhetorical utterance, the *genus iudiciale*. He pays particular attention to this aspect of forensic oratory when addressing the topic of refutations in book v. It is always important in a court of law to consider how exactly the prosecution has spoken. If our opponent has argued with little vehemence, it may be best to speak in similar terms when turning to

53 Quintilian 1920–2, III.VII.25, vol. I, p. 476: 'ut pro temerario fortem, pro prodigo liberalem, pro avaro parcum vocemus; quae eadem etiam contra valent'.

54 Quintilian 1920–2, III.VIII.32, vol. I, p. 494: 'quod nos honestum, illi vanum, ambitiosum, stolidum ... vocant'.

55 *Ad C. Herennium* 1954, III.III.6, pp. 166–8: 'is qui contra dicet iustitiam vocabit, nos demonstrabimus ignaviam esse et inertiam ac pravam liberalitatem; quam prudentiam appellarit, ineptam et garrulam et odiosam scientiam esse dicemus; quam ille modestiam dicet esse, eam nos inertiam et dissolutam neglegentiam esse dicemus; quam ille fortitudinem nominarit, eam nos gladiatoriam et inconsideratam appellabimus temeritatem'.

the attack. But if he has used bitter and violent words, 'what we must do is to restate the case in more mitigating terms'.[56] For example, 'we can say in defence of someone of whom it has been claimed that he is promiscuous that "*it has been objected that his manner of living is a little too liberal*", and in the same way we can hope to redescribe an avaricious person as thrifty and a slanderer as someone who talks somewhat freely'.[57]

The Tudor rhetoricians generally present their discussions of this technique in the form of close paraphrases of Quintilian's account. Richard Sherry refers us directly to Quintilian's examples when examining, under the heading of 'Diminution', the process by which 'greate matters are made lyghte of by wordes, as when he was wel beaten by a knave, that knave wyll saye he dyd but a lytle stryke hym'.[58] Later he quotes (though without acknowledgment) the entire opening of Quintilian's section on *amplificatio*:

> The first way of increasyng or diminishing is by chaungynge the worde of the thynge, when in encreasyng we use a more cruell worde, and a softer in diminyshynge, as when we call an evyll man a thiefe, and saye he hathe kylled us, when he hathe beaten us. And it is more vehemente if by correccion we compare greater wordes wyth those that we put before, as: Thou haste broughte not a thyefe, but an extortioner, not an adulterer but a ravysher, etc.[59]

Like Quintilian, Sherry thinks that the best effects require a combination of word substitution with the figure of climax.

Thomas Wilson follows Quintilian even more closely – as well as using some of Aristotle's examples – in discussing the topic of redescription in *The Arte of Rhetorique*. He begins by observing that 'the firste kinde of Amplification is when by chaunging a woorde, in augmentynge we use a greater, but in diminishynge we use a lesse'.[60] Among the examples he gives of augmentation, he suggests that we 'call a naughtye felowe thiefe or hangemanne', or 'call one that is troubled with choler, and often angrye, a madde manne', or 'a pleasant gentilman a raylynge iester', or 'a covetous man a devill'. Among his examples of how to use the same device in extenuation, he suggests calling 'him that is a cruell or mercilesse man somewhat soore in iudgement', or 'a naturall foole a playne symple man', or 'a notable flatterer a fayre spoken man, a glutton a good felowe at hys

56 Quintilian 1920–2, V.XIII.25, vol. II, p. 326: 'eandem rem nostris verbis mitioribus proferamus'.

57 Quintilian 1920–2, V.XIII.26, vol. II, p. 326: 'et protinus cum quadam defensione, ut, si pro luxurioso dicendum sit, *Obiecta est paulo liberalior vita.* Sic et pro sordido parcum, pro maledico liberum dicere licebit.'

58 Sherry 1961, p. 61.

59 Sherry 1961, pp. 70–1.

60 Wilson 1554, fo. 66^{v}. Cf. fo. 69^{r}.

table, a spende all a liberall gentilman, a snudge or pynche penye a good husbande, a thriftye man'.[61]

After these pioneering discussions in the early 1550s, we find the same arguments and examples widely taken up.[62] When Henry Peacham, for example, published the first edition of his *Garden of Eloquence* in 1577, he included a long list of 'extenuating' redescriptions by way of illustrating how we can hope to 'excuse our own vices, or other mens whom we doe defend':

> Call him that is craftye, wyse; a covetous man, a good husband; murder, a manly deede; deepe dissimulation, singuler wisedome; pryde, cleanlynesse; covetousnesse, a worldly or necessarye carefulnesse; whoredome, youthful delight & dalyance; idolatry, pure religion; glotony and dronkennesse, good fellowship; cruelty, severity.[63]

Peacham's list obviously owes a good deal to Wilson's reading of Quintilian, but it includes one additional item worth underlining, if only because it can hardly fail to catch the eye of any reader of Shakespeare: the suggestion that someone might attempt to excuse an act of murder by redescribing it as a manly deed. 'When you durst do it, then you were a man' is the redescription Lady Macbeth offers Macbeth in her speech encouraging him to kill Duncan.[64]

Although it was widely agreed that this method of redescription was of immense rhetorical significance, there was some disagreement as to how it should be named and classified.[65] Aristotle's original suggestion in book III of the *Rhetoric* had been that, when we augment or diminish an action by redescribing it – as in excusing a crime by calling it a mistake – we should think of ourselves as employing a species of metaphor.[66] He was thus inclined to treat the device as one of the tropes of speech. But this was not a proposal that found much favour with the Roman theorists of eloquence. When Quintilian addresses the same question in book VIII, he first suggests that the technique of substituting *res pro re* should be regarded neither as a figure nor a trope, but rather as a distinct method of amplification.[67] He later observes, however, that 'when an act of temerity is called *courage*, or when luxury is called *liberality*, some writers want to say that these are

61 Wilson 1554, fos. 66^{v}, 67^{r}. Cf. Ascham 1970b, pp. 206–7.

62 For European discussions see Cox 1989.

63 Peacham 1971, sig. N, iiii^{v}.

64 Shakespeare 1988, *Macbeth*, I.vii.49, p. 981. Cf. Burton 1989, p. 47 and note.

65 The resulting confusions persist in modern scholarship. See for example Sonnino 1968, pp. 79–80, focusing solely, and misleadingly, on Hoskins. My own initial discussion (Skinner 1991) owed a debt both to Whigham 1984 and Cox 1989, and has since been interestingly developed in Condren 1994, esp. pp. 78–84.

66 Aristotle 1926, III.II.9–10, pp. 354–6.

67 Quintilian 1920–2, VIII.IV.1–14, vol. III, pp. 262–70.

instances of catachresis', as a result of which they classify the device as one of the tropes.[68] But he explicitly adds that he dissents from this judgment, since it is only proper to speak of catachresis when we adapt a neighbouring term to describe something for which no term exists at all.[69] Quintilian's own final suggestion – although he puts it forward with some hesitation[70] – is accordingly that the device ought probably to be grouped among the *schemata* or figures of speech. He adds that those who have argued for this classification have generally agreed 'that the name to be given to the figure in use when you call someone wise rather than astute, or courageous rather than overconfident, or careful instead of avaricious is παραδιαστολή',[71] a term he renders into Latin as *distinctio* and defines as 'the figure by means of which similar things are distinguished from each other'.[72]

When Quintilian speaks of those who have already used this term to define the technique of substituting *res pro re*, he may have been thinking of his elder contemporary P. Rutilius Lupus, who had published a treatise entitled *De figuris sententiarum et elocutionis* in about the year AD 20. Rutilius' *De figuris* is the earliest surviving example of a rhetorical genre that became very popular in the Renaissance, a genre in which the entire discussion centres on the topic of *elocutio*, and more specifically on the figures and tropes of speech. Rutilius' text as it has come down to us consists of forty-one sections arranged in two books. Each section is devoted to one of the figures, the names of which are given in transliteration from the Greek together with brief definitions and a number of illustrations in each case. Book I, section 4, is headed 'Paradiastole'. This *schema* can be defined, Rutilius says, as 'that which separates two or more things which may appear to have the same force, and teaches us how far they are distinct from each other'.[73] He adds a number of examples, most of which were subsequently repeated by Quintilian almost word for word. It is an instance of paradiastole, Rutilius explains, when you attempt to show 'that you should be recognised as wise rather than astute, or

68 Quintilian 1920–2, VIII.VI.36, vol. III, p. 320: 'Illa quoque quidam catachresis volunt esse, cum pro temeritate *virtus* aut pro luxuria *liberalitas* dicitur.'

69 Quintilian 1920–2, VIII.VI.34, vol. III, p. 320. For an excellent analysis of Quintilian's discussion see Parker 1990.

70 See Quintilian 1920–2, IX.III.65, vol. III, p. 482: 'an figura sit dubito'.

71 Quintilian 1920–2, IX.III.65, vol. III, p. 482: 'cui dant nomen παραδιαστολή ... Cum te pro astuto sapientem appelles, pro confidente fortem, pro illiberali diligentem.' For a discussion of paradiastole as a *figura*, with many helpful illustrations, see Kowalski 1928.

72 See Quintilian 1920–2, IX.III.65, vol. III, p. 482 on *distinctio*, 'qua similia discernuntur'.

73 Rutilius Lupus 1970, I.4: 'Hoc schema duas aut plures res, quae videntur unam vim habere, disiungit et quantum distent docet.'

courageous rather than over-confident, or careful rather than avaricious in your family affairs, or severe rather than malevolent'.[74]

This final suggestion – that the technique should be classed as a *schema* and given the name *paradiastole* – eventually won by far the widest acceptance. This is not to say that Rutilius' analysis was universally accepted by later Roman writers on the rhetorical arts. Iulius Rufinianus, for example, whose glossary *De figuris sententiarum et elocutionis* appeared in the course of the fourth century, offers a strongly contrasting account.[75] To a large extent, however, Rutilius' understanding of the concept prevailed. This development appears to have been due in part to the influence of the late Roman rhetorical treatise entitled *Carmen de Figuris vel Schematibus*. The *Carmen*, whose author has never been identified, discusses some sixty figures of speech, the thirty-eighth of which is given in Greek as παραδιαστολή and in Latin as *subdistinctio*. We have an example of paradiastole, the *Carmen* adds, 'when someone who is insanely reckless is called courageous, or when a prodigal is called a good fellow, or when an infamous person is called illustrious'.[76] An even more important conduit for transmitting the same understanding of paradiastole appears to have been Isidore of Seville's *Etymologiarum sive originum Libri* XX, perhaps the most widely used encyclopaedia of late antiquity. Isidore opens his treatise with a survey of the liberal arts, devoting book I to grammar and book II to rhetoric and dialectic. His discussion of rhetoric includes a survey of the figures of speech, and among these he duly mentions the *schema* of paradiastole. He begins by putting forward a new definition, claiming that 'we have an instance of paradiastole whenever we have to grasp what we say by interpretation'.[77] But in turning to illustrate this somewhat vague claim he draws his examples almost verbatim – as he duly acknowledges – from Rutilius' account. 'It is a case of paradiastole', he maintains, 'when, as Rutilius Lupus says, book I section 4, you call yourself wise rather than cunning, or courageous rather than heedless, or careful rather than parsimonious.'[78]

The first Renaissance rhetorician to present a similar analysis appears to have been Antonio Mancinelli in his *Carmen de Figuris* of 1493. Mancinelli's impressive survey begins by describing a number of purely grammatical

74 Rutilius Lupus 1970, 1.4: 'te pro astuto sapientem intelligenti, pro confidente fortem, pro inliberali diligentem rei familiaris, pro malivolo severum'.

75 See Rufinianus 1533, fo. 31ʳ, and cf. Skinner 1991, p. 6.

76 *Carmen de Figuris* 1863, p. 67: 'Dum fortem, qui sit vaecors, comemque vocat se/ Quom sit prodigus, et clarum qui infamis habetur.'

77 Isidore 1911, vol. 1, 1.21.9, sig. H, 1ʳ: 'Paradiastole est, quotiens id, quod dicimus, interpretatione discernimus.'

78 Isidore 1911, vol. 1, 1.21.9, sig. H, 1ʳ: 'Paradiastole est ... (cf. Rutil. Lup. 1, 4): "cum te pro astuto sapientem appellas, pro inconsiderato fortem, pro inliberali diligentem".'

figurae, after which he turns to the *tropi* and finally the *schemata* or figures of speech. His discussion of paradiastole, which is placed almost at the end of the book, begins with a definition in verse, followed by a number of examples in prose. As Mancinelli acknowledges, the resulting analysis owes everything to Quintilian's account. 'According to the testimony of Quintilian in book IX', Mancinelli explains, 'it is an example of paradiastole when you call yourself wise rather than astute, or courageous rather than over-confident.' To which he adds that 'it is similarly an example if I should call a prodigal man generous, or a reckless man brave, and so forth'.[79]

This analysis was in turn taken up and developed by Johann Susenbrotus, who refers specifically to Mancinelli in his section on paradiastole in his *Epitome troporum ac schematorum* of 1535.[80] It is true that Susenbrotus introduces a potentially confusing complication into his argument. He appears at one stage to suggest that, 'whenever we elevate a vice by redescribing it with the name of a neighbouring virtue', we should think of ourselves as employing the *schema* not of paradiastole but rather of meiosis, the 'diminishing' figure of speech.[81] Susenbrotus accordingly treats it as a case of meiosis 'when we call a cruel man slightly severe, or an imprudent person ingenuous, or a flatterer an affable companion',[82] although he had earlier given the impression that such examples should be classed as instances of paradiastole.[83]

If we turn, however, to those English rhetoricians who made use of Susenbrotus' account, we find that they generally managed to distinguish meiosis from paradiastole, while acknowledging the similarities between the two figures at the same time. Henry Peacham in the first edition of his *Garden of Eloquence* accepts that paradiastole is 'nye kin' to meiosis, but treats the latter as referring to the general technique of using 'a lesse word for a greater, to make the matter much lesse then it is'. By contrast, he reserves the term paradiastole – in a clear allusion to Susenbrotus – for cases in which 'by a mannerly interpretation we doe excuse our own vices, or other mens whom we doe defend, by calling them virtues'.[84] George Puttenham subsequently distinguishes between the two figures in virtually

79 Mancinelli 1493, sig. H, 1ʳ: 'Paradiastole sit teste Fabio libro nono quum te pro astuto sapientem appellas, pro confidente fortem ... sic prodigum dicim liberalem temerarium fortem & similia.'

80 Susenbrotus 1562, p. 46.

81 See Susenbrotus 1562, p. 78, on diminutio or meiosis, which we employ 'quoties vitium nomine vicinae virtutis elevamus'.

82 Susenbrotus 1562, p. 78: 'cum crudelem appellamus paulo severiorem: imprudentem simpliciorem: adulatorem, comem sive affabilem'.

83 Susenbrotus 1562, p. 46.

84 Peacham 1971, sig. H, iiiᵛ.

identical terms. When we make use of 'wordes and sentences of extenuation or diminution', we are employing the figure of '*Meiosis*, or the Disabler'.[85] But when 'such moderation of words tend to flattery, or soothing or excusing, it is by the figure *Paradiastole*'.[86] Angel Day briskly summarises the entire discussion in the appendix to the 1592 edition of his *English Secretary*. He considers the figures of paradiastole and meiosis together at the end of his section on 'Schemes Syntaxicall',[87] and observes that, whereas meiosis refers in general to a 'maner of disabling', paradiastole is the appropriate term for describing those cases in which 'with a milde interpretation or speech we color others or our owne faultes, as when wee call a subtill person, *wise*, a bold fellow, *couragious*, a prodigall man, *liberall*: a man furious or rash, valiant: a Parasite, a companion: him that is proud, Magnanimous: and suchlike'.[88]

VIRTUE AND VICE AS NEIGHBOURS

As well as showing us how to amplify our arguments by substituting *res pro re*, the classical rhetoricians offered an overwhelmingly influential explanation of why it will always be possible to propose such redescriptions with some show of plausibility. The clue is alleged to lie in recognising that many of the virtues, and many of the terms we consequently employ to describe and appraise human behaviour, constitute a mean between two extremes of vice.

It was of course Aristotle in book II of the *Nicomachean Ethics* who first made the doctrine of the mean central to moral argument. Turning in chapter 6 to ask how virtue should be characterised, he replied that it represents a state neither of insufficiency nor of superfluity for the agent, and can therefore be described as a mean between two vices, one of deficiency and the other of excess.[89] In book I of *The Art of Rhetoric* he developed the doctrine into a bridge between his moral and rhetorical thought. His crucial suggestion is that, if virtue is a mean, the virtues and vices must stand in a certain relationship of proximity. As Hobbes was to put it in translating the *Rhetoric*, they may be said to 'confine upon' one another: like neighbouring countries, they may be said to share certain confines or boundaries.[90] It is true that this conclusion seems in tension

85 Puttenham 1970, pp. 219–20.
86 Puttenham 1970, p. 184.
87 Day 1592, pp. 86–91.
88 Day 1592, pp. 90–1.
89 Aristotle 1985, pp. 43–4 and 49.
90 Hobbes 1986, p. 53. Hobbes's Latin MS translation of the *Rhetoric* (Chatsworth: Hobbes MS D.1) reads (p. 24): 'Confinia virtutibus vitia'.

with Aristotle's claim in the *Ethics* that the extremes of any virtue will always be opposed and indeed contrary to each other.[91] But Aristotle also stressed that, because every good quality lies at an intermediate point, it will generally bear some resemblance to one or other of its extremes. To cite his own examples, intermediate and commendable states such as courage and generosity will sometimes appear more like rashness and wastefulness.[92]

This was the conclusion that Aristotle chose to underline in the *Rhetoric*, and this was the conclusion that his admirers among the Roman rhetoricians subsequently reiterated, usually stating it in the form of the claim that every good quality will be found to have a 'neighbouring' or 'bordering' vice. Cicero expresses the doctrine in just these terms when discussing the key concept of *honestas* in book II of *De inventione*. The dispositions to be avoided if we wish to act well 'are not only the contraries of the virtues, as courage is of cowardice and justice of injustice, but also those which appear close to virtues, and to border on them, even though they are in fact a very long way from them'.[93] For example, 'diffidence is the opposite of courage and for that reason is a vice, but audacity is not its opposite but is similar and close to it, but is nevertheless a vice. So too with the other virtues, each of which will be found to have a vice bordering upon it.'[94]

Quintilian later outlines a similar argument, illustrating it specifically from the art of oratory. The first juncture at which he notes 'that there is a certain neighbourly quality between a number of virtues and vices' is when considering the merits of untrained orators in book II. There he quotes (although without acknowledgment) three of Aristotle's examples: 'slander can pass for frankness, recklessness for courage, extravagance for copiousness'.[95] He repeats the suggestion when discussing *ornatus* in book VIII, observing that 'this is the department of rhetoric in which the virtues and the vices are most evidently neighbours of each other'.[96] He reverts to the idea when speaking about the imitation of suitable stylistic models in book

91 Aristotle 1985, p. 49.

92 Aristotle 1985, p. 50.

93 Cicero 1949a, II.LIV.165, p. 332: 'sunt non ea modo quae his contraria sunt, ut fortitudini ignavia et iustitiae iniustitia, verum etiam illa quae propinqua videntur et finitima esse, absunt autem longissime'.

94 Cicero 1949a, II.LIV.165, p. 332: 'fidentiae contrarium est diffidentia et ea re vitium est; audacia non contrarium sed appositum est ac propinquum et tamen vitium est. Sic uni cuique virtuti finitimum vitium reperietur.'

95 Quintilian 1920–2, II.XII.4, vol. I, p. 284: 'Est praeterea quaedam virtutum vitiorumque vicinae ... maledicus pro libero, temerarius pro forti, effusus pro copioso accipitur'.

96 Quintilian 1920–2, VIII.III.7, vol. III, p. 214: 'in hac maxime parte sint vicina virtutibus vitia'. See also VIII.III.58, vol. III, p. 242.

x, at which point he warns us against the danger 'of merely attaining those vices of style which are closest to the virtues, achieving inflation instead of grandeur, meagreness instead of concision, recklessness instead of boldness' and so forth.[97] Finally, in presenting his sketch of the perfect orator in book XII he refers directly to Aristotle's doctrine of the mean and its relevance to oratory, 'in which conscientiousness can all too easily be denounced as dullness, while fluency can be denounced as sheer recklessness'.[98]

The Roman moralists and historians frequently discuss the affinities between good and evil in similar terms. When Livy in book XXII describes the opposition to Fabius Maximus' tactics against Hannibal, he observes that it is always possible 'to fabricate vices that lie in the neighbourhood of a person's virtues'.[99] Seneca echoes these sentiments in letter CXX of his *Epistulae morales*, in which his theme is how we acquire our knowledge of the good. 'As you know', he remarks, 'there are various vices that border upon the virtues, so that there is some similarity to rectitude even in things that are abandoned and debased. The man of extravagance counterfeits the man of liberality, while negligence imitates good-nature and recklessness imitates courage.'[100]

Due in large part to the influence of these authorities, similar allusions to the proximity of good and evil recur with some frequency among the poets and moralists of Renaissance England.[101] The figure of the count in Thomas Hoby's translation of Castiglione assures us that for every virtue we can always expect to find a 'nexte vice'.[102] Philip Sidney in his *Defence of Poesie* speaks of the 'nearnesse' of evil to good,[103] while Francis Bacon draws on the same imagery in a number of different works. He first does so in his fragment of 1597, 'Of the colours of good and evil', in which he considers a number of rhetorical 'sophisms'.[104] The seventh states that

97 Quintilian 1920–2, X.II.16, vol. IV, p. 82: 'et proxima virtutibus vitia comprehendunt fiuntque pro grandibus tumidi, pressis exiles, fortibus temerarii'.

98 Quintilian 1920–2, XII.IX.14, vol. IV, p. 444: 'quorundam cura tarditatis, quorundam facilitas temeritatis crimine laboravit'.

99 Livy 1929, XXII.XII.11, pp. 242: 'adfingens vicina virtutibus vitia'.

100 Seneca 1917–25, epistola CXX, vol. III, pp. 384–6: 'Sunt enim, ut scias, virtutibus vitia confinia, et perditis quoque ac turpibus recti similitudo est; sic mentitur prodigus liberalem ... Imitatur neglegentia facilitatem, temeritas fortitudinem.'

101 The movement may perhaps be said to culminate in John Wilkins's 'scientific' attempt to tabulate the apparent affinities between moral virtues and vices with a view to preventing confusion between them. See Wilkins 1668, pp. 206–13, and cf. Shapiro 1983, Skinner 1994.

102 Castiglione 1994, p. 37.

103 Sidney 1923, p. 26.

104 It was when he republished this material in *De Augmentis* in 1623 that he called them sophisms. See Bacon 1857b, p. 674.

'what is in the neighbourhood of goodness is good; what is remote from good is evil'.[105] Bacon puts forward no fewer than three 'reprehensions' of this proposition, the third of which claims that, on the contrary, evil often 'approacheth to good'.[106] He later makes a similar claim in his essay 'Of praise', in which he argues that those actions which most readily win the plaudits of the multitude are not the virtues themselves but rather the 'shews' or 'appearances that are similar to the virtues'.[107]

With these contentions about the neighbourly relations between virtue and vice, the writers we are considering arrive at their explanation of why it will always be possible to employ the figure of paradiastole to arouse the deepest emotions of an audience. It is precisely because of these associations and affinities, they claim, that a clever orator can always hope to challenge the proffered description of an action or state of affairs with some show of plausibility. For he can always hope to go some way towards excusing or extenuating an evil action by imposing upon it the name of an adjoining virtue. Conversely, he can always hope to denigrate or depreciate a good action by imposing upon it the name of some bordering vice.

It is in Aristotle's *Art of Rhetoric* that this inference is first explicitly drawn. If there is always a vice resembling every alleged virtue, we may be able to claim that the resemblance is actually an identity, thereby praising what had previously been condemned or condemning what had previously been praised.[108] Cicero later speaks in similar vein in the *De partitione oratoria,* emphasising how careful we must be 'not to find ourselves deceived by those vices which appear to imitate virtue'.[109] He goes on to offer a number of examples:

> Cunning is able to imitate prudence, while insensibility imitates temperance, pride in attaining honours and superciliousness in looking down on them both imitate magnanimity, extravagance imitates liberality and audacity imitates courage.[110]

Quintilian points to the same crucial inference in book VIII of his *Institutio oratoria,* taking his illustrations once more from the art of rhetoric itself. When we add *ornatus* to our speech, it is all too easy 'for those who speak badly to impose on what they are doing the name of the virtues'. This is

105 Bacon 1859, p. 85: 'Quod bono vicinum, bonum; quod a bono remotum, malum.'
106 Bacon 1859, p. 86.
107 See Bacon 1972, p. 156 on 'shews, and *species virtutibus similes*'.
108 Aristotle 1926, I.IX.28–9, pp. 96–8.
109 Cicero 1942b, XXIII.81, p. 370: 'ne fallant ea nos vitia, quae virtutem videntur imitari'.
110 Cicero 1942b, XXIII.81, p. 370: 'Nam et prudentiam malitia et temperantiam immanitas in voluptatibus asperandis et magnitudinem animi superbia in nimis extollendis et despicientia in contemnendis honoribus et liberalitatem effusio et fortitudinem audacia imitatur.'

because the element of *ornatus* is the aspect of eloquence in which 'the vices are above all the neighbours of the virtues'.[111]

The Roman poets and moralists echo the same arguments, laying their main emphasis on the disconcerting ease with which it is possible to cloak or hide our vices under the mantle of goodness. Ovid in his *Ars amatoria* emphasises the capacity of evil 'to hide itself by its proximity to goodness',[112] while Seneca reflects on the same tendency in a number of different passages in his *Epistulae morales*. When speaking in letter XCII about our disposition to measure the standards of morality by our own natures, he laments the readiness with which we are able 'to impose the name of virtue upon our vices'.[113] When discussing the sophistries of rhetoric in letter XLV, he warns us of the need 'to stamp everything with identifying marks that cannot possibily be disputed',[114] since we shall otherwise find 'that vices creep up on us under the name of virtues, with temerity hiding under the title of courage and timidity winning acceptance as cautiousness'.[115] Harking back to these discussions, St Augustine complains in his *Confessions* that far too many of the vices are liable to deceive us by imitating the virtues: pride passes for high spirits, ignorance and foolishness cloak themselves with the names of simplicity and innocence, while extravagance is able to hide under the shade of liberality.[116]

The same metaphors of deceit and concealment recur with no less frequency among the moralists and rhetoricians of Renaissance England. Hoby's translation of Castiglione's *Cortegiano* observes how often we find ourselves 'coverynge a vyce with the name of the next vertue to it, and a vertue with the name of the nexte vice'.[117] Sidney in his *Defence of Poesie* offers to 'turne *Ovids* verse' by way of reminding us that good things can 'lye hid, in nearnesse of the evill'.[118] Bacon in his 'Colours of good and evil' turns Ovid back again, first observing that 'evil approacheth to good sometimes for concealment, sometimes for protection', and then quoting Ovid's line: 'vice often hides itself by its proximity to goodness'.[119] Henry

[111] Quintilian 1920–2, VIII.III.7, vol. III, p. 214: 'cum in hac maxime parte [sc. ornatus] sint vicina virtutibus vitia, etiam qui vitiis utuntur, virtutum tamen iis nomen imponat'.

[112] Ovid 1979, II, line 662: 'Et lateat vitium proximitate boni.'

[113] Seneca 1917–25, epistola XCII, vol. II, p. 462: 'et vitiis nostris nomen virtutis imponimus'.

[114] Seneca 1917–25, epistola XLV, vol. I, p. 294: 'His certas notas inprime.'

[115] Seneca 1917–25, epistola XLV, vol. I, p. 294: 'Vitia nobis sub virtutum nomine obrepunt, temeritas sub titulo fortitudinis latet . . . pro cauto timidus accipitur.'

[116] Augustine 1912, vol. I, pp. 84–6.

[117] Castiglione 1994, p. 37.

[118] Sidney 1923, p. 26.

[119] Bacon 1859, p. 86 (slightly misquoting): 'saepe latet vitium proximitate boni'. Cf. Bacon 1915, p. 121.

Crosse underlines the same point in discussing the cardinal virtue of fortitude in his *Vertues Common-wealth*. He notes that 'many hide themselves under the wings of this *Vertue*', offering as an example the increasing prevalence of reckless swashbucklers who offer duels on the faintest pretext.[120] Later he generalises the argument in his attack on the figure of 'the cold Christian', a character recognisable by the fact that he aims to 'hide great vices under a thin colour of *Vertue*'.[121]

Among these images, the most popular speak of the propensity of wickedness to mask itself behind a veil of virtue. Thomas Nashe in his *Anatomie of Absurditie* expresses the hope that, if Englishmen would only become 'halfe so much Italianated as they are', the vices would no longer find it so easy to 'maske under the visard of vertue'.[122] William Leighton in *Vertue Triumphant* refers specifically to a number of vices that seek to deceive us by presenting themselves under the guise of prudence:

Against this vertue there are opposit
Foure vices cover'd underneath a vaile:
Resembling in some sort true signes of merit;
But not abiding touch, their purpose faile.
  Yet do they strive, and worke, and labour still,
  With goodly shews to worke the course of ill.[123]

Sir Thomas Lodge invokes the same metaphor in the preface to his translations of Seneca's moral treatises.[124] The reason why a heathen like Seneca is able to offer instruction to Christians – who ought to be ashamed of themselves – is that nowadays we perceive virtue 'but in a shadow, which serves for a vaile to cover many vices'.[125] Following up the implications of the imagery, Joseph Hall demands in his *Characters* that the veil be lifted to uncover the naked truth. 'Vertue is not loved enough, because shee is not seene; and Vice loseth much detestation, because her uglinesse is secret.'[126] Both should be 'strip't naked to the open view, and despoiled, one of her rags, the other of her ornaments, and nothing left them but bare pretence to plead for affection'.[127]

The poetry of the period reflects an even deeper preoccupation with the power of evil to cloak and disguise itself by taking refuge behind a mask of

120 Crosse 1603, sig. C, 1^{v}.
121 Crosse 1603, sig. H, 2^{v}.
122 Nashe 1958, p. 10.
123 Leighton 1603, sig. C, 8^{r}.
124 On Lodge see Salmon 1989, pp. 199–200.
125 Seneca 1614, sig. XX, 1^{r}.
126 Hall 1608, 'The Prooeme', p. 1.
127 Hall 1608, 'The Prooeme', pp. 2–3. On the pervasiveness of sexual metaphors (especially those concerned with uncovering to the gaze) in the moral and rhetorical texts of this period see Parker 1987, esp. pp. 127–32.

goodness. One of the earliest English poets to meditate on this theme was Sir Thomas Wyatt in the version he made in 1536 of Luigi Alammani's satire on court life.[128] Wyatt first mentions the familiar objection that courtiers are obliged to learn a number of hypocritical arts:

> Praise him for counsel that is drunk of ale;
> Grin when he laugheth that beareth all the sway,
> Frown when he frowneth and groan when he is pale,
> On other's lust to hang both night and day.[129]

Wyatt is not merely concerned to repudiate these talents; he is even more anxious to disclaim what he takes to be the more disquieting ability to redescribe the vices as virtues:

> None of these points would ever frame in me.
> My wit is naught. I cannot learn the way.
> And much the less of things that greater be,
> That asken help of colours of device
> To join the mean with each extremity:
> With the nearest virtue to cloak away the vice.[130]

The rhetorical technique Wyatt wishes to disavow is the one the rhetoricians had taken to follow from the Aristotelian doctrine of the mean.[131] Since there will always be a virtue resembling whatever vice we stand accused of, we can always hope to 'cloak away' the accusation by collapsing the distinction between the mean and its extremity.

The opening books of Edmund Spenser's *Faerie Queene* convey a similar sense of anxiety about the implications of Aristotle's argument. If virtue is a mean – as Spenser accepts[132] – then wickedness can always hope to present itself as goodness by claiming not to be the excess of a related virtue but rather to be that virtue itself. By such methods the false Duessa (who is 'double') manages to deceive the holy knight in book I, appearing to him in the form of Fidessa, a figure of true faith. Spenser ponders the difficulty of distinguishing the vices when they imitate the virtues so skilfully:

> What man so wise, what earthly wit so ware,
> As to descry the crafty cunning traine,
> By which deceipt doth maske in visour faire,
> And cast her colours dyed deepe in graine,

128 For Alammani, and a reprinting of the poem used by Wyatt, see Mason 1986, pp. 260–3. On Wyatt as courtier see Southall 1964, esp. chapter 6, pp. 67–77; Greenblatt 1980, esp. pp. 136–46. On poetry and courtliness see also Javitch 1978.

129 Wyatt 1978, p. 187, lines 52–5.

130 Wyatt 1978, p. 187, lines 56–60. For a discussion see Whigham 1984, p. 204.

131 On Wyatt and rhetoric see Hannen 1974. For helpful commentary on this part of Wyatt's poem see Mason 1986, pp. 283–9.

132 See *The Faerie Queene*, book II, canto II, in Spenser 1970, p. 76.

To seeme like Truth, whose shape she well can faine,
And fitting gestures to her purpose frame,
The guiltlesse man with guile to entertaine?
Great maistresse of her art was that false Dame,
The false *Duessa*, cloked with *Fidessaes* name.[133]

Alluding to the classical conception of a mask as a *persona*, Spenser implies that the deepest deceit consists of masking the vices so convincingly that virtue is actually impersonated.[134]

Of all the poets of this period, it is Shakespeare who alludes most frequently to the ease with which it is possible to clothe or disguise our vices as virtues. This is the approach Luciana recommends in *The Comedy of Errors* to the bewildered Antipholus at the moment when, supposing him to be her sister's husband, she upbraids him for his seeming coldness:

Muffle your false love with some show of blindness.
Let not my sister read it in your eye.
Be not thy tongue thy own shame's orator.
Look sweet, speak fair, become disloyalty;
Apparel vice like virtue's harbinger.[135]

Luciana expects Antipholus to acknowledge that the resemblances between virtue and vice are such that it will always be possible to put on a good 'show'.

By contrast, it is precisely the ability of evil to deceive us by appearing under the guise of good that perplexes Bassanio in the scene from *The Merchant of Venice* in which he confronts the three caskets and tries to choose between them. One is made of gold, one of silver and one of lead, and in one of them lies the portrait of Portia, the key to his happiness. Turning first to the golden casket, Bassanio decides to reject it:

So may the outward shows be least themselves.
The world is still deceived with ornament.
In law, what plea so tainted and corrupt
But, being seasoned with a gracious voice,
Obscures the show of evil? In religion,
What damnd error but some sober brow
Will bless it and approve it with a text,
Hiding the grossness with fair ornament?
There is no vice so simple but assumes
Some mark of virtue on his outward parts.[136]

133 Spenser 1970, I.VII.I, p. 34.
134 See Whitaker 1972, esp. pp. 103–4, 107–8.
135 Shakespeare 1988, *The Comedy of Errors*, III.ii.8–12, p. 266.
136 Shakespeare 1988, *The Merchant of Venice*, III.ii.73–82, p. 439.

By recalling the potentially deceiving character of rhetorical ornament, Bassanio is able to decide that the most ornamental of the three caskets is the one that ought most decisively to be set aside. The entire scene amounts to a meditation on the figure of paradiastole.

DISPARAGING VIRTUE AND EXCUSING VICE

When the classical rhetoricians consider the uses of paradiastolic redescription, they generally emphasise its value as a means of mitigation, a means of augmenting what can be said in favour of some particular action or of diminishing what can be said against it. This is certainly Aristotle's principal concern in *The Art of Rhetoric*. As we have seen, he is chiefly preoccupied with how we can hope to palliate or justify behaviour that may have been denounced as rude, arrogant, reckless, extravagant or in some other way blameworthy.[137] As Quintilian's examples suggest, he too is mainly interested in the technique as a method of extenuation or excuse. In book II he considers how one might hope to redescribe an action condemned as abusive, reckless or extravagant in such a way as to defend it; in book IV he similarly considers how one might hope to vindicate an action previously stigmatised as luxurious, avaricious or negligent.[138]

The same emphasis recurs among the moralists and historians of Greece and Rome. An early and extremely influential example can be found in book III of Thucydides' *History*, at the point where he describes the quarrels that arose in many of the Greek cities in the early years of the Peloponnesian war over the question of whether to support the Spartan or Athenian cause. For an English version of the passage in question, we can hardly do better than turn to the translation of Thucydides' *History* published by Hobbes in 1629. This contains an unsurpassable rendering of the section in which Thucydides explains how, with the spread of these seditions, many serious political shortcomings were exonerated. 'For inconsiderate boldness was counted true-hearted manliness', while 'a furious suddenness was reputed a point of valour'. As a result, 'he that was fierce, was always trusty; and he that contraried such a one was suspected'.[139]

There are fascinating echoes of this passage in a number of later attacks on the Athenian democracy. Plato speaks in remarkably similar vein in the passage from book VIII of the *Republic* in which he describes how the soul adjusts itself from an oligarchic to a democratic form of life. One symptom

137 Aristotle 1926, I.IX.28–9, pp. 96–8.
138 Quintilian 1920–2, II.XII.4, vol. I, p. 284, and IV.II.7, vol. II, pp. 90–2.
139 Hobbes 1975a, p. 222.

of this psychological decline is that many of the vices are redescribed and exculpated. The insolent begin to congratulate themselves on their good breeding, the licentious on their enjoyment of liberty, while the shameless pass off their conduct as true manliness.[140] Isocrates in his lament for the decay of Athenian democracy in the *Areopagiticus*[141] mounts a similar criticism. By contrast with the democracy under Solon and Cleisthenes, citizens are nowadays trained in such a way as to think of lawlessness as liberty, of insolence as truly democratic behaviour and of impudent speech as an indication of their concern for civic equality.[142]

We encounter the same emphasis yet again among the historians of Rome. The earliest to refer to the technique of paradiastolic redescription is Sallust in his *Bellum Catilinae*, who treats the device entirely as a method of extenuation and excuse. His main illustration occurs in the passage describing the debate in the Senate following the first discovery of Catiline's plot. Most speakers concentrated on what should be done with those already arrested, but Marcus Cato called for strong measures to forestall any further extortion or violence. Cato is represented as conceding that 'at this point someone is sure to call instead for mildness and clemency'.[143] But such a response, he is made to retort, will simply be an instance of the extent to which 'we have already lost the true names of things, such that the squandering of other people's goods is nowadays called liberality, while audacity in wrong-doing is called courage'.[144]

Pliny the younger, who studied under Quintilian, similarly alludes to the technique in the course of describing the return to good government following the tyranny of Domitian. He feels constrained to begin his 'vote of thanks' by emphasising that his panegyric on Trajan is sincerely meant, and not intended merely as a device for excusing neighbouring vices:

> There is no danger that in my references to his humanity he will see a reproach for arrogance; that he will suppose I mean extravagance by modest expenditure, and cruelty by forbearance; that I think him covetous and capricious when I call him generous and kind; profligate and idle instead of self-controlled and active, or that I judge him a coward when I speak of him as a brave man.[145]

140 Plato 1930–5, VIII.XIII.560, vol. II, pp. 296–8.

141 On which see Vickers 1989, pp. 9–11 and 149–59.

142 Isocrates 1929a, 20, pp. 114–16. Cf. the translation by Vives in Isocrates 1538, p. 280: 'non obtemperare legibus, libertatem: pro cacitatem linguae effrenem, aequalitatem legum: & horum omnium flagitiorum impunitam licentiam, felicitatem esse arbitrarentur'.

143 Sallust 1921a, LII.11, p. 102: 'Hic mihi quisquam mansuetudinem et misericordiam nominat.'

144 Sallust 1921a, LII.11, p. 102: 'Iam pridem equidem nos vera vocabula rerum amisimus. Quia bona aliena largiri liberalitas, malarum rerum audacia fortitudo vocatur, eo res publica in extremo sita est.'

145 Pliny 1969, 3.4, vol. II, p. 328. I have used the translation given at p. 329.

The reason for his confidence, Pliny ends by declaring, is that Trajan is someone 'whose virtues are not in fact lessened by bordering on any vices'.[146]

Of all the Roman historians, it is Tacitus who lays the strongest emphasis on paradiastolic redescription as a means of excusing vice, and with the publication of Henry Savile's translation of the *Histories* in 1591 his discussion became widely known to English readers.[147] There are three closely connected episodes in the *Histories* in which, with a characteristic shrug, Tacitus points to the technique of rhetorical redescription in play.[148] The first is in Otho's speech to the army attempting to rouse them against Galba. As Savile's rendering puts it, 'those things which other men account haynous faults, he tearmes them gentle remedies: cruelty he clokes with the name of severity; and wretched covetousnes he tearmeth provident sparing'.[149] Tacitus again refers to the technique when recounting the death of Galba shortly afterwards. 'By all men's opinions', as he puts it, Galba would have been judged 'capable of Empire, had he never bene Emperour'. Nevertheless, 'his honourable birth and the dangerous times covered the matter, entitling that wisdome, which in truth was but slouth'.[150] Finally, Tacitus speaks in similar terms when recording the ignominious end of Vitellius, Galba's immediate successor on the throne. Of this emperor, whom Tacitus views with unmitigated contempt, he first observes that 'without measure or judgement' he not only gave away his own property but 'lasht out other mens' at the same time. But in spite of this, Tacitus concludes in a formula strikingly reminiscent of Sallust, 'his favourers termed it curtesy and goodness', thereby 'construing vices for vertues'.[151]

Due in large measure to the influence of these discussions, a number of Tudor rhetoricians were led to conclude that the figure of paradiastole can actually be *defined* as a method of excusing the vices by redescribing them as virtues.[152] The crucial intermediary in this development appears to

146 Pliny 1969, 4.5, vol. II, p. 330: 'cuius virtutes nullo vitiorum confinio laederentur'.

147 On the European growth of interest in Tacitus see Burke 1969a, Schellhase 1976, Tuck 1993, pp. 39–45. For the origins of Tacitism in England see Salmon 1989, pp. 209–10, Womersley 1991. On the use of Tacitist ideas see Salmon 1989, Tuck 1993, pp. 104–19. On the reaction against Tacitism see Bradford 1983. On Savile's translation see Smuts 1994, esp. pp. 25–30.

148 There is also the moment in *Agricola* when, in Savile's translation, Tacitus speaks of those who 'when all is waste as a wildernesse, that they call peace'. See Tacitus 1591, p. 255. Tacitus' epigram ('ubi solitudinem faciunt, pacem appellant') is recalled by Burton when discussing rhetorical redescription. See Burton 1989, p. 45.

149 Tacitus 1591, p. 22.

150 Tacitus 1591, p. 28.

151 Tacitus 1591, p. 30.

152 The misunderstanding carried over into the definition of paradiastole in the *OED*. See Skinner 1991, p. 15, note 76.

have been Johann Susenbrotus in his *Epitome troporum ac schematorum* of 1535. Susenbrotus offers an unusually full analysis of the technique, in the course of which he declares that 'it is a case of paradiastole whenever, by means of a courteous interpretation, we give a favourable representation either to our own vices or to the vices of others by speaking of them in a flattering style'.[153] He adds a wide range of examples, mainly taken from the obvious classical sources, all of which corroborate his understanding of the device as a method of extenuating faults. The *figura* is said to be in use 'whenever you call yourself wise rather than cunning, or courageous rather than over-confident, or careful rather than parsimonious'.[154] It is also in use 'when we say of a prodigal man that he is liberal, or of a man of sheer temerity that he is courageous', or 'when we say of a miser that he is merely frugal, or of a haughty man that he is magnanimous, or when we describe a sycophant as a companion, or a dependant as a friend'.[155] 'In brief', Susenbrotus concludes, it is a case of paradiastole 'whenever vices display themselves under the guise of virtue'.[156]

Susenbrotus' analysis was adopted by most English rhetoricians of the later sixteenth century. When Wilson discusses 'the first kinde of Amplification' – that of 'augmentynge' or 'diminishynge' the force of an utterance 'by chaunging a woorde' – he assumes that the aim of speaking in this way will always be to 'give vices the names of virtues'.[157] When Peacham first attempts to pin down the figure of paradiastole in the 1577 edition of his *Garden of Eloquence*, he defines it as the technique we employ when 'we do excuse our own vices, or other mens whom we doe defend, by calling them vertues'.[158] Puttenham similarly lays it down that the point of using the device is that of 'moderating and abating the force of the matter by craft, and for a pleasing purpose'.[159] He accordingly proposes that the figure should be renamed 'the *Curry-favell*'.[160] His image, drawn from the grooming of horses, doubly hints at the idea of smoothing over blemishes or faults. To 'curry' means to smooth or comb out,[161] while Fauvel was

153 Susenbrotus 1562, p. 46: 'Paradiastole est cum civili interpretatione nostris aut aliorum vitiis assentando blandimur.'

154 Susenbrotus 1562, p. 46: 'Ut cum pro astuto sapientem appellas: pro confidente, fortem: pro illiberali, diligentem.'

155 Susenbrotus 1562, p. 46: 'cum item prodigum dicimus liberalem, temerarium fortem, avarum frugalem, fastidiosum magnanimum, adulatorem comem, assertorem amicum'.

156 Susenbrotus 1562, p. 46: 'Breviter, [paradiastole est] cum vitia sub virtutis specie sese ostendant.'

157 Wilson 1554, fos. 66^{v}–67^{r}.

158 Peacham 1971, sig. N, iiii^{v}.

159 Puttenham 1970, p. 185.

160 Puttenham 1970, p. 184.

161 Hence the expression *to curry favour*, which Hobbes uses on at least one occasion. See Hobbes 1840c, p. 416.

the name of the horse in Gervais de Bus's fourteenth-century poem, *Le roman de Fauvel*, whose initials spell out the vices of *Flatérie*, *Avarice*, *Vilanie*, *Variété*, *Envie* and *Lascheté*.[162]

Due no doubt to the weight of these theoretical pronouncements, the poets and moralists of Renaissance England largely concentrate on illustrating the power of moral redescriptions to mitigate and excuse. Wyatt even refers specifically to the flattering of Fauvel when listing the courtly wiles of those who 'join the mean with each extremity':

> As drunkenness good fellowship to call;
> The friendly foe with his double face
> Say he is gentle and courteous therewithal;
> And say that Favel hath a goodly grace
> In eloquence; and cruelty to name
> Zeal of justice and change in time and place.[163]

The count in Hoby's version of Castiglione's *Cortegiano* likewise assumes that, when someone tries to 'prayse or dysprayse accordynge to hys fansye', his purpose will normally be to excuse or justify, 'as in calling him that is sawcye, bold', or 'hym that is seelye, good', or 'him that is unhappye, wittie: and lykewyse in the reste'.[164] Castiglione implies that the use of such palliatives may be especially prevalent in Italy, a suggestion picked up by Hubert Languet: 'it is indeed due to Italian influence that nowadays we invert everything, giving the names of the virtues to the vices to such an extent that no one is ashamed to call stratagems, perfidy and cruelty by the names of prudence and magnanimity'.[165] Robert Burton speaks in similar vein when denouncing the abuses of the age at the start of *The Anatomy of Melancholy*. The public morality of our times is such that knavery is commonly redescribed as policy, while the private conduct of the rich is no better, their vaunted liberality being such that 'many times that word is mistaken', so that 'under the name of Bounty & Hospitality, is shrowded Riot and Prodigality'.[166]

It is obviously one-sided, however, to suppose that the technique of paradiastolic redescription can actually be *defined* – as Peacham claims – as an 'instrument of excuse'.[167] As Aristotle had originally made clear in the

162 Harman 1962, p. 121. Cf. Mason 1986, pp. 287–8.

163 Wyatt 1978, p. 188, lines 64–9.

164 Castiglione 1994, p. 37. But Castiglione also speaks of calling 'hym that is sober, drie', thereby acknowledging the possibility of using the technique to dispraise the virtues.

165 Languet 1633, letter XXXIII, pp. 103–4: 'Iam vero ex disciplina vestrae Italiae, invertimus omnia, & virtutum nomina vitiis indere [sic: *recte* induere] solemus, ita ut non pudeat, nos fraudes, perfidiam & crudelitatem, prudentiam & animi magnitudinem nominare.'

166 Burton 1989, pp. 97–8. See also Crosse 1603, sig. K, 1^r.

167 Peacham 1593, p. 169.

Rhetoric, there is no reason why the same technique should not be used to perform the opposite task of amplifying what can be said against a given course of action by depreciating its apparently virtuous qualities. To cite Aristotle's own example, it may be possible to denigrate the behaviour of a habitually cautious man by claiming that he is really a person of cold and designing temperament.[168] Hobbes's translation of the *Rhetoric* succinctly summarises the general point: the same device can equally well be employed to 'make the best of a thing' or else to 'make the worst of it'.[169]

Even before Aristotle proposed this analysis, a number of writers had already emphasised that moral redescriptions can equally well be used in disparagement. Thucydides in the famous passage on the civil wars in Greece observes that, in addition to excusing the vices, those fomenting sedition attempted to ensure that – as Hobbes's translation puts it – such virtues as modesty and provident deliberation were redescribed and denounced as 'the cloak of cowardice'.[170] Plato similarly maintains in book VIII of the *Republic* that the first stage in the degeneration of the human soul from its oligarchic to its democratic form is always signalled by an increased willingness to redescribe and belittle the virtues. Reverence comes to be viewed as folly, temperance as want of manhood, moderation in expenditure as sheer rusticity and meanness.[171]

Nor was this alternative possibility lost on the moralists and historians of ancient Rome. Seneca is chiefly concerned with excuses, but he also notes in letter XLV of his *Epistulae morales* that one of the ways in which 'we embrace evil things in place of good' is by decrying the virtues.[172] The illustration he offers – an apparent allusion to Thucydides – is that 'moderation can be redescribed as cowardice'.[173] A similar example – which Seneca may also have had in mind – had already been given by Livy in the passage explaining how we can hope 'to fabricate vices that lie in the neighbourhood of a person's virtues'. As we have seen, Livy had illustrated this contention from the behaviour of Fabius Maximus' subordinates at the time of his delaying tactics in the face of Hannibal's advance on Rome. 'Fabius' master of horse', Livy reports, 'was more enraged even than Hannibal was by these prudent measures.'[174] Evidently an orator as well as a soldier, he sought to discredit his leader by

168 Aristotle 1926, I.IX.28, p. 96.
169 Hobbes 1986, p. 109.
170 Hobbes 1975a, p. 222.
171 Plato 1930–35, VIII.XIII.560, vol. II, p. 298.
172 Seneca 1917–25, epistola XLV, vol. I, p. 294: 'Pro bonis mala amplectimur'.
173 Seneca 1917–25, epistola XLV, vol. I, p. 294: 'moderatio vocatur ignavia'.
174 Livy 1929, XXII.XII.12, p. 240: 'Sed non Hannibalem magis infestum tam sanis consiliis habebat quam magistrum equitum.'

offering a paradiastolic redescription of Fabius' dogged refusal to join battle. As Livy puts it, 'fierce and hasty in his judgments, and with an ungovernable tongue, he spoke of his commander at first among a few, and then openly among the troops, not as a man of deliberation but simply as lacking in energy, and not as cautious but rather as timorous'.[175]

Despite the one-sided understanding of paradiastole adopted by so many Renaissance rhetoricians, a number of Tudor poets and moralists remained fully alive to this alternative possibility. This is certainly clear from Wyatt's satire on court life. Although he begins by speaking of those who attempt 'with the nearest virtue to cloak away the vice', he immediately goes on to refer to the contrasting rhetorical possibility:

And, as to purpose likewise it shall fall,
To press the virtue that it may not rise.[176]

Having mentioned both stratagems, Wyatt concludes by exemplifying each of them:

And he that suffereth offence without blame
  Call him pitiful, and him true and plain
  That raileth reckless to every man's shame;
Say he is rude that cannot lie and feign,
  The lecher a lover, and tyranny
  To be the right of a prince's reign.[177]

The courtier not only knows how to excuse princely excess; he also knows how to use the same device to sneer at honesty and magnanimity.

If we turn to the moralists of the next generation, we find an even stronger disposition to emphasise the power of paradiastole to disparage the virtues. Ben Jonson's friend William Drummond argues in one of his sonnets (in a manner reminiscent of Wyatt) that the art is a specifically courtly one:

O! how more sweete is Birds harmonious Moane,
Or the hoarse Sobbings of the widow'd Dove;
Than those smooth whisperings neere a Princes Throne,
Which Good make doubtfull, doe the evill approve?[178]

Robert Burton makes a similar claim when lamenting the abuses of his age in *The Anatomy of Melancholy*. Although he chiefly stresses the propensity to excuse wickedness, he begins by emphasising the contrasting corruption of

175 Livy 1929, XXII.XIII.12, pp. 240–2: 'Ferox rapidusque in consiliis ac lingua immodicus primo inter paucos, dein propalam in volgus pro cunctatore segnem pro cauto timidus.'
176 Wyatt 1978, p. 187, lines 62–3.
177 Wyatt 1978, p. 188, lines 70–5.
178 Drummond 1976, sonnet 22, p. 111. See also Fowler 1992, p. 215.

those by whom 'honesty is accounted folly'.[179] But perhaps the most striking examples can be found in Lyly's *Euphues*. Lyly frequently refers to the device of paradiastole, and invariably emphasises its use as a means of denigrating virtue. When he speaks in his own person at the outset of his story about 'those of sharpe capacitie', one of his criticisms is that, if anyone seeks to 'argue with them boldly, then he is impudent: if coldly, an innocent'.[180] When the figure of Euphues later addresses his 'cooling' oration to his friend Philautus and to 'all fond lovers', one of his complaints against women is that they are too ready to redescribe the finest manly qualities in such a way as to depreciate them. If a man 'be cleanelye, then terme they him proude; . . . if bolde, blunt; if shamefast, a cowarde'.[181]

This apparent change of direction in the discussion of paradiastole may perhaps be attributable in part to the influence of Philemon Holland's translation of Plutarch's *Moralia*, which he issued as *The Philosophie, commonlie called, The Morals* in 1603. Plutarch had spoken in his essay on 'How a man may discerne a flatterer from a friend' of two contrasting ways in which flatterers habitually wreak their mischief. Some attempt to excuse their patrons' vices by redescribing them as virtues. But others operate in a more direct and dangerous way:

> Other flatterers there be, who like as Painters to set up their colours and to give them more beautifull light and lustre unto them, lay neere unto them others that be more darke and shadowe: so they in blaming, reprooving, reproching, traducing & deriding the contrarie vertues to those vices which are in them whom they meane to flatter, covertly and underhand do praise and approove those faults and imperfections that they have.[182]

Plutarch adds a number of examples to show how this can lead to a direct attack on the virtues:

> They will speake basely of Temperance and Abstinence, calling it rusticitie: and as for those that live justly and with a good conscience, contenting themselves with their estate, and therin reposing suffisance, those they will nickname heartlesse, and base minded folke, altogether insufficient to do or dare any thing.[183]

These illustrations – especially the allusions to baseness and rusticity – are strongly reminiscent of the account Plato had given of the degeneration of the human soul with the coming of democracy, and it may well be that

179 Burton 1989, p. 51.
180 Lyly 1868, p. 46.
181 Lyly 1868, p. 115. I have adjusted the punctuation. Ironically (in view of his dislike of Lyly) this recalls Sidney's lament at the end of sonnet 31. See Sidney 1922, p. 255.
182 Plutarch 1603, p. 94.
183 Plutarch 1603, p. 94.

one of the effects of Holland's translation was to give wider currency to these examples.

The popularity of Holland's translation soon made a visible difference to discussions about the ambiguous relationship of virtue and vice. One of the earliest indications of its direct influence – and one of the most interesting from the point of view of my present argument – occurs in the brief treatise of 1611 entitled *A Discourse Against Flatterie.* This was at first published anonymously, but was entered in Jaggard's catalogue of recent books in 1618 as the work of '*William Cavendish*, Knight',[184] in whose service Thomas Hobbes had been acting as tutor and secretary since 1608. Cavendish subsequently incorporated a revised and abbreviated version of his *Discourse* into his book of essays, *Horae Subsecivae*, which he published in 1620,[185] but his original discussion is at once fuller and includes a number of striking examples that were later removed.[186]

Cavendish begins by making the familiar point that the flatterer frequently works by redescribing the vices as virtues:

> Wherfore it is very dangerous to beleeve a flatterer: for under the person of a sweete friend he is a most bitter enemy, who increases all vices & settles them in us, either by consent, approbation or extenuation: as calling anger severity; fury, zeale; rashnesse, boldness; pride, fortitude; pusillanimitie, humility; covetousnesse, parcimony, or the like.[187]

Cavendish next turns to examine the converse possibility. Speaking once more of the flatterer, he goes on:

> Honesty to him is nice singularity; Repentance, superstitious melancholy; gravity, dulnesse; and all vertues an innocent conceit of the base minded.[188]

These are fascinating examples. The suggestion that a virtuously grave person might be subject to mockery for mere dullness echoes one of the cases mentioned by Plato in book VIII of the *Republic.* The example was rarely taken up in the Renaissance, however, and even Cavendish deleted this passage when revising his *Discourse* for republication in 1620.[189] This makes it all the more intriguing that, when speaking of moral redescription in chapter IV of *Leviathan*, Hobbes was to recur to the example of one

184 Jaggard 1941, p. 169.
185 On Cavendish's authorship see chapter 6, notes 185–6, *infra.*
186 The 1620 version also omits some long quotations and verse translations from Martial and Terence.
187 [Cavendish] 1611, p. 36. Cavendish later adds (p. 54) that flattery makes us 'account vertue to be vice'. See also [Cavendish] 1620, p. 442.
188 [Cavendish] 1611, pp. 41–2.
189 Nor does this passage bear any resemblance – save for the closing reference to 'the base minded' – to Holland's version of Plutarch.

person calling '*gravity* what another *stupidity*',[190] after which it became one of the stock instances of paradiastolic speech.[191]

Cavendish is especially interested in the technique of paradiastolic redescription as a method of disparaging virtue. He reverts to the point at a later stage in his discourse on flattery, drawing closely on Plutarch in describing the subtlest of flatterers in precisely these terms:

> If a man bee given to any vices, they will not commend them, but approve them by discommending the contrary virtues, as calling temperance rusticity, and such as live within their estates misers.[192]

He returns to the same theme once more in 1620 in another of the essays published in his *Horae Subsecivae*, the essay entitled 'Of detraction'.[193] A willingness to belittle the virtues is said to be essential to the character of the detractor:

> The Detractor, to anie laudable atchievement, will be sure to finde out wrong causes, and to good things, wrong names; as if a man be liberall, hee is prodigall; if parsimonious, covetous; if magnificent, ambitious; if courteous, then hee is of a weake and servile spirit; if grave, then proud; if considerate in danger, then a Coward; if valorous, rash; if silent, cunning; if a discourser, then one that loves to heare himselfe talke.[194]

It is, in short, typical of the Detractor to speak in such a way that 'Virtue (to which he gives the name of the confining *Vice*) may the lesse appeare'.[195]

Besides the possible influence of Holland's version of Plutarch, we need to take note of a further and perhaps more likely explanation for the apparent shift of emphasis in English discussions of moral redescription towards the end of the sixteenth century. It may be significant that these were the years in which, as Gabriel Harvey noted, English readers first began 'to be prettely well acquayntid with a certayne parlous booke' by Niccolò Machiavelli entitled *Il principe*.[196] For Machiavelli's book is one in which the technique of rhetorical redescription is not only put to sensational use, but is used specifically as a means of depreciating and undermining the so-called 'princely' virtues of clemency and liberality.

Machiavelli first employs the device in his reconsideration of princely

190 Hobbes 1991, p. 31.
191 See for instance South 1823a, p. 130. The example recurs in *Tristram Shandy* (see Sterne 1967, p. 55) and *Vanity Fair* (see Thackeray 1968, p. 159).
192 [Cavendish] 1611, pp. 106–7. This discussion, taken from Plutarch, is expanded in *Horae Subsecivae*. See [Cavendish] 1620, pp. 495–6.
193 See [Cavendish] 1620, pp. 52–73.
194 [Cavendish] 1620, p. 54.
195 [Cavendish] 1620, p. 55.
196 Harvey 1884, p. 79.

liberality in chapter 16. He prefaces his discussion by conceding that liberality is undeniably one of the most laudable of the virtues; a ruler who is miserly will always be blamed.[197] But he then declares – taking up an example used by Sallust and Tacitus – that much of the conduct of those usually held to be liberal ought rather to be redescribed and condemned as mere ostentatiousness.[198] To which he adds – echoing Sallust still more closely – that those who strive to uphold a reputation for liberality will soon find themselves driven 'to do everything they can possibly do to gain money for themselves'.[199] With these redescriptions, Machiavelli paves the way for the central argument of his chapter: that princes ought not to worry so much about being described as miserly or parsimonious.

Machiavelli's next chapter questions the princely virtue of clemency in the same way. He begins by acknowledging that cruelty is of course a vice. 'Every prince ought to want to be regarded as merciful and not as cruel.'[200] But he insists that many of the actions usually celebrated as instances of clemency ought rather to be redescribed in far less favourable terms. The avoidance of cruelty for which the Florentines congratulated themselves when they refused to punish the leaders of the uprising at Pistoia ought really to be recognised as an instance of over-indulgence.[201] Likewise, the clemency for which Scipio Africanus became famous in his campaigns against Hannibal was really an example of laxity.[202] As before, Machiavelli's redescriptions pave the way for his main and even more challenging argument: 'a prince ought not to worry too much about acquiring a reputation for being a cruel man'.[203]

One writer who may have had Machiavelli in mind when reflecting on what he took to be the growing tendency to disparage the virtues was Stefano Guazzo, whose *Civile conversazione* of 1574 appeared in an English translation by George Pettie and Bartholomew Young in the early 1580s.[204] The figure of Guazzo in the dialogue registers the anxiety:

> At this day the malice of men is so great, that they spare not the honour of whosoever it bee, whether Prince or private person, and thinke sinisterly and preposterously of all the good deedes which are wrought: in such sorte that if you addict your selfe to

197 Machiavelli 1960, p. 65, acknowledges that the quality is 'laudibilissima'.

198 Machiavelli 1960, p. 66, refers to the 'suntuosità' of those 'tenuto liberale'.

199 Machiavelli 1960, p. 66: 'fare tutte quelle cose che si possono fare per avere danari'.

200 Machiavelli 1960, p. 68: 'ciascuno principe debbe desiderare di esser tenuto pietoso e non crudele'.

201 See Machiavelli 1960, p. 69, claiming that it was really a case of 'troppa pietà'.

202 See Machiavelli 1960, p. 71, claiming that it was really a case of a 'natura facile'.

203 Machiavelli 1960, p. 69: 'Debbe per tanto uno principe non si curare della infamia di crudele'.

204 See Lievsay 1961, pp. 54–77.

devotion, and the exercise of charitie, you are taken for an hypocrite; if you be affable and courteous, you shalbe called a flatterer.[205]

The irony to which Guazzo points is that the art of rhetoric, intended as the brightest ornament of human discourse, is undermining instead of enhancing the conversation of mankind.

Of all the moralists of this period, it is Innocent Gentillet who is most emphatic in blaming Machiavelli for popularising the use of paradiastolic redescriptions to disparage the virtues. Gentillet's attack on Machiavelli was originally published in 1576, and first appeared in English as *A Discourse ... against Nicholas Machiavell the Florentine* in 1602. Gentillet promises in his preface to uncover the tricks Machiavelli uses 'to give colour unto his most wicked and damnable doctrines',[206] and in analysing chapters 16 and 17 of *Il principe* he several times mentions Machiavelli's use of paradiastole to provide such colouring. Commenting on the critique of liberality, he points out 'how Machiavell delights to mock & play with the most excellent vertues among men'.[207] Turning to the chapter on clemency, he again stresses how Machiavelli manages 'to call things with contrarie names' by implying that the great and indispensable virtue of clemency is really a vice.[208] The effect, Gentillet concludes, is 'to praise that which is to be despised and detested, to follow that which is to be fled, to love that which is to be hated', and above all 'to bring into a confusion the distinction of good and evil'.[209]

REDESCRIPTION AND ITS DANGERS

There is an obvious risk of underestimating the importance of moral redescription if we think of it simply as a figure of speech. Even those rhetoricians who classified the technique of paradiastole as one of the *figurae sententiarum* generally recognised that something of far greater significance was at stake. The deep question raised by the prospect of endless debate over actions and their descriptions was whether any evaluative terms can ever be applied without ambiguity, and whether in consequence any moral arguments can ever be resolved.

It is true that most Renaissance rhetoricians, professionally attuned as they were to the ideal of arguing *in utramque partem*, appear to have viewed these questions with equanimity. George Puttenham speaks with evident pride of paradiastole as one of the most valuable devices available to us for

205 Guazzo 1925, I, p. 38.
206 [Gentillet] 1602, sig. A, ii^{v}.
207 [Gentillet] 1602, p. 275, discussing maxim 22, pp. 275–99.
208 [Gentillet] 1602, p. 215, discussing maxim 8, pp. 199–215.
209 [Gentillet] 1602, p. 215.

helping 'to excuse a fault', 'to make an offence seeme lesse then it is' and in consequence to 'make the best of a bad thing, or turne a signification to the more plausible sence'.[210] Richard Beacon writes even more fulsomely in his dialogue of 1594, *Solon his Follie*, especially in his chapters discussing the art of persuasion as a means of promoting the reformation of government. When he turns to this topic in detail in book II, in which he considers 'how to winne, moove and dispose the affections of the people',[211] one of the techniques he particularly recommends for facilitating reform and avoiding discontent is that of learning how to speak paradiastolically. Closely following the account given by Plutarch in his life of Solon, Beacon makes the figure of Epimenides in the dialogue congratulate Solon on his achievements as a lawgiver, while reminding Solon that one of his most effective methods of persuasion was that 'you clothed things bitter and unpleasant with pleasing names; calling taxes, contributions; garrisons, gardes; prisons, houses; and such like: by the which pollicie, you made even things odious pleasing and acceptable to the people, and easily thereby persuaded the embracing thereof'.[212]

The evident pride taken by the rhetoricians in their ability to question the ordinary language of morality eventually became a standing accusation against them. We encounter the reproach as late as Berkeley's dialogue of 1732, *Alciphron or the Minute Philosopher*. The figure of Lysicles opens the discussion by assuring his astonished listeners that 'it would be endless to trace and pursue every particular vice through its consequences and effects, and shew the vast advantage they all are of to the public'.[213] His interlocutor Euphranor responds that 'I should wonder if men were not shocked at notions of such a surprising nature, so contrary to all laws, education, and religion.'[214] Lysicles retorts that 'they would be shocked much more' if 'a certain polite way of speaking' had not been introduced, 'which lessens much of the abhorrence and prejudice towards vice'.[215] As he explains, 'in our dialect, a vicious man is a man of pleasure, a sharper is one that plays the whole game, a lady is said to have an affair, a gentleman to be a gallant, a rogue in business to be one that knows the world'.[216] The

210 Puttenham 1970, pp. 184–5.

211 Beacon 1594, pp. 29–31. Canny 1987, pp. 167–73, and Peltonen 1994, pp. 477–80, 483–6, discuss the 'Machiavellian' context. For a tabulation of Beacon's invocations of Machiavelli see Anglo 1990, pp. 162–4.

212 Beacon 1594, p. 32. Beacon is using North's translation, which tells us that Solon managed 'to make certen things pleasaunt, that be hatefull, finely conveying them under culler of pleasing names. As calling whores, lemans: taxes, contributions: garrisons, gardes: prisones, houses.' See Plutarch 1580, pp. 94–5.

213 Berkeley 1871, p. 62.

214 Berkeley 1871, p. 62.

215 Berkeley 1871, pp. 62–3.

216 Berkeley 1871, p. 63.

stress on sexual promiscuity is new, but the point remains the same: that the technique of rhetorical redescription can always be brought to bear, as Euphranor observes, to suggest that vice is 'a fine thing with an ugly name'.[217]

As Berkeley's irony suggests, however, there was a strong feeling among critics of the art of rhetoric that this was one of the points at which the equivocal nature of the relationship between truth and eloquence revealed itself most alarmingly. The danger was said to be that of opening up a world of complete moral arbitrariness, a world in which there might be no possibility of agreeing about the application of evaluative terms, and no possibility in consequence of avoiding a state of unending confusion and mutual hostility.

These misgivings were as old as the art of rhetoric itself. One of the earliest writers to speak in such terms was Euripides, whose contemporaries included Gorgias and other leading sophists of the rhetorical school. As Quintilian was later to observe, Euripides was more interested than any of the other ancient dramatists in the rhetorical arts, and above all in the art of presenting moral dilemmas in the form of 'statements and replies'.[218] This makes it all the more significant that the young Thomas Hobbes should have produced a Latin translation of Euripides' *Medea*,[219] a play in which the power of eloquence to excuse evil is scrutinised in a way that gave the story a special standing among English humanists of the Renaissance. Sir Thomas Smith, John Lyly, George Puttenham, Isabella Whitney and Robert Burton all make special mention of it,[220] but the greatest humanist before Hobbes to devote himself to Euripides' version was George Buchanan, whom Montaigne was not alone in placing among the finest Latin poets of the age.[221] Buchanan's verse translation, first performed and published in 1543,[222] is particularly interesting for its rendering of the passage in which Jason, with a conscious show of manly confidence, bids farewell to Medea after forsaking her for the daughter of King Kreon. Medea first replies – in a speech invoking the very rhetorical figure we have been examining – by challenging Jason to admit that his account of his own behaviour is self-deceived:

217 Berkeley 1871, p. 63.

218 See Quintilian 1920–2, X.I.68, vol. IV, p. 38, on Euripides and the method of 'dicendo ac respondendo'.

219 See chapter 1, note 67, *supra*.

220 Smith, *Dialogue*, CUL MS Gg-3-34, p. 69, describes how Jason 'dyd forsake Medea', thereby behaving 'most unkyndly'. See also Lyly 1868, pp. 77, 92; Puttenham 1970, pp. 183, 211–12; Whitney 1992, p. 188; Burton 1989, pp. 112–13.

221 For this judgment see Montaigne 1893, p. 339.

222 McFarlane 1981, pp. 91–2, 119–20.

It is not courage, it is not confidence
To look injured friends closely in the face.
Rather it is the gravest of all the diseases
By which mankind is afflicted, shamelessness.[223]

Jason seeks to exculpate himself by responding in a similarly rhetorical style, arguing that his conduct has been in the best interests of Medea and their children. But this in turn provokes Medea to a violent outburst against the deceiving character of eloquence itself:

How much I differ from what is commonly felt! . . .
For anyone who glories in his power
To adorn evil by his style of speech
Will never hold back from any wickedness,
And is empty of wisdom.[224]

It is the presumed connection between eloquence and wisdom, and above all the ability of rhetoricians to conceal evil under the guise of good, that Medea denounces with the greatest vehemence.

The moralists and historians of the next generation were to reflect with even deeper hostility on the power of oratory to excuse the vices and disparage the virtues. When Thucydides considers the technique of moral redescription in book III of the *History*, he not only associates this 'art of assailing', as he calls it, with sedition and war, but argues that it has the effect of undermining the very possibility of moral argument. As Hobbes's translation puts it, by these means 'the received value of names imposed for signification of things' is 'changed into arbitrary'.[225] Thucydides points to the terrible consequences that ensued for the cities of Greece: 'he that could outstrip another in the doing of an evil act, or could persuade another thereto that never meant it, was commended'.[226]

It was within the circle of Socrates, however, that the most passionate attacks were mounted on the art of rhetoric, and especially on the

223 Euripides, *Medea*, 1715, II, p. 198, col. I:
NON fortitudo est ista, non fiducia,
Laesos amicos contueri cominus:
Sed morbus unus omnium gravissimus
Additus hominibus, impudentia.

224 Euripides, *Medea*, 1715, II, p. 199, col. I:
Quam nostra vulgo dissidet sententia! . . .
Nam quae iniqua comere
Se gloriatur lingua, non maleficio
Ullo abstinebit, ac vacua sapientiae est.

225 Hobbes 1975a, p. 222. As Hobbes rightly observes – by contrast with many recent translators – Thucydides' point is about the *value* of words, not their *meaning*. On this point cf. Wilson 1982.

226 Hobbes 1975a, p. 222. For a discussion of paradiastole in the passage see Kowalski 1928, pp. 171–2.

dangerous habit of redescribing the vices as virtues. As we have already seen, Plato insists in book VIII of the *Republic* that a willingness to offer such redescriptions is an obvious sign of corruption in the soul. It seems clear, moreover, that his account was intended as a satire on the Athenian government of his day. Isocrates puts forward very similar objections both in his *Areopagiticus* and later in his plea for a return to older democratic ways in his *Antidosis*. It is not merely a symptom, he declares, but a cause of Athens' decline that 'some of our people no longer use words in their proper meaning but wrest them from the most honourable associations and apply them to the basest pursuits'.[227]

The same sense of outrage is no less strongly marked among the Roman moralists and historians who comment on the phenomenon of paradiastolic speech. Sallust goes so far as to put into the mouth of Marcus Cato the claim that 'it is because the squandering of other people's goods is nowadays called liberality, while audacity in wrong-doing is called courage, that our republic has been reduced to its present extremity'.[228] Livy concludes his discussion of how it is always possible 'to fabricate vices that lie in the neighbourhood of a person's virtues' by declaring that this particular art of words 'is the worst art of all'.[229] Seneca likewise ends his account of how 'vices creep up on us under the name of virtues' with the warning that, 'with such developments, we find ourselves straying into grave danger'.[230]

Drawing directly on these authorities, the poets and moralists of the English Renaissance generally speak in tones of equal hostility. One denunciation of paradiastole to which they frequently recur is that of Thucydides. Hobbes was of course among those who helped to give wide currency to Thucydides' strictures, and Thucydides' argument may in turn have helped Hobbes to decide, when brooding about the impending political crisis of his own age, that the publication of his translation might be a means – as his prefatory epistle puts it – of offering 'profitable instruction', to those who 'have the managing of great and weighty actions'.[231] A generation before Hobbes's version appeared, however, Thucydides' attack on the dangers of paradiastole had already been made familiar to English readers. One conduit had been William Jones's translation of Lipsius' *Sixe Bookes of Politickes* in 1594.[232] Speaking of the

227 Isocrates 1929b, pp. 341–3.

228 Sallust 1921a, LII.11, p. 102: 'Quia bona aliena largiri liberalitas, malarum rerum audacia fortitudo vocatur, eo respublica in extremo sita est.'

229 On 'adfingens vicina virtutibus vitia' as 'pessima ars' see Livy 1929, XXII.XII.12, p. 242.

230 Seneca 1917–25, epistola XLV, vol. I, p. 294: 'in his magno periculo erramus'.

231 Hobbes, 1975a, epistle dedicatory, p. 4.

232 For this translation see Oestreich 1982, pp. 114–15.

need to understand the multitude, Lipsius had argued that rulers should pay particular attention to their fickleness, and above all to their disposition to confuse the language of vice and virtue to suit their own purposes. He had expressed the point in the form of a close paraphrase of the famous passage from book III of Thucydides' *History*. 'Whatsoever is moderate', the populace will say it 'hath a kind of slouthful cowardise; and whatsoever is circumspectly and providently handled, that sure they say is slow negligence: but whatsoever is rash and headie, that is deemed by them to be couragiously and valiantly enterprised.'[233]

For the fullest development of Thucydides' doubts, however, we must return to the version of Plutarch's *Moralia* published by Holland in 1603, and in particular to his rendering of Plutarch's essay on how to distinguish a true friend from a flatterer. As we have seen, one of the tests Plutarch had proposed for identifying flatterers is that they 'pervert' manners by 'giving to vices the name of virtues'.[234] By way of example, he adds a comment on the same passage from book III of Thucydides:

> Thucydides in his storie writeth: That during civill seditions and warres, men transferred the accustomed significations of words unto other things for to justifie their deeds: for desparate rashnesse, without all reason, was reputed valour, and called Love-friendship: provident delay and temporizing was taken for decent cowardise: Modestie and temperance was thought to be a cloke of effeminate unmanlinesse: a prudent and wary circumspection in all things was held for a generall slouth and idlenesse.[235]

Plutarch goes on to apply Thucydides' comments to the analogous and still more disgraceful case of false friends:

> According to which precedent, we are to consider and observe in flatterers, how they terme prodigalitie by the name of liberalitie; cowardise is nothing with them but heedfull warinesse; brainsicknesse they entitle promptitude, quicknesse and celeritie; base and mechanicall niggardise they account temperate frugalitie. Is there one full of love and given to be amorous? him they call a good fellow, a boun-companion, a man of a kinde and good nature. See they one hastie, wrathfull and proud withall? him they will have be hardie, valiant and magnanimous: contrariwise, one of a base minde and abject spirit they will grace with the attribute of fellow-like and full of humanity.[236]

With these observations, Holland not only put into currency an especially withering denunciation of paradiastole, but offered a number of new comments on the dangers of employing the technique.

The other classical warning against paradiastole that was widely taken

233 Lipsius 1594, p. 69. A marginal scholium refers us to 'Thuc.3.'
234 Plutarch 1603, p. 93.
235 Plutarch 1603, p. 93.
236 Plutarch 1603, p. 93.

up was Sallust's in the *Bellum Catilinae.* An early allusion can be found in Humfrey Braham's *The Institucion of a Gentleman* of 1555, which includes an account of 'suche abuses as have corrupted the better disposycyon of younge gentlemen' of recent times.[237] Braham specifically mentions the willingness to denigrate virtue and excuse vice, and cites 'the sayinge of the wyse Romayne Salust', who took note of 'the mysgovernaunce of many yonge gentylmen in Rome, whiche used to wrest the names of good thinges into the names of vices'.[238] We too, according to Braham, have by now 'loste the trew names of thinges, because the givyng away of other mens goodes is called liberalitie, & unshamefastnes in noughty thinges, is called high or gentle courage'.[239]

A similar though immeasurably more eloquent adaptation of Sallust's argument can be found in Ben Jonson's *Catiline*, first performed and published in 1611.[240] The chorus brings Act IV to a close with a denunciation of Cicero's detractors which ends by calling on Rome – exactly as Cato had done in the *Bellum Catilinae*[241] – to abandon the dangerous and corrupting habit of paradiastolic speech:[242]

> What age is this, where honest men,
>   Plac'd at the helme,
> A sea of some foule mouth, or pen,
>   Shall over-whelme?
> And call their diligence, deceipt;
>   Their vertue, vice;
> Their wachfulnesse, but lying in wait;
>   And bloud, the price.
> O, let us plucke this evill seede
>   Out of our spirits;
> And give, to every noble deede,
>   The name it merits.
> Lest we seeme falne (if this endures)
>   Into those times,
> To love disease: and brooke the cures
>   Worse, then the crimes.[243]

Like other moralists of the period, Jonson lays more emphasis on the

237 Braham 1555, sig. B, ii^r.
238 Braham 1555, sig. B, iii^v.
239 Braham 1555, sig. B, iiii^r.
240 See Barton 1984, p. 154; cf. Goldberg 1989, pp. 193–203.
241 On Jonson's appeals to – and 'recharacterisations' of – Sallust's account, see Ayres 1987, esp. pp. 210–18.
242 For a discussion see Lawry 1982, esp. pp. 399–400.
243 Jonson 1937, p. 526.

disparagement of virtue than on the excusing of vice, while stressing that both forms of corruption appear to be gaining ground.[244]

We should finally note that the poets and moralists were not alone in calling for an end to these practices. Perhaps most striking of all is the fact that some at least of the rhetoricians acknowledged that the art of eloquence may be said to over-reach itself when it encourages the confusion of virtue and vice. There are hints of this concession even among the leading rhetorical theorists of antiquity. When Cicero in the *De partitione oratoria* considers how the vices can be falsely represented as virtues, he adds a warning about the importance of ensuring that we never allow ourselves to be deceived by such appearances.[245] When Quintilian in book III of the *Institutio oratoria* first considers the possibility of redescribing a reckless man as courageous, or a prodigal man as generous, he insists that such deceptions are so dangerous and reprehensible 'that the good orator, who will also be a good man, must never make use of them unless he is perhaps led to do so by a concern for the public interest'.[246]

A similar note of warning is sounded by several English rhetoricians of the later sixteenth century. Even Puttenham feels constrained to admit that, when we employ the device of paradiastole, we may find ourselves speaking in terms 'more favorable and of lesse vehemencie then the troth requires'.[247] Henry Peacham makes the same point with far greater urgency. Although he contents himself in the 1577 edition of his *Garden of Eloquence* with a conventional definition of paradiastole, the second edition of 1593 attacks the use of the device in violent terms. 'Paradiastole', he now declares, is a 'faultie tearme of speech', which 'opposeth the truth by false tearmes and wrong names, as in calling dronkennesse good fellowship, insatiable avarice good husbandrie, craft and deceit wisedome and pollicie'.[248] This makes it nothing better than a technique 'for the better maintenance of wickednesse', one that helps promote 'selfe-love, partiall favour, blinde affection, and a shamelesse person'.[249]

By the end of the sixteenth century there was a widespread feeling that the technique of moral redescription had become too dangerous to tolerate. But this consensus was by no means matched by any clear sense

[244] It is worth observing that Jonson wrote a prefatory poem for Thomas Wright's *The Passions of the Mind in Generall* (see Wright 1971, p. lxv, and cf. Briggs 1989, p. 79) since it is one of Wright's complaints that 'at this present' rhetoricians 'cover stincking matters with fragrant flowers'. See Wright 1971, p. 99.

[245] Cicero 1942b, XXIII.81, p. 370.

[246] Quintilian 1920–2, III.VII, 25, vol. I, p. 476: 'Quod quidem orator, id est vir bonus, numquam faciet, nisi forte communi utilitate ducetur.'

[247] Puttenham 1970, p. 220.

[248] Peacham 1593, p. 168.

[249] Peacham 1593, p. 169.

of how to regulate it. While the poets and moralists continued to demand that it should be neutralised or outlawed from moral and political debate, the question of how this might be done remained one of the unanswered puzzles in moral philosophy. As we shall see, however, the puzzle was one that Hobbes specifically set himself to solve as part of his project of constructing a science of civil life.

Chapter 5

THE USES OF IMAGERY

The central question raised by the classical rhetoricians is how to speak and write in a 'winning' style. As we have seen, part of their answer is that we need to master the various techniques of redescription that serve to amplify our utterances. But their main answer is that we need to learn how to make effective use of the figures and tropes of speech.[1] As Cicero puts it in his *De partitione oratoria*, 'we must learn to employ words with the power to illuminate what is being described',[2] which in turn requires 'that they must be weighty, full, resonant', and 'above all used in a metaphorical way'.[3] Quintilian develops the argument at greater length in books VIII and IX of the *Institutio oratoria*. To achieve victory in the war of words, we must learn 'to increase or diminish at will what we want to say, to excite or subdue, to speak joyfully or severely, copiously or concisely, sharply or gently, magnificently or subtly, gravely or wittily'.[4] The best way to generate these various forms of amplification 'is by the right kind of metaphorical usages, as well as by the figures of speech, the right reflections, and finally the right type of arrangement'.[5] The closing chapter of book VIII examines the specific contribution made by the *tropi* to producing these effects, at which point Quintilian stresses that 'many of the tropes are used simply to increase and add *ornatus* to our utterances'.[6] The bulk of book IX is then given over to considering the contribution of the *schemata*, a discussion Quintilian summarises by saying that nothing does more to arouse the emotions of an audience than an apt use of figures, so that nothing 'more readily enables us to commend to our hearers what we are arguing, whether by winning approval for our

1 On the figures and tropes as 'expressive' see Vickers 1989, pp. 283–6, 294–339.

2 Cicero 1942b, XV.53, p. 350: 'verba ponenda sunt quae vim habeant illustrandi'.

3 Cicero 1942b, XV.53, p. 350: 'gravia, plena, sonantia ... in primisque translata'.

4 Quintilian 1920–2, VIII.III.40, vol. III, p. 232: 'augere quid velimus an minuere, concitate dicere an moderate, laete an severe, abundanter an presse, aspere an leniter, magnifice an subtiliter, graviter an urbane'.

5 Quintilian 1920–2, VIII.III.41, vol. III, p. 232: 'quo translationum genere, quibus figuris, qualibus sententiis, qua postremo collocatione'.

6 Quintilian 1920–2, VIII.VI.40, vol. III, p. 322: 'Cetera ... ad ornandam et augendam orationem assumuntur.'

conduct or prompting them to view the cause we are pleading in a favourable light'.[7]

The same assumptions recur in most of the English rhetorical handbooks of the sixteenth century. Thomas Wilson reiterates the point at the outset of his discussion of the tropes in *The Arte of Rhetorique.* 'An Oration is wonderfullye enriched when apte Metaphores are gotte and applied to the matter; neither can anye one perswade effectuouslye, and winne men by weyght of his Oration, withoute the helpe of woordes altered and translated.'[8] We recognise the force of this argument as soon as we reflect on the power of such figurative 'translations'. For we see that 'nothinge is more profitable for anye one that myndeth by hys utteraunce to stirre the hartes of menne either one waye or other'.[9] George Puttenham makes the same point at the start of his lengthy discussion of 'Ornament' in *The Arte of English Poesie.* He begins by explaining that 'this ornament then is of two sortes', one of which merely serves 'to satisfie & delight th' eare', while the other produces more impressive effects 'by certaine intendments or sence of such wordes & speaches inwardly working a stirre to the mynde'.[10] The surest way to stir the mind, he later adds, is by using 'figures sententious, otherwise called Rhetoricall'. They possess so much virtue and efficacy that, whether the orator aims 'to pleade, or to praise, or to advise', he can always hope to 'utter and also perswade both copiously and vehemently'.[11]

How can we hope to deploy the figures and tropes to arouse the emotions of an audience? Among the classical rhetoricians, it is Quintilian who offers the most comprehensive and influential response. It will accordingly be most convenient to take his discussion as our point of departure. He has two main suggestions to make, the first of which I shall discuss in the next two sections, while a discussion of his second suggestion will bring this chapter to a close.

CONVERTING AUDITORS INTO SPECTATORS

Quintilian puts forward his first suggestion in the course of analysing perorations in book VI, since it is in the peroration, he maintains, that we

7 Quintilian 1920–2, IX.I.21, vol. III, p. 358: 'Plurimum tamen ad commendationem facit, sive in conciliandis agentis moribus sive ad promerendum actioni favorem.' On *figurae* as the chief means by which 'ornatur oratio', cf. Quintilian 1920–2, X.V.3, vol. IV, p. 114.

8 Wilson 1554, fo. 92^{r}.

9 Wilson 1554, fo. 92^{v}.

10 Puttenham 1970, pp. 142–3.

11 Puttenham 1970, p. 196. Cf. also pp. 218, 222, 224, 240. For similar accounts of how to use the figures and tropes to 'stir' and 'move' the affections, and hence to persuade, see Sherry 1961, p. 22; Fenner 1584, esp. p. 173; Lyly 1868, esp. p. 137; Fraunce 1950, esp. p. 64.

must seek to excite our hearers to the highest pitch. He argues that it may be possible to employ figurative language with so much vividness and immediacy that our audience comes to 'see' what we are trying to describe, and is thereby roused to accept and endorse our vision of events. This is obviously a far from straightforward doctrine, and Quintilian himself acknowledges in a rare moment of hesitation that he finds it difficult to explain in any greater detail what he has in mind.[12] He nevertheless sets himself in book VI to develop a full analysis, beginning in chapter 2 with the arresting suggestion that our first step must be to cultivate the almost hallucinatory ability to form 'mental pictures' – what he also describes as *visiones* or, adapting the Greek term, *fantasias*. We must attempt, in advance of speaking, to conjure up appropriate visions in the mind's eye, so that 'images of things absent come to be present to the mind, in consequence of which we appear to see them before our very eyes'.[13] The indispensable talent is that of 'fancying', creating a *fantasia* of the scene or action we wish to describe.

Quintilian is drawing here on the familiar assumption that most of our conceptions ultimately derive from sensory impressions, and especially from visual impressions, which in turn become lodged in the memory as remembered pictures or 'ideas'. He adds that some people possess in abundance the further faculty – which anyone can acquire and cultivate – of being able to create images of things never seen but only 'imagined'.[14] He accordingly conceives of a powerful fancy or imagination as a capacity to put together composite images of things seen and remembered in such a way as to create novel visions in the mind's eye. Although he regards this ability essentially as 'a vice of the mind', a mere capacity for day dreaming,[15] he stresses that orators can put it to extraordinarily effective use. Suppose, for instance, I find myself pleading in a case of murder:

> Shall I not try to bring before my eyes everything that may plausibly be represented as taking place in such a case? Shall I not show the assassin suddenly bursting forth? Shall I not show the victim trembling, crying out, begging for mercy, taking to flight? Shall I not see the blow struck, the body felled?[16]

12 Quintilian 1920–2, VI.II.29, vol. II, p. 432.

13 Quintilian 1920–2, VI.II.29–30, vol. II, p. 432–4: 'imagines rerum absentium ita repraesentantur animo, ut eas cernere oculis ac praesentes habere videamur'. Cf. also Quintilian 1920–2, XI.III.62, vol. IV, p. 276.

14 Quintilian 1920–2, VI.II.30–1, vol. II, p. 434.

15 On 'hoc animi vitium' see Quintilian 1920–2, VI.II.30, vol. II, p. 434.

16 Quintilian 1920–2, VI.II.31, vol. II, p. 434: 'non omnia, quae in re praesenti accidisse credibile est, in oculis habebo? non percussor ille subitus erumpet? non expavescet circumventus? exclamabit vel rogabit vel fugiet? non ferientem, non concidentem videbo?'

Even if I have never witnessed a murder, I may be able to produce an exceptionally telling and emotionally arousing description if I can manage to put together such invented images to create a speaking likeness of the actual scene.

About this ability to 'imagine' Quintilian has two principal points to make. The first is that, if we possess a powerful imagination, we shall find that we are capable of describing to others the images in our mind's eye with a corresponding degree of immediacy and force. Quintilian appears to believe, in other words, that it follows from the ability to conjure up vivid mental pictures that, when we come to communicate what we see, we shall find ourselves capable of doing so with commensurate vividness. 'It is this power of the mind', he explains, 'which above all makes people eloquent in their speech.'[17] His second point is that an orator possessed of this ability will not only be able to impose his view of the facts; since he will be capable of communicating his vision of the entire episode, he will be able to make his audience share his emotional response to it. 'It will be the speaker who is best able to summon up these images of things in the mind who will prove to be by far the most powerful in the production of emotional effects.'[18]

The Roman theorists employ a distinctive formula to summarise this line of argument. The most persuasive speakers, they maintain, will be those who turn their auditors into spectators. Cicero at the end of book I of *De inventione* stresses that, to be sure of winning a case, we must speak 'in language that does as much as possible to place the event in question before the eyes of our listeners'.[19] He later puts the same point into the mouth of Crassus in book III of the *De oratore*. One of the most effective methods of moving an audience is 'when we offer an explanation of the events under examination with so much clarity that it is almost as if we render visible the way in which they were actually carried out'.[20] Quintilian subsequently develops the argument in a number of different passages in the *Institutio oratoria*. When discussing how to lay out a narrative in book IV, he observes that 'it is extremely helpful if we can manage to present a credible picture of the events in question of such a kind as will lead our hearers to feel that it is as if they had actually been present at the

17 See Quintilian 1920–2, X.VII.15, vol. IV, p. 140, on the power to conjure these *imagines* as the *vis mentis* which *disertos facit*. Cf. Cocking 1991, pp. 28–32.

18 Quintilian 1920–2, VI.II.30, vol. II, p. 434: 'Has [imagines] quisquis bene conceperit, is erit in adfectibus potentissimus.'

19 Cicero 1949a, I.LIV.104, p. 156: 'rem verbis quam maxime ante oculos eius apud quem dicitur ponimus'. See also Cicero 1942b, VI.20, p. 326.

20 Cicero 1942a, III.LIII.202, vol. II, p. 160: 'explanatio rerumque quasi gerantur sub aspectum paene subiectio'.

scene'.[21] When he turns to the topic of *ornatus* in book VIII, he praises Cicero's prodigious capacity 'for offering an image of an event so that it seems painted in words',[22] and adds that 'it is a great quality in oratory to be able to present our views on any issue about which we are speaking not merely with clarity but in such a way that the scene appears to become visible'.[23] Like the poets, whom Horace in a celebrated phrase had compared with painters – *ut pictura poesis*[24] – the orator's power to speak persuasively is held to depend on his ability 'to appeal to the eyes of the mind'.[25]

Quintilian encapsulates his argument in a turn of phrase that proved to have exceptional resonance. A good orator will not only state or narrate his case; he will 'hold forth' the facts so that they can be, as it were, visually inspected.[26] As Hobbes was later to put it with elegant ambiguity in *Leviathan*, he will present the facts in such a way that they are 'preferred'.[27] Quintilian's chapter on narrative in book IV singles out Cicero for his ability 'not so much to offer an account of the facts as to hold them out to us'.[28] His discussion of perorations in book VI again refers to Cicero's mastery of the technique 'by which we seem not so much to describe an event as to hold it forth to be inspected'.[29] And in his survey of *ornatus* in book VIII he includes several further references to the importance of being able 'not merely to explain things but to hold them out to the eyes of the mind'.[30] It is a crucial characteristic of eloquence, he concludes, 'that it not only speaks of things but manages clearly and plainly to hold them forth'.[31]

These formulations proved so influential that, among English writers of the Renaissance, we frequently find the power of eloquence defined as an ability to 'figure' or 'set forth' an argument or else (in a later usage even

21 Quintilian 1920–2, IV.II.123, vol. II, p. 116: 'Multum confert adiecta veris credibilis rerum imago, quae velut in rem praesentem perducere audientes videtur.'

22 Quintilian 1920–2, VIII.III.63, vol. III, p. 246: 'rerum imago quodammodo verbis depingitur'.

23 Quintilian 1920–2, VIII.III.62, vol. III, p. 244: 'magna virtus est res de quibus loquimur clare atque, ut cerni videantur, enuntiare'. Cf. Quintilian 1920–2, VIII.III.81, vol. III, p. 256, on the capacity *ponendi rem ante oculos*.

24 'A poem is like a picture.' Horace 1929, p. 480, line 361. For the fact that the dictum recalls Aristotle's *Rhetoric* (Aristotle 1926, III.XII.5, p. 422), and should be understood in rhetorical terms, see Trimpi 1973.

25 Quintilian 1920–2, VIII.III.62, vol. III, p. 244: 'oculis mentis ostendi'.

26 On this capacity to 'hold forth' (*ostendere*) see Quintilian IV.II.114, vol. II, p. 112; VI.II.32, vol. II, p. 434; VIII.III.62, vol. III, p. 244; VIII.III.86, vol. III, pp. 258–60.

27 Hobbes 1991, p. 484.

28 Quintilian 1920–2, IV.II.114, vol. II, p. 112: 'non tam narraret quam ostenderet'.

29 Quintilian 1920–2, VI.II.32, vol. II, p. 434: 'non tam dicere videtur quam ostendere'.

30 Quintilian 1920–2, VIII.III.62, vol. III, p. 244: 'non exprimi et oculis mentis ostendi'.

31 Quintilian 1920–2, VIII.III.86, vol. III, pp. 258–60: '[eloquentia] de quibus dicat, clare atque evidenter ostendere'.

closer to Quintilian's) as a talent for 'holding forth'. These phrases recur prominently in Sidney's restatement of the Aristotelian theory of mimesis in his *Defence of Poesie.*[32] The poet begins with an '*Idea*, or fore conceit of the worke', which is 'seene by the eyes of the mind'.[33] He then displays his skill by representing or 'figuring forth' his perceptions in the form of a 'speaking picture', one of such liveliness that 'we seeme not to heare' but 'clearly to see' what has been figured forth.[34] Ben Jonson provides a fine summary of the same theory in his *Discoveries*:

> *Poetry*, and *Picture*, are Arts of a like nature; and both are busie about imitation. It was excellently said of *Plutarch*, *Poetry* was a speaking Picture, and *Picture* a mute Poesie. For they both invent, faine and devise many things, and accommodate all they invent to the use, and service of nature.[35]

A number of Tudor rhetoricians had already spoken in similar terms about the ability of poets and orators to make us witnesses of the events they describe. Henry Peacham, for example, explains in the 1593 version of his *Garden of Eloquence* that good orators are able 'by a diligent gathering together of circumstances, and by a fit and naturall application of them', to 'expresse and set forth a thing so plainly and lively, that it seemeth rather painted in tables, then declared with words'. The effect of managing to 'set forth' an argument with this degree of clarity is that 'the hearer shall thinke that he doth plainly behold the matter described'.[36]

The argument we have been considering is thus that, if we wish to excite the emotions, we must learn how to hold forth images of the truth.[37] To this the classical rhetoricians add that, if we wish to hold forth such an image, we must learn how to make appropriate use of the figures and tropes of speech, and above all the master tropes of simile and metaphor. The author of the *Ad Herennium* underlines this further and crucial claim with his habitual trenchancy when discussing the topic of *elocutio* in book IV. One of the best ways 'to place something *ante oculos*, before our very eyes'[38] is by using metaphors, 'as for instance when we say: "the uprising suddenly awoke Italy with terror"'.[39] He later observes

32 On Sidney's use of Aristotle's *Poetics* see Heninger 1984.

33 Sidney 1923, pp. 7–8.

34 Sidney 1923, pp. 9, 14, 15. On Sidney's view of poetry as 'figuring forth' see Weiner 1978, esp. pp. 43–7.

35 Jonson 1947, pp. 609–10.

36 Peacham 1593, pp. 134–5; for further examples see Gent 1981.

37 Rossi 1968, pp. 178–85, describes Bacon (p. 181) as taking up this view of rhetoric as a method 'of creating "visible" images of mental concepts'. It seems a misconception to regard Bacon as an enemy of images and the imagination. For this contention see McCreary 1973, but for a corrective see Harrison 1968, Vickers 1968 and Vickers 1991, esp. pp. 251–3.

38 The phrase appears to be taken from Aristotle. See Aristotle 1926, III.x.6, p. 398.

39 *Ad C. Herennium* 1954, IV.XXXIV.45, p. 342: By *translatio* it is possible 'rei ante oculos ponendae

that similes can frequently produce a comparable effect, since they enable us 'to embellish, to teach, to make the matter more open or to place it before our eyes'.[40] Quintilian agrees that one of the best methods 'of presenting an image of things as a means of explaining them' is by using similes.[41] He subsequently notes that metaphors provide an even more powerful means 'of deeply moving the feelings and drawing special attention to things and placing them before our very eyes'.[42] He ends by adding that a large number of *schemata* can also be used to yield the same result. They have a capacity 'to give such a form to things by means of the words employed as to leave the impression that they have been seen rather than heard'.[43]

These assumptions were widely echoed by the rhetoricians of the English Renaissance. When Richard Sherry, for example, considers the trope of metaphor in his *Treatise of Schemes and Tropes*, his reason for commending it as the chief virtue of speech is that 'none perswadeth more effecteouslye, none sheweth the thyng before our eyes more evidently', and in consequence 'none moveth more mightily the affections'.[44] This view of figurative language as a means of holding forth an image of the truth became so deeply entrenched that the figures and tropes eventually came to be described simply as 'imagery'. While this usage only became standard in the course of the eighteenth century, we already find Puttenham alluding to the idea that poets and orators have a special talent for suggesting resemblances 'by Pourtrait or Imagery'.[45] Peacham in his *Garden of Eloquence* goes on to itemise a number of figures with the distinctive property of conveying 'a visible and lively image', while adding in a further reference to the theory of mimesis that 'the Orator imitateth the cunning painter', since his skill in deploying the figures and tropes is such that 'cunning and curious images are made'.[46]

A man of good fancy or imagination is accordingly seen as the possessor of two closely connected abilities. He is skilled at conjuring up images or pictures in his mind's eye. But he is also skilled – in consequence of this

causa, sic: "Hic Italiam tumultus expergefecit terrore subito"'. Cf. Cicero 1942a, III.XL.160–1, vol. II, pp. 124–6; Cicero 1942b, VI.20, p. 326.

40 *Ad C. Herennium* 1954, IV. XLV.59, p. 376: 'aut ornandi causa aut probandi aut apertius dicendi aut ante oculos ponendi'. See also IV.XLVIII.62, p. 384.

41 Quintilian 1920–2, VIII.III.72, vol. III, p. 250: 'ad exprimendam rerum imaginem compositae'.

42 Quintilian 1920–2, VIII.VI.19, vol. III, p. 310: 'Nam translatio permovendis animis plerumque et signandis rebus ac sub oculos subiiciendis reperta est.'

43 Quintilian 1920–2, IX.II.40, vol. III, pp. 396–8: 'quaedam forma rerum ita expressa verbis, ut cerni potius videatur quam audiri'.

44 Sherry 1961, p. 40.

45 Puttenham 1970, p. 241 and cf. pp. 243, 244. See also Sidney 1923, p. 29.

46 Peacham 1593, pp. 134, 146. Cf. pp. 135, 139, 151, 167.

clarity of mental vision – at communicating these images in correspondingly incisive figures and tropes, and especially in fresh and illuminating similes and metaphors. By his use of similes he prompts his hearers to see that unfamiliar things are similar to things they already know about, thereby enabling them to grasp the unfamiliar with a new sense of understanding and clarity. By his use of metaphors he contrives to suggest, even more daringly, that things unfamiliar are in a certain sense identical with more familiar things, thereby enabling his audience to 'see' even more clearly how to incorporate them into their existing frameworks of belief.

TEMPERING IMAGINATION WITH JUDGMENT

Besides arguing that the figures and tropes provide us with the best means of transforming auditors into spectators, the classical rhetoricians enunciate a set of rules for employing figurative language to produce this effect, their aim being to help the orator to speak in moving and persuasive ways. The adoption of these rules gave rise to an aesthetic that was destined to exercise an overwhelming influence in shaping the neo-classicism of the Renaissance. The rules affirm that, if our use of figures and tropes is to have its fullest emotional impact, two contrasting requirements must be satisfied. The first is that the orator must never look for his imagery too close at hand. He must at all costs avoid hackneyed figures and familiar turns of phrase, since these will obviously lack the power to amplify his arguments and augment the swelling scene. Rather they will cause his oration to 'fall flat'. Instead he must ensure, as Aristotle had originally emphasised in the *Rhetoric*, that his images (as Hobbes's translation puts it) are 'farre fetcht'.[47] Since his aim is to jolt his audience into seeing things in a new way, he must conjure up a range of tropes and figures that are correspondingly surprising and memorable. He therefore needs to make them 'unalike' and 'unproportionable'.[48]

The Roman theorists similarly speak of the need for the fancy to roam far afield to bring back new and challenging figures and tropes of speech. Crassus declares in book III of the *De oratore* that our figurative language will never seem striking unless our images are *longe repetita*, fetched from a considerable distance.[49] Quintilian in his analysis of *ornatus* in book VIII likewise insists in his discussion of similes that 'the more far-fetched they are, the greater will be the sense they bring back of novelty and

47 Hobbes 1986, p. 110.
48 Hobbes 1986, p. 117.
49 Cicero 1942a, III.XXXIX.160, vol. II, p. 124.

unexpectedness'.[50] Drawing on these authorities, the rhetoricians of Renaissance England likewise underline the importance of surprise. Wilson observes in *The Arte of Rhetorique* that 'menne counte it a poynte of witte to passe over suche woordes as are at hande, and to use suche as are farre fetcht and translated'. He goes on to explain, very much in the spirit of Quintilian, how the employment of figurative language, and especially the principal tropes, can serve to rouse and persuade an audience. A startling metaphor produces a far more suggestive and enlightening effect than ordinary speech, since 'the hearer is led by cogitacion', and 'thinketh more by remembraunce of a word translated then is there expreslye spoken'. An unusual simile can also lead us to a better understanding of a novel or difficult argument, since we often find that 'the whole matter seemeth by a similitude to be opened'.[51] Bacon comments in similar vein in *The Advancement of Learning*. Referring in particular to the art of poetry, and alluding to Horace's comparison of the poet with the painter, he remarks that there is a sense in which poetry is 'extremely licensed', so that it 'doth truly refer to the imagination'. This is due to the fact that, 'being not tied to the laws of matter', it is able to trespass more widely than such laws allow, and can even 'join that which nature hath severed, and sever that which nature hath joined'.[52]

The poets themselves frequently encapsulate the idea of the fancy's roaming quality in the claim that the imagination, like Pegasus, may be said to 'take wing', so that we may speak of 'flights of fancy'. Ben Jonson assures us in *Discoveries* that this is the true poetical rapture; this is what 'the Poets understood by their Helicon, Pegasus, or Parnassus'.[53] John Marston similarly makes the figure of Feliche in his *Antonio and Mellida* speak of 'the soul's swift Pegasus, the fantasy'.[54] The same image recurs in an anonymous set of verses written in the 1620s in praise of the poets of the age, in the course of which the worthy eulogist puts together two writers whose talents might be thought somewhat disparate:

> Ingenious *Shakespeare*, *Massinger*, that knowes
> The strength of plot to write in verse and prose,
> Whose easie Pegassus will amble ore
> Some threescore miles of fancy in an houre.[55]

50 Quintilian 1920–2, VIII.III.74, vol. III, p. 252: 'Nam quo quaeque longius petita est, hoc plus adfert novitatis atque inexspectata magis est.'
51 Wilson 1554, fo. 91^r^.
52 Bacon 1915, p. 82.
53 Jonson 1947, p. 637.
54 Marston 1965, *Antonio and Mellida*, III.ii.43, p. 41.
55 Ingleby 1879, p. 134.

A strong fancy involves an untiring capacity to fly long distances in search of exotic verbal felicities.[56]

The second and contrasting requirement the orator must satisfy is that of knowing how to range freely without getting lost. Although he must be prepared to roam at large, he must avoid merely wandering about (*extra vagans*) in an 'extravagant' way, and must take care not to travel so far as to end up outside the ordinary world (*ex orbe*) in a state of mere 'exorbitancy'.[57] He must have a good fancy, but he must never allow himself to become merely fanciful. If the images he brings back and holds forth are excessively far fetched, he will fail to produce any answering mental picture in the minds of his audience, and will fail in consequence to rouse and persuade them to see things from his point of view.

For this second rule the Roman theorists are again indebted to Aristotle's analysis of the tropes in *The Art of Rhetoric*. As Hobbes's version puts it, 'a *Metaphor* ought not to be so farre fetcht as that the Similitude may not easily appeare'.[58] The most revealing tropes will be unproportionable, but they must never be disproportionate. Aristotle explains why excessive disproportion is always displeasing in the course of describing what it is about a successful metaphor that gives pleasure:

> Metaphors please; for they beget in us by the *Genus* or by some *common thing* to that with another, a kind of *Science*: as when an *Old Man* is called *Stubble*; a man suddainely learnes that hee growes up, flourisheth and withers like Grasse, being put in minde of it by the qualities common to *Stubble* and to *Old men*.[59]

The most powerful metaphors are accordingly those which are 'drawne from *Proportion*' so as to establish surprising but revealing connections between disparate things.[60]

Cicero and Quintilian repeat that, while we must avoid clichés, we must never allow our imagery to become *longius petitus*, unduly far fetched.[61] Quintilian underlines the moral at a number of different points in discussing *ornatus* in book VIII. We must never lapse into obscurity, remembering that the whole purpose of adding *ornatus* is to engender a greater and not a lesser degree of clarity than ordinary speech.[62] Above all we must strive to avoid that special form of obscurity which results from

56 Cf. Cook 1981, esp. pp. 228–9.
57 Cf. Rossky 1958, esp. pp. 54–64.
58 Hobbes 1986, p. 109.
59 Hobbes 1986, p. 115.
60 Hobbes 1986, p. 116.
61 For this phrase see Quintilian 1920–2, VIII.V.20, vol. III, p. 292, and cf. Cicero 1942a, III.XLI.163, vol. II, p. 126.
62 Quintilian 1920–2, VIII.III.73–5, vol. III, pp. 250–2.

over-ambitious straining after novel tropes. This risk, Quintilian thinks, is especially liable to afflict those who make extensive use of metaphor:

While a moderate and appropriate use of the trope of metaphor makes our speech more illuminating, frequent use serves at once to obscure what we are saying and to weary our hearers, while continuous use causes our language to degenerate into mere enigmas and allegories.[63]

The danger to be avoided at all costs is that of using the figures and tropes to puzzle instead of enlighten our audience.[64]

The same warnings are loudly voiced by the rhetoricians of Tudor England. This is perhaps slightly ironic, since they quickly gained a reputation for encouraging an absurdly inflated and euphuistic form of writing based, as Henry Crosse complains, on 'fine phrases, Inkehorn-termes, swelling words, bumbasted out with the flocks of sundry languages'.[65] But this was by no means their intention, even though it may have been a foreseeable consequence of their emphasis on the glories of the Ciceronian Grand Style. We already find Sherry insisting at the start of his *Treatise of Schemes and Tropes* that, 'of these thynges that we put in eloquucion, lette thys be the fyrste care, to speake evidentlye after the dignity and nature of thynges', so that 'everye thynge may seme to be spoken purelye, apertlye and clerelye'.[66] Wilson similarly insists at the outset of *The Arte of Rhetorique* that the orator must 'utter his mind in plain wordes, suche as are usually received, and tell it orderly, without goyng aboute the busshe'.[67] As a result of these commitments, the Tudor rhetoricians sharply repudiate the use of riddles, 'strong lines' and dark or enigmatic turns of phrase.[68] Sherry warns that 'in speakynge and Wrytynge nothyng is more folyshe than to affecte or fondly to laboure to speake darkelye',[69] while Wilson opens his section on elocution by demanding that 'among al other lessons, this should first be learned, that we never affect any straunge ynkehorne termes', nor take the art of rhetoric 'to stande wholy upon darke woordes'.[70]

63 Quintilian 1920–2, VIII.VI.14, vol. III, pp. 306–8: 'Ut modicus autem atque opportunus eius [sc. metaphor] usus illustrat orationem, ita frequens et obscurat et taedio complet, continuus vero in allegorias et aenigmata exit.'

64 Quintilian 1920–2, VIII.VI.52, vol. III, p. 330.

65 See Crosse 1603, sig. N, 4^{r}, who also complains (sig. O, 4^{v}) of 'wandering imaginations' who 'follow their owne fancies'.

66 Sherry 1961, pp. 19–20.

67 Wilson 1554, fo. 1^{v}.

68 For two later discussions of riddles and 'strong lines' see Burton 1989, pp. 13, 17, and Jonson 1947, pp. 622–4.

69 Sherry 1961, p. 12.

70 Wilson 1554, fo. 86^{r-v}. For a complaint (also from the 1550s) to the effect that the *figurae,* described as the lights of speech, are really shadows, see Jewel 1850, p. 1286: 'figurae ... lumina vocant (mihi tenebrae potius videntur)'.

Like their classical authorities, the Renaissance writers draw the moral that, while we must be prepared to fetch our figurative language from afar, we must never allow ourselves to fall into merely exorbitant or extravagant speech. Sidney's *Defence of Poesie* points to the irony that some writers travel such great distances in their imagination to bring back 'far fette words' that their discoveries 'seeme monsters', or at least 'straungers to anie poore Englishman'.[71] Puttenham repeats the attack on 'inkhorne termes' and 'speeches misticall and darke or farre fette', commenting with particular hostility on those who would 'rather fetch a word a great way off then to use one nerer hand to expresse the matter aswel & plainer'.[72] Speaking specifically of metaphor, Peacham adds that we must never allow the underlying simile to be so 'farre fetcht, as from strange things unknowne to the hearer' that we merely bewilder our audience.[73]

These writers generally summarise the two contrasting principles of their aesthetic by stressing that we must never make an inept, indiscreet or indecorous use of figures and tropes; we must always take care to temper and adjust our language to suit the time, the place and the persons concerned. The fullest statement of this doctrine is owed to Quintilian, who lays it down in book VIII that 'we must recognise that no speech can be said to embody genuine *ornatus* if it lacks aptness in any way'.[74] He returns to the point in his detailed description of the figures of speech in book IX. On the one hand we must avoid mere tameness and the associated danger of bathos. 'When a case needs to be fought by calling on terror, hatred and compassion, who can tolerate a speaker who confines his expressions of rage, pity and entreaty to neat antitheses and balanced cadences?'[75] On the other hand we must avoid any impression of excess. 'While the use of figures adds *ornatus* to our speech when they are appropriately deployed, they become totally unsuitable if they are sought after too much.'[76] The basic rule is one of decorum: 'we should know what is required in the matter of place, person and time in delivering any speech'.[77]

While the prose theorists of Renaissance England exhibit a wide spectrum of stylistic allegiances, ranging from Tacitean laconicism to the fullest Ciceronian opulence, they all agree about the need to avoid these

71 Sidney 1923, p. 42.

72 Puttenham 1970, pp. 145, 147, 183, 245. For earlier attacks on inkhorn terms see Vos 1976.

73 Peacham 1593, pp. 14, 16, 145, 147, 249.

74 Quintilian VIII.III.15, vol. III, p. 218: 'sciamus nihil ornatum esse quod sit improprium'.

75 Quintilian IX.III.102, vol. III, p. 506: 'Ubi vero atrocitate, invidia, miseratione pugnandum est, quis ferat contrapositis et pariter cadentibus ... irascentem, flentem, rogantem?'

76 Quintilian 1920–2, IX.III.100, vol. III, p. 504: '[Figurae] ornent orationem opportune positae, ita ineptissimas esse, cum immodice petantur.'

77 Quintilian 1920–2, IX.III.102, vol. III, p. 504: 'Sciendum vero in primis, quid quisque in orando postulet locus, quid persona, quid tempus.'

cardinal sins of indiscretion and ineptness.[78] This is one of the commitments explicitly announced by John Lyly, perhaps the most notorious exponent of the neo-Ciceronian Grand Style. Addressing the theme of true eloquence in *Euphues*, he stresses that the height of ineptitude lies in failing to think about the character of the persons we wish to impress. We need above all to remember that 'they that study to please the multytude are sure to displease the wise'.[79] The same commitment is no less strongly expressed by Francis Bacon, whose *Essays* mark him by contrast as a self-conscious opponent of neo-Ciceronian magniloquence.[80] He makes the point with particular emphasis in analysing the *genus iudiciale* in his essay 'Of judicature'. One of the main objections we can fairly level against the eloquence of advocates is that, in addition to producing 'cunning counsel, gross neglect, slight information', they are excessively prone to 'indiscreet pressing, or an over-bold defence'.[81] Of all these warnings, however, the most celebrated comes from Shakespeare in the scene where Hamlet instructs the visiting troupe of actors on how to deliver the lines he has written for them. On the one hand, as he admonishes the First Player, it is essential to avoid mere tameness. But on the other hand, even in a whirlwind of passion 'you must acquire and beget a temperance that may give it smoothness'.[82] Nothing must be done in an exorbitant or inappropriate way. 'Suit the action to the word, the word to the action, with this special observance: that you o'erstep not the modesty of nature.'[83] A well-educated humanist, Hamlet lays down a set of precepts closely modelled on the doctrines of Quintilian.

The injunction to avoid ineptness is also expressed in positive terms. The golden rule for aspiring orators is to temper their flights of fancy with discretion and judgment. Enunciating the rule at the end of book VI, Quintilian begins by admitting that 'it is no more possible to teach good judgment by rules of art than it is to teach the sense of taste or smell'.[84] Nevertheless, 'nothing is of greater importance, not merely in the art of speaking, but in the whole conduct of life, than the possession of a sound judgment, in the absence of which all formal instruction will be given in vain'.[85] Only if we cultivate a sense of discretion, and hence a capacity for

78 Cf. Rossky 1958, esp. pp. 67–73; on decorum as a social as well as aesthetic ideal see Javitch 1978, pp. 50–4, 144–5.

79 Lyly 1868, p. 136.

80 On Bacon as 'anti-Ciceronian' see Vickers 1968, esp. pp. 103–15.

81 Bacon 1972, p. 164.

82 Shakespeare 1988, *Hamlet*, III.ii.7–8, p. 671.

83 Shakespeare 1988, *Hamlet*, III.ii.17–19, p. 671.

84 Quintilian 1920–2, VI.V.I, vol. II, p. 514: 'nec magis arte traditur [sc. iudicium or concilium] quam gustus aut odor'.

85 Quintilian 1920–2, VI.V.II, vol. II, p. 520: 'nihil esse non modo in orando, sed in omni vita prius consilio, frustraque sine eo tradi ceteras artes'.

speaking with true judgment, can we hope to ensure 'that our speech is suitably adapted to places, times and persons' in the manner required by perfect eloquence.[86]

This positive injunction likewise commanded a broad measure of assent among the prose theorists of Renaissance England.[87] We find it echoed on the one hand among the defenders of the highest neo-Ciceronian style. Lyly, for example, insists on the rule when speaking out in *Euphues* against the practice of extempore oratory. His main objection is that, in the hands of beginners, such orations will be sure to lack the essential qualities of discretion and aptness. He does not wish 'to condemne this exercise of the wit', but he 'woulde not have any young scholler openly to exercise it, but when he shall grow both in age and eloquence, insomuch as hee shall through great use and good memory bee able aptly to conceive and readily to utter any thing'.[88] The same point is made by many writers of strongly contrasting stylistic allegiances. Bacon, for example, begins his essay 'Of discourse' by castigating the error of those who 'desire rather commendation of wit' than the cultivation of discretion and good judgment. The avoidance of inept and indiscreet speech is so important that we may even say that 'discretion of speech is more than eloquence'.[89] As before, however, it is Shakespeare who provides the finest summary of the conventional wisdom by making it the nerve of Hamlet's speech to the First Player to 'let your own discretion be your tutor'.[90] Nothing must be 'overdone, or come tardy off'. Concluding his advice in a turn of phrase remarkably reminiscent of *Euphues*, Hamlet reminds the actors that any falling away in either direction, 'though it make the unskilful laugh, cannot but make the judicious grieve; the censure of the which one must in your allowance outweigh a whole theatre of others'.[91]

The classical rhetoricians summarised these contentions in the form of two pervasive images, both of which were much elaborated by their Renaissance followers. The first suggests that an orator who makes effective use of the figures and tropes will be able not merely to avoid the dullness of flat description but to imitate the brightness of life itself. Cicero makes particular play with images of light in his analysis of *ornatus* in the final book of *De oratore*, in which Crassus speaks of metaphor as 'a method

86 Quintilian 1920–2, VI.V.11, vol. II, p. 520: 'aptare etiam orationem locis, temporibus, personis'.

87 For a full analysis see Tuve 1947, pp. 192–247. On analogies beween order in discourse and social order see Parker 1987, esp. pp. 97–125.

88 Lyly 1868, p. 136.

89 Bacon 1972, pp. 12, 103.

90 Shakespeare 1988, *Hamlet*, III.ii.16–17, p. 671.

91 Shakespeare 1988, *Hamlet*, III.ii.24–28, p. 671.

of adding brightness to our speech',[92] adding in a purple passage much invoked in the Renaissance that 'this makes it possible in the highest degree to mark out and illuminate what we are saying with stars of light'.[93]

The significance of Cicero's imagery stems from the equation it implies between light and enlightenment. The brilliance of metaphor, as Crassus puts it, 'serves to illuminate that which we wish to be understood', and thereby 'enables us to present our case in a clearer way'.[94] The connection was one that Cicero's admirers among the Tudor rhetoricians were especially quick to exploit.[95] Wilson opens his section on exornation in *The Arte of Rhetorique* by affirming that 'when a thynge full ofte can not be expreste by an apte and mete woorde, we do perceyve (when it is spoken by a woorde translated) that the likenes of that thynge whiche appeareth in an other worde, muche lighteneth that which we woulde most gladly have perceyved'.[96] Peacham in the 1593 version of *The Garden of Eloquence* similarly declares that 'eloquence is the light and brightnesse of wisedome', and that metaphors in particular 'give pleasant light to darke things, thereby removing unprofitable and odious obscuritie'.[97]

The other image put into currency by the classical rhetoricians speaks of the power of figures and tropes to clothe our arguments in gorgeous colours, thereby rendering the naked truth more appealing and attractive. This is not to say, Quintilian warns, that our use of *ornatus* should produce the kind of colour that comes from the employment of deceptive dyes.[98] It is a grave mistake to suppose that our arguments will necessarily look better 'if they glow with a complexion that is not their own, as opposed to that which an uncorrupted Nature is able to give them'.[99] Rather we shall cease to sound persuasive if it becomes obvious that we are decking out our arguments in false colours, just as a woman will cease to seem attractive if it becomes obvious that her apparent beauty is owed to cosmetics.[100] If we can manage, however, to appear natural while

92 Cicero 1942a, III.XL.161, vol. II, p. 126: '[translatio] lumen affert orationi'.

93 Cicero 1942a, III.XLIII.170, vol. II, p. 134: 'quod maxime tanquam stellis quibusdam notat et illuminat orationem'. Cf. Farnaby 1970, p. 20, marginal scholium: 'Metaphora ... lumen & stella sit orationis.'

94 Cicero 1942a, III.XXXVIII.155 and III.XXXIX.157, vol. II, p. 122. '[translatio] illustrat id quod intelligi volumus', so that metaphors 'clariorem faciunt rem'. Cf. *Ad C. Herennium* 1954, IV.XXIII.32, p. 308.

95 Tuve 1947, pp. 29–33.

96 Wilson 1554, fo. 91r.

97 Peacham 1593, sig. AB, iiv and p. 13.

98 Quintilian 1920–2, VIII.III.6, vol. III, p. 214. Cf. Quintilian 1920–2, VIII, Proemium 20, vol. III, p. 188.

99 Quintilian 1920–2, II.V.12, vol. I, p. 250: 'non suo colore nitidis ... quam possit tribuere incorrupta natura'.

100 Quintilian 1920–2, II.V.11–12, vol. I, p. 250.

employing the art that conceals art, we can hope to add greatly to the persuasiveness of our case.[101] 'We must vary and diversify our speech with a thousand figures, but we must do so in such a way that our orations appear entirely the products and children of nature, and in no way artificially manufactured at all.'[102]

The force of this second image derives from the connection it implies between the use of highly coloured speech and the capacity to render our arguments more 'colourable'. We can hope to use the colours of rhetoric to paint over any imperfections in our case, thereby rendering it more plausible and appealing to our audience by lending it at least a gloss or varnish of truth.[103] Quintilian merely hints at the connection, but a number of his admirers among the Tudor rhetoricians eagerly seize on it. Wilson declares that the figures and tropes enable us to amplify our arguments with so much beauty 'that reason semeth to bee clad in purple', whereas in their absence it appears to be 'walkyng afore, bothe bare and naked'.[104] This is why we must not hesitate to 'commende and beautifie oure talke wyth divers goodlye coloures and delightful translations'.[105] Puttenham likewise insists on the value of 'ornament' as a means of making the truth more attractive, and underlines the alleged parallel with the artful enhancement of feminine beauty in a manner evidently designed to appeal particularly to his courtly audience. He begins by explaining – with the customary allusion to Horace's *ut pictura poesis* – what he means by the process of adding 'ornament' to our speech:

> This ornament we speake of is given to it by figures and figurative speaches, which be the flowers as it were and colours that a Poet setteth upon his language by arte, as the embroderer doth his stone and perle, or passements of gold upon the stuffe of a Princely garment, or as th' excellent painter bestoweth the rich orient coulours upon his table of pourtraite.[106]

He goes on to argue, very much in the spirit of Quintilian, that we must of course be sure to apply these colours in such a way as to disguise art with art:

> If the same coulours in our arte of Poesie (as well as in those other mechanicall artes) be not well tempered, or not well layd, or be used in excesse, or never so litle disordered or misplaced, they not onely give it no maner of grace at all, but rather do

101 Quintilian 1920–2, IX.IV.5, vol. III, p. 508 and IX.IV.120, vol. III, p. 574.
102 Quintilian 1920–2, V.XIV.32, vol. II, p. 366: 'mille figuris variet ac verset ... [sed] ut ea nasci et ipsa provenire natura, non manu facta'.
103 See Tuve 1947, pp. 61–78; Plett 1975, pp. 144–50.
104 Wilson 1554, fo. 85^v. Cf. fos. 63^r and 89^v.
105 Wilson 1554, fo. 810 (*recte* $90)^r$. Cf. fos. 86^r and 111^v.
106 Puttenham 1970, p. 138.

disfigure the stuffe and spill the whole workmanship, taking away all bewtie and good liking from it.[107]

So long, however, as we apply the tinctures of rhetoric with discretion and judgment, we can hope to 'delight and allure as well the mynde as the eare'. This is because 'a certaine noveltie and strange maner of conveyance' will serve to render our utterances 'nothing the more unseemely or misbecomming, but rather decenter and more agreable to any civill eare and understanding'.[108]

Puttenham is mainly addressing the poets at this juncture, and it is among the poets that we find the implications of his imagery most fully explored. They continue to insist on the importance of discretion, and thus on the need to avoid o'erstepping the modesty of nature. As Sidney puts it in criticising the euphuistic versifiers of his day, we must never permit 'that hony-flowing Matrone *Eloquence*' to become 'apparelled, or rather disguised, in a Courtisanlike painted affectation'.[109] Ben Jonson later speaks out against such meretriciousness in tones of even deeper disgust:

But now nothing is good that is naturall: Right and naturall language seemes to have the least of the wit in it; that which is writh'd and tortur'd, is counted the more exquisite. Cloath of Bodkin, or Tissue, must be imbrodered; as if no face were faire, that were not pouldred, or painted? No beauty to be had, but in wresting and writhing our owne tongue?[110]

If we are to paint, Jonson insists, we must make sure that we confine ourselves to natural hues.[111]

While the poets are opposed to such garishness, they are equally emphatic that we can never hope to speak persuasively if we fail or refuse to lay on the colours of rhetoric in such a way as to help our arguments to look their best. Spenser points to the tragic consequences of one such failure in the course of narrating, in book II of *The Faerie Queene*, the history of the early British kings. King Leyr in old age called upon his three daughters to tell him 'which of them most did love her parentage':

The eldest *Gonorill* gan to protest,
That she much more than her owne life him lov'd:
And *Regan* greater love to him profest,
But *Cordeill* said she lov'd him, as behoov'd:
Whose simple answere, wanting colours faire
To paint it forth, him to displeasance moov'd,

107 Puttenham 1970, p. 138.
108 Puttenham 1970, p. 137. On Puttenham's 'artificial' writing cf. Knauf 1967.
109 Sidney 1923, p. 42. The image seems to be taken from Tacitus 1970, 26.1, p. 300.
110 Jonson 1947, p. 581. Cf. Norbrook 1984, pp. 186–7.
111 Jonson 1947, p. 581.

That in his crowne he counted her no haire,
But twixt the other twaine his kingdome whole did shaire.[112]

A true humanist, Spenser feels obliged to warn us that even the most honourable speeches are liable to miscarry if we remain content to present them in a pallid or undecorated style.

By contrast, Shakespeare in his many allusions to the value of rhetorical colouring prefers to emphasise its power to brighten even the darkest deeds. When Sir William Catesby in *Richard III* presents the duke of Gloucester with the head of the murdered Hastings, the deceiving Richard recalls how much he himself has been deceived:

I took him for the plainest harmless creature
That breathed upon the earth, a Christian,
Made him my book wherein my soul recorded
The history of all her secret thoughts.
So smooth he daubed his vice with show of virtue.[113]

Extending the image of highly coloured speech, Richard leaves us with the disquieting thought that, even if a painting is no better than a daub, it may nevertheless be sufficient to deceive.

PROVOKING LAUGHTER AND SCORN

I turn finally to Quintilian's second suggestion about the best means of employing figurative language to amplify the force of our utterances and thereby arouse the emotions of our audience. Although he acknowledges that what he proposes to say may appear trivial,[114] he insists on its importance for anyone hoping to achieve victory in the war of words. His contention is that the figures and tropes can also be used to provoke laughter, and that this represents an exceptionally potent means of undermining our adversaries. So far is Quintilian from supposing this further suggestion to be inconsequential that he declares in book x that 'the use of humour, together with the ability to inspire pity, are undoubtedly the two means of stirring the emotions that have the greatest impact of all'.[115]

Quintilian opens his discussion by distinguishing two different ways in which a talent for inducing laughter may be used to 'disarm' and win over an audience. By speaking amusingly we can hope in the first place to divert attention from any weak points in our argument. The underlying

112 Spenser 1970, *The Faerie Queene*, II.x.28, p. 121.
113 Shakespeare 1988, *Richard III*, III.v.24–8, p. 204.
114 Quintilian 1920–2, VI.III.8, vol. II, p. 442.
115 Quintilian 1920–2, X.I.107, vol. IV, p. 60–2: 'Salibus certe et commiseratione, qui duo plurimum in adfectibus valent.'

suggestion, already put forward in the *De oratore*,[116] is that if we can manage to divert our hearers we may be able to prevent them from lapsing into boredom or hostility. 'By moving our judges to laughter we can dissolve their harsher feelings'[117] and 'sometimes even refresh and restore them when they have fallen into a state of satiety or fatigue'.[118] Still more important, 'we can often succeed by these means in diverting their attention from the facts of the case'.[119]

The deep influence of this argument on Renaissance thought is attested by the fact that, by the middle of the seventeenth century, the idea of speaking 'divertingly' had come to be identified with speaking in an amusing or entertaining style. However, neither Cicero nor Quintilian takes this to be the most important reason for seeking to provoke laughter, and neither of them supposes that the figures and tropes have anything to contribute to this kind of wit. Both limit themselves to observing that, if we wish to refresh or distract our hearers, the best way of doing so will probably be to insert some humorous anecdotes into our speech.[120] Quintilian cites a number of examples from Cicero's orations, adding that the main rule to be observed in telling such stories is that 'the whole exposition must be presented with elegance and charm, and that the speaker must ensure that his own contribution is the most humorous part of all'.[121]

Of greater significance according to Quintilian is the other way in which we can hope to wield the weapon of humour to defeat our adversaries. To understand his further argument, we need to begin, as Quintilian does, by asking what range of feelings may be said to find their natural expression in laughter. Aristotle had given an arresting answer in the course of discussing the emotions in *The Art of Rhetoric*, a discussion to which Quintilian appears to be much indebted. The essence of Aristotle's argument is that laughter is almost invariably an expression of scorn or contempt. He first hints at this

116 Quintilian is deeply indebted to Cicero's discussion, as he acknowledges at several points. See Quintilian 1920–2, VI.III.1–8 and 39–44, vol. II, pp. 438–42 and 458–62. Both writers in turn appear to be reliant on a lost Greek literature *De ridiculis* mentioned in Cicero 1942a, II.LIII.217, vol. I, p. 356. For conjectures about these sources see Grant 1924, pp. 13–39. On the discussion of humour in *De oratore* see Michel 1960, pp. 271–84, Monaco 1964 and Wisse 1989, pp. 301–12.

117 Quintilian 1920–2, VI.III.1, vol. II, p. 438: 'risum iudicis movendo et illos tristes solvit adfectus'. See too Quintilian 1920–2, VI.III.9, vol. II, p. 442.

118 Quintilian 1920–2, VI.III.1, vol. II, p. 438: 'aliquando etiam reficit et a satietate vel a fatigatione renovat'.

119 Quintilian 1920–2, VI.III.1, vol. II, p. 438: 'animum ab intentione rerum frequenter avertit'.

120 Cicero 1942a, II.LIX.240–2, vol. I, pp. 376–8; Quintilian 1920–2, VI.III.39–44, vol. II, pp. 458–62.

121 Quintilian 1920–2, 'in his omnibus cum elegans et venusta exigitur tota expositio, tum id festivissimum est quod adiicit orator'.

thesis in book I, chapter 11, where he affirms that among the things that give pleasure are 'ridiculous Actions, Sayings and Persons'.[122] He makes the point still more explicitly at the end of book II, chapter 12, the passage in which he discusses the manners of youth. There he roundly declares that '*Jesting* is witty Contumely', having already informed us that '*Contumely*, is the disgracing of another for his owne pastime'.[123]

Quintilian's argument is based on very similar premises. He too stresses that laughter 'has its source in things that are either deformed or disgraceful in some way',[124] adding that 'those sayings which excite ridicule are often false (which is always ignoble), are often ingeniously distorted and are never in the least complimentary'.[125] But while these remarks are reminiscent of Aristotle, they owe a more immediate debt to the discussion of laughter in the *De oratore*, the most elaborate of the surviving discussions from antiquity. The figure of Caesar in Cicero's dialogue speaks at length about the situations that cause amusement, this being the first question to which he turns when persuaded in book II to speak about the concept of the laughable – *De facetiis*.[126] He begins by offering a restatement and elaboration of Aristotle's point:

> The proper field and as it were the province of laughter (this being our first question) is restricted to matters that are in some way either disgraceful or deformed. For the principal if not the sole cause of mirth are those kinds of remarks which note and single out, in a fashion not in itself unseemly, something which is in some way unseemly or disgraceful.[127]

Crassus explains that the kind of unseemliness he has in mind can either be moral or physical. He first suggests that 'materials for ridicule can be found in the vices observable in people's behaviour, provided that the people concerned are neither especially popular nor figures of real tragedy'.[128] To which he adds that 'further materials especially suitable for making jokes are provided by ugliness and physical deformity'.[129]

122 Hobbes 1986, p. 57.

123 Hobbes 1986, pp. 70, 86.

124 Quintilian 1920–2, VI.III.8, vol. II, p. 442, quoting Cicero 1942a, II.LVIII.236, vol. I, p. 372: '[Risus] habet sedem in deformitate aliqua et turpitudine'.

125 Quintilian 1920–2, VI.III.6, vol. II, p. 440: 'ridiculum dictum plerumque falsum est (hoc semper humile), saepe ex industria depravatum, praeterea nunquam honorificum'.

126 Cicero 1942a, II.LVII.233, vol. I, p. 370.

127 Cicero 1942a, II.LVIII.236, vol. I, p. 372: 'Locus autem et regio quasi ridiculi (nam id proxime quaeritur) turpitudine et deformitate quadam continetur; haec enim ridentur vel sola, vel maxime, quae notant et designant turpitudinem aliquam non turpiter.'

128 Cicero 1942a, II.LIX.238, vol. I, p. 374: 'materies omnis ridiculorum est in istis vitiis quae sunt in vita hominum neque carorum neque calamitosorum'. For a discussion of Cicero's views about the limits of ridicule, see Grant 1924, pp. 76–87.

129 Cicero 1942a, II.LIX.239, vol. I, p. 374: 'Est etiam deformitatis et corporis vitiorum satis bella materies ad iocandum'.

For Cicero and Quintilian, it follows that to laugh is almost always to laugh *at* someone. As Quintilian puts it – juggling *ridere* and *deridere* – 'mirth is never very far removed from derision'.[130] The most basic feeling to which laughter gives expression is accordingly said to be disdainful superiority.[131] When we laugh, we are usually glorying or triumphing over others as a result of having come to see that, by comparison with ourselves, they are suffering from some contemptible weakness or infirmity. 'The most ambitious way of glorying', as Quintilian puts it, 'is to speak derisively.'[132]

One of the most important conduits for the transmission of this argument to Renaissance England was Castiglione's *Il libro del cortegiano*. With the publication of Hoby's translation in 1561, Castiglione's lengthy analysis in book II of 'merrie conceits and Jestes' entered the mainstream of English moral and rhetorical thought.[133] Drawing in particular on the *De oratore*,[134] Castiglione reiterates that the feelings which find their natural expression in laughter are chiefly those of scorn and contempt. He goes so far as to suggest that, if we are to ensure that 'the Jest shal have any grace', it is indispensable that it should 'be seasoned with this deceit, or dissimulacion, or mockinge, or rebukinge, or comparason'.[135] This is because 'the hedspring that laughing matters arrise of, consisteth in a certein deformitie or ill favourednesse, bicause a man laugheth onlie at those matters that are disagreeing in themselves, and (to a mans seeminge) are in yll plight'.[136]

Although Gabriel Harvey specifically mentions Castiglione's discussion,[137] most Tudor rhetoricians appear to have drawn their understanding of laughter directly from their Roman sources. Thomas Wilson, who is singled out by Harvey[138] for including in his *Arte of Rhetorique* a special section on 'delityng the hearers and stirryng them to laughter',[139] refers us to Cicero and Quintilian for the view that 'where the jest is aptly applied', the aim will almost always be to ensure that someone is 'laughed

[130] Quintilian 1920–2, VI.III.8, vol. II, p. 442: 'a derisu non procul abest risus'.

[131] This came to be the most widespread understanding of laughter in Renaissance thought. Spinoza may have been the first post-Renaissance philosopher to question these assumptions when he insisted – echoing Terence – on a sharp distinction between laughter as derision and as a pure expression of joy. See Spinoza 1985, p. 572.

[132] Quintilian XI.I.22, vol. IV, p. 166: 'Ambitiosissimum gloriandi genus est etiam deridere'.

[133] Castiglione 1994, pp. 150–98.

[134] See Castiglione 1994, p. 150, marginal scholium: 'This discourse of Jestes is taken out of Cicero *de Orat.* lib.ii.'

[135] Castiglione 1994, p. 188.

[136] Castiglione 1994, p. 155.

[137] Harvey 1913, p. 114.

[138] Harvey 1913, p. 114.

[139] Wilson 1554, fo. 47^r.

to scorne'.[140] Wilson repeats that when we laugh we are almost always directing our mirth at 'the fondnes, the filthiness, the deformitee and all suche evill behavior as we see to be in other'.[141] To stimulate laughter, we therefore need to 'touche handsomely and wittely some especiall fault or fonde behavior in some one body or some one thing'.[142] Puttenham speaks in similar vein when he turns at the end of his section on ornament to examine 'things that move a man to laughter'. He agrees that the main occasions for mirth are given by 'scurrilities & other ridiculous behaviours'. This is due to the fact that 'in every uncomlinesse there must be a certaine absurditie and disproportion to nature' which means that 'we may decently laugh'.[143] A fuller treatment can be found in Sidney's *Defence of Poesie*, towards the end of which he launches an attack on writers of comedy for mistakenly supposing that laughter is an expression of delight. The truth is, he retorts, that laughter and delight 'have as it were a kinde of contrarietie'. We take delight 'in thinges that have a conveniencie to our selves', whereas laughter 'almost ever commeth of thinges moste disproportioned to our selves and nature'. As a result, 'laughter hath onely a scornfull tickling'. For example, 'we are ravished with delight to see a faire woman, and yet are farre from being mooved to laughter'. By contrast, 'wee laugh at deformed creatures, wherein certainly we cannot delight'.[144] Bacon summarises the underlying assumption with characteristic briskness in his essay 'Of boldness': 'absurdity be the subject of laughter'.[145]

The poets connect laughter even more closely with feelings of condescension and contempt. One figure who is always able to laugh, according to Sir Thomas Wyatt, is the lover who has sufficiently recovered from his passion to recognise his own previous absurdity:

> Lo, how desire is both sprung and spent!
> And he may see that whilom was so blind,
> And all his labour now he laugh to scorn,
> Meshed in the briars that erst was all to-torn.[146]

But Wyatt here reverses the usual *topos*: it was generally the *belle dame sans merci* who was pictured as laughing her suitors to scorn. Colin Clout, the lovelorn shepherd's boy in Spenser's *Shepheardes Calendar*, complains of exactly this treatment:

140 Wilson 1554, fo. 74r.
141 Wilson 1554, fo. 74v.
142 Wilson 1554, fo. 74v.
143 Puttenham 1970, p. 291.
144 Sidney 1923, pp. 40–1.
145 Bacon 1972, p. 36.
146 Wyatt 1978, p. 96.

I love thilke lasse, (alas why doe I love?)
And am forlorne, (alas why am I lorne?)
Shee deignes not my good will, but doth reprove,
And of my rurall musick holdeth scorne.
Shepheardes devise she hateth as the snake,
And laughes the songes, that *Colin Clout* doth make.[147]

Shakespeare brings the two *topoi* together in *Much Ado About Nothing* when Benedict sagely reflects that our affections are so fickle that it is all too easy for the first of these stock characters to become transformed into the second:

I do much wonder that one man, seeing how much another man is a fool when he dedicates his behaviours to love, will, after he hath laughed at such shallow follies on others, become the argument of his own scorn by falling in love.[148]

It merely adds to the comedy that the complacent Benedict is about to discover the truth of this observation in his own case.

The poets are no less emphatic that, since laughter mainly expresses derision, to laugh is to glory over others, to give vent to feelings of triumphant superiority. The phrase 'They laugh that win' became proverbial in Elizabethan England, and as early as 1562 we find John Heywood using it as the basis for one of his 'epigrammes upon proverbs', although his purpose is to warn us that such glorying may easily turn out to be vainglorious:

They laugh that win, falsely to win and keepe,
Winners may laugh when they have cause to weepe.[149]

This kind of hubristic amusement was commonly associated with the cynical and worldly-wise as they contemplate the depths of human folly and ingenuousness. The king in *Love's Labour's Lost* warns Longueville and Dumaine to expect this kind of laughter from Biron when he learns of their amorous entanglements:

What will Biron say when that he shall hear
Faith so infringèd, which such zeal did swear?
How will he scorn, how will he spend his wit!
How will he triumph, leap, and laugh at it![150]

Such glorying, the poets especially warn us, must above all be expected

147 Spenser 1970, p. 422.
148 Shakespeare 1988, *Much Ado About Nothing,* II.iii.7–11, p. 549.
149 Heywood 1867, p. 163. The distracted Othello quotes the proverb: see Shakespeare 1988, *Othello*, IV.i.121, p. 842.
150 Shakespeare 1988, *Love's Labour's Lost*, IV.iii.143–46, p. 294.

from the figure of the stony-hearted mistress. John Dowland pictures her mocking her suitor as he voices his despair:

> Gentle love draw forth thy wounding dart,
> Thou canst not pearce her heart,
> For I that do approve:
> By sighs and teares more hote then are thy shafts:
> Did tempt while she for triumps laughs.[151]

With this image of the rejected and ridiculed lover, Dowland brings his lyric to a close.

Of all the writers from this period who analyse the phenomenon of laughter, it is Burton in *The Anatomy of Melancholy* who makes the strongest connection between laughter and ridicule.[152] This forms one of the major themes in his opening address to his readers in the person of Democritus Junior, the laughing philosopher *redivivus*. Burton contrasts Democritus with Heraclitus, who 'out of a serious meditation of mens lives, fell a weeping, and with continuall teares bewailed their miserie, madnesse, and folly'.[153] By contrast, Democritus 'burst out a laughing' as soon as he turned his attention to the consideration of man's lot. The reason for his 'ironicall passion' was that he rightly perceived man's utter absurdity.[154] Most ridiculous of all, Burton later explains, is the fact that 'not acknowledging our owne errors, and imperfections, wee securely deride others, as if we alone were free, and spectators of the rest'.[155] We need to recognise that we are all equally foolish and equally deserving of being laughed to scorn.

If laughter at once reflects and excites such profound feelings of disdain, it is hardly surprising that the theorists of rhetoric should have viewed it as such a potentially lethal weapon of debate. For it follows that, if we can manage to expose our opponents as laughable, we can hope to bring them into contempt, thereby undermining and depreciating their arguments while augmenting our own case at their expense. This is the promise that Cicero holds out in book II of the *De oratore*. Humour, as Antonius observes in describing Crassus' conduct as an advocate, can be used as a powerful means of offence as well as defence.[156] The figure of Caesar later underlines the point in explaining why he thinks 'it is obviously appro-

151 Dowland 1597, song 17, sig. I, 1v.
152 But see also Jonson 1947, pp. 643–4.
153 Burton 1989, p. 32.
154 Burton 1988, p. 33. On Burton's wish to prevent us from distancing ourselves from this absurdity see Fish 1972, pp. 303–32.
155 Burton 1989, p. 57.
156 Cicero 1942a, II.LV.222–5, vol. I, pp. 360–4.

priate for an orator to attempt to move his audience to mirth'.[157] He first emphasises the power of laughter to augment our own cause:

> The ability to arouse hilarity always enables an orator who knows how to excite it to win the goodwill of his audience, because everyone admires the kind of acumen involved, which can often be manifested in a single word.[158]

As well as winning goodwill, laughter can equally well be used to challenge our adversaries:

> The same talent is of even greater value in replying to your opponent's arguments, although it is also of great value in attacking them, since humour can be used to break up his case, to obstruct his arguments, to make light of his cause, to deter him from speaking and to turn aside what he has said.[159]

Quintilian subsequently places an even greater emphasis on this latter point, arguing that the primary value of humour 'is that we can use it either to reprehend, or turn aside , or make light of, or repel, or deride our opponents'.[160]

Among the Tudor rhetoricians, it is Thomas Wilson who displays the greatest interest in these arguments. Drawing on Cicero's analysis,[161] he presents a still stronger statement of the wounding and depreciating power of wit. 'Some thinke it a trifle', he concedes, to cultivate the gift of 'delityng the hearers and stirryng them to laughter'.[162] But this is to underestimate the talent involved, for 'it appeareth that thei whiche wittely can be pleasant, & when time serveth can give a mery answere or use a nipping taunte, shal bee able to abashe a righte worthy man & make hym at his wittes ende'. 'I have knowen some', he goes on, 'so hit of the thumbes that thei could not tell in ye world whether it were beste to fighte, chide, or to go their waie.' Nor should this surprise us, 'for wher ye iest is aptly applied, the hearers laugh immediately; & who would gladly be laughed to scorne?'[163] It is thus of great importance to be able to confront an opponent with 'some pleasant iest'. By these means we can hope to

157 Cicero 1942a, II.LVIII.236, vol. I, p. 372: 'est plane oratoris movere risum'.

158 Cicero 1942a, II.LVIII.236, vol. I, p. 372: 'vel quod ipsa hilaritas benevolentiam conciliat ei, per quem excitata est; vel quod admirantur omnes acumen uno saepe in verbo positum'.

159 Cicero 1942a, II.LVIII.236, vol. I, p. 372: 'maxime respondentis, nonnunquam etiam lacessentis; vel quod frangit adversarium, quod impedit, quod elevat, quod deterret, quod refutat'.

160 Quintilian 1920–2, VI.III. 23, vol. II, p. 448: 'aut reprehendimus aut refutamus aut elevamus aut repercutimus aut eludimus'.

161 Wilson 1554, fo. 75[r–v] includes a long though unacknowledged quotation from Cicero's analysis of laughter in book II of *De oratore*.

162 Wilson 1554, fo. 74[r].

163 Wilson 1554, fo. 74[r].

'extenuate and diminishe his doynges' to 'dashe hym out of countenaunce' and even to 'laugh him to skorne out right'.[164]

But how can an orator hope to incite his hearers to laughter and thereby stimulate such powerful feelings of contempt? This brings the classical theorists to their central point. The most effective method according to Cicero and Quintilian is to exploit a distinctive range of figures and tropes of speech.[165] First they emphasise that a number of the tropes can readily be adapted to derisive use. Cicero observes in *De oratore* that similes and metaphors can frequently be used to spark off laughter, since an imaginative orator can always hope to think up comparisons of a scornful or ludicrous character.[166] The *Ad Herennium* makes the same point, mentioning the comparison of a slow-witted adversary to a snail as an instance of 'a simile used to excite contempt'.[167] Quintilian adds that another trope peculiarly well-suited to derisive use is hyperbole, and cites as an example Publius Oppius' remark about the Lentuli family to the effect that, because their children are always smaller than their parents, 'we may expect their line to die out by way of birth'.[168]

More important is the fact that a number of tropes possess an inherently ridiculing character. One instance is aestismus, the trope we use when we mockingly exploit some ambiguity in a word or turn of phrase. Quintilian offers several examples, including the remark made by Claudius Nero about a dishonest slave: 'no one was more trusted in my house, for nothing was locked or sealed to him'.[169] Among the mocking tropes the most effective is said to be *ironia*, which Cicero defines as the form of speech we use 'when the whole drift of your oration shows that you are joking in a solemn way, speaking throughout in a manner contrary to your thoughts'.[170] Quintilian agrees that 'even at its most austere, irony can properly be defined as a kind of joking',[171] and later instances the ridicule Cicero heaped on Clodius by assuring him 'believe me, your integrity has cleared you of blame, your modesty has rescued you, your previous life has

164 Wilson 1554, fo. 75^r.

165 For a listing of such figures, with illustrations taken from Terence, see Herrick 1950, pp. 189–214.

166 Cicero 1942a, II.LXV.261–3, vol. I, pp. 394–6. Cf. Quintilian 1920–2, VI.III.65–71, vol. II, pp. 474–6.

167 On the use of similes *in contemptionem* see *Ad C. Herennium* 1954, IV.XLIX.62, p. 386.

168 Quintilian 1920–2, VI.III.67, vol. II, p. 474: 'cum assidue minores parentibus liberi essent, *nascendo interiturum*'.

169 Quintilian 1920–2, VI.III.50, vol. II, p. 464: 'nulli plus apud se fidei haberi, nihil ei neque occlusum neque signatum esse'.

170 Cicero 1942a, II.LXVII.269, vol. I, p. 402: 'cum toto genere orationis severe ludas, cum aliter sentias ac loquare'. On this view of irony see Knox 1989, pp. 9–18.

171 Quintilian 1920–2, VI.III.68, vol. I, p. 474: 'etiam quae severissime fit, ioci prope genus est'.

stood you in good stead'.[172] As Quintilian puts it, Cicero's irony consists of 'speaking in derision by saying the opposite of what is to be understood'.[173]

These observations were much amplified by the rhetoricians of Renaissance England. One of the tropes they discuss at greater length is aestismus, which as Wilson observes is often used to give 'just occasion of muche laughter'.[174] Henry Peacham provides the most extensive analysis of the trope in the 1593 edition of his *Garden of Eloquence*. We have an example of aestismus when 'a word having two significations is exprest in the one and understood in the other', or when 'a saying is captiously taken and turned to another sense'.[175] Peacham instances the story of Diogenes, who was asked 'what he would take for a knocke upon his pate' and replied 'that he would take an helmet'.[176] As Puttenham had earlier emphasised, the point of the device is to produce 'a kinde of mock' in which the words are 'spoken in plain derision'.[177]

The Tudor rhetoricians also provide a more extended account of irony.[178] Sherry defines *ironia* as 'a mockyng whiche is not perceived by the wordes',[179] while Puttenham adds that it represents the best means to 'dissemble when ye speake in derision or mockerie'.[180] Peacham underlines the point when discussing the special value of the trope, explaining that it 'pertaineth chiefly to reprove by derision and illusion and also to iest and move mirth by opposing contraries'.[181] To these observations Sherry, Peacham and Day add some remarks about sarcasm,[182] contrasting it with irony by treating it not as a mocking inversion but (in Sherry's words) as a more direct method 'of iesting or scoffinge bytynglye'.[183] Peacham agrees that any 'bitter kind of derision' can be described as a sarcasm, and cites a number of Biblical instances, including the command 'Sing us one of your songs of Sion', which 'was uttered in

172 Quintilian 1920–2, VIII.VI.56, vol. III, p. 332: 'Integritas tua te purgavit, mihi crede, pudor eripuit, vita anteacta servavit'.

173 Quintilian 1920–2, VIII.VI.56, vol. III, p. 332: 'in risu quodam contraria dicuntur iis quae intelligi volunt'.

174 Wilson 1554, fo. 76v. Cf. Sherry 1961, p. 46.

175 Peacham 1593, p. 34.

176 Peacham 1593, p. 34.

177 Puttenham 1970, pp. 190–1. Cf. Farnaby 1970, p. 22 and marginal scholium, characterising aestismus as *iocus urbanus* and as a species of irony.

178 Irony is often described simply as 'the mocking trope'. See Fenner 1584, sig. D, 2r–v; Fraunce 1950, pp. 4, 10. On whether the mockery need be derisive see Knox 1989, pp. 78–94.

179 Sherry 1961, p. 45.

180 Puttenham 1970, p. 189; cf. also p. 154.

181 Peacham 1593, p. 36.

182 On Renaissance distinctions between irony and sarcasm see Knox 1989, appendix C, pp. 170–7.

183 Sherry 1961, p. 46. See also Farnaby 1970, p. 22.

scornful and insulting maner against the poore Israelites being captives in Babylon'.[184]

These writers also examine a number of mocking tropes not mentioned by their classical authorities. One is charientismus, the device we use according to Puttenham when we 'give a mocke under smooth and lowly wordes'.[185] Puttenham cites as an example the 'myld and appeasing mockery' of the man who overheard another saying of him 'thou art sure to be hanged ere thou dye' and replied 'sir, I know your maistership speakes but in iest'.[186] A second mocking trope is diasyrmus, which we employ according to Sherry 'when we make lyghte of and dyspyse great argumentes brought agaynst us' by setting them aside as beneath our notice.[187] Peacham, drawing on Sherry's analysis, adds that the best way of achieving this tone is 'either by some base similitude or by some ridiculous example to which the adversaries obiection or argument is compared, whereby it is either made ridiculous or at least much disgraced'.[188] The relationship between this trope and the derisive use of similes is not made entirely clear, but Peacham refuses to explain further, observing that the device is so regrettably familiar that no examples need be adduced.[189] A third mocking trope is said to be mycterismus, which is held to involve *pronuntiatio* as well as *elocutio* in that it requires, as Sherry puts it, 'some gesture of the face'.[190] Puttenham explains that we employ this trope 'when we give a mocke with a scornfull countenance as in some smiling sort looking aside or by drawing the lippe awry, or shrinking up the nose', one instance being that of the man who 'said to one whose wordes he beleved not, no doubt Sir of that'.[191] As Peacham adds in his section on the value of the device, it can be described as 'a privie kind of mocke' which 'serveth to represse pride, rebuke folly and taunt vice'.[192]

We need finally to note that, in addition to surveying the mocking tropes, the classical rhetoricians argue that a number of figures or *schemata* can equally well be adapted to produce a derisory effect. Once again it is Quintilian who provides the fullest account. Among the *figurae verborum* he particularly singles out various patterned forms of speech – such as anaphora and antithesis – by which we can hope to contrive a tone of

184 Peacham 1593, pp. 37–8. Cf. Puttenham 1970, pp. 189–90; Day 1592, p. 85.
185 Farnaby 1970, p. 22 later underlined the point, defining charientismus as the substitution of smooth for hard words: 'Dat Charientismus pro duris mollia verba.'
186 Puttenham 1970, p. 191. Cf. Day 1592, p. 86.
187 Sherry 1961, p. 61.
188 Peacham 1593, pp. 39–40.
189 Peacham 1593, p. 40.
190 Sherry 1961, p. 46. The same was often held to be true of irony: see Knox 1989, pp. 58–77.
191 Puttenham 1970, p. 191.
192 Peacham 1593, pp. 38–9.

disparagement or ridicule.[193] And among the *figurae sententiarum* he mentions meiosis or ironical understatement as a device especially susceptible of being applied in a contemptuous or reproachful way.[194]

These observations were likewise taken up and extended by the rhetoricians of Tudor England. They begin by echoing Quintilian's remarks about meiosis as a form of mockery, while placing considerably more emphasis on the point. Sherry observes that we make use of this figure whenever 'greate matters are made lyghte of by wordes'.[195] Puttenham agrees that the chief use of this figure is to 'diminish and abbase a thing by way of spight or mallice, as it were to deprave it'.[196] He later adds that the essence of the technique consists of extenuating or diminishing an argument so as 'to bring our adversaries in contempt'.[197] Peacham repeats that meiosis is essentially a means to 'diminish and pul downe', since it is generally used 'when a lesse word is put for a greater to make the thing appeare lesse then it is'. We mock a learned doctor by calling him a pretty scholar, or someone who has sustained a grievous wound by calling it a mere scratch.[198]

Besides reiterating these claims, the Tudor rhetoricians consider a number of other figures particularly well adapted to arousing contempt. The followers of Ramus place a distinctive emphasis on *permissio* and *concessio*, sometimes describing the latter as synchoresis. Dudley Fenner stresses that the first of these is used 'when mockinglie we give liberties to any deed' and the second 'when an argument is mockingly yeelded unto'.[199] Abraham Fraunce similarly speaks of *concessio* or 'graunting' as the device we employ 'when we jestingly admit of anie speech or argument'.[200] Charles Butler devotes a whole chapter to the technique under the heading of synchoresis. This is the figure we invoke 'when a statement or an argument is seemingly accepted', but when 'that which we concede is harmful to the person to whom the concession is made'.[201]

A second example of a figure especially well-suited to malicious or contemptuous use is said to be aposiopesis.[202] According to Fenner's definition, 'a keeping of silence or Aposiopesis is when the course of the

193 Quintilian 1920–2, IX.III.29, vol. III, pp. 460–2.
194 Quintilian 1920–2, VI.III.93–5, vol. II, pp. 488–90.
195 Sherry 1961, p. 61.
196 Puttenham 1970, p. 185
197 Puttenham 1970, p. 219.
198 Peacham 1593, p. 168.
199 Fenner 1984, sig. E, 1^v.
200 Fraunce 1950, p. 104.
201 Butler 1629, Book 1, chapter 33, sig. M, 4^v to sig. N, 1^r: 'Synchoresis est, cum dictum aliquod aut argumentum condonatur ... [sed] cum id concedimus, quod ei cui conceditur, nocet'.
202 On this figure, especially in Quintilian, see Dalimier 1989.

sentence begon is so stayed, as thereby some part of the sentence not being uttered, may be understood'.[203] Puttenham notes that the device can readily be used as a threat, since we can give the impression, 'when we begin to speake a thing, and breake of in the middle way', that 'we were ashamed, or afraide to speak it out'.[204] Angel Day adds in similar vein that, when we use this figure and thereby 'stop our speech on a sodaine', we can easily leave the impression that we are in 'discontented moode'.[205] Peacham carries the point still further in the 1593 edition of his *Garden of Eloquence*, observing in his 'Caution' on the use of the device that we can all too easily use it 'in malice', since we can hope by our silence to leave 'the venome of some false suspicion behind it'.[206]

The last and perhaps the most important of the ridiculing figures according to these writers is tapinosis. Sherry informs us that this is the name of the technique in play 'when the dygnitye of the thyng is diminyshed by basenes of the worde, as if we shuld say to a greate prynce or a kynge: if it please your mastershypp'.[207] Puttenham and Peacham both view the technique essentially as a means of belittling or undermining our opponents' arguments. Puttenham refers to the technique in tones of unusual sententiousness, condemning it as a 'vicious maner of speach', a means to 'diminish and abbase', to 'speake untruly and injuriously by way of abbasement'.[208] Peacham expresses himself no less censoriously, referring to 'that fault of speech, which is usually called Tapinosis, that is when the dignitie or majestie of a high matter is much defaced by the basenesse of a word'.[209]

We should note in conclusion that Henry Peacham in the 1593 edition of *The Garden of Eloquence* discusses two further mocking figures scarcely mentioned by his predecessors. The first is leptotes,[210] which 'taketh the positive' by 'denying the superlative', as when we scornfully say of someone not wise at all that 'he is not the wisest man in the world'.[211] Peacham observes that, although the main use of this figure is to enable us to speak with becoming modesty, it is also susceptible of being used with malice and arrogance.[212] The other mocking figure he singles out is apodioxis, the device by which 'the Orator reiecteth the obiection or argument of his

203 Fenner 1584, sig. D, 4v.
204 Puttenham 1970, p. 166.
205 Day 1592, p. 87.
206 Peacham 1593, p. 118. See also Fraunce 1950, p. 80; Butler 1629, sig. M, 1r.
207 Sherry 1961, p. 34.
208 Puttenham 1970, pp. 185, 259.
209 Peacham 1593, p. 168.
210 Puttenham 1970, p. 184 and Day 1590, p. 90, had previously mentioned it, but without treating it as a mocking figure.
211 Peacham 1593, p. 150. Cf. *Ad C. Herennium* 1954, IV.XXXVIII.50, pp. 354–6.
212 Peacham 1593, p. 151.

adversaries as thinges needlesse, absurde, false or impertinent to the purpose'.[213] Again Peacham observes that, while it may often be appropriate to turn away an opponent's objections in this way, the technique is all too easily adapted 'to reject them with derision or scorningly'.[214]

I have been concerned in part I of this book with the teaching of rhetoric in the grammar schools of Thomas Hobbes's youth, and more broadly with the place of the *ars rhetorica* in Tudor political argument. I have been speaking of a period when conscientious grammar school pupils were expected to master the names, the definitions and the applications of all the figures and tropes we have been examining, and thereafter to take advantage of their special rhetorical properties to lend additional emphasis, or clarification, or alternatively an element of satire and ridicule to their speech. By the time of Hobbes's maturity, the deployment of these techniques had become a matter of second nature to the educated, and was already beginning to give rise – not least in the works of Hobbes himself – to that distinctive tone of ironic condescension which has left its mark on the writing of English philosophy ever since. The extent to which the lessons of the classical *ars rhetorica* had become assimilated and internalised is explicitly underlined in an anonymous pamphlet of 1673 attacking the scornful and ridiculing temper of the times:

> One may observe a sort of Natural Rhetorick, even among the Common professors of the Art of Railling; they have their Figures, Graces, and Ornaments peculiar to their kind of Speech, though they do not distinguish or use them Grammatically.[215]

By this stage, as the writer complains, a century of rhetorical instruction in the schools had made it possible even for those without any first-hand acquaintance with the *ars rhetorica* to learn its most subversive tricks. No one any longer needs to know 'the names of *sarcasmus*, *aestismus*, *micterismus*, *antiphrasis*, *charientismus*, or *ironia*'.[216] Even without such knowledge, everyone understands how to indulge in 'their Dry *Bobs*, their Broad *Flouts*, Bitter *Taunts*, their Fleering *Frumps*, and Privy *Nips*', thereby ridiculing and undermining the best features of the age.[217] Among these scoffers, by far the most dangerous was commonly held to be Thomas Hobbes, the monster of Malmesbury;[218] and it is Hobbes's use of the *ars rhetorica* in his civil science that I next wish to examine in part II of this book.

213 Peacham 1593, p. 185.
214 Peacham 1593, p. 185.
215 *Raillerie* 1673, pp. 40–1.
216 *Raillerie* 1673, p. 41.
217 *Raillerie* 1673, p. 41.
218 For an anonymous attack, also from 1673, on 'the fantastical definitions of the self-conceited *Malmsbury* Philosopher', see *Reflexions*, pp. 6–7.

Part II

HOBBES AND THE IDEA OF A CIVIL SCIENCE

Chapter 6

HOBBES'S EARLY HUMANISM

HOBBES'S HUMANIST CAREER

Thomas Hobbes died at Hardwick Hall in Derbyshire on 4 December 1679.[1] By that time the Royal Society had been incorporated for nearly twenty years, and many of the most celebrated English contributions to the scientific revolution had been in print for a generation or more. William Harvey had published his findings about the circulation of the blood in his *Exercitatio Anatomica* in 1628.[2] John Napier, Isaac Barrow[3] and John Wallis[4] had all completed their most important mathematical work by the middle years of the century, Napier first announcing his discovery of logarithms as early as 1614.[5] William Gilbert's *De Magnete* had appeared even earlier,[6] while Robert Boyle began his physical experiments in the course of the 1640s, eventually publishing his proof of the phenomenon still known as Boyle's law in the second edition of his *New Experiments Physico-Mechanical Touching the Air* in 1662.[7]

Hobbes not only lived long enough to learn about all these discoveries, but also to take an active part in debating their significance. He discusses Gilbert's claim that the earth is a magnet in the course of his lengthy manuscript of 1642–3 on Thomas White's *De mundo*,[8] a work in which he also voices for the first time his partially sceptical views about the idea of a vacuum.[9] He held numerous meetings with Harvey in the early

1 James Wheldon, Hobbes's last amanuensis, supplied John Aubrey with details about Hobbes's final illness and death, which Aubrey added to his biography. See Aubrey 1898, I, pp. 382–3.

2 See Harvey 1628.

3 Barrow's *Lectiones* on optics and geometry were collected and published in 1669, by which time he had resigned his professorship. See Barrow 1669.

4 See Wallis 1656a.

5 See Napier 1614.

6 See Gilbert 1600.

7 See Boyle 1662, esp. pp. 57–68. For a discussion see Shapin and Schaffer 1985, pp. 168–9. For a survey of science in early seventeenth-century England see Feingold 1984.

8 BN, Fonds Latin MS 6566A, fos. 98^{r}–102^{v}. Cf. Hobbes 1973, pp. 182–4. For the date of this manuscript see Jacquot and Jones 1973, pp. 43–5.

9 BN, Fonds Latin MS 6566A, fos. 23^{r}–24^{v}. (The MS is misbound at this point.) Cf. Hobbes 1973, pp. 121–5.

and refers admiringly to Harvey's work in the epistle dedicatory to the English version of *De Corpore* as a rare instance of a new scientific theory becoming universally accepted during its author's own lifetime.[11] Soon afterwards he published a strong attack on Boyle's account of the vacuum in his *Dialogus Physicus* of 1661,[12] prompting Boyle to issue a dignified but stinging rejoinder in the second edition of his *New Experiments* in the following year.[13] Even more unwisely, he attempted to dismiss the value of Wallis's *Arithmetica Infinitorum* in his *Six Lessons* of 1656, declaring that he had 'wholly and clearly confuted' Wallis's line of reasoning.[14] This brought an immediate and contemptuous response,[15] giving rise to an acrimonious pamphlet war with Wallis and his associates that continued to rumble on for the next twenty years.[16]

As a result of these and many similar interventions, Hobbes's commentators have generally treated him not merely as one of the more vociferous polemicists of the scientific revolution in England, but as someone whose intellectual formation was itself a product of the scientific developments spanning the century. This, for example, is how Sorell expresses the point in the opening paragraph of his study of Hobbes:

> Thomas Hobbes's philosophical ideas were formed by two great upheavals of the 17th century. One was local, political, dangerous, and as Hobbes believed, deeply irrational. This was the English Civil War. The other was largely Continental, benefited people in obvious ways, showed what reason could accomplish when properly guided and applied. This was the upheaval in scientific ideas that Hobbes thought had been started by Galileo. Mainly on the strength of writings occasioned by the first upheaval Hobbes claimed to have contributed something important to the second.[17]

Although this view of Hobbes as 'formed' by the scientific revolution is widely shared, it is part of my purpose to suggest that there is something misleading about it. That it yields at best a partial picture of Hobbes's intellectual development becomes clear as soon as we consider how his career and interests actually unfolded in the period before 1642, the year in which he published his first major treatise, *De Cive*, and suddenly rose (as he himself boasted) to a position of international fame.[18] If we re-examine

10 Aubrey 1898, I, p. 337; cf. Blackbourne 1839, p. xxxvii.

11 Hobbes 1839d, p. viii.

12 Hobbes 1845a; for a discussion see Shapin and Schaffer 1985, pp. 112–54 and for a translation of the *Dialogus* Shapin and Schaffer 1985, appendix, pp. 345–91.

13 See Boyle 1662; on his rejoinder see Shapin and Schaffer 1985, pp. 169–207.

14 Hobbes 1845g, p. 187. Hobbes later observed that Wallis's book was 'all nought from the beginning to the end'. See Hobbes 1845h, p. 383.

15 See Wallis 1656b, esp. pp. 41–50.

16 Robertson 1886, pp. 167–85, still provides the best brief outline of the dispute.

17 Sorell 1986, p. 1.

18 See Hobbes 1839b, p. xc, line 154.

Hobbes's life and studies during his earlier years of obscurity, and if we reflect on the range of works he published prior to the appearance of *De Cive*, we find that his intellectual formation was overwhelmingly indebted not to the culture of science but rather to the humanist literary culture we have so far examined.[19]

Perhaps the most obvious reflection of Hobbes's humanist allegiances can be observed in his choice of career. As we saw in chapter 2, the most usual pattern of employment for humanist intellectuals in Renaissance England was either to act as teachers of the *studia humanitatis* in the grammar schools and universities, or else to serve as tutors and secretaries in the households of the gentry and nobility. Hobbes was no exception, and in the years following his graduation from Oxford in 1608[20] he served on three separate occasions as tutor and companion to the heirs of leading English landed families.[21]

Hobbes owed the first of these appointments to the fact that William Cavendish, the first baron of Hardwick, found himself in a quandary in 1608 over the education of his son and heir, who also bore the name William Cavendish. Although the younger William was barely eighteen years old,[22] he had been married in April 1608[23] to Christian, only daughter of Lord Bruce of Kinloss, James I's Master of the Rolls.[24] Anxious to ally the Bruces with the English aristocracy, the king had encouraged the match and may even have made a contribution to Christian's dowry.[25] William's bride was only twelve years of age,[26] but his marriage debarred him from attending a university,[27] and his father decided that a tutor would have to be found. However, the young William had views of his own about tutors, including the belief 'that he should profitt more in his learning if he had a scholar of his owne age to wayte on him then if he had

19 As noted in the introduction (note 13), the importance of humanist literary culture in Hobbes's intellectual development was originally emphasised by Strauss 1963, esp. pp. 30–43, and Reik 1977, esp. pp. 25–34. More recent commentators who have taken up the point include Johnston 1986, pp. 3–25; Tuck 1989, pp. 1–11 (see also Tuck 1993, pp. 279–83), and Schuhmann 1990, pp. 332–6.

20 On Hobbes's date of graduation (5 February 1607, i.e. 1608 our style) see Aubrey 1898, I, p. 330. Why Hobbes took five years to complete the bachelor's course is not known. The usual period of residence was four years. See Fletcher 1986, pp. 165–6.

21 For an important account of the aristocratic milieu in which Hobbes lived and its effect on his intellectual development see Thomas 1965, esp. pp. 191–214.

22 Bickley 1911, p. 41.

23 Bickley 1911, p. 41. See also Malcolm 1994, p. 807.

24 Malcolm 1994, pp. 806–7.

25 Pomfret 1685, pp. 23–4, maintained that the king gave her £10,000. The claim has often been repeated, but Malcolm 1994, p. 807, notes its inherent dubiousness.

26 Malcolm 1994, p. 807.

27 A point helpfully stressed in Rogow 1986, p. 57.

the information of a grave doctor'.[28] Evidently bowing to his wishes, his father approached Sir James Hussey, the former principal of Magdalen Hall, to ask whether he had anyone to recommend.[29] Hussey wrote suggesting the name of Hobbes,[30] who was about to graduate and was less than three years older than his prospective charge. The Cavendishes appear to have accepted Hobbes at once, for he informs us in his *Vita Carmine Expressa*, the verse autobiography he composed in 1672,[31] that 'as the result of a letter of recommendation from the Head of my College, I went as soon as I left Oxford to the great and splendid mansion of the Cavendish family and entered their service'.[32]

Neither in his verse autobiography nor in his prose *Vita* of 1676[33] does Hobbes make any mention of what he taught the young William, and Aubrey implies that he may have acted more as a servant and companion than a tutor in the strict sense. 'He was his lordship's page, and rode a hunting and hawking with him, and kept his privy-purse.'[34] After following this way of life for several years, Hobbes and Cavendish departed on a tour of France and Italy.[35] It has generally been assumed that they left in 1610[36] and stayed abroad for five years, only returning to England in the course of 1615. This is not only inherently improbable, however, but appears to be a mistake.[37] The young Cavendish, whose father made him a quarterly allowance of £50, was still receiving payments in London up to the beginning of 1614.[38] Hobbes too was still in London at this time, for in the absence of Lord Hardwick's steward the payment of Cavendish's

28 Aubrey 1898, I, p. 330.

29 Aubrey 1898, I, p. 330.

30 Hobbes 1839b, p. lxxxvii, line 65. But Hobbes implies that it was the incumbent rector who recommended him. This would have been John Wilkinson, who succeeded Hussey in c.1605. See Aubrey 1898, I, p. 330, and cf. Blackbourne 1839, p. xxiii.

31 Hobbes 1839b, p. lxxxv, gives the date.

32 Hobbes 1839b, p. lxxxvii, lines 63–5:

Oxonium linquo, servitum me fero in amplam
Gentis Candisiae conspicuamque domum;
Rectoris aulae commendat Epistola nostrae.

Chatsworth: Hobbes MS A.6, a copy of the *Vita* in the hand of James Wheldon, contains numerous corrections by Hobbes. Where these seem significant, I have added the revised lines in square brackets.

33 Hobbes 1839a. For the date see Aubrey 1898, I, p. 372, who states that he himself commissioned the work.

34 Aubrey 1898, I, pp. 330–1.

35 Hobbes 1839a, p. xiii. Hobbes 1839b, p. lxxxviii, line 86, adds that they also visited Germany.

36 First stated in Blackbourne 1839, p. xxiv, and repeated ever since.

37 Malcolm 1984, pp. 49, 120, was the first to point out the error, although it continues to be repeated.

38 Hardwick MS 29 shows quarterly payments made in February 1611 (i.e. 1612 our style) (p. 222) and February 1613 (i.e. 1614 our style) (p. 364). Cavendish may also have spoken in Parliament in the spring of 1614. See Malcolm 1981, p. 319.

allowance was made directly to Hobbes 'at London' in February 1614.[39] He and Cavendish appear to have gone abroad later in the same year, spending the winter in Venice (where Hobbes seems to have been impressed by the opera)[40] and returning by way of Paris[41] in the summer of 1615.[42] By this time Cavendish was twenty-five years old, and any pedagogical duties Hobbes may originally have been discharging must long since have ceased. Nevertheless, Hobbes remained in Cavendish's household as 'domesticall servant and Secretary',[43] leaving only after the sudden death of his former pupil at the age of thirty-eight on 20 June 1628.[44] Rounding off his own account of this period, Hobbes remarks that 'this was by far the happiest time of my life, and nowadays the recollection of it frequently gives me sweet dreams'.[45]

Hobbes's second appointment as tutor and travelling companion began in 1629, and arose indirectly out of the death of William Cavendish in the previous year. William, whose father had been created earl of Devonshire in 1618,[46] and whom he had succeeded as second earl in 1626,[47] was now succeeded in turn by his ten-year-old son, yet another William Cavendish. The second earl's young widow Christian, who managed to obtain ward-

39 Hardwick MS 29, p. 364: 21 February 1613 (i.e. 1614 our style): 'To M^r^. Hobbes by my Lo: appoyntment in paymente of Sir William Cavendyshe his qrtly allowance to end at mid sommer nexte fifty pounds'. The page heading states that the payment was made 'at London in Travises absence'. Henry Travis, previously steward to Bess of Hardwick, countess of Shrewsbury, had become Lord Hardwick's steward.

40 Hobbes 1971a, p. 47. But his knowledge of what he describes as sung drama may date from the 1630s.

41 When Cavendish was sent, in October 1615, the first in a series of seventy-six news-letters from Fulgenzio Micanzio, whose acquaintance he had made in Italy, Micanzio noted that Cavendish had been staying in Paris, while assuming that he would by now be back in London. The translation of his first letter, marked 'Venice Octob. 30. 1615' begins: 'Most worthy S^r^ By what you advise, by your most welcome letter from Paris, this of mine will arrive to doe you humble reverence, about the time of your being backe at Court.' See Chatsworth: Hobbes MS 73.Aa, p. 1; cf. Gabrieli 1957, appendix, pp. 243–50, and Malcolm 1984, pp. 49–50.

42 There is a gap in the payment of William Cavendish's allowance between midsummer 1614 and July 1615. By the latter date, however, he was available to receive a special payment of £200 (and another in December), possibly to defray additional costs incurred abroad. See Hardwick MS 29, pp. 453, 458.

43 This is how Hobbes is legally described in an indenture of 1627 (Hardwick MS 301/15) drawn up between himself and his former pupil.

44 Bickley 1911, p. 43. On his will and death see also Malcolm 1994, pp. 807–8. A year before he died, he gave Hobbes a twenty-one-year lease on a manor in Yorkshire for an annual rent of £20; in 1638 this was converted by the third earl into a hundred-year tenancy at a peppercorn rent. For the indentures see Hardwick MSS 301/15 and 301/16.

45 Hobbes 1839b, p. lxxxviii, lines 71–2:

Pars erat illa meae multo dulcissima vitae,
Et nunc saepe mihi somnia grata facit.

46 See Bickley 1911, p. 39, who adds that Cavendish reputedly paid £10,000 for the title.

47 The first earl died, aged seventy-three, on 3 March 1626. Bickley 1911, p. 42 and note.

ship over her son,[48] might perhaps have been expected to appoint Hobbes to fill the same tutorial role as he had filled in the case of her late husband. But she seems at first to have been averse to any such scheme, and evidently turned to another young graduate of Oxford, George Aglionby, to take charge of her son's education.[49] Hobbes tells us in his verse *Vita* that this treatment left him feeling neglected,[50] but in another and earlier recollection he says that it actually led to his being discharged.[51] Whatever the cause, the consequence was that he felt obliged 'to leave the home that I had come to enjoy only too much'.[52]

At this juncture he was rescued by one of the Cavendishes' neighbours, Sir Gervase Clifton, who was looking for someone to accompany his seventeen-year-old son and heir Gervase on a tour of France.[53] Hobbes appears to have been very glad to obtain the post, for his letters of this period, as well as his later prose *Vita*, speak of Sir Gervase in tones of fulsome gratitude.[54] He duly took the young Gervase to Paris at the start of 1629,[55] after which they travelled to Geneva via Lyons and on to Orleans.[56] A plan to winter in Venice was abandoned because of the Mantuan war,[57] and they returned to England before the end of 1630, at which point Hobbes's employment with the Clifton family seems to have come to an end.[58]

Hobbes's third and final stint as a tutor spanned what he describes as

48 Bickley 1911, p. 44.

49 Malcolm 1994, pp. 777–8 and 808. Cf. Hobbes 1994, letter 3, pp. 7–8, which suggests that Aglionby was serving in the countess's household in a tutorial capacity.

50 Hobbes 1839b, p. lxxxviii, line 91.

51 Chatsworth: Hobbes MS D.6, fo. 3: 'Thomas Hobbes ... was upon ye death of his said Lord & Master discharged.'

52 Hobbes 1839b, p. lxxxviii: 'Deinde domo placita nimium ... abivi.'

53 On Sir Gervase see Malcolm 1994, pp. 820–3. Malcolm suggests (p. 821) that it may have been on the recommendation of the Welbeck Cavendishes that Hobbes gained his appointment as tutor to Sir Gervase's son.

54 Hobbes's verse *Vita* makes no mention of his employment by Clifton, but the prose *Vita* describes him as 'the noblest of men'. See Hobbes 1839a, p. xiv, and cf. letter 8 in Hobbes 1994, p. 17. Hobbes's good opinion of Sir Gervase seems to have been widely shared: see Malcolm 1994, p. 823.

55 See letter 4 in Hobbes 1994, pp. 10–11 (Hobbes to Sir Gervase Clifton, April 1630), stating that they have just arrived in Geneva from Paris. Hobbes claimed in his verse *Vita* that, after leaving the employment of the Devonshires, he spent eighteen months in Paris. See Hobbes 1839b, p. lxxxviii, line 92. This must be a slight exaggeration, as Hobbes was still in London in November 1628. (See letter 2 in Hobbes 1994, p. 6.) But it suggests that, if he and the young Gervase set out for France in 1629 (as the prose *Vita* states, p. xiv), they must have left very early in the year.

56 See letters 4, 5, 6 and 7 in Hobbes 1994, pp. 10–16. As these make clear, Hobbes and Gervase were in Geneva during April and May, and in Orleans during July and August.

57 See letter 4 in Hobbes 1994, p. 11.

58 As letter 8 in Hobbes 1994, p. 17, makes clear, Hobbes was definitely back in England by November 1630.

'seven painstaking years' between 1631 and 1637.[59] During this period he acted once again for the Cavendishes, evidently returning to their service as a result of the good offices of Sir Gervase Clifton. A letter of November 1630 from Hobbes to Sir Gervase implies that the latter had given the countess of Devonshire a good report of Hobbes's conduct in his employment, and that this had caused the countess to change her mind and appoint Hobbes after all as tutor to her son, who was now almost thirteen years old.[60] Hobbes adds in his prose *Vita* that he began teaching the young earl in 1631,[61] and that they studied together for three years before setting out – for the third time, in Hobbes's case – on an extended tour of the continent.[62]

Hobbes chooses to highlight these travels in his verse *Vita*, emphasising that he and his pupil by no means spent their whole time reading books.[63] But he seems to have taken his pedagogical duties very seriously, and he gives a revealing account of the curriculum he drew up for the young Cavendish. This makes it clear that he saw his basic duty as that of inculcating the three primary elements of the traditional *studia humanitatis*: grammar, rhetoric and poetry. Although he adds that he taught the young earl some logic, arithmetic and geography,[64] he stresses that they began 'by learning the meaning of the speech used by the Romans, and how to join Latin words together in the proper way';[65] that they moved on to consider 'how orators write, and by means of what art rhetoricians are accustomed to deceive the uninitiated'; and that they also made a study 'of how poetry is composed'.[66] As Hobbes explicitly points out, what he provided for his pupil was thus an education *in literis*, in the traditional humanistic ideal of 'good letters'.[67]

As we saw in chapter 2, those employed by the nobility and gentry on the strength of their mastery of the *studia humanitatis* were normally expected to serve not merely as tutors but as agents, secretaries and sometimes even as

59 Hobbes 1839b, p. lxxxix, line 103.

60 Hobbes 1994, p. 17.

61 Hobbes 1839a, p. xiv. This is confirmed in the *Narration* of 1639: see Chatsworth: Hobbes MS D.6, fo. 3^r.

62 Hobbes 1839a, p. xiv; cf. letter 11 in Hobbes 1994, p. 21.

63 Hobbes 1839b, p. lxxxix, lines 105–6.

64 Hobbes 1839b, p. lxxxix, lines 99–101.

65 Hobbes 1839b, p. lxxxviii, lines 95–6:

Hunc Romanarum sensus cognoscere vocum;
Jungere quoque decet verba Latina modo.

66 Hobbes 1839b, p. lxxxviii, lines 97–8:

Fallere quaque solent indoctos rhetores arte;
Quid facit orator, quidque poeta facit.

67 Hobbes 1839a, p. xiv.

legal and financial advisers to the families retaining them. It is a further indication of the traditional way in which Hobbes and the Cavendishes viewed his place in their household that, when his talents as a teacher were not required, it was chiefly in these other and time-honoured roles of the hired humanist that he found himself employed.

During his two decades of service to the second earl between 1608 and 1628, it is clear that Hobbes increasingly acted as Cavendish's personal secretary.[68] This was certainly the style in which he preferred to be described. When he translated the letters that Cavendish received from Fulgenzio Micanzio after returning from Venice in 1615, he identified himself at the beginning of the correspondence as 'Secretary to ye Lord Cavendysh'.[69] When he published his translation of Thucydides in 1629, he referred to himself on the title page as 'Secretary to ye late Earle of Devonshire'.[70] And when he presented the dowager countess of Devonshire with a number of legal requests on behalf of her son at the time of the latter's majority in 1639, he spoke once more of 'having been Secretary to her Husband'.[71]

As secretary to the second earl, Hobbes at first appears to have performed a number of rather menial duties. Aubrey notes with evident distaste that 'his lord, who was a waster, sent him up and downe to borrow money, and to gett gentlemen to be bound for him, being ashamed to speake him selfe'.[72] It is also clear that, although Hobbes counted by this time as a member of Cavendish's establishment, his salary sometimes depended on the willingness of Cavendish's father to settle his son's debts.[73] During the 1620s, however, Hobbes gradually acquired a position of greater responsibility. His chief labours on behalf of Cavendish in the early 1620s arose out of his patron's interest in the Virginia Company and its subsidiary, the Somers Island company,[74] of which Cavendish's father had become a member in 1615.[75] We first hear of Hobbes's employment in

68 Malcolm 1981, p. 297, notes his changing role.

69 Chatsworth: Hobbes MS 73.Aa: vellum-bound volume of letters, marked on flyleaf: 'Translated out of the originall Italian letters by Th: Hobbes secretary to ye Lord Cavendysh'. Cf. Bush 1973.

70 Hobbes 1629, title page; cf. Macdonald and Hargreaves 1952, p. 1.

71 Chatsworth: Hobbes MS D.6, fo. 3r.

72 Aubrey 1898, I, p. 347. Cavendish was undoubtedly a waster on a grand scale: see Malcolm 1994, p. 807.

73 Hardwick MS 29: Hobbes was paid £5.15s.0d in a settlement of Cavendish's debts in 1618 (p. 536) and £49.4s.0d in a further settlement in 1619 (p. 627).

74 Both of which Hobbes mentions in *Leviathan*. See Hobbes 1991, p. 159.

75 Bickley 1911, p. 39. By that time Lord Hardwick had been investing in Virginia and other overseas ventures for several years. See Hardwick MS 29: the first reference to Virginia (p. 213) dates from 1611; in subsequent years Lord Hardwick regularly invested over £2,000 p.a. in 'adventures by sea'. See p. 270 (for 1612), p. 345 (for 1613) and p. 383 (for 1614).

this connection in 1622. The records of the Virginia Company for that year state that, at a meeting of the company court held on 19 June, 'it pleased the right Hono^{ble} the Lord Cavendish to passe over one of his shares of land in Virginia unto m^{r} Hobbs wch beinge allowed of by the Auditors was also approved and ratified by the Court'.[76]

Cavendish's aim in making this grant was clearly to enlist Hobbes on his side in the increasingly acrimonious quarrels dividing the company at this time. These disputes became so serious that the company was obliged to submit to a judicial investigation of its affairs in 1623, and finally to the revocation of its charter and the transfer of Virginia to the crown in the following year.[77] Hobbes's presence undoubtedly strengthened Cavendish's hand in these arguments, but it is ironic that the most lasting consequence of Hobbes's attendance at the company's meetings may well have been to quicken his interest in the *studia humanitatis*, and especially in the classical art of eloquence. This possibility is suggested by the fact that one of the other members of the Virginia company was Dr Theodore Goulston. Goulston was a Fellow of the Royal College of Physicians, and the Virginia Company made some use of his scientific expertise, putting him on a committee in 1620 to examine the possibility of making wine in the colony[78] and involving him in 1621 in the appointment of a ship's doctor.[79] As we saw in chapter 1, however, Goulston was also a celebrated scholar of the humanities, who had issued in 1619 the first Latin translation of Aristotle's *Art of Rhetoric* to be published in England. Hobbes undoubtedly encountered Goulston at the meetings of the Virginia Company's court: they were present together for the first time at a court meeting on 2 April 1623,[80] and Hobbes was evidently sitting next to Goulston when names were taken at the meeting of 28 April 1624.[81] It is tempting (although perhaps not very profitable) to wonder whether the two men may have conversed about the subject matter of Goulston's latest book.

Whatever personal benefits Hobbes may have gained from attending these meetings, his principal reason for being there was of course to act as Cavendish's agent and representative. He seems to have discharged this duty with considerable assiduity. Between his admission in the summer of 1622 and the recall of the company's charter in May 1624 he attended no

76 Kingsbury 1906–35, II, p. 40. I owe this reference to Malcolm 1981, p. 298, an exceptionally valuable article to which my own discussion is deeply indebted. Hobbes's former pupil had acquired the style of Lord Cavendish on the elevation of his father to the earldom of Devonshire in 1618.

77 Craven 1932, pp. 265–91 and 316–18.

78 Kingsbury 1906–35, I, p. 403.

79 Kingsbury 1906–35, I, p. 523.

80 Kingsbury 1906–35, II, pp. 340–1.

81 Kingsbury 1906–35, II, pp. 533–4.

fewer than thirty-seven meetings of the company and its Somers Island subsidiary,[82] in addition to serving on at least one of its committees.[83] It is clear, moreover, that he played a useful role as someone whom Cavendish could rely on to take his side in debates about the company's affairs. For example, when the quarter court of 27 November 1622 was asked to approve the indentures making grants of land in Somers Island, it was Cavendish who moved – 'after a verie longe disputation' – that the indentures be accepted. When this proposal was put to the vote, there were found to be twenty-one in favour and twenty against. The fact that Hobbes duly voted on Cavendish's side made, in this instance, all the difference.[84]

If we turn from the early to the late 1620s, we encounter further evidence that Hobbes continued to act as agent for the Cavendishes and a representative of their interests. The most striking example relates to Charles I's so-called Forced Loan of 1626. The Privy Council resolution on this levy not only called on local magnates to subscribe generously, but also to support the government in its efforts to raise the tax from others.[85] The Cavendishes duly complied with both requirements,[86] and from a letter of September 1627 to Edward Nicholas, secretary to the duke of Buckingham, we learn that Hobbes was one of those whom they employed to travel round Derbyshire cajoling people into making their payments. A number of persons are listed in the letter as having promised but not yet contributed, but against one of the sums it is noted that it has been 'paid since that tyme to Mr Hobs Secreatary to the Earle of Devonshire'.[87] It is worth adding that this method of collection proved a resounding success, eventually netting over a quarter of a million pounds for the Exchequer.[88] In a modest way Hobbes helped to promote the policy of raising extra-parliamentary revenues that he later defended so vigorously in *The Elements of Law*.[89]

While Hobbes seems to have remained primarily in the employment of the Cavendishes throughout the 1620s, his skills as a humanist – and especially his exceptional command of Latin – led to his being engaged at some point as secretary to Francis Bacon.[90] It is not clear how this

82 Malcolm 1981, p. 298.
83 Kingsbury 1906–35, IV, p. 48.
84 Kingsbury 1906–35, II, pp. 159–60.
85 Cust 1987, pp. 3, 46–9, 101–2.
86 Devonshire at first refused to subscribe (October 1626), but paid by the end of the year. See Cust 1987, pp. 3, 101–2 and note.
87 State Papers 16/79, p. 67 (repaginated on microfilm as p. 105). Letter to Edward Nicholas, 30 September 1627. Cf. Sommerville 1992, p. 170.
88 Cust 1987, p. 92.
89 Hobbes 1969a, p. 140.
90 See Blackbourne 1839, p. xxv. On Bacon and the Cavendishes see also Gabrieli 1957 and Malcolm 1984, pp. 47–54.

secondment arose, but it must have taken place at some time between Bacon's dismissal from the Lord Chancellorship in May 1621 and his death in 1626.[91] One of Bacon's chief projects during these years was to turn his earlier vernacular works into Latin. He issued an extended version of *The Advancement of Learning* as *De Dignitate et Augmentis Scientiarum* in 1623, and at the same time began to translate some of his *Essays* into Latin. For this latter undertaking he needed some assistance, and according to Aubrey it was Hobbes who supplied it. Aubrey not only records that 'The Lord Chancellour Bacon loved to converse' with Hobbes, but that Hobbes 'assisted his lordship in translating severall of his Essayes into Latin, one, I well remember, is that *Of the Greatnes of Cities*'.[92] Aubrey also informs us that Hobbes acted as one of Bacon's amanuenses, and rapidly became Bacon's favourite. His lordship 'was wont to have him walke with him in his delicate groves where he did meditate: and when a notion darted into his mind, Mr. Hobbs was presently to note it downe, and his lordship was wont to say that he did it better then any one els about him; for that many times, when he read their notes he scarce understood what they writt, because they understood it not clearly themselves'.[93]

During his second spell of service to the Cavendishes in the 1630s Hobbes no longer appears to have described himself formally as a secretary. Nevertheless, it is clear that he continued to act as agent and adviser to the family throughout this period. We first catch a glimpse of him serving in this capacity in 1634, although he is acting on this occasion not for his principal employer but for his cousin and neighbour, the earl of Newcastle. He writes to Newcastle from London on 26 January 1634 as follows:

> My first businesse in London, was to seeke for Galileos dialogues; I thought it a very good bargaine, when at taking my leave of your Lordship I undertooke to buy it for you, but if yo[r] Lo[P] should bind me to performance it would be hard enough, for it is not possible to get it for mony; There were but few brought over at first, and they that buy such bookes, are not such men as to part wth them againe. I heare say it is called in, in Italy, as a booke that will do more hurt to their Religion then all the bookes have done of Luther and Calvin, such opposition they thinke is betweene their Religion, and naturall reason. I doubt not but the Translation of it will here be publiquely embraced, and therefore wish extreamely that D[r] Webbe would hasten it.[94]

91 The Cavendishes, however, had known Bacon for a considerable time. As solicitor general in 1612 he had been involved in the contempt case against the countess of Shrewsbury (Spedding 1868, pp. 294–7). Malcolm 1984, p. 50, notes that, in a letter of March 1616, Micanzio thanks the young Cavendish (Hobbes's pupil) for having put him in touch with Bacon.

92 Aubrey 1898, I, p. 331.

93 Aubrey 1898, I, p. 70, 83.

94 See letter 10 in Hobbes 1994, p. 19.

Here we see Hobbes discharging one of the most dignified and time-honoured roles of the humanist, that of keeping his patrons informed about the latest books and trying to make suitable purchases for their libraries.

When Hobbes's duties as a tutor finally came to an end in 1637,[95] the third earl retained him in much the same capacity as his father had done, as someone to whom he could turn for advice and loyal support in his financial and even his legal affairs. This emerges most clearly from a document of 1639 which appears to have been drawn up by Hobbes and is signed by him and the third earl at the foot of each alternate page. It is dated 12 April 1639 and carries the title *A Narration of ye Proceedings both Publique & Private concerning ye Inheritance of ye Right Honble William Earle of Devonshire.*[96] The third earl, who had come of age in October 1638,[97] was facing a number of financial difficulties arising from the fact that, when his father had succeeded in 1626, he had found his inheritance heavily encumbered by the first earl's legendary extravagance.[98] His response had been to introduce a Bill into the House of Lords allowing him the exceptional expedient of breaking some family entails to meet his debts.[99] After his death in 1628 his widow Christian made use of this permission to undertake extensive retrenchment and rationalisation of the Devonshire estates.[100] As soon as her son came of age he demanded an audit of his mother's stewardship,[101] and in consequence of its findings entered into a serious quarrel with her about the management of his patrimony. The countess had acted on the assumption that, if she disposed of an estate to discharge debts upon it, and if this resulted in a surplus, she had the right to make use of the spare money to purchase other estates of which she became sole proprietor.[102] Moreover, she seems to have taken the view that she retained such rights of disposal even after the end of her son's minority, and even appears to have contemplated the sale of Devonshire House, the family's most important property in London.[103]

The young earl was so incensed by his mother's behaviour that he planned to start legal proceedings against her. When Hobbes was consulted, he refused to countenance such a drastic step. He takes considerable credit upon himself for this advice, and it is striking that he

95 Hobbes 1839b, p. lxxxix, line 103, notes the length of his service in this role.
96 Chatsworth: Hobbes MS D.6. For a discussion see Malcolm 1994, pp. 815–16.
97 Malcolm 1994, pp. 809, 815.
98 See Malcolm 1994, p. 807, who notes that the second earl was scarcely less extravagant.
99 See Bickley 1911, p. 43 and cf. Malcolm 1994, p. 807.
100 For details see Malcolm 1994, p. 808.
101 Rogow 1986, p. 113.
102 See Pomfret 1685, pp. 30–2, and Bickley, p. 45.
103 Rogow 1986, p. 114.

actually refers to himself at this juncture, in traditional humanist vein, as the young earl's counsellor. The *Narration* ends by pointing out that the earl is 'living at this present in ye house of his said Mother', and adds that 'the said Thomas Hobbes hath counselled him, & doth still counsell him to continue so; & not to commence any suite against her'.[104] Hobbes characteristically adds that 'for this information ye said Thomas Hobbes neyther hath receaved nor demanded, nor expecteth any reward, but onely ye testimony of having performed ye part of a faithfull Tutor, & to be justified against aspersions to ye contrary'.[105]

Nevertheless, Hobbes made use of his position as a faithful tutor to take sides in the dispute with extraordinary boldness, especially for someone with no legal training. He announced himself unhappy in the first place with the basic principles underlying the Act of 1628. From the point of view of the present earl, the *Narration* observes, it is 'worthy ye considering that by this Act ye undoubted property he had in his estate was wthout pretence of benefitt to ye Publique, wthout Crime, & against his Will taken from him'.[106] Hobbes further contends that, even if the Act be regarded as legally admissible, it cannot be equitable for the earl's mother to treat the proceeds of any estates sold under its provisions as her own property. On the contrary, 'it might well be presumed, that his Father did intend, after ye augmentation of ye joynture of ye said Countesse his Wife', that 'if any overplus did remaine out of ye revenue of ye estate wthout touching ye said joynture, the same should be wholly to ye benefitt of his sonne ye said Earle'.[107] Finally, Hobbes specifically addresses the question of Devonshire House, declaring that there can be no question of its being treated as one of the properties capable of being sold. This is because 'in ye Act of Parlam^{t}. it is put downe as a motive to cause ye said Earle to pay his Fathers debts, that ye said debt was partly contracted by ye purchase of Devonshire house'. It must therefore be 'against equity & ye expectation of ye Parlam^{t}. that ye same, or any part thereof should be devised from him either for ever, or for any time at all'.[108]

A year after this fracas, the young earl made a further and more public attempt to employ Hobbes as a counsellor and spokesman for his family and local interests. He tried to have Hobbes returned as member of Parliament for Derbyshire in the so-called Short Parliament of 1640, seeking to place him in the seat that the second earl, Hobbes's original

104 Chatsworth: Hobbes MS D.6, fo. 6.
105 Chatsworth: Hobbes MS D.6, fo. 6. The *Narration* ends with these words.
106 Chatsworth: Hobbes MS D.6, fo. 6.
107 Chatsworth: Hobbes MS D.6, fo. 5.
108 Chatsworth: Hobbes MS D.6, fo. 5.

pupil, had held for five years before succeeding to his title in 1626.[109] The evidence concerning this scheme comes from a letter written by Sir John Coke to his eldest son on 26 January 1640.[110] Coke had just been dismissed from his post as secretary of state in Charles I's increasingly unpopular government. He was about to retire to Derbyshire, where he had been proprietor since 1626 of estates close to those of the Cavendishes. He wrote to tell his son that, although Hobbes was the earl of Devonshire's nominee in the forthcoming elections, 'Mr Fulwood telleth me that Derbymen are resolved to give no way to the election of Mr Hobs'.[111] Coke's informant is identifiable as Christopher Fulwood, who was certainly well-placed to know the mood of the local electorate. The eldest son of Sir George Fulwood of Middleton, Christopher Fulwood was a lawyer who resided out of term in Derbyshire, where he had been serving for some time as a justice of the peace.[112] Fulwood's view, Coke goes on to inform his son, is that 'your brother may be introduced' instead of Hobbes if the earl of Devonshire's attempt to promote the latter's candidature is blocked. 'But I shall not persuade him' Coke cautiously adds, 'to put himself in contestation against my lord. Only if you find that Hobs cannot prevail, do what you can for your brother, and write speedily how they stand affected, that we may co-operate also from hence.'[113]

The tone of Coke's letter is knowing, but his eldest son appears to have had a better understanding of the Derbyshire voters. When the election took place it was he himself who was returned as Member for the county rather than any of the candidates who had been discussed. By a final irony that can scarcely have been pleasing either to Hobbes or the Cavendishes, the young Coke promptly lent his active support to the Parliamentary cause – the very cause his father had opposed throughout his long public career. Years later Hobbes was to point out with deep bitterness in *Behemoth* that, when electing members of Parliament, 'it is usuall with the Freeholders in the Counties, and with tradesmen in the Cities and Burroughs to choose, as near as they can, such as are the most repugnant to the giving of Subsidies'.[114]

Within a few months of this reverse, Hobbes found himself the victim of an even more ironic turn of events. The Parliament of 1640, in which he had doubtless hoped to speak in favour of the government, launched a campaign of such hostility against the crown and its supporters that

109 Bickley 1911, p. 42.
110 See Warrender 1983, p. 4 and note.
111 Coke 1888, II, p. 251.
112 See *DNB*, *sub* Fulwood, Christopher.
113 Coke 1888, II, p. 251.
114 St John's College Oxford MS 13, p. 114. The word 'the' before 'giving' is crossed out as an afterthought. Cf. Hobbes 1969b, p. 121.

Hobbes instead began to fear for his life.[115] He suddenly resolved in November 1640 to leave for France,[116] thereby embarking on a period of exile that lasted over eleven years.

Hobbes's decision to seek sanctuary abroad – where he was shortly joined by the earl of Devonshire, and later by the earl of Newcastle[117] – appears to have been due in part to the fact that he had become so closely identified with the Cavendishes, who had in turn become associated with the hated policies of the court. The third earl of Devonshire remained strongly attached to the party of Charles I, and even voted in the House of Lords in 1640 against the attainder of the earl of Strafford, the chief architect of Charles's non-parliamentary government of the 1630s.[118] His cousin, the earl of Newcastle, a prominent courtier and a still more strident royalist, had been serving since 1638 as 'governor' to the young prince of Wales.[119] When civil war broke out in 1642, he went to the remarkable lengths of raising and leading a private army for the king, a service for which he was immediately rewarded with a marquisate.[120]

Meanwhile Hobbes had given ample evidence on his own account of his dislike of Parliaments and his preference for the royalist cause. Not only had he helped to collect the Forced Loan, the legality of which had been questioned even by the judges;[121] two years later, in publishing his translation of Thucydides, he had appended an introductory essay pointing with obvious admiration to the fact that Thucydides had despised and detested the public assemblies of his day. Hobbes focuses on three aspects of Athenian democracy which Thucydides had particularly criticised, describing them in terms highly insulting to any committed supporter of parliamentary rule:

> For his opinion touching the government of the state, it is manifest that he least of all liked the democracy. And upon divers occasions he noteth the emulation and contention of the demagogues for reputation and glory of wit, with the crossing of each other's counsels, to the damage of the public; the inconsistency of resolutions, caused by the diversity of ends and power of rhetoric in the orators; and the desperate actions undertaken upon the flattering advice of such as desired to attain, or to hold what they had attained, of authority and sway amongst the common people.[122]

115 Sommerville 1992, pp. 119.
116 The suddenness of his resolve is attested by the letter he sent from Paris to Lord Scudamore in April 1641. See letter 35 in Hobbes 1994, pp. 114–15. Cf. also Hobbes 1840c, p. 414.
117 Malcolm 1994, pp. 814, 816.
118 Pomfret 1685, pp. 42–3.
119 Malcolm 1994, p. 814.
120 Malcolm 1994, p. 814.
121 Cust 1987, pp. 3, 101–2.
122 Hobbes 1975b, p. 13. Hobbes later repeated this judgment in *De Cive*. See Hobbes 1983a, x.xi, p. 178, on the fact that 'contrariis sententiis orationibusque pugnant aequales oratores'.

Hobbes later reiterated that 'what I found pleasing in Thucydides beyond all other historians was the fact that he demonstrated how inept democracy is, and how much wiser is the rule of a single man than that of a multitude'. This is why, he explains, 'I decided to translate him, in order to make him speak to the English about the need to avoid the rhetoricians whom they were at that time planning to consult.'[123]

As soon as the Short Parliament met in April 1640, political attitudes of this complexion began to come under dangerous fire. Roger Maynwaring, who as chaplain to Charles I had preached in favour of the Forced Loan,[124] was immediately singled out for attack and imprisoned by order of the Long Parliament later in the year.[125] Since Hobbes believed that, as he informed Aubrey, Maynwaring had 'preached his doctrine', he may well have been right to fear the same fate, although it seems slightly self-important on his part to have assumed that his views were sufficiently well known to make him a target in the same way.[126] Nevertheless, he fell into a characteristic state of deep anxiety, writing to Lord Scudamore from the safety of Paris in April 1641 that 'the reason I came away was that I saw words that tended to advance the prerogative of kings began to be examined in Parlament', and 'I knew some that had a good will to have had me troubled'.[127] Aubrey makes essentially the same point, although he allows himself a touch of sly bathos in reporting the slightly inglorious end to this phase of Hobbes's career. Seeing Maynwaring and others sent to the Tower, 'then thought Mr. Hobbes, 'tis time now for me to shift for my selfe, and so withdrew into France and resided at Paris'.[128]

HOBBES'S HUMANIST STUDIES

If Hobbes's pattern of employment up to 1640 points to his essentially humanist allegiances, this impression is amply confirmed if we turn to the range of studies he pursued during the same period. As we saw in chapter 1, by the time of his arrival at Oxford in 1603 he had already acquired a

123 Hobbes 1839b, p. lxxxviii, lines 80–4:

> Sed mihi prae reliquis Thucydides placuit.
> Is Democratia ostendit mihi quam sit inepta
> [Is Democratiam docuit me quam sit inepta,]
> Et quantum coetu plus sapit unus homo.
> Hunc ego scriptorem verti, qui diceret Anglis,
> [Hunc ego scriptorem feci ut loqueretur ad Anglos]
> Consultaturi rhetoras ut fugerent.

124 Sommerville 1986, pp. 127–9.

125 Sommerville 1992, pp. 17–18, 80–1.

126 Aubrey 1898, 1, p. 334.

127 See letter 35 in Hobbes 1994, p. 115. Cf. Zagorin 1978.

128 Aubrey 1898, 1, p. 334.

sufficient command of the classical languages to have completed a Latin translation of Euripides' *Medea*. Nor did he allow himself, if his verse *Vita* is to be believed, to be much distracted from his interest in humane letters by the scholastic curriculum he was obliged to follow to obtain his bachelor's degree. He assures us that he sedulously attended his lessons in logic, even though his teacher was no more than a beardless youth and the lessons struck him as inherently absurd. But he adds that he soon stopped going to his classes in physics, and explains that 'I turned instead to more agreeable studies, and began in particular to revolve in my mind once more the books to which I had earlier been introduced, but which I still did not know very well.'[129]

These literary pursuits by no means came to an end after he left Oxford to join the Cavendish household in 1608. It is true that, according to the prose *Vita*, they were seriously interrupted for a while. 'During the year that followed I spent almost the whole of my time with my master in the city, as a result of which I forgot most of the Latin and Greek I had ever known.'[130] After returning from his European tour in 1615, however, Hobbes seems to have settled down to a regular and scholarly mode of life. He informs us that 'my master provided me with leisure throughout these years, and supplied me in addition with books of all kinds for my studies'.[131] Hobbes appears to have made particularly good use of the pocket-sized volumes published by the Dutch firm of Elzevir (who were later to issue *De Cive* in this format). He liked to carry them around with him, Aubrey reports, so that he could 'read in the lobbey, or antechamber, whilest his lord was making his visits'.[132] As his autobiographies make clear, the books he was reading largely centred on the five canonical disciplines of the *studia humanitatis*: grammar, rhetoric, poetry, history and civil philosophy.

Hobbes stresses in his prose *Vita* that, upon his return from his first foreign trip, he began by setting himself a course of reading specifically designed to recover and extend his mastery of the classical languages. 'As

129 Hobbes 1839b, p. lxxxvii, lines 51–2:
Ergo ad amoena magis me verto, librosque revolvo,
Queis prius instructus, non bene doctus eram.
[Queis prius edoctus, non bene doctus eram.]

130 Hobbes 1839a, p. xiii: 'Anno sequente, cum domino suo in urbe perpetuo fere degens, quod didicerat linguae Graecae et Latinae, magna ex parte amiserat.'

131 Hobbes 1839b, p. lxxxviii, lines 73–4:
Ille per hoc tempus mihi praebuit otia, libros
Omnimodos studiis praebuit ille meis.'
[Ille per hos annos mihi praebuit otia, libros
Omnimodos studiis suppeditatque meis.]

132 Aubrey 1898, I, p. 331.

soon as I got back to England, I started carefully to read over the works of a number of poets and historians, together with the commentaries written on them by the most celebrated grammarians.'[133] He adds that 'my aim was not to learn how to write floridly, but rather to learn how to write in an authentically Latin style, and at the same time how to find out which particular words possessed the power best suited to my thoughts'.[134] He must have begun to recover his knowledge of Greek during the same period, Lucian being one of the authors on whom he seems to have concentrated. He alludes to Lucian's version of the fable of Hercules in *Leviathan*, and in the appendix added to the Latin edition of 1668 he refers to him admiringly as an excellent writer of Greek.[135]

No doubt as part of this process, Hobbes appears to have renewed his acquaintance with the classical theorists of eloquence at the same time. He must have made a close study of Aristotle's *Art of Rhetoric* either at this juncture or in the early 1630s, given that his English paraphrase of the text was in print by 1637. He must also have read, or more probably reread, the major treatises on Roman rhetorical theory in the course of the 1620s. Previous studies of Hobbes's intellectual development have tended to leave the impression that his detailed knowledge of ancient eloquence may have been limited to Aristotle's *Rhetoric.*[136] But in the introduction to his translation of Thucydides in 1629 Hobbes makes it clear that he was no less familiar with a number of leading works of Roman rhetorical thought. He not only refers familiarly to Cicero's *Orator*, *De optimo oratore* and *De oratore*, but he also quotes from each of these texts.[137] Finally, it seems likely that it was during the same period that he immersed himself in Quintilian's *Institutio oratoria*, a treatise to which he makes reference in several of his later works.[138]

There is plentiful evidence that Hobbes was also much preoccupied in the 1620s with the third element in the traditional *studia humanitatis*, the study of classical poetry. He informs us in his verse *Vita* that he read a great deal of ancient poetry and drama at this time, specifically mentioning Horace, Virgil and Homer among the poets, together with Euripides, Sophocles, Plautus and Aristophanes among the dramatists.[139] Aubrey

133 Hobbes 1839a, pp. xiii–xiv: 'Itaque cum in Angliam reversus esset, Historicos et poetas (adhibitis grammaticorum celebrium commentariis) versavit diligenter.'

134 Hobbes 1839a, p. xiv: 'non ut floride, sed ut Latine posset scribere, et vim verborum cogitatis congruentem invenire'.

135 See Hobbes 1668, p. 346 on Lucian as 'bonus author linguae Graecae'.

136 See for example Strauss 1963, pp. 35, 41–2, Shapiro 1980, pp. 148–50.

137 Hobbes 1975b, pp. 10, 18–19, 26–7.

138 See the allusions in Hobbes 1971a, esp. pp. 49–51; various references in Hobbes 1991 (e.g. p. 176) and the invocation of Quintilian's judgment on Lucan in Hobbes 1844, p. viii.

139 Hobbes 1839b, p. lxxxviii, lines 77–8.

confirms that, although Hobbes in later life possessed relatively few books, his visitors could always expect to find copies of Homer and Virgil on his table.[140] Aubrey also lets slip that, before embarking on his translation of Thucydides, Hobbes 'spent two years in reading romances and playes, which he haz often repented and sayd that these two yeares were lost of him'.[141] Hobbes himself makes no mention of these literary diversions, but it is perhaps suggestive that, when examining the phenomenon of 'Learned madnesse' in chapter 10 of *The Elements of Law*, the example he chooses to discuss is that of Don Quixote.[142]

Hobbes adds in his verse *Vita* that this was a time when he read many other poets.[143] One of these must have been Lucan, whose *Pharsalia* he cites in his essay on heroic poetry and praises for having achieved 'the height of Fancie'.[144] A second must have been Ovid, whom he might have been expected to mention among his favourite poets, especially as he modelled his verse *Vita* so closely on Ovid's autobiography. Not only does he imitate Ovid's elegiac couplets, occasionally even echoing a turn of phrase,[145] but he presents his personality in remarkably similar terms. Like Ovid he speaks in tones of mingled injury and self-justification of his many enemies and how he has learned to overcome or endure them; and like Ovid he lays particular emphasis on the sadness of exile and the embittering treachery of former friends.

It is also noteworthy that, according to Aubrey, Hobbes was very much in the company of poets at this time. Aubrey tells us that, as a schoolboy in Wiltshire in 1634, he first encountered Hobbes when the latter returned to his native county in the summer of that year to visit his old schoolmaster, Robert Latimer, who was by that time teaching Aubrey himself. Aubrey recalls being much impressed by Hobbes, who 'was then a proper man, briske, and in very good habit', and that 'his conversation about those times was much about Ben: Jonson, Mr. Ayton, etc.'[146] The name of Ben Jonson scarcely needs glossing, but it is worth noting that 'Mr. Ayton' must have been Sir Robert Ayton, a kinsman of the second earl of Devonshire's

140 Aubrey 1898, I, p. 349.
141 Aubrey 1898, I, p. 361.
142 BL Harl. MS 4235, fo. 42^{v}. Cf. Hobbes 1969a, p. 52.
143 Hobbes 1839b, p. lxxxviii, line 79.
144 Hobbes 1844, p. vii. Hobbes also mentions Lucan in his *Answer* to Davenant. See Hobbes 1971a, p. 46.
145 Compare, for example, Ovid 1988 line 20 with Hobbes 1839b, p. lxxxvi, line 28; Ovid 1988, line 56 with Hobbes 1839b, p. xc, line 154; Ovid 1988 line 132 with Hobbes 1839b, p. xcix, line 369.
146 Aubrey 1898, I, p. 332.

wife.[147] Ayton was a prolific writer in Latin as well as English verse, much given to the poetry of regret and unrequited love.[148] Aubrey elsewhere informs us that Ayton 'was a great acquaintance' of Hobbes's,[149] and that Hobbes submitted the draft of his translation of Thucydides to Ayton as well as Jonson so that they could 'give their judgment on his style'.[150]

Hobbes became friendly with several other poets during the same period. By far the greatest of these was John Donne, whom he first encountered as a fellow member of the Virginia Company in the early 1620s. Hobbes and Cavendish both went to hear Donne preach a sermon to the company in November 1622,[151] and Hobbes attended a number of meetings of the company's court at which Donne was also present.[152] Hobbes also made the acquaintance of Edmund Waller and Sir William Davenant around this time, later renewing these friendships in Paris in the course of the 1640s.[153] There too he met Abraham Cowley, who in turn 'bestowed on him', as Aubrey puts it, 'an immortal pindarique ode'.[154] Cowley's poem is striking not merely for its tone of extreme veneration, but for the emphasis it places on Hobbes's specifically literary talents and achievements. The fifth stanza runs:

> I little thought before,
> (Nor being my *own self* so *poor*
> Could comprehend so vast a *store*)
> That all the *Wardrobe* of rich *Eloquence*,
> Could have afforded half enuff,
> Of *bright*, of *new*, and *lasting* stuff,
> To cloath the mighty *Limbs* of thy *Gigantique Sence*.
> Thy solid *Reason* like the *shield* from Heaven
> To the *Trojan Heroe* given,
> Too strong to take a mark from any mortal dart,
> Yet shines with *Gold* and *Gems* in every part,
> And *Wonders* on it grav'd by the learn'd hand of *Art*
> A *shield* that gives delight
> Even to the *enemies* sight,
> Then when they're sure to *lose* the *Combat by't*.[155]

The shield of Hobbes's reasoning not only protects his philosophy against

147 Aubrey 1898, I, p. 365.
148 See the entries in Fowler 1992, pp. 76–86.
149 Aubrey 1898, I, p. 25.
150 Aubrey 1898, I, p. 365.
151 Malcolm 1981, p. 303.
152 Kingsbury 1906–35, II, pp. 244–6, 300–1, 390–1.
153 Aubrey 1898, I, pp. 206, 369–70.
154 Aubrey 1898, I, p. 368.
155 Cowley 1949, p. 44.

its enemies; like the armour of Demoleos in the *Aeneid*, it shines with so much brilliance as to be *decus et tutamen*, a thing of beauty as well as a means of defence.

It is evident from Hobbes's autobiographies that he also devoted himself after his return to England in 1615 to the fourth of the five elements in the *studia humanitatis*, the study of history. He informs us that 'in my early years I was drawn by my natural bent to the historians no less than to the poets',[156] and explains that this made him turn 'to our own historians as well as to those of Greece and Rome'.[157] He does not tell us which English historians he read, but he emphasises in both his autobiographies that, among the Greeks, 'it was Thucydides who pleased me above all the rest'.[158] Aubrey reveals that, among the historians of Rome, Hobbes chiefly admired Caesar, and particularly his *Commentarii*.[159] He adds that Hobbes never abandoned these early interests, and that in later life it was not uncommon to find him reading 'some probable historie'.[160]

Hobbes must in addition have made a close study of several other classical historians. This is evident from *The Elements of Law*, in which he reveals a detailed knowledge of Sallust's *Bellum Catilinae*;[161] it is also evident from *Leviathan*, in which he puts Plutarch's life of Solon to elegant though unacknowledged use.[162] But the same point emerges most clearly from his translation of Thucydides. One of the distinctive features of Hobbes's edition is his attempt to locate all the place-names mentioned in Thucydides' text. Hobbes entered the names on a map of ancient Greece which he drew himself, and which he arranged to have engraved and inserted into his book.[163] He explains in his opening address that he was able to discover the location of all the towns and villages 'by travel in Strabo, Pausanias, Herodotus and some other good authors'.[164] His

156 Hobbes 1839a, p. xx: 'Natura sua, et primis annis, ferebatur ad lectionem historiarum et poetarum.'

157 Hobbes 1839b, p. lxxxviii, lines 75–6:

> Vertor ego ad nostras, ad Graecas, atque Latinas
> Historias.

158 Hobbes 1839b, p. lxxxviii, line 80:

> Sed mihi prae reliquis Thucydides placuit.

Cf. also Hobbes 1839a, p. xiv.

159 Aubrey 1898, I, p. 331.

160 Aubrey 1898, I, p. 349.

161 BL Harl. MS 4235, fo. 131[r–v]. Cf. Hobbes 1969a, pp. 175–6.

162 The discussion of 'cobweb laws' in chapter XXVII of *Leviathan* is taken from Plutarch's life of Solon, evidently in North's translation. See Hobbes 1991, p. 204 and cf. Plutarch 1580, p. 89, speaking of Anacharsis' amusement at Solon's aspiration to frame laws 'to bridell mens covetousnes and injustice. For such lawes, sayed he, do rightly resemble the spyder's cobwebbes.'

163 See Hobbes 1629, in which 'The Mappe of Antient Greece' is tipped in after sig. c, 4[v].

164 Hobbes 1975a, p. 9.

index confirms that he made extensive use of all these authorities, and also read a number of other historians with the same purpose in mind. One of these was Appian, whose account of the Roman civil wars he mentions at several points.[165] A second was Polybius, whose *Histories* he refers to with some frequency.[166] But the most important was Livy, whose authority he invokes on dozens of occasions, drawing his information from at least ten different books of the history.[167]

During the long period of reading that followed Hobbes's return to England in 1615, he also seems to have taken a special interest in the fifth and culminating element in the traditional *studia humanitatis*, the study of moral and civil philosophy. His reading must at least have encompassed Lipsius' *De Doctrina Civili*, which he quotes in the introduction to his translation of Thucydides,[168] as well as Bacon's *Essays*, which he helped to translate. He must have known More's *Utopia* and Bodin's *Six livres de la république*, both of which he mentions in *The Elements of Law*, the latter in tones of considerable respect.[169] We learn in addition from one of his letters to the earl of Newcastle that he began reading John Selden's *Mare Clausum* as soon as it was published in 1635,[170] and from references in *The Elements of Law* that by 1640 he had mastered a number of classical texts in *scientia civilis*, including Aristotle's *Politics* and the works of Cicero and Seneca.[171]

It is in some ways even more striking that Hobbes's pupil William Cavendish should have taken such a remarkably professional interest in *scientia civilis* at the same time. As we saw in chapter 4, Cavendish made his debut as a writer on moral philosophy in 1611, when his *Discourse Against Flatterie* was published by the London firm of Walter Burre. Although the *Discourse* appeared anonymously, it was known to the booksellers as Cavendish's work,[172] and was dedicated to his father-in-law, Lord Bruce of Kinloss.[173] The epistle dedicatory further informs us that it was Lord Bruce 'for whose sake, and at whose commaundment is [sic] was first undertaken'.[174] The book was originally 'the worke of your will', the

165 See for example Hobbes 1629, sig. b, 2^v^.

166 Hobbes 1629, sig. c, 1^r^, sig. c, 2^r^ and sig. c, 3^r^.

167 Book 4 is cited at sig. c, 1^r^; book 8 at sig. c, 2^r^; book 9 at sig. c, 2^v^; book 28 at sig. c, 3^r^; book 31 at sig. c, 2^r^; book 32 at sig. b, 4^v^; book 42 at sig. b, 4^r–v^; book 44 at sig. b, 2^r^ and at many subsequent points; book 48 at sig. b, 3^r^, etc.

168 Hobbes 1975b, p. 27.

169 Hobbes 1969a, pp. 30, 172.

170 See letter 18 in Hobbes 1994, p. 32. Hobbes and Selden were fellow members of Magdalen Hall Oxford, and became friends towards the end of Selden's life. See Aubrey 1898, I, p. 369.

171 Hobbes 1969a, pp. 170, 174, 177.

172 See chapter 4, note 184, *supra*.

173 See [Cavendish] 1611, sig. A, 2^r^: 'To the honorable Gentleman the Lord Bruce, Baron of Kinlosse'.

174 [Cavendish] 1611, sig. A, 2^r^.

epistle goes on, and is now 'brought forth under your protection'.[175] There seems no reason to doubt – as some scholars have done[176] – that Cavendish was the principal author of the *Discourse*.[177] But if it is true that the work was commissioned by his formidable father-in-law, it would hardly have been surprising if Cavendish had called upon his tutor to help him make a satisfactory job of it.

After returning from his travels in 1615, Cavendish continued to read and write on similar themes. The first outcome was a set of ten short pieces[178] to which he gave the Baconian title of *Essayes* and which he presented to his father in the form of a manuscript volume inscribed from 'Your Lordships mos observant and dutifull sonne W. Cavendisshe'.[179] Hobbes must already have been acting as Cavendish's secretary by this time, for the volume is actually in Hobbes's hand,[180] although it includes corrections by Cavendish in addition to the signature claiming the volume as his own work.[181] Again there seems no reason to assume that Hobbes rather than Cavendish must have been the real author,[182] especially as some of the essays contain opinions diametrically opposed to those later expressed by Hobbes on the same subjects.[183] As in the case of the *Discourse*, however, it is hard to believe that Cavendish would not have discussed the contents of the volume with his former tutor, particularly as the opening essays are all devoted to issues so close to Hobbes's heart: 'Arrogance', 'Ambition', 'Affectation', 'Detraction' and 'Selfe-will'.[184]

Cavendish's final contribution to *scientia civilis* took the form of his volume of essays entitled *Horae Subsecivae* or 'Leisure hours'. This collection was first published anonymously by Edward Blount in 1620,[185] although

175 [Cavendish] 1611, sig. A, 2^v and 3^r.

176 Kennet 1708, p. 5, claimed that the anonymous *Horae Subsecivae* (1620) – which includes a version of the *Discourse* of 1611 – was written by Gilbert Cavendish, eldest son of the first earl, who died before 1618. Others have claimed the *Horae* (and *a fortiori* the *Discourse*) for Hobbes. See, most recently, Harwood 1986, p. 26 and note. On the *Horae* see notes 182–185, *infra.*

177 One of the findings of the computer analysis reported in Reynolds and Hilton 1993, p. 369.

178 Malcolm 1981, p. 321, suggests that these were probably drafted before 1610, although later revised to take account of Cavendish's foreign travels, including as they do a description of Rome.

179 Chatsworth: Hobbes MS D.3, p. vi.

180 Correctly noted in Strauss 1963, p. xii and note, and more recently in Wolf 1969 and Harwood 1986, p. 26 and note.

181 Hobbes MS D.3 has corrections at pp. 5, 13, 15, 22, 48, 58, etc., and Cavendish's signature at p. vi.

182 As claimed in Wolf 1969, pp. 113–31.

183 For example, on the value of studying history. See chapter 7, note 64, *infra.*

184 Chatsworth: Hobbes MS D.3, title page.

185 [Cavendish] 1620. An addition to the title-page of the annotated copy at Chatsworth (marked 'Bookcase 31, Shelf H') reads: 'written by Cavendysh'. Rogow 1986, p. 250, claims that the annotations are all in Hobbes's hand, but this is not correct.

when the firm of Legatt and Crooke registered the same work for republication in 1637 they described it as 'Lord Cavendishes *Essaies*'.[186] The first half of the *Horae* contains twelve short pieces entitled 'Observations', and consists of a slightly extended version of the manuscript volume of essays already presented by Cavendish to his father.[187] The second half is given over to four longer 'Discourses', the third of which is a revised and abbreviated version of the *Discourse Against Flatterie* originally published in 1611.[188] No doubt Cavendish and Hobbes discussed the contents of this collection as well, and it appears that Hobbes may actually have written some of the discourses, although the rest of the volume is Cavendish's work.[189] But in spite of the help he gave, Hobbes seems to have been activated by something deeper than mere flattery when, in the dedication to his translation of Thucydides, he assured the son of his former pupil that his father had always been seriously devoted to 'that kind of learning which best deserveth the pains and hours of great persons, history and civil knowledge'.[190]

HOBBES'S HUMANIST WRITINGS

The strongest evidence that we should think of Hobbes's intellectual formation essentially as that of a humanist is provided by the range of works he published prior to the appearance of his first major treatise, *De Cive*, in 1642. If we turn to his writings from this early period, we find that he not only contributed to all five of the recognised humanist disciplines, but that his published works were wholly confined to these distinctively humanist genres.

Hobbes initially made a contribution of exceptional importance to the first of the five elements in the traditional *studia humanitatis*, the study of the classical languages. This took the form of his translation of Thucydides' history, which appeared as *Eight Bookes of the Peloponnesian Warre* in 1629.[191] Hobbes concedes in his opening address that Thucydides' text has already been translated into English, and that he has seen a copy of this earlier version, which Thomas Nicolls had issued in 1550.[192] But Hobbes objects

186 Arber 1875–94, IV, p. 362.

187 The two pieces added to the earlier collection of ten 'Essayes' (Chatsworth: Hobbes MS D.3) are entitled 'Of a Country Life' and 'Of Religion'.

188 This appears as 'Against Flattery' at pp. 419–503. The other three 'Discourses' are entitled 'Upon the begining of Tacitus', 'Of Rome' and 'Of Lawe'.

189 See the computer analysis reported in Reynolds and Hilton 1993 pp. 366, 369 and figure 6 in appendix 3, p. 378.

190 Hobbes 1975a, p. 3.

191 Henry Seile, the publisher, entered the book in the Stationers' Register on 18 March 1628 (i.e. 1629 our style). Arber 1875–94, III, p. 161.

192 See Hobbes 1975a, p. 8, and cf. Schlatter 1975, pp. xi–xii.

that Nicolls's rendering is not merely full of inaccuracies, but offends against a more fundamental tenet of humanism by failing to make use of the best available texts. Nicolls had been content to work from a French translation (published by Claude de Seyssel in 1527) which in turn derived from Lorenzo Valla's Latin edition of the 1450s.[193] But Valla's translation, as Hobbes observes, 'was not without some errors', and was in any case taken from 'a Greek copy not so correct as now is extant'. When Nicolls based his English version on these already shaky foundations, the outcome was that 'by multiplication of error', Thucydides was 'at length traduced, rather than translated into our language'.[194] By contrast, Hobbes stresses, he has taken care to ensure that his own version reflects the highest standards of humanist textual scholarship. He has worked directly from Thucydides' original Greek, using the newly corrected edition of Aemilius Porta; and he has supplemented Porta's text with an up-to-date scholarly apparatus, 'not neglecting any version, comment, or other help I could come by'.[195] The outcome, Hobbes proudly announces, is a version as free as possible from errors, for 'I can discover none, and hope they be not many.'[196] There can be no doubt that his philological achievement was a considerable one, and was duly recognised as such. The translation was reprinted in 1634 and again in 1648,[197] and Hobbes assures us in his prose *Vita* that the experts received it 'with no small praise'.[198]

Soon afterwards Hobbes made an important contribution to the second discipline in the *studia humanitatis* when he published his translation of Aristotle's *Art of Rhetoric.* As we have seen, Hobbes originally encountered the editor of the *Rhetoric*, Dr Theodore Goulston, at meetings of the Virginia Company as early as 1623. But it appears to have been as part of his duties as tutor to the third earl of Devonshire in the early 1630s that Hobbes made a close study of Goulston's text.[199] He seems to have begun by translating sections of it into Latin, evidently dictating them to his pupil as a comprehension exercise.[200] He then turned this Latin version into English, publishing it anonymously as *A Briefe of the Art of Rhetorique* in

193 Schlatter 1975, pp. xi–xii. Cf. Thucydides 1564.
194 Hobbes 1975a, p. 8.
195 Hobbes 1975a, p. 8.
196 Hobbes 1975a, p. 8.
197 The publisher in 1634 was Richard Mynne, and in 1648 Laurence Sadler. See Macdonald and Hargreaves 1952, p. 2.
198 Hobbes 1839a, p. xiv: 'cum nonnulla laude'.
199 For the evidence that Hobbes used Goulston's text see Harwood 1986, pp. 21–2, 50, 99–100.
200 It was Robertson who first identified as the third earl's dictation book the volume, now at Chatsworth, which contains a Latin version of the *Briefe* of Aristotle's *Rhetoric* eventually published in English by Hobbes in 1637. See Robertson 1886, p. 29 and note, and cf. Harwood 1986, pp. 1–2 and Malcolm 1994, p. 815. The dictation book (Chatsworth: Hobbes MS D.1) is signed 'W. Devonshire' twice on the inside covers and frequently elsewhere. It is

1637.[201] This was the first English version of Aristotle's *Rhetoric* to be printed, and Hobbes's achievement in truncating, reshaping and supplementing the text[202] was clearly recognised at the time not merely as an exercise in grammar but as a contribution to the study of rhetoric as well. When the publisher Thomas Maxy reissued the *Briefe* in 1651, he went so far as to describe it as one of the three treatises indispensable for any reader needing 'a compendium of the arts of logic and rhetoric in the English tongue'.[203]

The third element in the *studia humanitatis* was the study and imitation of classical poetry, a genre to which Hobbes made an ambitious contribution in the course of his first period of service with the Cavendishes. He wrote and presented to the second earl of Devonshire, around the year 1627, a poem of some five hundred Latin hexameters entitled *De Mirabilibus Pecci, Carmen.*[204] According to Aubrey he offered it to his patron as a new year's gift, and received £5 for it.[205] Hobbes's poem, describing the 'wonders' of the Peak district in Derbyshire, was first published (according to Anthony à Wood) in c.1636,[206] and was thus the earliest piece of Hobbes's own writing – apart from his essay on Thucydides – to appear in print.

The most striking feature of Hobbes's poem is its continual use of themes and motifs derived from classical epic verse. This admittedly gives rise to a tone of unfortunate bathos in several passages, but from the perspective of the present argument the important point is that the aspiration is such a typically humanist one. The poem centres on the Homeric idea of a memorable journey, describing a trip from the earl of Devonshire's seat at Chatsworth to the neighbouring town of Buxton and

also signed 'Thomas Hobbes' inside the back cover. The book is in the third earl's handwriting, with headings, corrections and additions by Hobbes.

201 There seems no doubt about Hobbes's authorship. When his publisher, Andrew Crooke, entered the book in the Stationers' Register on 1 February 1636 (i.e. 1637 our style) he announced it as being 'by T:H:'. See Arber 1875–94, IV, p. 372. This was the formula Hobbes used in acknowledging the first edition of *De Cive*. See Hobbes 1983a, p. 76. Aubrey 1898, I, p. 359 confirms that the *Briefe* is by Hobbes, 'though his name be not to it'.

202 On these changes see Harwood 1986, esp. pp. 7, 13, 17, 19–20; Rayner 1991, pp. 87–91.

203 See Hobbes 1651. The other two treatises were a Ramist logic attributed to Robert Fage and the chapters on rhetoric from Dudley Fenner's *The Artes of Logike and Rethorike*, 1584. This led to the ascription of Fenner's treatise to Hobbes, an ascription accepted by Anthony à Wood (see Wood 1691–2, p. 480) and repeated by Molesworth in his edition of Hobbes's *English Works*. Ong 1951 definitively established the facts, but the mistake continues to be made. (See for example Sacksteder 1984, pp. 30, 42–3; Tuck 1989, p. 56.) Dodd 1952, pp. 36–9, considers it 'not impossible' that Hobbes edited the 1651 collection, but I agree with Harwood that this is extremely improbable, especially as Hobbes was still in France at the time. See Harwood 1986, p. 7, and note.

204 The manuscript copy at Chatsworth (Hobbes MS A.1) is partly in Hobbes's hand (most of p. 7, all of p. 8, top half of p. 9).

205 Aubrey 1898, I, p. 360.

206 Wood 1691–2, p. 479: 'printed at *Lond.* about 1636'.

its surrounding countryside. Recounting seven wonderful episodes – the ancient magic number – Hobbes permits himself copious use of the classical trope to the effect that he cannot hope to do justice to his extraordinary experiences. He nevertheless attempts to describe them, and in doing so repeatedly ornaments his verses with Virgilian echoes and references. The groves of Chatsworth are cooler than Virgil's beeches;[207] the fountains in its gardens are finer than the sacred font of Callirhoe;[208] the descent into the vaporous depths of Elden Hole is similar to Aeneas' visit to the underworld;[209] the robber's cave visited at the end of the journey is reminiscent of the Gorgon's lair.[210]

There are signs that Hobbes may in later life have felt somewhat embarrassed by this effort. When he produced his important essay on the theory of poetry in the form of his *Answer* to Sir William Davenant's preface to *Gondibert* in 1650, he began by declaring with some emphasis that 'I am not a Poet.'[211] Even more strikingly, when John Wallis sneered at 'the ribauldry in your obscene Poem *De Mirabilibus Pecci*' in his *Due Correction for Mr Hobbes* in 1656,[212] Hobbes may have surprised him by replying that 'my verses of the Peak' are 'as ill in my own opinion as I believe they are in yours'.[213] Nevertheless, the *De Mirabilibus Pecci* proved a considerable success. It was reprinted in 1666 and again in 1675,[214] and was reissued together with a facing-page verse translation in 1678, although the publisher felt obliged to point out that this was done 'without the knowledge of Mr. Hobs'.[215] By this time, moreover, the poem had attracted some remarkably distinguished readers.[216] It was one of three books by Hobbes that John Locke possessed,[217] and appears to have been the only one of Hobbes's works that Isaac Newton ever bought.[218]

Throughout the early part of his career, Hobbes also took an active interest in the fourth of the humanistic disciplines, the writing of history. It is true that he only became an historian himself in much later life. His *Behemoth*, on the history of the civil wars, and his *Historical Narration*

207 Hobbes 1845d, p. 325, line 16.
208 Hobbes 1845d, p. 326, line 31.
209 Hobbes 1845d, p. 334, lines 298–9.
210 Hobbes 1845d, p.339, lines 503–4.
211 Hobbes 1971a, p. 45.
212 Wallis 1656b, p. 3. Wallis was no doubt thinking of Hobbes's description of the Peak as a woman's body and as *Orci culum*. See Hobbes 1845d, p. 332, lines 177–8.
213 Hobbes 1845h, p. 389.
214 Macdonald and Hargreaves 1952, pp. 4–5.
215 Hobbes 1845d, p. 324.
216 Including Robert Burton, whose copy is inscribed 'Ex dono Authoris'. Kiessling 1988, p. 154.
217 Harrison and Laslett 1965, p. 155. (Locke also owned *Leviathan* and *Problemata Physica*.)
218 Harrison 1978, item 785, p. 161.

Concerning Heresy were both completed in the latter part of the 1660s.[219] But we already find him displaying considerable historical erudition in his edition of Thucydides, particularly in the footnotes and marginal glosses he appended to the text. There are learned references to the pattern of alliances at the outbreak of the Peloponnesian war, the nature of Greek religious observances, the methods of waging the war itself, and so forth.[220] As his introductory address points out, moreover, he decided to embark on his translation for reasons of a pre-eminently humanist kind. One reason he gives is his wish to show that Thucydides discharged 'the principal and proper work of history' more effectively than anyone else, that of seeking 'to instruct and enable men, by the knowledge of actions past, to bear themselves prudently in the present and providently towards the future'.[221] A further reason is that we can hope to learn something of importance from the fact that Thucydides 'least of all liked the democracy'.[222] This latter message is powerfully underscored by the frontispiece produced for Hobbes's edition by the engraver Thomas Cecill.[223] The degree of Hobbes's involvement in this visual rendering of Thucydides' alleged theme is not known, but the iconography is no less suggestive than in the more famous cases of *De Cive* and *Leviathan*. To the left, under the figure of King Archidamus of Sparta, we see a ruler taking counsel with seven wise noblemen, one of whom examines an open book. To the right, under the figure of Pericles of Athens, we see a demagogue haranguing a crowd, many of whom are ragged and lame.[224] The effect is to associate Thucydides with one of the central tenets of English Renaissance humanism: that wise and virtuous noblemen represent the best and most natural 'governors' in any well-ordered state.[225]

The early part of Hobbes's career culminated in the production of two major treatises of civil philosophy, traditionally the fifth and final element in the *studia humanitatis*. The first to appear was *The Elements of Law, Naturall and Politique*[226] which he completed on 9 May 1640, less than a week after the dissolution of the Short Parliament by Charles I.[227] Hobbes dedicated

219 Macdonald and Hargreaves 1952, pp. 39–40, 64–5, 72–3.
220 Hobbes 1975a, pp. 576, 577, 578, 581, 583.
221 Hobbes 1975a, p. 6.
222 Hobbes 1975b, p. 13.
223 The frontispiece is signed 'T. Cecill sculp.' On Thomas Cecill, who also engraved the frontispiece of Bacon's *Sylva Sylvarum*, see Corbett and Lightbown 1979, p. 185.
224 Hobbes 1629, title page. Cf. Macdonald and Hargreaves 1952, plate II.
225 It is suggestive that Hobbes MS D.1 (i.e. the earl of Devonshire's dictation-book) has inscribed inside its cover: 'that vertue is the true nobilitie'.
226 This is the form in which the title appears in the two best manuscripts. See BL Harl. MS 4235 and cf. Chatsworth: Hobbes MS A.2.B (except that the latter reads 'Elementes').
227 Parliament was dissolved on 5 May: see Robertson 1886, p. 52. The epistle dedicatory to *The Elements* is signed 'May the 9th. 1640'. See BL Harl. MS 4235, fo. 2^{v} and cf. Hobbes 1969a,

The Elements to the earl of Newcastle, expressing the hope in his prefatory epistle that Newcastle might be in a position to bring the book to the attention of 'those whom the matter it containeth most nearly concerneth'.[228] *The Elements* only appeared in print some ten years later, when its chiefly epistemological chapters were pirated as a separate treatise entitled *Humane Nature*, while its later political sections were published as *De Corpore Politico*.[229] It is clear, however, that the full text enjoyed a fairly wide circulation in 1640.[230] Hobbes himself informs us in his *Considerations* that 'though not printed, many Gentlemen had copies', characteristically adding that his was the first treatise in which anyone 'had ventured to write in the King's defence'.[231]

Hobbes made his second and even more important contribution to civil science when he published his *Elementorum Philosophiae sectio tertia de Cive* at Paris in April 1642.[232] He tells us in his *Considerations* that he completed the book in 1641 after fleeing from England at the end of the previous year.[233] But his labours were to some degree those of a translator, since *De Cive* mainly consists of an expanded version of the political chapters of the *Elements*, together with a fuller treatment of religious issues at the end. The *De Cive* was the first of Hobbes's political works to be published, and the fact that he wrote it in Latin appears to have given it a wide and immediate readership. He was later to boast in his *Considerations* that 'I know no book more magnified than this is beyond the seas.'[234]

Looking back over his long life in his verse *Vita*, Hobbes chose to bring the story of his early career to an end at this point, observing in typically humanist vein that fame had been the spur, and that fame was what he had now achieved. 'My book', he concludes, 'gave pleasure to the learned, and was indeed altogether original; it was translated into various languages

p. xvi. As Tönnies recognised, this was the work described by Hobbes in his *Considerations* of 1662 as the 'little treatise in English' which he completed and circulated in 1640. See Tönnies 1969a, pp. v–viii, and cf. Hobbes 1840c, p. 414.

228 See BL Harl. MS 4235 fo. 2^{r-v}, and cf. Hobbes 1969a, pp. xv–xvi.

229 See Hobbes 1650a and Hobbes 1650b. For the publishing history of these texts see Tönnies 1969a, pp. v–ix, and cf. Macdonald and Hargreaves 1952, pp. 10–12. Tönnies was the first to issue the complete treatise in the form in which Hobbes wrote it. See Hobbes 1969a.

230 An unusual number of manuscripts survive, including four among the Harleian manuscripts in the British Library, one more in the British Library and three at Chatsworth. See Tönnies 1969, pp. viii–ix and Warrender 1983, p. 3 and note.

231 Hobbes 1840c, p. 414.

232 For the title see Warrender 1983, p. 36, and for the date and circumstances of publication see Warrender 1983, pp. 5–8.

233 Hobbes 1840c, pp. 414–15; for the precise date of completion (1 November 1641) see Hobbes 1983a, p. 76.

234 Hobbes 1840c, p. 415.

and read with praise, as a result of which my name became widely known among many nations.'[235]

HOBBES'S RHETORICAL STYLE

I turn finally to examine in greater detail the two works Hobbes wrote and published during his 'humanist' period: the essay of 1629 entitled 'Of the Life and History of Thucydides' and the poem, *De Mirabilibus Pecci*, first printed in c.1636. When considering these works it is important to bear in mind the leading assumptions about the presentation of literary texts that the humanists of the English Renaissance had put into currency by this time. One was that all public utterances must conform to one or other of three rhetorical genres, those of demonstrative, deliberative or forensic speech. The other was that all such utterances must be organised according to the rules of the *ars rhetorica*, the rules governing the invention, disposition and ornamentation of persuasive arguments. If we examine Hobbes's early writings with these considerations in mind, we find that they are constructed almost entirely in the light of these standard rhetorical rules.

It is striking in the first place that, in his essay on Thucydides, Hobbes views the *History* essentially as a rhetorical achievement, analysing it wholly in terms of the concepts bequeathed by the classical theory of eloquence. He begins by declaring that 'two things are to be considered' in the appraisal of Thucydides' work, one being the quality of his elocution and the other the extent of his truthfulness.[236] Turning first to the question of truth, Hobbes treats this as equivalent to asking about Thucydides' powers of *inventio*. We need to know how much effort Thucydides expended in trying 'to find the truth of what he relateth'. Hobbes's answer is unambiguous: Thucydides exhibited 'as much diligence in search of the truth (noting every thing whilst it was fresh in memory, and laying out his wealth upon intelligence) as it was possible for a man to use'.[237] Next Hobbes turns to elocution, the concept lying at the heart of the classical theory of eloquence. He first speaks of Thucydides' *dispositio*, but mainly concerns himself with *elocutio* in the strict sense of analysing the characteristics of Thucydides' style. Following standard rhetorical practice, he subdivides this topic into three components, considering in turn the

235 Hobbes 1839b, p. xc, lines 152–4:

> Qui placuit doctis, et novus omnis erat;
> Versus et in varias linguas cum laude legebatur,
> Gentibus et late nomine notus eram.

236 Hobbes 1975b, pp. 16–17.

237 Hobbes 1975b, p. 17.

perspicuity, the strength and the propriety of Thucydides' prose. He ends by invoking the authority of a number of ancient rhetoricians – particularly Cicero – to underline his own judgment that Thucydides must be accounted the greatest of all historians no less for the presentation than for the content of his thought.[238]

Still more striking is the extent to which Hobbes's early writings are constructed according to the rules of the *ars rhetorica.* Consider first his poem *De Mirabilibus Pecci* of c.1627. This is wholly designed as an exercise in epideictic or demonstrative oratory. As we saw in chapter 1, the purpose of writing in this genus was supposed to be that of producing a *laudatio* or a *vituperatio.* Moreover, as Rainolde's *Foundacion of Rhetorike* had particularly emphasised, we can hope to direct such praises or censures not merely at persons but at a wide range of inanimate objects, including 'Castles. Toures. Gardeins. Stones.'[239] Hobbes's *De Mirabilibus Pecci* is a *laudatio* of exactly this kind. The first 'wonder' he describes is Chatsworth, which he praises for its fame and size.[240] The second is the Peak itself, which he commends for its splendour and frightening appearance.[241] The third is Mam Tor, the 'maimed rock', which he admires for its sheer scale.[242] And so on. The poem concludes, admittedly with something of an anti-climax, with a *laudatio* addressed to the robber's cave near Buxton, which is described as a place well worth visiting.[243]

Hobbes's essay on Thucydides is constructed even more precisely along rhetorical lines.[244] It too is clearly intended in part as a contribution to the *genus demonstrativum,* since it opens with the *laudatio* we have already considered in which Hobbes extols Thucydides' veracity and excellence of style. But it is mainly designed as an exercise in the *genus iudiciale,* and takes the form of a polemical engagement with Thucydides' detractors, especially Dionysius of Halicarnassus, in which Hobbes seeks to overthrow their criticisms by putting the other side of the case.

As Hobbes develops his plea for the defence, he follows with remarkable exactitude the rules laid down by such classical handbooks as the *Ad Herennium* for the invention and disposition of forensic arguments. It will be best to begin by recalling the exact content of these rules, since this will

238 Hobbes 1975b, p. 17, 18–19. For a comparison between Thucydides and Hobbes on the art of rhetoric see Johnson 1993, pp. 68–71, 141–3.

239 Rainolde 1564, fo. xxxvii.

240 Hobbes 1845d, p. 325, lines 4–5.

241 Hobbes 1845d, p. 330, lines 179, 183.

242 Hobbes 1845d, p. 332, line 238.

243 Hobbes 1845d, p. 339, line 472: 'dignissima visu'.

244 Reik 1977, pp. 44–52, discusses Hobbes's essay, but without analysing its rhetorical features.

provide us with a benchmark against which we can hope to indicate the meticulous care with which Hobbes conforms to their requirements.

The *Ad Herennium* starts by declaring that, whenever we speak or write in the *genus iudiciale*, we must be sure to present our argument in six consecutive steps. We must of course open with a suitable introduction or exordium. This ought to be as brief and direct as possible, unless the issue under consideration is in some way dishonourable, in which case a more subtle or indirect approach may be required.[245] The next three parts of a judicial oration are the *narratio*, the *divisio* and the *distributio*.[246] The *narratio* is the section in which we lay out whatever information we take to be relevant to the case. It needs to be kept as short and perspicuous as the case allows, and needs in addition to present the facts in the right order and under the most appropriate headings. The *divisio*, which ought to come next, allows us to introduce a distinction between the issues over which we are in agreement with our adversaries and those which remain in dispute. Lastly, the *distributio* is the name of the section in which we enumerate the principal claims we intend to put forward, taking care to ensure that there are no more than three of them. After this we come to the *confirmatio* and *confutatio*, the sections in which we attack our opponent's position and develop our own side of the case.[247] We must aim at this juncture to call on as many arguments as there are *causae* or issues on which we may be asked to speak. But there is one argument we must be sure to use, since it applies in every type of case. This consists of offering a justifying motive for the action we are defending, or alternatively (if we are engaged in prosecuting) of insisting by way of a general *accusatio* that no such motive can be adduced. Having argued our case in this way, it only remains to add a *peroratio* in which we summarise and amplify our previous statements. This *amplificatio* will be most effective if we can draw on a series of *loci communes* or common 'places' of argument. Among these, the most impressive will generally be those drawn from the authority of ancient usage or the works of acknowledged experts whose opinions can be shown to chime with the arguments already set out.[248]

When Hobbes turns in the final section of his essay to defend Thucydides against his detractors, he follows with almost mechanical exactitude this entire set of rhetorical rules.[249] His exordium, just as the *Ad Herennium* had demanded, is as brief as possible. As we have seen, it simply

245 *Ad C. Herennium*, I.III.4 to I.VII.11, pp. 8–22.
246 *Ad C. Herennium*, I.VIII.12 to I.X.17, pp. 22–30.
247 *Ad C. Herennium*, I.X.18 to I.XVII.27, pp. 32–54.
248 *Ad C. Herennium*, II.XXX.47 to II.XXXI.50, pp. 144–52.
249 Page references to Hobbes's discussion are hereafter given in brackets in the text, all references being to Hobbes 1975b.

affirms that that 'two things are to be considered' in Thucydides' writings, his elocution and his truthfulness (p. 16). Before proceeding further, however, Hobbes duly pauses (as Cicero had particularly advised)[250] to add an observation of the highest sententiousness, one that he expresses in his most sonorously antithetical style. 'For in *truth* consisteth the *soul*, and in *elocution* the *body* of history. The latter without the former, is but a picture of history; and the former without the latter, unapt to instruct' (p. 16).

'But let us see', Hobbes goes on, 'how our author hath acquitted himself in both' (p. 16). Hobbes's tone shifts at once to the informal and conversational as he supplies us, again as concisely as possible, with a *narratio* of the relevant facts. The facts relating to Thucydides' truthfulness are said to be three in number: that his veracity has never been impugned; that he had no motive for lying; and that he had all the necessary means to find out the truth (p. 17). The facts about his *elocutio* – which Hobbes arranges under suitable headings as the *Ad Herennium* demands – are of two kinds: those concerned with method, and those concerned with style (p. 17). The relevant facts about Thucydides' method are that he employed a strict narrative form, interspersing it with orations in the deliberative mode, while the most salient fact about his style is that it has always been commended by 'the judgment of divers ancient and competent judges' (p. 18).

Hobbes next passes to the third element in the classical theory of *dispositio*, the *divisio* or statement of the issues over which he agrees and disagrees with his adversaries. He concedes that there is one important point of agreement between himself and Thucydides' most vociferous opponent, Dionysius of Halicarnassus. This stems from the fact that Dionysius is prepared to acknowledge the remarkable 'purity and propriety' of Thucydides' style (p. 18). Hobbes's main concern, however, is of course with the other side of the *divisio* – with the places where he remains in disagreement with Dionysius, who 'hath taken so much pains, and applied so much of his faculty in rhetoric, to the extenuating of the worth' of Thucydides' masterpiece (p. 19).

As we have seen, the next step is supposed to take the form of a *distributio*, a preliminary enumeration of the chief points remaining to be debated. This is the one moment at which Hobbes shows himself less than totally obedient to the classical rules. Rather than listing the elements of his case against Dionysius, he contents himself with observing in general terms that he will next examine and respond to 'the principal objections he maketh' (p. 19). Since Hobbes goes on to consider four main objections,

[250] Cicero 1949a, I.XVIII.25, pp. 50–2.

however, it may well be that his reason for limiting himself to this minimal form of *distributio* is that he would otherwise have been obliged to disclose that he was breaking a more important rhetorical rule by considering four arguments rather than the maximum of three that classical decorum allowed.

When Hobbes turns to the four arguments in question, however, he reverts to following the classical rules with absolute fidelity. He provides us, that is, with a *confirmatio* and a *confutatio*, outlining Dionysius' criticisms and dismissing them at the same time. First he attacks Dionysius' claim that Thucydides failed to choose a satisfactory theme, and that Herodotus ought on those grounds to be preferred. Herodotus' theme, Hobbes retorts, was such that he constantly found himself obliged 'to write of those things, of which it was impossible for him to know the truth'. Thucydides, by contrast, only wrote of matters about which he possessed first-hand knowledge, and which he knew would be profitable to posterity (pp. 19–20). Hobbes next addresses Dionysius' objection that, as an Athenian, Thucydides ought not to have placed the responsibility for starting the war so firmly on the shoulders of his fellow countrymen. Hobbes answers by reminding us of Thucydides' other and higher obligation: he wrote, as an historian must, 'not as a lover of his country but of truth' (p. 21). Dionysius' third criticism is that Thucydides' strictly narrative approach is hard to follow. To this Hobbes replies that it is nevertheless the most natural approach, and is unlikely to give difficulty to any moderately attentive reader (pp. 22–3). Finally, Hobbes offers a fascinating response to Dionysius' suggestion that Thucydides ought to have discussed the real causes of the war before considering the pretexts given for it (pp. 23–4):

> The reprehension is absurd. For it is plain, that a cause of war divulged and avowed, however slight it be, comes within the task of the historiographer, no less than the war itself. For without a pretext, no war follows ... In a word, the image of the method used by Thucydides in this point, is this: 'The quarrel about Corcyra passed on this manner; and the quarrel about Potidaea on this manner': relating both at large: 'and in both the Athenians were accused to have done the injury. Nevertheless, the Lacedaemonians had not upon this injury entered into a war against them, but that they envied the greatness of their power, and feared the consequences of their ambitions.'

To this paraphrase Hobbes adds a single crushing rejoinder: 'I think a more clear and natural order cannot possibly be devised' (p. 24).

After this *confutatio*, Hobbes summarises his argument in exactly the manner recommended by the *Ad Herennium*. He asks himself, that is, what justifying motive Dionysius could possibly have had for criticising

Thucydides so unrelentingly. His answer, witheringly scornful and grimly humorous, offers a fine example of the kind of response most admired by the classical theorists of eloquence (p. 26):

> What motive he had to it, I know not; but what glory he might expect by it, is easily known. For having first preferred Herodotus, his countryman, a Halicarnassian, before Thucydides, who was accounted the best; and then conceiving that his own history might perhaps be thought not inferior to that of Herodotus: by this computation he saw the honour of the best historiographer falling on himself. Wherein, in the opinion of all men, he hath misreckoned. And thus much for the objections of Denis of Halicarnasse.

The carefully calculated bathos of the closing sentences echoes the absurdity of attempting to undermine Thucydides' fame.

The final element in a forensic argument is of course the *peroratio*. As we have seen, the writers of classical textbooks such as the *Ad Herennium* had popularised the view that the strongest way to round off a speech is by invoking the best authorities as witnesses on one's side. Once again, this is exactly what Hobbes does. Among ancient experts he calls on Demosthenes, Cicero and Lucian, all of whom he cites in support of his contention that Thucydides was the greatest historian of all (pp. 26–7). Among contemporary witnesses he singles out Justus Lipsius, declaring that 'the most true and proper commendation' of Thucydides is to be found in Lipsius' *De doctrina civili*. He focuses in particular on Lipsius' observation that 'Thucydides, who hath written not many nor very great matters, hath perhaps yet won the garland from all that hath written on matters both many and great' (p. 27). Hobbes clearly found Lipsius' epigram highly apposite, and with it he rests his case.

Chapter 7

HOBBES'S REJECTION OF ELOQUENCE

THE TURN AWAY FROM HUMANISM

While Hobbes was initially formed by the rhetorical culture of Renaissance humanism, there is no doubt that in the 1630s he began to desert the *studia humanitatis* in favour of a different kind of *scientia*, and at the same time to react strongly against his earlier intellectual allegiances. The explanation usually offered for this change of direction focuses on Aubrey's much-quoted anecdote about Hobbes's sudden discovery of geometrical method:

> Being in a gentleman's library in . . . , Euclid's Elements lay open, and 'twas the 47 El. libri I. He read the proposition. 'By G–,' sayd he, 'this is impossible!' So he reads the demonstration of it, which referred him back to such a proposition; which proposition he read. That referred him back to another, which he also read. Et sic deinceps, that at last he was demonstratively convinced of that trueth. This made him in love with geometry.[1]

Aubrey states that this epiphany occurred when Hobbes was forty years old, thereby implying that the library in question must have been that of the Devonshires.[2] But Hobbes himself tells us in his prose *Vita* that it was in the course of his visit to France with the son of Sir Gervase Clifton in 1629 that 'I first began to look into Euclid's *Elements*.'[3] Hobbes's account tallies with Aubrey's, however, in treating the moment as one of far-reaching significance. 'I was delighted by Euclid's method', Hobbes goes on, 'as a result of which I read his work with the utmost diligence, not simply on account of its theorems, but also as a guide to the art of reasoning.'[4]

1 Aubrey 1898, I, p. 332. Hobbes confirms the story in Hobbes 1660, pp. 154–5. (The edition used by Molesworth omits this passage.)

2 Aubrey 1898, I, p. 332.

3 Hobbes 1839a, p. xiv: 'inspicere coepit in Elementa Euclidis'. This version is repeated in Wood 1691–2, p. 477. Pacchi 1968 argues for a date between 1625 and 1628 on the strength of Chatsworth: Hobbes MS E.2, a booklist of nearly 900 titles. See Pacchi 1968, pp. 7–10 and 23. But Hobbes's connection with this list – which was drawn up, as Malcolm has shown, not by Hobbes (as Pacchi assumed) but by Robert Payne – remains unclear. See Malcolm 1994, p. 874.

4 Hobbes 1839a, p. xiv: 'delectatus methodo illius, non tam ob theoremata illa, quam ob artem ratiocinandi, diligentissime perlegit'.

If we turn, however, to Hobbes's correspondence of the 1630s, we come upon a second and contrasting reason for his change of intellectual direction. He was evidently much intrigued and increasingly captivated by the scientific experiments then being conducted at Welbeck Abbey under the aegis of the third earl of Devonshire's cousins, the earl of Newcastle and his younger brother, Sir Charles Cavendish.[5] Sir Charles, Aubrey informs us, 'was a little, weake, crooked man, and nature not having adapted him for the court nor campe, he betooke himselfe to the study of the mathematiques, wherin he became a great master'.[6] His elder brother was more a man of action, but he too took a serious interest in philosophy and the sciences. His scientific studies in the 1630s seem to have owed their direction in part to Robert Payne, whom he employed at Welbeck from 1632 notionally as his chaplain but at the same time to assist him in his experiments.[7] One of Payne's early papers for Newcastle was a study of 'the Motions of a Horse'[8] but his chief interest lay in optics and more generally in the phenomenon of light. He may possibly have written the so-called *Short Tract*, often attributed to Hobbes, in which a number of questions about colour, vision and light are discussed.[9] By 1634 Payne was in correspondence with Walter Warner about the problem of refraction,[10] and Warner in turn urged Payne to send his observations on the subject to Hobbes.[11] Hobbes's replies indicate that, although an admirer of Warner's scientific abilities,[12] he felt considerable scepticism about the experiments on which Warner claimed to be engaged.[13] Hobbes's correspondence also reveals that by this time he was conducting optical experiments himself. A note of May 1636 from Sir Charles Cavendish to Walter Warner mentions a paper on the problem of refraction which he

5 See Jacquot 1952; Tuck 1989, pp. 11–13; Malcolm 1994, pp. 802–3, 813–14.

6 Aubrey 1898, I, p. 153.

7 Malcolm 1994, p. 873.

8 Until recently (see for example Rogow 1986, p. 121, Tuck 1989, p. 13) this was attributed to Hobbes, but Malcolm 1994, pp. 813–14, notes that the treatise is in Payne's hand and regards him as the probable author.

9 See BL Harl. MS 6796, esp. fos. 297^{r}, 301^{v} and 303^{v} (on colour); fo. 302^{v} (on vision); fos. 300^{v} and 301^{v} (on light); cf. Hobbes 1988, pp. 13, 26, 30, 38. Tönnies suggested the title: see Hobbes 1969a, appendix I, p. 193. Bernhardt 1988, pp. 88–92, insists on Hobbes's authorship, but Malcolm 1994, p. 874, argues that 'since it is in Payne's own hand, it can plausibly be attributed to him'. It is conceivable, however, that Payne was merely acting as a copyist, as in the case of Hobbes MS E.2 (on which see note 3, *supra*).

10 See Warner to Payne, 17 October 1634, BL Birch MS 4279, fo. 307^{r}. Cf. Cavendish to Warner, BL Birch MS 4444, fo. 93^{r}, evidently of around the same date.

11 Warner to Payne, BL Birch MS 4279, fo. 307^{r}: 'For the problem of refractions, wch you write of, I pray you by any meanes send it to Mr Hobbes.'

12 See letter 19 in Hobbes 1994, pp. 33–4.

13 See letters 16 and 19 in Hobbes 1994, pp. 28–9 and 34. Cf. Cavendish to Warner, BL Birch MS 4444, fo. 93^{r}, thanking Warner for two tracts on optics but noting 'some doutes which Mr Payen & I have of some things in these tracts'.

had lately received together with a letter from Hobbes.[14] Hobbes also wrote to the earl of Newcastle from Paris in June 1636 to say that Descartes's friend Claude Mydorge had just sent Sir Charles a treatise on refraction, adding that he would like to know what the *virtuosi* at Welbeck thought of it.[15] A few weeks later he wrote to Newcastle once again to criticise with remarkable confidence both Warner's and Mydorge's experiments. 'For the optiques I know Mr Warner and Mr Mydorge are as able men as any in Europe, but they do not well to call their writings demonstrations, for the grounds and suppositions they use, so many of them as concerne light, are uncertayne and many of them not true.'[16] It would seem that Hobbes had already formulated his fundamental principle to the effect that purely experimental demonstrations cannot be said to count as scientific proofs.

If we shift our attention from Hobbes's correspondence to his autobiographies, we come upon a third and possibly a still more conclusive reason for his change of intellectual direction in the 1630s. His new interests appear to have been quickened above all by the contacts he made with Marin Mersenne in Paris in 1634 and again in 1636. Mersenne was Hobbes's age, and had been educated at the Jesuit College of La Flèche, where he had been a fellow pupil of Descartes.[17] He joined the order of Minim Friars in 1611, and from 1619 lived in the Convent of the Annunciation in Paris.[18] There he became the centre of a scientific community of which Hobbes provides a moving sketch in his verse *Vita*:

> Mersenne was my faithful friend, and was a learned man, wise and outstandingly good. His cell was regarded by everyone as preferable to the Schools with their Professors puffed up with ambitiousness. If anyone discovered a new principle or an interesting inference, it was to Mersenne that they brought it ... He in turn would discuss the problem with any of the learned who wished, either going over it with them at once or leaving them to mull it over at home. Among these many discoveries, he published the best, always signing them with their author's name. Mersenne was the axis around which every star in the world of science revolved.[19]

14 Cavendish to Warner, BL Birch MS 4407, fo. 186^r^: 'I received latelie a letter from Mr Hobbes where amongst other things he sent me this paper heer inclosed which is an experiment of the place of the Image of a thing.'

15 Letter 18 in Hobbes 1994, p. 32. Warner expresses considerable faith in Hobbes's capacity to negotiate with Mydorge. See Warner to Payne, BL Birch MS 4279, fo. 307^r^: 'I would be very glad to see Mons Mydorges way, if he make a secret of it, I doubt not but Mr Hobbes will know how to trafik with him.'

16 Letter 19 in Hobbes 1994, pp. 33–4.

17 Dear 1988, pp. 12–13, 15–16.

18 Dear 1988, p. 14.

19 Hobbes 1839b, p. xci, lines 165–70 and 173–8:

Mersennus, fidus amicus;
[Mersennus, tempore frater]

Welcomed by Mersenne into this circle, Hobbes subsequently re-established contact with several of its members during his exile in the 1640s, continuing to correspond with some of them even after his return to England in 1651.[20]

Hobbes states in his prose *Vita* that it was during his stay in Paris between 1634 and 1635 that he first encountered Mersenne and 'communicated with him daily about my thoughts'.[21] These meetings appear to have aroused in Hobbes an almost obsessional interest in the laws of physics, and above all in the phenomenon of motion. He tells us that, after setting out for Italy with the young earl of Devonshire in the autumn of 1635,[22] 'I began to think about the nature of things all the time, whether I was on a ship, in a coach, or travelling on horseback.' As a result, 'I came to the conclusion that there is only one thing in the whole world which is real, although it is undoubtedly falsified in many ways.' This single reality is motion, 'which is why anyone who wishes to understand physics must first of all make a study of the laws of motion'.[23] Through his conversations with Mersenne, Hobbes appears to have arrived at the governing assumption of his later philosophy.

Vir doctus, sapiens, eximieque bonus.
[Sed doctus, sapiens, egregieque bonus]
Cuius cella scholis erat omnibus anteferenda
Professorum omnes ambitione tument.
[Quotquot circuitus totius orbus habet]
Illi portabat, si dignum forte porisma
Reppererat quisquam, principiumve novum. . . .
Ille dedit doctis, qui vellent, rursus ut illud
Vel statim possent, vel trutinare domi.
Edidit e multisque inventis optima quaeque;
[Edit ex multis inventis optima quaeque]
Signans authoris nomine quidque sui.
Circa Mersennum convertebatur ut axem
Unumquodque artis sidus in orbe suo.

20 See Hobbes 1994 and for a discussion Skinner 1966a.

21 Hobbes 1839a, p. xiv: 'cogitatis suis cum Reverendo Patre Marino Mersenno . . . quotidie communicatis'. This is confirmed in Blackbourne 1839, p. xxviii. Cf. Hobbes 1839b, p. xc, line 127, which speaks of communicating with Mersenne 'anew' on returning to Paris in 1636 after wintering in Italy. Hobbes was in Paris for at least a year between autumn 1634 and 1635. See letters 12 to 16 in Hobbes 1994, pp. 22–30. On the importance of this visit see Brandt 1928, pp. 149–60.

22 Letter 16 (August 1635) shows Hobbes still in Paris. See Hobbes 1994, pp. 28–9. Letter 17 (April 1636), sent from Florence, speaks of having arrived there after a stay in Rome. See Hobbes 1994, pp. 30–1.

23 Hobbes 1839b, p. lxxxix, lines 109–12 and 119–20:

Ast ego perpetuo naturam cogito rerum,
Seu rate, seu curru, sive ferebar equo.
Et mihi visa quidem est toto res unica mundo
Vera, licet multis falsificata modis: . . .
Hinc est quod, physicam quisquis vult discere, motus
Quid possit, debet perdidicisse prius.

It is possible that Hobbes received some further encouragement during his trip to Italy. According to Aubrey, he managed to arrange a meeting with Galileo, by then living in bereaved and sightless retirement near Florence. Aubrey merely states that it was 'when he was at Florence' that Hobbes and Galileo met, adding that Hobbes 'extremely venerated and magnified' Galileo, 'and not only as he was a prodigious witt, but for his sweetnes of nature and manners'.[24] Hobbes underlines this judgment in his critique of White's *De mundo*, in the course of which he refers to Galileo as 'the greatest philosopher not merely of our own but of any age'.[25] Aubrey assigns no date to the encounter, but if it took place it must have been at some point between April 1636, when Hobbes set out from Rome for Florence, and June of the same year, by which time he was definitely back in Paris.[26]

It is strange, however, that Hobbes makes no mention of any such meeting in either of his autobiographies. He lays all his emphasis on the fact that, as the verse *Vita* puts it, 'after we returned to the high walls and magnificent buildings of Paris I was able to communicate anew with Mersenne about the questions concerning the motion of things that I had been turning over in my mind'.[27] The length of this second stay expanded in Hobbes's mind as he recalled it. Although it lasted four or five months at the most,[28] he assures us that 'it was after eight months that I returned to my native country and began to think about linking my thoughts together into a connected whole'.[29] The exaggeration no doubt reflects the importance Hobbes attached to this phase of his life. For it was at this juncture, he adds, 'that Mersenne approved my arguments and recommended me to many people, as a result of which I began to be numbered from this time among the ranks of the philosophers'.[30]

24 Aubrey 1898, I, p. 366.

25 BN MS Fonds Latin 6566A, fo. 91^{v}: 'non modo nostri, sed omnium saeculorum philosophus maximus'. Cf. Hobbes 1973, p. 178.

26 See letters 17 and 18 in Hobbes 1994, pp. 30–3.

27 Hobbes 1839b, pp. lxxxix–xc, lines 125–8:

> Rursusque redimus ad alta
> Moenia Lutetiae, tectaque magnifica.
> Hic ego Mersennum novi, communico et illi
> De rerum motu quae meditatus eram.

28 Hobbes was still in Florence in the spring of 1636, but back in England by early October. See letters 17, 20 and 21 in Hobbes 1994, pp. 30–1, 36–8.

29 Hobbes 1839b, p. xc, lines 131–2:

> In patriam rursus post menses octo reversus,
> De connectendis cogito notitiis.
> [De connectendis cogito quae scieram.]

30 Hobbes 1839b, p. xc, lines 129–30:

> Is [sc. Mersenne] probat, et multis commendat; tempore ab illo
> Inter philosophos et numerabar ego.

Back in England in October 1636, Hobbes seems to have suffered a psychological crisis. For some time he had been expressing anxiety and frustration as he tried to work out his new ideas in a systematic way. He wrote to Newcastle in 1634 to apologise for the fact that his patron's continual favours 'make me ashamed of my dull proceedinge'.[31] He wrote in even more self-critical mood to Sir Gervase Clifton in 1635 to complain of 'sterility of matter, and infelicity of brayne'.[32] He wrote again to Newcastle later in the same year to express a fear that 'if the world saw my little desert, so plainely as they see yor great rewards, they might thinke me a mountibancke'.[33] By the time of his return to England in the following year, he seems to have felt an acute sense of urgency about the need to devote himself to the new vocation he had found. Writing again to Newcastle, he reiterated his frustration at the prospect of returning to his old duties with the Devonshires. The earl and his mother 'do both accept so wel of my service as I could almost engage my selfe to serve them as a domestique all my life'. But 'the extreame pleasure I take in study overcomes in me all other appetites'. He felt his dilemma to be a stark one. 'I am not willing to leave my Lord so, as not to do him any service that he thinkes may not so well be done by another; but I must not deny my selfe the content to study in ye way I have begun.' He frankly admits that his best prospect will be to give up his position with the Devonshires and enter Newcastle's service instead. 'I cannot conceave I shall do any where so well as at Welbecke, and therefore I meane if yor Lo^{p} forbid me not, to come thither as soone as I can, and stay as long as I can without inconvenience to yor lo^{p}.'[34]

Hobbes must in the event have been granted the leisure he craved by the earl of Devonshire. For he remained in the earl's household, and in the course of the next two years he managed to surmount his intellectual crisis by dint of an extraordinary burst of activity, in the course of which he sketched the outlines of his entire philosophy. It was during this period, his verse *Vita* explains, that he hit upon the fundamental insight 'that the whole *genus* of philosophy is made up of just three parts: *Corpus*, *Homo*, *Civis*, body, man and citizen'.[35] Armed with these basic categories, he found himself able 'to move from the various types of motion to the variety of things, that is, to different species and elements of matter, and

31 Letter 10 in Hobbes 1994, p. 19.
32 Letter 14 in Hobbes 1994, p. 26.
33 Letter 16 in Hobbes 1994, p. 28.
34 Letter 21 in Hobbes 1994, p. 37.
35 Hobbes 1839b, p. xc, lines 137–40:

Nam philosophandi
Corpus, Homo Civis continet omne genus.

from there to the internal motions of men and the secrets of the heart, and from there, finally, to the blessings of government and justice'.[36] With this outline firmly established, 'I decided to write three separate books on each of these issues, and started to collect my materials day by day.'[37] There is little evidence that he made much progress with the first of these projected volumes – the one on bodies – during this period.[38] But he seems to have assembled a great deal of information for the second – on man – which he eventually published as *De Homine* in 1658.[39] And he actually completed the final section on the blessings of government and justice. As we saw in chapter 6, he initially circulated a version of this text as the second part of *The Elements of Law* in 1640; he subsequently issued it in a revised and extended form – with a title indicating its place in his intended trilogy – as *Elementorum Philosophiae sectio tertia de Cive* in 1642.[40]

During the 1630s Hobbes not only turned away from the *studia humanitatis*; he also turned against the humanistic disciplines, and above all against the idea of an art of eloquence. By a peculiar irony, he first expressed his misgivings about humanist rhetorical culture in the course of translating Aristotle's *Art of Rhetoric*. Aristotle begins by declaring that rhetoric is a highly useful art, because it helps those making legal judgments to arrive at verdicts congruent with justice and truth.[41] While purportedly translating this passage, Hobbes inserts a wholly different claim, undermining Aristotle's argument at the same time. The study of rhetoric, he grudgingly observes, 'brings with it at least this profit, that making the pleaders equal in skill, it leaves the oddes onely in the merit of the cause'.[42] He goes on to add a number of limiting remarks for which there is no warrant in

36 Hobbes 1839b, p. xc, lines 133–6:

> Motibus a variis feror ad rerum variarum
> Dissimiles species, materiaeque dolos;
> Motusque internos hominum, cordisque latebras:
> Denique ad imperii iustitiaeque bona.

37 Hobbes 1839b, p. xc, lines 139–40:

> Tres super his rebus statuo conscribere libros;
> Materiemque mihi congero quoque die.

38 Such evidence as survives is assembled in Tuck 1988b.

39 *De Homine*, caps. 2 to 9, are on optics, the topic on which Hobbes had completed his Latin MS treatise in 1640. See BL Harl. 6796, fos. 193–266. On the dating see Tönnies 1969, xii–xiii; Tuck 1988b, pp. 23–4, and Malcolm's additional evidence in Hobbes 1994, pp. liii–lv. By 1646 Hobbes had also completed an English MS treatise on optics: see BL Harl. MS 3360. As Robertson 1886, p. 59n., first noticed, the nine chapters on vision in BL Harl. MS 3360, fos. 73^r to 193^r, are virtually identical with the discussion in *De Homine* (i.e. in Hobbes 1839c, caps. 2 to 9, pp. 7–87).

40 Warrender 1983, pp. 5–8.

41 Aristotle 1926, I.I.12, p. 10.

42 Hobbes 1986, p. 39.

Aristotle's text. There is nothing in Aristotle corresponding to Hobbes's contention in chapter 1 that judges are incapable of following scientific proofs, and that advocates are consequently obliged to take 'the *Rhetoricall*, and shorter way'.[43] Nor is there anything corresponding to Hobbes's claim in chapter 2 that rhetoric is a purely self-serving art. Aristotle had noted that the aim of rhetoricians is to persuade,[44] but Hobbes insists that rhetoric can be defined as 'that Faculty, by which wee understand what will serve our turne'.[45] Most blatantly, there is nothing in Aristotle corresponding to Hobbes's sneering conclusion – later repeated in *De Cive* – that rhetoricians are only interested in victory and not in truth.[46]

It is in *The Elements*, however, and even more in *De Cive*, that Hobbes makes fully clear his dislike and suspicion of the rhetorical arts, and more generally of the rhetorical culture of Renaissance humanism. It would be no exaggeration to say that one of his principal purposes in both these works is to challenge and overturn the central tenets of the *ars rhetorica*. Not only does he repudiate the fundamental rhetorical assumption that all forensic and deliberative arguments must be organised around the categories of *inventio* and *elocutio*; he also seeks to discredit the underlying ideal of the *vir civilis*, and hence the theory of citizenship associated with the classical art of eloquence. The remaining sections of this chapter will consider in detail these aspects of Hobbes's campaign to outlaw the art of rhetoric from the domain of civil science.

THE ATTACK ON *INVENTIO*

When discussing the topic of *inventio*, most classical and Renaissance writers on rhetoric had begun by offering the same piece of advice. They had generally assumed that, in any work of a forensic or deliberative character, we must start by securing so far as possible the goodwill and favourable attention of our audience. As we saw in chapter 3, they usually added that the best means of putting our hearers in a receptive mood will be to establish our credit and reputation as a 'probable' witness. We must claim to have something novel to say, or declare that our arguments will be of special benefit to the community, or devise some other means of showing that we deserve to be trusted and believed.

By the end of the sixteenth century we already encounter an explicit

43 Hobbes 1986, pp. 39–40.
44 Aristotle 1926, I.2.I, p. 14.
45 Hobbes 1986, p. 40. The phrase 'serving one's turn' was in common use by this time as a means of stigmatising self-interested behaviour. See Kempe 1966, p. 196, Plutarch 1603, p. 103, and Hobbes's own use of the phrase in Hobbes 1840c, pp. 418–19.
46 Hobbes 1986, p. 41; cf Hobbes 1983a, XII.XII, p. 193.

rejection of this assumption as an obvious irrelevance in the case of science, a contention that reached its climax in the motto of the Royal Society, which enjoins us not to trust anyone's word: *nullius in verba.* Whatever may be necessary in legal or political argument, it is claimed, there is no need in reporting scientific findings to establish one's ethos in this way, since the force of the argument should be such as to persuade anyone capable of following it. The claim is first put forward in the case of mathematical reasoning. When John Dee, for example, contributed his so-called Mathematical Preface to Billingsley's translation of Euclid's *Elements* in 1571,[47] he concluded by insisting that 'if vertuous zeale, and honest Intent provoke and bring you to the reading and examining of this Compendious treatise, I do not doute, but, as the veritie thereof (according to our purpose) will be evident unto you: So the pith and force thereof, will persuade you.'[48] During the next generation the same anti-rhetorical topos can be found in a much wider range of English scientific treatises. Gilbert declares in the Preface to *De Magnete* that 'although many things in our reasonings and hypotheses may possibly seem rather hard to accept at first, since they are different from common opinion, I do not doubt that hereafter they will acquire authority from the demonstrations themselves'.[49] Harvey in his *Exercitatio Anatomica* likewise insists that in science what matters is the evidence itself, not who happens to be presenting it. This is the perspective of all true philosophers, 'who never find themselves such wise men, so full of wisdom or assured of their own sense, but that they give place to the truth from whomever and from wherever it may come'.[50]

A decade later, Hobbes carries the same argument a long step further. He maintains that the establishment of ethos is an irrelevance not merely in the natural sciences – a claim that many rhetoricians had been willing to concede – but in the moral sciences as well. His translation of Aristotle's *Art of Rhetoric* accordingly omits the entire section in which Aristotle speaks of the crucial importance of taking steps to make a good impression on one's audience.[51] And in the epistle dedicatory to *De Cive* – at the very point where he might have been expected to establish his own ethos – he instead congratulates his dedicatee, the earl of Devonshire, for refusing to

47 Dee signed his preface (sig. A, iiii^v) 'February 9th. 1570', i.e. 1571 our style.

48 Dee 1571, sig. A, iiii^v.

49 Gilbert 1600, sig. *, ii^v: 'Multa in rationibus & hypothesibus prima facie, duriora forsan videbuntur, cum sunt a communi opinione aliena; non diffido tamen quin postea ex demonstrationibus ipsis authoritatem tandem nanciscentur.'

50 Harvey 1628, p. 7: 'nunquam se tam σοφος, sapientia plenos reperiunt, an suo sensu abundant, quin veritati, a quocunque & quandoququnque venerit, locum dent'.

51 Aristotle 1926, II.I.1–4, pp. 168–70.

pay attention to 'such matters as the reputation of writers, the alleged novelty of their arguments, or the outward splendour of their style'.[52] He adds that, like his patron, he reserves his admiration not for the status of authors 'but for the firmness of their arguments themselves'.[53] He concludes by taking his stand – very much as Dee had done – on the principle that the establishment of ethos is unnecessary, since 'there is a certain thread of reason which, when we are guided by it, serves in itself to bring us to the clearest light'.[54]

After considering the question of ethos, classical and Renaissance writers on rhetoric had generally turned to the concept of 'invention' in the strict sense, discussing the 'places' in which we can hope to discover (*invenire*) the most persuasive arguments. As we saw in chapter 3, their handling of this topic was largely governed by their sense that the goal of all public utterances should be that of guiding action in some appropriate way. In forensic oratory the goal is that of persuading our hearers to arrive at a just judgment, while in deliberative oratory it is that of persuading them to decide on a course of action at once expedient and honourable. The surest means of forging these crucial links between theory and practice was said to be that of accommodating our arguments to the beliefs already held by our audience. We need to draw as many 'commonplaces' as we can from the best-known teachers of moral and political philosophy, invoking their precepts and applying them to the case in hand.

Hobbes is perfectly willing to accept that in civil science we are seeking a form of knowledge capable of yielding wise guidance in practical affairs. He is even prepared to endorse the cardinal humanist belief that *scientia civilis* is the master science, and that no one lacking such knowledge can count as genuinely wise.[55] At an early point in *The Elements*, however, he insists on a distinction ignored by exponents of the *studia humanitatis* between two types of knowledge, only one of which can be said to give rise to *sapientia* or wisdom in its full and proper sense. One kind of knowledge, he explains, can be described as experience of fact.[56] This has its origins in sense and is shaped by the operations of memory, experience being 'nothing else but remembrance of what antecedents have been followed with what consequents'.[57] Such knowledge undoubtedly yields a form of

52 Hobbes 1983a, epistle dedicatory, p. 76: 'neque celebritate authorum, neque novitate sua, neque specie orationis'.

53 Hobbes 1983a, epistle dedicatory, p. 76: 'sed firmitudine rationum'.

54 Hobbes 1983a, epistle dedicatory, p. 75; 'filum quoddam rationis, cuius ductu evaditur in lucem clarissimam'.

55 BL Harl. MS 4235, fos. 131^v–132^r. Cf. Hobbes 1969a, p. 176.

56 BL Harl. MS 4235, fo. 25^v. Cf. Hobbes 1969a, p. 26.

57 BL Harl. MS 4235, fo. 19^r. Cf. Hobbes 1969a, p. 15.

wisdom, since it gives rise to an ability 'to conjecture by the present, of what is past, and what to come'.[58] The name usually given to this essentially practical form of wisdom is prudence, which in turn explains why we expect those who are old – who have more experience – to be more prudent than the young.[59] To be contrasted with this, however, is the kind of knowledge generally known as science, which alone gives rise to wisdom in the proper meaning of the term – the meaning we signal when we speak of 'sapience'.[60] This second type has some beginnings in sense, but consists not in experience of fact but in 'knowledge of the truth of propositions, and how things are called'.[61] It is based not on factual evidence but on the 'evidence' we may be said to possess of propositional truths. This in turn consists of our experience – or, to speak more exactly, our understanding – 'of the proper use of names in Language'.[62] When we speak of possessing knowledge of this kind, what we are claiming is that, from some basis in sense, we have arrived at some evidence of truth by way of having correctly grasped the meanings of some relevant terms.[63]

From the vantage-point of this distinction, Hobbes goes on to attack two of the most cherished assumptions of humanist civil science. He first argues that, if our aim is to acquire the form of knowledge that yields authentic wisdom, we cannot hope to proceed in the manner recommended by humanist writers on *scientia civilis*, namely by seeking to elicit the knowledge in question from a study of history. The idea of history as, in Elyot's phrase, a teacher of wisdom or sapience had long been a central tenet of English humanism, and had recently been restated by Hobbes's own pupil, William Cavendish, in his *Horae Subsecivae* of 1620. The 'principall use' of studying the past according to Cavendish is 'to enforme and enable the judgement, and furnish a man with discretion, and wisdome'.[64] Hobbes maintains, by contrast, that history is simply the name we give to 'the Register we keepe in bookes' of 'the Experience of the effects of thinges',[65] and that such experience 'concludeth nothing universally'.[66] But universal conclusions are precisely what we stand in need of if our knowledge is to make us wise. It follows that history cannot be a teacher of wisdom or sapience. While it is true that 'this taking of signes from experience, is that wherein men do ordinarily think the

58 BL Harl. MS 4235, fo. 131^{v}. Cf. Hobbes 1969a, p. 176.
59 BL Harl. MS 4235, fo. 19^{v}. Cf. Hobbes 1969a, p. 16.
60 BL Harl. MS 4235, fos. 26^{r} and 132^{r}. Cf. Hobbes 1969a, pp. 26, 176.
61 BL Harl MS 4235, fos. 24^{v}–25^{r}. Cf. Hobbes 1969a, p. 24.
62 BL Harl. MS 4235, fo. 25^{r}. Cf. Hobbes 1969a, p. 24.
63 BL Harl. MS 4235, fos. 25^{v}–26^{r}. Cf. Hobbes 1969a, pp. 25–6.
64 'Of Reading History' in [Cavendish] 1620, p. 207.
65 BL Harl. MS 4235, fos. 25^{r} and 131^{v}. Cf. Hobbes 1969a, pp. 24–5, 176.
66 BL Harl. MS 4235, fo. 19^{v}. Cf. Hobbes 1969a, p. 16.

difference stands betweene man and man in wisedome', the fact is that 'this is an errour, for these signs are but Conjecturall, and according as they have often or seldome failed, so their assurance is more or lesse; but never full and evident'.[67]

So sure is Hobbes that the image of Clio as a teacher of wisdom is based on a confusion that he goes to considerable lengths in *The Elements* and *De Cive* to avoid relying on historical illustrations or arguments. When he considers in chapter IX of *De Cive* why the first *Dominium* over children lies in the mother rather than the father, he uses the occasion to emphasise that women are also capable of bearing *Dominium* over political communities.[68] But whereas a writer like Bacon, examining the same issue in *The Advancement of Learning*, had felt it natural to make extensive reference to the recent instance of Queen Elizabeth,[69] Hobbes makes no reference to any individual instances at all – a clear reflection of his basic assumption that, as he was later to express it in *Behemoth*, historians can provide us with examples of fact but never with arguments of right.[70] The same scruple is even more apparent in his discussion in chapter x of *De Cive* of whether monarchy should be considered the best form of government. He first notes that most of the information we possess about this question comes 'from examples and testimonies', that is, from the evidence of history.[71] But he immediately adds that we ought not to make any use of such evidence, 'since it cannot be said to be based on genuine arguments'.[72] Rather than pretending that history is capable of yielding general truths, he prefers to admit that his own predilection for monarchy 'is not a doctrine I have demonstrated, but merely one I have stated as a matter of probability'.[73]

It is true that some English humanists had allowed that the study of history is perhaps better described as a source of prudence than of wisdom in the strictest sense. These writers had invariably assumed, however, that the virtue of prudence – which they often equated with wisdom[74] – is crucial to the proper conduct and understanding of civic life. Sir Thomas Elyot, for example, had offered an elaborate encomium to prudence in

67 BL Harl. MS 4235, fo. 19v. Cf. Hobbes 1969a, p. 16.
68 Hobbes 1983a, IX.II–VII, pp. 122–4.
69 Bacon 1915, pp. 47–9.
70 St John's College Oxford MS 13, p. 72. Cf. Hobbes 1969b, p. 76 and see also Hobbes 1991, p. 490.
71 Hobbes 1983a, X.III, p. 172: 'exemplis & testimoniis'.
72 Hobbes 1983a, X.III, p. 172: 'quia id non rationibus ... faciunt'.
73 Hobbes 1983a, 'Praefatio ad Lectores', p. 83: 'non demonstratam sed probabiliter positam esse'.
74 See for example Blundeville 1570, sig. D, 3v; Valerius 1571, sig. D, ivv and sig. F, 1v; Robinson 1579, sig. H, 8v. Cf. Wilson 1554, fo. 17v.

book I of the *Governor*, describing it as indispensable and peculiar to man on the grounds that it forms 'the porch of the noble palace of man's reason, whereby all other virtues shall enter'. This is why prudence 'is named of Aristotle the mother of virtues; of other philosophers it is called the captain or mistress of virtue'. The reason is that 'by her diligence she doth investigate and prepare places apt and convenient, where other virtues shall execute their powers or offices'.[75]

By contrast with this humanist understanding, Hobbes dethrones the quality of prudence with remarkable brusqueness from a place of any significance in civil science.[76] Far from seeing it as a key to rationality and a means of activating the other virtues, he defines it in chapter 4 of *The Elements* as 'nothing else but Conjecture from Experience'.[77] Even more deflatingly, he adds that, since prudence amounts to nothing more than a capacity to learn from experience, it is not in the least a quality peculiar to man; it is a quality in which 'brute Beasts also participate'.[78]

This almost satirically anti-humanist conclusion is simply an aspect of Hobbes's more general belief that the concept of an experimental science is an oxymoron. This is not to say that Hobbes ever sought to discourage the performing of experiments. On the contrary, in his final statement of 'the principles and method of natural philosophy' in the *Decameron Physiologicum* of 1678 he even insists that 'you must furnish yourself with as many experiments (which they call phenomenon) as you can'.[79] Hobbes's objection is only to the belief that this process can ever serve in itself to yield scientific truths.[80] He first makes the point in *The Elements*, but he expresses it most forcefully in the opening chapter of his critique of Thomas White's *De mundo*. The theme of Hobbes's introductory chapter is that every science worthy the name 'must be treated in such a way that the truth of what is concluded can be known by necessary inference'.[81] From this axiom he derives a number of inferences:

It is necessary that Philosophy should be treated logically. For the goal of students of Philosophy is not to move the emotions but to know with certainty. So Philosophy has nothing to do with Rhetoric. Moreover, the goal is to know the necessity of consequences and the truth of universal propositions. So Philosophy has nothing to do

75 Elyot 1962, p. 79.
76 This point is excellently brought out in Kahn 1985, pp. 153–4, 161–2, 178–9, as well as in Rossini 1987; Rossini 1988, pp. 185–91, 204–9, and Hampsher-Monk 1992, pp. 2, 15–18.
77 BL Harl. MS 4235, fo. 19ᵛ. Cf. Hobbes 1969a, p. 16.
78 BL Harl. MS 4235, fos. 25ᵛ–26ʳ. Cf. Hobbes 1969a, p. 26.
79 Hobbes 1845h, chapter 2, pp. 82–8, at p. 88.
80 On this point see Shapin and Schaffer 1985, p. 129, and Boonin-Vail 1994, pp. 26–30.
81 BN Fonds Latin MS 6566A, fo. 6ᵛ, para. 3: 'ita tractanda sit ut eorum quae concluduntur veritas necessaria illatione cognoscatur'. Cf. Hobbes 1973, p. 107.

with history. Much less has it anything to do with Poetry, which narrates individual events, and in addition professedly neglects the truth.[82]

Hobbes rejects the pretensions not merely of history but of all the humanistic disciplines, each of which is shown in turn to be ill adapted to the production of genuine knowledge.

Hobbes's second line of attack on the humanist approach to *scientia civilis* is a more general one. If, he maintains, we wish to acquire and communicate a genuine knowledge and understanding of civic affairs, it is a fundamental error to proceed by way of accommodating our arguments to generally accepted beliefs and their expression in common speech. He launches a frontal assault, in other words, on the doctrine of *loci communes*, the doctrine lying at the heart of Renaissance ideas about the 'invention' of persuasive arguments.

This is not of course to say that Hobbes's was a lone voice raised in this period against the theory of commonplaces. As with the alleged importance of establishing ethos, the idea that we ought to seek knowledge by following the precepts of accredited authorities had already been severely criticised by many scientific writers of the early seventeenth century. Bacon makes it his chief complaint in the preface to his *Novum Organon* that even the leaders of the sciences 'still have not dared to abandon their adherence to received beliefs' but 'continue to rely on accepted opinions and customs'.[83] By contrast, he insists, his own philosophy 'makes no effort to flatter the intelligence by dealing in preconceived ideas'.[84] Gilbert concludes the preface to *De Magnete* by speaking even more contemptuously of 'those sworn to uphold the opinions of others'.[85] His own work is addressed 'to you alone, true admirers of philosophy and open-minded men, who search for knowledge not only in books but in things themselves'.[86] Harvey speaks in a similarly elevated tone in the epistle dedicatory to his *Exercitatio Anatomica*:

82 BN Fonds Latin MS 6566A, fo. 6^{v}, para. 3: 'necesse est ut tractetur [sc. Philosophia] logice. Finis enim Philosophiae studentium non est commovere, sed certo scire, neque ergo spectat ad Rhetoricam; et scire necessitatem consequentiarum veritatemque propositionum universalium; non ergo spectat ad historicam: multo minus ad Poeticam, nam et haec facta singularia narrat, et praeterea veritatem ex professo negligit.' Cf. Hobbes 1973, p. 107.

83 Bacon is speaking here in the general preface to the *Instauratio Magna*, which forms the introduction to his *Novum Organon*. See Bacon 1857c, p. 128: 'nec illi a receptis prorsus desciscere ausi sunt' but 'verum dum opinionibus et moribus consulitur'.

84 Bacon adds this in the preface to the *Novum Organon*. See Bacon 1857c, p. 153: 'neque ex praenotionibus intellectui blanditur'. Cf. Gilbert 1600, sig. *, ii^{v}, treating it as a matter of pride that his findings 'differ from what is commonly believed' ('sunt a communi opinione aliena').

85 Gilbert 1600, sig. *, ii^{v}: 'iuratis in aliorum sententias'.

86 Gilbert 1600, sig. *, ii^{v}: 'vobis tantum vere Philosophantibus, viris ingenuis, qui non in libris solum, sed ex rebus ipsis scientiam quaeritis'.

True Philosophers never become addicted to upholding the traditions and precepts of anyone else in such a way as to lose their own liberty, but rather seek to maintain their faith in their own eyes. Nor do they ever give their word to Mistress Antiquity in such a way as to relinquish their friend the truth openly, deserting her in the sight of all.[87]

Harvey recurs to the point in the opening chapter of his treatise, insisting that 'I myself seek to learn and teach anatomy not from books but from dissections, not from the opinions of philosophers but from the fabric of nature.'[88]

What is distinctive about Hobbes's argument in *The Elements* and *De Cive* is his insistence that the same considerations apply no less to the human than the natural sciences. He begins by recalling – though hardly in the most neutral terms – the rival rhetorical assumption that we ought to accommodate our arguments so far as possible to received beliefs. Chapter 5 of *The Elements* warns us against the misleading character of discourse 'derived from the Custome and Common use of Speech'.[89] Chapter 13 contains a more specific warning against writers on 'Policy, Government, and Lawes', who are particularly prone to 'take for principles those opinions which are already vulgarly received' and to 'take up Maximes from their Education, and from the authority of men'.[90] Chapter 8 of part II refers yet more specifically to the methods recommended by the theorists of eloquence, who 'derive what they would have to be believed, from somewhat believed already'.[91] By the time he comes to his analysis of the art of rhetoric in *De Cive*, we find Hobbes pronouncing in tones clearly intended to elicit our scorn that the basic assumption of those who speak with *eloquentia* is that our arguments should be 'accommodated to the passions of our hearers',[92] and that we ought therefore 'to construct our speeches out of whatever opinions, no matter of what kind, already happen to be generally believed'.[93]

Hobbes's main purpose in recalling these features of the doctrine of *inventio* is to introduce his objections to them. He has two connected objections to raise, the first of which states that this approach cannot even point us in the direction of discovering new and certain truths. The reason,

87 Harvey 1628, p. 7: 'Nec ita traditionibus & praeceptis quorumcunque addicti, inservire se patiuntur Philosophi, & libertatem perdunt, ne oculis propriis fidem adhibeant, nec ita in verba iurant antiquitatis magistrae, ut veritatem amicam in apertis relinquant, & in conspectus omnium deserant.'

88 Harvey 1628, p. 8: 'Non ex libris sed ex dissectionibus, non ex placitis Philosophorum, sed fabrica naturae discere & docere Anatomen profitear.'

89 BL Harl. MS 4235, fo. 22^{v}. Cf. Hobbes 1969a, p. 21.

90 BL Harl. MS 4235, fo. 52^{r-v}. Cf. Hobbes 1969a, pp. 66, 67.

91 BL Harl. MS 4235, fo. 132^{v}. Cf. Hobbes 1969a, p. 177.

92 Hobbes 1983a, XII.XII, p. 192: 'ad affectus accommodato'.

93 Hobbes 1983a, XII.XII, p. 193: 'ex iam receptis opinionibus, qualescunque eae sint, orationem texit'.

as chapter 13 of *The Elements* explains, is that if we 'take for principles those opinions which are already vulgarly received' we shall not only be relying on beliefs that may be true or false, but on beliefs that are almost certain to be false, simply because they will be the opinions of ordinary men.[94] Hobbes directly repudiates, in other words, the widespread humanist assumption to the effect that, if a given belief has been accepted *ab omnibus*, this in itself gives us some reason for espousing it. He later underlines his scepticism in the course of discussing Aristotle's moral theory at the end of chapter 18. By drawing on opinions 'which were generally believed in his time', Aristotle grounded his theory on a set of principles he had no reason to endorse, and had some reason to believe were 'not very likely to be accurate'.[95] Developing the point in *De Cive*, Hobbes gives a number of further instances. Anyone who relies 'on opinions that are already commonly received' is relying on opinions 'which for the greatest part are usually erroneous'.[96] For example, when Aristotle declared that man is a political animal, he made use of 'an axiom which, while accepted by very many people, is nevertheless false'.[97] Similarly, when he defined liberty in terms of dominion, he argued 'according to the custom of his time' and thereby introduced a serious confusion into his theory of government.[98] The approach characteristic of the rhetoricians is in short 'disjoined from a true knowledge of things, and hence from wisdom or sapience'.[99]

Discussing the art of rhetoric in chapter x of *De Cive*, Hobbes restates this first criticism in more general terms. Even if the commonplaces invoked by rhetoricians should happen to be true, their willingness to accept such maxims without testing their acceptability still amounts to a betrayal of *recta ratio*, a decision 'to put forward their opinions merely by the exercise of a violent impetus of the mind'.[100] This in turn leads him to respond directly to Quintilian's contention that, while good orators naturally aim at victory, they only aim at victory for the truth. Hobbes retorts that those who aim at victory thereby disclose that they do not care about the truth. 'The goal of eloquence, as all the masters of Rhetoric teach, is not the truth but victory, so that truth is only attained by accident.'[101]

94 BL Harl. MS 4235, fo. 52^{r-v}. Cf. Hobbes 1969a, p. 66.

95 BL Harl. MS 4235, fo. 71^{v}. Cf. Hobbes 1969a, p. 94.

96 See Hobbes 1983a, x.xi, p. 178, on 'opinionibus iam vulgo receptis, quae maxima ex parte erroneae esse solent'.

97 Hobbes 1983a, i.ii, p. 90: 'Axioma, quamquam a plurimis receptum, falsum tamen [est]'.

98 See Hobbes 1983a, x.viii, p. 176, on Aristotle arguing 'consuetudine temporis'.

99 See Hobbes 1983a, xii.xii, p. 193, on eloquentia as 'separata a rerum scientia, hoc est, a sapientia'.

100 Hobbes 1983a, x.xi, p. 178: 'non recta ratione, sed impetu animi sententias ferri'.

101 Hobbes 1983a, x.xi, p. 178: 'cuius [sc. eloquentia] finis (ut magistri Rhetoricae omnes docent) non veritas est (nisi per accidens) sed victoria'.

This conclusion brings Hobbes to his second objection to the theory of commonplaces. If, as he puts it in chapter 13 of *The Elements*, we remain content to 'take the habitual discourse of the tongue for ratiocination', the effect will not be to supplement *ratio* with *oratio* as the masters of rhetoric contend; it will simply be to elide the first into the second, thereby condemning us to move within the circle of our pre-existing passions and prejudices.[102] Hobbes introduces this argument with a direct allusion to Cicero's ideal of the orator as a man whose special talent is that of underpinning *ratio* with *oratio*, reason with powerful speech. So prevalent is this ideal, Hobbes replies, that 'Ratio, now, is but Oratio, for the most part. Wherein Custome hath so great a power, that the minde suggesteth onely the first word, the rest follow habitually, and are not followed by the minde.'[103] The outcome is that those now accepted as experts on moral and civil science are the merest *Dogmatici*, who 'with passion press to have their opinions passe every where for truth'.[104] Later he names the dogmatics he chiefly has in mind: 'Aristotle, Cicero, Seneca, and others of like authority', who 'have followed the autority of other men, as we doe theires'.[105]

It is of course true, Hobbes concedes, that dogmatism is not necessarily incompatible with truth. A dogmatic discourse may happen to furnish evidence of truth in the form of words correctly used and correctly linked, since it may happen that in naming things we 'name them aright by chance'.[106] But this cannot possibly count as a means of acquiring genuine *scientia* or knowledge. To say that we possess a knowledge of something, it is not sufficient to be able to speak the truth about it; it is also necessary to know that we are speaking the truth. If, by contrast, we merely happen to name things aright by chance, then we 'are not said to have Science, but Opinion', not knowledge but continuing uncertainty.[107] Hobbes summarises these contentions in the form of a spectacularly offensive dismissal of the rival claims about *inventio* embodied in the theory of eloquence. The figure of the orator, he concludes, is really no better than a parrot. 'For if the words alone were sufficient, a Parrott might be taught as well to knowe a truth, as to speak it.'[108]

102 BL Harl. MS 4235, fo. 52ᵛ. Cf. Hobbes 1969a, p. 67.
103 BL Harl. MS 4235, fo. 23ᵛ. Cf. Hobbes 1969a, p. 23. This strongly recalls an argument in the preface to Bacon's *Novum Organon*: 'mens ex quotidiana vitae consuetudine, et auditionibus et doctrinis inquinatis occupata' – 'due to the custom and conversations of everyday life, the mind is continually filled with debased beliefs'. See Bacon 1857c, p. 152.
104 BL Harl. MS 4235, fo. 52ᵛ. Cf. Hobbes 1969a, p. 67.
105 BL Harl. MS 4235, fo. 132ᵛ. Cf. Hobbes 1969a, p. 177.
106 BL Harl. MS 4235, fo. 132ʳ. Cf. Hobbes 1969a, p. 176.
107 BL Harl. MS 4235, fo. 132ʳ. Cf. Hobbes 1969a, p. 176.
108 BL Harl. MS 4235, fo. 25ᵛ. Cf. Hobbes 1969a, p. 25. The example was a standard one in

Hobbes reserves a word of special contempt for the most extreme expression of the rhetorical assumption that we ought so far as possible to accommodate our arguments to accepted beliefs. As we saw in chapter 3, this had given rise to a style of writing known as the *cento*, a genre of texts composed entirely of *sententiae* pieced together from the best authorities. Burton had provided a notable example in *The Anatomy of Melancholy*, and had recommended the method as an appropriate one to adopt in a decaying world in which all the best thoughts have already been thought. By contrast, when Hobbes mentions the genre in *The Elements*, it is in the context of illustrating the various forms of insanity. 'For a man contynually to speak his minde in a Cento of other mens Greeke and Latine Sentences', he concludes, is a sign of so much dejection of mind as to count as an instance of learned madness.[109]

THE ATTACK ON *ELOCUTIO*

Besides repudiating the theory of *inventio*, Hobbes launches an attack in *The Elements* and *De Cive* on the other leading feature of the *ars rhetorica*, the theory of *elocutio*. As before, he associates his critique with an account of the salient features of the doctrine involved. He first mentions, and indeed endorses, the emphasis placed by the classical theorists of rhetoric on the fact that most human emotions are of an inherently fickle and hence a pliable character. As we saw in chapter 3, Cicero had particularly stressed in the *De oratore* that actions commended by one person are always liable to be condemned by others, and this sentiment had been widely echoed by the more sceptical theorists of eloquence in the Renaissance. Hobbes reiterates precisely the same arguments, appropriating a number of Cicero's formulae and embroidering them at the same time. He initially makes the point in the epistle dedicatory to *De Cive*, where he treats it as a principal sign of our failure to construct a genuine science of politics that we find 'the same action praised by some people and denounced by others',[110] and 'the same man approving of something which he condemns at a different time'.[111] He repeats the claim towards the end of chapter III, where he observes in discussing the laws of nature that we not only find 'that one person praises, that is, calls good, something that another person

discussions about the possibility of possessing words without answering concepts. See Ashworth 1981, esp. pp. 315–16.

109 BL Harl. MS 4235, fo. 42ᵛ. Cf. Hobbes 1969a, p. 52. Hobbes's claim that the use of the genre implies depression is interesting in view of his friendship (on which see Malcolm 1994, p. 875) with Robert Burton, famous both for his *cento* and his dejection of mind.

110 Hobbes 1983a, epistle dedicatory, p. 75: 'alii laudent, alii vituperent eandem actionem'.

111 Hobbes 1983a, epistle dedicatory, p. 75: 'idem nunc probet quae alio tempore damnat'.

denounces as evil; we very often find the same person praising and blaming the very same action at different times'.[112] He further extends the argument when discussing the concept of civil law in chapter XIV. 'The diversity of human emotions', he now declares, 'is enough to ensure that we find one man calling something good which another calls evil, we find the same man calling something good which he soon afterwards calls evil, and we find the same man saying of the same attribute that it is good in him but evil in someone else.'[113]

Hobbes also reminds us why the classical and Renaissance theorists of *elocutio* had treated this emotional pliability as a matter of such importance. According to the crucial play on words lying at the heart of their argument, the best way of moving an audience towards the acceptance of our point of view will be to move them emotionally, to speak in such a way as to leave them 'greatly moved'. Hobbes first alludes to this pivotal doctrine in chapter 2 of part II of *The Elements* when discussing the behaviour of democratic assemblies. It is all too easy, he warns, for powerful orators to rouse and move the passions of their hearers in such a way as 'to inclyne and sway the assembly to their owne ends'.[114] But it is in *De Cive*, and especially in the analysis of sedition in chapter XII, that he refers most explicitly to the idea of eloquence as a moving force. He begins by reiterating that, as the theorists of rhetoric acknowledge, the aim of eloquent speakers is to win round their auditors and thereby attain victory.[115] But the most effective way of shifting or moving an audience is by acting as a *commotrix*, 'a mover of the passions of the soul, an arouser of such passions as hope, fear, anger and sorrow'.[116] Eloquence can indeed be defined as that power which 'by moving the minds of men, makes everything appear to them to be just as they conceived it to be in consequence of having had their minds moved'.[117] Hobbes's argument, like that of the rhetoricians, accordingly culminates in an image of eloquence as a *vis* or physical force. As *The Elements* puts it, 'Eloquence is nothing else but the power of winninge beliefe of what we say, and to that end we must have Aide from the passions of the

112 Hobbes 1983a, III.XXXI, p. 119: 'quod hic *laudat*, id est, appellat *bonum*, alter *vituperat* ut *malum*; immo saepissime idem homo diversis temporibus idem & *laudat* & *culpat*'.

113 Hobbes 1983a, XIV.XVII, p. 213: 'diversitate affectuum contingit, ut quod alter *bonum*, alter *malum*; & idem homo quod nunc *bonum*, mox *malum*; & eandem rem, in seipso *bonam*, in alio *malam* esse dicat'.

114 BL Harl. MS 4235, fo. 88ᵛ. Cf. Hobbes 1969a, p. 120.

115 Hobbes 1983a, XII.XII, pp. 192–3.

116 Hobbes 1983a, XII.XII, p. 192: 'affectuum animi (quales sunt spes, metus, ira, misericordia) commotrix'.

117 Hobbes 1983a, XII.XII, p. 193: 'commovendo animos, facit apparere omnia, qualia ipsi animis prius commotis ea conceperant'.

Hearer.'[118] We can therefore speak, *De Cive* adds, of *eloquentia potens*,[119] of eloquence as an efficacious and potent force. So great is this force, *The Elements* maintains, that in the hands of a speaker endowed 'with eloquence and reputation' it is sufficient 'to make that lawe to day, which another by the very same meanes shall abrogate to morrow'.[120]

Hobbes next recalls a further connected claim put forward by the classical and Renaissance theorists of *elocutio*. They had invariably argued that the surest means of arousing the fickle feelings of an audience and moving them to accept one's point of view will be by stretching or amplifying the truth. They had argued, that is, that the distinctive capacity of powerful speakers lies in knowing how to exaggerate what can be said in favour of a cause and how to extenuate anything that can be said against it, thereby quelling or inflaming the passions of their auditors at will. Hobbes not only ratifies this account of the orator's art, but takes pains in both *The Elements* and *De Cive* to echo the precise vocabulary employed by the rhetoricians themselves. He first does so in the context of discussing the emotions in chapter 9 of *The Elements*. 'Of all the passions of the minde, these two, Indignation & Pitty, are most easily raised and increased by Eloquence.' The reason is that 'the aggravation of the Calamity, and Extenuation of the Fault, augmenteth pitty', while 'the Extenuation of the worth of the person, together with the magnifying of his success (which are the parts of an Oratour) are able to turn these two passions into Fury'.[121] He makes a similar claim when comparing the virtues and shortcomings of monarchy, aristocracy and democracy. Democracy suffers from the gravest shortcomings, one of which arises from the fact that 'when thinges are debated in great assemblyes' everyone concerned 'indeavoureth to make whatsoever he is to sett forth for Good, better; and what he would have apprehended as Evill, worse, as much as is possible; to the end his Counsell may take place'.[122] The whole discussion is later summarised in the section on the art of eloquence in part II, chapter 8. Rhetoricians not only 'derive what they would have to be believed from somewhat believed already, but also by aggravations and Extenuations make good, and bad, right and wronge, appeare greate or lesse, according as it shall serve their turnes'.[123] Hobbes ends by stressing that these techniques of *amplificatio* are capable of having an extraordinarily 'moving' effect. 'Such is the power of Eloquence, as many tymes a man is made to believe thereby, that he

118 BL Harl. MS 4235, fo. 132ᵛ. Cf. Hobbes 1969a, p. 177.
119 Hobbes 1983a, XII.XII, p. 193.
120 BL Harl. MS 4235, fo. 105ᵛ. Cf. Hobbes 1969a, p. 143.
121 BL Harl. MS 4235, fo. 35ʳ⁻ᵛ. Cf. Hobbes 1969a, p. 41.
122 BL Harl. MS 4235, fo. 104ᵛ. Cf. Hobbes 1969a, p. 141.
123 BL Harl. MS 4235, fo. 132ᵛ. Cf Hobbes 1969a, p. 177.

sensibly feeleth smart and dammage, when he feeleth none, and to enter into rage and indignation, without any other Cause, than what is in the words and passion of the Speaker.'[124]

The same arguments are reiterated and further developed in *De Cive.* Hobbes initially reverts to the question of *amplificatio* in the course of discussing, in chapter v, the Aristotelian proposition that creatures other than man – and especially bees – can be classified as political animals. One reason for doubting this contention is that 'although such animals appear to have some use of the voice to indicate their feelings among themselves, they lack that particular art of words which is necessarily required if the motions of the mind are to be aroused in such a way that good can be represented to the mind as better, and evil as worse, than is really the case'.[125] But it is in chapter x, when discussing the different forms of government, that Hobbes chiefly speaks of *amplificatio,* although he is much less concerned than in the corresponding chapter of *The Elements* to preserve even a semblance of neutrality. 'The gift of eloquence', he now affirms, 'lies in being able to make good and evil, expedient and inexpedient, honourable and dishonourable appear to be greater or less than they are in fact, and in being able to make injustice appear to be justice in whatever way appears conducive to the purposes of the speaker himself.'[126] The same point is even more intemperately expressed in chapter xii. We are now told that those who possess the gift of *eloquentia* 'are able to turn foolish listeners into madmen, are able to make that which is bad seem worse and that which is honest seem bad, and are able to amplify hope and extenuate dangers beyond anything reasonable'.[127]

Hobbes also recalls the account given by the theorists of *elocutio* of the means by which we can hope to amplify our utterances in such a way as to move an audience. They had argued that the most effective technique will be to 'ornament' our arguments with the figures and tropes of speech. Hobbes first discusses this method of adorning the truth when analysing the emotions and their connections with intelligence in chapter 10 of *The Elements.* He asks himself about the specific means by which 'both poets

124 BL Harl. MS 4235, fos. 132^{v}–133^{r}. Cf. Hobbes 1969a, p. 177.

125 Hobbes 1983a, v.v, p. 133: 'animantia bruta, utcunque possint vocis suae usum aliquem habere ad significandum inter se affectus suos, carent tamen illa verborum arte, quae necessario requiritur ad perturbationes animi concitandas, nimirum, qua Bonum, Melius; Malum Peius repraesentatur animo, quam revera est.'

126 Hobbes 1983a, x.xi, pp. 177–8: 'Eloquentiae autem munus est *Bonum* & *malum, utile* & *inutile, Honestum* & *inhonestum,* facere apparere maiora vel minora quam revera sunt, & *Iustum* videri, quod *iniustum* est, prout ad finem dicentis videbitur conducere.'

127 Hobbes 1983a, xii.xii, p. 193: 'auditores suos, ex stultis insanos reddere possunt; quod facere possunt, ut quibus male est, Peius, quibus recte, male esse videatur; quod spem amplificare, pericula extenuare, praeter rationem iidem possunt'.

and orators have it in their power to make things please or displease, and shew well or ill to others, as they like themselves'. He responds that this ability depends above all on learning to cultivate the kind of fancy or imagination that enables us to produce 'gratefull Similies, Metaphors and other Tropes'.[128] He repeats the point in the chapters on the art of eloquence in *De Cive.* Chapter x observes that 'one reason why a large assembly is ill-suited for deliberation'[129] is that its members will be all too liable to fall under the sway of rhetoricians who make long speeches 'which they deliver to their hearers in a style filled up as much as possible with *ornatus* and rendered graceful by their *eloquentia*'.[130] Chapter XII adds that the principal means by which such rhetoricians are able to act as movers and shakers of the passions is 'by using words in a fashion at once metaphorical and at the same time accommodated to the emotions of their audience'.[131]

While these remarks are purportedly exegetical, Hobbes makes little attempt to disguise the fact that his chief purpose is to remind us of the position he wishes to challenge and undermine. His main concern is to establish that all these methods of ornamenting and thereby amplifying the truth are irrelevant and indeed inimical to the construction of a genuine science of civil life.

Such a rejection of *ornatus*, and more generally of *elocutio*, was not of course unparalleled. Even the rhetoricians had conceded that, at least in the case of scientific and especially mathematical reasoning, the techniques of powerful speaking will generally be out of place. When Thomas Wilson asks at the start of his *Arte of Rhetorique* about the range of disciplines in which an orator can hope to display his skills, he makes the concession in emphatic terms:

> Now Astronomie is rather learned by demonstracion, then taught by any greate utteraunce. Arithmetique smally nedeth the use of eloquence, seeyng it maie be had wholy by nombryng onely. Geometrie rather asketh a good square, then a cleane flowyng tongue, to set out the arte. Therfore an Orators profession, is to speake onely, of all suche matters as maie largely be expounded, for mannes behove, and maie with muche grace be set out, for all men to heare theim.[132]

If we ask what constellation of topics remain to be embellished with *eloquentia*, Wilson answers – in a close paraphrase of the *Ad Herennium* – that

128 BL Harl. MS 4235, fo. 41r. Cf. Hobbes 1969a, p. 50.
129 Hobbes 1983a, X.XI, p. 177: 'Alia causa quare magnus coetus ad deliberationem minus idoneus est.'
130 Hobbes 1983a, X.XI, p. 177: 'audientibus quantum potest ornatam gratamque eloquentia reddere'.
131 Hobbes 1983a, XII.XII, p. 192: 'ex usu verborum metaphorico, & ad affectus accommodato'.
132 Wilson 1554, fo. 1r.

orators are limited to 'those questions, whiche by lawe and mannes ordinaunce are enacted, and appoynted for the use and profite of man'.[133]

During the early seventeenth century this concession was taken up and elaborated by many English writers on the natural sciences.[134] Gilbert assures us in *De Magnete* that he will not even trouble to address himself 'to the ridiculous corrupters of the good arts', among whom he specifically numbers 'the grammaticists, the sophists and the mere ranters'.[135] 'I myself', he insists in contrast, 'have not introduced into this work any embellishments of *eloquentia*, nor have I added any *ornatus* to my words. I have merely aimed to examine difficult and unknown matters in such a style and by the use of such words as are necessarily required to render what I say clearly intelligible.'[136] A similar approach informs Bacon's programmatic writings on the natural sciences. Bacon was of course a student of rhetoric, and in his own contributions to the *studia humanitatis* a practitioner as well.[137] But he too draws a sharp distinction between the human sciences (in which the art of rhetoric has an important place) and the reporting of scientific findings (in which it has no place at all). He makes the point with particular emphasis in the *Parasceve*, the preliminary aphorisms he wrote as an introduction to his cherished project of a series of 'natural histories' of scientific subjects. These histories, he explains in aphorism 2, must be written 'in such a way as not to subserve the pleasures of the reader'.[138] What this means, he adds in aphorism 3, is that the style in which they are written 'must be discharged of everything superfluous'.[139] This requires two principal rules to be observed: 'first, all ancient authorities and citations and opinions of authors must be omitted altogether'; and secondly, 'everything concerned with the ornamentation of speech, with the use of similitudes, with the whole thesaurus of *eloquentia* and other such inanities must be absolutely avoided'.[140]

It is important to add that there was a long tradition of hostility even within the humanistic disciplines to the exaggerated use of highly orna-

133 Wilson 1554, fo. 1[r].

134 Cf. the excellent discussion in Shapiro 1983, chapter 7, pp. 227–66.

135 Gilbert 1600, sig. *, ii[v]: 'absurdissimis bonarum artium corruptoribus, literatis idiotis, grammaticis, sophistis rabulis'.

136 Gilbert 1600, sig. *, iii[r]: 'Neque huic operi ullum eloquentiae fucum aut verborum ornatum attulimus, sed hoc tantum fecimus, ut res difficiles & incognitae tractarentur a nobis, ea dicendi forma, iisque verbis necessario requisitis, ut intellegi dilucide queant.' Cf. Shapiro 1983, pp. 230, 232–3.

137 A point forcefully made in Vickers 1985, esp. pp. 11–14.

138 Bacon 1857a, p. 396: 'se non lectoris delectationi ... debere inservire'.

139 Bacon 1857a, p. 396: 'onerari superfluis'. Cf. Shapiro 1983, pp. 233–5.

140 Bacon 1857a, p. 396: 'Primo igitur facessant antiquitates et citationes aut suffragia authorum ... Quae vero ad ornamenta orationis et similitudines et eloquentiae thesaurum et huiusmodi inania spectant omnino abiiciantur.'

mented and emotional speech. A number of ancient rhetoricians had expressed the fear that excessive addiction to *ornatus* might have the ironic consequence of producing an absurd instead of an impressive effect. Cicero was ridiculed in the closing years of his career for the 'asiatic' and affected character of his prose, and in his *Orator* he sought to defend himself, not without considerable querulousness, against this wounding charge.[141] But the younger generation remained unconvinced, and in Tacitus' *Dialogus de oratoribus* the figure of Aper is made to speak with evident approval of those who criticise Cicero's style as inflated, bombastic and full of superfluities.[142]

The same scruples recurred in the English Renaissance, especially in the face of the growing popularity of rhetorical ornament in Elizabethan prose. Such sensitivities found expression in a series of images – and two in particular – that gained extensive currency. One alludes to the classical view that, since eloquent speech is meant to move and delight, it ought to be harmonious and refined. This can lead, it was objected, to a style so delicate as to be cloying, so sweet as to be sugary. This is Bacon's criticism in *The Advancement of Learning*, at the start of which he explains how the 'delicate and polished kind of learning' promoted by Roger Ascham and his disciples at Cambridge 'grew speedily to an excess':

> For men began to hunt more after words than matter; more after the choiceness of the phrase, and the round and clean composition of the sentence, and the sweet falling of the clauses, and the varying and illustration of their works with tropes and figures, than after the weight of matter, worth of subject, soundness of argument, life of invention or depth of judgment.[143]

Bacon's criticism was undoubtedly influential, but it merely reaffirms a well-entrenched dislike of rhetorical excess, a dislike especially evident among Elizabethan writers of a puritan cast. Thomas Becon in the preface to his collected works of 1564 had already attacked 'babbling orators' for corrupting the education of English youth, and had referred sarcastically to the prevalence of 'their sugared and ornate eloquence'.[144] Raphe Lever in the 'Forespeach' to his *Arte of Reason* of 1573 had likewise denounced the 'Ciceronians & suger tongued fellowes' in terms very similar to those subsequently used by Bacon. They 'labour more for finenes of speech, then for knowledge of good matter', as a result of which they 'oft speake

141 Cicero 1962b, esp. XXVIII, pp. 374–8, and XLI, 142, p. 416.

142 Tacitus 1970, 18.4, p. 278. For this 'atticist' attack on Cicero's 'asiatic' exuberance see Leeman 1963, pp. 136–67.

143 Bacon 1915, p. 24.

144 Becon 1843, pp. 10, 29.

much to small purpose, and shaking forth a number of choice words, and picked sentences, they hinder good learning, with their fond chatte'.[145]

The other popular image of distaste drew on the classical idea of *ornatus* as a means of clothing the naked truth in courtly and appealing dress. Such apparel, it was argued, can readily become so garish as to remind us not of a courtly lady but a prostitute. We already encounter the objection in Tacitus' *Dialogus de oratoribus*, in which the figure of Messala declares that 'it is far better to clothe your speech in a homespun toga than to deck it out in the dyed garments of courtesans'.[146] As we saw in chapter 5, Messala's argument resurfaces in Sidney's attack on those who present 'that hony-flowing Matrone *Eloquence* apparrelled, or rather disguised, in a Courtisanlike painted affectation'.[147] But Sidney's criticism is merely the best-known of numerous attacks on excessive verbal finery. Gabriel Harvey had already spoken in similar vein of those who declaim with 'a curtizan Tongue'.[148] Mulcaster had also pointed to the ease with which the art of eloquence can be abused, especially by those who, 'in *speeche* delicate and divine', give 'false & coloured informations, to serve their own turnes'. The right approach, Mulcaster insists, must be to follow those who 'have preferred plaine trueth before painted colours'.[149]

Hobbes's attack on the use of *ornatus* in *The Elements* and *De Cive* is clearly indebted to such criticisms.[150] But at the same time he carries the repudiation of rhetorical ornament very much further. What he denounces is not the exaggerated use but the very presence of *ornatus* in expository prose, and not merely in the natural sciences but in the *studia humanitatis* as well. He insists in particular that, since *scientia civilis* is genuinely a science, we have no need to supplement its findings with the techniques of persuasion any more than in the other scientific disciplines.

He reverts, in other words, to the most extreme version of the classical attack on rhetoric, the version associated in the minds of Cicero and Quintilian with Socrates' criticisms in the *Gorgias*. As we saw in chapter 2, they had both reported Socrates as claiming that the art of rhetoric is so entirely out of place in the moral as well as the other sciences that, if anyone speaks in a manner calculated to persuade, then it follows that they cannot be said to teach. The Roman rhetoricians had viewed this line of attack as the one they most of all needed to deflect, and among

145 Lever 1573, sig. **, 1v.
146 Tacitus 1970, 26.1: 'adeo melius est orationem vel hirta toga induere quam fucatis et meretriciis vestibus insignire'.
147 Sidney 1923, p. 42.
148 Harvey 1913, p. 189.
149 Mulcaster, 1888, pp. 160–1.
150 His pupil repeats the attack. See 'Of Affectation' in [Cavendish] 1620, esp. p. 49.

Renaissance writers it was widely agreed that Quintilian had succeeded in deflecting it, and so in establishing that there is no necessary incompatibility between teaching on the one hand and persuasion on the other. He was held to have shown that the rhetorician's highest task is *docere, suadere et delectare*: to teach, to persuade and to delight all at once.

Without deigning to go into the merits of Quintilian's argument, Hobbes simply reverts to the very claim that Quintilian had sought to contradict, reviving once again the Socratic objection that the techniques of teaching and persuading are irreconcilable. He first makes the point in the course of analysing what it means to teach in chapter 13 of *The Elements*. Teaching he defines as the act of 'begetting in another the same Conceptions that we have in our selves'. To which he adds that 'if the Conceptions of him that teacheth continually accompany his wordes, beginning at something from experience, then it begetteth the like evidence in the Hearer that understandeth them, and maketh him knowe some thinge, which he is therefore said to LEARNE'.[151] The 'infallible signe' of genuine teaching is accordingly that everyone teaches the same, and that there are no contradictory arguments.[152] If, by contrast, we employ the techniques of persuasion, we merely 'aime at getting opinion from Passion'.[153] But to achieve this result 'any premises are good enough to inferre the desired conclusion', because we are merely seeking to 'instigate' beliefs, to prompt our audience to share whatever opinions we already happen to hold.[154] 'There is therefore a great deale of difference betweene Teaching and Persuadinge, the signs of this being Controversie, the signe of the former, Noe-Controversie.'[155]

De Cive takes it for granted that this distinction has been established. Hobbes contents himself with recalling Quintilian's claim that a true rhetorician will always aim to teach and persuade at the same time, a contention to which he responds with the lie direct: 'the product of eloquence is not teaching, it is simply persuasion'.[156] He subsequently underlines the conclusion in his critique of Thomas White's *De mundo*, the opening chapter of which contains an anatomy of the uses of speech:

There are four proper ends of speech. Either we want to teach, that is, to demonstrate the truth of some universal proposition, which is done first by explaining the definitions of names in order that ambiguity may be excluded – the process known as definition – and next by drawing necessary consequences from the definitions, as mathematicians

151 BL Harl. MS 4235, fo. 51r. Cf. Hobbes 1969a, p. 64.
152 BL Harl. MS 4235, fo. 51r. Cf. Hobbes 1969a, p. 65.
153 BL Harl. MS 4235, fo. 53r. Cf. Hobbes 1969a, p. 68.
154 BL Harl. Ms 4235, fo. 53r. Cf Hobbes 1969a, p. 68.
155 BL Harl. MS 4235, fo. 52v. Cf Hobbes 1969a, p. 66.
156 Hobbes 1983a, X.XI, p. 178: 'munus [eloquentiae], non docere, sed suadere'.

do. Or else we want to narrate something, or else to move our hearer's mind towards doing something, or finally we may want to glorify deeds and, by celebrating them, to hand down their memory to posterity. The art by means of which the first is achieved is Logic; the second, History; the third, Rhetoric; the fourth, Poetry.[157]

The effect of Hobbes's typology is again to draw a categorical distinction between teaching and persuasion, and hence between the arts of logic and rhetoric.

Hobbes is not content, however, merely to recapitulate the Socratic attack on the incapacity of rhetoricians to teach. He proceeds in both *The Elements* and *De Cive* to expand his argument into a detailed indictment of the techniques of *elocutio* as described by the classical and Renaissance theorists of eloquence. As we saw in chapters 4 and 5, these theorists had generally focused on three distinct methods by which we can hope to amplify the truth in such a way as to teach and persuade at the same time. We can hope to manipulate the definitions of key terms, taking advantage of the fact that many definitions are not clearly settled. We can hope to make use of paradiastolic redescriptions, thereby exaggerating or extenuating the worth of particular actions or states of affairs. And we can hope to lend additional force and persuasiveness to our arguments by clothing them in highly coloured figures and tropes of speech.

Hobbes fully accepts that these are the principal means available to us for amplifying the force of our utterances. When he turns in chapter 5 of *The Elements* to consider the phenomenon of language and its capacity to refer to things, these are precisely the techniques he singles out.[158] When he discusses them, however, he distances himself as far as possible from the rhetorical assumption that these are the methods we need to cultivate if we are to write and speak with maximum effectiveness. On the contrary, he describes these very techniques as the leading causes of the errors we habitually make in attempting to describe and apprehend our world.[159] He treats them in consequence as a list not of the aids but of the barriers to successful teaching and communication in the human no less than the natural sciences.

157 BN MS Fonds Latin 6566A, fo. 6r: 'Dicentium autem fines honesti quatuor sunt. Vel enim volumus docere, id est demonstrare veritatem dicti alicuius universalis, quod fit 1° explicando nominum deffinitiones, ut excludatur aequivocum, id quod dicitur definire; deinde ex deffinitionibus texendo consequentias necessarias, ut faciunt Mathematici, vel volumus aliquid narrare, vel animum auditoris commovere ad aliquid agendum, vel denique volumus facta nobilitare, et celebrando tradere memoriae posterorum. Ars qua 1um perficitur, Logica est; ars secundi, Historica; tertii, Rhetorica; quarti, Poetica.' Cf. Hobbes 1973, p. 106.

158 He also notes in more general terms that men are subject 'to Paralogisme or Fallacy in reasoning'. BL Harl. MS 4235, fo. 24r. Cf. Hobbes 1969a, p. 23.

159 Besides these linguistic errors he mentions 'deceptions of Sense'. BL Harl. MS 4235, fo. 24r. Cf. Hobbes 1969a, p. 23.

When Hobbes lists these 'causes of error' in *The Elements*, he begins with the problem of definition, with 'how unconstantly names have bene settled'.[160] He later develops the point in *De Cive*, insisting in two different passages on the overwhelming importance of defining the key terms of a science of justice. He first raises the issue in chapter VI, when surveying the rights of sovereignty; he takes it up again in chapter XIV, when examining the relations between natural and civil law. As we saw in chapter 4, similar issues of definition had greatly preoccupied the classical writers on eloquence, who had mainly drawn their examples from Aristotle's *Nicomachean Ethics* and *Art of Rhetoric*. Aristotle had considered four main cases, all of which were subsequently appropriated by Quintilian: theft (*furtum*), murder (*homicidium*), adultery (*adulterium*) and sacrilege (*sacrilegium*). Hobbes refers in *De Cive* to precisely the same range of examples. Chapter VI adds an allusion to legal injury (*iniuria*), but his other instances are *furtum*, *homicidium* and *adulteria*.[161] Chapter XIV drops the discussion of *iniuria*, thereby concentrating entirely on Aristotle's and Quintilian's examples of *furtum*, *adulterium* and *homicidium*.[162] While Hobbes reminds us of these familiar illustrations, however, his purpose in citing them is as far as possible from that of the theorists of eloquence. Whereas they had been interested in showing us how the definitions of such key terms can be manipulated for rhetorical purposes, one of Hobbes's chief ambitions in developing his science of politics is to find some means of placing such definitions entirely beyond the reach of eloquence.

The second cause of error mentioned in chapter 5 of *The Elements* is ambiguity. We not only need to reckon with 'how unconstantly names have been settled' but also with 'how subject they are to equivocation'.[163] At this juncture Hobbes refers us back to an earlier section of the chapter, in which he had already outlined three possible sources of such confusing ambiguity. The first is that some terms have an inherently polysemic character. For example, the word *faith* 'sometymes signifieth the same with belief'; but sometimes it 'signifieth particularly that belief which maketh a Christian'; and sometimes it instead 'signifieth the keepinge of a Promise'.[164] Later in *The Elements*, and again in *De Cive*, he adds the further and more politically charged example of the word *people*, which is likewise said to have 'a double signification'. Sometimes 'it signifieth only a number of men, distinguished by the place of their habitation, as the

[160] BL Harl. MS 4235, fo. 24^r^. Cf. Hobbes 1969a, p. 23.
[161] Hobbes 1983a, VI.XVI, pp. 145–6.
[162] Hobbes 1983a, XIV.X, p. 210.
[163] BL Harl. MS 4235, fo. 24^r^. Cf. Hobbes 1969a, p. 23.
[164] BL Harl. MS 4235, fo. 22^r–v^. Cf. Hobbes 1969a, p. 20.

people of England'. But sometimes 'it signifieth a person civil, that is to say, either one man, or one Council, in the will whereof is included and involved the will of every one in particular'.[165] As Hobbes stresses, this latter instance reveals with particular clarity how this form of equivocation can be exploited by unscrupulous rhetoricians to their own advantage. Those who fail or refuse to distinguish between the two significations are able to 'attribute such rights to a dissolved multitude, as belong only to the people virtually contained in the body of the commonwealth'.[166]

The other two sources of equivocation are both said to stem from the capacity of the *ars rhetorica* to introduce deliberate ambiguities into the conversation of mankind. Some of these, Hobbes maintains, can be traced specifically to the art of *pronuntiatio*, the fourth of the five *partes* in the classical theory of eloquence. As we saw in chapter 1, a mastery of *pronuntiatio* had generally been held to embrace two elements: an ability to pronounce our words in such a way as to lend them a particular meaning and emphasis; and an ability to accompany them with appropriate gestures and bodily movements. Hobbes contends that these rhetorical skills are capable of altering the meanings of utterances so pervasively that 'there is scarce any word that is not made Equivocall by divers Contexture of speech, or by diversity of pronunciation and gesture'.[167] Later he adds that bodily movement and variations of intonation can change the meaning of what we say to such a degree that 'it must be extreme hard to find out the opinions and meanings of those men that are gone from us long ago, and have left us no other signification thereof but their books'. The reason is that, 'though words be the signes we have of one another's opinions and Intensions', we nevertheless find that 'the equivocation of them is so frequent according to the diversity of contexture, and of the Company wherewith they go', that we can hardly hope to provide convincing interpretations if we lack 'the presence of him that speaketh' and 'our sight of his action' as aids to understanding his utterances.[168]

The other way in which the practitioners of rhetoric introduce equivocations into our speech is by encouraging us to employ the techniques of *elocutio*, and especially the figures and tropes of speech. Hobbes is especially concerned about the master trope of metaphor, since 'all Metaphors are (by profession) Equivocall'.[169] He recurs to this anxiety at several different points. When discussing man's cognitive powers in chapter 10 of *The*

165 BL Harl. MS 4235, fo. 91^{r-v}. Cf. Hobbes 1969a, p. 124.
166 BL Harl. MS 4235, fo. 91^{v}. Cf. Hobbes 1969a, p. 125.
167 BL Harl. MS 4235, fo. 22^{v}. Cf. Hobbes 1969a, pp. 20–1.
168 BL Harl. MS 4235, fo. 53^{v}. Cf. Hobbes 1969a, p. 68. See also Hobbes 1983a, XVII.XVIII, p. 278.
169 BL Harl. MS 4235, fo. 22^{v}. Cf. Hobbes 1969a, p. 20.

Elements, he stresses that one of the most important means by which adepts of the *ars rhetorica* deceive us into accepting their conclusions is by making use of 'gratefull Similies' and 'other Tropes'.[170] When examining the art of rhetoric in chapter XII of *De Cive*, he raises the same objection with much greater ferocity. He now insists that the power of *eloquentia* to act 'as a mover and arouser of the passions of the soul' depends entirely on 'the use of words in a metaphorical way'.[171] The effect is that, although rhetoricians speak 'with powerful eloquence', theirs is an eloquence 'separated from a proper knowledge of things'.[172]

The third and last of the linguistic causes of error listed in chapter 5 of *The Elements* is the use of paradiastolic redescriptions. When we employ evaluative terms, our choice is 'diversified by Passion' to such an extent that we find 'scarce two men agreeing what is to be called good, and what evill, what Liberality, what Prodigallity, what Valour, what Temerity'.[173] Hobbes reverts to the same claim in chapter 7, in the course of discussing the definition of good and evil. So powerfully do the passions enter and affect our descriptions that, in the case of these two crucial terms, we generally apply them *simply* in line with our emotional attitudes. 'Every man for his owne part calleth that which pleaseth and is delightfull to himself GOOD, and that EVILL which displeaseth him.' But this leads to ambiguities of the utmost seriousness. For it means that, so long as 'every man differeth from other in Constitution', everyone will 'differ also one from another concerning the common Distinction of Good and Evill'.[174]

Hobbes finds little more to say in *The Elements* about these 'passionate words'. But in *De Cive* he discusses them at length, and in doing so provides a full account of the phenomenon of paradiastolic speech. He first reverts to the topic at the end of chapter III, where he reiterates that 'it is necessary to understand that *good* and *evil* are names imposed on things to signify the appetite or aversion of those by whom the things in question are named'.[175] He elaborates the point at the start of chapter VII when discussing the names given to different forms of government. 'Men are accustomed, in naming things, to signify not merely the things themselves, but at one and the same time their own passions, such as love, hatred,

170 BL Harl. MS 4235, fo. 41r. Cf. Hobbes 1969a, p. 50.

171 See Hobbes 1983a, XII.XII, p. 192, claiming that the capacity of *eloquentia* to serve as 'affectuum animi ... commotrix' arises 'ex usu verborum metaphorico'.

172 See Hobbes 1983a, XII.XII, p. 193, on '*eloquentia potens*, separata a rerum scientia'.

173 BL Harl. MS 4235, fo. 24r. Cf. Hobbes 1969a, p. 23.

174 BL Harl. MS 4235, fo. 27v. Cf. Hobbes 1969a, p. 29.

175 Hobbes 1983a, III.XXXI, p. 119: 'Sciendum igitur est, *bonum* & *malum* nomina esse rebus imposita ad significandum appetitum, vel adversionem eorum a quibus sic nominantur.'

anger and so forth.'[176] It follows that, in social description, the terms we employ will often perform the function not merely of describing, but also of expressing and soliciting a certain evaluative attitude towards whatever is described. Hobbes adds a number of examples to bring out more clearly the fact that there are two contrasting classes of such terms, and that 'good' and 'evil' are their respective paradigm cases. He first observes in his analysis of law in chapter XIV that 'the names given to some things are such that they are usually taken in a bad sense'.[177] From the perspective of the speaker, the application of such names provides a means of describing something and at the same time of expressing a feeling of aversion for it. For instance, to speak of *theft* or *adultery* is to speak of certain acts, and at the same time to say that they are sins.[178] But there are other words – the most obvious being 'the general names of the virtues and human powers' – which 'cannot be taken in a bad sense'.[179] If we invoke them, we shall be understood to be commending whatever actions or states of affairs we use them to describe. It is true that the direction of such appraisive terms may not always be entirely clear, simply because the value of the activities they describe may not always be agreed. As Hobbes puts it in drily humorous tones, when we say, for example, 'that someone is a philosopher, or an orator, or suchlike', we are speaking of avocations 'which are held by some people in honour and by others in contempt'.[180] But some cases are perfectly unambiguous. When we say 'that someone is good, beautiful, brave, just, and suchlike', we are using terms 'the use of which invariably implies that some acknowledgment of ability and virtue is being made'.[181]

Hobbes is pointing to the same crucial fact about language that the classical theorists of eloquence had emphasised: some descriptive terms also serve, *eo ipso*, to evaluate what they describe. He also follows the classical theorists in explaining how we can hope to use these terms to challenge the appraisal of particular actions and states of affairs. He provides an explanation, that is, of why it will always be possible to claim with some show of plausibility that – to cite his own examples – an action described as liberal (and hence as commendable) can be redescribed as

176 Hobbes 1983a, VII.II, p. 150: 'Solent enim homines per nomina, non res tantum, sed & proprios *affectus*, puta *amorem odium*, *iram*, &c. una significare.'

177 Hobbes 1983a, XIV.XVII, p. 214: 'quibus nomina imponunt, quae in malam partem accipi solent'.

178 Hobbes 1983a, XIV.XVII, p. 214.

179 Hobbes 1983a, XV.XI, p. 224: 'nomina *virtutum* & *potentiarum* generalia, quae in malam partem accipi non possunt'.

180 Hobbes 1983a, XV.XI, p. 224: 'quod sit Philosophus, quod Orator, & similia, quae apud alios in honore, aliis contemptui habentur'.

181 Hobbes 1983a, XV.XI, p. 224: 'Ut *Bonus*, *Pulcher*, *Fortis*, *Iustus* & similia ... quibus agnitio potentiae & virtutis semper subintelligitur.'

prodigal and thereby condemned; or why an action described as valorous (and again as commendable) can similarly be redescribed as a case of sheer temerity and so condemned.

Hobbes's explanation carries us back to an argument originally put forward by Aristotle. As we saw in chapter 4, Aristotle had maintained that many of the vices may be said to border on the virtues, in consequence of which we can hope to minimise or even obliterate the distinctions between them. Hobbes initially adopts this formula,[182] although he later prefers the slightly different metaphor invoked by the Roman theorists of eloquence, who had generally spoken of the vices and virtues as neighbours. This is the formula he invokes when he turns to the topic of rhetorical redescription in chapter III of *De Cive.* He begins by conceding that 'everyone will agree to speak in praise of these virtues of which we have spoken'.[183] Nevertheless, 'people will still disagree about their character, and about the sort of thing in which each of these qualities may be said to reside'.[184] This is because, 'whenever a good action proves displeasing to someone else, that person will impose upon the action in question the name of some neighbouring vice'.[185] And 'by the same token, disgraceful actions which please people can similarly be redescribed with the name of a virtue'.[186] It is due, in short, to this 'neighbourly' relationship between so many of the virtues and vices that 'it comes about that one and the same action can be praised by some, and described as a virtue, while others censure it and convert it into a vice'.[187] Although it remains unclear how 'good' and 'evil' can be subjected to rhetorical redescription – since they appear to be the names not of neighbourly but of diametrically opposed qualities – the generally Aristotelian direction of Hobbes's thinking is unmistakable.

Besides explaining how rhetorical redescription is possible, Aristotle had offered a number of illustrations of the phenomenon, several of which had proved to be almost as influential as his analysis itself. One was that of redescribing (and hence commending) an extravagant action as an instance of liberality. This too is one of Hobbes's favourite examples, although he could just as easily have taken it from a wide range of intermediate sources. As we saw in chapter 4, a number of Roman writers had already

182 Hobbes 1986, p. 53.

183 Hobbes 1983a, III.XXXII, p. 120: 'consentiant omnes in laude dictarum virtutum'.

184 Hobbes 1983a, III.XXXII, p. 120: 'tamen dissentiant adhuc de earum natura, in quo nempe, unaquaeque earum consistat'.

185 Hobbes 1983a, III.XXXII, p. 120: 'Quoties enim cuiquam displicet aliena bona actio, ei actioni imponitur nomen alicuius vitii vicini'.

186 Hobbes 1983a, III.XXXI, p. 120: 'similiter nequitiae quae placent, ad virtutem aliquam referuntur'.

187 Hobbes 1983a, III.XXXII, p. 120: 'Unde evenit eandem actionem ab his laudari & virtutem appellari, ab illis culpari & vitio verti.'

made use of it, including Sallust and Tacitus among the historians as well as Cicero and Quintilian among the theorists of eloquence. So too had a number of Renaissance rhetoricians, including Mancinelli, Susenbrotus and, among English writers, Wilson, Puttenham and Peacham. Hobbes first recurs to the example in chapter 5 of *The Elements,* when he complains about the impossibility of gaining agreement about what constitutes liberality as opposed to prodigality.[188] He recurs to it once again at the end of chapter III of *De Cive,* reiterating that the question of 'what constitutes true liberality' has been turned by the followers of Aristotle into a topic of apparently endless debate.[189]

Another of Aristotle's illustrations had been that of redescribing a reckless action as a case of genuine courage. This too is one of Hobbes's favourite examples, although again he could have taken it from a large number of intermediate authorities, including Cicero, Seneca and Quintilian and, among Renaissance writers on *elocutio,* Mancinelli, Susenbrotus and Peacham. Hobbes first makes use of a similar illustration in the introduction to his translation of Thucydides.[190] He subsequently repeats it in chapter 5 of *The Elements,*[191] reverting to it yet again in chapter III of *De Cive,* where he remarks that one of the unsolved disputes in moral philosophy centres on the question of what actions should be counted as instances of authentic courage.[192]

As in the case of the other rhetorical techniques he considers, Hobbes's analysis of paradiastolic redescription is simply a prelude to a denunciation of the technique and the dangers of using it. As with so many of his contemporaries, the main danger he foresees is that a world of complete moral arbitrariness will be conjured up, a world in which there will be no possibility of reaching any rational agreement about the application of evaluative terms, and no prospect in consequence of avoiding a state of unending confusion and mutual hostility. He first registers this fear in his translation of Thucydides' history. Thucydides' famous passage on rhetorical redescription begins by explaining – in Hobbes's rendering – that 'the received value of names imposed for signification of things was changed into arbitrary'.[193] Hobbes adds a gloss in the margin immediately opposite this sentence which reads, in minatory tones: 'The manners of the

188 BL Harl. MS 4235, fo. 24r. Cf. Hobbes 1969a, p. 23.

189 See Hobbes 1983a, III.XXXII, p. 120, on '[quod] facit *liberalitatem*' and the endless debates about such questions among those who accept the Aristotelian assumption that *virtus* lies *in mediocritate.*

190 Hobbes 1975b, pp. 12–13.

191 BL Harl. MS 4235, fo. 24r. Cf Hobbes 1969a, p. 23.

192 Hobbes 1983a, III.XXXII, p. 120.

193 Hobbes 1975a, p. 222.

seditious'.[194] He makes his anxieties even clearer in *The Elements of Law*. When discussing the Renaissance ethic of glory in chapter 9, he observes that those who dislike the pursuit of glory rename it pride, while those who admire it retort that their critics are poor and dejected.[195] When analysing the concept of sovereignty in part II, chapter I, he similarly remarks that those who hate the form of 'absolute subjection' necessary for the preservation of peace seek to redescribe and thereby condemn it as slavery.[196]

To these examples Hobbes adds a number of general expressions of disquiet about the dangerous implications of paradiastolic speech. When discussing the concept of civil law in part II chapter 10 of *The Elements*, he not only warns that there are deep and inevitable differences between us as to 'what is to be called Right, what Good, what vertue', but adds that wherever such disputes arise we cannot hope to avoid 'quarrells and breach of Peace'.[197] He expresses the same fears in even graver tones in *De Cive*. When analysing the laws of nature in chapter III, he repeats that so long as there are disputes about how these laws relate to the description of individual actions 'these will always give rise to quarrels among the parties concerned'.[198] Later in the same chapter he explains why these quarrels are so disastrous. He first reminds us that 'the words *good* and *evil* are names imposed on things to indicate either the desire or the aversion of those by whom the things in question are named'.[199] However, 'the desires of men are diverse, depending as they do on the diversity of their temperaments, their customs and their attitudes'.[200] The inevitable outcome is that, 'wherever *good* and *evil* are measured by the mere diversity of present desires, and hence by a corresponding diversity of yardsticks, those who act in this way will find themselves living in nothing better than a state of war'.[201] Nor is it easy to see how we can rescue ourselves from this state. Hobbes adds this last and most pessimistic conclusion in his discussion of civil law in chapter 14. 'It is simply not possible that the question of which actions are to be described as blameworthy, and which as not being blameworthy, can be decided by the consent of individual

194 Hobbes 1629, p. 198. Cf. Hobbes 1975a, p. 580.

195 BL Harl. MS 4235, fos. 32^{v}, 33^{v}. Cf. Hobbes 1969a, pp. 37, 38.

196 BL Harl. MS 4235, fo. 84^{r}. Cf. Hobbes 1969a, pp. 114–15.

197 BL Harl. MS 4235, fo. 141^{v}. Cf. Hobbes 1969a, p. 188.

198 Hobbes 1983a, III.XX, p. 115: 'ex quibus sequetur pugna inter partes'.

199 Hobbes 1983a, III.XXXI, p. 119: '*bonum* & *malum* nomina esse rebus imposita ad significandum appetitum, vel adversionem eorum a quibus sic nominantur'.

200 Hobbes 1983a, III.XXXI, p. 119: 'Appetitus autem hominum pro diversis eorum temperamentis, consuetudinibus, opinionibusque, diversi sunt.'

201 Hobbes 1983a, III.XXXI, p. 119: 'Sunt igitur tamdiu in statu belli, quam *bonum* & *malum* prae appetituum praesentium diversitae, diversis mensuris metiuntur.'

men, for it will never be the case that they will find themselves pleased and displeased by the same things.'[202]

It seems appropriate to end this account of Hobbes's attacks on *inventio* and *elocutio* with his own dismissive summaries of the doctrines concerned. As we have seen, the classical rhetoricians had maintained that, by inventing the most persuasive arguments and articulating them according to the rules of *elocutio*, we can hope to unite *oratio atque ratio*, reason with powerful speech. Hobbes responds that, if we proceed in this manner, the result will not be a union of reason with speech but a form of speech beyond reason: not *oratio atque ratio*, but *oratio praeter rationem.*[203] The rhetoricians had added that, if we develop our arguments in accordance with their rules, the effect will be to yoke together wisdom and eloquence. As Quintilian had put it, the two will become *iuncta* or joined; as Ascham had added, they will never be 'a sonder'. Hobbes retorts that the practitioners of rhetoric not only fail to join wisdom with eloquence; they almost invariably bring it about that the one is *disiungitur* or sundered from the other.[204]

THE ATTACK ON THE *VIR CIVILIS*

Hobbes's attack on humanist civil science is not confined to the rhetorical codes in which it was expressed. He also sets himself to discredit the ideal of citizenship underlying the classical and Renaissance theory of eloquence. As we saw in chapter 2, the classical rhetoricians had sought to equate the figure of the good orator with the good citizen, the *bonus civis* who willingly serves his community by pleading for just verdicts in the courts and beneficial policies in the assemblies. We also saw how this ideal of active citizenship was revived in the English Renaissance, in the course of which it came to be connected with a mastery of the *studia humanitatis* and employed to foster and legitimise the involvement of the nobility and gentry in the business of government.

Hobbes shows himself acutely and uncomfortably aware of the extent to which this specific political agenda underlay the revival of classical eloquence in Renaissance England. When he discusses the *ars rhetorica* in part II chapter 5 of *The Elements*, and again in chapter x of *De Cive*, he does so in the context of criticising the theory and practice of democratic government. And when he returns to the figure of the rhetorician in part II

202 Hobbes 1983a, XIV.XVII, p. 213: 'fieri non potest, ut quae facta culpanda, quae non culpanda sint consensu singulorum quibus non eadem placent & displicent definiatur'.
203 Hobbes 1983a, XII.XII, p. 193.
204 Hobbes 1983a, XII.XII, p. 193.

chapter 8 of *The Elements*, and once more in chapter XII of *De Cive*, his discussion is mainly aimed at stigmatising the art of rhetoric as a cause of the dissolution of commonwealths.[205] His principal concern throughout these chapters is to confront and repudiate the connections drawn by the classical and Renaissance theorists of eloquence between a mastery of rhetoric and a capacity for good citizenship.

Hobbes opens his critique by reminding his readers, most explicitly in *De Cive*, of the views generally expressed by the rhetoricians about the ideal of the *vir civilis*. He first observes that questions about rhetoric and its political implications arise most obviously in the case of democratic communities.[206] The defining characteristic of such communities is that everyone has a role to play in public deliberations, in consequence of which everyone needs to know how to make speeches in the style known to rhetoricians as the *genus deliberativum*.[207] But anyone who aspires to have their advice adopted by a popular assembly will find it necessary to speak not just with wisdom and *scientia*, but also with powerful *eloquentia*.[208] This is because they will need to be able not merely to give their reasons for preferring a certain course of action, but at the same time (and here Hobbes invokes the terminology of the *ars rhetorica*) to 'hold them forth' to their audience with suitable emphasis.[209]

Hobbes's main purpose in recalling these arguments is as usual to remind us of the position he hopes to undermine. His ensuing attack is rendered all the more pointed by the fact that, as the title of his treatise indicates, he too takes himself to be writing *de cive*, about the ideal of citizenship. He can hardly have been unaware that most political writers of the English Renaissance who had focused on the ideal of the *vir civilis* had drawn a sharp distinction between citizens and mere subjects. They had generally described the citizen as an active, participative figure, someone capable of helping to frame the laws as well as administer them. As Elyot had put it, a true citizen can be described as a 'governor', someone with a duty of acting together with his sovereign and 'as it were aiding him in the distribution of justice'.[210] By contrast, they had viewed the figure of the subject in wholly passive terms as someone whose sole duty, as the word implies, is that of living in obedient subjection to the laws.[211]

205 See the excellent discussion in Whelan 1981, esp. pp. 59–60. Cf. also Harwood 1986, pp. 16–17.
206 Hobbes 1983a, X.IX, pp. 176–7.
207 See Hobbes 1983a, X.XI, p. 176, on the role of citizens 'in deliberationibus'.
208 Hobbes 1983a, X.XI, pp. 177–8.
209 See Hobbes 1983a, X.IX, p. 176, on the need for one's reasons to be 'publice ostentandi'.
210 Elyot 1962, p. 13.
211 For an excellent discussion of 'subject' and 'citizen' see Condren 1994, pp. 91–114.

Given the importance of this contrast, it seems clear that Hobbes's purpose in calling his first treatise on politics *De Cive*, or *The Citizen*, must have been to arouse a number of expectations with the intention of disappointing them. The essence of his argument – couched in what must have struck his original readers as a pure oxymoron – is that citizens and subjects are one and the same.[212] He first hints at this contention in the opening chapters of part II of *The Elements*. Because 'in the making of a commonwealth, a man subjecteth his will to the power of others', it follows that 'every member of the body politic is called a SUBJECT (viz.), to the Soveraigne'.[213] Later he explicitly fuses the two concepts when discussing the dual signification of the term *people* in chapter XII of *De Cive*. As soon as a multitude consents to be governed by the will of one representative person, 'the members of the *Multitude* are thereby converted into citizens, that is to say, into subjects'.[214] He subsequently insists on the same interchangeability of terms when analysing the concept of treason in chapter XIV. Treason can be defined, he maintains, as that crime by which obedience is refused to a representative Person by 'a citizen, that is to say, a subject'.[215]

When Hobbes turns to criticise the contrasting ideal of the *vir civilis*, he proceeds in much the same way as in his attack on the theory of *elocutio*. He simply reverts, that is, to a number of anti-rhetorical arguments which had originally been voiced in classical antiquity, and which the Roman rhetoricians had supposed themselves to have overcome. As we have seen, one such argument had emphasised the ignorant, passionate, prejudiced character of the multitude, with the resulting openness of popular assemblies to manipulation by rhetoricians for their own factional ends. We first find Hobbes reiterating these claims in his edition of Thucydides. When he explains in his introduction why the historian 'least of all liked the democracy', he particularly stresses Thucydides' detestation of the demagogues in the Athenian assemblies 'with their crossing of each other's counsels, to the damage of the public'.[216] When he translates the passage from book III in which Cleon upbraids his fellow citizens in the assembly, he interposes a further judgment of a similar kind. Cleon tells the Athenians that 'you are excellent men for one to deceive with a speech of a new strain, but backward to follow any tried advice; slaves to strange things, contemners

212 See further Dietz 1990 and Condren 1994, pp. 98–100.
213 BL Harl. MS 4235, fo. 78v. Cf. Hobbes 1969a, p. 104.
214 Hobbes 1983a, XII.XII, p. 190: '*Multitudo* vero, cives sunt, hoc est subditi.'
215 See Hobbes 1983a, XIV.XX, p. 216 on the 'civis seu subditus'.
216 Hobbes 1975b, p. 13.

of things usual'.[217] Hobbes adds in a marginal gloss: 'the nature of the multitude in council, lively set forth'.[218]

The same position is taken up in chapter x of *De Cive*, in which Hobbes offers three reasons for doubting whether large assemblies can ever be safely entrusted with the conduct of government. He begins by observing that, 'if we are to deliberate rightly about everything conducive to the safety of our community, it is necessary to have a proper knowledge not only of internal but of external affairs'.[219] But the sad truth is that 'very few people in a large assembly of men can be expected to possess such knowledge, since most of them will be unversed in, not to say incapable of, understanding any such matters'.[220] This leads to 'the second reason for believing that large assemblies are unsuitable for deliberation'.[221] Due to their sheer size, they inevitably encourage the worst demagogues and rhetoricians, since 'everyone who wishes to explain his views finds it indispensable to present them in the form of a long and continuous speech'.[222] Finally, the ascendancy of such orators in turn gives rise to factions and mutual hostilities. Here Hobbes recalls – and virtually repeats – the arguments put forward in his introduction to his translation of Thucydides. Such factions develop because 'orators of equal skill oppose each other with contrary opinions and speeches', as a result of which 'the vanquished hates the victor', with consequences 'damaging to the commonwealth'.[223]

Hobbes also picks up a second and still more powerful strand of anti-rhetorical argument originally stemming from discussions of citizenship in antiquity. This was the suggestion that rhetoric is an inherently seditious and dangerous art. Sallust's account of Catiline's conspiracy, magnificently retold for early Jacobean audiences in Ben Jonson's *Catiline*, was regarded by Hobbes's generation as a classic illustration of the point. A man of small wisdom but of great eloquence – as Sallust had described him – Catiline was regarded as a terrible reminder of the ease with which the art of rhetoric in the wrong hands can be used to betray and ruin the most flourishing commonwealths.

217 Hobbes 1975a, p. 196.
218 Hobbes 1975a, p. 580.
219 Hobbes 1983a, x.x, p. 177: '[si] ad recte deliberandum de omnibus quae ad salutem civitatis conducunt, cognitu necessaria sunt non modo ea quae intus, sed etiam ea quae foris sunt'.
220 Hobbes 1983a, x.x, p. 177: 'Haec autem quia paucissimi cognoscunt in numeroso coetu hominum, maxima ex parte, talium rerum imperitorum, ne dicam incapacium.'
221 Hobbes 1983a, x.xi, p. 177: 'Alia causa quare magnus coetus ad deliberationem minus idoneus sit.'
222 Hobbes 1983a, x.xi, p. 177: 'unusquisque eorum qui sententiam suam explicant, necesse habet perpetua & longa uti oratione'.
223 Hobbes 1983a, x.xi, p. 178: 'contrariis sententiis orationibusque pugnant aequales oratores, victus victorem . . . odit . . . civitati damnosum'.

As we saw in chapter 2, the Roman rhetoricians had expended a great deal of energy in attempting to allay such fears about the dangers of eloquence. They had sought in particular to insist that a true orator, who seeks victory only for the truth, can never be other than a good and trustworthy citizen. But Hobbes simply reverts to the very criticisms they had tried to rebut. When in chapter XII of *De Cive* he discusses how commonwealths collapse, he inserts a scathing attack on the traditional syllabus of the *studia humanitatis* as a nursery of sedition. He gives a contemptuous summary of the standard humanist curriculum, describing it as a matter of studying 'the works of Historians, Rhetoricians, writers on political science and other books that can easily be read'.[224] He then observes even more contemptuously that those who pursue these studies 'come to think of themselves as so well trained in the relevant kinds of talent and doctrine as to be fully equipped to administer matters of the highest significance'.[225] One serious consequence of this folly is that 'many people who are themselves well-affected towards the commonwealth nevertheless co-operate, as a result of their ignorance of practical affairs, in inclining the minds of their fellow-citizens to *sedition*'.[226] They do so because they spend so much time 'in preaching doctrines compatible with treasonous opinions to adolescents in the schools and to the whole populace in the Churches'.[227]

Hobbes's other and principal contention is that Sallust was unquestionably right to connect the practice of rhetoric with the subversion of commonwealths. He develops this argument in part II chapter 8 of *The Elements*, where he begins by alluding to the efforts of the ancient rhetoricians to answer this charge. No doubt, he remarks, 'it seemeth a contradiction to place small judgment and greate eloquence, or, as they call it, powerfull speaking, in the same Man'.[228] The concession is liable to strike a modern reader as puzzling, since there is obviously nothing *contradictory* about the suggestion that someone might at once be a powerful speaker and a person of weak judgment. But the puzzle is readily solved if we think of Hobbes's way of putting the point as a reference to classical theories of eloquence. With their claim that good orators necessarily make good citizens, the ancient rhetoricians had certainly done their best to

224 Hobbes 1983a, XII.X, p. 191: 'Historicorum, Oratorum, Politicorum aliorumque librorum facile lectionem'.

225 Hobbes 1983a, XII.X, p. 191: 'Inde autem contingit, ut ad res maximi momenti administrandas & ab ingenio & a doctrina instructos se esse arbitrentur.'

226 Hobbes 1983a, XII.XIII, p. 193: 'Ad disponendum civium animos ad *seditiones*, multi etiam eorum qui bene erga civitatem affecti sunt ... per inscitiam cooperantur'.

227 Hobbes 1983a, XII.XIII, p. 193: 'dum doctis opinionibus conformem doctrinam adolescentibus in scholis & omni populo e cathedris insinuant'.

228 BL Harl. MS 4235, fo. 131[r]. Cf. Hobbes 1969a, p. 175.

imply that it would indeed be contradictory to suppose that someone might be eloquent without at the same time being wise. Hobbes responds that, if we reflect on the character of those who encourage sedition, we shall find that they invariably possess three qualities. They are 'discontented themselves'; they are 'men of meane judgment and Capacity'; and they are 'Eloquent men or good Oratours'.[229] This is the moment at which he cites the example of Catiline, 'who was Authour of the greatest sedition that ever was in Rome'.[230] As he reminds us, quoting the famous epigram, 'it was noted by Sallust' that Catiline possessed 'Eloquence sufficient, but little wisedome'.[231] To which Hobbes adds in his own most epigrammatic style that 'perhaps this was said of Catiline, as he was Catiline: but it was true of him as an Authour of Sedition. For the Conjunction of these two qualityes made him not Catiline, but Seditious.'[232]

To justify this unqualified rejection of humanist pieties, and at the same time to show us 'how want of wisedome and store of Eloquence may stand together',[233] Hobbes next reminds us of what he had said in chapter 5 about wisdom and knowledge. The knowledge that makes us wise derives from 'the remembrance of the names or appellations of things, and how everything is called'. Such knowledge 'is generally called Science, and the Conclusions thereof Trueth'.[234] But 'no Authour of Sedition can be wise in this acceptation of the word'.[235] For since 'no pretence of sedition can be right or just', it follows that all the authors of sedition must be ignorant of a true understanding of justice, and must therefore be unwise. We must rather expect them to 'name thinges not according to their true and generally-agreed-upon names, but call right and wronge, good and bad,[236] according to their passions' in the hope of arousing the same passions in others.[237] But as we have seen, those who are most guilty according to Hobbes of naming things 'according to their passions' are the practitioners of the art of rhetoric. He accordingly feels justified in claiming that he has proved his case:

This considered, together with the businesse that he hath to doe who is the Authour of Rebellion, (viz) to make men believe that their Rebellion is Just, their discontents

229 BL Harl. MS 4235, fo. 131r. Cf. Hobbes 1969a, p. 175.
230 BL Harl. MS 4235, fo. 131r. Cf. Hobbes 1969a, p. 175.
231 BL Harl. MS 4235, fo. 131r. Cf. Hobbes 1969a, p. 175.
232 BL Harl. MS 4235, fo. 131v. Cf. Hobbes 1969a, p. 175.
233 BL Harl. MS 4235, fo. 131v. Cf. Hobbes 1969a, pp. 175–6.
234 BL Harl. MS 4235, fo. 132r. Cf. Hobbes 1969a, p. 176.
235 BL Harl. MS 4235, fo. 132r. Cf. Hobbes 1969a, pp. 176–7.
236 BL Harl. MS 4235, fo. 132v inserts 'everythinge' at this point, but the hyperbole is crossed out in Hobbes's hand.
237 BL Harl. MS 4235, fo. 132v. Cf. Hobbes 1969a, p. 177.

grounded upon great Injuryes, and their Hopes great; there needeth noe more to prove, there can be no Authour of Rebellion, that is not an Eloquent and powerfull Speaker, and withall (as hath bene said before) a man of little wisedome.[238]

The repudiation of humanist values is as sweeping as possible. Whereas Cicero and his followers had seen the figure of the powerful orator as a benefactor to cities and a means of preserving them, Hobbes professes to find an intrinsic connection between the practice of eloquence and the destruction of civic life.

To round off his attack, Hobbes adds a series of comments on the self-congratulating imagery used by classical and Renaissance theorists of eloquence to dramatise their vision of citizenship. As we saw in chapter 2, they frequently spoke of the power of eloquence to captivate and carry away an audience. Hobbes enthusiastically picks up the suggestion that rhetoric is a seductive and bewitching art, but only as a prelude to reworking the familiar metaphors in grimly sardonic terms. He concludes his attack in *The Elements* by declaring that the power of eloquence 'is as the witchcraft of Medea'.[239] His allusion, as he explains, is to the story of the daughters of Pelias, king of Thessaly, who wished 'to restore theire ould decrepit father to the vigour of his youth'. They sought the counsel of Medea, who advised them to chop him in pieces 'and sett him a boilyng with I knowe not what herbes in a Cauldron'. The effect of Medea's deliberative oratory proved fatal; as Hobbes remarks with studied understatement, Pelias' foolish daughters 'could not make him revive againe'.[240] But the reason for their folly, as Hobbes makes clear in repeating the anecdote in *De Cive*, is that they were *ducti*[241] – they were seduced or carried away – by the spellbinding power of Medea's eloquence. Hobbes brings part II chapter 9 of *The Elements* to a close by pointing the moral of the tale:

So when Eloquence and want of Judgment goe together, want of judgment, like the Daughters of Pelias, consenteth, through Eloquence, which is as the witchcraft of Medea, to cut the Common wealth in pieces, upon pretence or hope of reformation, which when things are in Combustion, they are not able to effect.[242]

Hobbes not only treats the power of eloquence as a form of bewitchment, but alludes to the idea – subsequently so much emphasised by Burke – that orators are firebrands capable of setting the commonwealth ablaze.

When discussing 'the causes and generation of cities' in chapter V of *De*

238 BL Harl. MS 4235, fo. 133^r. Cf. Hobbes 1969a, p. 177.
239 BL Harl. MS 4235, fo. 133^r. Cf. Hobbes 1969a, p. 178.
240 BL Harl. MS 4235, fo. 133^r. Cf. Hobbes 1969a, p. 178.
241 Hobbes 1983a, XII.XIII, p. 193.
242 BL Harl. MS 4235, fos. 133^{r-v}. Cf. Hobbes 1969a, p. 178.

Cive, Hobbes picks up the two other figures of speech beloved of the rhetoricians and proceeds to modify them in equally sardonic style. He first alludes to the simile comparing the force of eloquence with the power of music to excite and charm. As Sidney had confessed in his *Defence of Poesie*, one often finds, even when listening to nothing more elevated than an old ballad, that one's heart is 'mooved more then with a Trumpet'.[243] Hobbes readily agrees that 'the tongue of man is indeed like a trumpet'.[244] But he adds at once that 'it is a trumpet of sedition and war'.[245] The second and even more familiar image had spoken of eloquence as a force of nature. As we have seen, Quintilian had thrice likened Pericles' impact on the Athenian assembly to that of a thunderstorm. Hobbes dutifully repeats that 'it is said of Pericles that with his orations he thundered and flashed lightning'.[246] But he immediately adds that, as a consequence of these thunderings, 'the whole of Greece was brought to a state of collapse'.[247]

Hobbes's argument culminates in a view of citizenship and its obligations diametrically opposed to the image of the *vir civilis*. The Roman rhetoricians and their Renaissance followers had emphasised the public duties of citizens to such a degree as to encourage an almost philistine rejection of the values associated with the scholarly and contemplative life. As we saw in chapter 2, Vives had gone to the extreme of claiming that all the 'excellencies' of human existence stem from *negotium* rather than *otium*, and that anyone desirous of benefiting his community must avoid any deep commitment to the merely abstract and speculative sciences. Hobbes always insists, by contrast, that the most important duties of citizenship lie in the private and not in the public sphere. He accordingly treats the ideal of the *vir civilis* as little better than the portrait of an ignorant and conceited meddler.[248] The point is pressed with withering scorn in the chapter on forms of government in *De Cive*. 'The only reason why anyone devotes himself to public rather than to family affairs is because the former appear to provide him with an opportunity for displaying his eloquence.'[249] By these means, 'such a man can hope to acquire the reputation of being clever and prudent, and can thereby hope, on returning home, to enjoy a triumph among his friends, his parents and his family for having conducted

243 Sidney 1923, p. 24.
244 Hobbes 1983a, v.v, p. 133: 'hominis autem lingua tuba quaedam [est]'.
245 Hobbes 1983a, v.v, p. 133: 'tuba quaedam belli est & seditionis'.
246 Hobbes 1983a, v.v, p. 133: 'dicitur Pericles suis quondam orationibus, tonuisse, fulgurasse'. Cf. Quintilian 1920–2, II.XVI.19, vol. I, p. 324.
247 Hobbes 1983a, v.v, p. 193: '& confudisse [sic; *recte* confundisse] totam *Graeciam*'.
248 Hobbes 1975b, pp. 12, 14.
249 Hobbes 1983a, x.xv, p. 179: 'Nihil enim est propter quod non malit quisquam *rei familiari* potius, quam *publicae* vacare, praeterquam quod locum esse videt facundiae suae.'

himself so impressively'.[250] For Hobbes, such vanities are the merest childishness, a view he makes brutally clear when citing the example of Coriolanus, 'who took joy from his own warlike deeds simply because the praises he won appeared to please his mother'.[251]

Hobbes's still more pressing objection is that the humanists are mistaken in their beliefs about the 'excellencies' of human life. These are the products, he insists, not of *negotium* but of just those speculative pursuits which the humanists despise. This is the contention with which he introduces his analysis of the sciences in chapter 13 of *The Elements*.[252] Suppose we ask who have been 'the Authours of all those excellencyes wherein we differ from such savage people as are now the inhabitants of divers places in America'.[253] The answer is that we owe these advances entirely to 'those men who have taken in hand to Consider nothing else but the Comparision of magnitudes, numbers, tymes, and Motions, and their proportions one to another'.[254] It is wholly due to their efforts, and not in the least to the meddling habits of humanist intellectuals, that we no longer follow a wild and warlike way of life. Hobbes goes on to give a detailed account of how their intellectual achievements have enabled us to rise above the miseries of our natural state:

For from the studyes of these men hath proceeded whatsoever cometh to us for our ornament by navigation. And whatsoever we have beneficiall to humaine society by the division, distinction, and purtraying of the face of the earth. Whatsoever also we have by the accompt of tymes & foresight of the Course of heaven. Whatsoever by measuringe distances, Plaines, and sollids of all sorts. And whatsoever we have either Elegant or defensible in building. All of which supposed away, what doe we differ from the wildest of the Indians?[255]

The distinctive vocabulary of classical humanism is cunningly put to work to press home the anti-humanist point. Of course we want elegance and ornament; of course we want foresight and the production of things beneficial to society. But these are the fruits of *otium*, the outcome of 'difficult and profound speculation'[256] of exactly the kind that Cicero's *De officiis*, the Bible of the humanists, had sought to discountenance by attacking those who devote themselves 'to obscure and difficult things'.[257]

250 Hobbes 1983a, x.xv, p. 179: 'qua possit ingenii & prudentiae existimationem acquirere, & domum reversus apud amicos, parentes, uxoresque, res bene gesta, triumphare'.

251 Hobbes 1983a, x.xv, p. 179; 'sicut olim Marco Coriolano omnis a factis bellicis iucunditas in eo sita erat, quod videret laudes suas placere matri'.

252 The point is later restated in Hobbes 1971b, p. 123.

253 BL Harl. MS 4235, fo. 51^{v}. Cf. Hobbes 1969a, p. 65.

254 BL Harl. MS 4235, fo. 51^{v}. Cf. Hobbes 1969a, p. 65.

255 BL Harl. MS 4235, fo. 51^{v}. Cf. Hobbes 1969a, pp. 65–6.

256 BL Harl. MS 4235, fo. 52^{r}. Cf. Hobbes 1969a, p. 66.

257 Cf. Cicero 1913, I.VI.19, p. 20 on 'res obscuras atque difficiles'.

The view of citizenship associated with the classical theory of eloquence may be said to reach its climax with the contention that the *bonus orator* is not merely a *vir bonus* and a *bonus civis* but is arguably the most humane of men, the man in whom the distinctive attributes of humanity attain their highest peak. Cicero and Quintilian had both maintained that, in order to see why this is so, we need only reflect that the quality which makes us most truly human is not so much our faculty of *ratio* or reasoning as our unique power of *oratio* or speech. To Quintilian the implications had seemed obvious:

> But if it is true that we receive from the gods nothing finer than this power of speech, what can possibly be more worth cultivating with effort and labour, or in what regard can we more desire to exceed our fellow-men, than in the exercise of that very power by which men exceed the animals?[258]

Quintilian's analysis accordingly culminates in the claim that, as Cicero had already put it at the start of *De inventione*, the greatness of the orator derives from the fact that 'he is the man who is pre-eminent over all other men in the very quality that makes men pre-eminent over the beasts'.[259]

When Hobbes outlines his theory of language in chapter 5 of *The Elements*, he presents his argument in the form of a commentary on exactly these complacencies. It is true, he retorts, that 'the Invention of names hath bene necessary for the drawing of men out of ignorance', and that it is due to 'the benefitt of words and Ratiocination' that men 'exceed brute beasts in knowledge'.[260] However, it is likewise due to the invention of names and our capacity to communicate them in speech that we acquire the connected ability 'to multyply one untruth by another'. So while it is true that men exceed the animals as a result of possessing the benefits of speech, it is no less true that 'by the Incommodities that accompany the same they exceed them also in errours'.[261] The final and most deflating thought Hobbes leaves with us is that the figure of the rhetorician is the man most likely to lower us beneath the level of the beasts.

258 Quintilian 1920–2, II.XVI.17, vol. I, p. 324: 'Quare si nihil a dis oratione melius accepimus, quid tam dignum cultu ac labore ducamus, aut in quo malimus praestare hominibus, quam quo ipsi homines ceteris animalibus praestant?'

259 Cicero 1949a, I.IV.5, p. 12: 'is qui qua re homines bestiis praestent ea in re hominibus ipsis antecellat'.

260 BL Harl. MS 4235, fo. 23v. Cf. Hobbes 1969a, p. 22.

261 BL Harl. MS 4235, fo. 23v. Cf. Hobbes 1969a, p. 22.

Chapter 8

HOBBES'S SCIENCE OF POLITICS

THE REPLACEMENT OF ELOQUENCE BY SCIENCE

Hobbes not only supplies us in *The Elements* and *De Cive* with a critique of the classical theory of eloquence and its associated conception of civil science. He also lays out his own contrasting prescriptions for the construction of a genuine science of politics independent of the rhetorical arts. He first puts forward his positive programme in chapter 6 of *The Elements*, in which he outlines what he calls the four steps of science[1] that need to be followed if we wish to attain the kind of knowledge that will make us wise. *De Cive* adds that the tracing of these *vestigia* or footsteps[2] can in turn be described as a matter of following *recta ratio* or right reasoning.[3] While Hobbes preserves this familiar terminology, however, he is far from viewing *recta ratio* in traditional terms as an unerring intuition or faculty.[4] As he makes clear when explaining how controversies in religion differ from those in science, he thinks of it simply as a method, 'a way of searching out the truth'.[5] There is thus a sense in which it is highly fallible, for the approach it prescribes can always be followed with greater or lesser intelligence. 'The reasonings of men are sometimes right and sometimes wrong, with the result that what is concluded and held to be true is sometimes the truth and is sometimes erroneous.'[6] Nevertheless, even for Hobbes there remains a sense in which *recta ratio* can properly be described as unerring. If we duly follow the four steps of science, we cannot fail to arrive at true *scientia*, a genuine knowledge or understanding of the issues involved.

1 Hobbes first speaks of these '4 stepps' in BL Harl. MS 4235, fo. 25^{v}. Cf. Hobbes 1969a, pp. 26 and 66.

2 Hobbes 1983a, epistle dedicatory, p. 75. Bacon similarly speaks of *vestigia* in the *Novum Organon*. See Bacon 1857c, p. 129.

3 Hobbes 1983a, XVI.I, p. 234 and XVI.IX, p. 238.

4 A point excellently emphasised in Malcolm 1983 and Malcolm 1991, pp. 523–4.

5 See Hobbes 1983a, XVII.XXVIII, p. 279, on *ratio* as a method for 'veritatis investigatio'.

6 Hobbes 1983a, XVII.XII, p. 261: 'Sed ratiocinationes hominum, interdum rectae interdum erroneae sunt, & proinde id quod concluditur & tenetur pro veritate, quandoque veritas, quandoque error est.'

According to chapter 6 of *The Elements*, the first step in this quest for authentic knowledge must be to start 'from some beginning or principle of sense'.[7] Although we are seeking true conceptions, we cannot hope to 'remember those Conceptions without the thing that produced the same by our Senses'.[8] Hobbes is here conceding that the scientific principles at which we eventually arrive must be rooted in some form of experimental evidence or at least of sensory awareness.[9] He never denies that the natural sciences need to proceed by way of collecting such observations and experiments. What he objects to – later so vociferously in his polemics against the Royal Society[10] – is any suggestion that such experiments are sufficient in themselves to make a science. What makes a science, Hobbes always insists, is the placing of such empirical data within an appropriate conceptual and explanatory framework.[11] And this framework, according to *The Elements*, takes the form of the three remaining steps of science.

We take the first of these steps when we ensure that the things we perceive, and consequently seek to conceptualise, are all consistently named. *The Elements* merely observes that this requires us to assign agreed names to things,[12] but *De Cive* expands the point into a claim about the indispensability of providing accurate definitions of key terms.[13] Hobbes first couches the argument in this form when introducing his analysis of the laws of nature in chapter II: 'the only proper method to follow if we wish to leave no space for contrary disputes is to begin with definitions and the exclusion of ambiguity'.[14] He underlines the implications in his chapter on the interpretation of Scripture: 'the one and only road to *scientia* is by way of *definitions*'.[15] Having grasped the meanings of key terms, we are ready to take the next step, which consists of joining names together 'in such manner as to make true propositions'.[16] Hobbes further elaborates in chapter XVIII of *De Cive*, offering as an illustration the claim that theft is an instance of injury. 'As long as we remember what things are called *Theft*,

7 BL Harl. MS 4235, fo. 25[v]. Cf. Hobbes 1969a, p. 26.

8 BL Harl. MS 4235, fo. 25[v]. Cf. Hobbes 1969a, p. 26.

9 This is not to say that the external world need remain in existence. If I have once formed conceptions based on sense, these will remain even if the world is annihilated. See BL Harl. MS 4235, fo. 11[v], and cf. Hobbes 1969a, p. 2.

10 See esp. Hobbes 1840c, pp. 436–7.

11 For a classic discussion see Brandt 1928, pp. 221–7. The point is valuably developed in Sorell 1986, pp. 4–7, 21–8, and Boonin-Vail 1994, pp. 21–34.

12 BL Harl. MS 4235, fo. 25[v]. Cf. Hobbes 1969a, p. 26.

13 For a helpful discussion of this step see Danford 1980, esp. pp. 113–16.

14 Hobbes 1983a, II.I, p. 98: 'Methodus scilicet qua incipitur a definitionibus & exclusione aequivoci, propria eorum est qui locum contra disputandi non reliquunt.'

15 Hobbes 1983a, XVIII.IV, pp. 284–5: 'unica via ad *scientiam* est *per definitiones*'.

16 BL Harl. MS 4235, fo. 25[v]. Cf. Hobbes 1969a, p. 26. (Cf. also p. 66.)

and what things are called *injury*, we shall be able to understand from the words themselves whether or not it is true that *Theft is injury*.'[17] This is because '*Truth* is the same as *a true proposition*, and a *proposition* is *true* wherever *the name following*, which logicians call the *Predicate*, is included within the range of reference of *the name Preceding*, which they call the *subject*.'[18] After learning to join names together in this syllogistic style, we are ready for the final step of science. This is described in *The Elements* as a process of linking propositions 'in such manner as they be concluding'.[19] Hobbes subsequently clarifies this somewhat gnomic observation in *De Cive*, in which he describes the fourth step as that of tracing the logical and material implications of joining true propositions to each other.[20] As he puts it in chapter XIV, the whole process of reasoning by *recta ratio* can thus be summarised by saying that 'it consists of beginning with the most evident principles and constructing a discourse by continually drawing out necessary consequences'.[21] He summarises yet again in chapter XVIII, in which the process of *ratiocinatio* is described as 'a matter of drawing out consequences from a starting-point based in our experiences'.[22]

There is nothing particularly original or distinctive about this general conception of science. The ideals of certainty and of demonstration from evident principles had after all been central to the Aristotelian tradition, and in this respect there are important continuities with Galileo's conception of demonstrative science. There are likewise obvious analogies with the outlook of Mersenne and his circle, and even more with the view of scientific method developed by Descartes.[23] It is true that Hobbes begins not with indubitable intuitions, as Descartes had done, but rather with unambiguous definitions. But he fully endorses Descartes's sense that all the genuine sciences proceed deductively, and that their goal must be the attainment of knowledge in the form of demonstrative certainty.

A still closer parallel can be drawn between Hobbes's methodology and that of a number of English scientific writers who had already

17 Hobbes 1983a, XVIII.IV, pp. 283–4: 'si meminerimus, quid sit quod vocatur *Furtum*, & quid *iniuria*, *sciemus*, ex ipsis vocibus, an verum sit, *Furtum esse iniuriam*'.

18 Hobbes 1983a, XVII.IV, p. 284: 'Veritas idem est, quod *vera propositio*; *vera* autem est *propositio* in qua *nomen consequens* quod vocatur a logicis *Praedicatum*, complectitur amplitudine sua *nomen Antecedens* quod vocatur *subiectum*.'

19 BL Harl. MS 4235, fo. 25[v]. Cf. Hobbes 1969a, p. 26.

20 For the fact that 'demonstration' in Hobbes is a matter not of quantifying but of providing chains of entailment, see Hanson 1990.

21 As Hobbes 1983a, XIV.XVI, p. 213, puts it, a claim is 'recte ratiocinetur' when 'incipiens a principiis evidentissimis texat discursum ex consequentibus continuo necessariis'.

22 See Hobbes 1983a, XVII.XII, p. 261, on *ratiocinatio*: 'id est, texendo consequentias initio sumpto ab experientiis'.

23 On continuities with the Aristotelian tradition see Jardine 1988, esp. pp. 708–11. On parallels with Mersenne and Descartes see Hanson 1990, esp. pp. 597–600, 611–14.

focused on mathematical methods and the prestige associated with them. John Dee had eulogised the axiomatic approach in his lengthy preface to Billingsley's translation of Euclid's *Elements of Geometry* in 1571. The defining characteristic of 'Mathematicall reasoninges' is that 'a probable Argument is nothyng regarded'. The special virtue of 'an Argument exactly and purely Mathematical' is that 'only a perfect demonstration of truthes certaine, necessary and invincible, universally and necessarily concluded is allowed as sufficient'.[24] The ensuing generation witnessed a widespread acceptance of this ideal of reasoning as a model for the experimental no less than the strictly mathematical sciences. Gilbert in his *De Magnete* begins by pointing out that, 'in the discovery of secret things and in the quest for hidden causes, stronger reasons result from surer experiments and demonstrated arguments than from probable conjectures and from following what pleases the generality of the Philosophers'.[25] He insists that he has respected this principle, proceeding 'from true demonstrations and from experiments that appeal to the senses as clearly as if one were pointing with the finger'.[26] As a result, he has succeeded in establishing a new and genuinely demonstrative science. 'Just as geometry rises up from certain simple and readily understood foundations to conclusions of the greatest difficulty, whereby the ingenious mind ascends above the ether: so too does our magnetic doctrine and science.'[27] Yet more strikingly, Bacon voices a similar admiration for mathematical methods in *The Advancement of Learning*. Discussing the various 'Idols' that interfere with the progress of science, he ends by considering 'the false appearances that are imposed upon us by words, which are framed and applied according to the conceit and capacities of the vulgar sort'. Even when 'we think we govern our words', we often find that they 'shoot back upon the understanding of the wisest, and mightily entangle and pervert the judgment'. The solution lies in recognising that 'it is almost necessary in all controversies and disputations to imitate the wisdom of the mathematicians, in setting down in the very beginning the definitions of our words and terms that others may know how we accept and understand them, and whether they concur with us or no'. Unless we follow these precautions, 'we are sure to end

24 Dee 1571, sig. [figure of pointing hand], iiii^{v}.

25 Gilbert 1600, sig. *, ii^{r}: 'in arcanis inveniendis, & abditis rerum causis perquirendis, ab experimentis certioribus, & argumentis demonstratis, validiores existant rationes, quam a probabilibus coniecturis, & vulgo Philosophantium placitis'.

26 Gilbert 1600, sig. *, ii^{r}: 'veris demonstrationibus, & manifeste sensibus apparentibus experimentis, tanquam digito designare'.

27 Gilbert 1600, sig. *, ii^{v}: 'Et veluti geometria a minimis quibusdam & facillimis fundamentis, ad maxima & difficillima assurgit; quibus mens ingeniosa, supra aethera scandit: ita doctrina nostra & scientia magnetica ...'

there where we ought to have begun, which is, in questions and differences about words'.[28]

While Hobbes's view of scientific method is not unfamiliar, his account is nevertheless remarkable for the assurance and polemical force with which he insists that civil science can and ought to be classified among the demonstrative sciences. He insists, that is, that his four steps of science are no less applicable in moral than in mathematical reasoning. It follows that we can hope to construct an authentic science of politics capable of proving its conclusions with certainty. We are not restricted to dealing in probabilities as the theorists of rhetoric and the followers of Aristotle had alike supposed.

The opening of Hobbes's first treatise on civil science announces this commitment in dramatic terms. The drama begins with the title, *The Elements of Law.* This is surely intended to recall *The Elements of Geometry*, the name Billingsley had given to Euclid's great treatise when he translated it in 1571. Hobbes's first move, in other words, is to associate his own treatise in the minds of his readers with one of the most celebrated works of deductive reasoning ever written. The epistle dedicatory continues in no less dramatic style. Hobbes is explicit in claiming that he has discovered the principles of a fully demonstrative science 'of Justice & Policy in generall', and that he will be able to explain for the first time 'the true and only foundation of such Science'.[29] He reiterates the promise in the epistle dedicatory to *De Cive.* By contrast with all previous writers on *scientia civilis*, he now declares, 'I have followed a proper principle of teaching', as a result of which 'it seems to me that I have succeeded in this brief work in demonstrating the character of moral virtue and the elements of civic duties by connecting them together in a completely self-evident way'.[30] Looking back on *De Cive* in his *De Corpore* of 1655, Hobbes stressed once more that his original work was based on principles of teaching as opposed to persuasion, and that he was able in consequence to demonstrate his conclusions as opposed to merely stating them in probable terms. It would thus be legitimate to say, as he adds in an oft-quoted boast, that the scientific study of politics is 'no older ... than my own book *De Cive*'.[31]

28 Bacon 1915, p. 134. Cf. also Bacon's positive injunction, in the preface to the *Novum Organon*, that 'certitudinis gradus constituamus, sensum per reductionem quandam tueamur' – that 'we must hold to the evidence of the senses, suitably corrected, and then build up progressive stages of certainty'. See Bacon 1857c, p. 151.

29 BL Harl. MS 4235, fo. 2^{r-v}. Cf. Hobbes, 1969a, pp. xv, xvi.

30 Hobbes 1983a, epistle dedicatory, pp. 75–6: 'commodo usus sit docendi principio ... inde virtutis moralis officiorumque civilium Elementa, in hac opella, evidentissima connexione video mihi demonstrasse'.

31 Hobbes 1839d, p. ix.

A number of recent commentators have interpreted Hobbes's drive towards demonstrative certainty in the moral sciences as a response to the growing popularity of Pyrrhonian scepticism and associated arguments of a supposedly relativist kind.[32] I have been arguing, by contrast, that his project is best understood as a reaction not to scepticism as an epistemological doctrine but rather to the modes of argument characteristic of the rhetorical culture of Renaissance humanism. Hobbes is seeking to replace the dialogical and anti-demonstrative approach to moral reasoning encouraged by the humanist assumption that there are two sides to any question, and thus that in the moral sciences it will always be possible to argue on either side of the case. He is chiefly reacting, in short, against what the English version of *De Cive* calls the 'rhetorication' of moral philosophy.[33] One of his fundamental purposes is to transcend and supersede the entire rhetorical structure – the structure of *inventio*, *dispositio* and *elocutio* – on the basis of which the humanist conception of *scientia civilis* had been raised. To understand his own vision of civil philosophy, we need to see it as framed in large part as an alternative to these prevailing humanist orthodoxies, and as an attempt to replace them with a theory of politics based on authentically scientific premises.

Hobbes first announces these commitments in the superbly confident epistle dedicatory to *The Elements*, in which he directly confronts the two basic presuppositions of humanist civil science. One of these, as we have seen, is that *ratio* or reason possesses no inherent power to move or persuade. This was taken to be one of the grounds for concluding that an effective civil science must be based on a union of reason and eloquence. To this Hobbes rejoins that reason no less than passion must be recognised as one of 'the two principall parts of our Nature', and that the power of reason is sufficient, even in matters of justice and policy, to give rise to a form of learning 'free from controversies and dispute'.[34]

The other humanist presupposition was that, in debates about justice and policy, it will always be possible to construct a 'probable' argument *in utramque partem*, and that the involvement of our passions and interests will

32 For suggestions about the influence of epistemological scepticism on the development of Hobbes's thought see Pacchi 1965, esp. pp. 63–9, 97–100, 179–83, and Battista 1966, esp. pp. 22, 53, 135, 145, 172–5. The argument has been elevated into an orthodoxy by more recent commentators. See for example Battista 1980; Missner 1983; Sarasohn 1985; Kahn 1985, esp. pp. 154, 181; Sorell 1986, esp. pp. 63–7; Tuck 1988a and Tuck 1989, esp. pp. 64, 93, 102 (and cf. Tuck 1993, pp. 285–98); Hampsher-Monk 1992, esp. pp. 4–6; Hanson 1993, esp. 644–5; Flathman 1993, esp. pp. 2–3, 43–7, 51–2. On this literature see also the introduction, notes 42, 43, 44, *supra*.

33 Hobbes 1983b, p. 26.

34 BL Harl. MS 4235, fo. 2^{r}. Cf. Hobbes 1969a, p. xv.

be such that we can never hope to avoid such arguments or finally resolve them with anything approaching demonstrative certainty. This was taken to be a further reason for concluding that we must always be prepared to make use of the moving force of eloquence to win round an audience. To these contentions Hobbes responds even more polemically. He concedes that anyone writing about justice and policy will be dealing with issues in which he 'compareth Men, & medleth with their Right and Profitt'. But he insists that it is nevertheless possible 'to reduce this doctrine to the rules and infallibility of Reason'. Despite the fact that our passions will be involved, we can still aspire 'to put such Principles down for a foundation, as Passion not mistrusting, may not seek to displace'. We can therefore hope, simply by force of scientific reasoning, to build up a set of political principles which, as Hobbes revealingly puts it, will be 'inexpugnable'– incapable of being dislodged or overthrown by any opposing force.[35]

Hobbes makes it no less clear in the body of *The Elements* that his aim is to counteract the presuppositions of humanist civil science. Against the view that reason is impotent in the absence of powerful speaking he insists in chapter 17 that reason is capable of dictating conclusions, of obliging us to follow particular arguments.[36] To this he adds in the opening chapter of part II that 'reason teacheth us' about such matters as the value of government.[37] But as he has explained in chapter 13, to teach is to beget in the minds of others a conception they will have no inclination to dispute. What he is again affirming is thus that reason is capable of producing conclusions beyond controversy or doubt. He insists, moreover, that these dictates of reason are such that even those of the meanest capacity can hope to follow them without difficulty.[38] This leads him to repudiate with considerable asperity the rhetorical assumption that we must always make a special effort, as Cicero had put it, to win the attention and consent of our audience. Reversing the usual argument, Hobbes declares that 'if reasoning aright I winne not Consent (which may very easily happen) from them that being confident of their owne Knowledge weigh not what is said, the fault is not mine but theirs'. This is because 'as it is my part to show my reasons, so it is theirs to bring attention'.[39]

It is true, Hobbes later concedes, that some people suffer from 'a fault of the minde' which he labels 'INDOCIBILITY, or difficulty of being taught'. This is due to the fact that, 'when men have once acquiesced in untrue

35 BL Harl. MS 4235, fo. 2^{r}. Cf. Hobbes 1969a, p. xv.
36 See BL Harl. MS 4235, fos. 67^{v}, 70^{r}, and cf. Hobbes 1969a, pp. 89, 92.
37 BL Harl. MS 4235, fo. 85^{v}. Cf. Hobbes 1969a, p. 116.
38 BL Harl. MS 4235, fos. 23^{r}, 52^{r}. Cf. Hobbes 1969a, pp. 22, 66.
39 BL Harl. MS 4235, fo. 11^{r-v}. Cf. Hobbes 1969a, pp. 1–2.

opinions, and registered them as authenticall records in their minds', it becomes 'no lesse impossible to speak intelligibly to such men than to write legibly upon a paper already scribbled over'.[40] But Hobbes is far from regarding indocibility as an insuperable barrier to the construction of a science of politics. As he observes in the same passage, 'if the mindes of men were all of white paper, they would almost equally be disposed to acknowledge whatsoever should be in right method, and right ratiocination delivered unto them'.[41] Nor is this merely a utopian prospect, for while 'opinions which are gotten by Education, and in length of tyme are made habituall, cannot be taken away by force, and upon the suddaine', they can nevertheless be taken away by the same means by which they were acquired, that is, 'by tyme and Education'.[42] Hobbes's highly optimistic conclusion is thus that, if the true principles of civil science were taught in the universities, we should quickly find 'that younge men, who come thither voyd of prejudice, and whose mindes are yet as white paper', would readily adopt them and teach them in turn to the generality of the people.[43]

Hobbes also returns to the attack he had earlier mounted in the epistle dedicatory on the assumption that, in matters of civil science, we are restricted to the presentation of merely 'probable' arguments. The opening chapter of *The Elements* begins by reaffirming that, when we are told that 'true knowledge' is impossible to acquire in matters of justice and policy, this merely reveals 'that they which have heretofore written thereof have not well understood their owne subject'.[44] The fact is that we can lay down 'necessary and demonstrable rules' about how to produce peace and good government.[45] We can hope in consequence to construct a science 'from which proceed the true and evident conclusions of what is right and wronge, and what is good and hurtfull to the being and welbeing of mankinde'.[46] The contrast drawn at the end of *The Elements* is accordingly between science and rhetoric, not between science and Pyrrhonian scepticism. As Hobbes puts it himself, the contrast is between those who aspire to write 'concerning morallity and policy demonstratively' and those who have merely 'insinuated their opinions by eloquent Sophistry'.[47]

If we turn from *The Elements* to *De Cive*, we encounter a still more

40 BL Harl. MS 4235, fo. 42ʳ. Cf. Hobbes 1969a, p. 51.
41 BL Harl. MS 4235, fo. 42ʳ. Cf. Hobbes 1969a, p. 51.
42 BL Harl. MS 4235, fo. 137ᵛ. Cf. Hobbes 1969a, p. 183.
43 BL Harl. MS 4235, fo. 138ʳ. Cf. Hobbes 1969a, pp. 183–4.
44 BL Harl. MS 4235, fo. 11ʳ. Cf. Hobbes 1969a, p. 1.
45 BL Harl. MS 4235, fo. 128ʳ. Cf. Hobbes 1969a, p. 171.
46 BL Harl. MS 4235, fo. 132ʳ. Cf. Hobbes 1969a, p. 176.
47 BL Harl. MS 4235, fo. 138ʳ. Cf. Hobbes 1969a, p. 183.

confident effort to challenge and supersede the presuppositions of humanist civil science. Hobbes is even more emphatic that *ratio* possesses an inherent power to persuade and convince, and thus that the idea of a union between reason and eloquence is an irrelevance. He first assures us in his epistle dedicatory – in a direct allusion to the rival rhetorical doctrine – that he aims to persuade his readers 'by the firmness of *rationes* and not by any outward display of *oratio*'.[48] He speaks at several subsequent points about the 'dictates' of right reason, and thus about its power to order, command and enforce particular conclusions upon us.[49] Finally, when examining the duties of sovereigns in chapter XIII he adds that 'the opinions they need to insert into the minds of men' can and ought to be inserted 'not by commanding but by teaching, not by fear of penalties but by perspicuity of reasons'.[50] The implication is unmistakable: if *ratio* is sufficient to insert opinions into the minds of men, there is no place for the techniques of persuasion associated with the art of eloquence.

Hobbes also reiterates his earlier attack on the belief that, in matters of justice and policy, we can only hope to discuss the issues in a 'probable' way, since it will always be possible to mount a case *in utramque partem*. The epistle dedicatory begins by identifying, as the position to be overcome, the view that in discussions about justice an effective argument 'can always be sustained on either side of the case'– *utraque pars tueatur*.[51] Hobbes mentions that orators habitually 'fight with contrary opinions and speeches',[52] and alludes to the view that in politics (as Quintilian had conceded) we can only hope to arrive at conclusions 'worthy of being debated'.[53] But he retorts that, so long as we follow the footsteps of science, we can hope to argue 'in such a way that no space is left for contrary disputes'.[54] We can hope to present our conclusions demonstratively, to argue in such a way that our conclusions are not merely defended as probable but are systematically proved.[55]

Hobbes summarises these contentions in a passage of magnificent

48 Hobbes 1983a, epistle dedicatory, p. 76: 'neque specie orationis, sed firmitudine rationum'.

49 See Hobbes 1983a, II.II, p. 100, and XV.IV, p. 221, on 'dictamina rectae rationis'; III.XIX, p. 115, on how 'ratio iubet'; III.XXVII, p. 118, and XV.XIV, p. 227, on how 'ratio dictat'; XV.XV, p. 229, on how 'ratio imperat'.

50 Hobbes 1983a, XIII.IX, p. 198: 'opiniones non imperando, sed docendo, non terrore poenarum, sed perspicuitate rationum animis hominum inseruntur'.

51 Hobbes 1983a, epistle dedicatory, p. 75.

52 Hobbes 1983a, X.XII, p. 178: 'contrariis sententiis orationibusque pugnant'.

53 Hobbes 1983a, XII.X, p. 191. For Quintilian's concession see ch. 2 note 256, *supra*.

54 See Hobbes 1983a, II.I, p. 98, on the methods 'qui locum contra disputandi non relinquunt'.

55 Hobbes is very free with the claim that his conclusions in *De Cive* are not merely probable but are demonstrated. See for example Hobbes 1983a, VII.IV, p. 152; XV.I, p. 219. Both his commitment and mode of expression strongly recall Bacon's preface to the *Novum Organon*, which ends with the proclamation that his aim is 'non belle et probabiliter opinari, sed certo et ostensive scire' – 'not to offer merely probable opinions in an elegant style, but to know demonstratively and with certainty'. See Bacon 1857c, p. 154.

effrontery in chapter XII, his chapter on the dissolution of commonwealths. He recurs to the idea that wisdom can be acquired 'by contemplating things as they are in themselves', and 'by gaining an understanding of words in their true and proper definitions', thereby ensuring that our statements of belief are founded on appropriate principles.[56] If we proceed in this manner, we shall be able to produce 'an expression of any propositions or conceptions in our mind which is at once *perspicua* and *elegans*'.[57] As a consequence, we shall be able to express ourselves not merely with wisdom but with true *eloquentia*.[58]

The ability to speak with eloquence, and hence to offer an explication of our beliefs at once elegant and perspicuous, was of course exactly what the theorists of rhetoric had always promised to those capable of mastering the techniques of *inventio*, *dispositio* and *elocutio*. But Hobbes insists that the key to elegance and perspicuity lies not in studying the art of rhetoric but in following the footsteps of science. With this contention he finally turns the tables on the rhetoricians and their theory of persuasive speech. He willingly accepts their central contention that eloquence is indispensable to civil science. But he insists that genuine eloquence arises from 'the Art of logic, not the Art of rhetoric'.[59] It follows that, when we acknowledge the indispensability of eloquence, we are merely saying that it is necessary to reason logically;[60] we are not in the least saying that it is necessary to call on the artificial aids associated with 'that form of powerful eloquence which is separated from a true knowledge of things'.[61]

THE FEATURES OF A SCIENTIFIC STYLE

Besides laying out his positive conception of civil science in *The Elements of Law* and *De Cive*, Hobbes is at pains to practise his own precepts, and thus to present us with a genuinely scientific analysis of justice and policy. This in turn means that he takes considerable care to avoid constructing his argument along the lines recommended by the theorists of eloquence. He makes no effort to establish ethos, to win attention and goodwill at the

56 See Hobbes 1983a, XII.XII, p. 192 for the claim that *sapientia* 'oriturque partim a rerum ipsarum contemplatione, partim a verborum in propria & definita significatione acceptorum intelligentia'.

57 Hobbes 1983a, XII.XII p. 192: 'sententiae & conceptuum animi perspicua & elegans'.

58 Hobbes 1983a, XII.XII, p. 192.

59 See Hobbes 1983a, XII.XII, p. 193 on true *eloquentia* as a product of mastering the *ars logica*, not the *ars rhetorica*.

60 Sorell 1986, pp. 134–5, in an otherwise excellent discussion, seems to me to miss Hobbes's point when he argues that Hobbes in this passage 'leaves room for a respectable type of eloquence'.

61 Hobbes 1983a, XII.XII, p. 193: '*eloquentia potens*, separata a rerum scientia'.

outset by presenting himself as a 'probable' witness. Rather he speaks in his prefatory epistles in such a way as to undercut the expectations of those familiar with such rhetorical strategies. The epistle dedicatory to *The Elements* says nothing about its author's credentials, claiming instead that anyone capable of following the argument will be sufficiently convinced. The epistle dedicatory to *De Cive* goes even further, directly challenging the rhetorical doctrine that all writers should begin by advertising their special expertise on the issues to be discussed. Hobbes observes that 'I know with what labour and diligence I have undertaken this investigation into the truth',[62] but adds that he prefers to say nothing about his qualifications or what he thinks he has achieved. We ought instead to acknowledge, he insists, that 'due to self-love, we place a less than fair estimate on the value of our own works'.[63]

It is also striking that Hobbes pays no attention to the specific prescriptions associated with the theory of *inventio*. As well as mounting his theoretical attack on the injunction to 'accommodate' our arguments to accepted beliefs, he exhibits a studious disregard for the implications of the injunction when he comes to develop his own case. He is sparing to the point of disingenuousness in referring to accredited authorities, and makes no effort to buttress his conclusions by appealing to the common 'places' of argument. This is not to say that he has no use for aphorisms and commonplaces. He is in fact conspicuously fond of them, and in both *The Elements* and *De Cive* he makes considerable play with maxims and expressions of a proverbial kind. A number of these, especially in *De Cive*, are taken from the legal and political writers of ancient Rome. For example, in chapter III he mentions 'the ancient saying' that *volenti non fit iniuria*, that no injury is done to the willing,[64] and in chapter V he similarly refers to 'the well-worn saying' that laws are silent in time of war: *inter arma silere leges*.[65] Besides mentioning such legal tags, Hobbes shows a marked fondness, especially in *The Elements*, for commonplaces in the strict sense of popular maxims expressed in an epigrammatic style. He concludes his analysis of the four steps of science by quoting the Socratic injunction *nosce teipsum*, know thyself.[66] A favourite saying among English humanists, this had already been described by Ascham as a 'wise proverbe'[67] and by Elyot

62 Hobbes 1983a, epistle dedicatory, p. 76: 'Quantum laboris diligentiaeque in veritate investiganda adhibitum sit.'

63 Hobbes 1983a, epistle dedicatory, p. 76: 'inventa nostra omnes prae amore minus recte aestimamus'.

64 Hobbes 1983a, III.VII, p. 111: 'Vetus est: *volenti non fit iniuria*.'

65 Hobbes 1983a, V.II, p. 131: 'Tritum est *inter arma silere leges*.'

66 BL Harl. MS 4235, fo. 24^{r}. Cf. Hobbes 1969a, p. 24.

67 Ascham 1970c, p. 111.

as 'an excellent and wonderful sentence'.[68] Hobbes offers a further example in chapter 12, in which he refers to the adage 'The world is governed by opinion.'[69] This too had become a popular maxim by the end of the sixteenth century, and occurs in probably its best-known form in Marston's *What You Will.*[70] A third example can be found in chapter 16, at the beginning of which Hobbes mentions the 'Common saying' that 'nature maketh nothing in vaine.'[71] Originally Aristotelian in provenance, this expression had likewise attained wide currency, and is cited in Gabriel Harvey's *Letter-Book*[72] as well as in Bacon's *De Augmentis.*[73]

While Hobbes makes frequent use of such popular commonplaces, he presents them in a fashion that must have struck his original readers as almost unthinkably arrogant and paradoxical. He never cites them, as the theory of *inventio* required, to lend additional force to his own arguments. Rather he treats his own arguments as a yardstick for measuring their value. When he refers to the dictum 'no injury is done to the willing', he offers as a reason for endorsing it the fact that 'its truth can be derived from my own principles'.[74] When he declares that 'laws are silent in times of war', he similarly points out that, if we reflect on his own analysis of the state of nature, we shall find that 'this well-worn saying is also a true one'.[75] The homely maxims he favours in *The Elements* are handled in a similar way. If we treat the injunction 'Know thyself' as a way of summarising his own analysis of the four steps of science, we shall find ourselves agreeing that it is 'a precept worthy the reputation it hath gotten'.[76] If we take the proverb 'The world is governed by opinion' as a means of paraphrasing his own theory of the will, we shall find it easy to accept that the proverb says something 'truly and properly'.[77] If we regard the proposition that 'nature maketh nothing in vain' as a restatement of his own belief that the laws of nature are merely precepts of reason, we shall have no difficulty in acknowledging that this 'Common saying' is also 'most certaine'.[78] The rhetorical

68 Elyot 1962, pp. 164–5.

69 BL Harl. MS 4235, fo. 50r. Cf. Hobbes 1969a, p. 63.

70 Marston 1934–9, *What You Will*, I.i.18–19, p. 37:

all that exsists,
Takes valuation from oppinion.

71 BL Harl. MS fo. 62v. Cf. Hobbes 1969a, p. 81.

72 See Harvey 1884, p. 123: 'Nature, they tell us / Doth nothinge in vayne.'

73 Bacon 1857b, p. 787: nature 'nihil facti frustra'. Cf. p. 570, where Aristotle is credited with the doctrine.

74 Hobbes 1983a, III.VII, p. 111: 'Veritatem tamen dicti liceat ex principiis nostris derivare.'

75 Hobbes 1983a, V.II, p. 131: 'Tritum est ... & verum est, non modo de *legibus civilibus*, sed etiam *de lege naturali*, si non ad animum sed ad actiones referatur.'

76 BL Harl. MS 4235, fo. 24r. Cf. Hobbes 1969a, p. 24.

77 BL Harl. MS 4235, fo. 50r. Cf. Hobbes 1969a, p. 63.

78 BL Harl. MS 4235, fo. 62v. Cf. Hobbes 1969a, p. 81.

approach to commonplaces is reversed in every case: rather than asking us to accept his arguments because they can be 'accommodated' to accepted beliefs, Hobbes asks us to endorse those beliefs because they can be shown to follow from his own arguments.

More generally, Hobbes makes no concession to the governing assumption of the theory of *inventio*, the assumption that there will always be two sides to every question,[79] and thus that we can only hope to proceed in civil science by considering alternatives and trying to harmonise them. Hobbes's manner of proceeding in *The Elements* and *De Cive* offers the strongest possible contrast with these humanist principles. He presents his argument in *The Elements* in wholly deductive style, numbering his paragraphs and constantly referring us back to what he has 'showed' or 'demonstrated'[80] as well as forwards to what he regards as necessary consequences.[81] He adopts the same approach with even greater confidence in *De Cive*, in which he again numbers his paragraphs and continually draws our attention to what follows from what he has already established or *ostensum*,[82] and what consequences ineluctably flow from what he has already proved or *demonstratum*.[83]

Most striking of all is the extent to which Hobbes bypasses the prescriptions associated with the theory of *elocutio*.[84] He explicitly draws attention to this feature of his writing in the epistle dedicatory to *The Elements*, in which he slyly recalls the rhetorical precept to the effect that we should always apologise for the shortcomings of our *elocutio* by emphasising its rough-and-ready state. The style of his own treatise, he duly concedes, 'is therefore the worse, because I was forced to consult when I was writing more with Logick then with Rhetorick'.[85] What he succeeds in conveying by this cunning adaptation of a familiar trope of modesty is that the task of laying the foundations of a civil science is one in which the art of rhetoric has no necessary place.

It is true that, in line with the theoretical stance adopted in chapter 10 of *The Elements*, Hobbes occasionally introduces an extended simile to

79 A point well brought out in Sorell 1990b.

80 See BL Harl. MS 4235, fos. 74v, 84v, 86v, 103v, 115r, 122v, 128v, 130r, 134v. Cf. Hobbes 1969a, pp. 99, 115, 117, 139–40, 155, 164, 172, 174, 179.

81 See BL Harl. MS 4235, fos. 62r, 87v, 129v. Cf. Hobbes 1969a, pp. 81, 119, 173.

82 Hobbes 1983a, x.iv, p. 173; xi.ii–iii, p. 182; xii.i, p. 185; xiii.ix, p. 198; xv.v, p. 221; xvii.xxvii, p. 277, etc.

83 Hobbes 1983a, vii.iv, p. 152; xv.xvii, p. 230 etc., and cf. xv.i, p. 219, on what has been 'comprobatum'.

84 A point well noted in Smith 1994, p. 36. This is not of course to deny that Hobbes uses more informal methods of emphasis (definitions, use of summaries, etc.) on which see Sorell 1990a.

85 BL Harl. MS 4235, fo. 2v. Cf Hobbes 1969a, p. xvi.

establish in the minds of his readers a set of connections they might otherwise have missed. The early sections of *The Elements* provide us with a number of such 'similitudes'. In chapter 3, for example, he explains the impact of external objects on the brain by analogy with the effects of wind on water,[86] while in chapter 9 he summarises his theory of the passions by comparing the life of the emotions with a race.[87] *De Cive* contains a number of explanatory tropes of a similar kind. Chapter III likens our different social dispositions to the different materials required for a building,[88] while chapter XIII compares the role of spies in preserving commonwealths with the movements of a spider in its web.[89]

Hobbes scarcely makes any attempt, however, to deploy the resources of *ornatus* in either of the ways that Quintilian and his followers had particularly recommended. As we saw in chapter 5, they had pointed out in the first place that many of the figures and tropes can be employed as a means of ridiculing and undermining our adversaries. It is true that Hobbes occasionally permits himself a touch of grim humour when contemplating the crimes and follies of mankind.[90] But he is far from making systematic use of such techniques, and on more than one occasion he expresses a keen distaste for those who go out of their way to write and speak in tones of ridicule or contempt. When he analyses the passions in chapter 9 of *The Elements*, he treats the habit of deriding others as a sign of vaingloriousness and lack of magnanimity. A man must be 'of little worth to think the Infirmityes of another sufficient matter for his tryumph'.[91] This prompts him to classify those who like to laugh at others as pusillanimous, since they merely gain 'affectation of Glory from other mens Infirmityes, and not from any ability of their own'.[92]

The other suggestion put forward by Quintilian and his followers had been that the figures and tropes can be used to convert mere auditors into spectators. We can hope, that is, to exploit the devices of *ornatus* in such a way as to enable our audience suddenly to 'see' what we want them to understand. Hobbes undoubtedly makes some gestures in this direction in *The Elements*. When discussing the relationship between evidence and truth he suggests that we should think of it 'as the sappe is

86 BL Harl. MS 4235, fo. 15^{r-v}. Cf Hobbes 1969a, p. 8.

87 BL Harl. MS 4235, fos. 39^{v} to 40^{r}. Cf. Hobbes 1969a, pp. 47–8.

88 Hobbes 1983a, III.IX, p. 112.

89 Hobbes 1983a, XIII.VII, p. 197.

90 See for example the use of meiosis in this way in BL Harl. MS 4235, fo. 25^{r} (cf. Hobbes 1969a, p. 25) and of litotes at Hobbes 1983a, XVII.XII, p. 261.

91 BL Harl. MS 4235, fo. 36^{r}. Cf. Hobbes 1969a, p. 42.

92 BL Harl. MS 4235, fo. 39^{v}. Cf. Hobbes 1969a, p. 47.

to the tree'.[93] When seeking to explain how it comes about that 'the passions of those that are singly moderate, are altogether vehement', he offers as an analogy the behaviour of 'a great many Coales' which 'though but warme asunder, being put together inflame one another'.[94] There are one or two further gestures of a similar kind in *De Cive*. When illustrating the shortcomings of large assemblies, he observes that the effects of faction are such that the laws 'are left floating in one direction or another as if they are on top of the waves'.[95] And when pointing to the dangers associated with over-mighty subjects, he describes them as 'needing to be stroked like horses given to ferociousness'.[96]

The remarkable feature, however, of Hobbes's use of *ornatus* in *The Elements* and *De Cive* is that, save for these few exceptions, he makes no effort to coin fresh images at all. So far is he from wishing to exploit the resources of *ornatus* to help us 'see' new connections that his figures and tropes are almost invariably familiar to the point of triteness. He tells us, for example, about the light of reason and the mind as a *tabula rasa*;[97] about the body politic and head of state;[98] about wounding words and the need to weigh opinions in the balance;[99] and so on. Apart from these and a few other equally comfortable clichés, he makes almost no use of *ornatus* in *The Elements* or *De Cive* at all. This is not to deny that both works contain some purely verbal effects of memorable brilliance, most of which depend on the exploitation of such *figurae verborum* as climax, epanodos and especially antithesis.[100] But the entire range of the *figurae sententiarum* anatomised by Quintilian and his followers is left virtually unexplored.

The outcome is a prose embodying a degree of austerity that even Hobbes's Tacitist contemporaries rarely sought to achieve. Hobbes's resolute refusal to engage with the rhetorical techniques so central to classical and Renaissance civil science must have occasioned a considerable shock of surprise to his original readers. The shock is one he clearly intended to administer. His literary manner amounts to a further declaration that his theory 'of Justice & Policy in generall' is not intended as a contribution to the *studia humanitatis* at all, but a further addition to the growing corpus of the new sciences.

93 BL Harl. MS 4235, fo. 25^{v}. Cf. Hobbes 1969a, p. 25.

94 BL Harl. MS 4235, fos. 104^{v}–105^{r}. Cf. Hobbes 1969a, p. 142.

95 Hobbes 1983a, X.XIII, p. 178: 'tanquam super undas huc illuc fluctuent'.

96 Hobbes 1983a, XIII.XII, p. 201: 'sicut equo propter ferociam'.

97 See BL Harl. MS 4235, fos. 42^{r}, 74^{v}, 138^{r} and cf. Hobbes 1969a, pp. 51, 99, 184.

98 See BL Harl. MS 4235, fos. 11^{r}, 78^{v}, 82^{r}, 102^{r}, 125^{r}, 131^{r} and cf. Hobbes 1969a, pp. 1, 104, 111, 138, 168, 175.

99 Hobbes 1983a, XII.XI, p. 192 and XIII.XVI, p. 204.

100 For examples from *The Elements*, see BL Harl. MS 4235, fo. 2^{r} (epanodos); 71^{r}, 141^{v} and 143^{v} (antithesis); 100^{v} and 130^{v} (climax). Cf. Hobbes 1969a, pp. xv, 94, 137, 175, 188, 190.

THE SCIENTIFIC ANALYSIS OF JUSTICE

Hobbes's desire in *The Elements* and *De Cive* to present his readers with an authentically scientific theory of politics is most ambitiously reflected in his attempt to analyse the fundamental concepts of civil life according to the so-called steps of science.[101] Among these concepts the most important according to Hobbes is the virtue of justice. Not only does he describe *The Elements* as an enquiry into the nature 'of Justice & Policy in generall', but he subsequently speaks of *De Cive* in very similar terms, declaring in the epistle dedicatory that his principal aim is to conduct 'an inquisition into natural justice',[102] and adding in the preface to the 1647 edition that the theme of his treatise is *scientia iustitiae.*[103] For Hobbes, in short, the ability to deliver a scientific analysis of justice lies at the heart of any civil science worthy the name.

This in turn means, according to Hobbes's own theory of moral science, that his task is a twofold one. He needs in the first place to arrive at a definition of justice capable of satisfying his conditions of scientific adequacy. He needs a definition, that is, which uses words in their generally accepted meanings; which avoids equivocation or ambiguity; and which enables instances of justice and injustice to be picked out by the application of some purely empirical criterion, thereby forestalling any distorting influences of passion or prejudice. The second task is then to show that, in the light of such a definition, it is possible to demonstrate that a number of 'necessary consequences' follow from it which are at once politically substantial and at the same time logically inescapable.

Although Hobbes makes a preliminary effort to practise these precepts in *The Elements*, he develops his argument with much greater rigour and clarity in the pages of *De Cive*. It would not be too much to say that in the latter work the definition of justice and the elucidation of its necessary consequences together make up the backbone of the work. Hobbes first introduces his definition in the course of surveying the laws of nature in chapters II, III and IV. He begins to pursue its implications in analysing the concept of covenanting in chapters V, VI and VII. And he deduces a further set of necessary consequences when discussing the authority of sovereigns and the dissolution of commonwealths in chapters XII, XIII and XIV.

101 The fact that Hobbes's procedures follow his canons for civil science is excellently brought out in Johnston 1986 and Sorell 1990b.

102 See Hobbes 1983a, epistle dedicatory, p. 75, speaking of devoting 'cogitationes meas ad inquisitionem iustitiae naturalis'.

103 Hobbes 1983a, 'Praefatio ad Lectores', p. 78.

Hobbes initially presents his definition of justice in the second part of his survey of the laws of nature in chapter III. Having stated it, however, he immediately adds a qualification to ensure that his use of the term is free from ambiguity. The reason for this caution, he explains, is that 'these words *Just* and *Unjust*, and likewise *Justice* and *Injustice* are in fact equivocal, because they mean one thing when attributed to Persons and another when attributed to Actions'.[104] This makes it crucial to emphasise, he adds, that his own concern is basically with the concept of justice as a property and hence a predicate of actions, and not with the separate idea of justice or righteousness as an attribute of persons, a usage he goes so far as to dismiss as a usurpation of the term.[105]

Focusing on the justice and injustice of actions, Hobbes next proceeds to apply the technique he had characterised in *The Elements* as that of discovering 'how thinges are named by generall agreement'.[106] He proceeds, in other words, to investigate the etymology and common usage of the terms *just* and *unjust* when applied to human actions. He begins by pointing out that, when people refuse to accept that a given action is just – when they say that it is *iniusta* or unjust – they are saying in effect that it interferes with some particular *ius* or right, and is therefore an instance of *iniuria* or legal injury.[107] 'It thus appears that the name *injury*' – and hence injustice – 'was originally attributed to any action or omission that was done without right.'[108] But to say of an action or omission that it was done *sine iure*, without right, is to say that the *ius* or right of performing or omitting it 'must have been transferred from the person performing or omitting it to someone else'.[109] As Hobbes has already laid down in chapter II, however, to speak of transferring the right of doing or omitting an action to some other person is equivalent to speaking of covenanting with that person to assign them that right.[110] From this examination of the origins and application of the word *iniuria* Hobbes is accordingly able to arrive at his definition of what it means to act justly or unjustly. An action

104 Hobbes 1983a, III.V, p. 110: 'Nomina haec *Iustum* & *Iniustum*, sicut & *Iustitia* & *Iniustitia* aequivoca sunt; aliud enim significant cum Personis, aliud cum Actionibus tribuuntur.'

105 Hobbes 1983a, III.V, p. 110, says that the words 'iustitia' and 'iniustitia' are 'usurpantur' when applied *de personis*. Boonin-Vail fails to take note of this passage, in consequence of which he seems to over-state his case when he claims that 'Hobbes's moral theory is primarily concerned with just people, rather than with just actions'. See Boonin-Vail 1994, pp. 111–12. Since Hobbes stresses, however, that it is important to make a habit of acting virtuously, his account of virtuous actions might be said to culminate in a theory of character.

106 BL Harl. MS 4235, fo. 132^r. Cf. Hobbes 1969a, p. 176.

107 Hobbes 1983a, III.III, p. 109.

108 Hobbes 1983a, III.III, p. 109: 'Videturque *iniuriae* nomen, inde actioni vel omissioni tribui, quia *sine iure est.*'

109 Hobbes 1983a, III.III, p. 109: 'ab eo qui agit vel omittit, translatum antea in alium fuerat'.

110 Hobbes 1983a, II. V–XIV, pp. 100–4.

is injurious and hence unjust 'if it involves the violation of a *Covenant* or the taking back of a gift, either of which invariably involves some action or failure to act'.[111] By contrast, an action is just if it involves no such infraction of a promise or covenant.[112] 'When the word *Just* is attributed to *Actions*, it means that the action was performed by right', and thus that no transfer of right and hence no violation of covenant was involved.[113] As an immediate corollary, Hobbes adds that we cannot therefore speak of injury or injustice in the absence of a promise or covenant. 'No injury can be done to anyone unless some *covenant* has been made with them, or unless some gift has been given to them, or unless something in the form of a *covenant* has been promised to them.'[114]

This, then, is Hobbes's proposal for bringing the 'passionate' and contested names *just* and *unjust* within the ambit of science. The power of his analysis stems from the fact that, if an unjust act is simply an act involving a breach of covenant, and if a just act is simply an act involving no such breach, then the question of whether a given action is properly to be evaluated as an instance of justice or injustice becomes, as Hobbes's scientific method requires, a purely empirical one: the moral question of whether the behaviour was just or unjust reduces to the factual question of whether its performance involved any breach of promise or covenant.

Having put forward this definition and protected it from distortion, Hobbes is ready to take the next and decisive step of science. He is ready, that is, to trace the necessary consequences of his definition, and hence to reveal what specific political implications follow from accepting his analysis of justice in terms of the performance of covenants.

Before we can turn to these implications, however, we need to take account of Hobbes's views about the role of covenants in the formation of commonwealths. Hobbes consistently argues that the act of covenanting forms the only legitimate means of 'instituting' a civil association of any kind. But his treatment of covenanting is less developed in *The Elements* than in *De Cive*. In *The Elements* he still holds to the assumption made familiar by such early seventeenth-century writers on natural law as Suarez that all commonwealths must originally have been democracies, and that some additional covenants must have been undertaken to convert them into other types of regime.[115] In *De Cive*, by contrast, he presents a

111 Hobbes 1983a, III.III, p. 109; '*Pacti* violatio sicut & dati repetitio (quae semper sita est in aliqua actione, vel omissione).'

112 The fact that Hobbes also stresses this converse point is well emphasised in Gauthier 1969, p. 45.

113 'Cum *Actionibus* tribuuntur, idem significat *Iustum*, quod iure factum.'

114 Hobbes 1983a, III.IV, p. 109: 'iniuriam nemini fieri posse nisi ei quicum initur *pactum*, sive cui aliquid dono datum est, vel cui *pacto* aliquid est promissum'.

115 BL MS 4235, fo. 87[r]. Cf. Hobbes 1969a, p. 118.

more systematic view of covenanting, beginning in chapter v by furnishing a general analysis of the *pacta* underlying all forms of civil association and using this analysis as an introduction to a series of separate chapters on monarchy, aristocracy and democracy.

Hobbes first lays it down in chapter v of *De Cive* that, when a multitude of individuals come together to institute a commonwealth, they covenant to allow the will of one person to represent or stand for the wills of all:

> Because a *conspiring* of many wills to the same end is not sufficient for the conservation of peace and stable defence, it is necessary that in those matters which are indispensable for peace and defence there should be *one will* to stand for the wills of all. But this cannot be done unless every individual is willing to subject his *will* to that of *someone else* – either a *single Man* or a single *Council* – so that whatever that person *wills* in matters indispensable to the common peace shall be taken to be the *will* of everyone in general and of each individual in particular.[116]

Hobbes is careful to add that we should not think of a multitude as coming together in the form of a single body to agree with one voice to accept an individual or council as their representative. We cannot properly speak of a multitude as constituting a single body until some individual or council has been appointed to represent them. It is only by acquiring a representative will, and thus a sovereign, that a body of people ceases to be a mere multitude.[117] It follows that the only means by which a body of people can perform the act of covenanting is by mutually agreeing – each individual with everyone else – to accept the terms of a *pactum* that will bind them all:

> This submission of the *Wills* of each individual to *the will of a single man* or *Council* takes place when each and every individual person obliges himself by means of a Covenant with each and every other individual person not to resist the *will* of that *man* or *Council* to whom he submits himself.[118]

Hobbes's doctrine is thus that the act of instituting a commonwealth takes place when everyone covenants with everyone else to relinquish the right of private judgment in matters pertaining to the being and well-being of the commonwealth, agreeing to assign the exercise of that right to a

116 Hobbes 1983a, v.vi, p. 133: 'Quoniam igitur *conspiratio* plurium voluntatum ad eundem finem non sufficit ad conservationem pacis, & defensionem stabilem, requiritur ut circa ea quae ad pacem et defensionem sunt necessaria, *una* omnium sit *voluntas*. Hoc autem fieri non potest, nisi unusquisque *voluntatem* suam, alterius *unius*, nimirum, unius *Hominis*, vel unius *Concilii*, *voluntati*, ita subiiciat, ut pro *voluntate* omnium & singulorum, habendum sit, quicquid de iis rebus quae necessariae sunt ad pacem communem, ille voluerit.'

117 These points are well emphasised in Malcolm 1991, pp. 541–2.

118 Hobbes 1983a, v.vii, p. 133: '*Voluntatum* haec submissio omnium illorum *unius hominis voluntati*, vel unius Concilii, tunc fit; quando unusquisque eorum unicuique caeterorum se Pacto obligat, ad non resistendum voluntati illius hominis, vel illius Concilii cui se submiserit.'

sovereign representative.[119] As soon as such a sovereign is chosen, the commonwealth is duly instituted in the form of a single body united by virtue of having acquired a soul or *anima* to act on its behalf.

With these definitions of justice and covenanting firmly in place, Hobbes is ready to deduce their necessary consequences. He first turns to this task in chapter VII, the argument of which can be summarised as follows. He has shown that, when we institute a civil association, we do so by covenanting between ourselves to decide who shall be sovereign. It follows that no covenants pass between sovereigns and their subjects. But he has also shown that, when we speak of injury and injustice, we are speaking about the violation of covenants. It follows that no actions taken by sovereigns against their subjects can ever be counted as instances of injury or injustice. This crucial inference is drawn in section XIV in Hobbes's most self-consciously demonstrative style:

> Because we have shown above, in articles 7, 9 and 12 that those who are installed in *supreme power* in commonwealths are not bound by any covenants to anyone, it follows that they cannot do any *injury* to their subjects. For *injury*, according to the definition given above in the third article of chapter III, is nothing other than the violation of covenants.[120]

This is not to deny, Hobbes adds, that 'it is possible for *a sovereign people*, or *an aristocratic assembly*, or a *Monarch* to transgress in various ways against other laws of nature'.[121] It is possible for them to do so 'by acting with *cruelty*, or *iniquity*, or *contumely*, or by indulging in other vices that do not fall under the strict and accurate meaning of the term *injury*'.[122] As Hobbes makes clear, however, this by no means reduces his original claim to a technicality. For to deny that a sovereign who behaves iniquitously is behaving unjustly or injuriously is to embrace the most absolutist version of the doctrine of reason of state. It is to declare that, as our representative will, our sovereign must be obeyed even in iniquitous commands so long as he judges them indispensable to the preservation of the being and well-being of the commonwealth.

It is in chapter XII, however, when discussing the dissolution of

119 Hobbes does not, however, describe the sovereign in *De Cive* as a representative: he first speaks of 'the Person representative' in *Leviathan*. See Hobbes 1991, esp. chapter 19, pp. 129–38.

120 Hobbes 1983a, VII.XIV, p. 155: 'Quoniam ostensum est supra, articulis 7.9.12. eos qui *summum* in civitate *imperium* adepti sunt, nullis cuiquam pactis obligari, sequitur eosdem nullam civibus posse facere *iniuriam*. Iniuria enim, per definitionem supra alatam capite tertio, articulo tertio, nihil aliud est quam pactorum violatio.'

121 Hobbes 1983a, VII.XIV, p. 155: 'Potest tamen & *populus, & curia optimatum, & Monarcha* multis modis peccare contra caeteras leges naturales.'

122 Hobbes 1983a, VII.XIV, p. 155: 'ut *crudelitate, iniquitate, contumelia*, aliisque vitiis, quae sub hac stricta & accurata *iniuriae* significatione non veniunt'.

commonwealths, that Hobbes gives his fullest attention to the implications of his scientific analysis of justice. He does so in a passage of exceptional pugnacity in which he seeks to demonstrate that, if we reflect on the implications of his definition, we shall come to see that a number of widely accepted political theories are not merely dangerously irrational but demonstrably false.

He begins by examining the claim that in any civil association it is always possible to make a categorical distinction between just and unjust laws. This contention had lain at the heart of the natural-law tradition, and had generally been accepted without question by humanist political writers of Renaissance England. As Elyot had declared in *The Governor*, an act 'can by no means be lawful' if it is in any way 'repugnant to justice'.[123] Hobbes attempts to demonstrate, by contrast, that this doctrine is not merely incoherent but is inconsistent with the very existence of a stable commonwealth. He has shown, he claims, that every sovereign possesses the sole right to make and enforce laws. But he has also shown that no sovereign acquires this right from the terms of a covenant. It only makes sense, however, to speak of injustice where the terms of a covenant have been violated. It follows that no subject can ever legitimately question the justice of a law. All subjects must recognise, on the contrary, that in civil associations the measure of justice is furnished by the laws themselves. The character of civil associations is such that 'the civil laws constitute the rules of what is *good* and *evil*, *just* and *unjust*, *honourable* and *dishonourable*, from which it follows that whatever the legislator commands is to be taken as *good*, and whatever he forbids is to be taken for *evil*'.[124] The very idea of a duty on the part of sovereigns to ensure that their laws are just embodies a reversal of the true relationship between law and justice. 'The question of what is *just* and *unjust* depends on the right of the sovereign, in consequence of which all legitimate rulers cause those things which they command to be just by way of commanding them, and cause those things which they forbid to be unjust by way of forbidding them.'[125]

Hobbes next considers the closely connected claim that our duty of obedience is owed only to sovereigns who command justly. This too had originally been a classical doctrine, but had gained new prominence in the sixteenth century as a result of the constitutional conflicts associated with

123 Elyot 1962, p. 169.

124 Hobbes 1983a, 'Regulas *boni* & *mali*, *iusti* & *iniusti*, *honesti* & *inhonesti* esse leges civiles, ideoque quod legislator praeceperit, id pro *bono*, quod vetuerit, id pro *malo* habendum esse.'

125 Hobbes 1983a, XII.1, p. 186: 'Quod *iusta* vel *iniusta* sit, a iure imperantis provenit. Reges igitur legitimi quae imperant iusta faciunt imperando, quae vetant vetando iniusta.' Malcolm 1983 valuably emphasises Hobbes's radically voluntarist conception of law.

the Lutheran reformation.[126] A sworn enemy of constitutionalism, Hobbes seeks to demonstrate that the falsity of this argument follows immediately from his analysis of law and justice. He has shown that all laws enacted by legitimate sovereigns are *ex hypothesi* just. It follows as a necessary consequence that 'the opinion therefore of those who teach *that subjects commit a sin whenever they carry out any commands of their Princes which appear to them to be unjust* is an erroneous one, and one that must be numbered among those by which civil obedience is overturned'.[127]

Hobbes ends by challenging the traditional distinction between lawful rulers and tyrants, and especially the alleged implication that it must be legitimate not merely to disobey tyrannical rulers but if possible to assassinate them. He regards this doctrine as typical of classical and humanist theories of government, associating it above all 'with *Plato, Aristotle, Cicero, Seneca, Plutarch* and all the other admirers of the Greek and Roman anarchies'.[128] Despite this lofty pedigree, he treats the defence of tyrannicide as dangerous and irrational in the highest degree. He has shown that the act of instituting a commonwealth involves relinquishing the right of private judgment in public affairs, since it involves recognising the need to assign that right to a sovereign to exercise on our behalf. But this is what makes it irrational to insist on a continuing right to dispose of our sovereigns if they appear to be behaving tyrannically. For this is to argue 'that you as a private person can take back to yourself the capacity to judge *good* and *evil*'.[129] And this is to lay claim to the very discretion we agreed to relinquish when we covenanted to become subjects. The outcome of failing to recognise this inconsistency, Hobbes declares, 'is an opinion utterly pernicious to all commonwealths, and above all to *Monarchies*'.[130] As he solemnly concludes, 'the effect of this doctrine is that any king whatever, whether good or evil, becomes exposed to condemnation by the judgment, and to strangulation by the hand, of every assassin in the world'.[131]

126 For a fascinating account of this background and Hobbes's reaction to it, see Thomas 1993, esp. pp. 44–6.

127 Hobbes 1983a, XII.II, p. 187: 'Opinio igitur eorum qui docent, *peccare subditos, quoties mandata Principum suorum, quae sibi iniusta videntur esse, exequuntur*, & erronea est, & inter eas numeranda quae obedientiae civili adversantur.'

128 Hobbes 1983a, XII.III, p. 187; '*Platone, Aristotele, Cicerone, Seneca, Plutarcho*, caeterisque Graecae & Romanae Anarchiae fautoribus.'

129 Hobbes 1983a, XII.III, p. 187: 'tu privatus existens, cognitionem ad te trahas *boni* & *mali*'.

130 Hobbes 1983a, XII.III, p. 187: 'pernitiosa vero civitatibus, praesertim vero *Monarchiis*, opinio haec sit'.

131 Hobbes 1983a, XII.III, p. 187: 'per eam quilibet Rex, sive malus sive bonus, unius sicarii & iudicio condemnandus, & manu iugulandus exponitur'.

THE SCIENCE OF VIRTUE AND VICE

Hobbes is far from supposing that his analysis of justice is sufficient in itself to entitle him to the name of a political scientist. As we have seen, he acknowledges at the outset of *The Elements* that his goal must be to provide a fully demonstrative account 'of Justice & Policy in generall'. He makes the point still more emphatically in the epistle dedicatory to *De Cive*, in which he declares that a genuine science of politics must encompass not merely the principles of natural justice but 'the Elements of moral virtue and civic duties' as well.[132] It is true that in *The Elements* he finds little to say about these other virtues, save for a brief discussion at the end of chapter 17.[133] But in *De Cive* he introduces a systematic distinction between the concept of justice and the other qualities indispensable to the maintenance of civic life. Chapter II is entitled 'The law of nature concerning contracts', and concentrates on the idea of covenanting and hence on the virtue of justice.[134] Chapter III is entitled 'The remaining laws of nature', and focuses on a further series of virtues that need to be treated scientifically if a full-scale *scientia civilis* is to be formulated.[135]

It had of course been one of the central preoccupations of English moral philosophy throughout the sixteenth century to list and analyse the different virtues required for a commonwealth to flourish in peace. As we saw in chapter 2, Sir Thomas Elyot in *The Governor* had furnished one of the earliest and most influential of these discussions, singling out four qualities held to be of particular significance. One was said to be humanity; a second was mercy, which Elyot associated with placability and the avoidance of wrath; a third was amity, under which Elyot included trust, friendship and the avoidance of ingratitude; and the last was affability, which for Elyot involved modesty of demeanour, a willingness to recognise a certain human equality and a corresponding willingness to avoid behaving in haughty or prideful ways.

Hobbes's enumeration of the leading social virtues echoes that of Elyot and his humanist followers with remarkable closeness. He puts forward a tentative list in chapter 17 of *The Elements*, in which he mentions such attributes as equity, gratitude, temperance and prudence.[136] But he presents his definitive statement at the end of chapter III of *De Cive*, at which point he declares that the virtues indispensable to civil life are

132 Hobbes 1983a, epistle dedicatory, 'virtutis moralis officiorumque civilium Elementa'.
133 BL Harl. MS 4235, fo. 71^r–v^. Cf. Hobbes 1969a, p. 94.
134 Hobbes 1983a, p. 98: 'caput II: De lege naturae circa contractus'.
135 Hobbes 1983a, p. 107: 'caput III: De legibus naturae reliquis'.
136 BL Harl. MS 4235, fo. 71^r^. Cf. Hobbes 1969a, p. 94.

modestia or modesty; *aequitas* or equity; *fides* or trust; *humanitas* or humanity; and *misericordia* or mercy.[137]

According to Hobbes, the project of constructing a *scientia civilis* is essentially that of giving a scientific analysis of these particular virtues and the contributions they make to civil peace. Although the point has rarely been made by Hobbes's commentators, this makes it clear that for Hobbes the central problem of civil science is that of showing how to transcend the perspectives of humanist culture by providing an analysis of these virtues according to the canons of science.[138] The problem of doing so is said to take the same form as in the case of the basic social virtue of justice. We need in the first place to define the terms we use to describe the virtues in question, ensuring that our definitions are at once respectful of common usage and at the same time purged of ambiguity. We also need to discover some purely empirical criterion for identifying instances of each virtue, so that the terms we apply to describe them remain free of distortion by passion or prejudice. We again need to ensure, in other words, that we supplement our definitions with a scientific test capable of placing beyond dispute the question of whether a given action ought or ought not to be classed as an instance of a particular virtue or vice.

As we saw in chapter 7, Hobbes views these tasks as peculiarly difficult in the case of the terms we employ to describe and appraise moral behaviour. This is the problem he outlines at the end of chapter III of *De Cive*.[139] The root of the difficulty lies in the fact that the names of the virtues and vices are generally 'imposed on things in order to indicate either the desire or the aversion of those by whom the things in question are named'.[140] But as he has already stressed, and now repeats, 'the desires of men are diverse, depending as they do on the diversity of their temperaments, their customs and their attitudes'.[141] This is nowhere more evident than 'in the things pertaining to life's public activities, where we not only find one person *commending* (that is, calling *good*) something that another person *denounces* (that is, calls *evil*); in very many cases we find the same person at different times both *praising* and *censuring*

137 Hobbes 1983a, III.XXXI, p. 120.

138 That Hobbes is in this sense a theorist of the virtues has, however, been powerfully argued in Boonin-Vail, 1994, esp. pp. 106–23, where generous acknowledgment is made to my own attempt (Skinner 1991) to sketch a similar case. One ought also to take note – as Boonin-Vail duly does – of similar arguments in Sorell 1988 and Dietz 1990. Cf. also Gert 1988.

139 Here I draw on my discussion in Skinner 1991, esp. pp. 33–5.

140 Hobbes 1983a, III.XXXI, p. 119: 'imposita ad significandum appetitum, vel adversionem eorum a quibus sic nominantur'.

141 Hobbes 1983a, III.XXXI, p. 119: 'Appetitus autem hominum pro diversis eorum temperamentis, consuetudinibus, opinionibusque, diversi sunt.'

the same thing'.[142] The outcome is that, even when people agree about the definitions of the virtues, 'they may still disagree about their nature and about the sort of thing in which each of these qualities may be said to reside'.[143] The remaining problem, in short, is the one identified and exacerbated by the rhetorical technique of paradiastolic redescription: we may still disagree about whether or not some particular action deserves to be described by the name of one of the virtues.

Hobbes also emphasises the dangerous implications of these disagreements for the stability of commonwealths. As he puts it in the same passage, 'so long as *good* and *evil* are measured by the mere diversity of present desires, and hence by a corresponding diversity of yardsticks, those who act in this way will find themselves still living in a state of war'.[144] Unless we can find a scientific method of overcoming the problems raised by the technique of rhetorical redescription, and thus of stabilising the language of moral appraisal, we shall find ourselves condemned to discovering at first hand how quickly political anarchy follows from anarchy in the use of evaluative terms.[145]

It is true that there is a sense according to Hobbes in which these problems can easily be solved. He presents his solution in chapter XVII of *De Cive* in the course of discussing how we can hope to find answers to the numerous questions not covered by the law of Christ. He first considers how to proceed in cases where there is controversy over the correct definition of some morally significant term. The only possible remedy is for the sovereign to impose his own definition and use his authority to forbid any further argument.[146] He then proposes the same solution in the case of controversies stemming from the use of paradiastolic redescriptions. Hobbes recognises that such disputes will not be about definitions[147] but

142 Hobbes 1983a, III. XXXI, p. 119: 'in iis rebus quae pertinent ad actiones vitae communes, ubi quod hic *laudat*, id est, appellat *bonum*, alter *vituperat* ut *malum*; immo saepissime idem homo diversis temporibus idem & *laudat* & *culpat*'.

143 Hobbes 1983a, III.XXXII, p. 120: 'tamen dissentiant adhuc de earum natura, in quo nempe, unaquaeque earum consistat'.

144 Hobbes 1983a, III.XXXI, p. 119: 'Sunt igitur tamdiu in statu belli, quam *bonum* & *malum* prae appetituum praesentium diversitate, diversis mensuris metiuntur.'

145 Although it has not I think been recognised that, as Hobbes's examples make clear, he is referring specifically to the problem of paradiastole, the fact that he sees a close connection between moral ambiguity and civil strife has been widely noted. See Shapiro 1980, esp. p. 151; Whelan 1981; Missner 1983, esp. pp. 410–11, and the more general comments in Jones 1951, pp. 123–5.

146 See the discussion *de definitionibus* in Hobbes 1983a, XVII.XII, p. 261.

147 It might be argued, however, that in the crucial passage (XVII.XII) Hobbes is not completely clear, since his view of what it means to argue about definitions might appear to embrace both types of dispute. Elsewhere, however, he marks a clear distinction between disputes about definitions and disputes about their application and use. See for example BL Harl. MS 4235 fo. 142^r. (Cf. Hobbes 1969a, p. 189.)

about 'whether someone has reasoned aright' in the application of some particular evaluative term.[148] But the only possible remedy will again be for the sovereign to decide. Only if he brings his authority to bear as a final arbiter will it be possible to forestall the endless quarrelling that will otherwise ensue.

Hobbes adds an example – later repeated and much developed by Locke[149] – in order to clarify this draconian reaction to the dangers of paradiastolic speech. He first mentions it in part II chapter 10 of *The Elements*, later repeating it in chapter XVII of *De Cive*.[150] The example relates to the concept of *humanitas*, one of the five leading social virtues he had earlier itemised. He begins by noting that in certain circumstances a question may arise as to whether someone should be regarded as fully human. The situation he considers is 'that in which a woman gives birth to an infant of a strange and deformed shape'.[151] When such an infant is born, 'there will be a question as to whether it can rightly be described as a man'.[152] This is not of course a question about the definition of the word *man*. As Hobbes remarks, 'we have no reason to go to the Aristotelian definition, according to which Man is a rational Animal'.[153] The question is whether the infant's condition is such that it deserves to be classified as an instance of a rational animal, and hence as a man. As Hobbes indicates, much may depend on whether this powerfully normative description is applied or withheld. For example, if it is decided that the infant is rightly to be described as fully human, then it cannot lawfully be killed.[154] How then is the question to be resolved?

Hobbes reiterates his basic contention that 'no one can possibly doubt that it must be the sovereign who makes the judgment'.[155] He must use his absolute authority to arbitrate, and his subjects must accept his arbitration – as in all matters pertaining to the being and well-being of the commonwealth – as final and beyond appeal.[156] Hobbes states the conclusion as firmly as possible in the final chapter of *The Elements of Law*:

148 Hobbes 1983a, XVII.XII, p. 261: 'an quis recte ratiocinatus'.

149 See Locke 1979, III.VI.25, pp. 452–4 and IV.IV. 13–16, pp. 569–73.

150 See BL Harl. MS 4235, fo. 142r (and cf. Hobbes 1969a, p. 189) and Hobbes 1983a, XVII.XII, pp. 261–2.

151 Hobbes 1983a, XVII.XII, p. 261: 'si mulier partum ediderit formae insolitae'. For the phrase 'strange and deformed' see BL Harl. MS 4235, fo. 142r, and cf. Hobbes 1969a, p. 189.

152 Hobbes 1983a, XVII.XII, p. 261: 'nascitur quaestio an partus sit homo'.

153 Hobbes 1983a, XVII.XII, p. 261: 'nulla habita ratione definitionis Aristotelicae, quod, Homo sit Animal rationale'.

154 Hobbes 1983a, XVII.XI, p. 261. Cf. Skinner 1991, p. 54.

155 Hobbes 1983a, XVII.XII, p. 261: 'Nemo dubitat quin iudicabit civitas'; more exactly, the judgment is made by the 'Person' of the *civitas*, and thus by the sovereign. On these equivalences see Hobbes 1983a, V.IX–XII, pp. 89–90.

156 For the fact that the sovereign acts in such circumstances as an arbitrator, see BL Harl. MS

Consequently the civill Lawes are to all subjects the measures of their Actions, whereby to determine whether they be right or wronge, profittable or unprofittable, vertuous or vitious, and by them the use, and definition of all names not agreed upon, and tending to Controversie, shall be established.[157]

This is the moral to be drawn not just from the story of the strange birth but from all other such cases.

It still remains, however, to ask whether the sovereign's ruling need be arbitrary in the pejorative sense,[158] or whether there is any scientific test by means of which the correctness or otherwise of applying any particular evaluative term can be vindicated. It is Hobbes's belief, as chapter III of *De Cive* makes clear, that he has in fact discovered such a test. This means that he has succeeded, he proclaims, in finding a remedy for a problem which no philosopher has hitherto been able to solve.[159] As a result, he has been able to place on a genuinely scientific footing the analysis not merely of justice but of all the other leading virtues of civic life. This is what entitles him, as he later declares in *Leviathan*, to be hailed as the inventor of 'the science of Vertue and Vice'.[160]

To understand Hobbes's solution to the problems raised by rhetorical redescription, we need to begin by recalling three connected arguments that go to make up the psychological grounding of his theory of the state. He first claims that, by necessity of nature, we all desire to avoid that greatest enemy of nature, death. This being so, it is natural for us to act to preserve ourselves, with the result that no such actions can be stigmatised as contrary to right.[161] His second and deeply pessimistic contention is that, since we are all more or less equal, the state in which we attempt to exercise this equal right of self-preservation will prove to be a state of war.[162] Worse than this, it will prove to be a war of all against all, a *bellum omnium in omnes*.[163] His third and more optimistic suggestion is that, as soon as this danger becomes apparent, all of us will recognise the need to avoid

4235, fos. 68^v–69^r and cf. Hobbes 1969a, pp. 90–1. Hobbes may have had in mind that, as his own translation of Aristotle's *Rhetoric* puts it, actions of equity require one to submit 'to the sentence of an Arbitrator, rather then of a Judge'. See Hobbes 1986, p. 62. On the other hand, he prefers to speak in *De Cive* of *iudicium* or judgment. See Hobbes 1983a, VI.IX, p. 139, and XIV.XVII, pp. 213–14. Whichever way Hobbes' conceives of the sovereign's role, it would seem that, within a Hobbesian polity, subjects would merely be informed rather than taught about the character of moral discourse.

157 BL Harl. MS 4235, fo. 142^r. Cf. Hobbes 1969a, p. 189.

158 As is implied – wrongly I now feel – in Skinner 1991, pp. 54–6.

159 Hobbes 1983a, III.XXXII, p. 120.

160 Hobbes 1991, p. 111.

161 See BL Harl. MS 4235, fos. 54^v–55^r. Cf. Hobbes 1969a, pp. 70–1, and Hobbes 1983a, I.VIII–X, pp. 94–5.

162 BL Harl. MS 4235, fos. 56^v–57^r. Cf. Hobbes 1969a, p. 73.

163 Hobbes 1983a, I.XII, p. 96.

war and seek peace in the name of preserving ourselves. This is at once a natural reaction and is further prompted by our capacity to foresee the unintended consequences of our unfettered behaviour. We may thus speak of it both as a dictate of reason and as a law of nature. It follows that the fundamental dictate of reason, and hence the first law of nature, must be *quaerere pacem*, to seek peace as the only means of preserving ourselves from death.[164]

To this analysis Hobbes adds a further suggestion which is only adumbrated in *The Elements* but is systematically explored in chapter III of *De Cive*. If the fundamental law of nature prescribes the seeking of peace, the rest of the laws of nature must prescribe ancillary lines of conduct similarly dictated by reason for attaining a secure and peaceable life. Describing these further laws in chapter III, Hobbes proceeds to itemise a number of specific courses of action we must be sure to follow if war is to be avoided and peace maintained. Always accept gifts in such a spirit that their donors will have no cause to regret giving them.[165] Always be helpful to others and not harsh or troublesome.[166] Always ensure that punishments have an eye not to past evils but to future good.[167] Never deny the natural equality of others or attempt in prideful ways to claim superiority over them.[168] And always be willing to grant to others whatever rights we claim for ourselves.[169]

If we act in these ways, we shall be doing everything that reason commands for the preservation of peace.[170] We shall thus be obeying the full range of the laws of nature. But we shall also be upholding the virtues indispensable to social life.[171] For we shall at the same time be exhibiting the attributes of modesty, equity, trust, humanity and mercy. By accepting gifts in such a spirit that their donors have no cause to regret giving them we shall be showing trust and avoiding ingratitude.[172] By acting helpfully to others and not being harsh or troublesome we shall be acting humanely

164 BL Harl. MS 4235 fos. 57^v–58^r. Cf. Hobbes 1969a, pp. 74–5; Hobbes 1983a, I.XIII–XV, pp. 96–7.

165 Hobbes 1983a, III.VIII, p. 111.

166 Hobbes 1983a, III.IX, p. 112.

167 Hobbes 1983a, III.XI, p. 113.

168 Hobbes 1983a, III.XIII, pp. 113–14.

169 Hobbes 1983a, III.XIV, p. 114.

170 The laws of nature are accordingly dictates of reason. It is true that Hobbes also describes them as commands of God. But he never says – *pace* Warrender 1957 and Hood 1964 – that we obey them because they are commands of God. It is reason that commands us to obey them. See further Skinner 1964 and 1988b.

171 The point is first made in BL Harl. MS 4235, fo. 71^r. (Cf. Hobbes 1969a, p. 94.) But for a clearer analysis, based on Hobbes's list of the five key social virtues, see Hobbes 1983a, III.VIII–XIV, pp. 111–14, and XXXII, p. 120.

172 On *ingratitudo*, see Hobbes 1983a, III.VIII, p. 112.

and avoiding the vice described by Cicero as *inhumanitas.*[173] By ensuring that punishments have an eye not to past evils but future good we shall be exhibiting mercy and avoiding cruelty.[174] By acknowledging the natural equality of others we shall be acting equitably and avoiding the sin of pride.[175] And by granting to others the rights we claim for ourselves we shall be conducting ourselves with appropriate modesty.[176]

Hobbes's fundamental contention is thus that the list of actions prescribed by reason for the maintenance of peace is identical with the traditional list of the leading social virtues. He announces this crucial finding in chapter III, section XXXI:

> By a precept of reason, peace is recognised to be good, from which it follows by the same reason that all the courses of action necessary for the preservation of peace must be good. So *modesty*, *equity*, *trust*, *humanity* and *mercy*, which we have demonstrated to be necessary for peace, must at the same time be *good practices* or habits of mind, that is to say, they must be *virtues*. The moral *Law*, therefore, because it prescribes the means to peace, also and *eo ipso* prescribes *good practices* or *virtues*, and is for that reason called the *moral* law.[177]

There is a complete homology, in short, between the dictates of reason and the requirements of morality. 'Reason never changes its goal, which consists of *peace* and *defence*, nor its means of attaining that goal, which consists of the virtues of the mind we have described above.'[178]

As Hobbes himself emphasises, however, it is important to understand what he is claiming and what he is not claiming about the social virtues and the maintenance of peace. He is not claiming that any virtuous action will prove to be a means to self-preservation as a result of being a means to peace. As he explains in chapter III, section XXXII, 'while *the laws of nature* comprise the sum of *moral* Philosophy, in this argument I have only considered those of its precepts which pertain to our conservation from dangers that arise out of civil discord'.[179] There are other virtues which contribute to our preservation not because they help to maintain peace,

173 On being *inhumanus*, see Hobbes 1983a, III.IX, p. 112.

174 On *crudelitas*, see Hobbes 1983a, III.XI, p. 113.

175 On *superbia*, see Hobbes 1983a, III.XIII, p. 114.

176 On being *immodestus*, see Hobbes 1983a, III.XIV, p. 114.

177 Hobbes 1983a, III.XXXI, p. 120: 'Praecipiente ratione pacem esse bonam, sequitur eadem ratione, omnia media ad pacem necessaria bona esse, ideoque *modestiam*, *aequitatem*, *fidem*, *humanitatem*, *misericordiam*, (quas demonstravimus ad pacem esse necessarias) *bonos* esse *mores*, sive *habitus*, hoc est, *virtutes*. *Lex* ergo eo ipso quod praecipit media ad pacem, praecipit *bonos mores*, sive *virtutes*. Vocatur ergo *moralis*.'

178 Hobbes 1983a, III.XXIX, p. 119: 'Ratio tamen eadem neque finem mutat, quae est *pax* & *defensio*, neque media, nempe animi virtutes eas quas supra declaravimus.'

179 Hobbes 1983a, III.XXXII, p. 120: 'Sunt igitur *leges naturales* summa Philosophiae *moralis*, cuius praecepta hoc loco ea tantum tradidi, quae pertinent ad conservationem nostram, contra pericula quae a discordia oriuntur.'

but rather because a disposition to ignore them will directly threaten our life. One such virtue is temperance, 'which is a precept of reason because intemperance has the effect of bringing on diseases and death'.[180] Another is courage, which is likewise a precept of reason because a failure to act courageously may in certain circumstances cause us to forfeit our life.[181]

As Hobbes makes clear, however, he certainly wishes to affirm the converse of this argument. He wishes to claim, that is, that any action which can be shown to conduce to the maintenance of peace is entitled on that account to be described by the name of a virtue. He is thus concerned in effect to insist on three connected truths. The first is that the list of laws of nature is identical with the list of actions prescribed by reason for preserving our lives. The second is that those actions which contribute to preserving our lives by way of maintaining peace can in turn be described as instantiations of one or other of the leading social virtues of modesty, equity, trust, humanity and mercy. The third is that what entitles these qualities to be regarded as virtues is the fact that they conduce to the maintenance of peace. The vital inference, as he puts it in chapter III, section XXXII, is that 'the goodness of such actions lies in the fact that they contribute to peace, just as actions that contribute to discord are for that reason evil'.[182]

It remains to explain why this inference is of such importance for the science of politics. The answer is that it provides a key to solving the problems raised by the technique of rhetorical redescription in the case of all the leading virtues of social life. For it provides us with an unambiguous criterion, and hence a scientific test, by means of which we can hope to put an end to arguments about the correct application of all such evaluative terms.

Hobbes introduces this part of his argument by emphasising the widespread acceptance of the rival doctrine to the effect that virtue lies in a mean between opposing vices. It remains 'the common opinion', as he remarks in chapter 17 of *The Elements*, that 'vertue consisteth in mediocrity, and vice in extremes'.[183] He repeats the observation in chapter III of *De Cive*. Philosophers 'have wanted to believe that the nature of the *virtues* is to be found in a certain kind of *mediocrity* between two *extremes*, while the vices are to be found in the *extremes* themselves'.[184]

180 Hobbes 1983a, III.XXXII, pp. 121: 'praeceptum rationis est, quia intemperantia tendit ad morbos & interitum'.

181 Hobbes 1983a, III.XXXII, p. 121.

182 See Hobbes 1983a, III.XXXII, p. 120, on the fact that philosophers hitherto have failed to observe that 'bonitatem actionum in ea sitam esse, quod in ordine ad pacem; malitiam in eo quod in ordine ad discordiam essent'.

183 BL Harl. MS 4235, fo. 71[r–v]. Cf. Hobbes 1969a, p. 94.

184 Hobbes 1983a, III.XXXII, p. 120: 'Voluerunt enim naturam *virtutum* in *mediocritate* quadam inter duo *extrema* sitam esse, vitia vero in ipsis *extremitatibus*.'

It is Hobbes's thesis that the solution to the difficulties created by rhetorical redescription depends on recognising that this standard theory of the virtues is false. As he puts it in chapter 17 of *The Elements*, 'as for the common opinion that vertue consisteth in mediocrity, and vice in extremes, I see no ground for it, nor can find any such mediocrity'. He concedes that 'this doctrine of mediocrity is Aristotles', but retorts that this scarcely gives us a reason for accepting it. Aristotle's opinions about virtue and vice 'are no other than those which were received then, and are still by the generality of men unstudied, and therefore not very likely to be accurate'.[185] The corresponding passage in *De Cive* is even more dismissive. Hobbes now asserts that the entire theory of the mean 'is plainly false',[186] and adds that it has misled philosophers ever since Aristotle, 'who have constructed *a moral Theory* which is not merely separated from *the moral law* but is inconsistent in itself'.[187]

The reason for this failure, Hobbes goes on, is that moral philosophers who focus on the idea of the mean are betrayed into overlooking the connection between virtuous actions and the maintenance of peace. They fail to appreciate that, as he has just explained, the goodness of such actions lies in the fact that they contribute to peace, just as actions which contribute to discord are for that reason evil. This is why philosophers have found no remedy for the problems posed by the fact that 'whenever a good action is performed by someone which is displeasing to someone else', it can always be rhetorically redescribed 'by the name of some neighbouring vice', while 'disgraceful actions which please people can similarly be redescribed with the name of a virtue'.[188] They have failed to see that the qualities of modesty, equity, trust, humanity and mercy deserve to be characterised as virtues not because they approximate to a mean but because they conduce to peace.[189]

Armed with this insight, we can solve the problems raised by the technique of rhetorical redescription at a stroke. Of any action whose moral quality may be in dispute, we need only ask whether the effect of the action will or will not be conducive to the maintenance of peace. As Hobbes expresses it, we need only enquire into the 'cause' or end

185 BL Harl. MS 4235, fo. 71^{r-v}. Cf. Hobbes 1969a, p. 94.

186 Hobbes 1983a, III. XXXII, p. 120: 'quod est aperte falsum'.

187 Hobbes 1983a, III. XXXII, p. 120: '*moralem Philosophiam* condiderunt a *morali lege* alienam, & sibi non constantem'.

188 Hobbes 1983a, III.XXXII, p. 120: 'Quoties enim cuiquam displicet aliena bona actio, ei actioni imponitur nomen alicuius vitii vicini; similiter nequitiae quae placent, ad virtutem aliquam referuntur.'

189 See Skinner 1991, esp. pp. 51–2.

towards which the action in question may be said to contribute. If the end is that of peaceful and sociable living, then we cannot rightly withhold from the action the name of a virtue. For as Hobbes has just told us, the goodness of such actions 'lies in the fact that they contribute to peace'.[190]

Hobbes underlines this conclusion by re-examining a number of classic instances in which the application of the technique of paradiastolic redescription had seemed especially hard to block off. One is that of someone performing an act of extreme daring, where the question is whether the behaviour deserves to be commended as an instance of true courage or condemned as mere recklessness. Another is that of someone making a gift, where the question is whether this is necessarily to be appraised as an act of genuine liberality or whether it might be more appropriate to speak on the one hand of prodigality or on the other hand of parsimoniousness. The problem can be solved in these and all other apparently intractable cases, Hobbes declares, by the imposition of his simple scientific test. 'An act of daring is to be commended, and under the name of *courage* is to be taken for a virtue – however extreme the daring may have been – in any instance in which the cause is approved.'[191] So too with liberality. 'It is not the quantity of anything offered as a gift – whether great, small or middling – that constitutes *liberality*, but the cause for the sake of which the gift was made.'[192] The cause must of course be sociability and peace. As Hobbes summarises in chapter 17 of *The Elements*, 'the summe of vertue is to be sociable with them that will be sociable and formidable to them that will not. And the same is the sum of the Lawe of Nature, for in being sociable, the Lawe of nature taketh place by way of peace and society.'[193]

When Hobbes in old age came to reflect on his work as a moral philosopher, the achievement he particularly singled out was his discovery of a test for deciding whether any given action ought or ought not to be described by the name of a virtue. 'Before my work', his prose *Vita* declares, 'nothing had ever been written in Ethics except for some commonly-received arguments. But I succeeded in deriving the habits of men from an examination of human nature, the character of the virtues and the vices from the law of nature, and the goodness and evil of

190 Hobbes 1983a, III.XXXII, p. 120: 'quod in ordine ad pacem'.

191 Hobbes 1983a, III.XXXII, p. 120: 'Nam audere, laudatur, & nomine *fortitudinis* pro virtute habetur, quamquam extremum sit, si causa approbetur.'

192 Hobbes 1983a, III.XXXII, p. 120: 'Quantitas item rei quae dono datur, sive magna, sive parva, sive media sit, non facit *liberalitatem*, sed donandi causa.'

193 BL Harl. MS 4235, fo. 71^{v}. Cf. Hobbes 1969a, p. 95.

actions from the civil law.'[194] Hobbes viewed his main achievement, in short, as that of having created for the first time an objective science of virtue, a science grounded on the laws of nature and hence on the paramount moral imperative of seeking peace.

194 Hobbes 1839a, p. xix: 'In Ethicis ante illum nihil scriptum est, praeter sententias vulgares. At ille mores hominum ab humana natura, virtutes et vitia a lege naturali, et bonitatem maliciamque actionum a legibus civitatum, derivavit.'

Chapter 9

HOBBES'S RECONSIDERATION OF ELOQUENCE

THE RETURN TO CIVIL SCIENCE

When Hobbes reissued *De Cive* in a revised and expanded form in 1647, he added a new 'Praefatio ad Lectores' in which he explained that, by publishing the original version in 1642, he had broken the sequence in which he had initially intended to present his system of philosophy. As we saw in chapter 6, he came to the conclusion in the course of the 1630s that the elements of philosophy can be divided into three principal parts: body, man and citizen. Following this discovery, as the 1647 'Praefatio' recounts, he decided to write three corresponding books, 'in the first of which I would have spoken of the body and its general properties', while the second would have examined 'Man and his particular faculties and emotions' and the third 'the State and duties of citizens'.[1] However, 'it happened that in the meantime my native country, a few years before the civil war broke out, began to seethe with questions about the right of Sovereignty and the obligations of citizens to obedience'.[2] This made it seem a matter of urgency to issue the volume on citizenship and its duties at once, in consequence of which 'the section which was to have been last in order appeared first in time'.[3]

After completing *De Cive* in November 1641,[4] Hobbes reverted to working on his philosophical system in the order in which he had originally conceived it. The first significant piece of writing to which this gave rise was his critical examination of Thomas White's *De mundo*.[5] 'The most

1 Hobbes 1983a, 'Praefatio ad Lectores', p. 82: 'in prima, de corpore proprietatibusque eius generalibus; in secunda, de Homine & facultatibus affectibusque eius speciatim; in tertia, de Civitate, civiumque officiis ageretur'.

2 Hobbes 1983a, 'Praefatio ad Lectores', p. 82: 'accidit interea patriam meam, ante annos aliquot quam bellum civile exardesceret, quaestionibus de iure Imperii, & debita civium obedientia'.

3 Hobbes 1983a, 'Praefatio ad Lectores', p. 82: 'Itaque factum est ut quae ordine ultima esset, tempore tamen prior prodierit.'

4 The epistle dedicatory is signed 'Parisiis Nov.1.1641'. See Hobbes 1683a, p. 76.

5 On this manuscript see Jacquot and Jones 1973, pp. 12–13.

learned Mr White', as Hobbes called him,[6] was an English Catholic priest and a fellow exile well-known to Hobbes,[7] whose *De mundo* had been published in the form of three dialogues – in imitation of Galileo[8] – in September 1642.[9] Hobbes drafted his reply during the winter of 1642 and spring of 1643,[10] producing a major work of forty chapters which he brought to a state of virtual completion, although he never published it. One reason for its non-appearance seems to have been that Hobbes intended to incorporate its arguments into the first section of his projected trilogy, his volume on body. This is corroborated by the fact that, when he eventually published this part of his system as *De Corpore* in 1655, he included a reconsideration of several of the issues originally examined in his critique of White, including such central topics as place, cause, motion, circular motion and the behaviour of heavenly bodies.[11]

Having disposed of *De mundo,* Hobbes moved on to a number of other projects of a mainly scientific character. Recalling this period of his life in his verse *Vita,* he remembered it as a time when 'for four years I thought night and day about the form of my book *De Corpore* and how it ought to be written'.[12] But in fact he appears to have engaged in a much wider range of scientific and metaphysical pursuits. According to Aubrey he not only 'went through a course of chymistry' at some point in the mid-1640s,[13] but also read Vesalius and conducted anatomical dissections with William Petty, who became Professor of Anatomy at Oxford in 1651.[14] He also continued to work on questions about the freedom of the will, a problem he had first broached in the closing chapters of his examination of White's *De mundo.*[15] Hobbes's interest in this issue was evidently rekindled by the arrival at Paris in April 1645 of Newcastle and a number of other royalist exiles,[16] including the future Archbishop of Armagh, John Bramhall. At Newcastle's invitation Hobbes engaged in a disputation with Bramhall about freedom and determinism, subsequently reiterating his arguments in the form of a letter to Newcastle apparently written in the

6 Hobbes 1840a, p. 236.
7 Jacquot and Jones 1973, pp. 22–5.
8 Jacquot and Jones 1973, pp. 12–13.
9 Jacquot and Jones 1973, p. 44.
10 Jacquot and Jones 1973, pp. 43–5.
11 Hobbes 1839d, chapters 7, 9, 15–16, 21–2, 25–6; cf. Hobbes 1973, chapters 4, 7, 14, 22, 30.
12 Hobbes 1839b, p. xci, lines 159–60:

Inde annis quatuor libri De Corpore formam,
Qua sit scribendus, nocte dieque puto.

13 Aubrey 1898, I, p. 336.
14 Aubrey 1898, I, pp. 336–7; cf. Strauss 1954, pp. 28–9, 39–40.
15 BN Fonds Latin MS 6566A, chapters XXXIII–XXXVIII, fos. 370r–444r; cf. Hobbes 1973, pp. 387–427.
16 Malcolm 1994, p. 814.

summer of 1645.[17] This proved to be the start of a long pamphlet war with Bramhall which came to an end on Hobbes's side only when he published the definitive statement of his position in *The Questions Concerning Liberty, Necessity, And Chance* in 1656.[18]

During these years Hobbes also kept up his interest in the science of optics, concentrating as before on the phenomenon of refraction and the mechanisms for producing it. He appears to have completed his Latin manuscript treatise on optics as early as 1640,[19] a section of which was published by Mersenne in his *Universae geometricae synopsis* in 1644 with a prefatory note ascribing the work 'to that excellent man and exceptionally subtle philosopher D. Hobs, who investigates refractions according to the right hypotheses'.[20] Soon after finishing this treatise Hobbes began to correspond with an increasingly irritable Descartes (Mersenne acting as intermediary) about the account of refraction offered in Descartes's *Dioptrique*.[21] Four years later, at the behest of Newcastle,[22] Hobbes returned to the topic again, producing his *Minute or First Draught of the Optiques*[23] in the second half of 1645.[24] Although this manuscript was never printed, Hobbes eventually incorporated nine of its chapters into his section on optics in the *De Homine*,[25] the second part of his philosophical trilogy, which he finally published in 1658.

Having finished these projects, Hobbes appears to have decided on a complete change of direction at the beginning of 1646. After an interval of over four years, he suddenly returned to the study of civil science. The

17 Sommerville 1992, pp. 173–4, notes that, although Bramhall did not read Hobbes's letter until April 1646, he spoke of having received it some time before. Jacquot and Jones 1973, p. 73, suggest that it was written during Hobbes's visit to Rouen in August 1645.

18 See Hobbes 1656, in which Hobbes's original arguments, Bramhall's objections and Hobbes's replies are printed together.

19 BL Harl. MS 6796, fos. 193^r–266^v, a Latin treatise in four chapters dealing with light, refractions, convex and concave figures and vision. For the dating of this manuscript see the introduction, note 22.

20 Dear 1988, p. 6. Cf. Hobbes 1845c, p. 216: 'viri nobilis subtilissimique philosophici D.[sic] Hobs, qui ex propriis hypothesibus refractiones prosequitur'.

21 See letters 29 and 30 in Hobbes 1994, pp. 54–80.

22 See BL Harl. MS 3360, fo. 2^r (Dedication 'To the right honourable the Marquise of Newcastle') and fo. 3^v, where Hobbes expresses the hope that the treatise 'will sufficiently give your Lo^{pp} satisfaction, in those quaeres you were pleased to make concerning this subject'.

23 BL Harl. MS 3360, fos. 1–193. Aubrey states that the illustrations were made by William Petty, 'which draughts Mr. Hobbes did much commend'. Aubrey 1898, I, p. 368 and II, p. 140. Some of the drawings are certainly spectacular, especially the one marked 'Of ^{y}e Organe of Sight' at fo. 6^r.

24 Although BL Harl. MS 3360, is signed (fo. 1^r) 'Thomas Hobbes at Paris 1646', the draft was evidently written in November 1645. See Jacquot and Jones 1973, pp. 72–3 and cf. letter 42 (June 1646) in Hobbes 1994, p. 133, which mentions the work and implies that it had been completed for some time.

25 See BL Harl. MS 3360, fos. 73^r–193^r and cf. Hobbes 1839c, caps. 2 to 9, pp. 7–87.

move was evidently prompted by Samuel Sorbière, who came forward at this juncture with the idea of a second edition of *De Cive*, offering to see a revised version through the press with the Amsterdam firm of Elzevir.[26] Hobbes responded to Sorbière's invitation in two ways.[27] He composed the important new 'Praefatio' in which he outlined for the first time his philosophical grand design,[28] and he inserted a large number of annotations into his text so that – as the 'Praefatio' puts it – 'I shall be able to amend, soften and explain anything that may have seemed erroneous, hard or obscure.'[29] Hobbes appears to have carried out these revisions in the early months of 1646, for in writing to Sorbière at the beginning of May he thanked him for a letter praising what he had done.[30] It took Sorbière longer than expected to see the resulting volume into print, but he was able to send Hobbes sample proofs by the end of October,[31] and the new edition was published in January 1647,[32] a further version appearing later in the same year.[33]

With his own part in this undertaking out of the way by the spring of 1646, Hobbes initially intended to return to his interrupted work on *De Corpore*. He assured Sorbière in May that within a month he would be retiring to Montauban to make certain that he finally completed his book.[34] During the intervening weeks, however, an event took place which made him change his plans and resolve instead to press on with his renewed work on civil science. According to his verse *Vita*, the climacteric moment came when 'Charles, the heir to the throne, appeared in Paris accompanied by a band of followers renowned for their arms and nobility.'[35] The young prince and his retinue arrived around the beginning of July, evidently full of news about the latest royalist defeats and the growing disposition of their enemies to regard their successes as signs of God's providence. Hobbes reports that 'I could not bear to hear such terrible crimes attributed to the commands of God', and concluded that 'although I had decided to write my book

26 See letters 40 and 41 in Hobbes 1994, pp. 125–30.
27 Warrender 1983, pp. 41–3.
28 Hobbes 1983a, 'Praefatio ad Lectores', pp. 77–84.
29 Hobbes 1983a, 'Praefatio ad Lectores', p. 84: 'si quae erronea, dura, obscurave esse viderentur, ea emendarem, mollirem atque explicarem'.
30 Letter 40 in Hobbes 1994, p. 126.
31 Letter 47 in Hobbes 1994, p. 143.
32 Letter 51 in Hobbes 1994, p. 154.
33 Warrender 1983, p. 12; cf. letter 54 in Hobbes 1994, pp. 161–2.
34 Letter 40 in Hobbes 1994, p. 127.
35 Hobbes 1839b, p. xcii, lines 183–5:

Ipse haeres regni Carolus, comitante caterva
Armis clarorum et nobilitate virum,
Lutetiam venit.

De Corpore, and had prepared all the materials, I would have to put it off'.[36] The highest priority, he now felt, was 'to write something that would absolve the divine laws'.[37] It was accordingly at this moment[38] that he began to compose the treatise which, 'under the name of *Leviathan*, now fights for all kings and all those who under whatever name bear the rights of kings'.[39]

By Hobbes's own admission, the composition of *Leviathan* at first proceeded very haltingly. 'For a long time I experienced great anxiety' and could only write 'a small amount at a time'.[40] He also suffered a number of frustrating delays arising from his loss of income in exile and his consequent need to earn his living as a tutor. For some time he had been teaching several children of exiled royalists, including one of the sons of Edmund Waller,[41] but the arrival of the court in the summer of 1646 greatly added to his burdens. He was almost immediately called upon to act as tutor in mathematics to the young Prince Charles, and found himself obliged – as he told Sorbière in a letter of October 1646 – to wait upon his royal pupil every day.[42] As he later put it in a rueful passage of the *Vita*, 'throughout the time when I was helping the Prince in his mathematical studies I was not always in a position to help myself in my own studies at all'.[43]

A year later he suffered a far more serious interruption when, in mid-August 1647, he fell dangerously ill. Mersenne wrote to Sorbière in early November to say that Hobbes had been contending with death for two or

36 Hobbes 1839b, p. xcii, lines 187–90:

> Tunc ego decreram *De Corpore* scribere librum,
> Cuius materies tota parata fuit.
> Sed cogor differre; pati tot tantaque foeda
> Apponi iussis crimina, nolo, Dei.

Hobbes may be guilty of slight exaggeration in claiming that by this time he had prepared *all* the materials for *De Corpore*. But he had certainly completed a draft of part I, and most of part II, of what he eventually published as *De Corpore* in Latin in 1655 and in English in 1656. The draft survives at Chatsworth as Hobbes MS A.10. Jacquot and Jones 1973 date the manuscript to 1645 (p. 86), while stressing (pp. 84–5) that Hobbes undoubtedly based it on earlier notes.

37 Hobbes 1839b, p. xcii, line 191:

> Divinas statuo quam primum absolvere leges.

38 The composition of *Leviathan* was begun, in other words, in July 1646. This is corroborated in Hobbes 1840c, p. 415.

39 Hobbes 1839b, p. xcii, line 200 speaks of the book which, 'nomine Leviathan',

> Militat ille Liber nunc Regibus omnibus, et qui
> Nomine sub quovis regia iura tenent.

40 Hobbes 1839b, p. xcii, line 192 notes that he was 'sollicitusque diu' and only able to write 'paulatim'.

41 Letter 39 in Hobbes 1994, pp. 124–5; cf. Malcolm 1994, p. 914.

42 Letter 45 in Hobbes 1994, p. 141.

43 Hobbes 1839b, p. xcii, lines 193–4:

> Namque mathematicae studiis dum Principi adessem,
> Non potui studiis semper adesse meis.

three months,[44] and Hobbes himself told Sorbière that at the height of his fever he had been unable to recognise the friends who came to visit him.[45] He later recalled that 'I was prostrated by my illness for fully six months, and prepared myself for the approach of death.'[46] These preparations included a confession of his religious faith to Dr John Cosin, the future Bishop of Durham, who was serving as chaplain to the Anglican members of Queen Henrietta Maria's household in Paris.[47] Hobbes began to recover in the early months of 1648,[48] but he was never the same man again. It was at this period, according to Aubrey, that he first began to suffer from 'the shaking palsey in his handes', a condition that left him restricted in movement and virtually unable to write for the last fifteen years of his life.[49]

After this crisis Hobbes seems to have worked steadily on *Leviathan* for over a year, aided no doubt by the fact that the removal of Prince Charles to Holland in the spring of 1648 brought his duties as the prince's tutor to an end. He was then interrupted yet again, less alarmingly but scarcely less importunately, by the somewhat egregious figure of the royalist poet Sir William Davenant. Davenant had been living in exile in Paris since 1646, devoting himself to the composition of his long-meditated 'Heroick Poem' *Gondibert*.[50] This was planned as an epic in five books, but the publication of the first three sections in 1651 aroused so much derision that the rest remained unwritten.[51] Davenant's preface to the published sections informs us that Hobbes not only did him the honour 'to allow this Poem a daylie examination as it was writing' but supplied him with many corrections and improvements.[52] As well as soliciting his help, Davenant invited Hobbes to respond to his preface, in which he had addressed 'his much honor'd friend, M. Hobbes'[53] on the subject of imagination and the art of poetry. Hobbes must by this time have been deeply immersed in *Leviathan*, but he nevertheless paused to oblige. His *Answer* to Davenant,

44 Letter 26 in Hobbes 1983a, p. 314.

45 Letter 56 in Hobbes 1994, p. 164.

46 Hobbes 1839b, p. xcii, lines 195–6:

> Dein per sex menses morbo decumbo, propinquae
> Accinctus morti.

47 BL Sloane MS 3930, fo. 2^r. Cf. Hobbes 1845e, p. 5.

48 This can be inferred from letter 56 in Hobbes 1994, p. 164, and from Hobbes 1939b, p. xcii, line 195.

49 Aubrey 1898, I, p. 352.

50 On Davenant's relationship with Hobbes see Thomas 1965, esp. pp. 208–11. For an appreciation of Davenant see Sharpe 1987, pp. 54–108.

51 Gladish 1971, p. ix.

52 Davenant 1971a, p. 3; cf. p. 24. On the preface and Hobbes's response see Hardison 1989, pp. 219–25.

53 Davenant 1971a, p. 3.

together with Davenant's original preface, were thereupon published together in 1650, a year before the appearance of the poem itself.[54]

Although Hobbes's *Answer* is brief, it is a text of great importance, containing as it does the clearest exposition of his theory of the fancy and its connections with reason and the methods of science. This makes it all the more unfortunate that it subsequently became a source of some embarrassment to Hobbes. As a result of including in it a fulsome eulogy of Davenant's poem, Hobbes found himself a butt of the satire to which the publication of *Gondibert* gave rise:

> *Waller* and *Cowly* tis true have prais'd my Book,
> But how untruly
> All they that read may look;
> Nor can old *Hobbs*
> Defend me from dry bobbs.[55]

Hobbes was clearly upset by the ridicule he incurred, as he made plain when asked some years later to add an introduction to Edward Howard's poem *The British Princes*. Although he accepted the invitation, he felt obliged to begin by observing, in markedly peevish tones, that 'My Judgment in *Poetry* hath, you know, been once already Censured by very good Wits, for commending *Gondibert*.'[56]

Despite the attentions of Sir William, the two years following Hobbes's recovery in early 1648 proved to be among the most fruitful of his intellectual life. By May 1650 his friend Robert Payne was able to inform Gilbert Sheldon that he had recently received a letter from Hobbes in which he had announced (in tones, one might add, of magnificent *sprezzatura*) that he was hoping shortly to complete a new 'trifle'. As Payne went on to explain, Hobbes's promised work 'is Politique in English, of which he hath finished thirty-seven chapters, intending about fifty in the whole'.[57] During the second half of 1650 – working at prodigious speed, and evidently dictating[58] – Hobbes completed the remaining ten of the forty-seven chapters into which he eventually divided *Leviathan*, and made arrangements for the manuscript to be printed in London by the firm of Andrew Crook,[59] who had published his *Briefe of the Art of Rhetorique*.[60]

54 Macdonald and Hargreaves 1952, pp. 24–5.
55 Davenant 1971b, p. 277.
56 See letter 184 in Hobbes 1994, p. 704.
57 See *Illustrations* 1848, p. 172. I owe this reference to B. S. Greenslade. Cf. Greenslade 1975, p. 310. It is not known which chapters Hobbes had completed.
58 For one point at which Hobbes would appear to have been dictating, see Hobbes 1991, p. 237, where he speaks of saying 'either I [i.e. Aye], or No'.
59 Hobbes was still in Paris while *Leviathan* was going through the press; he was back in London by February 1652. See Nicholas 1886, pp. 286–7.
60 Macdonald and Hargreaves 1952, pp. 7, 30.

Crook duly issued *Leviathan* in folio in April 1651,[61] the selling price (according to Payne) being eight shillings and sixpence.[62]

THE CONTINUING PURSUIT OF SCIENCE

Hobbes's restatement of his civil science in *Leviathan* embodies a number of important revisions and developments, the most fundamental and far reaching being a new view about the character of civil science itself. Both *The Elements of Law* and *De Cive* had been founded on the conviction that any genuine science of politics must aim to transcend and repudiate the purely persuasive techniques associated with the art of rhetoric. By contrast, *Leviathan* reverts to the distinctively humanist assumption that, if the truths of reason are to be widely believed, the methods of science will need to be supplemented and empowered by the *vis* or moving force of eloquence.

To say this, however, is by no means to say (as some scholars have done)[63] that *Leviathan* should be described as a work of rhetoric as opposed to a work of science. While it reflects a remarkable change of mind on Hobbes's part about the proper relations between *ratio* and *oratio*, the scientific aspirations of *The Elements* and *De Cive* nevertheless remain firmly in place. Furthermore, this is no less true of the revised edition of *Leviathan* issued in Latin in 1668 than of the original English version of 1651.[64]

One feature that remains constant is Hobbes's suspicion of any theory of politics dependent on the invocation of purportedly authoritative writers and books. Chapter IV of *Leviathan* reiterates that 'those men that take their instruction from the authority of books, and not from their own meditation' are 'as much below the condition of ignorant men, as men endued with true Science are above it' (p. 28).[65] Chapter VII explains that this is because their approach is incapable even in principle of supplying them with genuine knowledge. 'When a mans Discourse beginneth not at Definitions', but merely 'at some saying of another', the subject of his discourse 'is not so much concerning the Thing, as the Person', with the result that he can never hope to acquire anything more than opinions or

61 The dedication is signed 'Paris. *Aprill* 15/25. 1651.' By 6th May Payne was able to report to Sheldon that 'I am advertised from Oxf[ord,] that Mr Hobbes' book is printed and come thither: he calls it Leviathan.' *Illustrations* 1848, p. 223.

62 *Illustrations* 1848, p. 223.

63 See for example Taylor 1965, p. 35.

64 The Latin *Leviathan* generally echoes the new perspectives adopted in the English text. Where this is the case, I make no separate references to it. Sometimes, however, the Latin text expands or further emphasises Hobbes's arguments, and these additions are explicitly noted.

65 Note that, in this and subsequent page references to *Leviathan* in the body of the text, my citations come from Richard Tuck's edition (Hobbes 1991), by far the best available.

beliefs about the topic concerned (p. 48). As the review and conclusion adds, to rely on the reputation of any writer is therefore to reverse the proper relationship between reason and authority. Although the truth of a doctrine can give credit to many, it can never receive it from any writer (p. 490).

Hobbes likewise continues to insist that civil philosophy can and ought to aspire to the status of a genuine science. He first recurs to this fundamental belief in the 1647 'Praefatio' to *De Cive*, in which he speaks of a *scientia iustitiae*[66] and adds that he 'will demonstrate the doctrines of just and unjust and of good and evil with unassailable arguments'.[67] He proclaims once more in chapter XV of *Leviathan* that moral philosophy must take the form of 'the Science of what is *Good*, and *Evill*, in the conversation, and Society of man-kind' (p. 110). He brings book II to a resounding close with the claim that he has in fact 'put into order, and sufficiently or probably proved all the Theoremes of Morall doctrine', thereby articulating the principles of 'the Science of Naturall justice' (p. 254).

Hobbes also holds to his earlier account of what it basically means to proceed according to the footsteps of science. Again we are assured that the first step must be to enunciate a set of unambiguous definitions of key terms. This is the main contention put forward in chapter IV, which is entitled '*Of* Speech'. 'Seeing then that *truth* consisteth in the right ordering of names in our affirmations, a man that seeketh precise *truth*, had need to remember what every name he uses stands for; and to place it accordingly' (p. 28). It follows that 'in the right Definition of Names, lyes the first use of Speech; which is the Acquisition of Science: And in wrong, or no Definitions, lyes the first abuse; from which proceed all false and senseless Tenets' (p. 28). The point is underlined in the attack on 'vain philosophy' in chapter XLVI. Hobbes now speaks of 'a certain *Philosophia prima*, on which all other Philosophy ought to depend', adding that it 'consisteth principally in right limiting of the significations of such Appellations, or Names, as are of all others the most Universall: Which Limitations serve to avoid ambiguity and aequivocation in Reasoning; and are commonly called Definitions' (p. 463).

Once these definitions are settled, the next and crucial step must be to infer their necessary consequences. Hobbes initially recurs to this claim in chapter V, the chapter entitled '*Of* Reason, and Science'. He now declares that 'by this word *Reason*, when wee reckon it amongst the Faculties of the

66 Hobbes 1983a, 'Praefatio ad Lectores', p. 78.
67 Hobbes 1983a, 'Praefatio ad Lectores', p. 79: 'rationibusque firmissimis ostenderit, Doctrinas de justo & injusto, bono & malo'.

mind', we should understand 'nothing but *Reckoning* (that is, Adding and Subtracting) of the Consequences of generall names agreed upon for the *marking* and *signifying* of our thoughts' (p. 32). This enables him to restate and elaborate his earlier definition of science (p. 35):

> By this it appears that Reason is not as Sense, and Memory, borne with us; nor gotten by Experience onely, as Prudence is; but attayned by Industry; first in apt imposing of Names; and secondly by getting a good and orderly Method in proceeding from the Elements, which are Names, to Assertions made by connexion of one of them to another; and so to Syllogismes, which are the connexions of one Assertion to another, till we come to a knowledge of all the Consequences of names appertaining to the subject in hand; and that it is, men call SCIENCE.

As chapter VII later summarises, scientific knowledge can thus be characterised as 'Knowledge of the consequence of words' (p. 48).

The outcome of tracing the consequences of definitions is the production of demonstrative truths. This was the juncture at which Hobbes had insisted in *The Elements* and *De Cive* that his method transcends that of the rhetoricians, who can only hope to debate – *disserere* – the problems of civic life. He initially reaffirms the superiority of his own approach in a passage of marked aggression in the 'Praefatio' to the 1647 edition of *De Cive*. He first announces, in an evident allusion to the art of eloquence, that *non enim dissero sed computo*: 'I reckon, I do not merely debate.'[68] As a result, 'I am able to reach my conclusions and demonstrate my findings in the most self-evident style.'[69] He adds that 'there is only one argument in this entire book' – namely, his preference for monarchy – 'which is stated as a matter of probability as opposed to being demonstrated'.[70] The same commitment is no less emphatically reiterated in *Leviathan*. Chapter V affirms that what it means to master 'the Science of any thing' is to possess the capacity to 'demonstrate the truth thereof perspicuously to another'.[71] Chapter VIII infers that 'rigourous search of Truth' can therefore be equated with the quest for demonstrations (p. 52). Chapter XLVI stresses yet again that, by contrast with vain philosophy, 'nothing is produced by Reasoning aright, but generall, eternall and immutable Truth'.[72]

Of even greater importance is the fact that, when Hobbes proceeds in *Leviathan* to put these various precepts about scientific method into practice, he reaches almost exactly the same conclusions about the science

68 Hobbes 1983a, 'Praefatio ad Lectores', p. 82.

69 Hobbes 1983a, 'Praefatio ad Lectores', p. 82: 'evidentissime demonstro & concludo'.

70 Hobbes 1983a, 'Praefatio ad Lectores', p. 83: 'rem unam in hoc libro non demonstratam sed probabiliter positam'.

71 Hobbes 1991, p. 37; cf. Hobbes 1668, p. 24: 'perspicue demonstrare'.

72 Hobbes 1991, p. 458. The point is emphasised again in chapter I of the appendix to the Latin *Leviathan*. See Hobbes 1668, p. 338.

'of Justice & Policy in generall' as he had earlier reached in *De Cive* and *The Elements*. This applies most clearly to his renewed attempt to provide a scientific analysis of justice. Chapter XV repeats his former definitions of justice and injustice, relating both concepts to the notion of a covenant. 'When a Covenant is made, then to break it is *Unjust*: And the definition of INJUSTICE, is no other than *the not Performance of Covenant*' (p. 100). However, 'whatsoever is not Unjust, is *Just*', from which it follows 'that the nature of Justice, consisteth in keeping of valid Covenants' (pp. 100, 101). Next Hobbes turns, as before, to examine the nature of the covenants giving rise to commonwealths. Here he introduces an important refinement by declaring that such covenants have the effect of bringing into existence an artificial person. Although the notion of legal personality had been present in both the previous recensions of his political theory,[73] his analysis in chapter XVI of *Leviathan* of 'Persons, Authors *and things Personated*' is without parallel in any of his earlier works. Hobbes is chiefly interested in those 'Persons Artificiall' who may be said to 'have their words and actions *Owned* by those whom they represent' (p. 112). When this happens, 'the Person is the *Actor*; and he that owneth his words and actions is the AUTHOR: In which case the Actor acteth by Authority' (p. 112). When he goes on to ask in chapter XVII what form of covenant is needed to generate a commonwealth, this enables him to describe the required act of mutual agreement as the creation of just such an artificial person as a representative. The parties agree 'to appoint one Man or Assembly of Men to beare their Person; and every one to owne and acknowledge himself to be Author of whatsoever he that so beareth their Person shall Act, or cause to be Acted, in those things which concerne the Common Peace and Safetie; and therein to submit their Wills, every one to his Will, and their Judgements, to his Judgment' (p. 120). It follows that the commonwealth itself can be defined as 'One Person, of whose Acts a great Multitude, by mutuall Covenants with one another, have made themselves every one the Author, to the end he may use the strength and means of them all, as he shall think expedient, for their Peace and Common Defence' (p. 121).

While this notion of authorising an artificial person is an innovation,[74] Hobbes employs it to derive exactly the same consequences as he had earlier derived in *De Cive* from his definition of justice as the non-violation of covenants. The only difference is that, due to his ingenious reformulation of his argument, he is able to insist even more firmly that any attempt

73 BL Harl. MS 4235, fos. 77^{r}–80^{v}; cf. Hobbes 1969a, pp. 102–4, 108–10, and Hobbes 1983, I.IX–XII and VI.I–III, pp. 134–8.

74 A point well emphasised in Gauthier 1969, pp. 120–6.

to question his inferences will lead to self-contradiction, and will thus give rise not merely to error but to absurdity.

The first necessary consequence is that no action taken by a sovereign can ever be accounted an instance of injury or injustice. As chapter XVIII puts it, closely paraphrasing *De Cive*, 'whatsoever he doth, it can be no injury to any of his Subjects; nor ought he to be by any of them accused of Injustice' (p. 124). The reason, as Hobbes is now able to express it, is that 'every subject is by this Institution Author of all the Actions, and Judgments of the Soveraigne Instituted' (p. 124). It follows that 'he that complaineth of injury from his Soveraigne, complaineth of that whereof he himselfe is Author; and therefore ought not to accuse any man but himselfe' (p. 124). A further consequence is that no subject can lawfully complain about alleged injustices in the civil law. Since there can be no question of injustice in the absence of a covenant, there can be no question of injustice except within a commonwealth. Within a commonwealth, however, 'the measure of Good and Evill actions is the Civill Law; and the Judge the Legislator, who is alwayes the Representative of the Commonwealth'.[75] It follows, as *De Cive* had already intimated, that any claim to judge the justice of a law will involve an absurdity, that of claiming the right to question the standard of justice itself. The final consequence Hobbes draws is that no subject can ever lawfully pit his conscience against the law. Here he begins by laying it down that 'a mans Conscience, and his Judgement is the same thing' (p. 223). He then reminds us that, according to his theory of covenants, to say of a man that he is subject to the artificial person of a sovereign is to say that he must have covenanted to hand over his right of private judgment to be exercised on his behalf through the medium of the law. But this is to say that 'the Law is the publique Conscience', and that every subject 'hath already undertaken to be guided' by it (p. 223). Once again it follows that any attempt to question the sovereign's decisions merely leads to incoherence.

If we turn from Hobbes's analysis of justice to his wider concern with 'the science of virtue and vice', we encounter the same attempt to restate – and at the same time to revise and strengthen – the arguments already put forward in *The Elements* and *De Cive*. As we saw in chapter 7, these earlier

[75] Hobbes 1991, p. 223. Hobbes appears at first to have carried this conclusion even further, for in the presentation manuscript copy of *Leviathan*, evidently completed just before publication, another hundred words or so are added at this point. See BL Egerton MS 1910, fo. 108^{v}. Hobbes seems to have thought better of the addition, however, for the lines are heavily cancelled (and are illegible) and make no appearance in the printed text. This is the one major cancellation in the manuscript version of the text. On the manuscript see Tricaud 1979, esp. pp. 411–13; on its date see Tuck's valuable 'Note on the text' in Hobbes 1991, pp. xxvii–xxxvii.

works had located the chief obstacle to constructing a science of morality in the rhetorical technique of paradiastolic redescription, and hence in the capacity to make the vices appear as virtues and the virtues as vice. This is precisely the topic to which Hobbes reverts in analysing the relationship between the laws of nature and the moral virtues in chapter XV of *Leviathan*. He begins by offering a powerful restatement of the predicament giving rise to paradiastolic speech (p. 110):

> *Good*, and *Evill*, are names that signifie our Appetites, and Aversions; which in different tempers, customes and doctrines of men, are different: And divers men differ not onely in their Judgement, on the senses of what is pleasant and unpleasant to the tast, smell, hearing, touch, and sight; but also of what is conformable, or disagreeable to Reason, in the actions of common life. Nay, the same man, in divers times, differs from himselfe; and one time praiseth, that is, calleth Good, what at another time he dispraiseth, and calleth Evil.

While this account is strongly reminiscent of chapter III of *De Cive*, the discussion of rhetorical redescription in *Leviathan* includes a number of new features. Hobbes now describes the problem as stemming not merely from variations of temper and custom but also of interest. He initially introduces this point at the end of chapter IV, at the moment when he first explicitly broaches the problem of paradiastolic speech:

> For though the nature of that we conceive, be the same; yet the diversity of our reception of it, in respect of different constitutions of body, and prejudices of opinion, gives every thing a tincture of our different passions. And therefore in reasoning, a man must take heed of words; which besides the signification of what we imagine of their nature, have a signification also of the nature, disposition, and interest of the speaker.[76]

A second difference is that Hobbes illustrates the technique of rhetorical redescription with a new range of examples. He begins by arguing, as before, that the problems posed by the technique arise mainly in connection with 'the names of such things as affect us, that is, which please and displease us', and hence in connection with 'the names of Vertues and Vices' (p. 31). He then offers the following instances (p. 31):

> For one man calleth *Wisdome*, what another calleth *feare*; and one *cruelty*, what another *justice*; one *prodigality*, what another *magnanimity*; and one *gravity*, what another *stupidity*, *etc.*

This intriguing list is very different from anything to be found in *The Elements* or *De Cive*. As we have seen, Hobbes had previously contented himself with two familiar *topoi* from the rhetorical literature: the possibility of arguing about what should count as liberality as opposed to prodigality,

76 Hobbes 1991, p. 31. The Latin *Leviathan* speaks at this point 'de natura ingenio & affectibus hominis'.

and what should count as valour as opposed to temerity. He still alludes to the first of these examples in speaking of prodigality and magnanimity. But he now drops the other standard *topos* in favour of three new cases. One is similar to another stock example from the rhetorical literature: the possibility of debating whether a given action should be appraised as cruel or merely just. But the others are of considerably greater interest, since they are taken not from the usual rhetorical texts but from a number of leading moralists and historians of antiquity.

Consider first Hobbes's suggestion that an action praised by one person as wisdom might be stigmatised by someone else as fear or cowardice. This is not an example mentioned by any of the classical rhetoricians we have considered, nor by any of their Renaissance disciples. As we saw in chapter 4, however, this was precisely the illustration Livy had offered in reflecting on the 'neighbourly' relations between virtue and vice.[77] Even more revealingly, this was one of Thucydides' examples in the passage commenting on the process by which – in the words of Hobbes's translation – 'the received value of names' was 'changed into arbitrary' in the faction-ridden cities of Greece. One resulting misfortune was that 'provident deliberation' came to be seen as 'a handsome fear' and modesty as 'the cloak of cowardice'.[78]

Consider similarly Hobbes's suggestion that an action praised by some for its gravity might be criticised by others as mere stupidity.[79] Again this is not an example to be found in any of the classical or Renaissance textbooks on rhetoric. But it is strongly reminiscent of Plato's discussion in *The Republic* of the democratic disposition to reject as sheer folly any feelings of awe and reverence. And it is even more reminiscent of Montaigne's analysis of differences of custom in his *Apologie* for Sebond. As Florio translates the relevant passage, much of what we commend as civility would have been dismissed as folly by several ancient sects of philosophy.[80] For the closest parallel, however, we must turn to Hobbes's own pupil, William Cavendish, and his *Discourse Against Flatterie* of 1611. The flatterer, we are told, treats honesty as nice singularity, repentance as superstitious melancholy and gravity as mere dullness.[81] As we saw in chapter 4, Cavendish deleted this passage when he republished his essay in *Horae Subsecivae* in 1620. But it appears that, forty years after his original *Discourse* had appeared, his tutor remembered the example (which he may

77 Livy 1929, XXII.XII.12, pp. 240–2.
78 Hobbes 1975a, p. 222.
79 The Latin version of *Leviathan* speaks of *gravitas* and *stupor*. See Hobbes 1668, p. 19.
80 Montaigne, 1893, p. 299. Cf. Skinner 1991, pp. 27–8, 43–7.
81 [Cavendish] 1611, pp. 41–2.

of course have suggested in the first place) and decided to put it back into currency.

As well as examining once again the technique of rhetorical redescription, Hobbes repeats his earlier warnings about the dangers to which it gives rise. He begins by reiterating that 'the names of such things as affect us' – and above all the names of virtues and vices – 'are in the common discourses of men of *inconstant* signification' (p. 31). This is because 'seeing all names are imposed to signifie our conceptions; and all our affections are but conceptions; when we conceive the same things differently, we can hardly avoyd different naming of them' (p. 31). This implies that 'such names can never be the true grounds of any ratiocination' (p. 31). The disastrous consequences are spelled out at the end of the chapter on the virtues and laws of nature. So long as everyone applies the names of the virtues and vices according to their own passions and interests, we shall find ourselves 'in the condition of meer Nature', which 'is a condition of War' (p. 111). Political anarchy is the only possible outcome of disagreements about the application of evaluative terms.[82]

Turning to ask how these dangers can be overcome, Hobbes answers again as before. Since our use of evaluative language will inevitably be conditioned by our passions and interests, the only method of avoiding disputes and hostilities will be to appoint an arbitrator to decide how such language should be used. 'The parties must by their own accord, set up for right Reason, the Reason of some Arbitrator, or Judge, to whose sentence they will both stand, or their controversie must either come to blowes, or be undecided, for want of a right Reason constituted by Nature' (pp. 32–3). Hobbes later adds that in civil associations the arbitrator must in turn be the figure of the sovereign, and hence in effect the civil law. He concedes, as before, that 'in the condition of men that have no other Law but their own Appetites, there can be no generall Rule of Good, and Evill Actions' (p. 469). But in a commonwealth the situation is transformed, for 'Not the appetite of Private men, but the Law, which is the Will and Appetite of the State is the measure' (p. 469).

As before, however, this leaves Hobbes with the question of whether the sovereign's acts of arbitration need be arbitrary in the pejorative sense, or whether the problems raised by rhetorical redescription can be solved in an authentically scientific way. Here again he answers as before, although with considerably greater brevity. The basic point to grasp, he repeats, is that the list of the laws of nature is at once a list of theorems concerning what conduces to our peace and defence, and at the same time a list of the

[82] This point is excellently made in Whelan 1981, esp. p. 59.

traditional moral virtues. 'The way, or means of Peace, which (as I have shewed before) are *Justice, Gratitude, Modesty, Equity, Mercy* & the rest of the Laws of Nature, are good; that is to say, *Morall Vertues*; and their contrarie *Vices*, Evill' (p. 111). It follows that any actions conducive to peace will not merely be entitled to the name of a virtue, but will be entitled *on that account* to the name of a virtue. Hobbes's crucial contention is thus that 'the Writers of Morall Philosophie, though they acknowledge the same Vertues and Vices', fail to see 'wherein consisted their Goodnesse', since they fail to see 'that they come to be praised, as the means of peaceable, sociable, and comfortable living' (p. 111).

To appreciate this point is to arrive at an empirical test for deciding whether any given action is or is not entitled to the name of a virtue. The prerequisite for accepting this solution is of course to abandon the common but erroneous belief that what makes an action virtuous is the fact that it evinces 'a mediocrity of passions' (p. 111). We must recognise instead that the question to ask, of any action whose moral character may be in doubt, is whether the cause for which the action was undertaken was, or was not, the upholding of the means to a peaceable, sociable and comfortable life. If the action was inimical to such ends, we are bound to assign it the name of a vice; if it instead sought to uphold them, we cannot withhold from it the name of a virtue. It is, in short, the cause and not the degree of daring that makes true fortitude, just as it is the cause and not the value of a gift that makes true liberality. By applying this simple scientific test, the problems raised by the technique of rhetorical redescription can always be solved.

Hobbes never wavered from this solution,[83] and offered perhaps the best summary of it nearly twenty years later in *Behemoth*, his history of the civil wars. As the Hobbesian figure of 'A' observes in the opening dialogue, 'severall men praise severall customes, and that which is Vertue with one is blamed by others, and contrarily what one calls Vice, another calls Vertue, as their present affections lead them'.[84] Aristotle and his admirers have effectively prevented us from seeing how this difficulty can be remedied, since 'Their Doctrins have caused a great deale of dispute concerning Vertue and Vice, but no knowledge of what they are, nor any method of attaining Vertue, nor of avoiding Vice.'[85] This is because 'they estimate Vertue, partly by a mediocrity of the passions of men, and partly by that that they are Praised'.[86] Against this orthodoxy Hobbes affirms yet again

83 He presents it in the same form in the Latin *Leviathan*. See Hobbes 1668, p.79.
84 St John's MS 13, p. 41.
85 St John's MS 13, p. 40.
86 St John's MS 13, p. 40.

that 'it is not the Much or Little that makes an action vertuous, but the Cause. Nor Much or Little that makes an action Vicious, but its being unconformable to the Laws in such men as are subject to the Law, or its being unconformable to equity or charity in all men whatsoever.'[87] This enables him to conclude once more that 'In summe all actions and habits are to be esteemed good or evill, by their causes and usefullnesse in reference to the commonwealth, and not by their mediocrity nor by their being commended.'[88]

THE INDISPENSABILITY OF ELOQUENCE

Although Hobbes continued to pursue his scientific aspirations in *Leviathan*, he undoubtedly exhibits a new willingness in this final version of his civil philosophy to combine the methods of science with the persuasive force of eloquence. To say this, however, is by no means to say that Hobbes ever came to express any positive enthusiasm in *Leviathan* for the art of rhetoric. He continues to harbour many of his earlier anxieties about its deceiving nature and its potentially pernicious effects on the proper conduct of public life. When he asks himself in chapter XVII what makes it impossible for men to govern themselves by their own judgment, he lays an impressive amount of blame on the rhetorical technique of *amplificatio*, 'that art of words by which some men can represent to others that which is Good, in the likenesse of Evill; and Evill, in the likenesse of Good; and augment or diminish the apparent greatnesse of Good and Evill; discontenting men and troubling their Peace at their pleasure' (pp. 119–20). Later he focuses in particular on the dangers posed by rhetoricians in public assemblies. Chapter XIX declares that 'Orators, that is to say, Favourites of Soveraigne Assemblies, though they have great power to hurt, have little to save' (p. 132). And chapter XXV explains that this is due to the fact that 'the passions of men, which asunder are moderate, as the heat of one brand; in Assembly are like many brands, that enflame one another (especially when they blow one another with Orations) to the setting of the Common-wealth on fire, under pretence of Counselling it' (p. 181).

Hobbes never overcame these suspicions of the *ars rhetorica*, and continued to voice them nearly twenty years later at the outset of his *Dialogue Between a Philosopher and a Student of the Common Laws*. The figure of the philosopher admits, in answering an objection from the lawyer, that the art of rhetoric is indispensable in successful pleading, but he voices the

87 St John's MS 13, p. 40.
88 St John's MS 13, p. 41.

concession in such a way as to make plain his deep distrust of the art involved:

> A Pleader commonly thinks he ought to say all he can for the Benefit of his Client, and therefore has need of a faculty to wrest the sense of words from their true meaning; and the faculty of *Rhetorick* to seduce the Jury, and sometimes the Judge also.[89]

The image of rhetoric as seductive, a means of captivating and deceiving us, recurs yet again in Hobbes's verse *Vita*. When explaining why he decided to publish his edition of Thucydides, he states that 'my reason for translating this writer was in order to make him talk to the English about the need to escape from the clutches of the rhetoricians whom they were in the process of consulting at that time'.[90] And when speaking in praise of his friend Marin Mersenne, one of the reasons he gives for his admiration is that Mersenne was not only a learned man, but someone who wrote about his researches and those of his associates 'in a clear and correct style, innocent of any ambition or deceit, and innocent at the same time of any rhetorical figures or ambiguities'.[91]

Besides these general expressions of hostility, Hobbes includes in *Leviathan* a number of specific criticisms of the classical theory of eloquence. He renews his attack on *inventio*, concentrating as before on the doctrine of *loci communes* and the associated claim that specific arguments must always be supported by broader maxims of recognised sententiousness. He rounds off his discussion of science in chapter v with a forthright denunciation of exactly this approach. To allow oneself to 'be guided by generall sentences read in Authors' is nothing better than 'a signe of folly, and generally scorned by the name of Pedantry' (p. 37). Chapter xxv returns to the attack on 'rash and unevident inferences' of the kind 'fetched onely from Examples or authority of Books' (p. 180). The aim of speaking in this fashion is 'to be thought eloquent, and also learned in the Politiques' (p. 181). But the effect is to produce mere patchworks 'made up of the divers colored threds or shreds of Authors' (p. 181).

Hobbes also raises a number of doubts about rhetorical *elocutio*, insisting in particular on the need to avoid excessive use of the figures and tropes. A similar warning had been sounded by the classical rhetoricians themselves, but Hobbes places much greater emphasis on the range of circumstances

89 Hobbes 1971b, p. 56.

90 Hobbes 1839b, p. lxxxviii, lines 83–4. But here I have preferred Hobbes's emendation of his text in the Chatsworth manuscript. See Hobbes MS A.6:

> Hunc ego scriptorem feci, ut loqueretur ad Anglos,
> Consultaturi rhetoras ut fugerent.

91 Hobbes 1839b, p. xci, lines 171–2:

> Perspicuo et proprio sermone, carente figuris
> Rhetoricis, gnomis, ambitione, dolo.

in which he regards it as inappropriate and even dishonest to add *ornatus* to one's speech. He first lays it down that the tropes, and especially the master trope of metaphor, must never be used with the intention to deceive.[92] This is not to deny that the verbal ambiguities inherent in metaphor can be exploited in innocent ways.[93] Hobbes is even willing to allow that, as he puts it in discussing the intellectual virtues, 'in profest remissnesse of mind, and familiar company, a man may play with the sounds and aequivocall significations of words; and that many times with encounters of extraordinary Fancy' (p. 52). Nor should we fear that such ambiguities need act as serious barriers to communication, if only because metaphors are avowedly equivocal and thereby 'profess their inconstancy' (p. 31). Nevertheless, when people 'use words metaphorically; that is, in other sense than that they are ordained for; and thereby deceive others', we are bound to classify that particular use of *ornatus* as an abuse of speech (p. 26).

Hobbes also agrees with Quintilian that the figures and tropes must never be used in putting forward assertions and arguments. Anatomising the causes of absurd assertions in chapter v, he lists as the sixth possible cause 'the use of Metaphors, Tropes, and other Rhetoricall figures instead of words proper' (p. 35). This does little harm in ordinary conversation, but 'in reckoning, and seeking of truth, such speeches are not to be admitted' (p. 35). If we fail to limit our use of *ornatus* in this way, we shall mislead our readers as well as ourselves. Hobbes amuses himself by first using a simile and then a metaphor to underline his point. 'Metaphors, and senselesse and ambiguous words, are like *ignes fatui*; and reasoning upon them, is wandering amongst innumerable absurdities; and their end, contention, and sedition, or contempt' (p. 36).

Finally, Hobbes endorses Quintilian's additional warning that the figures and tropes must never be used in teaching or offering advice. He takes up this further point in discussing the role of advisers to princes in chapter xxv. There he begins by observing that the act of counselling is often confused with the rhetorical act of deliberation. As we saw in chapter 1, the rhetoricians had described the aim of speaking in the *genus*

92 Note that Hobbes's attack is on the use of metaphors *with the intention to deceive*, not on the use of metaphors *in themselves*, as is frequently but misleadingly claimed. See for example May 1959, p. 4; Wolin 1970, p. 38; Kahn 1985, p. 157; Shapiro 1980, p. 147; Whelan 1981, p. 71; Sacksteder 1984, p. 31. For a corrective see Prokhovnik 1991, pp. 110–17. This is clearer from the Latin than the English *Leviathan.* See Hobbes 1668, p. 14, arguing (my italics) that it is 'when words are used metaphorically, that is in another sense than ordained, and *when as a result of this* other people are deceived' that we have an abuse of speech: 'quando verbis utuntur metaphoricis, id est alio sensu quam ad quem ordinata sunt; atque ita alios decipiunt'.

93 See Hobbes 1991, p. 25, on 'playing with our words, for pleasure or ornament, innocently'.

deliberativum as that of persuading someone that a given course of action is at once *honestum* and *utile*. But as Hobbes emphasises, a person engaged in this form of counselling 'doth not deduce the consequences of what he adviseth to be done, and tye himselfe therein to the rigour of true reasoning; but encourages him that he Counselleth to Action' (p. 177). Such advisers 'have in their speeches a regard to the common Passions and opinions of men, in deducing their reasons; and make use of Similitudes, Metaphors, Examples and other tooles of Oratory to perswade their Hearers of the Utility, Honour or Justice of following their advice' (pp. 177–8). These procedures stand in contrast with the duties of a true counsellor. 'The office of a Counsellour, when an action comes into deliberation, is to make manifest the consequences of it, in such manner as he that is Counselled may be truly and evidently informed' (p. 179). A true counsellor must therefore 'propound his advise, in such forme of speech, as may make the truth most evidently appear; that is to say, with as firm ratiocination, as significant and proper language, and as briefly, as the evidence will permit' (pp. 179–80). We must recognise that '*all metaphoricall Speeches, tending to the stirring up of Passion*, (because such reasoning, and such expressions, are usefull onely to deceive, or to lead him we Counsell towards other ends than his own) *are repugnant to the Office of a Counsellour*', and must never be employed (p. 180). Whereas the humanists had above all seen themselves as advisers to the mighty, Hobbes exhibits scarcely less hostility to this traditional role than to the more obvious dangers posed by the presence of rhetorical firebrands in public assemblies.

Despite these doubts and criticisms, the fact remains that in *Leviathan* Hobbes abandons his earlier insistence that the art of rhetoric must be outlawed from the domain of civil science. Although he never came to view the *ars rhetorica* with positive favour, he undoubtedly came to believe in the inescapable need for an alliance between reason and eloquence, and hence between the art of rhetoric and the methods of science. This is a remarkable *volte face*, and one that stands in particular need of analysis and illustration in view of the widespread tendency among Hobbes's commentators to write as if the governing assumptions of his civil philosophy remained at all times fundamentally the same.[94] My aim in the rest of this chapter will accordingly be to outline Hobbes's new conception of civil

94 See for example Warrender 1957, p. viii; Raphael 1977, p. 13; Hampton 1986, p. 5; Rogow 1986, p. 126; Baumgold 1988, pp. 3, 11; Tuck 1989, p. 28; Sommerville 1992, p. 3. Cf. Burgess 1990, p. 683, stating that 'there are two major areas of change in Hobbes's thought' between *The Elements* and *Leviathan* without mentioning the change in Hobbes's view of *scientia civilis* itself.

science in *Leviathan*, while the next and final chapter will trace its impact on the presentation of his argument.

To understand why Hobbes reverts to the humanist ideal of a union between *ratio* and *oratio*, we need to begin by noting that *Leviathan* embodies a new and far more pessimistic sense of what the powers of unaided reason can hope to achieve.[95] Hobbes had previously insisted that *ratio* possesses an inherent capacity to persuade; it is capable, as *De Cive* had put it, of dictating and commanding us to accept whatever truths it finds out. However, by the time he returned to the study of civil science in the later 1640s, Hobbes had almost entirely lost this confidence. The first hint of this new scepticism can be found in one of the annotations to the 1647 edition of *De Cive*. Describing what we can hope to discover by the light of natural reason, he now lays a sombre emphasis on the fact that most people 'are either not accustomed to, or else not capable of, or else not interested in arguing properly'.[96] He subsequently enlarges on this insight in analysing the concept of reason in chapter v of *Leviathan*. First he observes that even those who understand how to argue properly are highly fallible and prone to self-deceit (p.32):

> And as in Arithmetique unpractised men must and Professors themselves may often erre and cast up false; so also in any other subject of Reasoning the ablest, most attentive and most practised men may deceive themselves and inferre false conclusions; Not but that Reason it selfe is alwayes Right Reason, as well as Arithmetique is a certain and infallible Art: But no one mans Reason, nor the Reason of any one number of men makes the certaintie; no more than an account is therefore well cast up because a great many men have unanimously approved it.

To this he adds, even more despondently, that most people have no understanding of right reasoning at all. At this juncture he revives a complaint not uncommon among scientific writers of the previous generation to the effect that ordinary people are actually afraid of the sciences. John Dee had lamented in his preface to Billingsley's translation of Euclid that anyone who devotes himself to mathematics is liable to be denounced as a 'coniurer'.[97] Hobbes makes the same complaint, declaring that most people are so far from understanding science 'that they know not what it is', the most obvious instance being the fact that 'Geometry they have thought Conjuring' – an 'Ars Magica', as the Latin *Leviathan* adds.[98]

95 A point excellently made in Missner 1983, esp. pp. 419–21. For analogous points see Whelan 1981, p. 71; Johnston 1986, pp. 98, 101–4; Condren, 1990, pp. 703–5.

96 Hobbes 1983a, XIV.XIX, Annotatio: 'qui recte ratiocinari non solent, vel non valent, vel non curant'.

97 Dee 1571, sig. A, 1v.

98 Hobbes 1991, p. 36; cf. Hobbes 1668, p. 23.

These observations about error and ignorance are reinforced at several later points. When discussing in chapter XXX how the generality of mankind learn their civic duties, Hobbes first reminds us of 'the deep meditation which the learning of truth, not onely in the matter of Naturall Justice, but also of all other Sciences necessarily requireth' (pp. 236–7). He then adds that it is hardly surprising to find so few people willing or able to undertake this kind of meditation. We can scarcely expect to encounter it among those 'whom necessity or covetousness keepeth attent on their trades and labour' (p. 236). Nor can we expect it among those 'whom superfluity or sloth carrieth after their sensuall pleasures' (p. 236). But the truth is, he adds with evident distaste, that these 'two sorts of men take up the greatest part of Mankind' (p. 236). The point is developed with still greater vehemence by the figure of the lawyer in Hobbes's later *Dialogue Between a Philosopher and a Student of the Common Laws*. 'You are not ignorant' the lawyer reminds the philosopher, 'of the force of an irregular Appetite to Riches, to Power, and to sensual Pleasures', and 'how it Masters the strongest Reason, and is the root of Disobedience, Slaughter, Fraud, Hypocrisie, and all manner of evil habits'.[99]

Hobbes also speaks in *Leviathan* with a new asperity and frustration of what follows from such neglect of reason and science. The most obvious outcome is that people fall 'vehemently in love with their own new opinions (though never so absurd)', and become 'obstinately bent to maintain them' (p. 48). A further consequence, as he later observes in discussing miracles, is that 'such is the ignorance and aptitude to error generally of all men, but especially of them that have not much knowledge of naturall causes' that they are susceptible of being deceived 'by innumerable and easie tricks' (p. 304). Worst of all, he adds in his critique of demonology, 'wee see daily by experience in all sorts of People, that such men as study nothing but their food and ease, are content to beleeve any absurdity, rather than to trouble themselves to examine it' (p. 454).

To these melancholy observations Hobbes adds a deeper reason for fearing that even the clearest scientific demonstrations may fail to convince. Even if people find it perfectly easy to follow a certain line of argument, they may still refuse to acknowledge its force if it happens to offend against their perceived sense of their own interests.[100] This stress in *Leviathan* on interests, and on their capacity to set aside the findings of science, not only introduces a new concept into Hobbes's civil philosophy, but one that bears much of the weight of his scepticism about the efficacy of rational argument.

99 Hobbes 1971b, p. 57.
100 A point well brought out in Whelan 1981, p. 66.

When Hobbes speaks of interests in *Leviathan*, he mainly uses the term in connection with political leaders and their sense of what conduces to the benefit of a commonwealth. He speaks, for instance, of a sovereign's duty 'to procure the common interest', and of an ambassador's 'to take for instruction that which Reason dictates to be most conducing to his Soveraigns interest'.[101] But he also uses the term to describe what individuals take to be in line with their profit or advantage. He speaks about pre-political multitudes and 'the difference of their interests'; about 'the diversity of Opinions and Interests' in public assemblies; and about factional groups who attempt to seduce such assemblies 'for their particular interest'.[102]

At first sight Hobbes appears to be arguing that reason remains the force guiding both public and private persons towards an appreciation of their interests. But he also maintains that conflicts can easily arise between individual perceptions of interest and a recognition of what reason dictates. His sceptical conclusion, stated with real bitterness, is that in these circumstances it is almost inevitable that the findings of reason will be set aside. In his survey of forms of government he concedes that in monarchies this can happen even in the case of the sovereign, since the bearer of the artificial person of the commonwealth will at the same time be an individual natural person. While such a ruler may be 'carefull in his politique Person to procure the common interest', he will nevertheless be 'more or no less carefull to procure the private good of himselfe, his family, kindred and friends; and for the most part, if the publique interest chance to cross the private, he preferrs the private: for the Passions of men are commonly more potent than their Reason' (p. 131). But Hobbes's main concern is with the same disposition as it affects ordinary citizens. He speaks in chapter XXV of corrupt counsellors who give advice in opposition to right reason because they are 'as it were bribed by their own interest' (p. 178). He adds later in the same chapter that entire assemblies can usually be expected to follow their interests rather than what they know to be reasonable, simply because 'in an Assembly of many there cannot choose but be some whose interests are contrary to that of the Publique; and these their Interests make passionate, and Passion eloquent, and Eloquence drawes others into the same advice' (p. 181).

Hobbes's basic insight is thus that interests contaminate the formation of beliefs, giving rise to a willingness to challenge even the most palpable truths of reason when interest and reason collide. He first enunciates this

101 Hobbes 1991, pp. 131, 188; cf. also p. 476.
102 Hobbes 1991, pp. 115, 118, 119, 164; cf. pp. 155, 159, 489.

general conclusion in tones of outrage towards the end of chapter II (p. 74):

> I doubt not, but if it had been a thing contrary to any mans right of dominion, or to the interest of men that have dominion, *That the three Angles of a Triangle, should be equall to two Angles of a Square*; that doctrine should have been, if not disputed, yet by the burning of all books of Geometry, suppressed, as farre as he whom it concerned was able.

The same kind of irrationality is subsequently illustrated at a number of different points. The analysis of religion in chapter XII concludes by listing a series of absurd beliefs and practices that owe their prevalence solely to the interests of the clergy.[103] The discussion of scriptural hermeneutics in chapter XXXVIII includes a reference to the capacity of people's interests 'to corrupt the interpretation of texts' (p. 316). The review and conclusion ends by predicting that similar prejudices will affect the reception of *Leviathan* itself. Although its conclusions are demonstrably true, their appearance 'in a time wherein the interests of men are changed' will be sure to inhibit their acceptance (p. 489).

These new doubts were to remain with Hobbes for the rest of his life. When he issued the English version of *De Corpore* in 1656, he began by observing in his grimmest tones that 'I am not ignorant how hard a thing it is to weed out of men's minds such inveterate opinions as have taken root there, and been confirmed in them by the authority of most eloquent writers.'[104] When he published *De Principiis et Ratiocinatione Geometrarum* a decade later, he signalled a yet further retreat from his earlier confidence in the powers of science. He had opened *The Elements of Law* by claiming that, although civil philosophy has hitherto amounted to mere dogmatism, the application of mathematical techniques will enable it to attain certainty. The *De Principiis* opens by declaring that he 'will show how even the writings of the geometers suffer from uncertainty and falsehood no less than the writings of those who have considered the problems of physics and moral philosophy'.[105] The verse *Vita* ends by speaking almost despairingly about his own inability to win assent even for doctrines he has demonstrated beyond any doubt. He mentions the publication of *De Cive* and the fact that it was received with praise. Then he suddenly bursts out: 'Yet who thinks any work of real value, however just its arguments may be, if it fails to fit with their present concerns?'[106] He speaks with equal

103 Hobbes 1991, p. 86.
104 Hobbes 1839d, p. 2.
105 Hobbes 1845b, p. 385: 'ubi ostenditur incertitudinem falsitatemque non minorem inesse scriptis eorum qam scriptis physicorum et ethicorum'.
106 Hobbes 1839b, p. xci, lines 157–9:

Sed quod consiliis praesentibus utile non est,
Quantumvis justum, quis putat esse bonum?

despondency about the reception of his *Six Lessons* of 1656. 'Although I criticise the new geometers as severely as they deserve, I have been unable to make any headway, simply because the error in question has been upheld by famous authors, so that my medicine can do nothing for their disease.'[107]

Given this ever-deepening scepticism about the power of reason to win assent, Hobbes found himself obliged in *Leviathan* to confront a new set of questions about the nature of *scientia civilis*, a set of questions he had earlier seen no reason to ask. If the findings of civil science possess no inherent power to convince, how can we hope to empower them? How can we hope to win attention and consent, especially from those whose passions and ignorance are liable to make them repudiate even the clearest scientific proofs?

These were of course exactly the questions that the classical and Renaissance theorists of eloquence had always addressed. As we saw in chapter 2, Cicero had furnished perhaps the most celebrated and influential answer in the opening pages of *De inventione*. He had laid it down that, if we are to attain wise and effective government, the faculty of *ratio* must never be neglected. But he had added that *ratio* in itself *parum prodesse* – can scarcely hope to produce much benefit.[108] He had inferred that, if the dictates of *ratio* and hence of *sapientia* are to have any effect, they will need to be empowered by the *vis* or moving force of *eloquentia*.[109] Developing the same line of argument, Quintilian had underpinned Cicero's mechanistic imagery by arguing that, if the claims of justice and truth are to be vindicated, it will always be necessary to use the force of eloquence to pull or draw – *trahere* – our fellow citizens towards accepting them.[110]

Returning in *Leviathan* to the humanist roots he had severed in *De Cive* and *The Elements*, Hobbes not only arrives at the same conclusions but expresses them in terms that echo with fascinating closeness these classical formulations of the case. He first hints at this new commitment in analysing the concept of power in chapter x. 'The Sciences are small Power', he now concedes, but 'Eloquence is Power', and is indeed to be numbered among the most eminent faculties of the human mind.[111] He

107 Hobbes 1839b, p. xcv, lines 276–8:

> Tango geometras, ut meruere, novos;
> Sed nil profeci, magnis authoribus error
> Fultus erat; cessit sic medicina malo.

108 See Cicero 1949a, I.I.I, p. 2 on *ratio* and how 'sine eloquentia parum prodesse civitatibus'.

109 Cicero 1949a, I.I.I, p. 2: 'urbes constitutas . . . cum animi ratione tum facilius eloquentia'.

110 Quintilian 1920–2, I.XIV.29, vol. II, p. 364.

111 Hobbes 1991, p. 62 and cf. p. 61.

develops the argument in chapter xxv, in the course of which he introduces the play on words lying at the heart of the classical and Renaissance *ars rhetorica.* The reason why eloquence is so powerful, he now explains, is that those who listen to eloquent speakers find themselves 'moved' to endorse their side of the argument (p. 181). The effect of eloquence can thus be described by saying – and here he actually invokes Quintilian's terminology – that it 'drawes' our hearers into accepting our point of view (p. 181).

A remarkable passage in the review and conclusion points the moral for the proper conduct of civil philosophy. Hobbes begins by associating the claims he now wishes to put forward with the two leading genera of rhetorical utterance: the *genus iudiciale*, here described as 'Pleadings'; and the *genus deliberativum*, here described as 'Deliberations' (p. 483). As we saw in chapter 1, the theorists of rhetoric had all agreed about the goals of such utterances. The aim of speaking in the *genus iudiciale* is that of persuading a court of law to arrive at a just verdict, while the aim of the *genus deliberativum* is that of helping public assemblies to arrive at resolutions useful and beneficial to the commonwealth. Hobbes refers to both these formulae in introducing his first argument, which makes the familiar point that we have no hope of attaining these goals without proper ratiocination, and hence without recognising that 'the faculty of solid Reasoning is necessary' (p. 483). He initially notes that, in the absence of such ratiocination, 'the Resolutions of men are rash, and their Sentences are unjust' (p. 483). Later he adds that his own reasoning in *Leviathan* can be viewed as an antidote to such recklessness, and hence as an exercise closely akin to the *genus deliberativum.* His principal ambition is 'to offer such Doctrines as I think True, and that manifestly tend to Peace and Loyalty, to the consideration of those that are yet in deliberation' about the settlement of the commonwealth (p. 490).

Hobbes's *volte face* comes with the statement of his second and strongly contrasting argument. It is worth repeating in full the passage in which it occurs (p. 483):

> In all Deliberations, and in all Pleadings, the faculty of solid Reasoning is necessary: for without it the Resolutions of men are rash, and their Sentences unjust: and yet if there be not powerfull Eloquence, which procureth attention and Consent, the effect of Reason will be little. But these are contrary Faculties; the former being grounded upon principles of Truth; the other upon Opinions already received, true, or false; and upon the Passions and Interests of men, which are different and mutable.

Hobbes's new contention is thus that, if the findings of civil science are to be credited, they will have to be proclaimed with eloquence, since reason cannot in itself hope to prevail.[112] With this dramatic concession, Hobbes not only announces his conversion to the rhetorical ideal of an alliance between *ratio* and *oratio* but again presents his conclusion in terms that closely echo those of the classical rhetoricians themselves. When he maintains that in the absence of eloquence 'the effect of reason will be little', he offers a virtual translation of Cicero's claim that *ratio parum prodesse*. And when he infers that reason will need to be supplemented with 'powerfull eloquence', he similarly alludes to Cicero's image of the *vis* or moving force of eloquent speech.

Hobbes later announced a further stage of his conversion in his *Dialogue* between the philosopher and lawyer.[113] As we saw at the start of chapter 2, the revival of the classical *ars rhetorica* in Tudor England had partly been motivated by a desire to improve the quality of preaching. The figure of the philosopher in the *Dialogue* recalls this concern at the outset of his analysis of the laws of heresy. Speaking of the various kinds of people who were members of the primitive church, he asks the lawyer to say 'of these sorts of Christians which was the most likely to afford the fittest Men to propagate the faith by Preaching, and Writing, or Publick or private Disputation; that is to say, who were the fittest to be made Presbyters and Bishops?'[114] The lawyer responds without hesitation by saying that the fittest were undoubtedly 'those who (*caeteris paribus*) could make the best use of *Aristotle's* Rhetorick, and Logick'.[115] Hobbes is now prepared to acknowledge that, in the preaching of religion no less than in the science of politics, the moving force of eloquence is indispensable if truth is to be effectively propagated.

In announcing this change of mind, Hobbes closely mirrors the language he had previously employed to mount the opposite case. He had declared in *The Elements* that, so long as his readers 'bring attention', it ought to be sufficient for him 'to show my reasons' to win assent.[116] In *Leviathan* he declares that the only way to win 'attention and consent' is to write with eloquence (p. 483). *The Elements* had concluded that, because rhetoricians 'derive what they would have to be believed from somewhat believed already' and in doing so 'must have Aide from the passions of the

[112] For helpful commentary on this crucial passage see Shapiro 1980, p. 157; Whelan 1981, p. 71; Johnston 1986, pp. 130–2; Barnouw 1988, pp. 3–4; Cantalupo 1991, pp. 20–3, 241–9; Prokhovnik 1991, pp. 120–2.

[113] On the new perspectives adopted by Hobbes in this text see the excellent discussion in Okin 1982.

[114] Hobbes 1971b, p. 125.

[115] Hobbes 1971b, p. 125. Cf. the appendix to the Latin *Leviathan*, in which Hobbes similarly notes (Hobbes 1668, p. 348) that those who rose to power in the early Church were those able 'potentius perorare': to orate more powerfully than the rest.

[116] BL Harl. MS 4235, fo. 11^{v}. Cf. Hobbes 1969a, pp. 1–2.

Hearer', the art of rhetoric must be outlawed from civil science.[117] *Leviathan* concludes that, although it is true that rhetoricians rely 'upon Opinions already received, true or false; and upon the Passions and Interests of men', the science of politics must nevertheless be founded on an alliance between reason and these apparently contradictory faculties (p. 483).

Hobbes is careful to add that it is only in civil science, not in the natural sciences, that such an alliance is necessary. This particular contrast between two different types of science is not explicitly drawn in *De Cive* or in *The Elements*; Hobbes first presents it in chapter IX of *Leviathan*, the chapter entitled '*Of the Severall* Subjects *of* Knowledge'.[118] He appends to his discussion an ambitious diagram, somewhat Ramist in appearance, in which he attempts to tabulate the full range of the authentic sciences. It is true that his terminology is not entirely consistent, since he distinguishes in his diagram between 'natural philosophy' and 'politics and civil philosophy', whereas in the review and conclusion he instead distinguishes between natural and moral science.[119] Some four years later, however, he clarified his position in the course of summarising the different parts of philosophy in chapter I of *De Corpore*. Again he discriminates between 'two parts of philosophy, called *natural* and *civil*', a contrast he takes to depend on whether the bodies under examination are natural or artificial.[120] But he now makes it clear that the subject matter of moral science is a knowledge of 'civil duties', and thus that in speaking of moral science he is speaking of '*politics*, or simply *civil philosophy*'.[121]

Having enunciated this basic distinction, Hobbes uses it to underline his new account of the relations between rhetoric and science. He reaffirms his earlier contention that in the natural sciences there can be no place for rhetorical display. He remarks somewhat tentatively in the review and conclusion of *Leviathan* that eloquence is 'not perhaps' suited to these disciplines,[122] but he restates his claim more forcefully in the opening chapter of *De Corpore*, in which he stresses that philosophy 'professedly rejects not only the paint and false colours of language, but even the very ornaments and graces of the same'.[123] *Leviathan* goes on to add that this

117 BL Harl. MS 4235, fo. 132ᵛ. Cf. Hobbes 1969a, p. 177.

118 Hobbes 1991, p. 60. He does, however, make the distinction in a preliminary form in the 1645 manuscript draft of *De Corpore*. See Chatsworth: Hobbes MS A.10, fo. 1ᵛ. For a valuable discussion of Hobbes's division of the sciences see Hood 1964, pp. 26–30.

119 Hobbes 1991, pp. 61, 483–4.

120 Hobbes 1839d, p. 11.

121 Hobbes 1839d, pp 10, 11. For Hobbes's earlier and partial formulation see Chatsworth: Hobbes MS A.10, fo. 1ᵛ.

122 Hobbes 1991, pp. 483–4.

123 Hobbes 1839d, p. 2. This observation does not appear in the 1645 draft of *De Corpore* which

suggests a categorical distinction between the methods appropriate to the natural and the moral sciences. Drawing this last and crucial inference, Hobbes reverts once more to the language he had used in *The Elements* to mount the opposite case. There he had argued that the art of rhetoric is almost inherently treasonous, and had emphasised 'how want of wise-dome, and store of Eloquence, may stand together'.[124] Now he affirms that reason and eloquence 'may stand very well together', and must indeed do so if our fellow citizens are to be convinced of the truths that civil science finds out (p. 484).

This account of the relationship between reason and rhetoric, and thus between science and eloquence, marks the final phase in Hobbes's progressive withdrawal from his commitment in *The Elements of Law* to the methodological unity of the moral and natural sciences. He first began to retreat from this position in the theoretical introduction to his Latin optical treatise of 1640, which opens with a sharp distinction between two different forms of science:

> The discussion of natural things differs greatly from the form of discussion appropriate to the other sciences. In the others, nothing is required or permitted in the way of foundations or first principles of demonstration other than definitions of words, by means of which Ambiguity can be excluded. But in the explication of natural phenomena another type of principle must necessarily be followed, which is called Hypothesis or supposition.[125]

Hobbes went on to introduce a second distinction between different forms of science in the new 'Praefatio ad Lectores' added to *De Cive* at the time of

begins at paragraph three of the printed version of 1656. See Hobbes 1839d, pp. 1–3, and cf. Chatsworth: Hobbes MS A.10 fo. 1^{r-v}. It might seem that, with this observation, Hobbes goes back on his distinction between natural and moral philosophy. As his ensuing examples suggest, however, and as he later appears to state, he seems to be thinking at this juncture in particular of 'natural philosophy and geometry'. See Hobbes 1839d, p. 7. It is perhaps worth stressing in addition that what Hobbes says is that philosophy *professedly* rejects the ornaments of language. Certainly Hobbes does not *actually* reject *ornatus* even in this passage, which comes immediately after a highly rhetorical exordium (absent from the 1645 draft) in which the cultivation of philosophy is compared, in an extended simile, with the improvement of agriculture, and in which the metaphor of wandering out of the way of reason is repeated from chapter v of *Leviathan*. See Hobbes 1839d, pp. 1–2, and cf. Hobbes 1991, p. 36.

124 BL Harl. MS 4235, fo. 131^{v}. Cf. Hobbes 1969a, pp. 175–6.

125 BL Harl. MS 6796, fo. 193^{r}: 'Rerum naturalium tractatio a caeterarum scientiarum tractatione plurimum differt. In caeteris enim fundamenta sive principia prima demonstrandi alia neque requiruntur, neque admittuntur, quam definitiones vocabulorum, quibus excludatur Amphibologia ... Sed in explicatione Conarum naturalium, aliud genus principiorum necessario adhibendum est, quod vocatur Hypothesis sive suppositio.' On this manuscript see note 19, *supra*. On the implications of the distinction see Brandt 1928, pp. 191–201, and Sorell 1986, esp. pp. 12–13, 21–4, 41–2. Cf. also Sorell 1988. Boonin-Vail 1994 appears to overlook the significance of the distinction when he claims (p. 115) that, for Hobbes, 'to say that ethics and physics are both sciences is to say that ethics is a branch of physics'.

its reissue in 1647. There he tells us that, while the natural sciences are purely mechanistic and anti-teleological in their procedures, the artificial bodies investigated by civil scientists are such that it remains inescapable to consider the purposes for which they are brought into existence.[126] Finally, *Leviathan* introduces the yet further distinction we have just examined. While repudiating the possibility of yoking reason and eloquence in the natural sciences, Hobbes now concludes that in the moral sciences they 'may stand very well together' (p. 484).

THE ELEMENTS OF RHETORIC REVALUED

Besides defending a humanist understanding of the relations between reason and rhetoric, Hobbes provides us in *Leviathan* with a detailed reassessment of the art of rhetoric and its constituent elements. He begins by offering a far more favourable account of the standing of rhetoric among the sciences. He had argued in *The Elements* that, when someone persuades us of something, they cannot properly be said to teach; they can only be said to work on our passions in such a way as to instigate a belief. He had also laid it down that the hallmark of any authentic science is that its findings can be demonstratively proved and taught. The inference is clear: the art of rhetoric, which operates by persuasion, cannot be numbered among the genuine sciences. Chapter v of *Leviathan* continues to insist that a 'certain and infallible' sign of possessing true knowledge is 'when he that pretendeth the Science of any thing can teach the same; that is to say, demonstrate the truth thereof perspicuously to another' (p. 37). But when Hobbes turns in chapter IX to analyse the concept of Science ('that is, knowledge of Consequences') he abandons this categorical distinction between teaching and persuading, and thereby his earlier attack on rhetoricians for merely 'getting opinion from passion'. He no longer thinks of rhetoric as basically concerned with tracing 'Consequences from the Passions of Men'. Rather he classifies it together with logic as one of the sciences concerned with tracing 'Consequences from *Speech*' (p. 61). He accordingly allows that 'Rhetorique' is the name of an authentic science, and goes on to define it – in a phrase that the author of *The Elements* would have dismissed as a blank oxymoron – as the science that uses speech to persuade (p. 61). The point is carried yet further in the Latin *Leviathan*, in which Hobbes feels able to group rhetoric together with ethics, logic and civil philosophy as

126 Hobbes 1983a, 'Praefatio ad Lectores', pp. 79–80. This distinction is excellently analysed in Malcolm 1990, esp. pp. 148–52.

among the sciences 'that arise out of the contemplation of Man and his Faculties'.[127]

Hobbes also reconsiders a number of his earlier fears about the subversive implications of the rhetorical arts. When discussing this topic in *The Elements* and *De Cive* he had issued a number of grave warnings about the disposition of trained orators to foment sedition among impressionable multitudes. As we saw in chapter 7, he had blamed Pericles' rhetorical prowess for hastening the destruction of Greece, and had singled out Catiline as the most terrible example of an eloquent orator deliberately using his skills to undermine civic peace. He had rounded off his discussion by telling the story of the daughters of Pelias, who foolishly adopted Medea's advice and chopped up their father in the hope of reviving him. The moral of the story was said to be that eloquence 'is as the witchcraft of Medea' – a power inciting us 'to cut the Common wealth in pieces'.[128]

If we turn to the corresponding chapter on the dissolution of commonwealths in *Leviathan*, we find these earlier accusations almost entirely withdrawn. There is no reference to Catiline or Pericles, no trace of the purple passages in which they had previously been condemned. Nor does Hobbes recur to his earlier contention that trained orators were largely responsible for the collapse of several ancient states. He now maintains that the commonwealths of antiquity usually came to grief as a result of their own inherent weaknesses of structure and statesmanship.[129] He still thinks of certain categories of people as especially liable 'to stirre up trouble and sedition' (p. 71), but he never reverts to his earlier image of the tongue of man as a trumpet of sedition, nor does he even mention the rhetoricians in listing the social groups most liable to act treasonously. Rather he lays the blame on 'needy men, and hardy'; on those 'not contented with their present condition'; and on 'men that are ambitious of Military command' (pp. 70–1).

A still more striking change is that, even when Hobbes dwells on the dangers of rousing and 'stirring' the fickle populace, he no longer speaks of trained orators as having a special tendency to produce these effects. He focuses instead on the hereditary nobility and those 'versed more in the acquisition of Wealth than of Knowledge', these being the groups he now considers especially prone to 'give their advice in long discourses, which

127 Hobbes 1668, p. 43: 'Ex contemplatione denique Hominis & Facultatum eis oriuntur Scientiae *Ethica*, *Logica*, *Rhetorica*, & tandem *Politica* sive *Philosophia Civilis*.' The claim in Shapiro 1983, p. 235, that 'Hobbes retained the distinction between science and rhetoric' is thus true only of the early Hobbes.

128 BL Harl. MS 4235, fo. 133[r–v]. Cf. Hobbes 1969a, p. 178.

129 See Hobbes 1991, pp. 225–6.

may and commonly do exite men to action but not governe them in it'.[130] And although he recounts the story of Pelias once more, he does so without making any allusion to the bewitching powers of eloquence. He draws a new and different moral from the tale, simply remarking that 'they that go about by disobedience to doe no more than reforme the Common-wealth, shall find they do thereby destroy it' (p. 234).

Not only does Hobbes withdraw these criticisms; he goes on to speak with positive respect of those possessing a talent for eloquence. Whereas he had previously attacked the selfish and destructive ambitions of trained orators, he now observes that eloquence is not merely one of the attributes for which men are most readily praised, but that it deserves to be regarded as honourable.[131] He reveals a similar change of heart when reflecting on the faculty of speech. *The Elements* had inverted the humanist *topos* to the effect that speech is man's greatest attribute, the quality raising him above the beasts. It is equally capable, Hobbes had retorted, of introducing us to errors of which the beasts are innocent, and hence of lowering us below their level at the same time. By contrast with this sardonic tone, *Leviathan* reverts to something closely resembling the rhetorical point of view.[132] Chapter III concludes by agreeing that 'the help of Speech and Method' is what enables our faculties to be 'improved to such a height as to distinguish men from all other living Creatures' (p. 23). And chapter IV opens with a conventional paean to the power of speech as 'the most noble and profitable invention of all other' (p. 24).

As well as reappraising the value of rhetoric, *Leviathan* includes a reconsideration of all the leading elements in the classical *ars rhetorica*: *inventio*, *dispositio*, *elocutio* and *pronuntiatio*. It is true that, like the classical rhetoricians themselves, Hobbes finds little to say about *pronuntiatio*, but it is noteworthy that even in this case he speaks without a trace of his former hostility. He had initially discussed the concept in his paraphrase of Aristotle's *Rhetoric*, at which point he had observed – in an addition to Aristotle's text – that it encompasses an ability to match our utterances not merely with apt gestures, but with the most appropriate '*Magnitude*, *Tone*, and *Measure* of the Voice'.[133] As we saw in chapter 7, however, when examining this aspect of rhetorical utterance in *The Elements* he dismissed these talents as nothing better than a means of introducing ambiguities into speech, and hence as one of the barriers erected by the art of rhetoric in the pathway of civil science. By contrast, chapter XXV of *Leviathan*

130 Hobbes 1991, p. 131. But cf. Hobbes 1668, p. 94, where orators are again mentioned.
131 See Hobbes 1991, p. 87 and cf. pp. 65–6.
132 Although a hint of the earlier sardonic passage remains: see Hobbes 1991, p. 28.
133 Hobbes 1986, p. 107.

includes an account of various circumstances in which a mastery of *pronuntiatio* may be vital to the proper functioning of families as well as commonwealths. Hobbes focuses on the situation in which someone with a right to issue orders may have a reason for wishing to avoid so far as possible the tone and language of command. The example he gives is that of a military leader who finds it necessary to call for some 'soure labour' to be performed (p. 178). In such circumstances it will sometimes be a dictate of necessity, and will always be a requirement of humanity, that the orders be issued in such a form that they can be taken not as acts of commanding but rather of counselling and offering advice. The way to achieve this effect is by practising the art of *pronuntiatio* or 'delivery', the art by means of which the bitter pill of obeying orders can be 'sweetned' (p. 178). This can best be done by using what Hobbes had described in his paraphrase of Aristotle as the right 'tone and measure', and what he now describes as the most suitable 'tune' of voice.[134] He now wishes to claim, in short, that in these circumstances a mastery of rhetorical *pronuntiatio* becomes imperative: those in a position to issue orders must understand how to modulate their words to convey the impression that they are speaking 'in the tune and phrase of Counsell rather than in harsher language of Command' (p. 178).

He also modifies his previous strictures on the rhetorical doctrines of *inventio* and *dispositio*. It is true that in this instance he largely repeats his earlier criticisms, speaking out as violently as ever against the assumption that the 'invention' of arguments involves the collection of commonplaces, the invocation of authorities or the accommodation of conclusions to received beliefs. But there is one aspect of *inventio* which is completely reappraised in his later works: the suggestion that we must always preface our arguments with an attempt to establish our ethos. The classical rhetoricians had insisted that, if there is to be any prospect of winning an argument, we must try to present ourselves at the outset as worthy of being heard on the question at issue, and hence as a 'probable' witness. They had added that, as Davenant was to remind Hobbes in his preface to *Gondibert*, we must therefore find some means of capturing both the attention and the confidence of our readers, whom we must seek 'to court, draw in, and keep with artifice'.[135]

Hobbes had explicitly denied the need for any such devices in *The Elements* and *De Cive*. But he evidently came to feel that he had needlessly deprived himself of a valuable literary technique. The first hint of this reappraisal can be found in his *Answer* to Davenant, in which he begins by remarking that he wants to tell the truth about Davenant's poem, which in

134 Hobbes 1986, p. 107; Hobbes 1991, p. 178.
135 Davenant 1971a, p. 24.

turn means that he wants to commend it. He also makes it clear that he plans to commend it essentially as a work of rhetoric, concentrating on Davenant's *inventio* or 'choyse of your Argument', *dispositio* or 'disposition of the parts' and *elocutio* or 'dignity and vigour of your expression'.[136] However, Hobbes goes on, he recognises that, even if he manages to tell the truth about all these aspects of Davenant's achievement, this will not be sufficient for his testimony to be believed. This is because 'I lie open to two Exceptions, one of an incompetent, the other of a corrupted witness. Incompetent because I am not a Poet; and corrupted with the Honor done me by your Preface.'[137] The only possible solution, he now admits, is to take steps in the face of these difficulties to establish his ethos or, as he puts it, to improve 'the weight and credit of my testimony'.[138]

Hobbes's tone in this passage is jocular, but he makes the same point in *Leviathan* with complete seriousness. In his review and conclusion he insists – in an evident allusion to the discussion of ethos in the *Ad Herennium* – that the techniques of the rhetorician are indispensable if we wish 'to procure attention' from an audience (p. 483). He still dislikes the fact that those who 'have gotten credit' with their hearers can often manage to 'draw' them 'to believe any thing' (p. 82). But he now lays repeated emphasis on the importance of winning the confidence of those whom we hope to persuade. Chapter x declares that a reputation for prudence can already be described as a form of power (p. 63). And chapter xii confirms that, whenever we forfeit credit or incur contempt, we place ourselves on the high road to losing power and influence (p. 85).

Hobbes adds an extended illustration of the importance of establishing ethos when discussing the rise and fall of organised religions in chapter xii. The passage in question has no parallel in any of his earlier works, but is strikingly reminiscent of Livy's discussion of Rome's early religious practices, a discussion subsequently elaborated by Machiavelli in book i of the *Discorsi*.[139] Hobbes's point, like Livy's, is that anyone who hopes to found a religion must begin by acquiring the greatest possible degree of credit and reputation with the multitude. He now suggests, that is, that the rise of new religions may depend less on the content of their creeds than on the success of their founders at establishing themselves in the eyes of the populace as persons of wisdom and sincerity (p. 84). He even goes to the extreme of suggesting that the springing up of new religions may sometimes be due entirely to 'the culture of such men as for such purpose are in

136 Hobbes 1971a, p. 45.
137 Hobbes 1971a, p. 45.
138 Hobbes 1971a, p. 45.
139 Machiavelli 1960, i.xi, pp. 160–3.

reputation' (p. 83). The successful establishment of ethos may be sufficient in itself to induce belief.

It is in relation to the theory of *elocutio*, however, that Hobbes changes his mind about the art of rhetoric in the most comprehensive way. His later writings present us in the first place with a new view of *perspicuitas*, one of the two main aspects of *elocutio* on which the Roman and Renaissance theorists of rhetoric had always concentrated. Hobbes had of course emphasised in all his earlier works the importance of speaking and writing with the greatest possible clarity. As we saw in chapter 8, however, when discussing the ideal of *perspicuitas* in *De Cive* he had sought to separate this stylistic virtue from any connection with the theory of eloquence. If we succeed in expressing ourselves with perspicuity and thus with genuine elegance, he had argued, this will not be because we have mastered an element of the *ars rhetorica*; it will on the contrary be because we have abandoned rhetoric in favour of logic and the footsteps of science.

If we turn to *Leviathan*, we encounter a no less emphatic insistence on the value of perspicuity. Hobbes proclaims in chapter v that 'the Light of humane minds is Perspicuous Words', adding that his own argument is laid out 'orderly and perspicuously', with the result that his treatise is 'clear' and 'not obscure'.[140] He makes a similar boast at several points in his controversy with Bramhall, in which he criticises his opponent for failing to write 'plain and perspicuous English', and insists by contrast that 'I have endeavoured all I can to be perspicuous',[141] and that 'in the examination of truth, I search rather for perspicuity than elegance'.[142] He notes Bramhall's condemnation of *Leviathan* as monstrous and dark,[143] but confidently retorts that 'he will find very few Readers that will not think it clearer than his Scholastique Jargon'.[144]

Hobbes also pays tribute in *Leviathan* to the closely connected virtue of writing 'shortly', a literary quality that had come to be widely prized. Ben Jonson had expatiated in his *Discoveries* on the merits of 'a strict and succinct style' in which 'you can take away nothing without losse, and that losse to be manifest'.[145] Thomas Sprat in his *History of the Royal Society* of 1667 was to praise the Fellows in similar vein for returning 'to the primitive purity, and shortness, when men deliver'd so many *things*, almost in an

140 Hobbes 1991, pp. 11, 36, 254, 490.
141 Hobbes 1840d, pp. 281, 371.
142 Hobbes 1841, p. 325.
143 Bramhall 1655, sig. A, had spoken of *Leviathan* as 'Monstrum horrendum, informe, ingens, cui lumen ademptum'.
144 Hobbes 1841, p. 26.
145 Jonson 1947, p. 623.

equal number of *words*'.[146] Hobbes first alludes to the same ideal in the Introduction to his translation of Thucydides, where he makes it clear that he regards the virtue of shortness as a quality less of concision than of density. He cites with approval Cicero's commendation of Thucydides as a writer 'so full of matter that the number of his sentences doth almost reach to the number of his words', and supports this judgment with a tribute of his own to Thucydides' fullness, pithiness and strength.[147] As with the value of perspicuity, moreover, Hobbes is convinced that he has succeeded in upholding the ideal himself. He brings part II of *Leviathan* to a close by expressing the hope that he may win sufficient readers to 'convert this Truth of Speculation into the Utility of Practice' (p. 254). To which he adds that his chief reason for regarding this hope as realistic is the fact that his treatise 'is short and I think clear' (p. 254).

When Hobbes praises perspicuity and shortness in *Leviathan*, however, he does so from a perspective completely at odds with the one he had earlier adopted in *De Cive*. He now accepts the very presupposition he had previously denied: that these literary virtues form an aspect of *elocutio*, and consequently that a writer who possesses them must be acknowledged to have mastered one of the leading elements in the art of rhetoric. He first announces this concession in his *Answer* to Davenant, in which he not only accepts that perspicuity must be classified as a feature of expression or elocution, but adds that the first sign of knowing a subject well is being able to write about it perspicuously.[148] He subsequently generalises the point in the review and conclusion of *Leviathan*, in which he declares in a rare trope of modesty that, although 'there is nothing I distrust more than my Elocution',[149] *Leviathan* must at least be acknowledged to possess the virtue of perspicuity, since it 'is not obscure' (p. 490). He now agrees, that is, that the perspicuity he claims for his own writing constitutes an aspect of elocution, and hence a feature of rhetoric. He never subsequently wavered from this judgment, as is evident from his final pronouncements on the question of style in his essay *Concerning the Virtues of an Heroic Poem* which he published as the preface to his translation of Homer's *Odyssey* in 1675. If a poem is written with perspicuity, he there asserts, and is at the same time well-constructed, 'this is usually called a good style'.[150]

146 Sprat 1959, p. 113.
147 Hobbes 1975b, p. 19.
148 Hobbes 1971a, p. 52.
149 Hobbes 1991, p. 490. Hobbes's commentators have generally taken this comment at face value. See for example Jones 1951, pp. 80–1; Reik 1977, p. 163; Shapiro 1980, p. 148. But Hobbes surely does not mean us to understand that he genuinely distrusts his literary talents: rather his trope of modesty calls them to our attention, as Silver 1988, p. 371, rightly notes.
150 Hobbes 1844, p. iv. Cf. Hobbes 1994, p. 704, for the claim that 'perspicuous language' is indispensable to 'the height of poetry'.

The other aspect of *elocutio* invariably treated at length by the rhetoricians was *ornatus*, the addition of 'ornament' or 'adornment' to our utterances in the form of figures and tropes. This brings us to the most important change of perspective in Hobbes's later writings on civil science. It is a change, moreover, that arguably stands in need of special emphasis, if only because Hobbes has recently been criticised by a surprising number of commentators for allegedly combining a theoretical hostility in *Leviathan* to the use of figures and tropes with an extensive use of exactly these resources of *ornatus* throughout his text.[151] This is held to give rise to 'a noteworthy disparity'[152] and even to 'obvious contradictions'[153] between his literary theory and his own practice. Hobbes is said to violate his own rules[154] to such an extent – to such a glaring and comical extent[155] – that we are left confronting a paradox: 'despite his vociferous polemics against metaphors', Hobbes 'is probably the most metaphorical of political philosophers'.[156]

As so often, however, the confusion seems to lie with Hobbes's critics rather than with Hobbes. What these unwisely condescending accusations overlook is the extent to which Hobbes changed his mind about his literary principles as well as his practice between the severely scientific prose of *The Elements* and the highly 'ornamental' style of *Leviathan*. What these critics consequently fail to register is the degree to which Hobbes's use of *ornatus* in *Leviathan* mirrors a new-found willingness to endorse a humanist understanding of the proper relationship between reason and eloquence.

The capacity to make effective use of *ornatus* is treated by Hobbes at all times as the distinctive product of a powerful imagination or fancy. He first makes the point when discussing different types of wit in *The Elements*, arguing that it is due to 'excellency of FANCY' that some people are able to discover 'gratefull Similies, Metaphors and other Tropes'.[157] He reiterates the claim – with special reference to poetry – in his *Answer* to Davenant, in the course of which he lays it down that 'fancy begets the ornaments of a poem'.[158] It follows that, if we wish to understand Hobbes's changing beliefs about the value and use of *ornatus*, we need to begin by sketching his theory of the imagination,[159] a theory first outlined in chapter 10 of *The*

151 For a corrective see Prokhovnik 1991, pp. 110–17, and some, at least, of the remarks in Cantalupo 1991, pp. 56–7.
152 May 1959, p. 4.
153 Kahn 1985, p. 157. For a critique of Kahn's analysis see Barnouw 1988, esp. pp. 15–17.
154 May 1959, p. 4; Shapiro 1980, p. 147; Sacksteder 1984, p. 31.
155 Wolin 1970, p. 38.
156 Whelan 1981, p. 71.
157 BL Harl. MS 4235, fo. 41^r. Cf. Hobbes 1969a, p. 50.
158 Hobbes 1971a, p. 49.
159 For a full analysis see Thorpe 1940, esp. pp. 79–117, and Reik 1977, pp. 138–57.

Elements and definitively unfolded in the opening three chapters of *Leviathan*.

Hobbes takes as his starting-point the fact that we all acquire conceptions in the mind from the objects around us.[160] These are originally begotten upon our organs of sense, but are capable of remaining in the mind even after the objects initially giving rise to them have been removed.[161] We generally describe these retained images as fancies or imaginations caused by the objects originally sensed. The faculty of imagination can therefore be defined as 'decaying sense', and at the same time as memory or reminiscence of the various objects we have perceived at different times.[162] When we recollect our experiences, we go through these images in the mind, comparing them, relating them and putting them together in new and 'compounded' forms. As *The Elements* explains, some people possess this ability only to a very limited extent, and may be said to suffer from a specific weakness of the mind called dullness. Others possess the ability to a marked and sometimes an almost frenzied degree, and these are the people who may be said to enjoy excellency of fancy.[163] Hobbes later underlines the point in his *Answer* to Davenant, in which he explains – in a striking echo of Descartes – that a powerful fancy can be described as the faculty that furnishes us with 'images of nature in the memory distinct and cleare', and consequently enables us 'to know well'.[164]

According to *The Elements*, a powerful fancy can therefore be defined as a reflection of two conjoined qualities. One is a 'quick Rangeing of minde', which Hobbes compares in chapter 4 with the purposeful ranging of spaniels in quest of a scent.[165] The other is a 'curiosity of Comparing' the various images that swarm into the mind as it ranges over the memories contained within it.[166] The characteristic outcome of encouraging the mind to roam in this systematic manner is the discovery of 'unexpected similitudes in things', while the characteristic expression of these novel and surprising connections takes the form of 'Similies, Metaphors, and other Tropes'.[167]

Hobbes's thesis is thus that the use of *ornatus* represents the natural way

160 See BL Harl. MS 4235, fos. 11^r–12^r (and cf. Hobbes 1969a, p. 2); Hobbes 1991, p. 13; Hobbes 1668, p. 3.

161 See BL Harl. MS 4235, fos. 12^r–13^r, 15^{r-v} (and cf. Hobbes 1969a, pp. 2–3, 8); Hobbes 1991, pp. 13, 15–16; Hobbes 1668, pp. 3–5.

162 Hobbes 1991, p. 15; Hobbes 1668, pp. 4–5.

163 BL Harl. MS 4235, fo. 41^r. Cf. Hobbes 1969a, p. 50.

164 Hobbes 1971a, p. 52.

165 BL Harl. MS 4235, fos. 18^v, 41^r. Cf. Hobbes 1969a, pp. 14, 50.

166 BL Harl. MS 4235, fo. 41^r. Cf. Hobbes 1969a, p. 50.

167 BL Harl. MS 4235, fo. 41^r. Cf. Hobbes 1969a, p. 50.

of expressing the imagery of the mind, a commitment that makes him one of the earliest writers in English to employ the general term 'imagery' to refer to the figures and tropes of speech.[168] Developing this view of the fancy in *The Elements*, he goes on to mark a sharp contrast between this faculty and the one that enables us to acquire genuine knowledge. The usual effect of finding unexpected similitudes is that those who do so are able to make things appear other than as they are; they are able 'to make things please or displease, and shew well or ill to others, as they like them selves'.[169] Hobbes consequently regards the products of the imagination not merely as potentially manipulative and deceptive, but as inimical to the methods of the authentic sciences. As chapter 10 of *The Elements* puts it, the virtue of the mind by means of which 'men attaine to exact and perfect knowledge' stands at the opposite pole from the fancy, since it takes the form of a capacity not for discovering similarities but for 'discerning suddainely dissimilitude in thinges that otherwise appeare the same'.[170] It is this contrasting faculty, usually known as judgment, which enables us, by way of making appropriate 'distinction of persons, places, and seasons' to offer 'continuall instruction' in the making of true and perspicuous discernments between different things.[171] It follows that, although the qualities of fancy and judgment can both be described as forms of wit, they remain opposed faculties. There is no place in *The Elements* for the possibility that the fancy might be capable of co-operating with the judgment in the production of knowledge and hence in the construction of a genuine science.

If we turn, by contrast, to the review and conclusion of *Leviathan*, we find Hobbes presenting this viewpoint as the one he now wishes to question and oppose.[172] Some people believe, he observes, that there is not only a 'contrariety of some of the Naturall Faculties of the Mind', but that this gives us grounds for doubting whether 'any one man should be sufficiently disposed to all sorts of Civill duty' (p. 483). The alleged contrariety on which he particularly focuses is between 'Celerity of Fancy' on the one hand and 'Severity of Judgment' on the other. Those who stress this contrast declare that any disposition to allow free rein to the fancy will lead us into moral confusion. The reason ('they say') is that 'Celerity of

168 Although Bacon in *The Advancement of Learning* had already spoken of 'images' and how they are 'figured'. See Bacon 1915, pp. 38, 40. On Bacon's theory of the imagination see Cocking 1984. For Hobbes's mentions of 'imagery' see Hobbes 1844, p. vi; Hobbes 1971a, p. 49; Hobbes 1994, p. 275.

169 BL Harl. MS 4235, fo. 41^{r}. Cf. Hobbes 1969a, p. 50.

170 BL Harl. MS 4235, fo. 41^{r-v}. Cf. Hobbes 1969a, p. 50.

171 BL Harl. MS 4235, fo. 41^{v}. Cf. Hobbes 1969a, p. 50.

172 As Cantalupo 1991, pp. 49–50, rightly notes, we cannot therefore speak simply of Hobbes's 'distrust of imagination', as some critics have done.

Fancy makes the thoughts less steddy than is necessary to discern exactly between Right and Wrong' (p. 483).

This is the difficulty that Hobbes now thinks it possible to overcome. He first hints at his solution in the *Answer* to Davenant, generously adding that he partly owes his new understanding to Davenant himself.[173] The right reaction, he now maintains, is to seek an alliance between reason and the imagination, so that 'the workemanship of Fancy' may be 'guided by the Precepts of true Philosophy'.[174] Whenever this has happened – whenever 'the Fancy of man has traced the wayes of true Philosophy' – the result has been to produce 'very marvellous effects to the benefit of mankind'.[175] Hobbes concedes that no such effects have so far been produced in the moral sciences. But the way forward lies in recognising that 'where these precepts fayle, as they have hetherto fayled in the doctrine of Moral vertue, there the architect (*Fancy*) must take the Philosophers part upon herselfe'.[176]

Although Hobbes appears in this passage[177] to be speaking in favour of an alliance between rhetoric and science, the exact direction of his argument is tentative and hard to follow.[178] If we turn to the review and conclusion of *Leviathan*, however, we find him proposing just such a solution in unambiguous terms. There is no reason, he now maintains, why the arguments of the moral philosophers should fail to persuade, and in consequence fail to have their appropriate and beneficial effects. This is because there is no reason why *ornatus*, the distinctive product of the fancy, should not be used to empower and thereby 'prefer' or 'hold forth' the findings of *ratio*, the distinctive work of the judgment. 'For wheresoever there is place for adorning and preferring of Errour, there is much more place for adorning and preferring of Truth, if they have it to adorn' (p. 484).

This is not to deny that fancy and judgment operate to some extent in different directions, and thus that it is difficult for the one to be employed to supplement and 'prefer' the other. But while these are 'indeed great difficulties', they are 'not impossibilities', for 'by Education and Discipline' these disparate talents 'may bee, and are sometimes, reconciled'. It is possible, that is, for judgment and fancy to 'have place in the same man', since the judgment can be 'fixed upon one certain Consideration' while the fancy is left 'at another time wandring about the world' (p. 483).

173 Hobbes 1971a, p. 54.
174 Hobbes 1971a, p. 49.
175 Hobbes 1971a, p. 49.
176 Hobbes 1971a, pp. 49–50.
177 For further discussion see Johnston 1986, pp. 90–1, and Prokhovnik 1991, pp. 94–6.
178 Although it seems to have been influential. See for example Blount 1971, p. 146.

Hobbes adds with a flourish that, if it seems too much to hope for such a convergence, its possibility can be demonstrated by pointing to the figure of his friend Mr Sidney Godolphin, the man to whom *Leviathan* is dedicated (p. 484):

I have known cleernesse of Judgment, and largenesse of Fancy; strength of Reason, and gracefull Elocution; a Courage for the warre, and a Fear for the Laws, and all eminently in one man; and that was my most noble and honored friend Mr. *Sidney Godolphin*; who hating no man, nor hated of any, was unfortunately slain in the beginning of the late Civill warre, in the Publique quarrell, by an undiscerned and an undiscerning hand.

Hobbes's statement embodies a moving and justly celebrated tribute to his friend,[179] but it also reflects a remarkable shift of intellectual allegiances. He now speaks in favour of the very alliance he had previously thought impossible: between fancy and judgment, and hence between the techniques of rhetoric and the methods of science.

But how can fancy hope to collaborate with reason to create a persuasive civil science? Hobbes replies that, for such a conjunction to be fruitful, the characteristic products of the fancy – the figures and tropes of speech – must satisfy two contrasting conditions on which the classical rhetoricians and their Renaissance followers had already pronounced at considerable length. Admittedly Hobbes is not yet ready to acknowledge that his views about *ornatus* and its place in *scientia civilis* are taken from these theorists of eloquence. On the contrary, he is at pains to underline his refusal to follow 'the custom of late time' by invoking the authority of 'ancient Poets, Orators and Philosophers' (p. 490). But if we turn to his much later essay on the virtues of heroic poetry, we not only find him citing Quintilian by name; we also find him referring explicitly to 'the ancient writers of eloquence' as a source of inspiration for his view of 'images' and their connection with 'the perfection and curiosity of descriptions'.[180]

According to the rhetoricians, the first prerequisite of an effective fancy is that the mind must range over the entire stock of its memories and experiences. As we saw in chapter 5, they generally expressed this desideratum by speaking of the need for the imagination, like Pegasus, to take wing and soar. Should Hobbes have needed any reminder of this familiar conceit, he would have found one ready to hand in Davenant's preface, which stresses the poet's capacity to 'mount his *Pegasus*, unhood his *Muse*' and take to flight.[181] The aim of encouraging such flights of

179 The Latin *Leviathan* transfers the tribute to the epistle dedicatory: see Hobbes 1668, sig. aaa, 2r.
180 Hobbes 1844, pp. vi, viii.
181 Davenant 1971a, p. 21; cf. also p. 18.

fancy, the rhetoricians had added, is to prevent the imagination from expressing itself in merely hackneyed images and worn-out turns of phrase. Aristotle had summarised the argument in a metaphor subsequently picked up by Quintilian and many of his followers: if the images produced by the fancy are to be memorable and persuasive, they must never be gathered from too close at hand; they must always be 'far-fetched'.[182]

Hobbes provides an influential restatement of this first element in the classical theory of style. The best summary of his position can be found in his analysis of the qualities of great poetry in his *Answer* to Davenant.[183] Where poetic fancy is truly effective, this is primarily because it possesses 'the strength and winges of *Pegasus*'.[184] A powerful imagination enables the poet 'to fly from one *Indies* to the other, and from Heaven to Earth, and to penetrate into the hardest matter and obscurest places, into the future and into her selfe, and all this in a point of time'.[185] It is crucial for poets to employ such resources of recollection and experience if they are to have any prospect of creating an 'admirable variety and novelty of metaphors and similitudes'.[186] It is crucial, in other words, for their imagery to be 'farre fetch't', so that their diction is never 'defac'd by time or sullied with vulgar or long use'.[187]

The second and contrasting[188] requirement of a good fancy was said to be that, while the mind must bring back new and surprising images, they must never be so far-fetched as to suggest that the imagination has merely been *extra vagans*, wandering out of its way and losing itself in extravagance. As we saw in chapter 5, the reason given by Quintilian and his followers for insisting with so much strictness on this second criterion was that any such 'exorbitant' imagery will be sure to fall short of the twin goals we must set ourselves in adorning our speech: that of brightening our arguments to make them clearer and more illuminating, and that of clothing the naked truth to make it more appealing and believable. If our figures and tropes are drawn from too far afield, neither of these purposes will be fulfilled. Rather than appearing fresh and arresting, our images will merely seem monstrous and deformed. Even worse, they will tend to darken rather than illuminate our meaning, producing mere confusion and puzzlement. Worst of all, they will fail to make our arguments more 'colourable', since their colours will not appear true to life; they will

182 Hobbes 1986, p. 110.
183 For a full analysis see Thorpe 1940, pp. 156–69.
184 Hobbes 1971a, p. 46.
185 Hobbes 1971a, p. 49.
186 Hobbes 1971a, p. 53.
187 Hobbes 1971a, p. 53.
188 But not contradictory, as implied in Cook 1981, p. 229.

merely look 'made up' in the fashion of painted courtesans, no longer alluring because so evidently false.

As before, Hobbes not only reiterates these arguments but expresses them in almost identical terms.[189] He presents his fullest analysis in discussing the characteristics of poetic imagination in his *Answer* to Davenant, where he begins by announcing his strong dissent 'from those that thinke the Beauty of a Poeme consisteth in the exorbitancy of the fiction'.[190] A poet must take care to speak only from his own experience, thereby ensuring that his 'coulor and shaddow' are taken 'out of his owne store'.[191] As long as we observe this rule, we shall be able to compose in 'the true and natural Colour'.[192] But if we rely on the imaginative experiences recorded in other people's books, we shall merely be dipping into 'the ordinary boxes of Counterfeit Complexion'.[193] Above all, we must ensure that, in striving for 'novelty of expression', we avoid 'the ambitious obscurity of expressing more then is perfectly conceaved; or perfect conception in fewer words then it requires'.[194] Dryden was later to castigate such obscurities as 'metaphysical', but Hobbes already dismisses them with no less confidence. 'Though they have had the honor to be called strong lines', they are 'in deed no better then Riddles, and not onely to the Reader, but also (after a little time) to the Writer himselfe darke and troublesome'.[195] (Ben Jonson had already warned that 'whatsoever looseth the grace and clearenesse converts into a Riddle'.)[196] Hobbes ends with a striking adaptation of the familiar injunction that our images must never be excessively far-fetched. We must at all costs avoid sounding like people who have just returned from travelling abroad, full of affected phrases and incapable even of translating their own speech.[197]

The remaining question is how these two contrasting requirements of a

189 Some critics have seen a change of mind at this point, since Hobbes had spoken in his translation of Aristotle's *Rhetoric* of the need for metaphors to be 'unproportionable'. See Hobbes 1986, p. 117, and cf. Watson 1955, p. 559, treating this as a 'metaphysical' commitment, a judgment endorsed in Cook 1981, pp. 229, 232. But Hobbes is paraphrasing Aristotle at this juncture, not speaking *in propria persona*. Moreover, he had already exhibited a 'neo-classical' commitment at earlier points in his paraphrase (see for example Hobbes 1986, pp. 109, 116). And when he eventually speaks in his own person –in his *Answer* to Davenant and in *Leviathan* – he reveals himself to be 'a passionate neo-classical', as Watson 1955, p. 559, rightly puts it. For critiques of Watson's argument see Gang 1956 and Prokhovnik 1991, pp. 90–100.

190 Hobbes 1971a, p. 51.

191 Hobbes 1971a, p. 50.

192 Hobbes 1971a, p. 51.

193 Hobbes 1971a, p. 51.

194 Hobbes 1971a, p. 52.

195 Hobbes 1971a, p. 52.

196 Jonson 1947a, p. 624.

197 Hobbes 1971a, p. 53.

good fancy can be simultaneously met. Hobbes responds, exactly as Quintilian had done,[198] that the answer lies in cultivating the virtue of discretion, the characteristic product of good judgment. He first outlines this solution in an exceptionally compacted passage of his *Answer* to Davenant:

> Time and education begets experience; Experience begets memory; Memory begets Judgement, and Fancy; Judgment begets the strength and structure; and Fancy begets the ornaments of a Poeme. The Ancients therefore fabled not absurdly in making memory the mother of the Muses.[199]

Having presented this summary, Hobbes pauses to construe and elaborate it. On the one hand, 'the Fancy, when any worke of Art is to be performed, findes her materials at hand and prepared for use, and needes no more then a swift motion over them, that what she wants, and is there to be had, may not lye too long unespied'.[200] But on the other hand the Judgment ('the severer Sister') needs to engage 'in grave and rigide examination of all the parts of Nature, and in registring by Letters, their order, causes, uses, differences and resemblances'.[201] So long as these two approaches are followed with equal vigour, we shall be able to create an effect of perfect discretion in our deployment of the figures and tropes, since the outcome will be a series of 'translations' at once new and far-fetched, but at the same time apt, comely and instructive.[202]

Hobbes extends the argument in chapter VIII of *Leviathan*, his chapter on the intellectual virtues, in which he distinguishes once more between fancy and judgment. When people observe 'the things that passe through their imagination', we may say of 'those that observe their similitudes, in case they be such as are but rarely observed by others' that they have 'a *Good Wit*; by which, in this occasion, is meant a *Good Fancy*' (p. 50). By contrast, 'they that observe their differences, and dissimilitudes; which is called *Distinguishing*, and *Discerning*, and *Judging* between thing and thing; in case such discerning be not easie, are said to have a *good Judgement*' (p. 51). As before, the central question concerns the proper relationship between the two faculties. The clue is said to lie in recognising that 'Judgment and Discretion is commended for it selfe, without the help of Fancy', whereas 'Fancy, without the help of Judgement, is not commended as a Vertue' (p. 51). The Latin *Leviathan* relaxes this stricture, observing instead that 'it is not usual' for pure flights of fancy to be praised in the absence of

198 As Thorpe 1940, p. 103, rightly points out.
199 Hobbes 1971a, p. 49.
200 Hobbes 1971a, p. 49.
201 Hobbes 1971a, p. 49.
202 Hobbes 1971a, p. 53.

judgment.[203] Both versions accept, however, that this is because – as Dryden was later to reiterate – 'without Stedinesse, and Direction to some End, a great Fancy is one kind of Madnesse'.[204] The implication is thus that the fancy must at all times be tempered and controlled by the judgment. This alone enables us – and here Hobbes appears to quote Quintilian – to attain the pivotal intellectual virtue of discretion, 'wherein times, places and persons are to be discerned' (p. 51). It follows that, when we speak of a man as having an excellent fancy, we are not merely describing his talent for discovering similitudes; we are also praising his capacity for observing 'Discretion of times, places and persons' and for committing himself to 'an often application of his thoughts to their End; that is to say, to some use to be made of them' (p. 51). Hobbes concedes that such a combination of intellectual virtues is extremely hard to achieve. But he now stresses that anyone who achieves it will be able to combine *ornatus* with *ratio* in a spectacularly persuasive way. For 'he that hath this Vertue will be easily fitted with similitudes that will please, not onely by illustration of his discourse, and adorning it with new and apt metaphors; but also by the rarity of their invention' (p. 51).

If we turn to Hobbes's final pronouncement on these issues in his essay on the virtues of heroic poetry, we find an even clearer endorsement of the same classical values. The only difference is that, in the twenty-five years that had elapsed since the completion of *Leviathan*, Hobbes had come to feel even more strongly that, while fancy is a valuable gift, it must never be put to extravagant use. He begins by observing that 'elevation of fancy' is 'generally taken for the greatest praise of heroic poetry', because 'men more generally affect and admire fancy than they do either judgment, or reason, or memory, or any other intellectual virtue'.[205] This in turn is due to the fact that fancy 'flies abroad swiftly to fetch in both matter and words', giving rise to 'that poetical fury which the readers, for the most part, call for'.[206] Despite the popularity of such outpourings, however, the praise of fancy in the absence of discretion and judgment remains a serious aesthetic mistake, because 'the virtues required in an heroic poem, and indeed in all writing published, are comprehended all in this one word – *discretion*'.[207] A powerful fancy is of course necessary for the creation of new and startling images, but 'if there be not discretion at home to distinguish which are fit to be used and which not, which decent

203 Hobbes 1668, p. 35: 'Phantasia sine *Iudicio* laudari raro solet.'

204 Hobbes 1991, p. 51; cf. Hobbes 1668, p. 35: 'nisi constans adsit cogitationum ad aliquem finem regulatio, Phantasia magna species quaedem est Insaniae'.

205 Hobbes 1844, p. v.

206 Hobbes 1844, p. v.

207 Hobbes 1844, p. iii.

and which undecent for persons, times and places, their delight and grace is lost'.[208]

With this theory of the imagination, Hobbes returns in a wide circle to the humanist allegiances of his youth. As often, his final position seems close to that of Bacon in *The Advancement of Learning.*[209] Bacon had already argued that reason will remain 'captive and servile' unless we employ 'eloquence of persuasions' to 'win the imagination from the affections' part, and contract a confederacy between the reason and imagination'.[210] If we can bring about this confederacy – if we can manage 'to apply reason to imagination for the better moving of the will' – we shall be able to discharge the fundamental 'duty and office of rhetoric', the end or purpose of which is 'to fill the imagination to second reason, and not to oppress it'.[211] Having initially rejected any such possibility of 'seconding' the methods of science with the products of the imagination, Hobbes eventually came round to endorsing exactly this point of view. As the review and conclusion of *Leviathan* puts it, 'if there be not powerful Eloquence, which procureth attention and Consent, the effect of Reason will be little' (p. 483). Bacon had added that we need not fear the consequences of such a confederacy between reason and the imagination, if only because 'speech is much more conversant in adorning that which is good than in colouring that which is evil'.[212] Hobbes ends by offering precisely the same reassurance. As we have seen, his reason for thinking that reason and eloquence 'may stand very well together' is that 'wheresoever there is place for adorning and preferring of Errour, there is much more place for adorning and preferring of Truth' (p. 484).

Hobbes rounds off his analysis of *ornatus* in chapter VIII of *Leviathan* by anatomising the varying roles that the figures and tropes ought ideally to play in the different humanistic disciplines. His aim in this crucial passage – which has no parallel in *The Elements* or *De Cive* – is to determine how far the resources of *ornatus* should be deployed if our aim is to combine the clearest methods of reasoning with the most persuasive effects. The outcome is a survey of what he takes to be the optimum relationship between fancy and judgment, and hence between *ornatus* and *ratio*, throughout the full range of the *studia humanitatis.*

208 Hobbes 1844, p. v.

209 Hobbes only once refers directly to Bacon in *Leviathan,* and only in the Latin version, which includes a critical allusion to the *New Atlantis.* See Hobbes 1668, p. 172. But in a number of places he seems close to Bacon's position in *The Advancement of Learning.* See for example Bacon 1915, pp. 31, 43, 126–8, 134, 153, 172.

210 Bacon 1915, p. 147.

211 Bacon 1915, p. 146.

212 Bacon 1915, p. 147.

He begins with poetry, which he now recognises as one of the modes in which knowledge in its fullest sense can be successfully communicated. He insists that good judgment is indispensable, since the workings of fancy 'ought not to please by Indiscretion', but he agrees that in this case 'the Fancy must be more eminent' (p. 51). Next he turns to history, in which 'the Judgement must be eminent', since the value of historical writing 'consisteth in the Method, in the Truth and in the Choyce of the actions that are profitable to be known' (p. 51). This is not to say, however, that the workings of fancy should be excluded. They remain necessary for 'adorning the stile', to which the Latin *Leviathan* adds that this specifically calls for the addition of *ornatus* to the actual narrative.[213] Hobbes then turns to examine the three genera of rhetorical utterance: the *genus demonstrativum*, the *genus iudiciale* and the *genus deliberativum*. First he considers the balance between fancy and judgment in the *genus demonstrativum*, that is, 'in Orations of Prayse and in Invectives' (p. 51). These require good judgment, but only to 'suggest what circumstances make an action laudable, or culpable' (p. 51). The predominant place must be occupied by the fancy, 'because the designe is not truth, but to Honour or Dishonour, which is done by noble or by vile comparisons' – to which the Latin *Leviathan* interestingly adds that the same results can be achieved by ridicule.[214] Next Hobbes turns to the *genus iudiciale*, that is, to 'Hortatives and Pleadings' (p. 51). The right balance between fancy and judgment in this case depends on whether your primary aim is to state the truth or disguise it. Earlier Hobbes had argued that the use of *ornatus* to disguise the truth must be classified as an abuse of speech (p. 26). He now accepts that there are bound to be cases in which deception 'serveth best to the Designe in hand', to which he adds that these are the cases in which the fancy will be 'most required' (p. 52). Finally, he considers the *genus deliberativum*, which he takes to encompass not merely the act of deliberating in the rhetorical sense of proffering public counsel, but also the pursuit of science or 'rigourous search of Truth' (p. 52). Here he remains closest to his earlier belief that, as he now expresses it, in these instances we can virtually say that 'Judgment does all' (p. 52). Certainly the master trope of metaphor must be 'utterly excluded', since metaphors 'openly professe deceipt', with the result that 'to admit them into Councell or Reasoning were manifest folly' (p. 52). Even here, however, Hobbes is far from his earlier contention that the techniques of rhetoric should be wholly eschewed. On the contrary, he assumes that even in this case our aim must be to establish the right relationship between reason and

213 Hobbes 1991, p. 51; cf. Hobbes 1668, p. 35 on the need for Phantasia 'in ornanda narratione'.
214 Hobbes 1991, p. 51. Cf. Hobbes 1668, p. 35.

eloquence. As we have seen, the relationship proposed in such classical textbooks as the *Ad Herennium* had assumed that certain features of *ornatus* – especially similes – will be useful in all forms of reasoning as means of rendering the understanding 'more open' (*apertior*) to the truth.[215] Hobbes takes up exactly this argument, concluding that even in the sciences we shall find that 'sometimes the understanding have need to be opened by some apt similitude', so that even in the most rigorous searches for truth 'there is so much use of Fancy' (p. 52). The Latin *Leviathan* goes even further, suggesting two additional reasons for introducing apt similitudes: either to ensure 'that those listening to us are able fully to follow what we are saying', or else to ensure 'that we reduce them to a state of greater docility'.[216]

With these changing views about the imagination, Hobbes contributed at different stages of his intellectual career to two contrasting strands of thought about fancy and judgment in later seventeenth-century England. His initial contention in *The Elements* that the two faculties are irreconcilable aligns him with a number of epistemologies of a broadly empiricist bent. If we consider, for example, the analysis of words and their abuses at the end of book III of John Locke's *Essay Concerning Human Understanding*, we find Locke reiterating that the operations of fancy, with their distinctive expression in figurative speech, are flatly incompatible with good judgment:

> If we would speak of Things as they are, we must allow, that all the Art of Rhetorick, besides Order and Clearness, all the figurative applications of Words Eloquence hath invented, are for nothing else but to insinuate wrong *Ideas*, move the Passions, and thereby mislead the Judgment.[217]

Locke later rejects with even greater force the possibility of an alliance between fancy and judgment in his essay *On the Conduct of the Understanding*, in which he invokes both the method and terminology of the *ars rhetorica* solely in order to repudiate them. 'The Custom of Arguing on any side', he declares, 'dimns the Understanding', to which he adds that 'there are so many ways of Fallacy, such Arts of giving Colours, Appearances and Resemblances by this Court dresser, the Phansie, that he who is not wary to admit nothing but Truth it self, very careful not to make his Mind subservient to any thing else, cannot but be caught'.[218]

By contrast, Hobbes's later belief that the virtue of discretion enables us to reconcile fancy and judgment serves to align him with the neo-classical

215 *Ad C. Herennium*, IV.XLVIII.61, p. 382.
216 Hobbes 1668, p. 36: 'ut ii qui audiunt, vel legunt, dociliores fiant'.
217 Locke 1979, III.X.34, p. 508.
218 Locke 1993, §32, pp. 99–100.

movement in aesthetics and its attack on 'metaphysical' extravagance. If we turn, for example, to Dryden's *Defence* of his essay on dramatic poetry, we encounter a very similar emphasis on the possibility as well as the necessity of tempering fancy with judgment. Dryden remains of the view that a powerful fancy is indispensable, since even the most accomplished compositions will otherwise lack nobility.[219] But fancy must always be controlled by reason and judgment:

> Fancy and Reason go hand in hand; the first cannot leave the last behind: and though Fancy, when it sees the wide gulf, would venture over, as the nimbler, yet it is withheld by Reason, which will refuse to take the leap, when the distance over it appears too large.[220]

Echoing one of Hobbes's favourite similes, Dryden adds in his epistle prefacing *The Rival Ladies* that we ought to acknowledge as one of the most important benefits of rhyme that 'it bounds and circumscribes the fancy', which is 'a faculty so wild and lawless, that like an high-ranging spaniel, it must have clogs tied to it, lest it outrun the judgment'.[221] After this it is not surprising to find Dryden admitting to Aubrey that he often made use of Hobbes's doctrines in his own works, nor to find him hailing Hobbes for his contributions to poetry no less than to philosophy.[222]

219 See the examples discussed in Thorpe 1940, esp. pp. 190–2, 211–14.

220 Dryden 1900, I, p. 128.

221 Dryden 1900, I, p. 8.

222 See Dryden 1900, I, p. 259, on 'our poet and philosopher of Malmesbury'. Cf. Aubrey 1898, I, p. 372. Elsewhere, however, Dryden was less complimentary. See Dryden 1900, II, p. 252.

Chapter 10

HOBBES'S PRACTICE OF RHETORIC

THE ESTABLISHING OF ETHOS

The conception of civil science embodied in *Leviathan* rests on the assumption that reason is of small power in the absence of eloquence. Hobbes's crucial inference is that, if truth is to prevail, the findings of science will have to be empowered by the persuasive techniques associated with the art of rhetoric. We next need to enquire into the extent to which these new theoretical commitments govern the presentation of Hobbes's mature civil science. How far is his later belief in the indispensability of eloquence mirrored in his employment of rhetorical techniques? How far do we find him calling on the methods of *inventio*, *dispositio* and *elocutio* to supplement his scientific demonstrations and lend them persuasive force?

As we have seen, Hobbes eventually endorsed one aspect of the rhetorical doctrine of *inventio*: the suggestion that, if there is to be any prospect of winning an argument, we must seek at the outset to gain the confidence of our audience by showing ourselves worthy of being heeded and believed. The rhetoricians had in turn suggested two main ways in which this can be done. One is by promising, as the *Ad Herennium* had put it, to say something at once novel and deserving of attention, and at the same time useful and important to the commonwealth. The other is by claiming, as Quintilian had later added, to be genuinely impartial on the issues under debate, and at the same time a person of accredited probity whose opinions can be trusted for moderation and modesty.

Hobbes had scorned this approach in the epistle dedicatory to *De Cive* in 1642, proclaiming that what matters is neither the standing of writers nor the novelty of what they write, but simply the power and weight of their arguments.[1] But by the time he came to issue the revised edition in 1647 he had completely changed his mind. His new preface opens with a direct apostrophe to his readers in the highest Ciceronian style, stressing his

[1] Hobbes 1983a, p. 76.

'probability' as a witness in a paraphrase of the classical theory of ethos so close as to echo its precise terminology:

Readers, I promise you such things here as, when they are usually promised, are recognised as commanding a Reader's attention in the highest possible degree, whether because of the Dignity and Usefulness of the Matter handled, or the propriety of the Method of handling it, or the author's motive for writing, or the probity of his judgment, or finally the Moderation revealed in what is written.[2]

The preface concludes with a further rhetorical declamation directly addressed to the reader in an even more high-flown imitation of the Ciceronian grand style:

If, then, you find that any of the things I have said are either less certain or are stated more sharply than is strictly necessary, I hope and pray, Readers, that you will agree to accept them with an open mind, since my concern is not with parties but rather with the cause of peace, and what I say is spoken, moreover, by someone who ought in fairness to be excused to some degree on account of his just feelings of grief for the present calamity of his native land.[3]

Once again, just as the *Ad Herennium* had advised, Hobbes emphasises the unimpeachability of his patriotism, his impartiality and his concern for the good of the commonwealth.

If we turn to the epistle dedicatory to *Leviathan*, we find Hobbes seeking to establish his ethos in scarcely less elevated tones. Again he stresses the relevance and importance of his arguments for the maintenance of peaceful government, pointing in particular to his 'endeavour to advance the Civill Power' and to prevent its authority from being impugned (p. 3). Again he emphasises his position as a man of no party, concerned to advance the good of his country while 'beset with those that contend on one side for too great Liberty, and on the other side for too much Authority', so that it is 'hard to passe between the points of both unwounded' (p. 3). And again he insists on his total impartiality as someone writing without fear or favour in defence of civil peace. He does so, moreover, in tones of calculated moderation, likening himself in a quaint trope of modesty 'to those simple and unpartiall creatures in the Roman Capitol, that with their noyse defended those within it, not because they were they, but there' (p. 3). To which he adds in the Latin

2 Hobbes 1983a, 'Praefatio', p. 77: 'Quae res attentam Lectionem promissae efficere maxime posse videntur, Rei tractandae Dignitas, & Utilitas, tractandi recta Methodus, causa & consilium in scribendo probum, scribentis denique Moderatio, eas, Lectores, vobis promitto.'

3 Hobbes 1983a, 'Praefatio', p. 84: 'Quapropter si aliqua inveneritis aut minus certa, aut magis quam necesse erat acriter dicta, cum non partium sed pacis studio, & ab eo dicta sint cuius propter patriae praesentem calamitatem dolori iusto aliquid condonari aequum est, ea ut aequo animo ferre dignemini, Lectores, oro postuloque.'

Leviathan, in a still loftier vindication of his moderation, that 'I cannot see any reason why either party should feel the least displeasure with me.'[4]

After the publication of *Leviathan*, Hobbes returned to his scientific and especially his mathematical pursuits. One might have expected a recrudescence at this point of his earlier belief that, in the natural if not in the moral sciences, the force of reason ought to be sufficient to convince an intelligent audience. Instead we find him voicing a no less urgent sense of the need to establish his ethos and to question the standing of his adversaries. He first strikes this note in the epistle dedicatory to *Six Lessons*, the attack on John Wallis's geometry which he appended to the English translation of *De Corpore* in 1656. Hobbes initially seeks to cast doubt on Wallis's credentials as a geometer, declaring that 'I have rectified and explained the principles of the science; *id est*, I have done that business for which Dr. Wallis receives the wages.'[5] At the same time he insists on his own standing as a teller of new truths, proclaiming that his findings are 'very singular', and that 'if you shall find those my principles of motion made good, you shall find also that I have added something to that which was formerly extant in geometry'.[6] He adopts a similar tone in dedicating his *Seven Philosophical Problems* to Charles II in 1662,[7] declaring that the fruits of his meditations on the causes of events are in many instances not commonly known, and assuring the king of the high importance of his work by claiming that 'this Contemplation of Nature (if not rendered obscure by empty termes) is the most noble employment of the minde that can bee to such as are at leasure from their necessary businesse'.[8]

It is in his more speculative works of the same period, however, that Hobbes displays the keenest anxiety to establish his ethos and undermine the credentials of his opponents. The epistle dedicatory to the English version of *De Corpore* opens with an exceptionally fulsome attempt to insist on the novelty and importance of his work. What he is publishing, he maintains, is 'a little book, but full; and great enough, if men count well for great'.[9] Moreover, it is 'clear and easy to understand, and almost new throughout, without any offensive novelty'.[10] But it is in his debate with John Bramhall, and especially in his summarising treatise of 1656 entitled *The Questions Concerning Liberty, Necessity and Chance*, that we encounter

4 Hobbes 1668, sig. aaa 1^{v}: 'Causam tamen cur pars utravis succensere mihi, nullam video.'
5 Hobbes 1845g, p. 185.
6 Hobbes 1845g, pp. 185, 189.
7 The 1662 text was entitled *Problemata Physica*; this was translated and published as *Seven Philosophical Problems* in 1682. See Macdonald and Hargreaves 1952, pp. 48–9.
8 BL Sloane MS 3930, fo. 1^{v}. Cf. Hobbes 1845e, p. 4.
9 Hobbes 1839d, p. vii.
10 Hobbes 1839d, p. vii.

Hobbes's most aggressive attempts to prove himself. He appears to have felt especially put on his mettle by the fact that, in examining the problem of predestination, he was addressing one of the most troublesome issues in post-Reformation theology. Furthermore, he was proposing to debate the question with a prominent theologian, a doctor of divinity from the University of Cambridge who had made his mark as a harsh and effective controversialist.[11] Faced with this challenge, Hobbes appeals more fully than ever to the strategies for establishing ethos recommended by the classical theorists of eloquence.

He may have felt emboldened to adopt this approach by the appearance in print two years earlier of the letter he had written in 1645 in criticism of Bramhall's views about the freedom of the will. The marquis of Newcastle had commissioned Hobbes's response, and this was the text that appeared – apparently without Hobbes's knowledge – under the title *Of Liberty and Necessity* in 1654.[12] At the outset of his *Questions Concerning Liberty* Hobbes explains how this came about. While he was living in Paris, a French gentleman asked him to allow a young English friend to make a translation of his 1645 letter. Hobbes acceded to the request, but later found that the young man – whom he describes as 'a nimble writer' – had taken a copy for himself.[13] This was the copy published in 1654 together with a prefatory epistle (presumably by the same nimble writer) addressed 'To the sober and discreet reader',[14] in which Hobbes's qualifications for writing on the subject of free will are proclaimed with an enthusiasm bordering on idolatry.

The epistle begins by arguing that the theologians with their endless quarrelling have discredited themselves as experts on the topic to be discussed:

> What shall we think of those vast and involuble volumes concerning *predestination, free-will, free-grace, election, reprobation*, &c., which fill not only our libraries but the world with their noise and disturbance, whereof the least thing we are to expect is *conviction*; every side endeavouring to make good their own grounds, and keep the cudgels in their hands as long as they can?[15]

The writer next seeks to persuade us that Hobbes's moderation and impartiality are by contrast indisputable. 'This great author' is 'a person, whom not only the averseness of his nature to engage himself in matters of

11 On Bramhall see Mintz 1962, pp. 110–23, and Daly 1971.

12 Macdonald and Hargreaves 1952, pp. 37–8. Cf. Hobbes's version of the story in Hobbes 1841, p. 2.

13 Hobbes 1841, pp. 25–6.

14 Hobbes 1840a, p. 231.

15 Hobbes 1840a, p. 234.

controversy of this kind, but his severer study of the *mathematics*, might justly exempt from any such skirmishes'.[16] We are then treated to a bravura passage in vindication of the novelty and significance of Hobbes's contribution to the debate:

I dare advance this proposition, how bold soever it may seem to some; that this book, how little and contemptible soever it may seem, contains more evidence and conviction in the matters it treats of than all the volumes, nay libraries, which the *priests, jesuits* and *ministers* have, to our great charge, distraction and loss of precious time furnished us with.[17]

The epistle concludes – very much in the style of Hobbes's 1647 preface to *De Cive* – with a hyperbolical apostrophe:

Thus much, Reader, I have thought fit to acquaint thee with, that thou mightest know what a jewel thou hast in thy hands, which thou must accordingly value, not by the bulk, but the preciousness. Thou hast here in a few sheets what might prove work enough for many thousand sermons and exercises; and more than the *catechisms* and *confessions* of a thousand *assemblies* could furnish thee with: thou hast what will cast an eternal blemish on all the *cornered* caps of the *priests* and *jesuits*, and all the *black and white* caps of the *canting tribe*; to be short, thou art now acquainted with that man, who, in matters of so great importance as those of thy salvation, furnishes thee with better instructions than any thou hast ever yet been acquainted with, what *professions*, *persuasion*, *opinion* or *church* soever thou art of; of whom and his works make the best use thou canst.[18]

To this the writer simply adds 'Farewell', as if challenging us to disagree if we dare.[19]

Hobbes later apologised to Bramhall for the fact that his young admirer had published his letter of 1645 without reference to the letter from Bramhall which had provoked it.[20] But it is striking that Hobbes never offered any apology for the style or content of the prefatory epistle, even though Bramhall in his *Defence of True Liberty* of 1655 specifically complained about its 'ignorant censures' and 'hyperbolical expressions'.[21] On the contrary, Hobbes devoted the introductory pages of *The Questions Concerning Liberty* to underlining his disciple's efforts by drawing once more on the precepts laid down by the classical theorists of eloquence for establishing one's ethos. First he calls attention in his slyest style to the novelty of his argument. The reader will find, he declares, that each contestant in the ensuing debate relies on the authority of Scripture, but that 'one of them is a learned School Divine, the other a man that doth not much admire that

16 Hobbes 1840a, pp. 234–5.
17 Hobbes 1840a, p. 236.
18 Hobbes 1840a, pp. 237–8.
19 Hobbes 1840a, p. 238.
20 Hobbes 1841, pp. 25–6.
21 See Hobbes 1841, p. 23.

kind of learning'.[22] Next he emphasises the public importance of his conclusions, insisting in aggressive tones on their relevance for the proper government of the commonwealth. The idea of free will is denounced as papist in origin, to which Hobbes adds that those members of the Anglican Church who have adopted it have largely done so for corrupt motives. 'The Doctors of the Roman Church' originally 'exempted from this dominion of God's Will, the Will of Man', and it is 'not many years since it began again to be reduced by Arminius and his followers, and became the readiest way to Ecclesiastical promotion'.[23] Hobbes goes so far as to imply that the Arminian doctrine, 'by discontenting those that held the contrary', was 'in some part the cause of the following troubles', so contributing to the downfall of the English monarchy.[24] Finally, he takes care to point out once again that he himself is a man of no party, but someone who has considered the issues from all possible points of view:

> You shall find in this little volume the questions Concerning *necessity*, *freedom* and *chance*, which in all ages have perplexed the minds of curious men, largely and clearly discussed, and the arguments on all sides, drawn from the authority of Scripture, from the doctrine of the schools, from natural reason, and from the consequences pertaining to common life, truly alleged and severally weighed.[25]

As before, the impression Hobbes aims to leave with us – exactly as the classical theory of ethos required – is of an independent thinker addressing an issue of public importance in a spirit of unimpeachable learning and integrity.

THE ADORNMENT OF TRUTH

Among the elements of the classical *ars rhetorica*, the element of *elocutio* is undoubtedly the one that Hobbes employs most systematically and effectively in *Leviathan*. He allows himself in the first place to profit from a minor and notably cynical piece of advice about persuasive presentation put forward by Aristotle in book III of *The Art of Rhetoric*. Discussing what Hobbes's own translation calls '*the* Convenience *or* Decencie *of* elocution',[26] Aristotle had pointed out that 'it conferres also to perswasion very much to use these ordinary formes of speaking, *All men know; Tis confessed by all; No man will deny* and the like'.[27] The reason is that 'the Hearer consents,

22 Hobbes 1841, 'To the Reader', unpaginated.
23 Hobbes 1841, pp. 1–2.
24 Hobbes 1841, p. 2.
25 Hobbes 1841, 'To the Reader'.
26 Hobbes 1986, p. 112.
27 Hobbes 1986, p. 113.

surprized with the feare to be esteemed the onely Ignorant man'.[28] The technique is one that can thus be used to lend credence even to the most doubtful arguments.

Hobbes makes no appeal to this aspect of *elocutio* in *The Elements* or *De Cive.* As his implacable adversary John Wallis duly pointed out, however, he later made ruthless use of his discovery that, as Wallis contemptuously put it, he can 'by a *Manifestum est,* save him the trouble of attempting a Demonstration'.[29] We first find Hobbes resorting to the device when revising *De Cive* for republication in 1647, suggesting at one point in his correspondence with Sorbière – who was seeing the volume through the press – that where he had written 'It has been shown in the previous section', this could be replaced with 'It is self-evident'.[30] He deploys the same stratagem with no less ruthlessness at several points in *Leviathan.* He first does so at the end of chapter XV in a passage which, while highly dubious in dialectical quality, is crucial to his purportedly scientific answer to the problem of paradiastolic speech. As we saw in chapter 9, he wishes to insist that, since peace is a great good, the qualities conducive to peace must also be recognised as good. He was undoubtedly aware, however, that the growing popularity of *raison d'état* theories of statecraft had made it highly contentious to assume without argument that actions liable to give rise to good consequences need necessarily be good in themselves. Hobbes's response is to turn to Aristotle's advice. Declaring that 'Peace is Good, and therefore also the way or Means of Peace', he confronts this obvious *non sequitur* by assuring us that 'all men agree on this', to which he adds for good measure in the Latin *Leviathan* that 'this is something that cannot be denied'.[31] He employs the same tactic at the start of book III, where he begins by declaring that the definitions from which he has so far inferred his conclusions are 'universally agreed on' (p. 255). Finally, he proclaims even more coercively in his review and conclusion that the laws of nature, on which he has based his entire argument, are so familiar and well-understood that 'no man that pretends but reason enough to govern his private family ought to be ignorant' of their requirements (p. 489).

Of all the aspects of *elocutio*, however, it is Hobbes's use of *ornatus* that makes the presentation of his argument in *Leviathan* so comprehensively different from *The Elements* and *De Cive.* As we saw in chapter 5, the rhetoricians had singled out one particular form of rhetorical 'ornament' which they regarded as useful and appropriate even in scientific discourse.

28 Hobbes 1986, p. 113.
29 Wallis 1662, p. 103.
30 See letter 42 in Hobbes 1994, p. 132.
31 Hobbes 1991, p. 111; cf. Hobbes 1668, p. 79: 'negari non potest'.

This was the technique of using the figures and tropes – especially the master tropes of simile and metaphor – to supplement the findings of reason by 'preferring' or 'holding forth' the truth in such a way as to enable it, so to speak, to be visually inspected. The image they had generally invoked to convey this thought had been that of turning one's readers into spectators, enabling them to 'see' the implications of unfamiliar arguments by offering them pictures to illustrate and thereby illuminate their significance.

Hobbes makes no mention of this idea in *The Elements* or *De Cive*, although he was undoubtedly aware of it.[32] By contrast, it occupies an important position in all his later pronouncements on the theory of style. He first refers to it in discussing the example of poetry in his *Answer* to Davenant. Davenant had already alluded in his preface to Horace's famous line comparing poetry with painting, adding that the business of the poet is to 'represent the Worlds true image often to our view'.[33] Hobbes picks up the visual metaphor, modifying it with an elegant play on the word 'lines', the materials out of which poems and drawings are alike composed:

> Poets are Paynters: I would faine see another Painter draw so true perfect and natural a Love to the Life, and make use of nothing but pure lines, without the helpe of any the least uncomely shaddow as you have done.[34]

There is no comparably direct reference to the doctrine of *ut pictura poesis* in *Leviathan*, but Hobbes gestures at its implications at several different points. He speaks in chapter VIII of the value to anyone engaged in ratiocination of using similes and metaphors to offer 'illustration of his discourse', conveying by his play on the word 'illustration' the idea of providing a picture and providing additional enlightenment at the same time (p. 51). Later in the same chapter he speaks of the way in which, even in the course of 'rigourous search of Truth', the understanding may be 'opened by some apt similitude', so hinting at the idea of displaying or exposing an argument to view (p. 52). He recurs more directly to the classical doctrine of mimesis in his late essay on the virtues of heroic poetry, in which he reiterates that 'a poet is a painter' and speaks in praise of Virgil for managing to 'set before our eyes the fall of Troy'.[35] He ends by suggesting that aspiring poets should 'paint actions to the understanding

32 He makes reference to it as early as his introduction to his translation of Thucydides in 1629. See Hobbes 1975b, pp. 7, 18.

33 Davenant 1971a, p. 4.

34 Hobbes 1971a, p. 50.

35 Hobbes 1844, p. vi.

with the most decent words, as painters do persons and bodies with the choicest colours, to the eye'.[36]

One of the systematic ways in which Hobbes exploits the resources of *ornatus* in *Leviathan* is precisely in accordance with this classical recommendation to employ the master tropes of simile and metaphor to 'prefer' or 'hold forth' the findings of science to the mind's eye. It is true that he makes almost no use of this technique in books III and IV, in which he appears to regard himself as engaged less in presenting new arguments than in offering, in best rhetorical style, a *confirmatio*[37] of what he has already established and a *refutatio*[38] of the conclusions put forward by his dialectical enemies. If we turn back to the first half of his treatise, however, we find him making extensive use of 'illustrative' similes and metaphors in his analysis of man and his imaginative faculties in book I, as well as in his theory of the commonwealth in book II.[39]

Hobbes begins to write in this style in his introduction, in which he quotes the Socratic injunction *nosce teipsum*. This he mistranslates as 'read thy self', thereby introducing a metaphor which he then applies to show us how to construct a civil science.[40] The image of reading a text is initially used to indicate the difficulties involved. To grasp the meaning of someone else's conduct is like trying to read the badly formed characters in a difficult piece of handwriting. This is why 'the characters of mans heart, blotted and confounded as they are with dissembling, lying, counterfeiting and erroneous doctrines, are legible only to him that searcheth hearts' (p. 10). The image is then used to suggest how these difficulties can be overcome. The approach we need to adopt is that of reading our own hearts, whose messages we can hope to decipher because we wrote them ourselves. The only way to 'learn truly to read one another' is in short to recognise that, because of 'the similitude of the thoughts and Passions of one man to the thoughts and Passions of another', anyone who 'looketh into himself and considereth what he doth' will be able to 'read and know what are the thoughts and Passions of all other men upon the like occasions' (p. 10). By means of such readings we can hope to build up a scientific understanding of social life.

Turning in his opening chapters to analyse the imagination, Hobbes

36 Hobbes 1844, p. vi.

37 Hobbes uses this precise language at the end of part III. See Hobbes 1991, p. 414.

38 Hobbes speaks at the start of part IV of the need to confute 'vain and erroneous Philosophy'. See Hobbes 1991, p. 418.

39 There have been several valuable studies of metaphor in *Leviathan*. See May 1959; Sacksteder 1984; Curtis 1988; Prokhovnik 1991. While I am indebted to these accounts, my aim is not to add to them, but to pursue a different though related enquiry, asking about Hobbes's underlying purposes in making use of particular metaphors.

40 Hobbes 1991, p. 10. For a discussion see Shapiro 1980, esp. pp. 149–51.

calls on two further tropes of a deliberately everyday nature to help us visualise and thereby understand the unfamiliar elements in his argument. He first proceeds in this fashion in chapter II, in which he describes how, after an object has been removed, 'wee still retain an image of the thing seen, though more obscure than when we see it' (p. 15). We can recognise what this process is like, he suggests, if we compare it with the behaviour of the sea when, 'though the wind cease, the waves give not over rowling for a long time'.[41] He offers a similar comparison at the start of chapter III when attempting to explain how it comes about that those motions which have 'immediately succeeded one another in the sense, continue also together after Sense', in such a way that 'the former comming again to take place and be praedominent, the latter followeth by coherence of the matter moved' (p. 20). We can hope to comprehend what is happening if we envisage 'the coherence of the matter moved' as taking place 'in such manner as water upon a plain Table is drawn which way any one of it is guided by the finger' (p. 20).

Of far greater significance is the sequence of images Hobbes invokes throughout books I and II to clarify successive elements in his theory of the commonwealth. He begins in chapter V with an extended simile designed to indicate why a scientific and demonstrable theory of civil associations is indispensable, and why it can never be satisfactory to rely on the cultivation of political prudence. To make the difference between these two approaches 'appeare more cleerly', he suggests that we visualise someone 'with an excellent naturall use and dexterity in handling his armes' confronting an opponent who has 'added to that dexterity an acquired Science, of where he can offend or be offended by his adversarie in every possible posture or guard' (p. 37). Hobbes's contention is that 'the ability of the former would be to the ability of the later as Prudence to Sapience; both usefull, but the later infallible' (p. 37). To which he adds in even more minatory tones that those who trust in civil affairs to rules of thumb and the authority of books 'are like him that trusting to the false rules of a master of Fence, ventures praesumptuously upon an adversary that either kills or disgraces him' (p. 37). The force of the simile derives from the implication that any purely prudential or experimental science of politics will be literally fatal to public security.

Hobbes employs a comparably extended simile in chapter XV to illuminate his account of the process by which commonwealths are formed. He starts by explaining that 'there is in mens aptnesse to Society a diversity of Nature, rising from their diversity of Affections' and that this

41 Hobbes 1991, p. 15. Hobbes had already used the image in *The Elements of Law*. See BL Harl. MS 4235, fo. 15^r, and cf. Hobbes 1969a, p. 8.

generates a distinct law of nature enjoining the virtue of 'compleasance', the virtue we display when we do our best to 'accommodate' ourselves to one another (p. 106). To clarify this difficult passage, and at the same time to underline his argument, Hobbes suggests that we can see what is at stake if we think of individuals in relation to civil associations as being like 'stones brought together for the building of an Aedifice'.[42] If there is a stone 'which by the asperity and irregularity of Figure takes more room from others than it selfe fills; and for the hardnesse cannot be easily made plain, and thereby hindereth the building, it is by the builders cast away as unprofitable and troublesome' (p. 106). If, by analogy, we come upon a man 'that by asperity of Nature will strive to retain those things which to himself are superfluous and to others necessary; and for the stubbornness of his Passions cannot be corrected', we ought to ensure that he too is 'left or cast out of Society as combersome thereunto' (p. 106). Hobbes's comparison offers a vivid commentary on the familiar contention that no society can hope to flourish unless its members all know their place.

If individuals constitute the building blocks of the commonwealth, it follows that the commonwealth itself can be viewed as a building, an implication Hobbes duly pursues in two further and closely connected tropes. One is a biblical allusion designed to bring home to us the dangers of failing to build scientifically. Those who 'have not sifted to the bottom, and with exact reason weighed the causes and nature of Common-wealths' are like men who 'lay the foundation of their houses on sand' for lack of understanding that 'the skill of making and maintaining Common-wealths consisteth in certain Rules, as doth Arithmetique and Geometry' (p. 145). Hobbes's second image reminds us that, even though a group of people may 'desire with all their hearts to conforme themselves into one firme and lasting edifice', their ignorance 'of the art of making fit Lawes to square their actions by', together with their lack 'of humility and patience to suffer the rude and combersome points of their present greatnesse to be taken off', will generally make it necessary for them to put their trust in someone of greater expertise.[43] 'They cannot', as he warns, 'without the help of a very able Architect be compiled into any other than a crasie building, such as hardly lasting out their own time must assuredly fall upon the heads of their posterity' (p. 221).

Hobbes next presents a range of contrasting (and hence partly mixed) metaphors designed to help us appreciate what kind of structure we bring into existence when we create a commonwealth. His argument at this

42 Hobbes 1991, p. 106. This strongly recalls the extended simile used by Quintilian at the start of book VII of the *Institutio oratoria*. See Quintilian 1920–2, VII, Proemium, vol. III, p. 2.

43 Hobbes 1991, p. 221. Cf. Hobbes 1991, p. 232.

stage differs very markedly from that of *The Elements* and *De Cive*, in which he had relied entirely on the traditional image of the commonwealth as a body politic with a sovereign as its soul.[44] It is true that *Leviathan* continues to invoke this well-worn trope. Hobbes declares in his introduction that 'the *Sovereignty* is an Artificiall *Soul*' giving 'life and motion to the whole body',[45] and subsequently pursues the implications of his analogy at somewhat tedious length.[46] Chapter XXII considers the position of corporations and other internal political 'systems', comparing them with 'the similar parts or Muscles of a Body naturall' (p. 155). Chapter XXIII discusses the role of public ministers, comparing them with various 'parts Organicall': those who judge or instruct are like 'the organs of Voice in a Body naturall'; those who execute the sovereign's judgments are like hands; those who are sent abroad as spies are like eyes; those who receive petitions are like ears; and so on.[47] Finally, Hobbes reverts to his earlier diagnosis in *The Elements* and *De Cive* of the sundry diseases of commonwealths. These are said to include excessive desire for change, which is like the itch; fear of ghostly authorities, which is like epilepsy; unwillingness to grant taxes, which resembles ague; and lastly civil war, which amounts to death.[48]

Alongside these familiar analogies, Hobbes introduces a fresh and very different metaphor that offers a much clearer indication of how he believes a commonwealth should be visualised. We should think of it, he suggests, not in organic terms as a natural body but in purely mechanistic terms as a machine.[49] The 'COMMONWEALTH OR STATE (in latine CIVITAS)' is accordingly described as 'an Artificiall Man' and compared with 'Engines that move themselves by springs and wheeles as doth a watch' (p. 9). Although we can still speak, if we like, of its heart, its nerves and its joints, we must recognise that the heart is 'but a *Spring*; and the *Nerves*, but so many *Strings*; and the *Joynts*, but so many *Wheeles*' (p. 9). These metaphorical transformations are crucial to Hobbes's argument, helping as they do to underpin his claim that commonwealths can in no sense be regarded as God-given creations or natural occurrences. They are wholly man-made contrivances, mechanisms we construct with the sole aim of furthering our own purposes. We may thus be said to stand in relation to them as God stands

44 BL Harl. MS 4235, fos. 11^r, 85^v, 102^r, 125^v, 131^r, 134^r, 139^r. Cf. Hobbes 1969a, pp. 1, 116, 138, 168, 175, 178, 184; Hobbes 1983a, VI.XIX, p. 148, and XII.I, pp. 185–6.

45 Hobbes 1991, p. 9; cf also pp. 153, 230, 398.

46 For a full survey see May 1959, pp. 84–97.

47 Hobbes 1991, pp. 166, 169.

48 Hobbes 1991, pp. 221, 225, 227, 229–30.

49 On Hobbes's mixture of organic and mechanistic imagery see Prokhovnik 1991, pp. 197–204. On the image of Leviathan as a machine see Roux 1981, pp. 110–12.

in relation to us. Just as God 'hath made and governes the World' by means of his art, so we in creating commonwealths imitate by our art 'that Rationall and most excellente worke of Nature, *Man*' (p. 9). We can even say that 'the *Pacts* and *Covenants* by which the parts of this Body Politique were at first made, set together and united resemble that *Fiat*, or the *Let us make man*, pronounced by God in the Creation' (pp. 9–10).

The frontispiece of *Leviathan* provides us with a celebrated portrayal of this artificial Person, whose body is formed out of those of myriad natural persons.[50] Hobbes had strangely foreshadowed the image at the end of his *Answer* to Davenant:

> I beleeve (Sir) you have seen a curious kind of perspective, where, he that lookes through a short hollow pipe, upon a picture conteyning diverse figures, sees none of those that are there paynted, but some one person made up of their partes, conveighed to the eye by the artificiall cutting of a glasse.[51]

When Hobbes came to anatomise the powers of this artificial person in *Leviathan*, he proceeded to superimpose a further and equally celebrated image designed to clarify the nature of the authority he wished to claim for the state. As his title-page declares, we should think of its 'Matter, Forme & Power' as those of Leviathan, the monster of the deep whom God describes in the book of Job. At the end of chapter XXVIII Hobbes duly reminds us of the relevant biblical passage (pp. 220–1):

> Hitherto I have set forth the nature of Man (whose Pride and other Passions have compelled him to submit himselfe to Government;) together with the great power of his Governour, whom I compared to *Leviathan*, taking that comparison out of the last two verses of the one and fortieth of *Job*; where God having set forth the great power of *Leviathan* calleth him King of the Proud. *There is nothing*, saith he, *on earth, to be compared with him. He is made so as not to be afraid. Hee seeth every high thing below him; and is King of all the children of pride.*

The contrast with *The Elements* and *De Cive* could scarcely be greater: there the powers of the state were described as those of a legal person; here the person has been transfigured into a monstrous beast.

Hobbes's famous image has the effect of presenting in visual terms a number of crucial features of his theory of the state. His simile (which is

50 Hobbes 1991, p. lxxiv. The image has been much discussed. On the artist see Brown 1978; Corbett and Lightbown 1979, pp. 219–30. On the design see Brandt 1987 (especially interesting on the centrality of the artificial person's heart, p. 177) and Prokhovnik 1991, pp. 130–48. For a full discussion of the metaphor and its portrayal see Smith 1994, pp. 155–9. Smith valuably emphasises that the frontispiece shows the commonwealth, not the sovereign as is so often assumed.

51 Hobbes 1971a, p. 55. For the background to Hobbes's interest in *perspectives curieuses*, see Baltrusaitis 1955 and the valuable discussion in Greenblatt 1980, pp. 17–21, and references at pp. 260–1.

how he thinks of it)[52] reminds us that public authority arises out of the deep in the sense that it arises out of our deepest fears. Among these, Hobbes continually insists, our greatest is the fear of death, which provides us with our main reason for constructing a commonwealth and agreeing to obey it.[53] His image also serves to underline the overwhelming scale and force of the state's authority. Although 'that great LEVIATHAN' is 'but an Artificiall Man', its strength and stature are immeasurably greater than those 'for whose protection and defence it was intended' (p. 9). This picture of vastness and potential violence additionally conveys a strong sense of how we ought to react to public power. We are instructed in chapter XVII to think of 'the generation of that great LEVIATHAN' as the bringing into being of a '*Mortall* God, to which we owe under the *Immortal God* our peace and defence' (p. 120). The impression we are left with is of an authority to be approached not merely with respect but with awe and reverence.

The last of Hobbes's running metaphors in book II of *Leviathan* dramatises the closely related concept of political obligation, arguably the central topic of the entire work. To show us how the concept should be understood, Hobbes presents us with a series of images of enslavement and physical constraint.[54] He initially declares at the beginning of chapter XVII that the relationship between citizens and the law is such that the law may be said to 'tye them by fear of punishment' (p. 117). He recurs to the metaphor in the following chapter, in which he first speaks of 'the untyed hands of that Man or Assembly of men that hath the Soveraignty' (p. 123) and later adds that subjects should regard the civil law as 'a coërcive Power to tye their hands from rapine and revenge' (p. 128). He reverts to the image in analysing the concept of liberty in chapter XXI, repeating it yet again when discussing the office of the sovereign in chapter XXX, where he concludes that 'the use of Lawes' is 'not to bind the People from all Voluntary actions; but to direct and keep them in such a motion, as not to hurt themselves by their own impetuous desires, rashness, or indiscretion'.[55]

Hobbes is extremely anxious to underline the metaphoricality of his discourse at this point. Just as we bring into existence an artificial man by covenanting to create a sovereign, so the bonds imposed by his sovereignty are correspondingly artificial in character. Hobbes gives expression to this crucial thought in a remarkable passage from chapter XXI in which he presents us with a version of Lucian's fable of Hercules:[56]

52 Hobbes 1991, p. 221, describes the image as a 'comparison'.
53 See Hobbes 1991, esp. p. 70 *et seq.*, on the implications of our 'Fear of Death and Wounds'.
54 These images make virtually no appearance in *The Elements of Law*, but are already present in *De Cive*. See Hobbes 1983a, II.XVIII, p. 105; XIV.III, p. 207; XIV.XI, p. 210.
55 See Hobbes 1991, p. 239, and cf. p. 147. See also p. 374 on the collar of civil subjection.
56 See Lucian 1913, esp. p. 65. On the Gallic Hercules see chapter 2, note 191, *supra*.

> But as men for the atteyning of peace, and conservation of themselves thereby, have made an Artificiall Man, which we call a Common-wealth; so also have they made Artificiall Chains, called *Civill Lawes*, which they themselves, by mutuall covenants, have fastned at one end to the lips of that Man, or Assembly, to whom they have given the Soveraigne Power; and at the other end to their own Ears. These Bonds in their own nature but weak, may neverthelesse be made to hold, by the danger, though not by the difficulty of breaking them.[57]

The passage is grotesquely at odds with Hobbes's usual expository style, but it draws on a *topos* much favoured by the rhetorical writers of his youth, the parallel with Puttenham's *Arte of English Poesie* being especially close.[58] At the same time, the imagery confirms Hobbes's earlier account of the promises, and hence the mutual bonds, by which we covenant with each other to institute a commonwealth. The bonds in question, as he had previously observed in a passage hovering between the metaphorical and the literal, 'have their strength, not from their own Nature, (for nothing is more easily broken than a mans word,) but from Feare of some evill consequence upon the rupture' (p. 93).

Hobbes introduces one final classical flourish when he adds that, from the point of view of powerful subjects, it follows that the binding force of law is no stronger – as Plutarch had remarked in his life of Solon[59] – than a cobweb to be brushed aside (p. 204). Once we recognise its fragility, we can also appreciate why Hobbes is so interested in metaphors of enslavement. Precisely because the bonds of law 'are in their own Nature weak', he wishes to articulate as vividly as possible the contention that we have a duty to think of them as inviolable. The implication he hopes to leave with us is that, if we are rational citizens, we shall treat the bonds of law as if they are genuine bonds, literally harnessing us to the performance of our duties while tying our hands from rapine and revenge.

THE PROVOCATION OF LAUGHTER

As well as explaining how the master tropes of simile and metaphor can be used to 'hold forth' our arguments, the classical theorists of rhetoric had spoken of a second means by which we can hope to call on the resources of *ornatus* to add persuasive force to the findings of reason and science. They had pointed to a number of ways in which we can hope to employ the figures and tropes to make our intellectual adversaries appear laughable,

57 Hobbes 1991, p. 147. The complaints in Silver 1988 pp. 369–70 about the 'ungainliness' of this 'outlandish' passage seem to stem from missing its allusiveness.

58 For Puttenham on Hercules as 'a lustie old man with a long chayne tyed by one end at his tong, by the other end at the peoples eares', see chapter 2, notes 194 to 196, *supra*.

59 Plutarch 1580, p. 89.

thereby undermining their arguments and advancing our own at the same time.

As we saw in chapter 5, the Roman rhetoricians were especially interested in laughter and the emotions expressed by it. According to their theory – which was taken over virtually without alteration by the rhetoricians of the Renaissance – to laugh is almost always to laugh *at* someone; laughter is a means of glorying over others and of indicating, almost involuntarily, a scornful sense of our own superiority. It follows that a talent for provoking laughter can be a lethal weapon of debate. To succeed in directing our wit in such a way as to arouse laughter against our opponents will be to succeed in causing them to be viewed with contempt, and will thus be a means of bringing their arguments into disrepute. In the words of the Psalmist (22: 7) they will be laughed to scorn.

Hobbes was fascinated by laughter and the kinds of wit and humour that provoke it. According to Aubrey he possessed an exceptionally quick wit himself, not only being 'of a cheerful and pleasant humour', but 'marvellous happy and ready in his replies', so much so that 'if trueth (uncommon) delivered clearly and wittily may goe for a saying, his common discourse was full of them'.[60] Hobbes was also preoccupied in a more theoretical spirit with the phenomenon of laughter, and especially with the range of emotions it may be said to express. He initially raises the question in anatomising the passions in *The Elements of Law*, subsequently developing essentially the same line of argument in chapter 1 of *De Cive* and in the definitive presentation of his theory of the passions in book 1 of *Leviathan*.

Hobbes opens the first of these discussions by announcing that the explanation he proposes to offer of the causes and occasions of mirth is an entirely original one:

> There is a passion, which hath no name, but the signe of it, is that distortion of the Countenance we call LAUGHTER, which is alwayes joy; but what joy, what we thinke, and wherein we tryumph when we laugh, hath not hitherto bene declared by any.[61]

This is a passage of remarkable effrontery, and makes one wonder a little at Hobbes's sense of his audience. Anyone acquainted with the classical *ars rhetorica* would have recognised at once that his ensuing analysis of laughter was scarcely original at all, but was overwhelmingly indebted to the theories of Cicero, Quintilian and their Renaissance followers.[62]

60 Aubrey 1898, I, pp. 340, 348, 356. Hobbes tells us that in company he liked to joke. See Hobbes 1839a, p. xxi.

61 BL Harl. MS 4235, fo. 35^{v}. Cf. Hobbes 1969a, p. 41.

62 Heyd 1982, esp. pp. 287–9, rightly stresses that Hobbes had predecessors, although without mentioning Roman rhetorical thought.

It is true that Hobbes adds one detail to the classical account. This stems from the emphasis he places on the importance of the novel and the surprising in the provocation of mirth. Speaking in his most mechanistic idiom – strongly reminiscent of the section *Du ris* in Descartes's *Les passions de l'âme*[63] – Hobbes insists that outbursts of laughter only occur when a sense of 'eminency' comes upon us with a feeling of suddenness. As he expresses the point in *The Elements*, 'for as much as the same thinge is no more ridiculous when it groweth stale or usuall, whatsoever it be that moveth Laughter, it must be new and unexpected'.[64]

Even this suggestion was not without precedent, for Vives had already put it forward in his *De Anima et vita* of 1538, in which he had stressed that laughter arises 'from a novel joy or delight',[65] and added that 'sudden and unexpected things have more effect on us and move us more quickly to laughter than anything else'.[66] Apart from emphasising this element of surprise, moreover, Hobbes's analysis of laughter is virtually identical with that of the Roman and Renaissance theorists of eloquence. His basic thesis, like theirs, is that 'the passion of Laughter proceedeth from a suddaine conception of some ability in himself that laugheth', and thus that 'men laugh at Jests, the witt whereof always consisteth in the Elegant discovering and conveying to our mindes some absurdity of another'.[67] What generally arouses the passion is 'the suddaine Imagination of our owne odds and eminence, for what is else the recommending our selves to our own good opinion, by comparison with another mans Infirmityes or absurditie?'[68] Like his classical authorities, Hobbes adds that the contemplation of other people's moral and physical deformities tends in particular to produce such feelings of ascendancy. 'Men laugh at the infirmityes of others, by comparison of which their owne abilityes are sett off and illustrated.'[69] Closely echoing Quintilian's further claim that this constitutes the most ambitious way of glorying over others, Hobbes ends with a famous definition:

> I may therefore conclude, that the passion of Laughter is nothyng else but a suddaine Glory arising from suddaine Conception of some Eminency in our selves, by Comparison with the Infirmityes of others, or with our owne formerly.[70]

63 Descartes 1988, art. 124, p. 153.
64 BL Harl. MS 4235, fo. 35^{v}. Cf. Hobbes 1969a, p. 41.
65 Vives 1964, III.x, p. 469: 'risus, qui ex affectu nascitur, de laetitia est, aut delectatione nova, surgit'.
66 Vives 1964, III.x, p. 469: 'insperata vero et subita plus afficiunt, citius commovent risum'.
67 BL Harl. MS 4235, fos. 35^{v}–36^{r}. Cf. Hobbes 1969a, pp. 41–2.
68 BL Harl. MS 4235, fo. 36^{r}. Cf. Hobbes 1969a, p. 42.
69 BL Harl. MS 4235, fo. 35^{v}. Cf. Hobbes 1969a, p. 41.
70 BL Harl. MS 4235, fo. 36^{r}. Cf. Hobbes 1969a, p. 42.

Although this has often been hailed as one of Hobbes's most characteristic pronouncements, it amounts to little more than a summary of Quintilian's argument.[71]

While Hobbes is greatly interested in laughter, we have seen that initially he declared himself very much opposed to the habit of laughing at others. Although he never explicitly criticises those with a talent for mockery, he conveys the impression in his early writings that he strongly disapproves of it. Here too the contrast with *Leviathan* is very marked. Although he still maintains that grieving or wounding others with a sharp tongue is an abuse of speech (p. 26), he now focuses on a number of circumstances in which he considers it appropriate and even necessary to permit oneself a certain licence in debate, including a licence to give vent to feelings of contempt. When discussing the laws of nature in chapter xv, he begins by conceding that any 'triumph' or 'glorying in the hurt of another' amounts to cruelty, but immediately adds that this is only true if the glorying is 'without reason' or 'to no end' (p. 106). More positively, he stoutly defends what he describes as 'the ordinary liberty of conversation', criticising the vaingloriousness of those who display an excessive proneness 'to interpret for contempt' the exercise of such liberties (pp. 205–6). He concludes with a strong attack on those who take offence 'from contumely in words or gesture, when they produce no other harme than the present griefe of him that is reproached' (p. 213). He insists that 'the true cause of such griefe' consists 'not in the contumely (which takes no hold upon men conscious of their own vertue) but in the Pusillanimity of him that is offended by it' (p. 213).

Despite this marked hardening of attitude, there remains a certain tension in *Leviathan* between Hobbes's precepts about the provocation of laughter and his own rhetorical practice. Apart from the exceptions he allows himself, his precepts remain comparable with those in *The Elements*, in which he had observed with distaste that a man must be 'of little worth, to think the Infirmityes of another sufficient matter for his tryumph'.[72] He repeats the charge in his *Answer* to Davenant, expressing it in tones of even sterner admonishment:

> Great persons that have their mindes employed on great designes, have not leasure enough to laugh, and are pleased with the contemplation of their owne power and vertues, so as they need not the infirmities and vices of other men to recommend themselves to their owne favor by comparison, as all men do when they laugh.[73]

71 Compare Quintilian 1920–2, XI.I.22, vol. IV p. 166, claiming that 'Ambitiosissimum gloriandi genus est etiam deridere' with Hobbes 1668, p. 29, claiming that 'Gloriatio subita Passio illa est, quae producit risum.'

72 BL Harl. MS 4235, fo. 36^{r}. Cf. Hobbes 1969a, p. 42.

73 Hobbes 1971a, p. 53.

The analysis of 'sudden glory' in chapter VI of *Leviathan* includes a still stronger and almost puritanical warning against the dangers of giving way to mirth (p.43):

> It is incident most to them, that are conscious of the fewest abilities in themselves; who are forced to keep themselves in their own favour, by observing the imperfections of other men. And therefore much Laughter at the defects of others is a signe of Pusillanimity. For of great minds, one of the proper works is to help and free others from scorn; and compare themselves onely with the most able.

For all these scruples, the fact remains that in *Leviathan* Hobbes directs a remorseless barrage of scornful comment against the alleged defects and imperfections of his intellectual adversaries. No aspect of *Leviathan* differs more sharply or revealingly from *The Elements* and *De Cive*. Apart from a number of sardonic touches, the earlier recensions of Hobbes's civil philosophy aspire to a style of studiously scientific neutrality. By contrast, *Leviathan* deploys the full panoply of techniques specifically recommended by the classical and Renaissance theorists of eloquence for arousing laughter and eliciting feelings of derision and contempt.[74]

A number of commentators have asked themselves why so many of Hobbes's original readers, most of whom had accepted *The Elements* and *De Cive* without difficulty, found themselves so deeply shocked and repelled by *Leviathan*.[75] It is perhaps surprising that Hobbes's change of polemical style has so rarely been cited as part of the explanation, especially as so many of his contemporaries remarked on it with such bitterness. Alexander Rosse in his *Leviathan drawn out with a Hook* of 1653 accused Hobbes of refusing to argue with his opponents, contenting himself with carping and laughing, adopting a posture of 'supercilious scorn', dismissing his critics 'with scorn and contempt'.[76] George Lawson in his *Examination* of 1657 likewise complained of Hobbes's 'fooleries and blasphemies'.[77] Thomas Tenison in his *Creed of Mr. Hobbes Examined* of 1670 denounced Hobbes as an 'insolent and pernicious writer', someone suffering not merely from 'weakness of head' but 'venome of mouth'.[78] Clarendon in his *Brief View* of 1676 similarly attacked Hobbes for exciting 'prejudice and contemt', and for seeking 'to lessen and vilifie' his

74 Cantalupo 1991 rightly points (pp. 191 and 236–9) to the elements of humour and satire in *Leviathan*. But he gives no account of the *figurae* recommended by the theorists of rhetoric for contriving such a tone, nor of Hobbes's use of these *figurae*.

75 See for example Tuck 1989, p. 29. But we must beware of assuming that *De Cive* had been well-received even among Hobbes's acquaintances. Deshommeaux remarked that it did not deserve to be criticised, only burned. See Jacquot and Jones 1973, p. 20.

76 Rosse 1653, pp. 81–2. On Rosse see Bowle 1969, pp. 17–21, 61–71.

77 Lawson 1657, p. 156. On Lawson and Hobbes see Condren 1989, pp. 173–80.

78 Tenison 1670, p. 2. For Tenison's attack see Mintz 1962, pp. 72–9.

adversaries.[79] He particularly singled out Hobbes's 'Comical mention of the power and goodness of God' in book III of *Leviathan*, and accused Hobbes's admirers of 'making themselves merry' with devout customs of speech.[80] John Dowel opened his *The Leviathan Heretical* of 1683 by explaining in tones of even deeper indignation 'how Capital a Delinquent is Mr Hobs, who hath by writeing endeavoured to render the sentiments of the best and most learned men ridiculous'.[81]

Hobbes never publicly admitted that he had gone too far in mocking his opponents, but he seems eventually to have conceded the charge. This is evident from the Latin *Leviathan* published in 1668. Although this version is in some ways an even more rhetorical text, it differs strikingly from the 1651 edition in suppressing a number of passages in which Hobbes had previously spoken in his most scornful and dismissive tones. Meanwhile, however, the English version of 1651 must rank among other things as a masterpiece of satire and invective, embodying as it does a systematic application of the techniques evolved by the theorists of rhetoric for speaking with ridicule and contempt. It is with Hobbes's exploitation of these techniques that the remaining sections of this chapter will be concerned.

THE SATIRISING OF OPPONENTS

We need to begin by considering Hobbes's employment of the master tropes of simile and metaphor as vehicles for satire. As we have seen, the classical and Renaissance rhetoricians had regarded these particular tropes – together with hyperbole – as especially well-adapted for expressing scorn and contempt. They had stressed that we can hope to use them not merely to picture or 'hold forth' our intellectual adversaries, but to picture them specifically as ludicrous, offering memorable images of their alleged absurdity.

Hobbes exploits this technique throughout *Leviathan*, especially in criticising the various sects and groups with whom he finds himself in deepest disagreement. He seeks in every instance to 'show' or portray his opponents – in advance of examining any of their arguments – as merely laughable. He first adopts the strategy when speaking in the early chapters of part I about those who put their faith in the authority of ancient books instead of in the methods of science. Chapter IV presents us with an image of this entire school of thought as little better than bird-witted. Bacon had

79 Clarendon 1676, p. 16. For an outline of Clarendon's attack see Bowle 1969, pp. 157–73.
80 Clarendon 1676, p. 18.
81 Dowel 1683, sig. A, 2v.

already invoked a similar metaphor in *The Advancement of Learning* to suggest the ineffectual flutterings of those who lack the ability to concentrate, and had added that 'if a child be bird-witted, that is, hath not the faculty of attention, the mathematics giveth a remedy thereunto'.[82] Hobbes reiterates the image when picturing those who distractedly flit about amid the contradictory texts of antiquity (p. 28):

They which trust to books, do as they that cast up many little summs into a greater, without considering whether those little summes were rightly cast up or not; and at last finding the errour visible, and not mistrusting their first grounds, know not which way to cleere themselves; but spend time in fluttering over their bookes; as birds that entring by the chimney, and finding themselves inclosed in a chamber, flutter at the false light of a glasse window, for want of wit to consider which way they came in.

The same passage develops a still more opprobrious image of muddled futility, portraying those who place their trust in learned doctors as persons of such stupidity as to be incapable even of counting their money correctly. 'A foole oft finds himselfe short of his reckonings' had become a proverbial expression by the time Hobbes was writing,[83] and he embroiders it in his most disdainful style (p. 29):

For words are wise mens counters, they do but reckon by them: but they are the mony of fooles, that value them by the authority of an *Aristotle*, a *Cicero*, or a *Thomas*, or any other Doctor whatsoever, if but a man.

The same metaphor[84] recurs in the chapter on counsel at the point where Hobbes is criticising the public behaviour of those 'who have the ambition to be thought eloquent, and also learned in the Politiques' (p. 181). Such people like to show off their knowledge of the best authorities, but they merely condemn themselves to the absurdity of producing 'motly orations, made of the divers colored threds or shreds of Authors' (p. 181). Their ambition, ironically enough, is to win applause – an irony recalling Jacques's aspiration in *As You Like it*:

O that I were a fool,
I am ambitious for a motley coat.[85]

What these orators forget, as Hobbes's metaphor reminds us, is that the wearing of motley identifies them as fools.

As the argument of *Leviathan* unfolds, Hobbes begins to concentrate on those admirers of antiquity who introduced the metaphysics of Aristotle

82 Bacon 1915, p. 151.
83 Cotgrave 1611, sig. Pp, v^r^.
84 Dascal 1976, esp. pp. 193–7, valuably discusses it, although he mistakenly calls it a simile.
85 Shakespeare 1988, *As You Like It*, II.vii.42–3, p. 637. Cf. Nashe 1985, p. 296, where it is said of the orator that the 'shreds of his sentences' are 'no more than a fool's coat of many colours'.

into the study of the Christian religion,[86] thereby giving rise to the discipline Hobbes describes as school divinity.[87] He focuses in particular on the distinctive jargon of the school divines, their 'insignificent Traines of strange and barbarous words' such as 'separate essences', 'intelligible species', 'infused faith' and the like.[88] Initially he attacks their use of this vocabulary to describe the indescribable attributes of God, thereby 'disputing Philosophically in stead of admiring, and adoring of the Divine and Incomprehensible Nature' (p. 467). But he mainly directs his hostility against their political aspirations, reserving his strongest condemnation for the evident ambition of the Catholic schoolmen to 'set up a *Supremacy* against the *Soveraignty*; *Canons* against *Lawes*; and a *Ghostly Authority* against the *Civill*'.[89]

Here too Hobbes prefaces his criticisms with a sequence of images designed to fix these opponents in the minds of his readers as figures of mere absurdity. His opening metaphor points to the emptiness and irrelevance of their supposed learning (p. 457):

> If a man would wel observe that which is delivered in the Histories, concerning the Religious Rites of the Greeks and Romanes, I doubt not but he might find many more of these old empty Bottles of Gentilisme, which the doctors of the Romane Church, either by Negligence, or Ambition, have filled up again with the new Wine of Christianity, that will not faile in time to break them.

Hobbes is alluding to a favourite New Testament parable: St Matthew (9: 17), St Mark (2: 22) and St Luke (5: 37–8) all report Christ's warning that, if new wine is placed in old bottles, the bottles will burst and the wine be spilled. Hobbes ingeniously elaborates the moral by implying, in his final and ambiguous phrase, that the superstitious doctors themselves, and not merely the bottles they have filled, will eventually be broken.[90]

The attack is kept up in the form of a response to an imagined critic who demands to know what purpose is served by examining the jargon of the theologians in a work of civil science. Hobbes answers with a simile conveying even more derisively the intellectual emptiness of school divinity (p. 465):

> It is to this purpose, that men may no longer suffer themselves to be abused by them that by this doctrine of *Separated Essences*, built on the Vain Philosophy of Aristotle,

86 Hobbes 1991, pp. 85, 418, 462, 472.

87 Hobbes 1991, e.g. pp. 463, 472.

88 Hobbes 1991, pp. 14, 34, 279, 465–6, 472, 477.

89 Hobbes 1991, p. 226; cf. also pp. 417–18, 465.

90 Cantalupo 1991, p. 222, remarks on the solemn effect produced by the string of monosyllables that bring the sentence to an end. For a full account of sentence structure in *Leviathan* see Roux and Gilibert 1980.

would fright them from Obeying the Laws of their Countrey, with empty names; as men fright Birds from the Corn with an empty doublet, a hat and a crooked stick.

With this richly scornful image Hobbes also hints at the idea of men of straw, while suggesting in a further play on words that their arguments are not merely mindless but dishonest – not merely empty but crooked.

We are later offered a different but equally dismissive picture of the school divines and their intellectual shiftiness. Hobbes introduces it in criticising their failure to see that the various epithets they apply to honour the name of God cannot possibly describe His nature (p. 467):

But they that venture to reason of his Nature, from these Attributes of Honour, losing their understanding in the very first attempt, fall from one Inconvenience into another, without end, and without number; in the same manner, as when a man ignorant of the Ceremonies of Court, comming into the presence of a greater Person than he is used to speak to, and stumbling at his entrance, to save himselfe from falling, lets slip his Cloake; to recover his Cloake, lets fall his Hat; and with one disorder after another, discovers his astonishment and rusticity.

Having initially reduced the Church's learned doctors to scarecrows, Hobbes now identifies them as country bumpkins. It is easy to sympathise with his frustration at their ignorance, especially when we recall that two of his most virulent clerical antagonists – first Rosse and later Whitehall – singled out what Rosse describes as Hobbes's vain and whimsical belief that the earth revolves around the sun.[91] Nevertheless, this was one of the moments at which Hobbes evidently came to feel that he had carried his insults too far, and in the Latin *Leviathan* these images of intellectual boorishness are both suppressed.[92]

Most of all, Hobbes likes to depict the school divines as benighted, as spiritual travellers overtaken by darkness. They are accordingly represented as among the most numerous and powerful inhabitants of the kingdom of darkness described in book IV.[93] One effect of their shady doctrines, especially as propagated by the Roman Catholic Church, is that they dim the clear light of reason and nature, thereby causing 'so great a Darknesse in mens understanding, that they see not who it is to whom they have engaged their obedience' (p. 420). Furthermore, by mixing religion with 'the vain and erroneous Philosophy of the Greeks', they obscure and even extinguish the light of Scripture.[94] Hobbes draws out the implications of the metaphor by suggesting that much of their resulting influence can be traced to the fact that ignorant people are often afraid of the dark.

91 Rosse 1653, p. 93; Whitehall 1679, p. 162.
92 Hobbes 1668, pp. 320–1.
93 On darkness as the 'controlling metaphor' of book IV see Cantalupo 1991, esp. pp. 196–8.
94 Hobbes 1991, p. 418. Cf. also p. 477.

Although the theologians have nothing more impressive to offer than 'the darknesse of Schoole distinctions, and hard words', the fact that 'the fear of Darknesse and Ghosts is greater than other fears' means that the Catholic Church can always rely on 'a party sufficient to Trouble and sometimes to Destroy a Commonwealth' (p. 227).

Such obscurantism is not merely ignorant but manipulative: the divines are full of dark purposes, their main concern being to keep us in the dark. This is the contention put forward in the opening chapter of part IV, '*Of Spirituall Darknesse from* misinterpretation *of Scripture*'. The faithful, 'who are the *Children of the Light*', find themselves confronted by '*a Confederacy of Deceivers, that to obtain dominion over men in this present world, endeavour by dark and erroneous Doctrines to extinguish in them the Light both of Nature and of the Gospell*' (pp. 417–18). The greatest deceiver is the pope, whom Hobbes portrays in an extension of his metaphor as forcing people to fight with each other in the dark without being able to distinguish friend from foe (p. 420):

> As often as there is any repugnancy between the Politicall designes of the Pope and other Christian Princes, as there is very often, there ariseth such a Mist amongst their Subjects, that they know not a stranger that thrusteth himself into the throne of their lawfull Prince, from him whom they had themselves placed there; and in this Darknesse of mind, are made to fight one against another, without discerning their enemies from their friends, under the conduct of another man's ambition.

So successfully have the divines raised these mists that 'wee are therefore yet in the Dark' (p. 418).

Hobbes summarises his objections by declaring, in a further extension of the metaphor, that 'the Enemy has been here in the Night of our naturall Ignorance, and sown the tares of Spirituall Errors' (p. 418). Here he alludes to the parable of the sower from St Matthew's gospel, thereby hinting at an even graver accusation against the school divines. When Christ's disciples asked him to interpret the parable, he replied that 'the tares are the children of the wicked one' and that 'the enemy that sowed them is the devil'.[95] We are left with the implication that the doctrines of the school divines are not merely obscurantist but diabolical.

These images culminate in a celebrated satire on the vacuous ghostliness of the papacy and the Roman Catholic Church (p. 480):

> From the time that the Bishop of Rome had gotten to be acknowledged for Bishop Universall, by pretence of Succession to St. Peter, their whole Hierarchy, or Kingdome of Darkenesse, may be compared not unfitly to the *Kingdome of Fairies*; that is, to the old wives *Fables* in England concerning *Ghosts* and *Spirits* and the feats they play in the night. And if a man consider the originall of this great Ecclesiasticall Dominion, he will

95 Matthew 13: 38–9.

easily perceive, that the *Papacy* is no other than the *Ghost* of the deceased *Romane Empire*, sitting crowned upon the grave thereof: For so did the Papacy start up on a Sudden out of the Ruines of that Heathen Power.

Two separate and equally dismissive metaphors are secreted within this famous passage. One reduces the papacy to a frightened animal suddenly 'starting up' amid the ruins of Rome, with the added implication that, since it is merely a ghost, we have no good reason to fear it at all. The other metaphor – following out the image of ghostliness – conveys a sense of the papacy as having no substance at all, and it is on this scornful note that Hobbes brings *Leviathan* to a close.[96] When we think about fairies, we think of '*Spirits* and *Ghosts*' which 'inhabite Darknesse, Solitudes, and Graves'. The school divines are similarly '*Spirituall* men, and *Ghostly* Fathers', who 'walke in Obscurity of Doctrine, in Monasteries, Churches and Church-yards' (p. 481). When we reflect on the reputed behaviour of fairies, we recall that they 'are said to take young Children out of their Cradles, and to change them into Naturall Fools, which Common people do therefore call *Elves*, and are apt to mischief' (p. 481). The school divines likewise 'take from young men the use of Reason, by certain Charms compounded of Metaphysiques, and Miracles, and Traditions, and Abused Scripture, whereby they are good for nothing else, but to execute what they command them'.[97] And just as the fairies 'have no existence, but in the Fancies of ignorant people', so the alleged power of the papacy 'consisteth onely in the Fear that Seduced people stand in, of their Excommunication; upon hearing of false Miracles, false Traditions, and false Interpretations of the Scripture' (p. 482).

A further group of clerical opponents whom Hobbes delights to identify satirically are the so-called Enthusiasts, whom he also characterises as the 'unlearned Divines'.[98] He first examines their distinctive beliefs in chapter XII, his chapter on the rise and fall of religious creeds. Such people generally claim to be 'possessed with a divine Spirit; which Possession they call Enthusiasme' (p. 81). They further claim that, due to this possession, God speaks directly in and through them, enabling them to prophesy and gain an insight into His desires (p. 81). When Hobbes turns in chapter XXIX to explain why commonwealths collapse, he devotes part of his analysis to examining the dangerous effects produced by such beliefs.[99] Those who

96 Thomas 1971, pp. 590–1, points out that Hobbes's scepticism embraces a wide range of popular beliefs about fairies and ghosts.

97 Hobbes 1991, p. 481. For a similar sentiment see Sprat 1959, p. 340.

98 Hobbes 1991, p. 224. On these groups and Hobbes's irritation with them see Smith 1989, pp. 72–8.

99 For Hobbes's fears about the politically unsettling effects of allegedly supernatural events see Johnston 1986, pp. 150–63, and cf. pp. 101–6.

hold them insist 'that Faith and Sanctity are not to be attained by Study and Reason, but by supernaturall Inspiration or infusion' of the kind that they alone experience (p. 223). This in turn means that they attempt to set themselves up as legislators, and at the same time 'do what they can to make men think that Sanctity and Naturall reason cannot stand together' (p. 224).

Here too Hobbes makes mocking use of simile and metaphor to fix in the minds of his readers the absurdity of his adversaries. He first examines their delusions in his *Answer* to Davenant, in which he likens them to 'unskillfull Conjurers' who, 'mistaking the rites and ceremonious points of their art, call up such spirits as they cannot at their pleasure allay againe'.[100] These tricks are not merely foolish but dangerous, since those who dabble in them generally produce 'subversion or disturbance' in the commonwealth.[101] Hobbes rounds off his image of bungled sorcery with a reference to the figure of paradiastole, the dangerous implications of which are seen to be the usual outcome of such meddling:

> For when they call unseasonably for *Zeale* there appeares a spirit of *Cruelty*; and when by the like error instead of *Truth* they rayse *Discord*; instead of *Wisedome*, *Fraud*; instead of *Reformation*, *Tumult*; and *Controversie* instead of *Religion*.[102]

By the time he came to write *Leviathan*, Hobbes's attitude had considerably hardened towards those who, as he sarcastically puts it, 'are possessed of an opinion of being inspired' (p. 54). His imagery now suggests that such people are not merely mischievous but insane. The point is brutally made in his analysis of the defects of the intellect, in which he not only insists that all enthusiasts are mad, but argues that 'if there were nothing else that bewrayed their madnesse; yet that very arrogating such inspiration to themselves, is argument enough' (p. 55). They resemble those inmates of Bedlam who at first entertain you with sober discourse, but end by assuring you that they are God the Father. As in this case, so with the enthusiast, 'you need expect no extravagant action for argument of his Madnesse' (p. 55).

While Hobbes devotes most of his satirical energies to ridiculing his clerical opponents, he is scarcely less scathing about his numerous political enemies. He reserves his deepest scorn for the lawyers and 'democraticall gentlemen' in the House of Commons, against whom he presses a number of serious charges. They undermine the scientific understanding of civil life by insisting on the barbarous study of precedent; they challenge the theory of absolute sovereignty with their foolish assumption that representative

100 Hobbes 1971a, p. 48.
101 Hobbes 1971a, pp. 48–9.
102 Hobbes 1971a, p. 48.

assemblies are indispensable; and they then employ the occasion of such assemblies to rouse the rabble against their lawful government.[103]

Hobbes had already spoken out against these groups in *De Cive* and *The Elements of Law*. But his earlier criticisms had been sober and serious in tone, whereas in *Leviathan* he prefaces his discussion with a series of images intended to reveal his adversaries as nothing better than futile and absurd. So withering are his comparisons that Clarendon felt moved in his *Brief View* to protest that Hobbes seemed bent on using 'light and scurrilous questions and instances' to 'expose the gravity and wisdom of all Government' to 'the mirth and contemt of all men'.[104]

Hobbes's similes are mainly designed to portray the lawyers and democratical gentlemen as immature and even infantile. He first points to their childishness when considering differences of customs, focusing in particular on their willingness to convert custom into a rule of action. They think 'that Unjust which it hath been the custome to punish; and that Just, of the impunity and approbation whereof they can produce an Example' (p. 73). This reduces them to the level of 'little children, that have no other rule of good and evill manners, but the correction they receive from their Parents and Masters' (p. 73). Later he generalises the attack to include all those who 'reprehend the actions and call in question the Authority of them that govern', and who are 'prone to all such Crimes as consist in Craft and in deceiving of their Neighbours' (p. 205). He warns us that 'those that deceive upon hope of not being observed do commonly deceive themselves', adding in his most derisive tones that this makes them 'no wiser than Children that think all hid by hiding their own eyes'.[105]

Hobbes later switches from picturing the democratical gentlemen as less than adult to picturing them as less than human, as animals of lethal viciousness. The change of tone from the discussion of the same topic in *The Elements* is remarkable. There Hobbes had proclaimed that 'Aristotle saith well' that 'noe man can partake of Liberty, but onely in a Popular Commonwealth'.[106] In *Leviathan* he declares that 'I cannot imagine how any thing can be more prejudiciall to a Monarchy, than the allowing of such books to be publikely read' as those which affirm 'that the Subjects in a Popular Common-wealth enjoy Liberty; but that in a Monarchy they are all Slaves'.[107] Such doctrines, Hobbes now insists, are nothing less then venomous, 'which Venime I will not doubt to compare to the biting of a

103 Hobbes 1991, pp. 73–4, 181–2.
104 Clarendon 1676, p. 132.
105 Hobbes 1991, p. 205. On the *topos* that those who try hardest to deceive others are most easily deceived see Knox 1989, pp. 115, 123.
106 BL Harl. MS 4235, fo. 126^{v}. Cf. Hobbes 1969a, p. 170.
107 Hobbes 1991, p. 226. Cf. Gauthier 1969, pp. 145–6.

mad Dogge', the effects of which are no less dangerous than 'when a Monarchy is once bitten to the quick by those Democraticall Writers that continually snarle at that estate' (p. 226).

Finally, in a further effort to indicate the absurdity of the democratical gentlemen, and especially their belief that government can best be carried on in large councils, Hobbes indulges in a rare attempt at satirical hyperbole (p. 182):

> A man that doth his businesse by the help of many and prudent Counsellours, with every one consulting apart in his proper element, does it best, as he that useth able Seconds at Tennis play, placed in their proper stations. He does next best, that useth his own Judgement only; as he that has no Second at all. But he that is carried up and down to his businesse in a framed Counsell, which cannot move but by the plurality of consenting opinions, the execution whereof is commonly (out of envy, or interest) retarded by the part dissenting, does worst of all, and is like one that is carried to the ball, though by good Players, yet in a Wheele-barrough, or other frame, heavy of it self, and retarded also by the inconcurrent judgements and endeavours of them that drive it; and so much the more, as they be more that set their hands to it; and most of all, when there is one or more amongst them, that desire to have him lose.

The extended simile is not perhaps very successful,[108] and Hobbes subsequently deleted it from the Latin *Leviathan.* But his intention remains clear enough: to 'hold forth' his political opponents – as he had earlier held forth his clerical enemies – as figures deserving of nothing better than ridicule and contempt.

THE EXPRESSION OF SCORN: THE TROPES

So far we have concentrated on Hobbes's employment of simile and metaphor to satirise his opponents by producing verbal pictures of their alleged absurdities. As we saw in chapter 5, however, the classical and Renaissance theorists of rhetoric had drawn attention to a second and more straightforward way in which we can hope to use the tropes to express our feelings of contempt. This further possibility was said to stem from the fact that several of the tropes possess an inherently ridiculing character. While the range of these so-called 'mocking tropes' remained a matter of debate, a number of neo-Ciceronian rhetoricians claimed to be able to distinguish as many as six of them: irony, sarcasm, aestismus, charientismus, diasyrmus and mycterismus.

Hobbes finds no place in *Leviathan* for charientismus or mycterismus, but

108 Attempting to translate *Leviathan* into French, François du Verdus wrote to Hobbes about this passage in 1656, saying that he had never seen anyone playing tennis in a wheel-barrow and asking 'whether it is played in that way in England'. See letter 100 in Hobbes 1994, p. 365.

he makes enthusiastic use of all the others in attacking his dialectical enemies. He displays a marked fondness for irony, the mocking trope *par excellence* according to the rhetoricians of his day.[109] He frequently appeals, that is, to commendatory terms to convey an underlying attitude of scorn.[110] Among the adversaries whom he ridicules in this fashion are the lawyers and democratical gentlemen who 'unsettle the Lawes with their publique discourse' (p. 205). It is rare, he observes, for such troublemakers to survive long enough to witness the results of their disturbances. To which he adds – in mocking reference to the language of conventional eulogy – that in consequence 'the benefit of their Crimes redoundeth to Posterity', the chief benefit being that new constitutional arrangements are foisted on those who never asked for them (p. 205). Later he speaks in similar vein about their theory that sovereign power may be divided. Thanking them for this alleged insight – which he describes as 'plainly and directly against the essence of a Common-wealth' – he emphasises that the lawyers are the experts to whom we are 'chiefly beholding' for this particular argument (p. 225).

It is in dealing with his religious antagonists that Hobbes makes fullest play with the inversions typical of ironic speech. He employs the technique against the Enthusiasts and their claim that God speaks to them directly, underpinning his irony with a stately invocation of anaphora, the figure of repetition (p. 256):

> When God speaketh to man, it must be either immediately; or by mediation of another man, to whom he had formerly spoken by himself immediately. How God speaketh to a man immediately may be understood by those well enough, to whom he hath so spoken; but how the same should be understood by another is hard, if not impossible to know.

He similarly ridicules the school divines by ironically commending the boldness of their arguments, especially about the nature of eternity (p. 466):

> For the meaning of *Eternity*, they will not have it to be an Endlesse Succession of Time; for then they should not be able to render a reason how Gods Will, and Praeordaining of things to come, should not be before his Praescience of the same, as the Efficient Cause before the Effect, or Agent before the Action; nor of many other their bold opinions concerning the Incomprehensible Nature of God.

109 On Hobbes's use of irony see the valuable comments in Roux 1981, pp. 103–13; Cantalupo 1991, esp. pp. 26–8, 255–6. For irony as 'the mocking Trope' see Fenner 1584, sig. D, 1^v, a description that came to be widely used.

110 For this understanding of irony as 'blaming by praise' see Butler 1629, sig. C, 3^r; Farnaby 1970, p. 21; Hoskins 1935, p. 30; Peacham 1593, p. 35; Puttenham 1970, p. 189; Sherry 1961, p. 45. Cf. Tuve 1947, pp. 184–5, 205–14, and Knox 1989, pp. 58–76.

Yet more daringly, Hobbes allows himself a similar tone of mockery in discussing the interpretation of Scripture. He does so in two remarkable passages which, perhaps not surprisingly, he later excluded from the Latin *Leviathan.* The first – in which he employs the less common technique of commending by way of ironically criticising – occurs in the discussion of the meaning of angels in the Bible. If we focus on the Old Testament, Hobbes remarks, it would seem that they are to be understood as nothing more than figments of our imagination induced by God. However, many passages in the New Testament 'have extorted from my feeble Reason an acknowledgment and beleef that there be also Angels substantiall and permanent'.[111] A similar but even broader irony marks the discussion of purgatory in chapter XLIV. Christ's own words, as reported in St Matthew's gospel, appear to make the existence of purgatory inconsistent with the world to come. 'But what then can bee the meaning of those our Saviours words' (p. 435)? Hobbes answers in tones of mocking deference to the school divines and their special aptitude for solving such puzzles:

> I confesse they are very hardly to bee reconciled with all the Doctrines now unanimously received: Nor is it any shame to confesse the profoundnesse of the Scripture to bee too great to be sounded by the shortnesse of humane understanding. Nevertheless, I may propound such things to the consideration of more learned Divines, as the text it selfe suggesteth.[112]

Hobbes's tone brings him remarkably close to concluding that, at both these crucial junctures, the Scriptures make no sense.

Besides using ironic inversion, Hobbes frequently permits himself the closely connected but cruder device of sarcasm. Among his favourite targets are again the Enthusiasts and their claims about inspiration and prophecy. When considering the nature of prophecy in *The Elements*, Hobbes had concluded, reasonably enough, that 'it is plaine, that they shall conjecture best that have most experience, because they have most

[111] Hobbes 1991, p. 278; cf. Hobbes 1668, p. 189. Martinich 1992, p. 252, commenting on this passage, assures us that Hobbes is here yielding ('with disarming candor') to 'the force of the New Testament, as one would hope a good Christian would do', since he 'felt compelled by the text of the New Testament to change his belief'. Here as elsewhere Martinich seems oblivious to Hobbes's use of irony to lend his apparent concessions a mocking undertone. My own view is that, despite Martinich's claim that he has at last provided the world with 'a historically informed and philosophically sensitive reading of *Leviathan*' (p. 333), his insensitivity to Hobbes's literary strategies vitiates much of his argument, especially about Hobbes's alleged religious commitments. As we have seen, Hobbes's contemporaries were better attuned to his rhetorical strategies and his use of them – as Clarendon complained – to excite prejudice and contempt. This in turn provides one reason for insisting (*pace* Martinich, pp. 354–61) that a study of Hobbes's contemporaries may not be irrelevant to an understanding of his thought.

[112] Hobbes 1991, p. 435; cf. Hobbes 1668, p. 302.

Signes to conjecture by'.[113] By contrast, the discussion in *Leviathan* strikes a jeering note. 'The best Prophet naturally is the best guesser; and the best guesser, he that is most versed and studied in the matter he guesses at' (p. 22). As John Whitehall declared in tones of outrage in his *Leviathan Found Out*, the implication of Hobbes's reformulation is that prophecy consists of guesswork and nothing more.[114]

The chief butts of Hobbes's sarcasm are the various scholastic admirers of Aristotle, especially the school divines. He sneers at their influence on the universities, which he sees as so pervasive that the study of philosophy in those august institutions 'is not properly Philosophy (the nature whereof dependeth not on Authors) but Aristotelity' (p. 462). He mocks their jargon, which pollutes the language with 'names that signifie nothing; but are taken up, and learned by rote from the Schooles, as *hypostatical*, *transubstantiate*, *consubstantiate*, *eternal-Now* and the like canting of Schoolemen' (p. 35). Above all he ridicules their beliefs about the physical world. Of their theory of motion, according to which 'heavy bodies fall downwards, out of an appetite to rest, and to conserve their nature in that place which is most proper for them', he observes that this commits the schoolmen to 'ascribing appetite, and Knowledge of what is good for their conservation, (which is more than man has) to things inanimate, absurdly' (p. 15). Of their theory of incorporeal substances he similarly remarks that, since 'Motion is change of Place, and Incorporeall Substances are not capable of Place', the schoolmen find it hard to explain 'how the ghosts of men (and I may adde of their clothes which they appear in) can walk by night' in visible yet incorporeal garments (p. 466).

As well as irony and sarcasm, a further mocking trope to which Hobbes is much addicted is diasyrmus. As we saw in chapter 5, this was the name given to the device enabling us to render an argument ridiculous by claiming that it bears a resemblance to an argument of unquestioned absurdity.[115] A sure sign of the trope's being in play is thus the presence of an introductory phrase of the form 'As if ...' or 'One might as well say ...' or some similarly derisive formula. One group of adversaries against whom Hobbes frequently wields this weapon are the ancient writers on moral and civil philosophy and their scholastic descendants in the universities. Analysing their concept of justice, he

113 BL Harl. MS 4235, fo. 19v. Cf. Hobbes 1969a, p. 16.

114 Whitehall 1679, p. 16. See also the anonymous tract of the same year entitled *The Spirit of Prophecy*, with its complaints (sig. a, 3r) about 'the Affronts Mr Hobbs hath cast, and Injuries he hath done to our religion' with his account of prophecy. Despite all this, Martinich 1992, p. 234, hopes to persuade us that Hobbes 'wants to make belief in genuine prophets as plausible as possible'.

115 See for example Sherry 1961, p. 61; Peacham 1593, p. 39.

explains that they divide the idea of just actions into commutative and distributive. The idea of distributive justice they in turn equate with 'the distribution of equall benefit to men of equall merit'. 'As if', Hobbes adds, 'it were Injustice to sell dearer than we buy; or to give more to a man than he merits' (p. 105). He uses the same device later in the chapter when examining the Aristotelian contention that some men are slaves by nature. Commenting on this doctrine in *The Elements*, he had noted that Aristotle 'putteth so much difference betweene the powers of Men by nature, that he doubteth not to sett downe as the grounde of all his Politiques, that some men are by nature worthy to governe and others by nature ought to serve'.[116] His paraphrase in *Leviathan* remains essentially the same, but his tone is remarkably different. First he supplements his original account with a sequence of sarcasms: Aristotle, we are now told 'maketh men by Nature, some more worthy to Command, meaning the wiser sort (such as he thought himselfe to be for his Philosophy;) others to Serve (meaning those that had strong bodies, but were not Philosophers as he)'. Then he adds a withering diasyrmus: 'as if Master and Servant were not introduced by consent of men, but by difference of Wit: which is not only against reason; but also against experience' (p. 107). He ends by deploying the same trope to encompass the full range of the ancient philosophical sects. He reminds us in his brief history of philosophy at the start of chapter XLVI that a number of intellectual coteries originally took their names from their meeting-places. 'They that followed *Plato*'s Doctrine, were called *Academiques*; The followers of *Aristotle*, *Peripatetiques*, from the Walk hee taught in; and those that *Zeno* taught, *Stoiques*, from the *Stoa*.' 'As if', he suddenly adds, 'we should denominate men from *More-fields*, from *Pauls-Church*, and from the *Exchange*, because they meet there often, to prate and loyter' (p. 460).

The enemies whom Hobbes most consistently targets with the trope of diasyrmus are the school divines. He first applies the device to ridicule their strained and often frankly ideological interpretations of the Scriptures. Chapter XXXVI considers the strange and much-debated opening of St John's gospel in which Christ is described as the Word made flesh. Hobbes notes that a number of divines have argued that what is meant by this proposition is that Christ is 'the Verbe of God'. But this is absurd: 'they might as well term him the Nown of God' (p. 289). Later he turns to the various biblical passages used by the divines to establish the pope's authority over civil sovereigns. One of their favourite texts is the New Testament reference to the two swords and the two luminaries, the

[116] BL Harl. MS 4235, fo. 67r. Cf. Hobbes 1969a, p. 88.

greater of which, they like to claim, 'signifies the Pope and the lesser the king'. 'One might as well inferre', Hobbes retorts, 'out of the first verse of the Bible, that by Heaven is meant the Pope, and by Earth the King: Which is not arguing from Scripture, but a wanton insulting over Princes' (pp. 428–9).

The same technique recurs in Hobbes's account of the relics of heathenism preserved by the divines among the practices of the Catholic Church. Chapter XLIV includes a discussion of pre-Christian rituals surviving in the sacraments, and especially in the sacrament of baptism, in the course of which 'the Priest blows thrice in the Childs face' and exhorts any unclean spirits to depart. 'As if', Hobbes comments, 'all Children, till blown on by the Priest were Daemoniaques' (p. 424). The ensuing chapter turns to the demonological theories propagated by the divines. When they form mental pictures of the dead in their imaginations, they like to claim that these are actually immaterial ghosts or demons at large in the world. But this is to argue, Hobbes replies, 'with just as much reason, as if one should say, he saw his own Ghost in a Looking-Glasse, or the Ghosts of the Stars in a River' (p. 441).

It is in analysing the 'vain philosophy' of the schoolmen that Hobbes employs the device of diasyrmus with the greatest freedom. (He later seems to have judged the freedom excessive, deleting virtually all the passages in question from the Latin *Leviathan*.)[117] He begins by focusing on one of the basic errors of school divinity, that of attempting to apply our ordinary concepts to describe the indescribable nature of God. This drives the divines to claim 'that by the Almighty power of God, one body may be at one and the same time in many places; and many bodies at one and the same time in one place'. 'As if', Hobbes sneers, 'it were an acknowledgment of the Divine Power to say that which is, is not; or that which has been, has not been' (p. 467). Next he turns to their theory of the will and their efforts to explain what causes us to act in particular ways. 'For cause of the Will', they assign 'the Capacity in generall that men have to will sometimes one thing, sometimes another', thereby 'making the *Power* the cause of the *Act*'. 'As if', he rejoins, 'one should assign for cause of the good or evill Acts of men, theire Ability to doe them' (p. 468). He concludes by examining the errors perpetrated by the divines in moral and civil philosophy. They argue that 'if a man doe an action of Injustice, that is to say, an action contrary to the Law, God they say is the prime cause of the Law, and also the prime cause of that, and all other Actions; but no cause at all of the Injustice; which is the Inconformity of the Action to the Law'.

[117] For his later and much abbreviated account see Hobbes 1668, pp. 320 *et seq.*

This for Hobbes is the acme of vain philosophy. 'A man might as well say, that one man maketh both a streight line, and a crooked, and another maketh their Incongruity' (p. 469).

Of all the mocking tropes, the one Hobbes chiefly favours is the subtler and more varied device of aestismus. Although this term has not survived in modern English dictionaries, it names a trope regarded by the Renaissance rhetoricians as having exceptional force. As we saw in chapter 5, it refers to the technique of describing our adversaries and their arguments by means of inherently ambiguous turns of phrase. If the words in question are taken in one way, they provide adequate descriptions; but if they are taken in another and no less proper sense, they instead produce a satirical effect.

As before, one of the groups against whom Hobbes delights in practising this technique are the Enthusiasts. When speaking in chapter III about those who accept the reality of prophecy, he makes play with the term *presumption* and its capacity to refer either to the belief that something will happen or else to the effrontery of presuming it.[118] He ends by observing that 'though it be called Prudence when the Event answereth our Expectation; yet in its own nature it is but Presumption'.[119] Later he speaks in similar but even more derisive vein about the supposed evidence in favour of prophecy and miracles. Drawing on the ambiguity inherent in the term *miracle*, which can either refer to a work of God or else (as Cotgrave's *Dictionarie* of 1611 puts it) a merely monstrous thing,[120] he indicates in his dryest tones that the capacity for true prophecy is indeed a miracle.[121] (He later thought better of the joke, which makes no appearance in the Latin *Leviathan*.) He appeals to the same device at the start of book III, where he alludes to the Enthusiasts and the *implicit* nature of their faith. To speak of believing something implicitly is to speak of possessing a high degree of trust and confidence in the doctrine concerned. But in seventeenth-century English the term could also be used to suggest that the belief in question may be self-deceiving and confused. Cotgrave's *Dictionarie*, for example, informs us

118 See Cotgrave 1611, sig. Sss, iii^{r-v}: 'to presume' can mean to 'thinke, weene, imagine', but also to 'thinke too well of himselfe, to arrogate'.

119 Hobbes 1991, p. 22. Cf. p. 37 for the unambiguous use of the term to mean presumptuousness, and pp. 47 and 98 for its unambiguous use to convey that something has been assumed. Had Martinich reflected on the studied ambiguity of Hobbes's language in chapter III, he might surely have reconsidered his claim about Hobbes's 'desire to preserve orthodoxy' in discussing prophecy. See Martinich 1992, p. 228.

120 Cotgrave 1611, sig. Ggg, 6^{r}.

121 Hobbes 1991, p. 84. Martinich 1992, p. 244, seems to me to miss the tone and point of this remark when he denies that Hobbes expressed any scepticism about the possibility of miracles. For a subtler commentary see Cantalupo 1991, pp. 163–6.

that 'an implicitie' can mean an 'intanglement, incombrance, obscure involution'.[122] There is thus a clear note of mockery underlying Hobbes's contention that the Enthusiasts and their followers, in seeking to formulate the principles of Christian politics, have been too willing to allow their natural reason 'to be folded up in the napkin of an Implicite Faith' (p. 255).

As usual, the adversaries against whom Hobbes is principally interested in wielding this weapon of ridicule are the school divines. He begins by turning against them the ambiguity inherent in the word *egregious*, which in seventeenth-century English could either mean exceptional or exceptionally absurd. (We read, for example, in Cockeram's *English Dictionarie* of 1623: '*Egregious.* Excellent, somtime vile, base.')[123] Hobbes slyly avails himself of this double meaning when he describes the whole tribe of schoolmen in chapter VIII as 'Egregious persons' (p. 59). Later he makes comparable use of the equivocal term *ghostly*, which could either mean devout and religious, or else insubstantial and unreal. 'The *Ecclesiastiques*', he assures us, are to be thought of as '*Spirituall* men, and *Ghostly* Fathers' (p. 481). A number of their key beliefs are later described in analogously mocking terms. When examining their doctrine of purgatory, Hobbes plays on the fact that the word *profit* can either mean (as Cotgrave's *Dictionarie* puts it) 'gaine, lucre' or else 'benefit, utilitie'.[124] We are told that the doctors of the Church conducted long debates about the location of 'the place which they were to abide in till they should be re-united to their Bodies in the Resurrection'. At first they supposed that 'they lay under the Altars', but 'afterward the Church of Rome found it more profitable to build for them this place of Purgatory' (p. 426). Finally, when discussing the papacy's claim to temporal jurisdiction, Hobbes similarly plays on the fact that the verb *to forge* can mean either to shape or to counterfeit. The secular authorities are to be blamed, he declares, for permitting such doctrines as that of papal supremacy 'to be forged in the Universities of their own Dominions' (p. 478).

Sometimes Hobbes is so anxious to make clear his contempt for the school divines that he opts for a cruder version of aestismus in which he explicitly draws attention to the ambiguities he is putting to satirical use. (He subsequently seems to have regretted the somewhat knockabout jokes that result, suppressing virtually all of them in the Latin *Leviathan.*) He indulges in one such moment of broad humour when discussing the concept of natural law. He remarks that the school divines generally

122 Cotgrave 1611, sig. Zz, iii^r. See also Bullokar 1967, sig. I, 1^r; Cockeram 1968, sig. F, 4^v.
123 Cockeram 1968, sig. D, 7^v. On Cockeram see Starnes and Noyes 1946, pp. 26–36.
124 Cotgrave 1611, sig. Sss, vi^r.

describe the laws of nature as unwritten laws, but adds that this appears to be a great mistake, since we see so many volumes published on this very subject by the divines themselves (p. 191). He introduces a comparably jocular note when examining Bellarmine's claims about the supremacy of the pope. Bellarmine maintains that the pope possesses supreme temporal authority over Christian princes indirectly. Hobbes retorts that this argument 'is denyed; unlesse hee mean by *Indirectly* that he has gotten it by Indirect means', that is, by underhand methods, in which case the argument can be granted (p. 394). Later he mocks the metaphysics of the school divines in a similar way. He points out that, when Aristotle describes himself as having written works of metaphysics, he is simply referring to his '*books written or placed after his naturall Philososophy*'. But when the school divines refer to the same works, they mean '*books of supernaturall Philosophy*: for the word *Metaphysiques* will bear both these senses'. 'And indeed', Hobbes cannot resist adding, 'that which is there written, is for the most part so far from the possibility of being understood, and so repugnant to naturall Reason, that whosoever thinketh there is any thing to bee understood by it must needs think it supernaturall' (p. 463). He even manages, in an analogous passage from chapter XLIV, to put together his two favourite mocking tropes – aestismus and diasyrmus – in a caricature of the doctrine he most of all despises in school divinity, the doctrine of transubstantiation. We should take note, he remarks, that this doctrine only arose in the course of the dark ages, a period so dark that 'men discerned not the Bread that was given them to eat'. Worse still, the priests ensured that the bread 'was stamped with the figure of Christ upon the Crosse, as if they would have men beleeve it were Transubstantiated, not only into the Body of Christ, but also into the Wood of his Crosse, and that they did eat both together in the Sacrament'.[125]

Of all Hobbes's uses of aestismus, the most striking occur in his discussions of the Christian faith. He first employs the device in surveying the rise and triumph of Christianity, which he characterises as a wonderful event. The term *wonderful*, in seventeenth-century English, could either refer to a genuinely marvellous happening or else to a merely disconcerting and unexpected one. The frequency of such ironic usages (Shakespeare is fond of them) suggests that more than a hint of the sardonic underlies Hobbes's account of the growth of Christianity. 'The Oracles ceased in all parts of the Roman Empire, and the number of Christians encreased wonderfully every day, and in every place, by the preaching of the Apostles and Evangelists' (p. 85).

[125] Hobbes 1991, p. 423. Cantalupo 1991 offers no commentary on this passage, but rightly notes (pp. 202–3) that in his other discussions of transubstantiation Hobbes adopts a deflating tone.

More remarkable is the way in which, when discussing the interpretation of Scripture, Hobbes exploits the ambiguity in the notion of *conspiracy*. To describe a number of persons as conspiring towards a certain end may of course mean no more than that they acted in co-operation. But the notion of conspiracy also carries with it an implication that the ends in question may be reprehensible. When, for example, groups of persons are described in the Old Testament as conspiring together, their purposes are invariably violent and usually murderous: we are told that Joseph's brothers conspired to slay him; that Jehu conspired against his master and slew him; that the servants of Joash made a conspiracy and slew him.[126] There is thus a considerable *frisson* attaching to Hobbes's use of the term to describe the books of the Bible and their various objectives. His original readers would undoubtedly have received a jolt from his observation that, 'although these books were written by divers men, yet it is manifest the Writers were all indued with one and the same spirit, in that they conspire to one and the same end' (p. 266).

Most remarkable of all is Hobbes's deployment of the colloquialism that speaks of *swallowing something whole*. By the time he was writing, this familiar metaphor was already in widespread use as a way of describing a gullible approach to the appraisal of beliefs and arguments. To swallow an argument was to accept it in an abject or credulous spirit, without making any proper efforts to chew over its plausibility. Thomas Nashe, for example, assures us in *The Unfortunate Traveller* that the only precept worth offering to those going abroad is 'Believe nothing, trust no man yet seem thou as thou swallowedst all, suspectedst none, but wert easy to be gulled by everyone.'[127] The duke in *Measure for Measure* invokes the same image, though far more solemnly, when accusing Angelo of deliberately forgetting his promise of marriage to Mariana. He declares that Angelo has 'swallowed his vows whole', meaning that he has failed to reflect on them at all.[128] Given the prevalence of such usages, it must be accounted one of the most daring moments in *Leviathan* when Hobbes announces at the outset of his analysis of Christian politics in chapter XXXII that 'the mysteries of our Religion' are like 'wholsome pills for the sick, which swallowed whole, have the vertue to cure; but chewed, are for the most part cast up again without effect' (p. 256). We are left with the implication that, if we wish to cleave to the central mysteries of Christianity, we have no alternative but to approach them in a spirit of abject credulousness.

126 See Genesis 13: 18; 2 Kings 10: 9; 2 Kings 12: 20.
127 Nashe 1985, p. 342.
128 Shakespeare 1988, *Measure for Measure*, III.i.228, p. 803.

THE EXPRESSION OF SCORN: THE FIGURES

We need finally to attend to the third way in which, as we saw in chapter 5, the techniques of *ornatus* can be used according to the classical and Renaissance rhetoricians to express and solicit contempt. Besides appealing to the so-called mocking tropes, we can hope to draw on a number of *schemata* or figures of speech to generate a tone of scorn or ridicule. We can even hope to produce these effects by means of various *figurae verborum*,[129] even though these devices rely for their rhetorical force on nothing more than a certain arrangement or patterning of words.

Quintilian had implied that a number of *figurae verborum* dependent on the opposition or repetition of particular words may be especially well adapted to satirical use, a suggestion developed by a number of neoclassical rhetoricians in Renaissance England. One such device, Henry Peacham had pointed out, is antithesis or *contentio*, the technique of juxtaposing words of strongly opposed meanings to create 'a proper coupling together of contraries'.[130] A second and comparable device, Richard Sherry had earlier emphasised, is epanaphora[131] or *repetitio*, the figure we employ when 'in lyke and diverse thynges we take our begynnyng continually at one & the selfe same word'.[132] As Sherry adds, this technique is particularly susceptible of being used with 'gravitie and sharpnes' as well as much pleasantness.[133]

Hobbes is exceptionally skilled at applying these *figurae verborum* to contrive a tone of sharpness and disparagement. He first does so when discussing the Enthusiasts and their wide range of foolish and dangerous beliefs. Speaking about their eagerness to equate their subversive arguments with the workings of conscience, he introduces an antithesis between *knowing* and *thinking* to underline his point. They wish to privilege their arguments to make it 'seem unlawfull to change or speak against them; and so pretend to know they are true, when they know at most, but that they think so' (p. 48). Later he deploys a satirical anaphora on the word *know* to dismiss their arguments about the afterlife. They possess no genuine knowledge of man's condition after death; they possess nothing

129 I know of no study of Hobbes's use of these figures. May 1959, Curtis 1988 and Prokhovnik 1991 restrict themselves to Hobbes's use of tropes. This restriction has encouraged some recent commentators (for example, Rayner 1991, pp. 92–5) to underestimate Hobbes's change of mind about classical rhetoric.

130 Peacham 1593, p. 160. Cf. Farnaby 1970, p. 23; Smith 1969, pp. 162 (*recte* 172)–75.

131 The shortening to anaphora, the modern term, first occurs in Fenner 1584, sig. D, 3^v^. Cf. Fraunce 1950, p. 40; Puttenham 1970, p. 198.

132 Sherry 1961, p. 47. For later but similar definitions see Wilson 1554, fo. 107^v^; Peacham 1593, p. 41; Hoskins 1935, p. 13; Butler 1629, sig. L, 1^v^.

133 Sherry 1961, p. 47.

more than 'a beliefe grounded upon other mens saying that they know it supernaturally, or that they know those, that knew them, that knew others, that knew it supernaturally' (p. 103). As William Lucy rightly remarked in his *Observations* on *Leviathan* in 1663, 'this is a most scornefull speech'.[134]

Hobbes makes use of the same *figurae* to attack the conduct of the lawyers and democratical gentlemen in Parliament. He introduces a sardonic antithesis into his discussion of the ambitions of those 'that are kinder to the government of an Assembly, whereof they may hope to participate, than of a Monarchy, which they despair to enjoy'.[135] He relies on the same technique when discussing the role of orators in public assemblies. He declares that such speakers, 'though they have great power to hurt, have little to save', explaining in a further antithesis that this is due to the fact that 'to accuse requires lesse Eloquence (such is mans Nature) than to excuse; and condemnation than absolution more resembles Justice' (p. 132).

It is in his running battle with the school divines that Hobbes appeals to anaphora and antithesis with the greatest frequency. He employs a sarcastic anaphora at the end of chapter II to describe their theory of the imagination:

> Some say the Senses receive the Species of things, and deliver them to the Common-sense; and the Common Sense delivers them over to the Fancy, and the Fancy to the Memory, and the Memory to the Judgment, like handing of things from one to another, with many words making nothing understood.[136]

He makes a subtler appeal to the same device in chapter XII, using a patterned repetition of the words *confess* and *define* to ridicule their efforts to explain the inexplicable nature of God. Those who have thought seriously about God's attributes 'choose rather to confesse he is Incomprehensible, and above their understanding; than to define his Nature by *Spirit Incorporeall*, and then confesse their definition to be unintelligible' (p. 77). He invokes the same device at the outset of his lengthy critique of Cardinal Bellarmine, in which he employs an emphatic anaphora (reiterating the word *and*) to outline Bellarmine's theory of the Church, after which he turns the argument against him in a conclusion of sudden and calculated bathos:

> If now it should appear, that there is no Coercive Power left them by our Saviour; but onely a Power to proclaim the Kingdom of Christ, and to perswade men to submit themselves thereunto; and by precepts and good counsell, to teach them that have submitted, what they are to do, that they may be received into the Kingdom of God

134 Lucy 1663, p. 232. On Lucy see Bowle 1969, pp. 23–5, 75–85.

135 Hobbes 1991, p. 123. Hobbes was unable to reproduce the antithesis in Latin, and substituted a different but still neater one: 'Coetui potius quam uni homini faventium; quia sub uno homine Vulgus sunt, sed sub coetu Regantis pars sunt.' See Hobbes 1668, p. 88.

136 Hobbes 1991, p. 19. The effect is even sharper in the Latin *Leviathan*: see Hobbes 1668, p. 8.

when it comes; and that the Apostles and other Ministers of the Gospel are our Schoolmasters and not our Commanders, and their Precepts not Laws but wholesome Counsells; then were all that dispute in vain.[137]

Hobbes is still more attracted by antithesis as a weapon in his battle with the school divines. He first turns the device against them in chapter III, which ends by declaring that their influence has reduced the study of metaphysics to little more than 'absurd speeches, taken upon credit (without any signification at all) from deceived Philosophers, and deceived or deceiving Schoolemen' (p. 24). Chapter VI ends in similar vein with a double antithesis mocking their views on the afterlife. 'What kind of Felicity God hath ordained to them that devoutly honour him, a man shall no sooner know than enjoy; being joyes that now are as incomprehensible as the word of Schoole-men *Beatificall Vision* is unintelligible' (p. 46). He recurs to the device in criticising their influence on the universities. He imagines two ripostes to his attack, the second of which accuses him of offering to teach the universities their own job. He responds with a grimly sardonic antithesis: 'to the later question, it is not fit nor needfull for me to say either I or No: for any man that sees what I am doing may easily perceive what I think'.[138] He appeals to the device once more in chapter XLII, using it to belittle the views of the divines about the use of excommunication as a punishment. When the godly impose this penalty, they merely condemn the accused to 'a leaving of their company, and having no more to doe with them'. But this, he adds in his most humorous tones, 'in many occasions might be a greater pain to the Excommunicant than to the Excommunicate' (p. 388).

Besides employing these techniques of contrast and connection, Hobbes directs a number of other purely verbal *figurae* against his dialectical enemies. One device of which he makes frequent use is *dubitatio*, the ironic expression of doubt or ignorance. Quintilian had classified this technique as a *figura verborum*, while adding that it comes very close to being a *figura sententiarum*, since the nature of the thought as much as the configuration of the words is responsible for the rhetorical effect.[139] Some English rhetoricians had assumed that the purpose of the device is to give voice to genuine uncertainties, in consequence of which they made no distinction between *dubitatio* and aporia.[140] But others recognised that, as Thomas

137 Hobbes 1991, p. 341. The final phrase appears to allude to I Corinthians 15: 14.

138 Hobbes 1991, p. 237. The effect is greatly heightened in the Latin *Leviathan* by means of assonance and alliteration. See Hobbes 1668, p. 161: 'nam qui legit quae scribo, facile intelligat quae sentio'.

139 Quintilian 1920–2, IX.III.87–8, vol. III, pp. 496–8.

140 See for example Sherry 1961, p. 54. (Note that this use of the term aporia considerably predates the first use recorded in the *OED*.) Sherry's understanding of *dubitatio* recurs in several Ramist rhetorics. See Fraunce 1950, p. 94; Butler 1629, sig. M, 2^v–3^r.

Wilson observes, the defining characteristic of *dubitatio* must be its disingenuousness. We are far from expressing any real uncertainty; we merely 'make the hearers beleve that the weight of our matter causeth us to doubte what were best to speake'.[141]

Hobbes is adept at manipulating *dubitatio* in this second and sardonic way. He uses it to attack the democratical gentlemen's claim that, even in monarchies, members of representative assemblies can exercise sovereign power. He dismisses the doctrine as incoherent, resulting as it does in the creation of two rival claimants to supreme authority. To which he somewhat archly adds that 'I know not how this so manifest a truth should of late be so little observed' (p. 130). He appeals to the same device in discussing the alleged evidence in favour of purgatory. The divines like to cite the passage from St Matthew's gospel about the penalties fixed for those who offend their brothers. Since only some offences are described as punishable by hell-fire, they claim that the rest must be punishable by consignment to purgatory. But as Hobbes demonstrates – in a typically humanist elucidation of meaning from context – the purpose of Christ's argument was merely to question various features of the Mosaic law. 'This considered', he adds, 'what can be drawn from this text, to maintain Purgatory, I cannot imagine' (p. 439).

A further *figura verborum* to which Hobbes is much addicted is epanodos. Among English rhetoricians, the Ramists had worked out the best definition of this figure, making it clear that it constitutes a kind of involuted antithesis. As Dudley Fenner explains in his *Artes of Logike and Rethorike*, 'Epanodos is when the same sound is repeated in the beginning and the middle, in the middle and the ende.'[142] Fenner's definition was repeated almost word for word by later Ramists such as Abraham Fraunce and Charles Butler,[143] eventually finding its way into Thomas Farnaby's popular textbook of 1625, the *Index Rhetoricus*.[144] Farnaby also repeats the passage from Virgil's eighth *Eclogue* already cited by Fraunce and Butler[145] to illustrate the figure:

Crudelis tu quoque, mater
Crudelis mater magis, an puer improbus ille?
Improbus ille puer: crudelis tu quoque, mater.[146]

141 Wilson 1554, fo. 98v. For this understanding see also Puttenham 1970, p. 226; Smith 1969, pp. 150–1.
142 Fenner 1584, sig. D, 3r.
143 Fraunce 1950, p. 46; Butler 1629, sig. L, 2v.
144 Farnaby 1970, p. 23.
145 Fraunce 1950, p. 47; Butler 1629, sig. L, 2v.
146 Farnaby 1970, p. 23, citing Virgil, *Eclogues*, VIII, lines 48–50. This was repeated in Smith 1969, p. 103.

As Virgil's lines arguably reveal, the problem of using the device is that of avoiding merely laboured and mechanical effects. Shakespeare implicitly comments on the risk when he makes Polonius say, speaking of Hamlet's apparent insanity:

> That he is mad, 'tis true; 'tis true 'tis pity,
> And pity 'tis, 'tis true.[147]

Polonius immediately excuses himself ('a foolish figure') but we are made to register the difficulty of employing it without falling into just such self-defeating artificiality.

Hobbes demonstrates, by contrast, that in the hands of a master rhetorician the device can be used as a powerful means of ridicule.[148] He first exploits it against his legal opponents and their habit of shifting between precept and precedent. 'They appeale from custome to reason, and from reason to custome, as it serves their turn; receding from custome when their interest requires it, and setting themselves against reason as oft as reason is against them.'[149] He recurs to the technique in attacking the figure of the Enthusiast, one of whose defining characteristics is the belief that God speaks to him in dreams. 'To say he hath spoken to him in a Dream is no more than to say he dreamed that God spake to him.'[150] He draws on it again in discussing the neo-Aristotelian theory of causation espoused by the school divines. 'In many occasions they put for cause of Naturall events their own ignorance; but disguised in other words: As when they say, Fortune is the cause of things contingent; that is, of things whereof they know no cause' (p. 468). Most daringly, he uses the same figure when considering the credibility of the Scriptures. The question of whether they are to be believed, he proposes, should be handled in the same way as with any other work of history. If, for example, '*Livy* say the Gods made once a Cow speak, and we believe it not; wee distrust not God therein, but *Livy*' (p. 49).

Of all the *figurae verborum*, the one that Hobbes invokes most frequently is *percontatio*, the technique of asking rhetorical questions. As Wilson explains in *The Arte of Rhetorique*, we have recourse to this device whenever we ask a

147 Shakespeare 1988, *Hamlet*, II.ii.98–9, p. 665.

148 He sometimes uses the device more good humouredly. See for example letter 24 in Hobbes 1994, p. 41.

149 Hobbes 1991, p. 73. This expands a remark from the epistle dedicatory to *The Elements of Law*. See BL Harl. MS 4235, fo. 2^{r}, and cf. Hobbes 1969a, p. xv. The device is also occasionally used in *De Cive*. See Hobbes 1983a, VIII.X, p. 163; X.XVIII, p. 180; XVI.I, p. 234.

150 Hobbes 1991, p. 257. Hobbes worked on this epigram, inserting 'dreamed' (in place of 'hath dreamt') at the last moment. See Hobbes 1991, p. 257 note. Given the opportunity for greater assonance, the Latin version is even more pointed. See Hobbes 1668, p. 174: 'Qui Deum in Somnio ad se loquutum esse dicit, Deum ad se loquutum esse somniasse se dicit.'

question not because we wish to know the answer, but merely 'because we would chide'; we engage, in short, in 'snappishe asking'.[151] Puttenham, who prefers to describe the technique as erotema, similarly observes that it can readily be used 'by way of skoffe',[152] while Peacham, who also speaks of erotema, goes so far as to add that it 'may aptly be compared to the point or edge of a weapon wherewith the Champion defendeth himselfe and woundeth his enemie'.[153]

The enemies Hobbes principally seeks to wound in this way are the school divines and their Aristotelian authorities. He first strikes at them in chapter VIII, at the end of which he quotes one of the chapter headings from a treatise by Francisco Suarez. 'When men write whole volumes of such stuffe, are they not Mad, or intend to make others so (p. 59)?' He returns to the charge in the course of responding to an imagined objection that his theory of political obligation will prove too difficult for ordinary people to understand. 'Shall whole Nations be brought to *acquiesce* in the great Mysteries of Christian Religion, which are above Reason', while refusing to accept an argument 'so consonant to Reason, that any unprejudicated man, needs no more to learn it, than to hear it (p.233)?' He throws out yet more rhetorical questions – the answers to which he has already made painfully clear – at the end of his survey of the ancient philosophical sects. 'But what has been the Utility of those Schools? what Science is there at this day acquired by their Readings and Disputings (p. 461)?' The same device reappears in the discussion of the scholastic doctrine of Separated Essences and the distinctions used to uphold it. 'Can any man', Hobbes bursts out, 'think that God is served with such absurdities (p. 466)?' The chapter ends in similar style with a denunciation of the errors perpetrated by the divines as a result of their reliance on 'false or uncertain History' (p. 473):

> What is all the Legend of fictitious Miracles, in the lives of the Saints; and all the Histories of Apparitions, and Ghosts, alledged by the doctors of the Romane Church, to make good their Doctrines of Hell and Purgatory, the power of Exorcisme and other Doctrines which have no warrant, neither in Reason, nor Scripture; as also all those Traditions which they call the unwritten Word of God; but old Wives Fables?

With this final and carefully controlled anti-climax Hobbes rests his case.

While the Renaissance rhetoricians had acknowledged that a number of *figurae verborum* can be used to contrive a tone of disparagement, they had placed far more emphasis on the capacity of the *figurae sententiarum* to

[151] Wilson 1554, fo. 58^{r}.
[152] Puttenham 1970, pp. 210–11.
[153] Peacham 1593, p. 106. Cf. also Sherry 1961, p. 52.

engender similar effects. As we saw in chapter 5, some had claimed that as many as six different figures are especially well-adapted to expressing and soliciting the specific *sententiae* of scorn and contempt: meiosis, synchoresis, aposiopesis, tapinosis, litotes and apodioxis. If we return to *Leviathan* with these further considerations in mind, we find Hobbes again revealed as a systematic practitioner of the art of rhetoric in the highest Renaissance style: there is not a single instance of these mocking figures that he fails to employ when dealing with his intellectual enemies.

It is true that he exploits these figures in widely varying degrees. He appeals only once to aposiopesis – the figure we invoke, as Dudley Fenner had explained, when we 'stay' the course of a sentence in such a way that the section we fail to utter is nevertheless understood.[154] But his use of the device provides us with a perfect example of the ease with which, as Henry Peacham had cautioned, it can be applied in malice.[155] Hobbes applies it in chapter XLVII in the course of discussing the issue of clerical celibacy. He had already examined this topic in *De Cive*, in which he had spoken in tones of unimpeachable gravity about the priestly way of life.[156] In *Leviathan*, by contrast, his tone is jocular in the extreme. He begins with a series of opprobrious comparisons between the Catholic priesthood and the fairies. The fairies only acknowledge one king; the priests only acknowledge the pope. The fairies live in enchanted castles; the priests have cathedral churches. The fairies cannot be made to answer for their crimes; the priests likewise vanish from the tribunals of justice. Then Hobbes adds his aposiopesis (p. 481):

> The *Fairies* marry not; but there be amongst them *Incubi*, that have copulation with flesh and bloud. The *Priests* also marry not.

Perhaps not surprisingly, he later thought better of the joke, which makes no appearance in the Latin *Leviathan*.

A second mocking figure Hobbes uses only sparingly is synchoresis, the pretence of yielding to an argument in order to disparage it with added force at a later stage. He employs it when considering Cardinal Bellarmine's contention that bishops receive their jurisdictions not from God but from the pope. He endorses Bellarmine's claim that 'if Bishops have their Jurisdiction *de Iure Divino* (that is, *immediately from God*) they that maintaine it, should bring some Word of God to prove it. But they can bring none' (p. 394). Then he comments: 'The argument is good; I have therefore nothing to say against it. But it is an argument no lesse good, to prove the

154 Fenner 1584, sig. D, 4^{v}.
155 Peacham 1593, p. 118.
156 Hobbes 1983a, XVIII.XIV, p. 293.

Pope himself to have no Jurisdiction in the Dominion of any other Prince' (p. 394). Later he uses the same technique to question Bellarmine's contention that the pope has a right to command temporal rulers to change their government. Bellarmine had offered as an alleged analogy the fact that a commonwealth may go so far as to depose a neighbouring prince 'and set another in his room, if it cannot otherwise defend it selfe against the injuries he goes about to doe them' (p. 398). This is certainly lawful, Hobbes allows; but 'by the same reason, it would be no lesse lawfull for a Civill Soveraign, upon the like injuries done or feared, to make warre upon the Spirituall Sovereign' (p. 398). And this, he adds with studied understatement, 'I beleeve is more than Cardinall Bellarmine would have inferred from his own proposition' (p. 398). Hobbes recurs to the device once more when objecting to the fact that the school divines 'impropriate the Preaching of the Gospell to one certain Order of men, where the Laws have left it free' (p. 472). 'If', he rejoins, 'I find my selfe amongst the Idolators of America, shall I that am a Christian, though not in Orders, think it a sin to preach Jesus Christ, till I have received Orders from Rome (p. 472)?' It will be retorted, he admits, that in these circumstances 'the necessity shall be esteemed for a sufficient Mission' (p. 472). Conceding that this is true, he adds that 'this is true also, that for whatsoever a dispensation is due for the necessity, for the same there needs no dispensation where there is no Law that forbids it' (p. 472).

By contrast with his sparing employment of aposiopesis and synchoresis, Hobbes makes repeated use of all the other mocking *figurae sententiarum* described by the Renaissance theorists of rhetoric. He makes considerable play with apodioxis, the figure we invoke when we repudiate an imagined objection that it would have been ludicrous to put forward.[157] As Clarendon bitterly noted in his *Brief View*, Hobbes is extremely fond of this device, constantly trying 'to put an objection into the mouth of a foolish adversary to make his readers merry'.[158] Hobbes first deploys the technique against the efforts of the Enthusiasts to find biblical authority for their claim to be directly inspired by God.[159] One of their favourite texts comes from the beginning of chapter 28 of Exodus, where the Lord says to the children of Israel, 'Thou shalt speak unto all that are wise hearted, whom I have filled with the spirit of wisdom, that they may make Aaron's garments to consecrate him' (28:3). Hobbes had originally examined this

157 The *OED* gives John Smith's *Mysterie of rhetorique unvail'd* (1657) (i.e. Smith 1969) as the first occurrence of the term. But it is well explicated in Peacham 1593, p. 185.

158 Clarendon 1676, p. 50.

159 Although there is one earlier use of the technique in *De Cive*. See Hobbes 1983, XVII.XII, p. 261, where it is said of Christ that he did not come into this world to teach logic. ('Neque enim venit in hunc mundum ut doceret *logicam*.')

passage in chapter 11 of *The Elements*, where he had explained that its meaning is simply that our faith 'is the work of the Spirit of God, in that sense, by which the Spirit of God giveth to one man wisedome and cunning in workmanship more then to another'.[160] But in *Leviathan* he renders the passage ludicrous by adding that, when God speaks of those 'whom I have filled with the spirit of wisedome to make garments', he does not mean 'a spirit put into them, that can make garments' (p. 57). The same device is used in discussing the passage from chapter 3 of Genesis in which God demands of Adam 'Who told thee that thou wast naked? Hast thou eaten of the tree, whereof I commanded thee that thou shouldest not eat?' (3: 11). Considering these questions in *De Cive*, Hobbes had contented himself with observing in plain terms that 'it is as if the Lord had asked: "How have you come to judge that the condition of nudity in which it seemed to me right to create you is a shameful one?" '[161] But in *Leviathan* the technique of apodioxis is used to reduce the discussion to absurdity. 'Whereas', Hobbes now observes, 'it is sayd, that having eaten, they saw they were naked; no man hath so interpreted the place, as if they had been formerly blind, and saw not their own skins' (p. 144).

Hobbes is even more addicted to the connected figures of meiosis and litotes. As we saw in chapter 5, meiosis was the term generally used by the rhetoricians to refer to humorous understatement, while litotes referred to the more specific technique of using an ironically mild-mannered negative to carry an affirmative force.[162] Hobbes initially calls on these figures to satirise the democratical gentlemen, fixing in particular on their admiration for the theories of liberty embodied in ancient treatises of statecraft. From these books 'they that live under a Monarch conceive an opinion, that the Subjects in a Popular Common-wealth enjoy Liberty; but that in a Monarchy they are all Slaves' (p. 226). He then adds a grim litotes: 'I say, they that live under a Monarchy conceive such an opinion; not they that live under a Popular Government: for they find no such matter' (p. 226). The same device is used to denounce the cynical martyrologies put forward by the school divines. 'To die for every tenet that serveth the ambition or profit of the Clergy', Hobbes responds, 'is not required' (p. 345). The subtler technique of meiosis is deployed against the same adversaries in the analysis of their views about baptism. Basing themselves on 1 Corinthians 15, the divines claim that in a sense we are baptised when

160 BL Harl. MS 4235, fo. 47^r. Cf. Hobbes 1969a, p. 59.

161 Hobbes 1983a, XII.1, p. 186: 'Quasi diceret, unde iudicasti nuditatem in qua visum est mihi te creare, inhonestatem esse.'

162 See Fenner 1584, sig. D, 2^v; Peacham 1593, p. 150; Smith 1969 (closely following Fenner) pp. 56, 69–70.

we fast, pray or give alms. But as Hobbes points out 'the word Baptisme is used (*Mar.*10.38. & *Luke.*12.50.) for being Dipped in ones own bloud'. To which he adds in tones of mock innocence that 'it is hard to say that Prayer, Fasting and Almes have any similitude with Dipping' (p. 437).

It is in discussing the interpretation of the Bible that Hobbes allows himself his most daring appeals to meiosis and litotes. (He later seems to have found them too daring, for they are mostly suppressed in the Latin *Leviathan.*) He uses meiosis to underline the improbability of supposing that the books of the Pentateuch were written by Moses himself. He refers us to Deuteronomy 34: 6, which claims that no one to this day knows the place of Moses's sepulchre. If Moses himself wrote this book, Hobbes points out, we should have to say that he spoke about his own sepulchre, while still alive, and prophesied that it would not be found. But this would be 'a strange interpretation' (p. 261). A comparable use of litotes underpins the discussion of whether Job was the author of the book of Job. Hobbes notes that, although the introduction and conclusion of the book are in prose, the whole of Job's complaint against the Lord is in verse. But 'Verse is no usuall stile' for those 'in great pain' (p. 264). He recurs to the device when expressing scepticism about the claim that those rewarded with eternal life will spend it in the *Coelum Empyreum.* Since there is no mention of any such place in the Scriptures, its existence 'is not easily to be drawn from any text that I can find' (p. 309). A still more derisive meiosis occurs in the explication of the famous passage from St Matthew's gospel (16.18) in which Christ says to Peter, *Tu es Petrus.* By this we are to understand, Hobbes explains, that the apostle's surname must have been Stone. We are not to understand that Christ was calling his disciple a stone, which would have been 'a strange and obscure speech' (p. 380). Finally, the figure is invoked yet again when Hobbes argues that, if we believe that Jesus will reign as an eternal king, we must also be committed to the belief that he has risen from the dead. The reason, he explains with mock patience, is that 'a dead man cannot exercise the Office of a King' (p. 411).

Of all the scornful *figurae sententiarum,* the one on which Hobbes principally relies is the contrasting and harsher device of tapinosis. This is the figure we employ when we make use of deliberately inappropriate and undignified terminology to belittle what we are talking about, thereby defacing high matters, as Henry Peacham had put it, by the use of base words.[163] Hobbes is especially fond of directing this weapon against his perennial enemies, the school divines. He first does so when attacking their

[163] Peacham 1593, p. 168. Cf. Puttenham 1970, pp. 259.

misuse of biblical texts to uphold their doctrine of purgatory. One text they like to cite is the passage from 1 Corinthians 3 in which St Paul speaks (v. 15) of those who will be saved as though by fire. But the divines are mistaken in supposing that St Paul is referring to the alleged fires of purgatory. He is speaking about the Day of Judgment, 'wherein the Elect shall not be consumed but be refined; that is, depose their erroneous Doctrines and Traditions, and have them as it were sindged off' (p. 436). This was one of the jokes that most upset Clarendon, who protests in his *Brief View* against the use of words 'so improper and unnatural' to describe such mighty events.[164] But the passage that most outraged Clarendon was Hobbes's use of tapinosis to scoff at the contention that God breathes grace into us, so that we may speak – as Aquinas had done – of 'infused' virtue.[165] Hobbes had initially considered this piece of school divinity in chapter XII of *De Cive*, observing that 'it is commonly taught that *Faith and sanctity are always infused or inspired into people*'.[166] At this juncture he responded with a sober and straightforward criticism: 'if this were true, I do not see why we are commanded to offer a justification for our faith, nor why each individual should not judge what it is right to do and to avoid from their own inspiration rather than from right reason or the precepts of those governing them'.[167] By contrast, his discussion in *Leviathan* centres on a derisive tapinosis based on the word *infused* and its two possible meanings – either spiritually instilled or literally poured out. To use the word *infused* in speaking of God's grace, Hobbes now contends, 'is an abuse of it; for those graces are Vertues, not Bodies to be carryed hither and thither, and to be powred into men as into barrels' (p. 279). Clarendon was greatly shocked. The text in question, he retorts, can hardly be explicated 'without saying, that good thoughts *are inspir'd, or infus'd*', so that Hobbes is simply making merry 'with that proper and devout custom of speaking', trying to make it 'the more ridiculous by turning into other words of the like signification'.[168]

Hobbes allows himself his freest use of tapinosis when discussing the

164 Clarendon 1676, p. 18. On Clarendon's reactions to Hobbes's political theory see Dzelzainis 1989.

165 See Aquinas 1969, I.II.63.4, p. 150, on 'whether moral virtues dwell in us by infusion' (*per infusionem*).

166 Hobbes 1983a, XII.VI, p. 189: 'Vulgo docetur, *Fidem & sanctitatem ... semper supernaturaliter hominibus infundi vel inspirari.*'

167 Hobbes 1983a, XII.VI, p. 189: 'Quod si verum esset, non video quare rationem fidei nostrae reddere iuberemur ... aut denique quare non unusquisque quid faciendum, & quid fugiendum sibi sit, ex propria potius inspiratione, quam ex praeceptis imperantium, aut recta ratione aestimaret.'

168 Clarendon 1676, pp. 17–18. On the association of wit with irreligiousness see Milburn 1966, pp. 268–312.

mysteries of the Christian faith. One problem which, as he says, has shaken the faith even of the saints is why evil has so often been permitted to triumph (p. 247). He pretends to approach the mystery in a serious frame of mind, putting forward as his main example the terrible sufferings endured by Job. But he then describes Job's experiences in language suited only to the handling of minor administrative complaints. He notes that Job at first attempted to 'expostulate with God'; that after a while God duly 'taketh up the matter'; and that Job's innocence is eventually 'approved'.[169] Hobbes later uses the technique even more deflatingly in examining the mystery of miracles in chapter XXXVII. 'By *Miracles*', he begins solemnly enough, 'are signified the Admirable works of God: & therefore they are also called *Wonders*' (p. 300). But he then offers an absurd example, further underlining its absurdity by means of a quizzical meiosis: 'Therefore, if a Horse, or Cow should speak, it were a Miracle; because both the thing is strange, & the naturall cause difficult to imagin.'[170] Yet more disdainful is his use of tapinosis to describe the mysterious nature of angels. (Too disdainful, he later seemed to have feared, for the passages are withdrawn from the Latin *Leviathan*.)[171] First he turns to the case of the angel that appeared to Abraham. This raises no difficulties, since the angel was merely a voice, which 'saves the labour of supposing any permanent Ghosts' (p. 276). This contrasts with the case of the angel that appeared to Moses. Although it was no more than a 'cloudy pillar', it 'stood at the dore of the Tabernacle' and 'talked with Moses', so that he found himself engaged in conversation with a cloud capable of motion and speech (p. 276). Most depreciating of all is Hobbes's use of tapinosis to analyse the concept of religion itself. Religion, he lays it down in chapter VI, can be defined as '*Feare* of power invisible, feigned by the mind, or imagined from tales publiquely allowed'.[172] This definition caused the greatest offence of all. John Whitehall called it a mockery of all faith,[173] while Sir Charles Wolseley in *The Reasonableness of Scripture-Belief* asserted that it showed more clearly than anything the iniquity of those

169 Hobbes 1991, p. 247. Cf. Martinich 1992, p. 158, claiming that Hobbes's intention in this passage is to assert orthodoxy.

170 Hobbes 1991, p. 300. Martinich 1992, p. 244, insists that, when discussing miracles, there is nothing sceptical about Hobbes's tone. But Martinich fails to mention the horse and the cow.

171 Martinich 1992, p. 252, argues that, had Hobbes wished to undermine belief in angels, 'he could either have dismissed talk of angels out of hand', or 'maintained his subtle demythologising interpretations throughout the New Testament'. But these are not the only possibilities. He could also have ridiculed the whole doctrine, which I am arguing is what he did.

172 Hobbes 1991, p. 42. Even Martinich 1992 finds 'difficulties' in this passage. But he manages to conclude (p. 59) that Hobbes's definition 'does not suggest any irreligion on his part'.

173 Whitehall 1679, p. 26.

who, 'by an empty prophane sort of discourse, which themselves call Wit', have disgraced the age.[174]

I end with Henry More of Christ's College Cambridge. When More examined the theological arguments of *Leviathan* in his *Immortality of the Soul* in 1662, one of the questions he asked himself was why Hobbes had been so 'copious in jearing' at his adversaries. 'One might well be amazed', More remarks, 'to observe such slight and vain arguing coming from so grave a Philosopher.'[175] He goes on to suggest, however, that we can easily account for Hobbes's ridiculing tone if we reflect that 'his peculiar eminency, as himself somewhere professes, lies in *Politicks*'.[176] Pursuing this explanation, More offers a fine summary of exactly the argument I have been seeking to develop about Hobbes's changing approach to civil science. When we engage in political debate, More suggests, it is no doubt indispensable to add as much as we can in the way of 'Rhetorications' to the statement of our case.[177] Hobbes had insisted in the epistle dedicatory to the English translation of *De Cive* that his main achievement had been to discredit and supersede the use of such 'successfull Rhetorications'.[178] As More observes, however, by the time Hobbes came to write *Leviathan* he had recognised that, in political argument, 'the humours and Bravadoes of Eloquence, especially amongst the simple, is a very effectuall and serviceable instrument'.[179]

174 Wolseley 1672, sig. A, 3^r–4^r.
175 More 1987, p. 56.
176 More 1987, p. 56.
177 More 1987, p. 56.
178 Hobbes 1983b, epistle dedicatory, p. 26.
179 More 1987, p. 56.

CONCLUSION: WHY DID HOBBES CHANGE HIS MIND?

Hobbes's conception of civil science in *The Elements of Law* and *De Cive* is founded on the belief that scientific reasoning possesses an inherent power to persuade us of the truths it finds out. By contrast, *Leviathan* declares that the sciences are small power, and reverts to the typically humanist assumption that, if we are to succeed in persuading others to accept our arguments, we shall have to supplement the findings of reason with the moving force of eloquence. A shift in outlook so profound and comprehensive clearly calls for an explanation. What made Hobbes change his mind about the idea of a civil science? What prompted him to adopt in *Leviathan* the very approach he had earlier repudiated?

One factor worth considering is that in *Leviathan* Hobbes evidently takes himself to be addressing a new type of audience, an audience at once broader and less well-educated than he had previously sought to reach. Although *The Elements* is in English, Hobbes explicitly tells us that his ambition in writing it was to insinuate its doctrines into the minds of 'those whom the matter it contayneth most neerly concerneth'.[1] *De Cive* is no less clearly intended for an elite, especially as it was written in Latin, a language which as Hobbes later observed 'is not commonly used by any Nation now in the world'.[2] By contrast with these narrow if lofty aspirations, Hobbes describes himself in the epistle dedicatory to *Leviathan* as offering his theory to the whole world, and reiterates in his final chapter that he plans to submit his work to the censure of his fellow-countrymen at large.[3]

A number of recent commentators have taken it for granted that Hobbes's desire to reach a wider audience must account for his changed literary strategies in *Leviathan*.[4] He is assumed to be following the ancient maxim to the effect that, while the open palm of rhetoric is needed for the vulgar, the closed fist of dialectic is sufficient for the learned. But this

1 BL Harl. MS 4235, fo. 2^{v}. Cf. Hobbes 1969a, p. xvi.
2 Hobbes 1991, p. 481.
3 Hobbes 1991, pp. 3, 482.
4 Johnston 1986, pp. 71–91, 130–2; Schoneveld 1987, pp. 112–14.

explanation fails to take account of the place in Hobbes's intellectual development of the Latin *Leviathan* of 1668. On the one hand this is obviously a further treatise intended for the learned. On the other hand it is arguably the most rhetorical of all Hobbes's works. It makes an even more extensive use of *ornatus* than the English version of 1651,[5] and employs a number of rhetorical devices not found in the earlier text, the most striking being the use of dialogue. The Latin *Leviathan* culminates in a long appendix of three chapters in which two figures called 'A' and 'B' debate in turn the meaning of the Nicene Creed, the history and character of heresy and the objections levelled against Hobbes's earlier statements of his theological beliefs.[6] Filled as these chapters are with appeals to history and discussions of ancient texts, they are at once more humanist in orientation and more rhetorical in idiom than anything in the English *Leviathan* of 1651.

It is doubtful, in short, whether considerations about audience go far towards explaining Hobbes's new concern in *Leviathan* to press home his scientific findings with the moving power of eloquence. Whether writing for a learned or a more popular audience, this concern remained with him throughout the latter part of his intellectual career. To explain his change of front between *The Elements* of 1640 and *Leviathan* of 1651, it seems more promising to focus on the fact that these were the precise years during which he was living in exile in France. Is it possible that this new and very different intellectual milieu affected his views about the writing of civil science?

The question seems especially worth asking when we reflect on the principal reason given in *Leviathan* for insisting that the sciences are small power, and thus that their findings need to be supplemented by the force of eloquence. As we saw in chapter 9, Hobbes came to believe that most people are moved less by force of reason than by their perceived sense of their own self-interest. By contrast with the optimism of *The Elements* and *De Cive*, he additionally insists in *Leviathan* that, if the requirements of reason collide with people's interests, they will not only refuse to accept what reason dictates, but will do their best to dispute or suppress even the clearest scientific proofs if these seem liable to affect their interests in an adverse way.[7]

This understanding of self-interest as a power greater than reason, and capable of overturning it, is scarcely to be found in English political

5 Hobbes's use of Latin permits, for example, a more extended use of antithesis and litotes. See Hobbes 1668, pp. 8, 196, 314, etc.

6 Hobbes 1668, pp. 328–46; 346–59; 359–65.

7 Hobbes 1991, esp. pp. 74, 233.

literature before the 1640s.[8] It is striking, however, that in the course of the 1630s this very doctrine rose to sudden and spectacular prominence in France.[9] Among its leading exponents was the Huguenot leader, the duc de Rohan, whose *De l'interest des princes et estats de la Chrestienté* was first issued in 1639[10] and was followed by his *Discours politiques* in 1646.[11] Some years before this, moreover, a number of publicists close to Richelieu had already begun to write about statecraft in similar terms. One was Jean de Silhon, whose *Ministre d'état* originally appeared in 1631 (with copious *éloges* to Richelieu);[12] another was Philippe de Béthune, whose *Conseiller d'état* was first published anonymously in 1633.[13]

The main concern of these writers is with the interests of princes,[14] but they also emphasise the need for individuals to learn how to guard and follow their own particular interests. Rohan lays it down that 'in affairs of State we must never let ourselves be carried away by unregulated desires, nor by violent passions that disturb us in so many different ways'.[15] We must always consider 'our own interest, guided by reason alone, which ought to be the rule of all our actions'.[16] Rohan still assumes that reason will enable us to form an understanding of our best interests and guide us to their fulfilment. But the stress on interest led these writers towards a different and contrasting conclusion which, a few years later, became pivotal to Hobbes's scepticism about the capacity of reason to move us. They insist, that is, that what moves princes and public figures is neither reason nor passion, but rather a sense – as Silhon puts it – of 'whatever passion their interest gives them'.[17] It follows, Béthune adds, that in dealing with such people we need 'to consider what, according to their

8 Gunn 1969, pp. 1, 36 and note. Hobbes makes one reference to 'interests' in the epistle dedicatory to *The Elements of Law*, but the term never recurs in the body of the text. The single occurrence is mistranscribed in Tönnies's edition as 'interest'. See Hobbes 1969a, p. xv, but cf. Hobbes MS A.2.B, p. iii and BL Harl. MS 4235, fo. 2^r, in both of which the word is clearly 'interests'.

9 This movement has been extensively discussed. See Thuau 1966, Church 1972, Pintard 1982. Cf. also Hirschman 1977, esp. pp. 31–42; Keohane 1980, pp. 168–82; McKenzie 1981; Tuck 1993, esp. pp. 82–94. For the Italian background see Viroli 1992, esp. pp. 238–80; Borrelli 1993, esp. pp. 63–222; Tuck 1993, esp. pp. 94–104, 120–4. On Hobbes and *ragione di stato* see Borrelli 1993, pp. 223–56, and Triomphe 1994.

10 Rohan 1639. Thuau 1966, p. 313, argues that the text was completed by 1634, although it remained unpublished until the year after Rohan's death in 1638.

11 Rohan 1646, title-page: 'Cy-devant non imprimez'.

12 Silhon 1631, sig. e, iv^r.

13 For the ascription to Béthune see Thuau 1966, pp. 238–40.

14 See for example Rohan 1646, pp. 107, 114, 117, 128.

15 Rohan 1639, pp. 132–3: 'en matiere d'Estat on ne doit se laisser conduire aux desirs desreglez ... ni aux passions violentes qui nous agitent diversement'.

16 Rohan 1639, p. 133: 'nostre propre interest; guidé par la seule raison, qui doit estre la regle des nos actions'.

17 Silhon 1631, p. 257: 'celle [passion] que l'interest leur donne'.

interests, their humours and their affairs of the moment they can reasonably desire'.[18] The conclusion to be drawn 'is that Reason of State is in effect nothing other than reason of interest'.[19] Rohan later points a similar moral in the much-quoted epigram introducing the first part of *De l'interest des princes*: 'Princes rule peoples, and interest rules princes.'[20]

These contentions open up the possibility of a collision between reason and interest, especially as these writers are anxious to stress that political leaders are prone to misperceive their interests and act in defiance of rationality. 'Where interest has been well or badly followed', Rohan observes, 'it has caused the ruin of some states and the grandeur of others.'[21] Once it is conceded that reason may conflict with interest, and that interest will generally prevail, the way lies open to the deeply sceptical conclusion on which Hobbes lays so much emphasis in *Leviathan*: that when someone decides that a certain belief or line of conduct is required by their interests, reason will have little hope of stopping them. This is already the implication Rohan leaves with us, going so far as to suggest in a moment of hyperbolical doubt that even eloquence can never hope to persuade us unless it happens to chime with our interests.[22]

What conclusions should we draw from the insight that reason may be unable to persuade us of the truths it finds out? As I stressed in chapter 9, Hobbes's answer in *Leviathan* is that, if the sovereignty of reason is to be maintained, we shall have to find some means of supplementing its findings with the arts of persuasion, and hence with the force of eloquence. Once again, it is striking to find the same inference drawn by a number of writers within the intellectual circles in which Hobbes began to move in Paris in the early 1640s. One name particularly worth mentioning in this context is that of François de La Mothe le Vayer, an exact contemporary of Hobbes's who became a close associate during the years of Hobbes's exile in France.[23] The son of an *avocat*, La Mothe le Vayer inherited and initially occupied the seat his father had acquired in the Parlement of Paris. Relinquishing his post to study philosophy, he went on to publish a series of *Considerations* in 1638 in which he compared the art of eloquence in

18 Béthune 1633, p. 326: 'considerer ce que raisonnablement selon leurs interests leur humeurs & les affaires du temps, ils peuvent desirer'.

19 Béthune 1633, p. 319: 'en effet Raison d'Estat n'est autre chose, que raison d'interest'.

20 Rohan 1639, p. 104: 'Les Princes commandent aux peuples, & l'interest commande aux Princes.'

21 See Rohan 1639, p. 105, on the fact that, insofar as interest 'a esté ou bien ou mal suivi, il a causé la ruine des uns ou la grandeur des autres [estats]'.

22 Rohan 1646, Discours v, p. 47: 'L'eloquence qui ne touche les interests de ceux qu'on veut persuader, a ordinairement peu d'effect envers eux.' Cf. Gunn 1966, p. 25.

23 For La Mothe le Vayer's connections with various of Hobbes's friends in Paris see Malcolm 1994, pp. 834, 836, 850.

antiquity and contemporary France and expatiated on the value of rhetoric in public life. Le Vayer's central contention is that, 'when there is a question of winning credibility among the most sensible people, or of convincing the most solid minds, and of coercing the most opinionated and incredulous, it is then we have need of the highest Eloquence'.[24] As long as we understand how to supplement reason with eloquence, we can always hope to speak persuasively: 'in an assembly of reasonable men', eloquence 'becomes a ruler of absolute power'.[25]

During the 1640s Le Vayer was appointed by Anne of Austria, Louis XIII's widow, as tutor to the young Louis XIV, who had succeeded to the throne in 1643 when less than six years old. For his illustrious pupil Le Vayer drew up a typically humanist syllabus of instruction, subsequently publishing it in instalments in the course of the 1650s. One of the first sections to be printed was entitled *La Rhétorique du Prince*. This provides an outline of the four traditional *elementa* of neo-Ciceronian rhetoric, concluding with an account of the importance of eloquence – and hence the art of rhetoric – in the proper conduct of public life. With greatly increased confidence, Le Vayer now insists not merely that eloquence is indispensable, but that its power is so overwhelming as to guarantee us whatever victories we seek. 'There is nothing', he concludes, 'that an army can accomplish with fire and sword that Eloquence cannot equally boast of being able to bring about in an assembly of reasonable men.'[26]

Another exponent of the rhetorical arts who may have had an influence on Hobbes at this period was Sir William Davenant. As we saw in chapter 9, Hobbes was in almost daily contact with Davenant while completing *Leviathan* at the end of the 1640s, and it was at this juncture that Davenant addressed the essay prefacing his heroic poem *Gondibert* to 'his much honor'd friend, M. Hobbes'.[27] Hobbes assured Davenant in his *Answer* that in a work shortly to see the light – by which he can only have meant *Leviathan* – Davenant would find extensive use made of his judgment.[28] What makes this exchange of civilities especially interesting is that one of Davenant's leading themes in his preface, as in many of his other works, was the importance of the rhetorical arts – especially the art of poetry – in

24 La Mothe le Vayer 1662a, p. 482: 'quand il est question de gagner creance parmi les plus habiles hommes, de convaincre les plus solides esprits, & de forcer les plus opiniastres & les plus incredules . . . c'est alors qu'il est besoin de la plus haute Eloquence'.

25 La Mothe le Vayer 1662a, p. 478: on how, in 'une assemblée d'hommes raisonnables', eloquence 'se rend maistresse absolue'.

26 La Mothe Le Vayer 1662b, p. 855: 'il n'y a rien que le fer & le feu executent dans une armée, dont l'Eloquence ne se puisse vanter de venir à bout dans une assemblée d'hommes raisonnables'.

27 Davenant 1971a, p. 3.

28 Hobbes 1971a, p. 54.

the regulation of civil life.[29] As he reminds Hobbes at the end of his preface, 'the weakest part of the people is their minds', so that we must stand ready to use the arts of persuasion to make them accept the truth.[30]

It seems probable that Hobbes may have been affected in the 1640s by all these writers, and more generally by the rhetorical culture of the *age d'éloquence* within which he was living during his years of exile in France.[31] Nevertheless, it must be admitted that there is something question-begging about pursuing this line of thought. We are not so much faced with the problem of explaining how Hobbes became aware of the arguments in favour of a union between reason and rhetoric, since he makes abundantly clear in *The Elements* and *De Cive* that he had never been unaware of these arguments at any point. What remains to be explained is why he should have come to accept them at the end of the 1640s when he had earlier repudiated them with so much vehemence.

Fortunately there is no need to speculate, for Hobbes supplies us with an answer himself. It was in consequence of brooding in the 1640s about the causes of the English civil war that he felt obliged to reconsider his views about the place of rhetoric in public debate. He first hints at this explanation in *Leviathan*, but it is in *Behemoth or the Long Parliament*[32] – the set of dialogues he wrote in the 1660s[33] on the causes and course of the revolution[34] – that he indicates most fully what prompted him to change his mind about the relations between reason and rhetoric, and hence about the idea of a civil science.

Behemoth lays the blame for the catastrophe of the 1640s on two groups above all. Hobbes mainly denounces the Presbyterians 'and other Fanatick Ministers',[35] going so far as to declare that the entire rebellion arose from 'the incitement of Presbyterian Ministers, who are therefore guilty of the death of all that fell in that Warre'.[36] He also inculpates the democratical

29 See Jacob and Raylor 1991, who reproduce and analyse Davenant's plans of 1654 'for advancement of moralitie' by means of musical drama, which (p. 245) will 'draw all by the Eares'. For further discussion see Smith 1994, pp. 87–8.

30 Davenant 1971a, p. 37.

31 On the *ars rhetorica* in France during this period, esp. in the Académie under Richelieu, see Fumaroli 1980, esp. pp. 647–60. Cf. Dear 1988, pp. 15–18, stressing the importance of rhetoric for Mersenne.

32 It is clear from the St John's College manuscript that this was Hobbes's intended title, although the first printed version (a pirated edition of 1679) was entitled *The History of the Civil Wars of England*. See St John's College MS 13, title page, and cf. Macdonald and Hargreaves 1952, p. 65.

33 For discussions of Hobbes's text, including the circumstances of its composition and publication, see Tönnies 1969b; MacGillivray 1970; Hartman 1978, pp. 233–300.

34 The term 'revolution' is not anachronistic here; it is Hobbes's own word for the upheavals of mid-century. See St John's MS 13, p. 189, and cf. Hobbes 1969b, p. 204.

35 St John's MS 13, p. 149. Cf. Hobbes 1969b, p. 159.

36 St John's MS 13, p. 89. Cf. Hobbes 1969b, p. 95. Still more forthrightly, Hobbes 1668,

gentlemen in the House of Commons,[37] insisting that they 'did no lesse desire a Popular government in the Civil State then these Ministers did in the Church'.[38]

Reflecting on their victory and how it came about, Hobbes draws two lessons from what he describes as the 'circular motion of the Soveraigne Power' between 1640 and 1660.[39] The first is that, in matters of public debate, reason and argument can scarcely hope to produce the least effect. He dramatises this deeply pessimistic conclusion in an exchange between the Hobbesian figure of 'A' and the more docile 'B' in the opening dialogue. The figure of 'A' begins with a rhetorical question:

> Why may not men be taught their duty, that is, the Science of Just and Uniust, as divers other Sciences have been taught from true Principles, and evident demonstration, and much more easily then any of those Preachers and Democraticall Gentlemen could teach Rebellion and Treason?[40]

There follows a remarkable passage – megalomaniac even by Hobbes's standards – in which 'A' answers his own question by claiming that this could in fact have been done:

> The Rules of *Just* and *Uniust* sufficiently demonstrated, and from Principles evident to the meanest capacity,[41] have not been wanting; and notwithstanding the obscurity of their Author, have shined not onely in this, but also in forraigne Countries to men of good education.[42]

Why then has this science been of no avail? Partly because so few people are well-educated, with the result that hardly anyone realised at the time that a scientific theory of politics had been made available. But mainly because most people learn their politics from divines in the pulpit, the very people who in this instance were preaching disobedience.[43] As a result, the true science of politics was 'cover'd and kept under here by a cloud of adversaries' to the terrible detriment of the commonwealth.[44] To this tirade the figure of 'B' adds a deeper point, drawing on the arguments

p. 359, claims that the Scottish war of 1639 'was revived in 1640 by the English Presbyterians' – 'instigantibus presbyterianis Anglicis anno 1640 resuscitatum'.

37 St John's MS 13, pp. 24, 26, 27. Cf. Hobbes 1969b, pp. 26, 28, 30–1.

38 St John's MS 13, p. 21. Cf. Hobbes 1969b, p. 23.

39 St John's MS 13, p. 189. Cf. Hobbes 1969b, p. 204. It was because of this circular motion that Hobbes thought of the events as a revolution.

40 St John's MS 13, p. 36. Cf. Hobbes 1969b, p. 39.

41 This phrase echoes chapter 13 of *The Elements of Law*, where Hobbes had spoken of 'principles evident even to the meanest Capacity'. BL Harl. MS 4235, fo. 52^{r}; cf. Hobbes 1969a, p. 66.

42 St John's MS 13, p. 36. Cf. Hobbes 1969b, p. 39.

43 For *Behemoth* on the dangers of private conscience to public peace see Lund 1992, esp. pp. 66–72.

44 St John's MS 13, p. 36. Cf. Hobbes 1969b, p. 40.

already put forward in *Leviathan* about the incapacity of reason and science to overcome the power of interest:

But who can teach what none have learn'd? Or if any man have been so singular, as to have studied the Science of Justice and Equity, how can he teach it safely, when it is against the interest of those that are in possession of the power to hurt him?[45]

Hobbes's first conclusion is thus that, faced with interest and ignorance, reason and science have little chance of being heard.

Hobbes next draws a contrasting and even more cheerless lesson from the debacle of the 1640s. Not only is reason impotent to persuade, but even the most absurd and pernicious doctrines, so long as they are put forward with sufficient rhetorical force, can always hope to triumph over the clearest scientific proofs. This is demonstrated in the first place by the success of the democratical gentlemen in the House of Commons. According to the witheringly scornful 'A', they had no arguments whatever on their side. They were men of utter absurdity, so that 'a Catalogue either of the Vices, or of the Crimes, or of the Follies of the greatest part of them that composed the long Parliament' would itself be so long that 'greater cannot be in the world'.[46] On the other hand they were undoubtedly men of enormous rhetorical skill. They had studied the writings of Aristotle and Cicero in youth, and 'from the love of their eloquence, fell in love with their Politicks'.[47] This made them 'great Haranguers',[48] and although they never formed a majority in the House of Commons 'yet by advantage of their eloquence' they 'were alwaies able to sway ye rest'.[49] The upshot was that, despite the weakness of their principles, their skill in oratory was sufficient to win over and thereby betray the people. They concentrated on 'seducing the multitude with Remonstrances from the Parliament House', and found no difficulty in cozening and imposing on the common people in the grossest possible way.[50] The figure of 'A' points the moral in his most caustic tones when describing their first major success, the attainder of the Earl of Strafford in 1641:

Impudence in Democraticall assemblies and[51] generally in all assemblies does almost all that's done, 'tis the Goddesse of Rhetorick, and carries proofe with it. For what

45 St John's MS 13, p. 36. Cf. Hobbes 1969b, p. 39.
46 St John's MS 13, p. 144. Cf. Hobbes 1969b, p. 155.
47 St John's MS 13, p. 40. Cf. Hobbes 1969b, p. 43.
48 St John's MS 13, p. 149. Cf. Hobbes 1969b, p. 158.
49 St John's MS 13, p. 3. Cf. Hobbes 1969b, p. 3.
50 St John's MS 13, pp. 110, 149. Cf. Hobbes 1969b, pp. 116, 158.
51 Hobbes crossed out a single word at this point, rendering it illegible. (Not even Paul Seaward – to whom I owe many thanks – has been able to read it.) See St John's MS 13, pp. 64–5.

ordinary man will not, from so great boldnesse of affirmation, conclude there is great probability in the thing affirmed?[52]

The same analysis is held to apply with even greater force in the case of the Presbyterians and their allies. According to 'A', these architects of the rebellion were not merely unreasoning and fanatical, but in some cases were actually insane. After listening to 'A's account of their beliefs and behaviour, 'B' adds his own crushing testimony to their incapacities. 'And yet converse with those Divinity disputers as long as you will, you will hardly find one in a hundred discreet enough to be imployed in any great affaire, either of Warre or Peace.'[53] Like the democratical gentlemen, however, they were undoubtedly rhetoricians of exceptional persuasiveness.[54] Hobbes makes the point with embittered emphasis in his opening dialogue, in which the figure of 'B', speaking of the Presbyterians, innocently asks 'how came their Power to be so great, being of themselves for the most part but so many poor Schollers?'[55] The Hobbesian figure of 'A' responds with a horrified tribute to the combined powers of *elocutio* and *pronuntiatio*, and thus to the persuasive force of rhetoric even when wholly disjoined from rational argument:

they so framed their countenance and gesture at the entrance into the Pulpit, and their pronuntiation both in their prayer and sermon, and used the Scripture phrase, whether understood by the people or not, as that no Tragoedian in the world could have acted the part of a right godly man better than these did, insomuch as a man unacquainted with such art, could never suspect any ambitious plot in them, to raise sedition against the State (as they then had designed) or doubt that the vehemence of their voice (for the same words with the usuall pronuntiation had been of little force) and forcednesse of their gesture and looks could arise from any thing else but zeal to the service of God.[56]

As in the case of the democratical gentlemen, Hobbes's crucial conclusion is that this degree of eloquence was sufficient in itself to seduce the multitude. The figure of 'B' declares at the end of the opening dialogue that this is what he now understands. He accepts that the Presbyterians 'preach'd us into the Rebellion', and later adds that their seditious outlook 'has been stuck so hard into the peoples heads and memories (I cannot say into their hearts, for they understand nothing in it, but that

52 St John's MS 13, pp. 64–5. Cf. Hobbes 1969b, pp. 68–9.
53 St John's MS 13, p. 135. Cf. Hobbes 1969b, p. 144.
54 For the fact that the radical puritans did indeed make self-conscious use of rhetorical techniques to move their audiences, see Smith 1989, esp. pp. 26–7, 308–13, on Perkins and Saltmarsh.
55 St John's MS 13, p. 19. Cf. Hobbes 1969b, p. 21.
56 St John's MS 13, p. 22. Cf. Hobbes 1969b, p. 24. For a discussion of this passage, and more generally of rhetoric in *Behemoth*, see Smith 1994, pp. 352–4.

they may lawfully Rebell) that I fear the Common wealth will never be cured'.[57] By the time we reach the final dialogue, the more forthright figure of 'A' is claiming that Presbyterian rhetoric is to blame for everything. 'The mischiefe proceeded wholly from the Presbyterian Preachers, who by a long practised Histrionick faculty, preached up the Rebellion powerfully.'[58]

To Hobbes, in short, the English revolution appears as a victory for the irrational but overwhelming power of neo-classical and antinomian rhetoric over the small power of science and rationality. As he puts it in the review and conclusion of *Leviathan*, the doctrines that poisoned 'the Fountains of Civill and Morall Doctrine' arose 'from the Venime of Heathen Politicians, and from the Incantation of Deceiving Spirits' (p. 491). This being so, it is hardly suprising to find him acknowledging in the same review and conclusion that, if the voice of reason is to have any prospect of being heard amid the clamour of obscurantism and error, it will need to speak the language of eloquence, the enormous power of which he no longer feels able to discount. He now makes it his highest hope that 'wheresoever there is place for adorning and preferring of Errour, there is much more place for adorning and preferring of Truth' (p. 484). Without such 'powerfull Eloquence', he now concedes, 'the effect of Reason will be little' (p. 483).

Hobbes treats the period between 1640 and 1660 as little more than a demented interruption of England's natural and civilised line of intellectual development. After the Restoration of 1660 this view became an orthodoxy, and was later enshrined as an important element in the national self-image known as the 'whig' interpretation of English history. The idea of the Interregnum as an era of superstition and lunacy was influentially fostered by the defenders of the new science, especially Thomas Sprat in his apologetic *History of the Royal Society* in 1667.[59] The corresponding demand for an end to such folly and obscurantism was vigorously put forward by the so-called latitudinarian divines of the same period. The 1660s saw the start of John Tillotson's polemic against the mysteries of Catholicism[60] as well as the beginnings of the movement led by his friend Edward Stillingfleet to develop a 'commonsense' version of the Anglican faith.[61] Some time before this outlook became widespread,

57 St John's MS 13, pp. 42, 53. Cf. Hobbes 1969b, pp. 46, 57.

58 St John's MS 13, p. 150. Cf. Hobbes 1969b, p. 159.

59 Sprat 1959, esp. pp. 53–4.

60 See McAdoo 1965, pp. 171–9 and Marshall 1985, esp. pp. 421–5 on Tillotson's Erastianism. Cf. Goldie 1990, esp. pp. 92–5, for Stillingfleet's comparable attack on popery and superstition.

61 See McAdoo 1965, pp. 179–87; Carroll 1975, esp. pp. 39–42.

however, Hobbes had already put forward a number of similar arguments.[62] He first presents them in *Leviathan*, in which he evenhandedly denounces the Roman Catholics and the fanatic sects for extinguishing the light of reason with their vain and absurd philosophies. He returns to the charge in his *Considerations* of 1662, upbraiding John Wallis and his puritan associates for having preached a set of principles that 'made both Oliver and the people mad'. 'You thought to make them mad', Hobbes goes on, 'but just to such a degree as should serve your own turn; that is to say, mad, and yet just as wise as yourselves.'[63] Finally, the figure of 'A' in *Behemoth* underscores the point with even greater violence:

> If in time as in place there were degrees of *high* and *low*, I verily beleeve that the highest of time would be that which passed between the years of 1640 and 1660. For he that thence, as from the divells mountain, should have looked upon the world, and observed the actions of men, especially in England, might have had a prospect of all kinds of Iniustice, and of all kinds of Folly that the world could afford, and how they were produced by their dams *hypocrisy* and *self-conceit*, whereof the one is double iniquity, and the other double folly.[64]

The entire period of the revolution is dismissed as nothing better than an era of collective insanity.

As well as emphasising the follies of his opponents, Hobbes cultivates a distinctive style in which to address their absurdities. It has been said, and rightly, that Hobbes was the first thinker to produce a comprehensive philosophical system in the English language.[65] It could equally well be said that, in teaching philosophy to speak English, Hobbes at the same time taught it a particular tone of voice. As we have seen, the tone is very much that of the sane and moderate *savant* beset on all sides by fanaticism and stupidity. We cannot expect reason to triumph, the tone implies, since the foolish and ignorant will always be in a majority. But we can at least hope to discomfit them by wielding the weapons of ridicule, deriding their excesses, sneering at their errors, drawing our readers into a scornful alliance against their general benightedness.

This tone of voice has been immensely influential in English philosophy. This was the tone that led Clarendon to protest that Hobbes scoffs at his opponents rather than making any attempt to argue with them.[66] This was

[62] For the suggestion that the ferocity of the attack on Hobbes owed something to the fact that his arguments were uncomfortably close to those of the so-called latitudinarians, see Marshall 1985; Malcolm 1988 (and cf. also Malcolm 1983). See also Goldie 1991a, esp. pp. 333–4; Goldie 1991b, esp. pp. 610–15.

[63] Hobbes 1840c, pp. 418–19.

[64] St John's MS 13, p. 1. Cf. Hobbes 1969b, p. 1.

[65] Sacksteder 1978, pp. 33–4.

[66] Clarendon 1676, esp. pp. 16–19.

the tone that prompted John Sergeant to complain in his *Reason against Raillery* that Tillotson dismisses the mysteries of the Catholic faith with sheer mockery as opposed to any effort at understanding.[67] This was the tone that Adam Smith admired in Hobbes,[68] as well as the tone in which his friend David Hume unrepentantly addressed the Anglican divines, seeking to undermine their theological arguments by parodying them with stately irony.[69] It remains the tone in which Hume's latter-day admirers – Bertrand Russell provides an eminent example – have continued to write the history of philosophy, presenting it as a sequence of more or less ludicrous misconceptions finally unmasked by their own unanswerable blend of civilised satire and unimpeachable rationality.

Hobbes was the first English philosopher to perfect and practise this style. I have argued that he learned it as a student of the classical art of rhetoric, and thus that his mature presentation of his political theory in *Leviathan* reflects an attempt to bring together the methods of science and the techniques of Renaissance humanism. The manner of writing philosophy to which this gave rise has in turn proved to be one of his enduring legacies.

67 For this ascription, and for Sergeant's debate with Tillotson, see Tavard 1978, esp. p. 233.

68 See Smith 1963, p. 56, defending Hobbes against Shaftesbury.

69 See Rivers 1993, esp. pp. 589–94.

BIBLIOGRAPHIES

MANUSCRIPT SOURCES

BIBLIOTHÈQUE NATIONALE, PARIS

Fonds Latin MS 6566A: *Hobs* [marked on spine; no title page].

THE BRITISH LIBRARY

Birch MS 4279, fo. 307r: Walter Warner to Robert Payne, 17 October 1634.

Birch MS 4407, fo. 186r: Sir Charles Cavendish to Walter Warner, 2 May 1636.

Birch MS 4444, fo. 93r: Sir Charles Cavendish to Walter Warner, 2 September [1636?].

Harl. MS 3360: *A Minute or First Draught of the Optiques.*

Harl. MS 4235: *The Elements of Law, Naturall and Politique.*

Harl. MS 6796, fos. 193–266: Latin optical treatise.

Harl. MS 6796, fos. 297–308: [*A Short Tract on First principles*].

Lansdowne MS 119, no. 2, fos. 13–16: *Orders for the School of St Edmunds Bury.*

Sloane MS 3930, fos. 1r–2r: *To the King* [Dedication of *Seven Philosophical Problems*].

Egerton MS 1910: *Leviathan Or the Matter, Forme, and Power of A Commonwealth Ecclesiastical and Civil.*

CAMBRIDGE UNIVERSITY LIBRARY

MS Mm. 1.48, pp. 394–413: Thomas Smith: *Oratio ... de Dignitate Legum atque Utilitate Studii Juris Civilis.*

MS Gg-3-34, pp. 1–82: Thomas Smith: *Dialogue about Qu. Elizabeth's Marriage.*

CHATSWORTH

Hardwick MS 29: *Book of Accounts: Begining 1608. Ending 1623.*

Hardwick MS 301/15: Counterpart of Indenture 'Betwene the Right Honoble William Earle of Devonshire on the one part, And Thomas Hobbes domesticall Servant and Secretary to the said Earle on the other parte', 4 August 1627.

Hardwick MS 301/16: Counterpart of Indenture 'Betweene the right Hoble William Earle of Devonshire of the one partie And Thomas Hobbes of London Esquire servaunt to the said Earle of the other partie', 24 February 1638 [i.e. 1639 our style].

Hobbes MS A.1: *Ad Nobilissimum Dominum Gulielmum Comitem Devoniae etc. De Mirabilibus Pecci, Carmen Thomas Hobbes.*

Hobbes MS A.2.B: *The Elementes of Law, Naturall and Politique.*

Hobbes MS A.6: Untitled. [MS of *Vita Carmine Expressa*, mainly in the hand of James Wheldon, with corrections by Hobbes. 10 folio pages]
Hobbes MS A.10: *Logica* and *Philosophia prima* [Draft of early chapters of *De Corpore*. 29 octavo pages].
Hobbes MS D.1: *Latin Exercises* [Bound manuscript volume, including *Ex Aristot: Rhet.*, pp. 1–143].
Hobbes MS D.3: *Essayes of 1 Arrogance 2 Ambition 3 Affectation 4 Detraction 5 Selfe=will 6 Masters and Servants 7 Expences 8 Visitations 9 Death 10 Readinge of Histories* [Bound manuscript volume, vi + 78pp.].
Hobbes MS D.6: *A Narration of y^e^ Proceedings both Publique & Private concerning y^e^ Inheritance of y^e^ Right Honble William Earle of Devonshire, from y^e^ time of y^e^ decease of his Grandfather, to this present* [8 folio pages].
Hobbes MS E.2: *Catalogue* [List of c 900 books in Bodleian Library. 40 16mo pages].
Hobbes MS 73.Aa: *Translations of Italian Letters* [Bound manuscript volume, 248pp., 34pp. blank at end. A collection of 76 letters from Fulgenzio Micanzio, inscribed on flyleaf in Hobbes's hand: 'Translated out of the originall Italian Letters by Th: Hobbes, secretary to ye Lord Cavendysh'].

PUBLIC RECORD OFFICE, LONDON

State Papers 16/79: letters and papers, 21 to 30 September 1627.

ST JOHN'S COLLEGE, OXFORD

MS 13: *Behemoth or the Long Parliament. By Thomas Hobbes of Malmsbury* [Fair copy in the hand of James Wheldon, with additions and excisions in the hand of Hobbes].

PRINTED PRIMARY SOURCES

Ad C. Herennium de ratione dicendi (1954). Ed. and trans. Harry Caplan, London.
Alciati, Andreae (1621). *Emblemata*, cum commentariis Claudii Minois [*et al.*], Padua.
Aphthonius (1508). *Progymnasmata* in *Rhetores*, ed. Aldus Manutius, Venice, pp. 1–17.
(c.1520). *Praeexercitamenta*, trans. and ed. Gentian Hervet, London.
(1575). *Progymnasmata partim a Rodolpho Agricola, partim a Ioanne Maria Catanaeo Latinitate donata*, London.
Aquinas, St Thomas (1969). *Summa Theologiae*. Vol. 23: *Virtue*, ed. W. D. Hughes, London.
Arber, Edward (ed.) (1875–94). *A Transcript of the Registers of the Company of Stationers of London, 1554–1640 AD*, 5 vols., London–Birmingham.
Aristotle (1926). *The 'Art' of Rhetoric*, trans. John Henry Freese, London.
(1985). *Nicomachean Ethics*, trans. Terence Irwin, Indianapolis.
Ascham, Roger (1864–65). *The Whole Works*, 3 vols., London.
(1970a). *A Report and Discourse written by Roger Ascham, of the affaires and state of Germany* in *English Works*, ed. William A. Wright, Cambridge, pp. 121–69.
(1970b). *The scholemaster* in *English Works*, ed. William A. Wright, Cambridge, pp. 171–302.
(1970c). *Toxophilus* in *English Works*, ed. William A. Wright, Cambridge, pp. 1–119.
Aubrey, John (1898). *'Brief Lives', chiefly of Contemporaries, set down by John Aubrey, between the years 1669 & 1696*, ed. A. Clark, 2 vols., Oxford.

Augustine, St (1912). *Confessions*, trans. William Watts, 2 vols., London.
Bacon, Francis (1857a). *Parasceve ad historiam naturalem et experimentalem* in *The Works of Francis Bacon*, ed. James Spedding, Robert Ellis and Douglas Heath, London, vol. I, pp. 367–411.
(1857b). *De Dignitate et Augmentis Scientiarum Libri IX* in *The Works*, ed. James Spedding, Robert Ellis and Douglas Heath, London, vol. I, pp. 423–837.
(1857c). *Novum Organon* in *The Works*, ed. James Spedding, Robert Ellis and Douglas Heath, London, vol. I, pp. 121–365.
(1859). 'Of the colours of good and evil' in *The Works*, ed. James Spedding, Robert Ellis and Douglas Heath, London, vol. VII, pp. 77–92.
(1915). *The Advancement of Learning*, ed. G. W. Kitchin, London.
(1972). *Essays*, introd. Michael J. Hawkins, London.
Barnes, Barnabe (1606). *Foure Bookes of Offices*, London.
Barrow, Isaac (1669). *Lectiones XVIII ... in quibus Opticorum Phaenomenon ... exponuntur. Annexae sunt Lectiones aliquot Geometricae*, London.
Barton, John (1634). *The Art of Rhetorick concisely and compleatly handled*, n.p.
Beacon, Richard (1594). *Solon his Follie, or a Politique Discourse, touching the Reformation of common-weales conquered, declined or corrupted*, Oxford.
Becon, Thomas (1843). *The Early Works*, ed. John Ayre, Cambridge.
(1844). *A New Catechism*, ed. John Ayre, Cambridge.
Berkeley, George (1871). *Alciphron, or The Minute Philosopher* in *The Works of George Berkeley*, vol. II, ed. Alexander Campbell Fraser, Oxford.
[Béthune, Philippe de] (1633). *Le Conseiller d'Estat*, Paris.
Blount, Thomas (1971). *The Academy of Eloquence*, ed. R. C. Alston, Menston.
Blundeville, Thomas (1570). *A very Briefe and profitable Treatise declaring howe many counsells, and what maner of Counselers a Prince that will governe well ought to have*, London.
(1574). *The true order and Methode of wryting and reading Hystories*, London.
Botero, Giovanni (1956). *The Reason of State*, trans. P. J. and D. P. Waley, London.
Boyle, Robert (1662). *A Defence of the Doctrine Touching the Spring and Weight of the Air* in *New Experiments Physico-Mechanical Touching the Air. The Second Edition. Whereunto is added A Defence of the Authors Explication of the Experiments, Against the Objections of Franciscus Linus, And, Thomas Hobbes*, London.
Braham, Humfrey (1555). *The Institucion of a Gentleman*, London.
Bramhall, John (1655). *A Defence of True Liberty from Ante-cedent and Extrinsecall Necessity*, London.
Brinsley, John (1616). *The First Book of Tullies Offices translated Grammatically*, London.
(1917). *Ludus Literarius or The Grammar Schoole*, ed. E. T. Campagnac, London.
Bullokar, John (1967). *An English Expositor*, ed. R. C. Alston, Menston.
Burton, Robert (1989). *The Anatomy of Melancholy*, ed. Thomas C. Faulkner, Nicholas K. Kiessling and Rhonda L. Blair, vol. I, Text, Oxford.
Butler, Charles (1629). *Rhetoricae Libri Duo*, London.
Camden, William (1605). *Remaines of a Greater Worke, concerning Britaine*, London.
Carmen de Figuris vel Schematibus (1863). In *Rhetores Latini Minores*, ed. C. Halm, Leipzig, pp. 63–70.
Castiglione, Baldassare (1994). *The Book of the Courtier*, ed. Virginia Cox, London.
[Cavendish, William] (1611). *A Discourse Against Flatterie*, London.

(1620). *Horae Subsecivae. Observations and Discourses*, London.

Cicero (1481). *Tullius de Amicicia translated ... by ... The Erle of Wurcestre* [ed.] William Caxton [Westminster], fos. 73^r^–100^v^.

(1534). *The thre bookes of Tullyes offyces bothe in latyne tonge & in englysshe lately translated by Roberte Whytinton poete laureate*, London.

(1550). *The Booke of freendeship*, trans. John Harryngton, London.

(1556). *Three bookes of dueties*, trans. Nicolas Grimalde, London.

(1574). *Rhetoricorum ... Ad C. Herennium, Libri IIII. ... [et] de Inventione Rhetorica, Libri II*, n.p.

(1577). *Foure Severall Treatises of M. Tullius Cicero: Conteyninge his most learned and Eloquente Discourses of Frendshippe: Old age: Paradoxes: and Scipio his Dreame*, trans. Thomas Newton, London.

(1913). *De officiis*, ed. and trans. Walter Miller, London.

(1923). *De amicitia*, ed. and trans. William A. Falconer, London.

(1931). *Pro T. Annio Milone oratio* in Cicero: *The Speeches*, ed. and trans. N. H. Watts, London.

(1942a). *De oratore*, ed. and trans. E. W. Sutton and H. Rackham, 2 vols., London.

(1942b). *De partitione oratoria*, ed. and trans. H. Rackham, London, pp. 310–420.

(1949a). *De inventione*, ed. and trans. H. M. Hubbell, London, pp. 1–346.

(1949b). *Topica*, ed. and trans. H. M. Hubbell, London, pp. 382–458.

(1962a). *Brutus*, ed. and trans. G. L. Henderson, revised edn., London, pp. 18–292.

(1962b). *Orator*, ed. and trans. H. M. Hubbell, revised edn., London, pp. 306–508.

Clarendon, Edward, Earl of (1676). *A Brief View and Survey of the Dangerous and pernicious Errors to Church and State, In Mr Hobbes's Book Entitled Leviathan*, Oxford.

Cockeram, Henry (1968). *The English Dictionarie*, ed. R. C. Alston, Menston.

Coke, Sir John (1888). 'Sir John Coke to his eldest son' in Historical Manuscripts Commission, *Twelfth Report, Appendix*, London, vol. II, pp. 250–1.

Cooper, Thomas (1565). *Thesaurus Linguae Romanae & Britannicae*, London.

Coote, Edmund (1968). *The English Schoole-maister*, ed. R. C. Alston, Menston.

Copland, Robert (c.1548). *The Art of Memory, that otherwyse is called the PHENIX*, London.

Cotgrave, Randle (1611). *A Dictionarie of the French and English Tongues*, London.

Cowley, Abraham (1949). 'To Mr Hobs' in Abraham Cowley: *Poetry & Prose*, ed. L. C. Martin, Oxford, pp. 42–5.

Cox, Leonarde (c.1530). *The Arte or Crafte of Rhethoryke*, London.

Crosse, Henry (1603). *Vertues Common-wealth: or the High-way to Honour*, London.

Daniel, Samuel (1963). *Musophilus, or Defence of all Learning* in *The Complete Works in Verse and Prose*, ed. Alexander B. Grosart, New York, vol. I, pp. 221–56.

Davenant, Sir William (1971a). 'The Author's Preface to his Much Honor'd Friend, M. Hobbes' in Sir William Davenant's *Gondibert*, ed. David F. Gladish, Oxford, pp. 3–44.

(1971b). *Gondibert an Heroick Poem*, ed. David F. Gladish, Oxford.

Davies, Sir John (1992). *Gulling Sonnets* in *The New Oxford Book of Sixteenth Century Verse*, ed. Emrys Jones, pp. 663–5.

Day, Angel (1592). 'A Declaration of such Tropes, Figures or Schemes, as for excellencie and ornament in writing, are specially used in this Methode' in *The Second Part of the English Secretary*, London, sig. M, 2^r^ and pp. 82–107.

(1967). *The English Secretary or Method of Writing Epistles and Letters*, ed. Robert O. Evans, Gainesville, Fl.

Dee, John (1571). 'Mathematical Preface' to Euclid, *The Elements of Geometrie*, trans. H. Billingsley, London, sig. iiii^{v} to sig. A iiii^{r}.

Descartes, René (1988). *Les passions de l'âme*, ed. Geneviève Rodis-Lewis, Paris.

Dowel, John (1683). *The Leviathan Heretical*, London.

Dowland, John (1597). *The First Booke of Songes or Ayres*, London.

Drayton, Michael (1953). 'To proverbe' from *Idea* in *Poems of Michael Drayton*, ed. John Buxton, London, vol. 1, pp. 2–18.

Drummond, William, of Hawthornden (1976). Sonnet 22: 'The praise of a solitarie life' from *Flowres of Sion* in *Poems and Prose*, ed. Robert H. Macdonald, London, p. 111.

Dryden, John (1900). *Essays of John Dryden*, ed. W. P. Ker, 2 vols., Oxford.

Dugard, William (1972). *Rhetorices Elementa*, ed. R. C. Alston, Menston.

Elyot, Sir Thomas (1962). *The Book named the Governor*, ed. S. E. Lehmberg, London.

Erasmus, Desiderius (1978a). *De Duplici copia verborum*, trans. Betty I. Knott in *Collected Works of Erasmus: Literary and Educational Writings II*, Toronto, pp. 279–660.

(1978b). *De ratione studii*, trans. Brian McGregor in *Collected Works of Erasmus: Literary and Educational Writings II*, Toronto, pp. 665–91.

Euclid (1571). *The Elements of Geometrie*, trans. H. Billingsley, London.

Euripides (1715). *Medea*, trans. George Buchanan in *Opera Omnia*, ed. Thomas Ruddimann, Edinburgh, vol. II, pp. 189–207.

Farnaby, Thomas (1970). *Index Rhetoricus*, ed. R. C. Alston, Menston.

Felippe, Bartolome (1589). *The Counseller: A Treatise of Counsels and Counsellers of Princes*, trans. John Thorius, London.

Fenner, Dudley (1584). *The Artes of Logike and Rethorike*, n.p. [?Middleburg].

Fraunce, Abraham (1950). *The Arcadian Rhetorike*, ed. Ethel Seaton, Oxford.

Fulwood, William (1571). *The Enemie of Idlenesse*, London.

[Gentillet, Innocent] (1602). *A Discourse upon the meanes of wel governing and maintaining in good peace, a kingdome, or other principalitie ... against Nicholas Machiavell the Florentine*, trans. Simon Patericke, London.

Gilbert, William (1600). *De Magnete, Magnetisque Corporibus*, London.

Goulston, Theodore (1619). *Aristotelis de Rhetorica seu arte Dicendi Libri Tres*, London.

Grataroli, Guglielmo (1562). *The Castel of Memorie*, trans. William Fulwood, London.

Guazzo, Stefano (1925). *The Civile Conversation*, trans. George Pettie and Bartholomew Young, ed. Sir Edward Sullivan, 2 vols., London.

Haechtanus, Laurentius (1579). *Μικροκοσμος: Parvus Mundus*, Amsterdam.

Hall, Joseph (1608). *Characters of Vertues and Vices: in two Bookes*, London.

Harvey, Gabriel (1577a). *Ciceronianus vel Oratio post reditum, habita Cantabrigiae ad suos Auditores*, London.

(1577b). *Rhetor, Vel duorum dierum Oratio, De Natura, Arte & Exercitatione Rhetorica*, London.

(1884). *Letter-Book of Gabriel Harvey, A.D. 1573–1580*, ed. Edward Scott, London.

(1913). *Marginalia*, ed. G. C. Moore Smith, Stratford-upon-Avon.

Harvey, William (1628). *Exercitatio Anatomica de motu cordis et Sanguinis in Animalibus*, Frankfurt.

Haward, Simon (1596). *Encheiridion Morale*, London.

Hawes, Stephen (1928). *The Pastime of Pleasure*, ed. William E. Mead, London.

Heywood, John (1867). *Three hundred epigrammes, upon three hundred proverbes* in *The Proverbs and Epigrams of John Heywood*, Manchester.

Hobbes, Thomas (1629). *Eight Bookes of the Peloponnesian Warre Written by Thucydides ... Interpreted ... By Thomas Hobbes*, London.

(1642). *Elementorum Philosophiae sectio tertia de Cive*, Paris.

(1650a). *Humane Nature: Or, The fundamental Elements of Policie*, London.

(1650b). *De Corpore Politico. Or The Elements of Law, Moral & Politick*, London.

(1656). *The Questions Concerning Liberty, Necessity, And Chance. Clearly Stated and Debated Between Dr. Bramhall Bishop of Derry, And Thomas Hobbes of Malmesbury*, London.

(1660). *Examinatio et Emendatio Mathematicae Hodierniae*, London.

(1668). *Leviathan, sive De Materia, Forma, & Potestate Civitatis Ecclesiasticae et Civilis* in *Thomae Hobbes Malmesburiensis Opera Philosophica Quae Latine scripsit, Omnia*, Amsterdam.

(1839a). *T. Hobbes Malmesburiensis Vita* in *Thomae Hobbes malmesburiensis opera philosophica quae latine scripsit omnia*, ed. Sir William Molesworth, London, vol. I, pp. xiii–xxi.

(1839b). *Thomae Hobbes Malmesburiensis Vita Carmine Expressa* in *Opera philosophica*, ed. Sir William Molesworth, London, vol. I, pp. lxxxi–xcix.

(1839c). *De Homine* in *Opera philosophica*, ed. Sir William Molesworth, London, vol. II, pp. 1–132.

(1839d). *Elements of Philosophy. The First Section, Concerning Body* in *The English Works of Thomas Hobbes of Malmesbury*, ed. Sir William Molesworth, London, vol. I, pp. v–xii, 1–532.

(1840a). *Of Liberty and Necessity* in *The English Works*, ed. Sir William Molesworth, London, vol. IV, pp. 229–78.

(1840b). *An Historical Narration Concerning Heresy and the Punishment Thereof* in *The English Works*, ed. Sir William Molesworth, London, vol. IV, pp. 385–408.

(1840c). *Considerations upon the Reputation, Loyalty, Manners, and Religion, of Thomas Hobbes of Malmesbury* in *The English Works*, ed. Sir William Molesworth, London, vol. IV, pp. 409–40.

(1840d). *An Answer to a Book Published by Dr. Bramhall* in *The English Works*, ed. Sir William Molesworth, London, vol. IV, pp. 279–384.

(1841). *The Questions Concerning Liberty, Necessity, And Chance* in *The English Works*, ed. Sir William Molesworth, London, vol. V, pp. 1–455.

(1844). 'Concerning the Virtues of an Heroic Poem', preface to *The Iliads and Odysses of Homer* in *The English Works*, ed. Sir William Molesworth, London, vol. X, pp. iii–x.

(1845a). *Dialogus Physicus de Natura Aeris* in *Opera philosophica*, ed. Sir William Molesworth, London, vol. IV, pp. 233–96.

(1845b). *De Principiis et Ratiocinatione Geometrarum* in *Opera philosophica*, ed. Sir William Molesworth, vol. IV, pp. 385–484.

(1845c). *Tractatus Opticus* in *Opera philosophica*, ed. Sir William Molesworth, London, vol. V, pp. 215–48.

(1845d). *De Mirabilibus Pecci, Carmen* in *Opera philosophica*, ed. Sir William Molesworth, London, vol. V, pp. 325–40.

(1845e). *Seven Philosophical problems ... with an Apology for Himself and his Writings* in *The English Works*, ed. Sir William Molesworth, London, vol. VII, pp. 1–68.

(1845f). *Decameron Physiologicum* in *The English Works*, ed. Sir William Molesworth, vol. VII, pp. 69–180.

(1845g). *Six Lessons to the Professors of the Mathematics* in *The English Works*, ed. Sir William Molesworth, vol. VII, pp. 181–356.

(1845h). *Marks of the Absurd Geometry, Rural Language, Scottish Church Politics, and Barbarisms of John Wallis* in *The English Works*, ed. Sir William Molesworth, vol. VII, pp. 357–400.

(1969a). *The Elements of Law Natural and Politic*, ed. Ferdinand Tönnies, second edn., introd. M. M. Goldsmith, London.

(1969b). *Behemoth or the Long Parliament*, ed. Ferdinand Tönnies, second edn., introd. M. M. Goldsmith, London.

(1971a). *The Answer of Mr. Hobbes to Sir Will. D'Avenant's Preface Before Gondibert* in Sir William Davenant's *Gondibert*, ed. David F. Gladish, Oxford, pp. 45–55.

(1971b). *A Dialogue Between a Philosopher and a Student of the Common Laws of England*, ed. Joseph Cropsey, Chicago.

(1973). *Critique du 'De mundo' de Thomas White*, ed. Jean Jacquot and Harold Whitmore Jones, Paris.

(1975a). *Hobbes's Thucydides*, ed. Richard Schlatter, New Brunswick.

(1975b). 'Of the Life and History of Thucydides' in *Hobbes's Thucydides*, ed. Richard Schlatter, New Brunswick, pp. 10–27.

(1983a). *De Cive: The Latin Version*, ed. Howard Warrender, Oxford: the Clarendon edition, vol. II.

(1983b). *De Cive: The English Version*, ed. Howard Warrender, Oxford: the Clarendon edition, vol. III.

(1986). *A Briefe of the Art of Rhetorique* in *The Rhetorics of Thomas Hobbes and Bernard Lamy*, ed. John T. Harwood, Carbondale and Edwardsville, pp. 33–128.

(1991). *Leviathan, or The Matter, Forme, & Power of a Common-wealth Ecclesiasticall and Civill*, ed. Richard Tuck, in Cambridge Texts in the History of Political Thought: Cambridge.

(1994). *The Correspondence*, ed. Noel Malcolm, 2 vols., Oxford: the Clarendon edition, vols. VI and VII.

[Hobbes, Thomas] (1637?). *A Briefe of the Art of Rhetorique*, London.

(1651). *A Brief of the Art of Rhetorick* in *A Compendium of the Art of Logick and Rhetorick in the English Tongue*, London, pp. 135–282.

[Hobbes, Thomas (?)] (1988). *Court traité des premiers principes: Le Short Tract on First Principles de 1630–1631*, ed. and trans. Jean Bernhardt, Paris.

Horace (1929). *De arte poetica* in *Horace*, ed. and trans H. Rushton Fairclough, pp. 450–88.

Hoskins, John (1935). *Directions for Speech and Style*, ed. Hoyt H. Hudson, Princeton.

Isidore of Seville (1911). *Etymologiarum sive originum Libri* XX, ed. W. M. Lindsay, 2 vols., Oxford.

Isocrates (1538). *Areopagitica Oratio*, trans. J. L. Vives in *Declamationes Sex*, Basel, pp. 277–95.

(1929a). *Areopagiticus*, ed. and trans. George Norlin, London, pp. 104–57.

(1929b). *Antidosis*, ed. and trans. George Norlin, London, pp. 184–365.

Jaggard, William (1941). *A Catalogue of such English Bookes, as lately have bene, and now are in*

Printing for Publication, ed. Oliver M. Willard in Stanford Studies in Language and Literature, Stanford, Cal.

Jewel, John (1850). *Oratio contra Rhetoricam* in *The Works of John Jewel*, ed. John Ayre, Cambridge, vol. IV, pp. 1283–91.

Jones, William (1967). *A Treatise of nobility*, ed. Alice Shalvi, London.

Jonson, Ben (1937). *Catiline his Conspiracy* in *Ben Jonson*, ed. C. H. Herford Percy and Evelyn Simpson, Oxford, vol. V, pp. 409–549.

(1947). *Timber: or, Discoveries Made upon Men and Matter* in *Ben Jonson*, ed. C. H. Herford Percy and Evelyn Simpson, Oxford, vol. VIII, pp. 555–649.

(1971). *Epicoene*, ed. Edward Partridge, London.

Kempe, William (1966). *The Education of children in learning* in *Four Tudor Books on Education*, ed. Robert D. Pepper, Gainesville, Fl., pp. 189–240.

Kingsbury, Susan M. (ed.), (1906–35). *The Records of the Virginia Company of London*, 4 vols., Washington, D.C.

La Mothe Le Vayer, François de (1662a). *Considerations sur l'eloquence françoise de ce temps* in *Oeuvres*, third edn., Paris, vol. I, pp. 429–84.

(1662b). *La Rhetorique de Prince* in *Oeuvres*, third edn., Paris, vol. I, pp. 827–55.

Languet, Hubert (1633). *Epistolae politicae et historicae scriptae ... ad... Philippum Sydnaeum*, ed. William Fitzer, Frankfurt.

Lawson, George (1657). *An examination of the political part of Mr Hobbs his Leviathan*, London.

Leighton, William (1603). *Vertue Triumphant, Or a lively description of the foure vertues cardinall*, London.

Lever, Ralphe (1573). *The Arte of Reason*, London.

Lipsius, Justus (1594). *Sixe Bookes of Politickes or Civil Doctrine*, trans. William Jones, London.

Livy (1929). *Ab urbe condita*, XXI–XXII, ed. and trans. B. O. Foster, London.

Locke, John (1979). *An Essay Concerning Human Understanding*, ed. Peter Nidditch, reprinted with corrections, Oxford.

(1993). *Of the Conduct of the Understanding*, ed. John Yolton, Bristol.

Lucian (1913). 'Heracles' in *Lucian*, ed. and trans. A. M. Harmon, vol. I, pp. 61–70.

Lucy, William (1663). *Observations, Censures and Confutations of Notorious Errours in Mr. Hobbes his Leviathan, and other his Books*, London.

Lyly, John (1868). *Euphues. The Anatomy of Wit*, ed. Edward Arber, London.

Machiavelli, Niccolò (1960). *Il Principe e Discorsi*, ed. Sergio Bertelli, Milan.

(1988). *The Prince*, ed. Russell Price and Quentin Skinner, in Cambridge Texts in the History of Political Thought: Cambridge.

Mancinelli, Antonio (1493). *Carmen de Figuris* in *Carmen de Floribus. Carmen de Figuris. De Poetica Virtute. Vitae Carmen*, Venice, sig. E, VIII^{r} to sig. H, I^{v}.

Marbeck, John (1581). *A Booke of Notes and Common places*, London.

Marston, John (1934–39). *What You Will* in *The Plays of John Marston*, ed. H. Harvey Wood, London, vol. II, pp. 227–95.

(1965). *Antonio and Mellida: The First Part*, ed. G. K. Hunter, London.

Melanchthon, Philipp (1522). *Institutiones Rhetoricae*, Basel.

Montaigne, Michel de (1893). *The Essayes of Michael Lord of Montaigne*, trans. John Florio, ed. Henry Morley, London.

More, Henry (1987). *The Immortality of the Soul*, ed. A. Jacob, Dordrecht.

More, Sir Thomas (1965). *Utopia [De optimo reipublicae statu deque nova insula Utopia]*, ed. Edward Surtz, S. J. and J. H. Hexter, London.

Mosellanus, Petrus (1533). *De Schematibus et tropis* in *De Figuris*, Venice, fos. 47^{v} to 60^{r}.

Mulcaster, Richard (1888). *Positions, wherin those primitive circumstances be examined, which are necessarie for the training up of children, either for skill in their booke, or health in their bodie*, ed. Robert H. Quick, London.

Napier, John (1614). *Mirifici Logarithmorum Canonis descriptio*, Edinburgh.

Nashe, Thomas (1958). *The Anatomy of Absurdity* in *The Works of Thomas Nashe*, ed. Ronald B. McKerrow, Oxford, vol. I, pp. 3–49.

(1985). *The Unfortunate Traveller* in *The Unfortunate Traveller and Other Works*, ed. J. B. Steane, London, pp. 251–370.

Nicholas, Sir Edward (1886). *Correspondence*. Vol. I: *1641–1652*, ed. George F. Warner, London.

Ovid (1979). *Ars Amatoria*, ed. and trans. J. H. Mozley, second edn., London.

(1988). *Tristia*, ed. and trans. A. L. Wheeler, revised G. P. Goold, London.

Peacham, Henry (1593). *The Garden of Eloquence*, London.

(1971). *The Garden of Eloquence*, ed. R. C. Alston, Menston.

Pemble, William (1633). *Enchiridion Oratorium*, Oxford.

Peter of Ravenna (1541). *Memoriae Ars quae Phoenix Inscribitur*, Vienna.

Plato (1930–35). *The Republic*, ed. and trans. Paul Shorey, 2 vols., London.

Pliny (1969). *Panegyricus* in *Letters and Panegyricus*, ed. and trans. Betty Radice, London, vol. II, pp. 322–546.

Plutarch (1580). *The Lives of the Noble Grecians and Romanes, Compared together*, trans. Thomas North, London.

(1603). *The Philosophie, commonlie called, The Morals*, trans. Philemon Holland, London.

Puttenham, George (1970). *The Arte of English Poesie*, ed. Gladys Willcock and Alice Walker, Cambridge.

Quintilian (1920–2). *Institutio oratoria*, ed. and trans. H. E. Butler, 4 vols., London.

Raillerie à la Mode Consider'd: or the Supercilious Detractor (1673). London.

Rainolde, Richard (1564). *A Booke called the Foundacion of Rhetorike*, London.

Rainolds, John (1988). *Oxford Lectures on Aristotle's Rhetoric*, ed. and trans. L. D. Green, London.

Ramée, Pierre de la [Petrus Ramus] (1964). *Dialectique (1555)*, ed. Michel Dassonville, Geneva.

Reflexions on Marriage, and the Poetick Discipline (1673). London.

Robinson, Richarde (c.1579). *The Vineyarde of Vertue*, London.

Rohan, Henri de (1639). *De l'interest des princes et estats de la Chrestienté*, Paris.

(1646). *Discours politiques*, n.p.

Rosse, Alexander (1653). *Leviathan drawn out with a Hook*, London.

Rufinianus, Iulius (1533). *De Figuris sententiarum & elocutionis liber* in *De Figuris*, Venice, fos. 23^{r}–35^{v}.

Rutilius Lupus, P. (1970). *De Figuris Sententiarum et Elocutionis*, ed. Edward Brooks Jr., Leiden.

Sallust (1921a). *Bellum Catilinae* in *Sallust*, ed. and trans. J. C. Rolfe, London, pp. 2–129.

(1921b). *Bellum Iugurthinum* in *Sallust*, trans. and ed. J. C. Rolfe, London, pp. 132–381.

Seneca (1569). *The Line of Liberalitie dulie directinge the wel bestowing of benefites*, London.
(1578). *The woorke of the excellent Philosopher Lucius Annaeus Seneca concerning Benefyting*, trans. Arthur Golding, London.
(1614). *The Workes both Morrall and Natural*, trans. Sir Thomas Lodge, London.
(1917–25). *Ad Lucilium Epistulae Morales*, ed. and trans. Richard M. Gummere, 3 vols., London.
(1928a). *De clementia* in *Moral Essays*, ed. and trans. John W. Basore, London, vol. I, pp. 356–449.
(1928b). *De ira* in *Moral Essays*, ed. and trans. John W. Basore, London, vol. I, pp. 106–355.
(1932). *De vita beata* in *Moral Essays*, ed. and trans. John W. Basore, London, vol. II, pp. 98–178.
(1935). *De beneficiis* in *Moral Essays*, ed. and trans. John W. Basore, London, vol. III.
S[ergeant], J[ohn] (1672). *Reason against Raillery: or, a Full Answer to Dr. Tillotson's Preface Against J. S.*, n.p.
Shakespeare, William (1988). *The Complete Works*, general eds. Stanley Wells and Gary Taylor, Oxford.
Sherry, Richard (1961). *A Treatise of Schemes and Tropes*, ed. Herbert W. Hildebrandt, Gainesville, Fl.
Sidney, Sir Philip (1922). *Astrophel and Stella* in *The Complete Works*, ed. Albert Feuillerat, Cambridge, vol. II, pp. 241–301.
(1923). *The Defence of Poesie* in *The Complete Works*, ed. Albert Feuillerat, Cambridge, vol. III, pp. 3–46.
Silhon, Jean de (1631). *Le Ministre d'Estat*. Paris.
Smith, Adam (1963). *Lectures on Rhetoric and Belles Lettres*, ed. John M. Lothian, London.
Smith, John (1969). *The mysterie of rhetorique unvail'd*, ed. R. C. Alston, Menston.
South, Robert (1823a). *The Fatal Imposture and Force of Words: Set Forth in a Sermon Preached on Isaiah* v. *20* in *Sermons Preached upon Several Occasions*, Oxford, vol. 4, pp. 108–38.
(1823b). *The Second Discourse on Isaiah* v. *20* in *Sermons Preached upon Several Occasions*, Oxford, vol. 4, pp. 203–88.
Spangenberg, Johann (1678). *Erotemata De Arte Memoriae seu Reminiscentiae* in *Variorum de Arte Memoriae*, Frankfurt, pp. 339–78.
Spenser, Edmund (1970). *Poetical Works*, ed. J. C. Smith and E. de Selincourt, Oxford.
Spinoza, Benedict de (1985). *Ethics* in *The Collected Works of Spinoza*, ed. and trans. Edwin Curley, Princeton, N.J., vol. I, pp. 408–617.
Spirit of Prophecy, The (1679). London.
Sprat, Thomas (1959). *History of the Royal Society*, ed. Jackson I. Cope and Harold Whitmore Jones, London.
Starkey, Thomas (1989). *A Dialogue between Pole and Lupset*, ed. Thomas F. Mayer, London.
Stephens, Thomas (1648). *Troposchematologia: Maximam partem ex indice Farnabii deprompta*, London.
Sterne, Laurence (1967). *The Life and Opinions of Tristram Shandy Gentleman*, ed. Graham Petrie, introd. Christopher Ricks, Harmondsworth.
Stockwood, John (1713). *The Treatise of the Figures*, London.

Susenbrotus, Johannes (1562). *Epitome troporum ac schematorum et grammaticorum & Rhetorum*, London.

Tacitus (1591). *The Ende of Nero and Beginning of Galba. Fower Bookes of the Histories of Tacitus. The Life of Agricola*, trans. Henry Savile, Oxford.

(1598). *The Annales of Cornelius Tacitus. The Description of Germanie*, trans. Richard Grenewey, London.

(1970). *Dialogus de oratoribus*, trans. W. Peterson, rev. M. Winterbottom in *Tacitus*, London, vol. I, pp. 230–347.

Talon, Omar (1631). *Rhetorica*, Cambridge.

Tenison, Thomas (1670). *The Creed of Mr. Hobbes Examined*, London.

Thackeray, William Makepeace (1968). *Vanity Fair*, ed. J. I. M. Stewart, London.

Thucydides (1564). *De Bello Peloponnesiaco libri octo, ex interpretatione Lorenzo Valla, recognita ab Henricus Stephanus*, Paris.

Valerius, Cornelius (1571). *The Casket of Jewels: Contaynynge a playne description of Morall Philosophie*, trans. I. C., London.

Vicars, Thomas (1621). *Cheiragogia: Manuductio ad Artem Rhetoricam*, London.

Vico, Giambattista (1948). *The New Science*, trans. Thomas Bergin and Max Fisch, Ithaca.

Virgil (1934–35). *Aeneid*, trans. H. Rushton Fairclough, 2 vols., London.

Vives, Juan Luis (1913). Vives: *On Education: A translation of the De tradendis disciplinis*, trans. and introd. Foster Watson, Cambridge.

(1964). *De Anima et vita* in *Opera Omnia*, London, vol. III, pp. 298–520.

Walker, Obadiah (1682). *Some instructions concerning the art of oratory*, second edn., Oxford.

Wallis, John (1656a). *Arithmetica Infinitorum* in *Opera Mathematicorum Pars Altera*, section III, Oxford, pp. 1–198.

(1656b). *Due Correction for Mr Hobbes*, Oxford.

(1662). *Hobbius Heauton-timorumenos*, Oxford.

Webbe, William (1904). *A Discourse of English Poetrie* in *Elizabethan Critical Essays*, ed. G. Gregory Smith, Oxford, vol. I, pp. 226–302.

Whitehall, John (1679). *The Leviathan Found Out*, London.

Whitney, Isabella (1992). 'To her unconstant Lover' in *The Penguin Book of Renaissance Verse 1509–1659*, selected by David Norbrook, ed. H. R. Woudhuysen, London, pp. 187–91.

Wilkins, John (1668). *An Essay Towards a Real Character And a Philosophical Language*, London.

Wilson, Thomas (1554). *The Arte of Rhetorique, for the use of all suche as are studious of Eloquence, sette forth in English*, n.p.

Wolseley, Sir Charles (1672). *The Reasonableness of Scripture-Belief*, London.

Wood, Anthony à (1691–92). *Athenae Oxoniensis*, 2 vols., London.

Wright, Thomas (1971). *The Passions of the Mind in Generall*, introd. Thomas O. Sloan, London.

Wyatt, Sir Thomas (1978). *The Complete Poems*, ed. R. A. Rebholz, Harmondsworth.

PRINTED SECONDARY SOURCES

Adolph, Robert (1968). *The Rise of Modern Prose Style*, Cambridge, Mass.

Alexander, Michael van Cleave (1990). *The Growth of English Education, 1348–1648: A Social and Cultural History*, London.

Altman, Joel B. (1978). *The Tudor Play of Mind: Rhetorical Inquiry and the Development of Elizabethan Drama*, Berkeley, Cal.

Anglo, Sydney (1977). 'The courtier: the Renaissance and changing ideals' in *The Courts of Europe: Politics, Patronage and Royalty 1400–1800*, ed. A. G. Dickens, London, pp. 33–53.

(1990). 'A Machiavellian solution to the Irish problem: Richard Beacon's *Solon his Follie*' in *England and the Continental Renaissance*, ed. Edward Chaney and Peter Mack, Woodbridge, pp. 153–64.

Ashworth, E. J. (1981). ' "Do Words Signify Ideas or Things?" The scholastic sources of Locke's theory of language', *Journal of the History of Philosophy*, 19, pp. 299–326.

Attridge, Derek (1986). 'Puttenham's perplexity' in *Literary Theory/Renaissance Texts*, ed. Patricia Parker and David Quint, Baltimore, Md., pp. 257–79.

Ayres, Philip J. (1987). 'The nature of Jonson's Roman history' in *Renaissance Historicism*, ed. Arthur F. Kinney and Dan S. Collins, Amherst, Mass., pp. 207–22.

Baldwin, T. W. (1944). *William Shakspere's 'Small Latine & Lesse Greeke'*, 2 vols., Urbana, Ill.

Baltrusaitis, Jurgis (1955). *Anamorphoses ou perspectives curieuses*, Paris.

Barnouw, Jeffrey (1988). 'Persuasion in Hobbes's *Leviathan*', *Hobbes Studies*, 1, pp. 3–25.

Barton, Ann (1984). *Ben Jonson, Dramatist*, Cambridge.

Bate, Jonathan (1994). 'The humanist *Tempest*' in *Shakespeare, La Tempête. Etudes critiques*, ed. Claude Peltrault, Besançon, pp. 5–20.

Battista, Anna Maria (1966). *Alle origini del pensiero politico libertino. Montaigne e Charron*, Milan.

(1980). 'Come giudicano la "politica" libertini e moralisti nella Francia del seicento' in *Il libertinismo in Europa*, Milan, pp. 25–80.

Baumgold, Deborah (1988). *Hobbes's Political Theory*, Cambridge.

Benhabib, Seyla (1992). *Situating the Self: Gender, Community and Postmodernism in Contemporary Ethics*, Cambridge.

Bernhardt, Jean (1988). 'Essai de commentaire' in Thomas Hobbes: *Court traité des premiers principes*, Paris, pp. 59–274.

Bickley, Francis (1911). *The Cavendish Family*, London.

Binns, J. W. (1990). *Intellectual Culture in Elizabethan and Jacobean England: The Latin Writings of the Age*, Leeds.

Blackbourne, R. (1839). 'Vitae Hobbianae Auctarium' in *Opera philosophica*, ed. Sir William Molesworth, London, vol. 1, pp. xxii–lxxx.

Bonner, Stanley F. (1977). *Education in Ancient Rome*, London.

Boonin-Vail, David (1994). *Thomas Hobbes and the Science of Moral Virtue*, Cambridge.

Borrelli, Gianfranco (1993). *Ragion di stato e 'Leviatano'*, Milan.

Bowle, John (1969). *Hobbes and his Critics*, second edn., London.

Box, M. A. (1990). *The Suasive Art of David Hume*, Princeton, N.J.

Bradford, Alan T. (1983). 'Stuart absolutism and the "utility" of Tacitus', *Huntington Library Quarterly*, 45, pp. 127–55.

Brandt, Frithiof (1928). *Thomas Hobbes' Mechanical Conception of Nature*, London.

Brandt, Reinhard (1987). 'Das Titelblatt des Leviathan', *Zeitschrift für Sozialwissenschaft*, 15, pp. 164–86.

Brennan, Joseph X. (1953). *The 'Epitome troporum ac schematorum' of Johannes Susenbrotus: Text, Translation, and Commentary*, PhD thesis, University of Illinois, Urbana, Ill.

(1960) 'The *Epitome troporum ac schematorum*: the genesis of a Renaissance rhetorical text', *Quarterly Journal of Speech*, 46, pp. 59–71.

Brett, Annabel S. (1994). *Subjective Right and Human Agency in Later Scholastic Thought c.1250–c.1560*, University of Cambridge, PhD no. 18626.

Briggs, John C. (1989). *Francis Bacon and the Rhetoric of Nature*, London.

Brown, Keith (1978). 'The artist of the *Leviathan* title-page', *British Library Journal*, 4, pp. 24–36.

Bruyère, Nelly (1984). *Méthode et dialectique dans l'oeuvre de La Ramée*, Paris.

Burgess, Glenn (1990). 'Contexts for the writing and publication of Hobbes's *Leviathan*', *History of Political Thought*, 11, pp. 675–702.

(1991). 'The impact on political thought: rhetorics for troubled times' in *The Impact of the English Civil War*, ed. John Morrill, London, pp. 67–83.

(1992). *The Politics of the Ancient Constitution: an Introduction to English Political Thought, 1603–42*, London.

Burke, Peter (1969a). 'Tacitism' in *Tacitus*, ed. J. A. Dorey, London, pp. 149–71.

(1969b). *The Renaissance Sense of the Past*, London.

Bush, Douglas (1973). 'Hobbes, William Cavendish, and "Essayes"', *Notes and Queries*, New Series, 20, pp. 162–4.

Campagnac, E. T. (1917). Introduction to John Brinsley: *Ludus Literarius or The Grammar Schoole*, London, pp. i–xxxvii.

Canny, Nicholas (1987). 'Identity formation in Ireland: the emergence of the Anglo-Irish' in *Colonial Identity in the Atlantic World, 1500–1800*, ed. Nicholas Canny and Anthony Pagden, Princeton, N.J., pp. 159–212.

Cantalupo, Charles (1991). *A Literary Leviathan: Thomas Hobbes's Masterpiece of Language*, Lewisburg.

Carr, Thomas M., Jr. (1990). *Descartes and the Resilience of Rhetoric*, Carbondale and Edwardsville.

Carroll, R. T. (1975). *The Common-sense Philosophy of Religion of Bishop Edward Stillingfleet, 1635–99*, The Hague.

Charlton, Kenneth (1965). *Education in Renaissance England*, London.

Chomarat, Jacques (1981). *Grammaire et rhétorique chez Erasme*, 2 vols., Paris,

Church, W. F. (1972). *Richelieu and Reason of State*, Princeton, N.J.

Clark, Donald L. (1948). *John Milton at St Paul's School*, New York.

Cocking, J. M. (1984). 'Bacon's view of imagination' in *Francis Bacon. Terminologia e fortuna nel XVII secolo*, ed. Marta Fattori, Rome, pp. 43–58.

(1991). *Imagination: a Study in the History of Ideas*, London.

Colie, Rosalie L. (1966). *Paradoxica Epidemica: the Renaissance Tradition of Paradox*, Princeton, N.J.

Collins, Stephen L. (1989). *From Divine Cosmos to Sovereign State: an Intellectual History of Consciousness and the Idea of Order in Renaissance England*, Oxford.

Collinson, Patrick (1967). *The Elizabethan Puritan Movement*, London.

Condren, Conal (1989). *George Lawson's 'Politica' and the English Revolution*, Cambridge.

(1990). 'On the rhetorical foundations of *Leviathan*', *History of Political Thought*, 11, pp. 703–20.

(1994). *The Language of Politics in Seventeenth-Century England*, London.

Conrad, F. W. (1992). 'The problem of counsel reconsidered: the case of Sir

Thomas Elyot' in *Political Thought and the Tudor Commonwealth*, London, pp. 75–107.

Cook, Elizabeth J. (1981). 'Thomas Hobbes and the "Far-Fetched"', *Journal of the Warburg and Courtauld Institutes*, 44, pp. 222–32.

Coorebyter, Vincent de (ed.) (1994). *Rhétoriques de la science*, Paris.

Corbett, Margery and Lightbown, Ronald (1979). *The Comely Frontispiece: the Emblematic Title-Page in England 1550–1660*, London.

Cox, Virginia (1989). 'Rhetoric and politics in Tasso's *Nifo*', *Studi Secenteschi*, 30, pp. 3–98.

(1992). *The Renaissance Dialogue*, Cambridge.

(1994). Introduction to Baldassare Castiglione: *The Book of the Courtier*, London, pp. xvii–xxxi.

Crane, William G. (1937). *Wit and Rhetoric in the Renaissance*, New York.

(1965). 'English rhetorics of the 16th century' in *The Province of Rhetoric*, ed. Joseph Schwartz and John A. Rycenga, New York, pp. 212–26.

Craven, Wesley Frank (1932). *Dissolution of the Virginia Company*, Oxford.

Crewe, Jonathan V. (1982). *Unredeemed Rhetoric: Thomas Nashe and the Scandal of Authorship*, London.

Cressy, David (1975). *Education in Tudor and Stuart England*, London.

Croll, Morris W. (1966). *Style, Rhetoric, and Rhythm*, Princeton, N.J.

Curley, Edwin (1988). '"I durst not write so boldly" or how to read Hobbes' theological-political treatise' in *Hobbes e Spinoza. Atti del Convegno Internazionale, Urbino*, ed. Daniela Bostrenghi, Naples, pp. 497–593.

Curtis, Cathy (1988). *Gone Fishing: Leviathan Drawn Out with a Metaphor*, MA Thesis, University of New South Wales.

Cust, Richard (1987). *The Forced Loan and English Politics 1626–1628*, Oxford.

Dalimier, Catherine (1989). 'Timides réflexions sur le sense du silence' in *Rhétorique et discours critiques*, Paris, pp. 27–32.

Daly, James W. (1971). 'John Bramhall and the theoretical problems of Royalist moderation', *Journal of British Studies*, 11, pp. 26–44.

Damrosch, Leopold (1979). 'Hobbes as Reformation theologian: implications of the freewill controversy', *Journal of the History of Ideas*, 40, pp. 339–52.

Danford, John W. (1980). 'The problem of language in Hobbes's political science', *The Journal of Politics*, 42, pp. 102–34.

Dascal, Marcelo (1976). 'Language and money: a simile and its meaning in 17th century philosophy of language', *Studia Leibnitiana*, 8, pp. 187–218.

Dassonville, Michel (1964). Introduction to Pierre de la Ramée: *Dialectique (1555)*, Geneva, pp. 7–46.

Dean, Leonard F. (1968). 'Francis Bacon's theory of civil history-writing' in *Essential Articles for the Study of Francis Bacon*, ed. Brian Vickers, Hamden, Conn., pp. 211–35.

Dean, Paul (1988). 'Tudor humanism and the Roman past: a background to Shakespeare', *Renaissance Quarterly*, 41, pp. 84–111.

Dear, Peter (1988). *Mersenne and the Learning of the Schools*, London.

Dewar, Mary (1964). *Sir Thomas Smith: a Tudor Intellectual in Office*, London.

Dietz, Mary G. (1990). 'Hobbes's subject as citizen' in *Thomas Hobbes and Political Theory*, ed. Mary G. Dietz, Lawrence, Kan., pp. 91–119.

Dillon, George L. (1986). *Rhetoric and Social Imagination*, Bloomington, Ind.

Dodd, Mary C. (1952). 'The rhetorics in Molesworth's edition of Hobbes', *Modern Philology*, 50, pp. 36–42.

Dowling, Maria (1986). *Humanism in the Age of Henry VIII*, London.

Draper, F. W. M. (1962). *Four Centuries of Merchant Taylors' School, 1561–1961*, London.

Duhamel, P. Albert (1952). 'Milton's alleged Ramism', *PMLA*, 67, pp. 1035–53.

Dzelzainis, Martin (1989). 'Edward Hyde and Thomas Hobbes's *Elements of Law, Natural and Politic*', *The Historical Journal*, 32, pp. 303–17.

Eisenach, Eldon J. (1982). 'Hobbes on church, state and religion', *History of Political Thought*, 3, pp. 215–43.

Elsky, Martin (1989). *Authorising Words: Speech, Writing, and Print in the English Renaissance*, London.

Elton, G. R. (1973). *Reform and Renewal: Thomas Cromwell and the Common Weal*, Cambridge.

Evans, Robert O. (1967). Introduction to Angel Day: *The English Secretary*, Gainesville, Fl., pp. v–xiii.

Fabricius, Johannes (1703). *Bibliotheca Latina*, London.

Feingold, Mordechai (1984). *The Mathematicians' Apprenticeship: Science, Universities and Society in England, 1560–1640*, Cambridge.

Ferguson, Arthur B. (1965). *The Articulate Citizen and the English Renaissance*, Durham, N.C.

(1979). *Clio Unbound: Perception of the Social and Cultural Past in Renaissance England*, Durham, N.C.

Fish, Stanley E. (1972). *Self-Consuming Artifacts: the Experience of Seventeenth-Century Literature*, London.

Flathman, Richard E. (1993). *Thomas Hobbes: Skepticism, Individuality, and Chastened Politics*, London.

Fletcher, J. M. (1986). 'The Faculty of Arts' in *The History of the University of Oxford*, vol. III, ed. James McConica, Oxford, pp. 157–99.

Fowler, Alastair, ed. (1992). *The New Oxford Book of Seventeenth-Century Verse*, Oxford.

Fox, Alistair (1986a). 'English humanism and the body politic' in Alistair Fox and John Guy, *Reassessing the Henrician Age*, Oxford, pp. 34–51.

(1986b). 'Sir Thomas Elyot and the humanist dilemma' in Alistair Fox and John Guy, *Reassessing the Henrician Age*, Oxford, pp. 52–73.

France, Peter (1972). *Rhetoric and Truth in France: Descartes to Diderot*, Oxford.

Fumaroli, M. (1980). *L'Age d'éloquence. Rhétorique et 'res literaria' de la Renaissance au seuil de l'époque classique*, Paris.

Fussner, F. Smith (1962). *The Historical Revolution: English Historical Writing and Thought, 1580–1640*, London.

G., J. (1881). *Memorials of Stonyhurst College*, London.

Gabrieli, Vittorio (1957). 'Bacone, la riforma e Roma nella versione hobbesiana d'un carteggio di Fulgenzio Micanzio', *English Miscellany*, 8, pp. 195–250.

Gang, T. M. (1956). 'Hobbes and the metaphysical conceit: a reply', *Journal of the History of Ideas*, 17, pp. 418–21.

Garcia, Alfred (1986). *Thomas Hobbes. Bibliographie internationale de 1620–1986*, Caen.

Gardner, Helen (ed.) (1972). *The New Oxford Book of English Verse*, Oxford.

Gauthier, David P. (1969). *The Logic of 'Leviathan': the Moral and Political Theory of Thomas Hobbes*, Oxford.

Gent, Lucy (1981). *Picture and Poetry, 1560–1620*, Leamington Spa.

Gert, Bernard (1988). 'The law of nature and the moral law', *Hobbes Studies*, 1, pp. 26–44.

Gierke, Otto von (1957). *Natural Law and the Theory of Society 1500 to 1800*, trans. Ernest Barker, Beacon edn., Boston, Mass.

Gilbert, Neal W. (1960). *Renaissance Concepts of Method*, New York.

Gladish, David F. (1971). Introduction to Sir William Davenant's *Gondibert*, Oxford, pp. ix–xlv.

Goldberg, Jonathan (1989). *James I and the Politics of Literature*, Stanford, Cal.

Goldie, Mark (1990). 'Danby, the bishops and the whigs' in *The Politics of Religion in Restoration England*, ed. Tim Harris, Paul Seaward and Mark Goldie, Oxford, pp. 75–105.

(1991a). 'The theory of religious intolerance in Restoration England' in *From Persecution to Toleration: the Glorious Revolution and Religion in England*, ed. Ole Peter Grell, Jonathan I. Israel and Nicholas Tyacke, Oxford, pp. 331–68.

(1991b). 'The reception of Hobbes' in *The Cambridge History of Political Thought 1450–1700*, ed. J. H. Burns and Mark Goldie, Cambridge, pp. 589–615.

Goldsmith, M. M. (1966). *Hobbes's Science of Politics*, New York.

(1990). 'Hobbes's ambiguous politics', *History of Political Thought*, 11, pp. 639–73.

Grafton, Anthony and Jardine, Lisa (1986). *From Humanism to the Humanities: Education and the Liberal Arts in Fifteenth- and Sixteenth-Century Europe*, London.

Grant, Mary A. (1924). *The Ancient Rhetorical Theories of the Laughable: the Greek Rhetoricians and Cicero* in University of Wisconsin Studies in Language and Literature 21: Madison, Wis.

Gray, Robert (1978). 'Hobbes's system and his early philosophical views', *Journal of the History of Ideas*, 39, pp. 199–215.

Green, Lawrence D. (1988). Introduction to John Rainolds: *Oxford Lectures on Aristotle's Rhetoric*, London, pp. 9–90.

(1994). 'Aristotle's *Rhetoric* and Renaissance views of the emotions' in *Renaissance Rhetoric*, ed. Peter Mack, London, pp. 1–26.

Greenblatt, Stephen (1980). *Renaissance Self-Fashioning: from More to Shakespeare*, Chicago, Ill.

Greenslade, B. D. (1975). 'The publication date of Hobbes's *Leviathan*', *Notes and Queries*, 220, p. 320.

Gunn, J. A. W. (1969). *Politics and the Public Interest in the Seventeenth Century*, London.

Guy, John (1980). *The Public Career of Sir Thomas More*, Brighton.

(1993). 'The Henrician age' in *The Varieties of British Political Thought 1500–1800*, ed. J. G. A. Pocock, Gordon J. Schochet and Lois G. Schwoerer, Cambridge, pp. 13–46.

Hamilton, A. C. (1977). *Sir Philip Sidney: a Study of his Life and Works*, Cambridge.

Hampsher-Monk, Iain (1992). *A History of Modern Political Thought: Major Political Thinkers from Hobbes to Marx*, Oxford.

Hampton, Jean (1986). *Hobbes and the Social Contract Tradition*, Cambridge.

Hannen, Thomas A. (1974). 'The humanism of Sir Thomas Wyatt' in *The Rhetoric of*

Renaissance Poetry from Wyatt to Milton, ed. Thomas O. Sloan and Raymond B. Waddington, London, pp. 37–57.

Hanson, Donald W. (1990). 'The meaning of "Demonstration" in Hobbes's science', *History of Political Thought*, 11, pp. 587–626.

(1993). 'Science, prudence, and folly in Hobbes's political theory', *Political Theory*, 21, pp. 643–64.

Hardison, O. B., Jr. (1962). *The Enduring Monument: a Study of the Idea of Praise in Renaissance Literary Theory and Practice*, Chapel Hill, N.C.

(1989). *Prosody and Purpose in the English Renaissance*, Baltimore. Md.

Harman, Alec (1962). *Man and His Music*. Part 1: *Mediaeval and Early Renaissance Music*, London.

Harrison, John (1978). *The Library of Isaac Newton*, Cambridge.

Harrison, John, and Laslett, Peter (1965). *The Library of John Locke*, Oxford.

Harrison, John L. (1968). 'Bacon's view of rhetoric, poetry, and the imagination' in *Essential Articles for the Study of Francis Bacon*, ed. Brian Vickers, Hamden, Conn., pp. 253–71.

Hartman, Mark (1978). *Contemporary Explanations of the English Revolution, 1640–1660*, University of Cambridge, PhD no. 10368.

Harwood, John T. (1986). Introduction to *The Rhetorics of Thomas Hobbes and Bernard Lamy*, Carbondale and Edwardsville, pp. 1–32.

Heninger, S. K., Jr. (1984). 'Speaking pictures: Sidney's rapprochement between poetry and painting' in *Sir Philip Sidney and the Interpretation of Renaissance Culture*, ed. Gary F. Waller and Michael D. Moore, London, pp. 3–16.

Herbert, Gary B. (1989). *Thomas Hobbes: the Unity of Scientific and Moral Wisdom*, Vancouver.

Herrick, Marvin T. (1926). 'The early history of Aristotle's *Rhetoric* in England', *Philological Quarterly*, 5, pp. 242–57.

(1950). *Comic Theory in the Sixteenth Century*, Urbana, Ill.

Hexter, J. H. (1961). 'The education of the aristocracy in the Renaissance' in *Reappraisals in History*, London, pp. 45–70.

Heyd, David (1982). 'The place of laughter in Hobbes's theory of emotions', *Journal of the History of Ideas*, 43, pp. 285–95.

Hirschman, Albert O. (1977). *The Passions and the Interests*, Princeton, N.J.

Hogrefe, Pearl (1967). *The Life and Times of Sir Thomas Elyot Englishman*, Ames, Ia.

Hood, F. C. (1964). *The Divine Politics of Thomas Hobbes*, Oxford.

Howell, Wilbur Samuel (1956). *Logic and Rhetoric in England, 1500–1700*, Princeton, N.J.

Hudson, Hoyt H. (1935). Introduction to John Hoskins: *Directions for Speech and Style*, Princeton, N.J., pp. ix–xi.

Hughes, Emrys, ed. (1992). *The New Oxford Book of Sixteenth-Century Verse*, Oxford.

Hungerland, Isabel C. and Vick, George R. (1973). 'Hobbes's theory of signification', *Journal of the History of Philosophy*, 11, pp. 459–82.

Hunter, G. K. (1962). *John Lyly: the Humanist as Courtier*, London.

Hutson, Lorna (1993). 'Fortunate travelers: reading for the plot in sixteenth-century England', *Representations*, 41, pp. 83–103.

Ijsseling, Samuel (1976). *Rhetoric and Philosophy in Conflict*, The Hague.

Illustrations (1848). 'Illustrations of the state of the church during the Great Rebellion', *The Theologian and Ecclesiastic*, 6, pp. 165–75, 217–26.

Ingleby, C. M. (ed.) (1879). *Shakespeare's Centurie of Prayse*, second edn., revised Lucy Toulmin Smith, London.

Jacob, James R. and Raylor, Timothy (1991). 'Opera and obedience: Thomas Hobbes and *A Proposition for Advancement of Moralitie* by Sir William Davenant', *The Seventeenth Century*, 6, pp. 205–50.

Jacquot, Jean (1952). 'Sir Charles Cavendish and his learned friends', *Annals of Science*, 3, pp. 13–27, 175–91.

Jacquot, Jean and Jones, Harold Whitmore (1973). Introduction to *Thomas Hobbes: Critique du 'De mundo' de Thomas White*, Paris, pp. 9–102.

James, Mervyn (1986). *Society, Politics and Culture: Studies in Early Modern England*, Cambridge.

Janson, Tore (1964). *Latin Prose Prefaces: Studies in Literary Conventions*, Stockholm.

Jardine, Lisa (1974). *Francis Bacon: Discovery and the Art of Discourse*, Cambridge.

(1977). 'Lorenzo Valla and the intellectual origins of humanist dialectic', *Journal of the History of Philosophy*, 15, pp. 143–64.

(1986). 'Gabriel Harvey: exemplary Ramist and pragmatic humanist', *Revue des sciences philosophiques et théologiques*, 70, pp. 36–48.

(1988). 'Humanistic logic' in *The Cambridge History of Renaissance Philosophy*, general ed. Charles B. Schmitt, Cambridge, pp. 173–98.

Jardine, Nicholas (1988). 'Epistemology of the sciences' in *The Cambridge History of Renaissance Philosophy*, general ed. Charles B. Schmitt, Cambridge, pp. 685–711.

Javitch, Daniel (1972). 'Poetry and court conduct: Puttenham's *Arte of English Poesie* in the light of Castiglione's *Cortegiano*', *Modern Language Notes*, 87, pp. 865–82.

(1978). *Poetry and Courtliness in Renaissance England*, Princeton, N.J.

(1983). '*Il cortegiano* and the constraints of despotism', in *Castiglione: The Ideal and the Real in Renaissance Culture*, ed. Robert W. Hanning and David Rosand, London, pp. 17–28.

Johnson, F. R. (1944). 'Two Renaissance text books of rhetoric: Aphthonius' *Progymnasmata* and Rainolde's *A Booke called the Foundacion of Rhetorike*', *Huntingdon Library Quarterly*, 5, pp. 427–41.

Johnson, Laurie M. (1993). *Thucydides, Hobbes, and the Interpretation of Realism*, DeKalb, Ill.

Johnson, Nan (1984). 'Ethos and the aims of rhetoric' in *Essays on Classical Rhetoric and Modern Discourse*, ed. Robert J. Connors, Lisa E. Ede and Andrea A. Lunsford, Carbondale and Edwardsville, pp. 98–114.

Johnston, David (1986). *The Rhetoric of 'Leviathan': Thomas Hobbes and the Politics of Cultural Transformation*, Princeton, N.J.

Jones, Richard Foster (1951). *The Seventeenth Century*, Stanford, Cal.

Joseph, Sister Miriam (1966). *Shakespeare's Use of the Arts of Language*, third edn., New York.

Jung, Marc-René (1966). *Hercule dans la littérature française du XVIe siècle*, Geneva.

Kahn, Victoria (1985). *Rhetoric, Prudence and Skepticism in the Renaissance*, Ithaca, N.Y.

Kavka, Gregory S. (1986). *Hobbesian Moral and Political Theory*, Princeton, N.J.

Kennedy, George (1969). *Quintilian*, New York.

(1972). *The Art of Rhetoric in the Roman World 300 BC–AD 300*, Princeton, N.J.

(1980). *Classical Rhetoric and its Christian and Secular Tradition from Ancient to Modern Times*, London.

Kennedy, William J. (1978). *Rhetorical Norms in Renaissance Literature*, New Haven, Conn.

Kennet, White (1708). *Memoirs of the Family of Cavendish*, London.

Keohane, Nannerl O. (1980). *Philosophy and the State in France: the Renaissance to the Enlightenment*, Princeton, N.J.

Kiessling, Nicolas K. (1988). *The Library of Robert Burton*, Oxford.

Kinney, Arthur F. (1986). *Humanist Poetics: Thought, Rhetoric, and Fiction in Sixteenth-Century England*, Amherst, Mass.

Kishler, Thomas C. (1976). 'Hobbes's *Answer* to Davenant: some aspects of the style', *Language and Style*, 9, pp. 130–8.

Knauf, David M. (1967). 'George Puttenham's theory of natural and artificial discourse', *Speech Monographs*, 34, pp. 35–42.

Knox, Dilwyn (1989). *Ironia: Medieval and Renaissance Ideas on Irony*, New York.

Kowalski, Georgius (1928). 'Studia rhetorica II: ad figurae ΠΑΡΑΔΙΑΣΤΟΛΗΣ historiam', *Eos*, 31, pp. 169–80.

Kristeller, P. O. (1979). 'Humanism and scholasticism in the Italian Renaissance' in *Renaissance Thought and its Sources*, ed. M. Mooney, New York, pp. 85–105.

Lanham, Richard A. (1976). *The Motives of Eloquence: Literary Rhetoric in the Renaissance*, New Haven, Conn.

Lawry, J. S. (1982). '*Catiline* and "the Sight of Rome in Us"' in *Rome in the Renaissance: the City and the Myth*, ed. P. A. Ramsey, Binghamton, N.Y., pp. 395–407.

Leach, A. F. (1905). 'Schools' in *The Victoria History of the County of Durham*, London, vol. I, pp. 365–413.

Leach, A. F. and Steele Hutton, E. P. (1907). 'Schools' in *The Victoria History of the Counties of England: Suffolk*, London, vol. II, pp. 301–55.

Lechner, Sister Joan Marie (1962). *Renaissance Concepts of the Commonplaces*, New York.

Leeman, A. D. (1963). *'Orationis Ratio': the Stylistic Theories and Practice of the Roman Orators Historians and Philosophers*, 2 vols., Amsterdam.

Lehmberg, S. E. (1961). 'English humanists, the Reformation and the problem of Counsel', *Archiv für Reformationsgeschichte*, 52, pp. 74–90.

Levy, F. J. (1967). *Tudor Historical Thought*, San Marino, Cal.

Lievsay, John Leon (1961). *Stefano Guazzo and the English Renaissance, 1575–1675*, Chapel Hill, N.C.

Lloyd, S. A. (1992). *Ideas as Interests in Hobbes's 'Leviathan': the Power of Mind over Matter*, Cambridge.

Logan, George M. (1983). *The Meaning of More's 'Utopia'*, Princeton, N.J.

Lund, William R. (1992). 'Hobbes on opinion, private judgment and civil war', *History of Political Thought*, 13, pp. 51–72.

Lupton, J. H. (1909). *A Life of John Colet, D.D.*, new edition, London.

Macdonald, Hugh and Hargreaves, Mary (1952). *Thomas Hobbes: a Bibliography*, London.

MacGillivray, Royce (1970). 'Thomas Hobbes's history of the English Civil War: a study of *Behemoth*', *Journal of the History of Ideas*, 31, pp. 179–98.

Maclean, Ian (1990). 'Philosophical books in European markets, 1570–1630: the case of Ramus', in *New Perspectives on Renaissance Thought*, ed. John Henry and Sarah Hutton, London, pp. 253–63.

(1992). *Interpretation and Meaning in the Renaissance: the Case of Law*, Cambridge.
Major, John M. (1964). *Sir Thomas Elyot and Renaissance Humanism*, Lincoln, Nebr.
Malcolm, Noel (1981). 'Hobbes, Sandys, and the Virginia Company', *The Historical Journal*, 24, pp. 297–321.
(1983). *Thomas Hobbes and Voluntarist Theology*, University of Cambridge, PhD no. 12565.
(1984). *De Dominis (1560–1624): Venetian, Anglican, Ecumenist and Relapsed Heretic*, London.
(1988). 'Hobbes and the Royal Society' in *Perspectives on Thomas Hobbes*, ed. G. A. J. Rogers and Alan Ryan, Oxford, pp. 43–66.
(1990). 'Hobbes's science of politics and his theory of science' in *Hobbes oggi*, ed. Andrea Napoli, Milan, pp. 145–57.
(1991). 'Hobbes and Spinoza' in *The Cambridge History of Political Thought 1450–1700*, ed. J. H. Burns and Mark Goldie, Cambridge, pp. 530–57.
(1994). 'Biographical register of Hobbes's correspondents' in *The Correspondence of Thomas Hobbes*, Oxford, pp. 777–919.
Marius, Richard (1985). *Thomas More: a Biography*, London.
Marsh, David (1980). *The Quattrocento Dialogue: Classical Tradition and Humanist Innovation*, London.
Marshall, John (1985). 'The ecclesiology of the Latitude-men 1660–1689: Stillingfleet, Tillotson and "Hobbism"', *Journal of Ecclesiastical History*, 36, pp. 407–27.
Martindale, Joanna (ed.) (1985). *English Humanism: Wyatt to Cowley*, London.
Martinich, A. P. (1992). *The Two Gods of Leviathan: Thomas Hobbes on Religion and Politics*, Cambridge.
Mason, H. A. (1986). *Sir Thomas Wyatt: a Literary Portrait*, Bristol.
Mathie, William (1986). 'Reason and rhetoric in Hobbes's *Leviathan*', *Interpretation*, 14, pp. 281–98.
May, Louis Francis, Jr. (1959). *A Literary Analysis of Thomas Hobbes' 'Leviathan'*. PhD, St Louis University.
Mayer, Thomas F. (1989a). *Thomas Starkey and the Commonweal*, Cambridge.
(1989b). Introduction to Thomas Starkey: *A Dialogue between Pole and Lupset*, London, pp. vii–xvii.
McAdoo, H. R. (1965). *The Spirit of Anglicanism*, London.
McConica, James K. (1965). *English Humanists and Reformation Politics*, Oxford.
(1986). 'The rise of the undergraduate college' in *The History of the University of Oxford*, vol. III, ed. James McConica, Oxford, pp. 1–68.
McCreary, E. P. (1973). 'Bacon's theory of imagination reconsidered', *Huntington Library Quarterly*, 36, pp. 317–26.
McFarlane, I. D. (1981). *Buchanan*, London.
McGregor, Brian (1978). Introductory note to *De ratione studii ac legendi interpretandique auctores* in *Collected Works of Erasmus*, vol. 24, Toronto, pp. 662–6.
McKenzie, Lionel A. (1981). 'Natural right and the emergence of the idea of interest in early modern political thought: Francesco Guicciardini and Jean de Silhon', *History of European Ideas*, 2, pp. 277–98.
McManamon, John M. (1989). *Funeral Oratory and the Cultural Ideals of Italian Humanism*, Chapel Hill, N.C.

Meerhoff, Kees (1994). 'The significance of Philip Melanchthon's rhetoric in the Renaissance' in *Renaissance Rhetoric*, ed. Peter Mack, London, pp. 46–62.

Metzger, Hans-Dieter (1991). *Thomas Hobbes und die Englische Revolution 1640–1660*, Stuttgart.

Michel, Alain (1960). *Rhétorique et philosophie chez Cicéron. Essai sur les fondements philosophiques de l'art de persuader*, Paris.

(1962). *Le 'Dialogue des orateurs' de Tacite et la philosophie de Cicéron*, Paris.

Miglior, Giorgio (1975). *Roger Ascham. La dottrina umanistica inglese e la sperimentazione nella prosa letteraria intorno alla metà del cinquecento*, Bari.

Milburn, D. Judson (1966). *The Age of Wit, 1650–1750*, London.

Mintz, Samuel I. (1962). *The Hunting of Leviathan*, Cambridge.

Missner, Marshall (1983). 'Skepticism and Hobbes' political philosophy', *Journal of the History of Ideas*, 44, pp. 407–27.

Monaco, G. (1964). *Cicerone. Il trattato de ridiculis*, Palermo.

Monfasani, John (1983). 'The Byzantine rhetorical tradition and the Renaissance' in *Renaissance Eloquence: Studies in the Theory and Practice of Renaissance Rhetoric*, ed. James J. Murphy, London, pp. 174–87.

(1987). 'Three notes on Renaissance rhetoric', *Rhetorica*, 5, pp. 107–18.

(1988). 'Humanism and rhetoric' in *Renaissance Humanism: Foundations, Forms, and Legacy*. Vol. III: *Humanism and the Disciplines*, ed. Albert Rabil, Jr., Philadelphia, Pa., pp. 171–235.

(1990). 'Lorenzo Valla and Rudolph Agricola', *Journal of the History of Philosophy*, 28, pp. 181–200.

Mooney, Michael (1985). *Vico in the Tradition of Rhetoric*, Princeton, N.J.

Morgan, John (1986). *Godly Learning: Puritan Attitudes towards Reason, Learning and Education, 1560–1640*, Cambridge.

Moss, Ann (1993). 'Printed commonplace-books in the Renaissance', *Journal of the Institute of Romance Studies*, 2, pp. 203–13.

Munz, Peter (1990). 'The rhetoric of rhetoric', *Journal of the History of Ideas*, 51, pp. 121–42.

Murphy, James J. (1974). *Rhetoric in the Middle Ages*, Berkeley, Cal.

(1981). *Renaissance Rhetoric: a Short-Title Catalogue of Works on Rhetorical Theory from the Beginning of Printing to AD 1700*, New York.

Myrick, K. O. (1935). *Sir Philip Sidney as a Literary Craftsman*, Cambridge, Mass.

Nadeau, Ray (1950). 'Thomas Farnaby: schoolmaster and rhetorician of the English Renaissance', *Quarterly Journal of Speech*, 36, pp. 340–4.

Nederman, Cary J. (1992). 'The union of wisdom and eloquence before the Renaissance: the Ciceronian orator in medieval thought', *Journal of Medieval History*, 18, pp. 75–95.

Nelson, John S., Megill, Allen and McCloskey, N. (eds.) (1987). *The Rhetoric of the Human Sciences*, Madison, Wis.

Nicolson, Marjorie Hope (1960). *The Breaking of the Circle: Studies in the Effect of the 'New Science' upon Seventeenth-Century Poetry*, revised edn., New York.

Norbrook, David (1984). *Poetry and Politics in the English Renaissance*, London.

(1992). Introduction to *The Penguin Book of Renaissance Verse, 1509–1659*, London, pp. 1–67.

(1994). 'Rhetoric, ideology and the Elizabethan world picture' in *Renaissance Rhetoric*, ed. Peter Mack, London, pp. 140–64.

Noreña, Carlos G. (1970). *Juan Luis Vives*, The Hague.

Oestreich, G. (1982). *Neostoicism and the Early Modern State*, trans. David McLintock, Cambridge.

Okin, Susan Moller (1982). '"The Soveraign and his Counsellours": Hobbes's reevaluation of Parliament', *Political Theory*, 10, pp. 49–75.

O'Malley, John W. (1983). 'Content and rhetorical forms in sixteenth-century treatises on preaching' in *Renaissance Eloquence*, ed. James J. Murphy, Berkeley, Cal., pp. 238–52.

Ong, Walter J. (1951). 'Hobbes and Talon's Ramist rhetoric in English', *Transactions of the Cambridge Bibliographical Society*, 1, pp. 260–9.

(1958a). *Ramus, Method, and the Decay of Dialogue*, Cambridge, Mass.

(1958b). *Ramus and Talon Inventory*, Cambridge, Mass.

(1965). 'Ramist rhetoric' in *The Province of Rhetoric*, ed. Joseph Schwartz and John A. Rycenga, New York, pp. 226–55.

(1982). *Orality and Literacy: the Technologising of the Word*, London.

Pacchi, Arrigo (1965). *Convenzione e ipotesi nella formazione della filosofia naturale di Thomas Hobbes*, Florence.

(1968). 'Una "biblioteca ideale" di Thomas Hobbes: Il MS E2 dell'Archivio di Chatsworth', *Acme*, 21, pp. 5–42.

Parker, Patricia (1987). *Literary Fat Ladies: Rhetoric, Gender, Property*, London.

(1990). 'Metaphor and catachresis' in *The Ends of Rhetoric: History, Theory, Practice*, ed. John Bender and David E. Wellberg, Stanford, Cal., pp. 60–73.

Patterson, Annabel M. (1970). *Hermogenes and the Renaissance: Seven Ideas of Style*, Princeton, N.J.

Peltonen, Markku (1994). 'Classical republicanism in Tudor England: the case of Richard Beacon's *Solon his Follie*', *History of Political Thought*, 15, pp. 469–503.

Percival, W. Keith (1983). 'Grammar and rhetoric in the Renaissance' in *Renaissance Eloquence*, ed. James J. Murphy, Berkeley, Cal., pp. 303–30.

Pintard, René (1982). *Le libertinage érudit dans la première moitié du XVIIe siècle*, second edn., Geneva.

Pitman, Margaret C. (1934). 'Studies in the works of Henry Peacham', *Bulletin of the Institute of Historical Research*, 11, pp. 189–92.

Plett, Heinrich F. (1975). *Rhetorik der Affekte. Englische Wirkungsästhetik im Zeitalter der Renaissance*, Tübingen.

Pocock, J. G. A. (1971). *Politics, Language and Time*, New York.

Pomfret, Thomas (1685). *The Life of ... Christian, Late Countess Dowager of Devonshire*, London.

Popkin, Richard H. (1979). *The History of Scepticism from Erasmus to Spinoza*, Berkeley, Cal.

(1982). 'Hobbes and skepticism', *History of Philosophy in the Making*, ed. Linus J. Thro, Washington, pp. 133–48.

Prokhovnik, Raia (1991). *Rhetoric and Philosophy in Hobbes's Leviathan*, London.

Raphael, D. D. (1977). *Hobbes: Morals and Politics*, London.

Rayner, Jeremy (1991). 'Hobbes and the rhetoricians', *Hobbes Studies*, 4, pp. 76–95.

Reik, Miriam M. (1977). *The Golden Lands of Thomas Hobbes*, Detroit.

Reynolds, Noel B. and Hilton, John L. (1993). 'Thomas Hobbes and authorship of the *Horae Subsecivae*', *History of Political Thought*, 14, pp. 361–80.

Rhodes, Neil (1992). *The Power of Eloquence in English Renaissance Literature*, London.

Rivers, Isabel (1993). '"Galen's Muscles": Wilkins, Hume, and the educational use of the argument from design', *Historical Journal*, 36, pp. 577–97.

Robertson, George Croom (1886). *Hobbes*, Edinburgh.

Rogow, Arnold A. (1986). *Thomas Hobbes: Radical in the Service of Reaction*, New York.

Rossi, Paolo (1968). *Francis Bacon: from Magic to Science*, trans. S. Rabinovich, London.

Rossini, Gigliola (1987). 'The criticism of rhetorical historiography and the ideal of scientific method: history, nature and science in the political language of Thomas Hobbes', in *The Languages of Political Theory in Early-modern Europe*, ed. Anthony Pagden, Cambridge, pp. 303–24.

(1988). *Natura e artificio nel pensiero di Hobbes*, Bologna.

Rossky, William (1958). 'Imagination in the English Renaissance: psychology and poetic', *Studies in the Renaissance*, 4, pp. 49–73.

Roux, Louis (1981). *Thomas Hobbes. Penseur entre deux mondes*, Saint-Etienne.

Roux, Louis and Gilibert, Hervé (1980). *Le Vocabulaire, la phrase et le paragraphe du 'Leviathan' de Thomas Hobbes*, Saint-Etienne.

Ryan, Lawrence V. (1963). *Roger Ascham*, London.

Saccone, Eduardo (1983). '*Grazia, sprezzatura, affettazione* in the *Courtier*', in *Castiglione: The Ideal and the Real in Renaissance Culture*, ed. Robert W. Hanning and David Rosand, London, pp. 45–67.

Sacksteder, William (1978). 'Hobbes: teaching philosophy to speak English', *Journal of the History of Philosophy*, 16, pp. 33–45.

(1982). *Hobbes Studies (1879–1979): a Bibliography*, Bowling Green, Oh.

(1984). 'Hobbes' philosophical and rhetorical artifice', *Philosophy and Rhetoric*, 17, pp. 30–46.

Salmon, J. H. M. (1989). 'Stoicism and Roman example: Seneca and Tacitus in Jacobean England', *Journal of the History of Ideas*, 50, pp. 199–225.

Sampson, Margaret (1990). '"Will You Hear What a Casuist He Is?" Thomas Hobbes as a director of conscience', *History of Political Thought*, 11, pp. 721–36.

Sarasohn, L. T. (1985). 'Motion and morality: Pierre Gassendi, Thomas Hobbes and the mechanical world-view', *Journal of the History of Ideas*, 46, pp. 363–79.

Saunders, H. W. (1932). *A History of the Norwich Grammar School*, Norwich.

Schellhase, Kenneth C. (1976). *Tacitus in Renaissance Political Thought*, London.

Schlatter, Richard (1975). Introduction to *Hobbes's Thucydides*, New Brunswick, pp. xi–xxviii.

Schmidt, Albert J. (1959–60). 'Thomas Wilson and the Tudor commonwealth: an essay in civic humanism', *Huntington Library Quarterly*, 23, pp. 49–60.

Schmitt, Charles B. (1972). *Cicero Scepticus: a Study of the Influence of the 'Academica' in the Renaissance*, The Hague.

(1983). *John Case and Aristotelianism in Renaissance England*, Kingston and Montreal.

Schoeck, Richard J. (1983). 'Lawyers and rhetoric in sixteenth-century England' in *Renaissance Eloquence: Studies in the Theory and Practice of Renaissance Rhetoric*, ed. James J. Murphy, London, pp. 274–91.

Schoneveld, C. W. (1987). '"Insinuations to the Will": Hobbes's style and intention in *Leviathan* compared to his earlier political works' in *Hobbes's 'Science of Natural Justice'*, ed. C. Walton and P. J. Johnson, Dordrecht, pp. 111–19.

Schuhmann, Karl (1990). 'Hobbes and Renaissance philosophy' in *Hobbes oggi*, ed. Andrea Napoli, Milan, pp. 331–49.

Scott, Izora (1910). *Controversies over the Imitation of Cicero as a Model for Style*, New York.

Seaton, Ethel (1950). Introduction to Abraham Fraunce: *The Arcadian Rhetorike*, Oxford, pp. vii–lv.

Seigel, Jerrold E. (1968). *Rhetoric and Philosophy in Renaissance Humanism: the Union of Eloquence and Wisdom, Petrarch to Valla*, Princeton, N.J.

Shapin, Steven and Schaffer, Simon (1985). *Leviathan and the Air-Pump: Hobbes, Boyle and the Experimental Life*, Princeton, N.J.

Shapiro, Alan E. (1973). 'Kinematic optics: a study of the wave theory of light in the seventeenth century', *Archive for the History of the Exact Sciences*, 11, pp. 133–266.

Shapiro, Barbara J. (1983). *Probability and Certainty in Seventeenth-Century England*, Princeton, N.J.

Shapiro, Gary (1980). 'Reading and writing in the text of Hobbes's *Leviathan*', *Journal of the History of Philosophy*, 18, pp. 147–57.

Sharpe, Kevin (1987). *Criticism and Compliment: the Politics of Literature in the England of Charles I*, Cambridge.

(1989). *Politics and Ideas in Early Stuart England*, London.

Shuger, Debora K. (1988) *Sacred Rhetoric: the Christian Grand Style in the English Renaissance*, Princeton, N.J.

Silver, Victoria (1988). 'The fiction of self-evidence in Hobbes's *Leviathan*', *ELH*, 55, pp. 351–79.

Simon, Joan (1979). *Education and Society in Tudor England*, Cambridge.

Skinner, Quentin (1964). 'Hobbes's *Leviathan*', *The Historical Journal*, 7, pp. 321–33.

(1965a). 'Hobbes on sovereignty: an unknown discussion', *Political Studies*, 13, pp. 213–18.

(1965b). 'History and ideology in the English Revolution', *The Historical Journal*, 8, pp. 151–78.

(1966a). 'Thomas Hobbes and his disciples in France and England', *Comparative Studies in Society and History*, 8, pp. 153–67.

(1966b). 'The limits of historical explanations', *Philosophy*, 41, pp. 199–215.

(1969). 'Thomas Hobbes and the nature of the early Royal Society', *The Historical Journal*, 12, pp. 217–39.

(1972a). 'The context of Hobbes's theory of political obligation' in *Hobbes and Rousseau*, ed. Maurice Cranston and Richard S. Peters, New York, pp. 109–42.

(1972b). 'Conquest and consent: Thomas Hobbes and the Engagement controversy' in *The Interregnum: the Quest for Settlement*, ed. G. E. Aylmer, London, pp. 79–98.

(1978). *The Foundations of Modern Political Thought*, 2 vols., Cambridge.

(1987). 'Sir Thomas More's *Utopia* and the language of Renaissance humanism' in *The Languages of Political Theory in Early-modern Europe*, ed. Anthony Pagden, Cambridge, pp. 123–57.

(1988a). *Meaning and Context: Quentin Skinner and his Critics*, ed. James Tully, Cambridge.

(1988b). 'Warrender and Skinner on Hobbes: a reply', *Political Studies*, 36, pp. 692–5.

(1989). 'The state' in *Political Innovation and Conceptual Change*, ed. Terence Ball, James Farr and Russell L. Hanson, Cambridge, pp. 90–131.

(1990a). 'Machiavelli's *Discorsi* and the pre-humanist origins of republican ideas' in *Machiavelli and Republicanism*, ed. Gisela Bock, Quentin Skinner and Maurizio Viroli, Cambridge, pp. 121–41.

(1990b). 'Thomas Hobbes on the proper signification of liberty', *Transactions of the Royal Historical Society*, 40, pp. 121–51.

(1991). 'Thomas Hobbes: rhetoric and the construction of morality', *Proceedings of the British Academy*, 76, pp. 1–61.

(1993). '*Scientia civilis* in classical rhetoric and in the early Hobbes' in *Political Discourse in Early Modern Britain*, ed. Nicholas Phillipson and Quentin Skinner, Cambridge, pp. 67–93.

(1994). 'Moral ambiguity and the Renaissance art of eloquence', *Essays in Criticism*, 44, pp. 267–92.

Slavin, Arthur J. (1970). 'Profitable studies: humanists and government in early Tudor England', *Viator*, 1, pp. 307–25.

Sloan, Thomas O. (1974). 'The crossing of rhetoric and poetry in the English Renaissance' in *The Rhetoric of Renaissance Poetry from Wyatt to Milton*, ed. Thomas O. Sloan and Raymond B. Waddington, London, pp. 212–42.

Smith, Nigel (1989). *Perfection Proclaimed: Language and Literature in English Radical Religion 1640–1660*, Oxford.

(1994). *Literature and Revolution in England 1640–1660*, London.

Smuts, Malcolm (1994). 'Court-centred politics and the uses of Roman historians, c.1590–1630' in *Culture and Politics in Early Stuart England*, ed. Kevin Sharpe and Peter Lake, London, pp. 21–43.

Sommerville, Johann P. (1986). *Politics and Ideology in England, 1603–1640*, London.

(1992). *Thomas Hobbes: Political Ideas in Historical Context*, New York.

Sonnino, Lee A. (1968). *A Handbook to Sixteenth-Century Rhetoric*, London.

Sorell, Tom (1986). *Hobbes*, London.

(1988). 'The science in Hobbes's politics' in *Perspectives on Thomas Hobbes*, ed. G. A. J. Rogers and Alan Ryan, Oxford, pp. 67–80.

(1990a). 'Hobbes's unaristotelian political rhetoric', *Philosophy and Rhetoric*, 23, pp. 96–108.

(1990b). 'Hobbes's persuasive civil science', *Philosophical Quarterly*, 40, pp. 342–51.

Southall, Raymond (1964). *The Courtly Maker: an Essay on the Poetry of Wyatt and his Contemporaries*, Oxford.

Spedding, James (1868). *The Letters and the Life of Francis Bacon*, London.

Spragens, Thomas A. (1973). *The Politics of Motion: the World of Thomas Hobbes*, London.

Springborg, Patricia (1975). '*Leviathan* and the problem of ecclesiastical authority', *Political Theory*, 3, pp. 289–303.

Starnes, De Witt T. and Noyes, Gertrude E. (1946). *The English Dictionary from Cawdrey to Johnson, 1604–1755*, Chapel Hill, N.C.

Steadman, John M. (1967). '*Leviathan* and Renaissance etymology', *Journal of the History of Ideas*, 28, pp. 575–6.

Stern, Virginia F. (1979). *Gabriel Harvey: his Life, Marginalia and Library*, Oxford.

Strauss, E. (1954). *Sir William Petty: Portrait of a Genius*, London.

Strauss, Leo (1963). *The Political Philosophy of Hobbes: its Basis and its Genesis*, trans. Elsa M. Sinclair, Phoenix edn., Chicago, Ill.

Tavard, George H. (1978). *The Seventeenth-Century Tradition: a Study in Recusant Thought*, Leiden.

Taylor, A. E. (1965). 'The ethical doctrine of Hobbes' in *Hobbes Studies*, ed. K. C. Brown, Cambridge, Mass., pp. 35–55.

Thomas, Keith (1965). 'The social origins of Hobbes's political thought' in *Hobbes Studies*, ed. K. C. Brown, Cambridge, Mass., pp. 185–236.

(1971). *Religion and the Decline of Magic*, London.

(1993). 'Cases of conscience in seventeenth-century England' in *Public Duty and Private Conscience in Seventeenth-Century England*, ed. John Morrill, Paul Slack and Daniel Woolf, Oxford, pp. 29–56.

Thorpe, Clarence DeWitt (1940). *The Aesthetic Theory of Thomas Hobbes*, Michigan.

Thuau, Etienne (1966). *Raison d'état et pensée politique à l'époque de Richelieu*, Paris.

Tinckler, John F. (1988). 'Praise and advice: rhetorical approaches in More's *Utopia* and Machiavelli's *The Prince*', *Sixteenth Century Journal*, 19, pp. 187–207.

Todd, Margo (1987). *Christian Humanism and the Puritan Social Order*, Cambridge.

Tönnies, Ferdinand (1969a). The editor's preface in *The Elements of Law Natural and Politic*, ed. Ferdinand Tönnies, second edn., introd. M. M. Goldsmith, London, pp. v–xiii.

(1969b). Preface in *Behemoth or the Long Parliament*, ed. Ferdinand Tönnies, second edn., introd. M. M. Goldsmith, London, pp. vii–xi.

Trease, Geoffrey (1979). *Portrait of a Cavalier: William Cavendish, First Duke of Newcastle*, London.

Trevor-Roper, H. R. (1957). 'Thomas Hobbes' in *Historical Essays*, London, pp. 233–8.

Tricaud, François (1971). 'Introduction du traducteur' in Thomas Hobbes: *Léviathan*, trans. and ed. François Tricaud, Paris, pp. xi–xxxvi.

(1979). 'Quelques éléments sur la question de l'accès aux textes dans les études hobbiennes', *Revue Internationale de Philosophie*, 33, pp. 393–414.

Trimpi, Wesley (1973). 'The meaning of Horace's *Ut pictura poesis*', *Journal of the Warburg and Courtauld Institutes*, 36, pp. 1–34.

Triomphe, Micheline (1994). 'Hobbes et la raison d'état' in *Raison et déraison d'état*, ed. Yves Charles Zarka, Paris, pp. 327–40.

Trousdale, Marion (1982). *Shakespeare and the Rhetoricians*, London.

Tuck, Richard (1979). *Natural Rights Theories: their Origin and Development*, Cambridge.

(1988a). 'Optics and sceptics: the philosophical foundations of Hobbes's political thought' in *Conscience and Casuistry in Early Modern Europe*, ed. Edmund Leites, Cambridge, pp. 235–63.

(1988b). 'Hobbes and Descartes' in *Perspectives on Thomas Hobbes*, ed. G. A. J. Rogers and Alan Ryan, Oxford, pp. 11–41.

(1989). *Hobbes*, Oxford.

(1993). *Philosophy and Government 1572–1651*, Cambridge.

Tully, James (1981). 'Current thinking about sixteenth- and seventeenth-century political theory', *The Historical Journal*, 24, pp. 475–84.

(1993). *An Approach to Political Philosophy: Locke in Contexts*, Cambridge.

Tuve, Rosemond (1947). *Elizabethan and Metaphysical Imagery: Renaissance Poetic and Twentieth-Century Critics*, Chicago, Ill.

Vasoli, C. (1968). *La dialettica e la retorica dell'umanesimo*, Milan.

Vicari, E. Patricia (1989). *The View from Minerva's Tower: Learning and Imagination in the Anatomy of Melancholy*, Toronto.

Vickers, Brian (1968). *Francis Bacon and Renaissance Prose*, Cambridge.

(1981). 'Rhetorical and anti-rhetorical tropes: on writing the history of *elocutio*', *Comparative Criticism*, 3, pp. 105–32.

(1983). '"The Power of Persuasion": images of the orator, Elyot to Shakespeare' in *Renaissance Eloquence*, ed. James J. Murphy, pp. 411–35.

(1985). 'The Royal Society and English prose style: a reassessment' in *Rhetoric and the Pursuit of Truth*, introd. Thomas F. Wright [William Andrews Clark Memorial Library Seminar Papers], Los Angeles, pp. 1–76.

(1988). 'Rhetoric and poetics' in *The Cambridge History of Renaissance Philosophy*, general ed. Charles B. Schmitt, Cambridge, pp. 715–45.

(1989). *In Defence of Rhetoric*, revised edn., Oxford.

(1991). 'Bacon among the literati: science and language', *Comparative Criticism*, 13, pp. 249–71.

(1994). 'Some reflections on the rhetoric textbook' in *Renaissance Rhetoric*, ed. Peter Mack, London, pp. 81–102.

Viroli, Maurizio (1992). *From Politics to Reason of State: the Acquisition and Transformation of the Language of Politics 1250–1600*, Cambridge.

Vos, Alvin (1976). 'Humanistic standards of diction in the inkhorn controversy', *Studies in Philology*, 73, pp. 376–96.

Wagner, Russell H. (1929). 'The text and editions of Wilson's *Arte of Rhetorique*', *Modern Language Notes*, 44, pp. 421–8.

(1960). 'Thomas Wilson's *Arte of Rhetorique*', *Speech Monographs*, 27, pp. 1–32.

Wallace, John M. (1968). *Destiny his Choice: the Loyalism of Andrew Marvell*, Cambridge.

Wallace, Malcolm W. (1915). *The Life of Sir Philip Sidney*, Cambridge.

Walmsley, Peter (1990). *The Rhetoric of Berkeley's Philosophy*, Cambridge.

Warrender, Howard (1957). *The Political Philosophy of Hobbes: his Theory of Obligation*, Oxford.

(1979). 'Political theory and historiography', *The Historical Journal*, 22, pp. 931–40.

(1983). Editor's introduction in *De Cive: The Latin Version*, ed. Howard Warrender, Oxford, pp. 1–67.

Watkins, J. W. N. (1965). *Hobbes's System of Ideas*, London.

Watson, George (1955). 'Hobbes and the metaphysical conceit', *Journal of the History of Ideas*, 16, pp. 558–62.

Watson, R. A. and Force, J. E. (1988). 'Publications of Richard H. Popkin 1950–1986 inclusive' in *The Sceptical Mode in Modern Philosophy*, ed. R. A. Watson and J. E. Force, Dordrecht, pp. 151–62.

Webster, Charles (1970). Introduction to *Samuel Hartlib and the Advancement of Learning*, Cambridge, pp. 1–72.

Weiner, Andrew D. (1978). *Sir Philip Sidney and the Poetics of Protestantism: a Study of Contexts*, Minneapolis, Minn.

Whelan, Frederick G. (1981). 'Language and its abuses in Hobbes' political philosophy', *American Political Science Review*, 75, pp. 59–75.

Whigham, Frank (1984). *Ambition and Privilege: the Social Tropes of Elizabethan Courtesy Theory*, Berkeley, Cal.

Whitaker, Mark (1988). 'Hobbes's view of the Reformation', *History of Political Thought*, 9, pp. 45–58.

Whitaker, Virgil K. (1972). 'The theological structure of the *Faerie Queene*, book 1' in *Essential Articles for the Study of Edmund Spenser*, ed. A. C. Hamilton, Hamden, Conn., pp. 101–20.

Wildermuth, Mark E. (1989). 'The rhetoric of Wilson's *Arte*: reclaiming the classical heritage for English Protestants', *Philosophy and Rhetoric*, 22, pp. 43–58.

Willcock, Gladys and Walker, Alice (1970). Introduction to *The Arte of English Poesie*, Cambridge, pp. ix–cii.

Wilson, John (1982). '"The customary meanings of words were changed" – or were they? A note on Thucydides 3.82.4', *Classical Quarterly*, 32, pp. 18–20.

Wilson, K. J. (1985). *Incomplete Fictions: the Formation of English Renaissance Dialogue*, Washington, D.C.

Wisse, Jakob (1989). *Ethos and Pathos from Aristotle to Cicero*, Amsterdam.

Wittgenstein, Ludwig (1958). *Philosophical Investigations*, trans. G. E. M. Anscombe, second edn., Oxford.

Wolf, Friedrich O. (1969). *Die Neue Wissenschaft des Thomas Hobbes ... Mit Hobbes' Essayes*, Stuttgart.

Wolin, Sheldon S. (1970). *Hobbes and the Epic Tradition of Political Theory*, ed. Richard E. Ashcraft [William Andrews Clark Memorial Library Seminar Paper], Los Angeles, pp. 1–55.

Womersley, David (1991). 'Sir Henry Savile's translation of Tacitus and the political interpretation of Elizabethan texts', *Review of English Studies*, 42, pp. 313–42.

Woolf, D. R. (1990). *The Idea of History in Early Stuart England: Erudition, Ideology and 'The Light of Truth' from the Accession of James I to the Civil War*, London.

Yates, Frances (1966). *The Art of Memory*, London.

Zagorin, Perez (1954). *A History of Political Thought in the English Revolution*, London.

(1978). 'Thomas Hobbes's departure from England in 1640: an unpublished letter', *The Historical Journal*, 21, pp. 157–60.

(1993). 'Hobbes's early philosophical development', *Journal of the History of Ideas*, 54, pp. 505–18.

Zappen, James P. (1983). 'Aristotelian and Ramist rhetoric in Thomas Hobbes's *Leviathan*: pathos versus ethos and logos', *Rhetorica*, 1, pp. 65–91.

INDEX